EYEWITNESS TRAVEL GUIDES

PARIS

EYEWITNESS TRAVEL GUIDES

PARIS

Main contributor: ALAN TILLIER

LONDON, NEW YORK,
MELBOURNE, MUNICH AND DELHI
www.dk.com

PROJECT EDITOR Heather Jones
ART EDITOR Janis Utton
EDITOR Alex Gray
DESIGNER Vanessa Hamilton
DESIGN ASSISTANT Clare Sullivan

CONTRIBUTORS
Chris Boicos, Michael Gibson, Douglas Johnson

PHOTOGRAPHERS
Max Alexander, Neil Lukas, Robert O'Dea

ILLUSTRATORS
Stephen Conlin, Stephen Gyapay,
Maltings Partnership

This book was produced with the assistance of
Websters International Publishers.

Reproduced by Colourscan, Singapore
Printed and bound by South China Printing Co. Ltd., China

First published in Great Britain in 1993
by Dorling Kindersley Limited
80 Strand, London WC2R 0RL

**Reprinted with revisions 1994, 1995, 1997 (twice),
1999, 2000, 2001, 2002, 2003, 2004, 2005, 2006, 2007, 2008**

Copyright © 1993, 2008 Dorling Kindersley Limited, London
A Penguin Company

A CIP CATALOGUE RECORD IS AVAILABLE FROM THE BRITISH LIBRARY.

ISBN 978 1 40532 106 8

FLOORS ARE REFERRED TO THROUGHOUT IN ACCORDANCE WITH FRENCH
USAGE; IE THE "FIRST FLOOR" IS THE FLOOR ABOVE GROUND LEVEL.

Front cover main image: Arc de Triomphe with Champs-Elysées

**The information in this
Dorling Kindersley Travel Guide is checked annually.**
Every effort has been made to ensure that this book is as
up-to-date as possible at the time of going to press. Some details,
however, such as telephone numbers, opening hours, prices, gallery
hanging arrangements and travel information are liable to change.
The publishers cannot accept responsibility for any consequences
arising from the use of this book, nor for any material on third-party
websites, and cannot guarantee that any website address in this book
will be a suitable source of travel information.
We value the views and suggestions of our readers very highly.
Please write to: Publisher, DK Eyewitness Travel Guides,
Dorling Kindersley, 80 Strand, London WC2R 0RL, Great Britain.

◁ Sacré-Coeur and the Butte Montmartre

CONTENTS

HOW TO USE THIS
GUIDE **6**

Henri II (1547–59)

INTRODUCING
PARIS

FOUR GREAT DAYS IN
PARIS **10**

PUTTING PARIS ON
THE MAP **12**

THE HISTORY OF
PARIS **16**

PARIS AT A GLANCE **42**

PARIS THROUGH
THE YEAR **62**

A RIVER VIEW
OF PARIS **66**

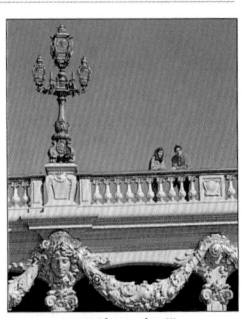

Pont Alexandre III

PARIS AREA BY AREA

ILE DE LA CITE AND ILE ST-LOUIS **76**

THE MARAIS **90**

BEAUBOURG AND LES HALLES **104**

TUILERIES QUARTER **116**

Opéra National de Paris Bastille

ST-GERMAIN-DES-PRES **134**

LATIN QUARTER **148**

JARDIN DES PLANTES QUARTER **160**

LUXEMBOURG QUARTER **168**

The Kiss by Rodin (1886)

MONTPARNASSE **174**

INVALIDES AND EIFFEL TOWER QUARTER **182**

CHAILLOT QUARTER **196**

CHAMPS-ELYSEES **204**

Sacré-Coeur in Montmartre

OPERA QUARTER **212**

MONTMARTRE **220**

FURTHER AFIELD **230**

EIGHT GUIDED WALKS **256**

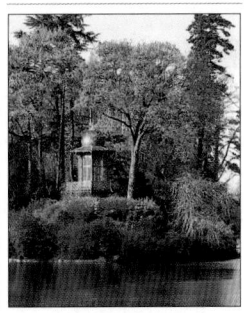

An island in the Bois de Boulogne

TRAVELLERS' NEEDS

WHERE TO STAY **276**

RESTAURANTS, CAFES AND BARS **292**

SHOPS AND MARKETS **320**

ENTERTAINMENT IN PARIS **340**

CHILDREN'S PARIS **360**

Noisettes of lamb

SURVIVAL GUIDE

PRACTICAL INFORMATION **366**

GETTING TO PARIS **376**

GETTING AROUND PARIS **382**

PARIS STREET FINDER **390**

GENERAL INDEX **424**

ACKNOWLEDGMENTS **444**

PHRASE BOOK **447**

The Panthéon

HOW TO USE THIS GUIDE

This Eyewitness Travel Guide helps you get the most from your stay in Paris with the minimum of practical difficulty. The opening section, *Introducing Paris*, locates the city geographically, sets modern Paris in its historical context and explains how Parisian life changes through the year. *Paris at a Glance* is an overview of the city's specialities. The main sightseeing section of the book is *Paris Area by*

Area. It describes all the main sights with maps, photographs and detailed illustrations. In addition, eight planned walks take you to parts of Paris you might otherwise miss.

Carefully researched tips for hotels, shops and markets, restaurants and bars, sports and entertainment are found in *Travellers' Needs*, and the *Survival Guide* has advice on everything from posting a letter to catching the metro.

PARIS AREA BY AREA

The city has been divided into 14 sightseeing areas. Each section opens with a portrait of the area, summing up its character and history, with a list of all the sights to be covered. These are clearly located by numbers on an *Area Map*. This is followed by a large-scale *Street-by-Street Map* focusing on the most interesting part of the area. Finding your way about the section is made simple by the numbering system used throughout for the sights. This refers to the order in which they are described on the pages that complete the section.

1 Area Map *For easy reference, the sights in each area are numbered and located on an area map. To help the visitor, the map also shows metro and mainline RER stations and car parks.*

2 Street-by-Street Map *This gives a bird's-eye view of the heart of each sightseeing area. The most important buildings are picked out in stronger colour, to help you spot them as you walk around.*

The Conciergerie 8 is shown on this map as well.

Colour-coding on each page makes the area easy to find in the book.

A locator map shows you where you are in relation to surrounding areas. The area of the *Street-by-Street Map* is shown in red.

Photographs of facades and distinctive details of buildings help you to locate the sights.

Sights at a Glance lists the sights in the area by category: Historic Streets and Buildings, Churches, Museums and Galleries, Monuments, and Squares, Parks and Gardens.

The area covered in greater detail on the *Street-by-Street Map* is shaded red.

Travel tips help you reach the area quickly.

Numbered circles pinpoint all the listed sights on the area map. The Conciergerie, for example, is **8**

A suggested route for a walk takes in the most attractive and interesting streets in the area.

Stars indicate the sights that no visitor should miss.

PARIS AT A GLANCE

Each map in this section concentrates on a specific theme: *Museums and Galleries, Churches, Squares, Parks and Gardens, Remarkable Parisians.* The top sights are shown on the map; other sights are described on the following two pages.

Each sightseeing area is colour-coded.

The theme is explored in greater detail on the pages following the map.

3 Detailed information on each sight
All important sights in each area are described in depth in this section. They are listed in order, following the numbering on the Area Map. Practical information is also provided.

4 Paris's major sights *These are given two or more full pages in the sightseeing area in which they are found. Historic buildings are dissected to reveal their interiors; and museums and galleries have colour-coded floor plans to help you find important exhibits.*

PRACTICAL INFORMATION

Each entry provides all the information needed to plan a visit to the sight. The key to the symbols used is on the inside back cover.

The Visitors' Checklist provides the practical information you will need to plan your visit.

Nearest metro station

Telephone number

Sight number

Opening hours

The facade of each major sight is shown to help you spot it quickly.

Conciergerie ➑

1 Quai de l'Horloge 75001.
Map 13 A3. **Tel** 01 53 73 78 50.
Ⓜ Cité. Apr–Sep: 9.30am–6pm daily.

Map reference to Street Finder at back of book

Address

Services and facilities available

Stars indicate the most interesting architectural details of the building, and the most important works of art or exhibits on view inside.

A timeline charts the key events in the history of the sight.

INTRODUCING PARIS

FOUR GREAT DAYS IN PARIS 10–11

PUTTING PARIS ON THE MAP 12–15

THE HISTORY OF PARIS 16–41

PARIS AT A GLANCE 42–61

PARIS THROUGH THE YEAR 62–65

A RIVER VIEW OF PARIS 66–73

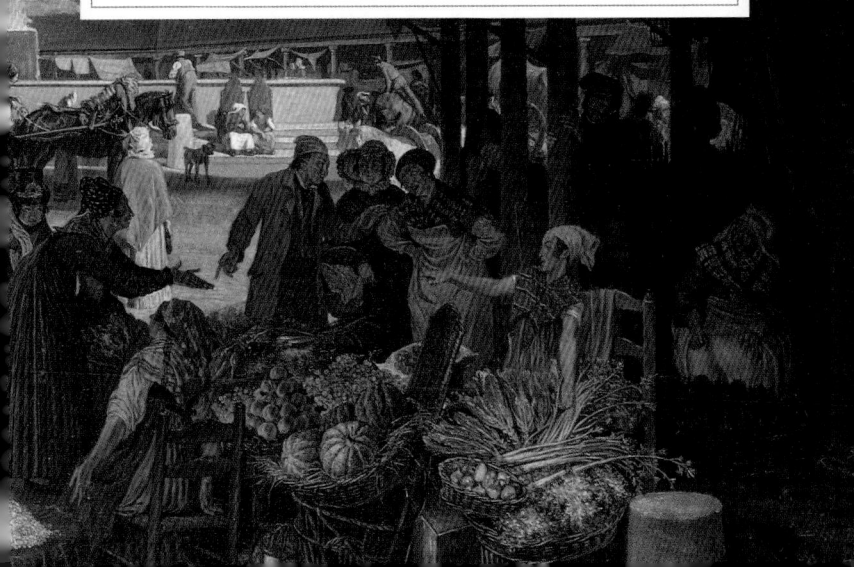

FOUR GREAT DAYS IN PARIS

Paris is a city packed with wonderful things to see and do. There may be a temptation to spend the trip in a café letting the French way of life wash over you, but it would be a shame to miss its treasures. Here are the best of the city's must-dos. Energetic sightseers should manage everything on these itineraries, but this selection can also be dipped into for ideas. All are reachable by public transport. Price guides are for two adults or for a family of two adults and two children, excluding meals.

Rodin's Thinker

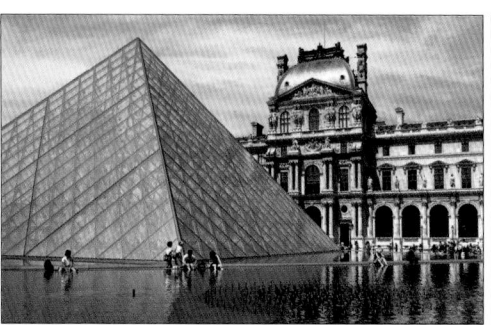

Pyramide du Louvre, from across the fountain pools

ARTISTIC TREASURES

- Fabulous art at the Louvre
- Lunch at chic Café Marly
- A visit to the Rodin sculpture garden or take in the Pompidou Centre
- Dine at Tokyo Eat

TWO ADULTS allow at least €60

Morning

Begin with the **Musée du Louvre** *(see pp122–9)*, one of the world's most impressive museums. Beat the crowds by using the little-known entrance at the Carrousel du Louvre (99 Rue de Rivoli). Save time by getting a floorplan and working out where you want to go and sticking to it.

Lunch

There are many cheap eateries nearby, but for a great lunch experience head to smart **Café Marly** *(see p304)*. On warm days sit in the outside gallery or revel in the cozy red velvet and gilt splendour of the interior.

Afternoon

Choose from three destinations for the afternoon. The fatigued should head to the sublime **Musée Rodin** *(see p187)* for a soothing stroll in the sculpture garden and a pensive moment next to *The Thinker*. Those seeking modern masterpieces should visit the **Pompidou Centre** *(see pp110–13)*, an intriguing inside-out building housing works from 1905 to the modern day. To go even more modern, explore the crop of galleries that are known as "Scene Est" in the 13th arrondissement (district). "Scene Est" is three roads full of cutting-edge galleries, with the **Rue Louise Weiss** *(Map 18 E4)* the most important and the Air de Paris gallery the most funky.

Evening

The **Palais de Tokyo** *(see p203)* is currently Paris' most fashionable exhibition space, with its multimedia displays open till midnight. After a quick tour around, stop at restaurant Tokyo Eat.

RETAIL THERAPY

- Buy foody treats at Le Bon Marché
- Lunch at a top department store restaurant
- Drinks and dinner at Kong

TWO ADULTS allow at least €25

Morning

One-stop shops for gourmets and gluttons include **Fauchon, Hediard** and **La Grande Epicerie** at **Le Bon Marché** *(see pp320–21)*. In fact, anything that is edible – as long as it's delicious – can be found here. Specialist shops include **Poilâne** for bread, **Richart** for chocolate, **Legrand** for wine and **Pierre Hermé** for cakes. Or head down the Rue Mouffetard, one of the city's best market streets.

Lunch

Shopaholics can eat in one of the main department stores. The World Bar at **Au Printemps**, designed by Paul Smith, is a super-cool eatery *(see pp320–21)*, for example.

Ultra-hip interior of Kong, which also has stunning rooftop views

The surrounding area is a busy shopping and eating hub, so you can combine the two with no difficulty.

Afternoon

Either shop on till you drop, or go esoteric and visit the **Musée de la Mode** at the Louvre *(see p121);* a true temple to fashion, dedicated to beautiful clothes and accessories. Boutique lovers should go to **Claudie Pierlot, Agnes B, Isabelle Marant, Vanessa Bruno** *(see pp324–7).*

Evening

Head for restorative drinks and dinner at **Kong** on top of Kenzo's flagship store and fashion shrine *(see pp317–8).*

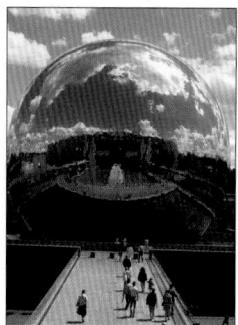

Reflections in La Géode, giant sphere at the Parc de la Villette

CHILD'S PLAY

• Explore Parc de la Villette
• See animals at the zoo at Jardin des Plantes
• Stop for a café lunch
• Go up the Eiffel Tower

FAMILY OF FOUR allow at least €130

Morning

Take receptive young minds to **Parc de la Villette**, which has an impressive children's programme. **La Cité des Sciences et de l'Industrie** (Science City) is packed with interesting interactive exhibits for budding Einsteins *(see pp236–9).* Family fun can be found at the **Ménagerie** *(see pp164)* in the Jardin des Plantes area where the zoo

is very popular. Even more exciting than the live animals for some are the skeletons and stuffed beasts in the **Muséum National d'Histoire Naturelle** *(see p167).*

Lunch

There are lots of cafés in the Jardin des Plantes area or a more formal lunch can be had at **Mavromatis** *(see p307).*

Afternoon

No child can resist a trip up the **Eiffel Tower**, so take them up in the afternoon for a proper view of the city, or wait until nightfall and time your trip to coincide with the changing of the hour when thousands of lights twinkle for ten minutes *(see pp194–5).* If there's time, take a tour of the waxworks at the **Grévin** museum *(see p218).* Most of the models are of French celebrities, but big international names in art and sport can also be spotted.

THE GREAT OUTDOORS

• Boat trip on the Seine
• Lunch on the Rue de Rivoli
• A walk to Luxembourg Garden
• Take a balloon ride

TWO ADULTS allow at least €65

Morning

For today's trip the metro is banned, so instead take the hop-on-hop-off bateaubus up the Seine. The first "stop" is near the **Eiffel Tower** so a quick look around the

Modern water sculpture and glasshouse, Parc André Citroën

Champ-de-Mars underneath Gustave Eiffel's monument is recommended *(see p191).* Continue on the bateaubus to the Louvre stop, jump off and wander around the **Jardin des Tuileries** *(see p130).*

Lunch

The tea salon **Angélina** *(see p318)* is a cut above other cafés on Rue de Rivoli. Leave space for the famous Mont Blanc cake of chestnut purée and cream.

Afternoon

Reboard the boat and head up to **Notre-Dame** *(see pp82–5),* then it's a good walk down the Boulevard St Michel to the **Jardin du Luxembourg** *(see p172).* There's lots to see – chess tables, beehives and donkey rides – and the **Musée du Luxembourg**, which hosts blockbuster shows. For a final blast of fresh air, cross the city to the **Parc André Citroën** and take a tethered balloon ride *(see p247).*

A floral display in the Jardin des Plantes

Putting Paris on the Map

Paris, the capital of France, is a city of over two million people covering 1,200 sq km (460 sq miles) of northern France. It is on the River Seine at the centre of the Ile-de-France, the region which is home to ten million people, around one-fifth of the French population. An important European business and cultural centre, it is the focus of activity in the north of France.

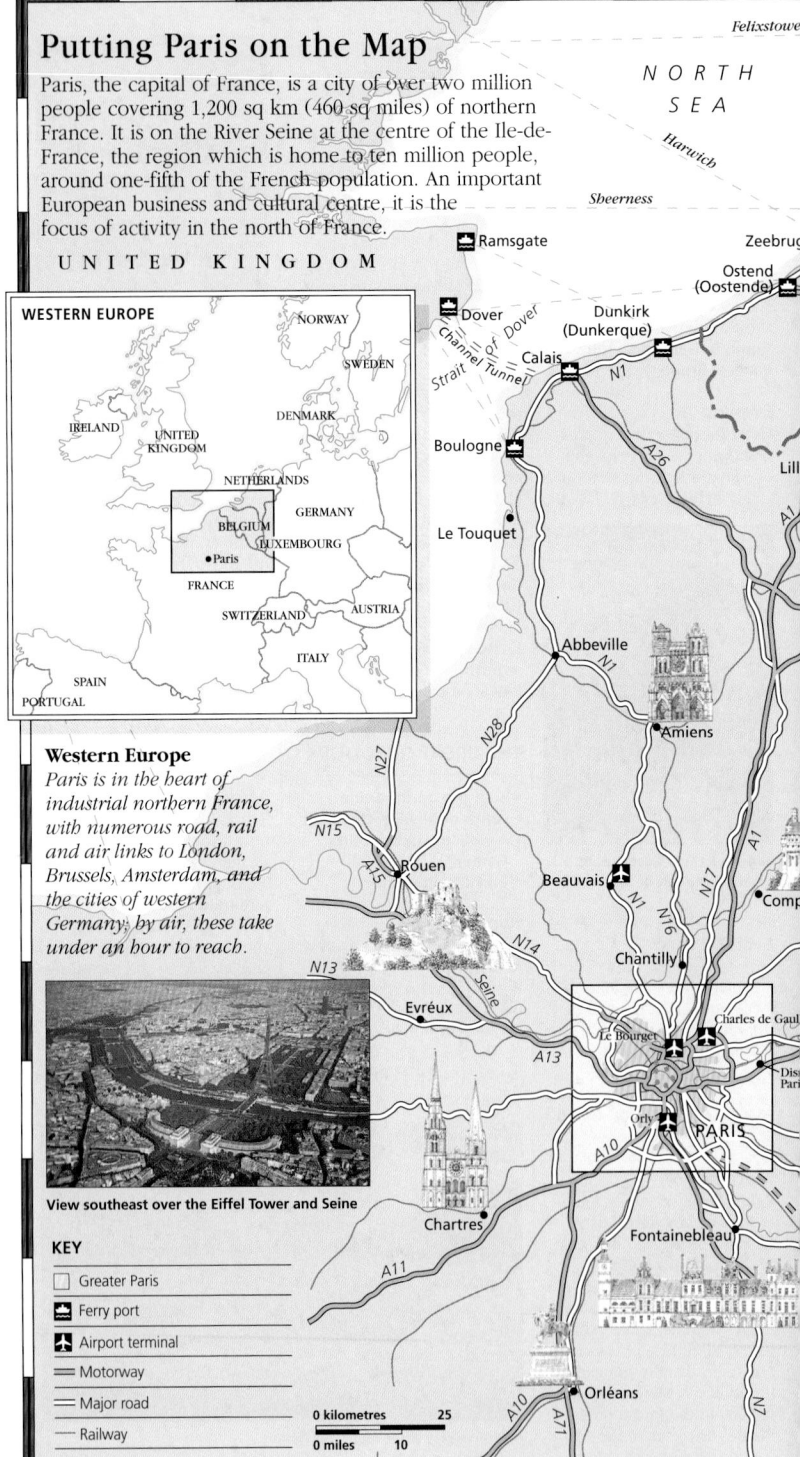

Western Europe

Paris is in the heart of industrial northern France, with numerous road, rail and air links to London, Brussels, Amsterdam, and the cities of western Germany; by air, these take under an hour to reach.

View southeast over the Eiffel Tower and Seine

KEY

☐	Greater Paris
⚓	Ferry port
✈	Airport terminal
═	Motorway
═	Major road
—	Railway

0 kilometres 25

0 miles 10

ILE-DE-FRANCE

Ile-de-France

The Ile-de-France includes the conurbation of Paris and many fascinating places such as Chartres and Versailles. Central Paris is bounded by the Périphérique ring road. Important sights outside central Paris are on pages 230–55.

Aerial view of central Paris

Central Paris

Napoleon's Arc de Triomphe

This book divides Paris into 14 areas, comprising central Paris and the nearby area of Montmartre. Most of the sights covered in the book lie within these areas, each one of which has its own chapter. Each area contains a range of sights that convey some of its history and distinctive character. The sights of Montmartre, for example, reveal its village charm and its colourful history as a thriving artistic enclave. In contrast, Champs-Elysées is renowned for its wide avenues, expensive fashion houses and opulent mansions. Most of the city's famous sights are within reach of the heart of the city and are easy to reach on foot or by public transport.

Dôme Church
The gilded Dôme Church (see pp188–9) lies at the heart of the Invalides.

Eiffel Tower
Named after the engineer who designed and built it in 1889, the Eiffel Tower is the city's best-known landmark (see pp194–5). It towers more than 320 m (1,050 ft) above Champ-de-Mars park.

KEY

▦	Star sights
Ⓜ	Metro station
🚇	SNCF (train) station
RER	RER station
⛴	Boat service boarding point
ℹ	Tourist information office

Musée du Louvre
Right in the heart of Paris, adjacent to the River Seine and the Tuileries garden, lies the city's most impressive museum, with an unrivalled collection of artifacts from around the world (see pp122–9).

Sacré-Coeur
Standing majestically above Montmartre is the striking basilica of Sacré-Coeur. Built between 1875 and 1914, it is dedicated to the sacred heart of Jesus (see pp226–7).

0 metres 800

0 yards 800

REPUBLIQUE FRANCAISE

LIBERTE EGALITE · FRATERNITE

THE HISTORY OF PARIS

The Paris conquered by the Romans in 55 BC was a small flood-prone fishing village on the Ile de la Cité, inhabited by the Parisii tribe. A Roman settlement soon flourished and spread on to the Left Bank of the Seine. The Franks succeeded the Romans, named the city Paris and made it the centre of their kingdom.

During the Middle Ages the city flourished as a religious centre and architectural masterpieces such as Sainte-Chapelle were erected. It also thrived as a centre of learning, enticing European scholars to its great university, the Sorbonne.

Paris emerged during the Renaissance and the Enlightenment as a great centre of culture and ideas, and under the rule of Louis XIV it also became a city of immense wealth and power. But rule by the monarch gave way to rule by the people in the bloody Revolution of 1789. By

Fleur-de-lys, the royal emblem

the early years of the new century, revolutionary fervour had faded and the brilliant militarist Napoleon Bonaparte proclaimed himself Emperor of France and pursued his ambition to make Paris the centre of the world.

Soon after the Revolution of 1848 a radical transformation of the city began. Baron Haussmann's grand urban scheme replaced Paris's medieval slums with elegant avenues and boulevards. By the end of the century, the city was the driving force of Western culture. This continued well into the 20th century, interrupted only by the German military occupation of 1940–44. Since the war, the city has revived and expanded dramatically, as it strives to be at the heart of a unified Europe.

The following pages illustrate Paris's history by providing snapshots of the significant periods in the city's evolution.

A map of Paris (about 1845)

◁ *Allegory of the Republic* (1848) by Dominique Louis Papety

Kings and Emperors in Paris

Paris became the power base for the kings of France at the beginning of the Capetian dynasty, when Hugh Capet ascended the throne. Successive kings and emperors have left their mark and many of the places mentioned in this book have royal associations: Philippe-Auguste's fortress, the Louvre Palace, is now one of the world's great museums; Henri IV's Pont Neuf bridge links the Ile de la Cité with the two banks of the Seine; and Napoleon conceived the Arc de Triomphe to celebrate his military victories. The end of the long line of kings came with the overthrow of the monarchy in 1848, during the reign of Louis-Philippe.

768–814 Charlemagne

743–751 Childéric III

716–721 Chilpéric II

695–711 Childebert II

566–584 Chilpéric I

558–562 Clotaire I

447–458 Merovich

458–482 Childéric I

674–691 Thierri III

655–668 Clotaire III

628–637 Dagobert I

954–986 Lothaire

898–929 Charles III, the Simple

884–888 Charles II, the Fat

879–882 Louis III

840–877 Charles I, the Bald

1137–80 Louis

987–996 Hugh Cape

1031–60 Henri I

1060–1 Philippe

400	500	600	700	800	900	1000	1
MEROVINGIAN DYNASTY				CAROLINGIAN DYNASTY		CAPETIAN DYNAS	
400	500	600	700	800	900	1000	

996–1031 Robert II, the Pious

986–987 Louis V

936–954 Louis IV, the Foreigner

888–898 Odo, Count of Paris

882–884 Carloman

877–879 Louis II, the Stammerer

814–840 Louis I, the Debonair

751–768 Pépin the Short

721–737 Thierri IV

711–716 Dagobert III

691–695 Clovis III

668–674 Childéric II

637–655 Clovis II

584–628 Clotaire II

562–566 Caribert

511–558 Childebert I

482–511 Clovis I

1108–37 Louis VI, the Fat

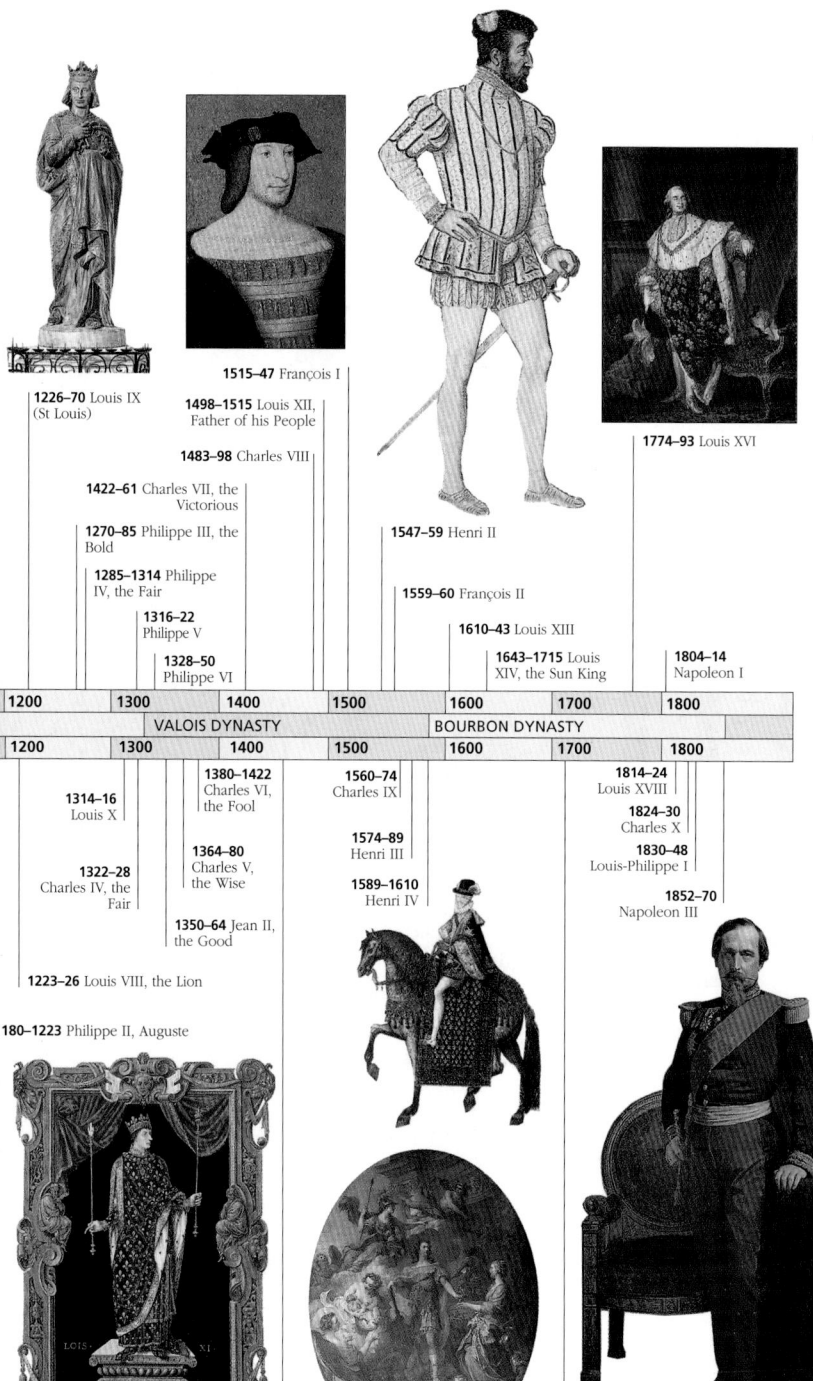

1226–70 Louis IX (St Louis)

1515–47 François I

1498–1515 Louis XII, Father of his People

1483–98 Charles VIII

1774–93 Louis XVI

1422–61 Charles VII, the Victorious

1270–85 Philippe III, the Bold

1547–59 Henri II

1285–1314 Philippe IV, the Fair

1559–60 François II

1316–22 Philippe V

1610–43 Louis XIII

1328–50 Philippe VI

1643–1715 Louis XIV, the Sun King

1804–14 Napoleon I

| 1200 | 1300 | 1400 | 1500 | 1600 | 1700 | 1800 |

VALOIS DYNASTY   BOURBON DYNASTY

| 1200 | 1300 | 1400 | 1500 | 1600 | 1700 | 1800 |

1380–1422 Charles VI, the Fool

1560–74 Charles IX

1814–24 Louis XVIII

1314–16 Louis X

1824–30 Charles X

1574–89 Henri III

1364–80 Charles V, the Wise

1830–48 Louis-Philippe I

1322–28 Charles IV, the Fair

1589–1610 Henri IV

1852–70 Napoleon III

1350–64 Jean II, the Good

1223–26 Louis VIII, the Lion

1180–1223 Philippe II, Auguste

1461–83 Louis XI, the Spider

1715–74 Louis XV

Gallo-Roman Paris

Paris would not have existed without the Seine. The river provided early peoples with the means to exploit the land, forests, marshes and islands. Recent excavations have unearthed canoes dating back to 4,500 BC, well before a Celtic tribe, known as the Parisii, settled there in the 3rd century BC, in an area known as Lutetia. From 59 BC, the Romans undertook the conquest of Gaul (France). Seven years later Lutetia was sacked by the Romans. They fortified and rebuilt it, especially the main island (the Ile de la Cité) and the Left Bank of the Seine.

Roman enamel brooch

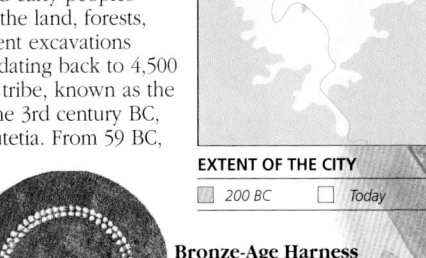

EXTENT OF THE CITY

▨ 200 BC   ☐ Today

Bronze-Age Harness
Everyday objects like harnesses continued to be made of bronze well into the Iron Age, which began in Gaul around 900 BC.

Iron Daggers
From the 2nd century BC, short swords of iron replaced long swords and were sometimes decorated with human and animal shapes.

Baths

Theatre

Forum

Present-day
Rue Soufflot

Glass Beads
Iron-Age glass beads and bracelets have been found on the Ile de la Cité.

Fired-Clay Vase
Pale ceramics with coloured decoration were common in Gaul.

Present-day
Rue St-Jacques

TIMELINE

Helmet worn by Gaulish warriors

4500 BC Early boatmen operate from the banks of the Seine

52 BC Labienus, Caesar's lieutenant, defeats the Gauls under Camulogenes. The Parisii destroy their own city

4500	400	200

Parisii gold coin minted on the Ile de la Cité

300 BC Parisii tribe settle on the Ile de la Cité

100 BC Romans rebuild the Ile de la Cité, and create a new town on the Left Bank

Roman Oil Lamp

The inhabitants of the densely populated Ile de la Cité derived comfort during the dark winter months from the warmth of central heating and the light from oil lamps.

Ile de la Cité

Gallo-Roman Goddess
Found in the arena, this head dates from the 2nd century AD.

Temple

WHERE TO SEE GALLO-ROMAN PARIS

Since the mid-19th century, excavations have yielded evidence of the boundaries of the Roman city which had as its central axes the present-day Rue St-Jacques and Rue Soufflot. In the Crypte Archéologique *(see p81)* under the square of Notre-Dame can be seen the remains of Gallo-Roman houses and Roman ramparts dating from the end of the 3rd century AD. Other Roman sites in Paris are the Arènes de Lutèce *(p165)* and the baths at the Musée de Cluny *(pp154 and 157)*.

The baths *(thermae)* at Cluny had three huge rooms of water with different temperatures.

Stage backdrop

Spectator seats

Arènes de Lutèce
This huge arena, built in the 2nd century AD, was used for circuses, theatrical performances and gladiatorial combat.

Ring Flask
From about 300 AD, this flask was found on the Ile de la Cité.

LUTETIA IN AD 200
Paris, or Lutetia, was laid out in a grid pattern with bridges linking the Ile de la Cité and the Left Bank.

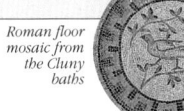

Roman floor mosaic from the Cluny baths

200 Romans add arena, baths and villas

285 Barbarians advance, Lutetia swept by fire

360 Julien, prefect of Gaul, is proclaimed Emperor. Lutetia changes its name to Paris after the Parisii

200

400

250 Early Christian martyr, St Denis, beheaded in Montmartre

451 Sainte Geneviève galvanizes the Parisians to repulse Attila the Hun

485–508 Clovis, leader of the Franks, defeats the Romans. Paris becomes Christian

Medieval Paris

Manuscript illumination

Throughout the Middle Ages, strategically placed towns like Paris, positioned at a river crossing, became important centres of political power and learning. The Church played a crucial part in intellectual and spiritual life. It provided the impetus for education and for technological advances such as the drainage of land and the digging of canals. The population was still confined mainly to the Ile de la Cité and the Left Bank. When the marshes *(marais)* were drained in the 12th century, the city was able to expand.

EXTENT OF THE CITY

▨ 1300	☐ Today

Sainte-Chapelle
The upper chapel of this medieval masterpiece (see pp88–9) was reserved for the royal family.

The Ile de la Cité, including the towers of the Conciergerie and Sainte-Chapelle, features in the pages for June.

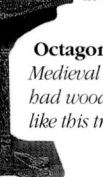

Octagonal Table
Medieval manor houses had wooden furniture like this trestle table.

Drainage allowed more land to be cultivated.

Weavers' Window
Medieval craftsmen formed guilds and many church windows were dedicated to their crafts.

A rural life was led by most Parisians, who worked on the land. The actual city only occupied a tiny area.

TIMELINE

512 Death of Sainte Geneviève. She is buried next to Clovis

725–732 Muslims attack Gaul

845–862 Normans attack Paris

500		700	800	900

543–556 Foundation of St-Germain-des-Prés

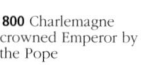

Golden hand reliquary of Charlemagne

800 Charlemagne crowned Emperor by the Pope

Notre-Dame
The great Gothic cathedrals took many years to build. Work continued on Notre-Dame from 1163 to 1334.

University Seal
The University of Paris was founded in 1215.

The Monasteries
Monks of many different orders lived in monasteries in Paris, especially on the Left Bank of the Seine.

The Louvre of Charles V
with its defensive wall is seen here from the Ile de la Cité.

The Nobility
From the mid-14th century, dress was considered to be a mark of class; noble ladies wore high, pointed hats.

A MEDIEVAL ROMANCE
It was in the cloisters of Notre-Dame that the romance between the monk Pierre Abélard and the young Héloïse began. Abélard was the most original theologian of the 12th century and was hired as a tutor to the 17-year-old niece of a canon. A love affair soon developed between the teacher and his pupil. In his wrath, Héloïse's uncle had the scholar castrated; Héloïse took refuge in a convent for the rest of her life.

THE MONTHS: JUNE AND OCTOBER
This illuminated prayer book and calendar, the Très Riches Heures (left and above), was made for the Duc de Berri in 1416. It shows many Paris buildings.

1010–22 Christians burn Jews and heretics

1167 Les Halles food market created on the Right Bank of the Seine

1253 The Sorbonne opens

1380 The Bastille fortress completed

Joan of Arc

1000 | **1100** | **1200** | **1300** | **1400**

1079 Birth of Pierre Abélard

1163 Work starts on Notre-Dame cathedral

1245 Work starts on Sainte-Chapelle

1226–70 Reign of Louis IX, St Louis

1215 Paris University founded

1430 Henry VI of England crowned King of France after Joan of Arc fails to defend Paris

Renaissance Paris

At the end of the Hundred Years' War with England, Paris was in a terrible state. By the time the occupying English army had left in 1453, the city lay in ruins, with many houses burned. Louis XI brought back prosperity and a new interest in art, architecture, decoration and clothes. During the course of the 16th and 17th centuries, French kings came under the spell of the Italian Renaissance. Their architects made the first attempts at town planning, creating elegant, uniform buildings and open urban spaces like the magnificent Place Royale.

Couple in fine courtly dress

EXTENT OF THE CITY

☐ 1590 ☐ Today

A Knight Preparing to Joust
The Place Royale was the setting for jousting displays well into the 17th century.

Printing Press (1470)
Religious tracts, mainly in Latin, were printed on the first press at the Sorbonne.

Jewel-Encrusted Pendant
A sign of the new prosperity, jewels became an important part of dress.

PLACE ROYALE
Built by Henri IV in 1609, with grand symmetrical houses round an open, central space, this was Paris's first square. Home to the aristocracy, it was re-named Place des Vosges in 1800 (see p94).

Pont Notre-Dame
This bridge with its row of houses was built at the start of the 15th century. The Pont Neuf (1589) was the first bridge without houses.

TIMELINE

1453 End of the Hundred Years' War with England

François I

1516 François I invites Leonardo da Vinci to France. He brings the *Mona Lisa* with him

1450	1460	1470	1480	1490	1500	1510	1520

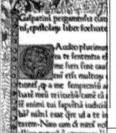

1469 First French printing works starts operating at the Sorbonne

1528 François I takes up residence in the Lou

16th-Century Knife and Fork Set
Ornate knife and fork sets were used in the dining rooms of the wealthy to carve joints of meat. Diners used hands or spoons for eating.

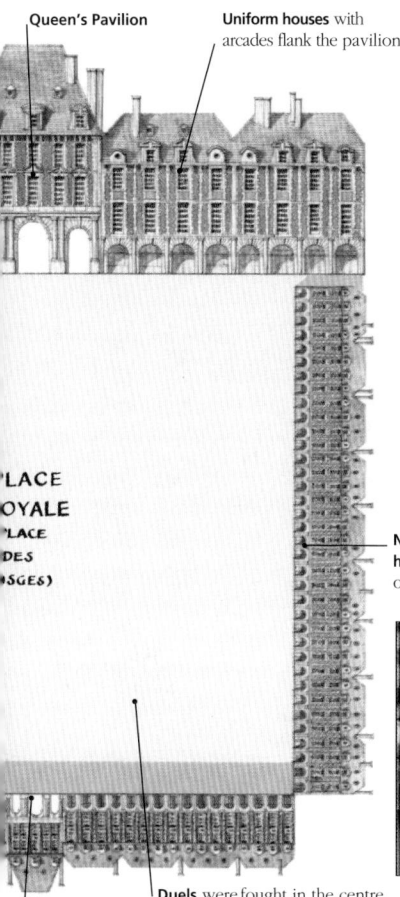

Queen's Pavilion

Uniform houses with arcades flank the pavilion.

'LACE
OYALE
'LACE
DES
'SGES)

Nine symmetrical houses line each side of the square.

King's Pavilion

Duels were fought in the centre of the square in the 17th century.

WHERE TO SEE RENAISSANCE PARIS TODAY

Besides the Place des Vosges, there are many examples of the Renaissance in Paris. Churches include St-Etienne-du-Mont *(p153)* and St-Eustache *(p114)*, as well as the Tour St-Jacques *(p115)*, the tower of a church no longer in existence. Mansions such as the Hôtel Carnavalet *(pp96–7)* have been restored, and the staircases, courtyard and turrets of the Hôtel de Cluny *(pp154–5)* date from 1485–96.

The rood screen of St-Etienne-du-Mont (about 1520) is of outstanding delicacy.

Walnut Dresser (about 1545)
Elegant carved wooden furniture decorated the homes of the wealthy.

Hyante and Climente
Toussaint Dubreuil and other artists took up Renaissance mythological themes.

1534 Ignatius of Loyola founds the Society of Jesus	**1546** Work starts on new Louvre palace; first stone quay built along Seine	**1559** Primitive street lanterns introduced; Louvre completed		**1572** St Bartholomew's Day massacre of Protestants	**1589** Henri III assassinated at St-Cloud, near Paris	**1609** Henri IV begins building Place des Vosges

30	1540	1550	1560	1570	1580	1590	1600

1534 Founding of the Collège de France	**1547** François I dies	**1589** Protestant Henri of Navarre converts to Catholicism, crowned as Henri IV	**1610** Henri IV is assassinated by Ravaillac, a religious fanatic
1533 Hôtel de Ville rebuilt	**1559** Henri II killed in a Paris tournament	**1589** Henri IV completes Pont-Neuf and improves capital's water supply	*The assassin Ravaillac*

The Sun King's Paris

The 17th century in France, which became known as *Le Grand Siècle* (the great century), is epitomized by the glittering extravagance of Louis XIV (the Sun King) and his court at Versailles. In Paris, imposing buildings, squares, theatres and aristocratic **Emblem of the Sun King** *hôtels* (mansions) were built. Beneath this brilliant surface lay the absolute power of the monarch. By the end of Louis' reign the cost of his extravagance and of waging almost continuous war with France's neighbours led to a decline in the monarchy.

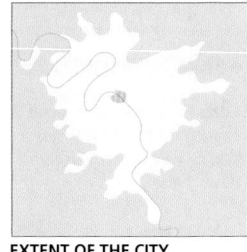

EXTENT OF THE CITY

▨ *1657*   ☐ *Today*

The mansard roof, with its slopes at both sides and both ends, came to typify French roofs of this period.

An open staircase rose from the internal courtyard.

Cross section of the living quarters

The Gardens of Versailles
Louis XIV devoted a lot of time to the gardens, which were designed by André Le Nôtre.

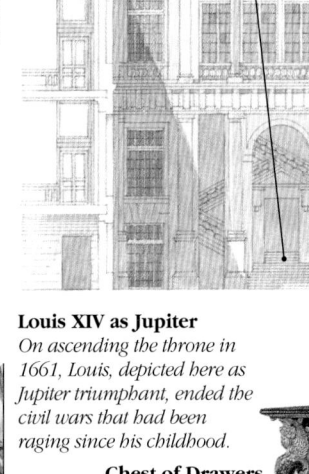

Louis XIV as Jupiter
On ascending the throne in 1661, Louis, depicted here as Jupiter triumphant, ended the civil wars that had been raging since his childhood.

The ground floor contained the servants' quarters.

Chest of Drawers
This gilded piece was made by André-Charles Boulle for the Grand Trianon at Versailles.

TIMELINE

1610 Louis XIII's accession marks the start of *Le Grand Siècle*	*Louis XIII*	**1624** Completion of Tuileries Palace	*Cardinal Mazarin* **1631** Launch of *La Gazette*, Paris's first newspaper	**1643** Death of Louis XIII. Regency under control of Marie de Médicis and Cardinal Mazarin	**1661** Louis XIV becomes absolute monarch. Enlargement of Château de Versailles begun
1610	**1620**	**1630**	**1640**	**1650**	**166**
1614 Final meeting of the Estates Council (the main legislative assembly) before the Revolution	**1622** Paris becomes an episcopal see	**1629** Richelieu, Louis XIII's first minister, builds Palais Royal **1627** Development of the Ile St-Louis	**1638** Birth of Louis XIV		**1662** Colbert, Louis XIV's finance minister, founds Gobelins tapestry works *Weaving frame*

Ceiling by Charles Le Brun
Court painter to Louis XIV, Le Brun decorated many ceilings like this one at the Hôtel Carnavalet (see p96).

Madame de Maintenon
When the queen died in 1683, Louis married Madame de Maintenon, shown here in a framed painting by Caspar Netscher.

Decorated Fan
For special court fêtes, Louis XIV often stipulated that women carry fans.

The Galerie d'Hercule with Le Brun ceiling

Formal Classical Garden

Dôme Church (1706)

HOTEL LAMBERT (1640)
In the 17th century, the aristocracy built luxurious town houses with grand staircases, courtyards, formal gardens, coach houses and stables.

Neptune Cup
Made from lapis lazuli with a silver Neptune on top, this cup was part of Louis' vast collection of art objects.

WHERE TO SEE THE SUN KING'S PARIS

Many 17th-century mansions such as the Hôtel Lambert still exist in Paris, but not all are open to the public. However, Hôtel des Invalides (*p187*), the Dôme Church (*pp188–9*), the Palais du Luxembourg (*p172*) and Versailles (*pp248–53*) give a magnificent impression of the period.

1667 Louvre built and observatory established

1682 Court moves to Versailles where it stays until the Revolution

1686 Le Procope, Paris's first café

1702 Paris first divided into 20 arrondissements (districts)

1715 Louis XIV dies

1670	1680	1690	1700	1710	

1692 Great famines due to bad harvests and wars

1670 Hôtel des Invalides built

1689 Pont Royal built

Statue of Louis XIV at Musée Carnavalet

Paris in the Age of Enlightenment

The Enlightenment, with its emphasis on scientific reason and a critical approach to existing ideas and society, was centred on the city of Paris. In contrast, nepotism and corruption were rife at Louis XV's court at Versailles. Meanwhile the economy thrived, the arts flourished as never before and intellectuals, such as Voltaire and Rousseau, were renowned throughout

Bust of François Marie Arouet, known as Voltaire

Europe. In Paris, the population rose to about 650,000: town planning was developed, and the first accurate street map of the city appeared in 1787.

EXTENT OF THE CITY

☐ 1720   ☐ Today

Nautical Instruments

As the science of navigation advanced, scientists developed telescopes and trigonometric instruments (used for measuring longitude and latitude).

18th-Century Wigs
These were not only a mark of fashion but also a way of indicating the wearer's class and importance.

COMEDIE FRANÇAISE
The Age of Enlightenment saw a burst of dramatic activity, and new theatres opened. Among them was the Comédie Française (see p120), still one of the most prestigious theatres in the world.

The auditorium, with 1,913 seats, was the largest in Paris.

TIMELINE

Fireman

1734 Fontaine des Quatre Saisons built

1748 Montesquieu's *L'Esprit des Lois* (an influential work about different forms of government) published

1720	1730	1740	1750

1722 City's first fire brigade founded

1751 First volume of Diderot's *Encyclopedia* published

Madame de Pompadour
Although generally remembered as the mistress of Louis XV, she was renowned as a patron of the arts and had great political influence.

Chocolate Pot
By the 18th century, bourgeois families could afford tobacco, tea, chocolate and coffee from Asia and the New World.

Vestibule with painted ceiling

Portico with Doric columns

The Catacombs
These were set up in 1785 as a more hygienic alternative to Paris's cemeteries (see p179).

WHERE TO SEE ENLIGHTENMENT PARIS

The district around the Rue de Lille, the Rue de Varenne and the Rue de Grenelle *(p187)* has many luxurious town houses, or *hôtels*, which were built by the aristocracy during the first half of the 18th century. Memorabilia from the lives of the great intellectuals Voltaire and Jean-Jacques Rousseau is in the Musée Carnavalet *(pp96–7)*, along with 18th-century interior designs and paintings.

Churches were built throughout the Enlightenment. St-Sulpice *(p172)* was completed in 1776.

Le Procope *(p140)* is the oldest café in Paris. It was frequented by Voltaire and Rousseau.

1757 First oil street lamps

1760 Place de la Concorde, Panthéon and Ecole Militaire built

1760

1762 Rousseau's *Emile* and the *Social Contract*

1764 Madame de Pompadour dies

1770

Rousseau, philosopher and writer, believed that humans were naturally good and had been corrupted by society.

1774 Louis XV, great grandson of Louis XIV, dies

1778 France supports American independence

1780

1782 First pavements built, in the Place du Théâtre Français

1783 Montgolfier brothers make the first hot-air balloon ascent

1785 David paints the *Oath of the Horatii*

Paris During the Revolution

A plate made in celebration of the Revolution

In 1789 most Parisians were still living in squalor and poverty, as they had since the Middle Ages. Rising inflation and opposition to Louis XVI culminated in the storming of the Bastille, the king's prison; the Republic was founded three years later. However, the Terror soon followed, when those suspected of betraying the Revolution were executed without trial: more than 60,000 people lost their lives. The bloody excesses of Robespierre, the zealous revolutionary, led to his overthrow and a new government, the Directory, was set up in 1795.

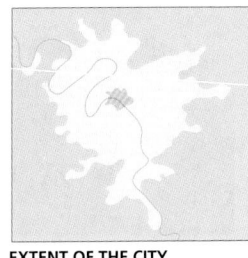

EXTENT OF THE CITY

▨ 1796	☐ Today

The prison turrets were set alight.

The French guards, who were on the side of the revolutionaries, arrived late in the afternoon with two cannons.

Declaration of the Rights of Man and the Citizen

The Enlightenment ideals of equality and human dignity were enshrined in the Declaration. This illustration is the preface to the 1791 Constitution.

Drawbridge

REPUBLICAN CALENDAR

The revolutionaries believed that the world was starting again, so they abolished the existing church calendar and took 22 September 1792, the day the Republic was declared, as the first day of the new era. The Republican calendar had 12 equal months, each subdivided into three ten-day periods, with the remaining five days of each year set aside for public holidays. All the months of the year were given poetic names which linked them to nature and the seasons, such as fog, snow, seed-time, flowers and harvest.

A coloured engraving by Tresca showing *Ventôse*, the windy month (19 Feb–20 Mar) from the new Republican calendar

TIMELINE

14 Jul Fall of the Bastille	**4 Aug** Abolition of feudalism			**10 Aug** The storming of the Tuileries
	26 Aug Declaration of the Rights of Man and the Citizen			
	17 Sep Law of Suspects passed: the Terror begins			
1789	**1790**	**1791**		**1792**

Cartoon on the three Estates: the clergy, the nobility and the awakening populace

Lafayette, Commander of the National Guard, takes his oath to the Constitution

17 Jul Champ de Mars massacre

25 A *La Marseilla* compos

5 May The Estates council meets

14 Jul Fête de la Fédération

Paper Money
Bonds, called assignats, *were used to fund the Revolution from 1790–93.*

La Marseillaise
The revolutionaries' marching song is now the national anthem.

The Sans Culottes
By 1792, the wearing of trousers instead of breeches (culottes) was a political symbol of Paris's artisans and shopkeepers.

"Patriotic" Chair
The back of this wooden chair is topped by red bonnets, symbol of revolutionary politics.

Wallpaper
Commemorative wallpaper was produced to celebrate the Revolution.

The dead and wounded totalled 171 by the end of the day.

Coin tower

Great court

Well court

Guillotine
This was used for the first time in France in April 1792.

STORMING OF THE BASTILLE
The Bastille was overrun on 14 July 1789 and the seven prisoners held there released. The defenders (32 Swiss guards, 82 wounded soldiers and the governor) were massacred.

...n Invasion ...e Tuileries **10 Aug** ...Overthrow ...of Louis XVI	**21 Jan** Execution of Louis XVI **Autumn** Robespierre in control of Committee of Public Safety	**16 Oct** Execution of Marie-Antoinette **24 Nov** Churches closed	**5 Apr** Execution of Danton and supporters **19 Nov** Jacobin Club (a revolutionary pressure group) closed	**22 Aug** New constitution: the Directory

1793	1794	1795

20 Sep Battle of Valmy **2–6 Sep** September massacres	**13 Jul** Assassination of Marat, founder of *L'Ami du Peuple,* the revolutionary newspaper	*Robespierre, revolutionary and architect of the Terror* **27 Jul** Execution of Robespierre

Napoleonic Paris

Napoleon Bonaparte was the most brilliant general in the French army. The instability of the new government after the Revolution gave him the chance to seize power, and in November 1799 he installed himself in the Tuileries Palace as First Consul. He crowned himself Emperor in May 1804. Napoleon established a

Napoleon's imperial crown

centralized administration and a code of laws, reformed France's educational system and set out to make Paris the most beautiful city in the world. The city was endowed with grand monuments and embellished with the spoils of conquest. His power was always fragile and dependent on incessant wars. In March 1814 Prussian, Austrian and Russian armies invaded Paris and Napoleon fled to Elba. He returned to Paris in 1815 but was defeated at Waterloo and died in exile in 1821.

EXTENT OF THE CITY

▨ 1810	☐ Today

Château de Malmaison
This was the favourite home of Josephine, Napoleon's first wife.

Ladies-in-Waiting hold Josephine's train.

Opaline-Glass Clock
The decoration on this clock echoed the fashion for draperies.

Elephant Project
This monument was planned for the centre of the Place de la Bastille.

Eagle's Flight
Napoleon's flight to Elba in 1814 was satirized in this cartoon.

TIMELINE

1799 Napoleon seizes power	**1800** Banque de France founded		**1812** Russian campaign ends in defeat	**1815** Waterloo; second abdication of Napoleon. Restoration of the monarchy
1797 Battle of Rivoli	**1802** Legion of Honour established			
1800	**1805**	**1810**	**1815**	**1820**
	1804 Napoleon crowned	**1806** Arc de Triomphe commissioned	**1814** Napoleon abdicates	**1821** Napoleon dies
1800 Napoleon returns from Egypt on his ship *L'Orient*			**1809** Napoleon divorces Josephine and marries Marie-Louise	*Napoleon's death mask*

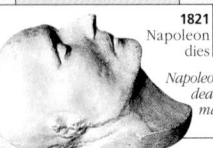

Bronze Table Top
Inlaid with Napoleon's portrait, this table marks the victory at Austerlitz.

Russian Cossacks in the Palais Royal
After Napoleon's defeat and flight in 1814, Paris suffered the humiliation of being occupied by foreign troops, including Austrians, Prussians and Russians.

Josephine kneels before Napoleon.

Napoleon holds the crown for his Empress, Josephine.

The Pope makes the sign of the cross.

The Arc de Triomphe du Carrousel was erected in 1806 and crowned with the horses looted from St Mark's, Venice.

WHERE TO SEE NAPOLEONIC PARIS

Many of the grand monuments Napoleon planned for Paris were never built, but two triumphal arches, the Arc de Triomphe (pp210–11) and Arc de Triomphe du Carrousel (p122), were a major part of his legacy. La Madeleine church (p216) was also inaugurated in his reign and much of the Louvre was rebuilt (pp122–3). Examples of the Empire style can be seen at Malmaison (p255) and at the Carnavalet (pp96–7).

NAPOLEON'S CORONATION
Napoleon's rather dramatic crowning took place in 1804. In this recreation by J L David, the Pope, summoned to Notre-Dame, looks on as Napoleon crowns his Empress just before crowning himself.

The Empress
Josephine was divorced by Napoleon in 1809.

1842 First railway line between Paris and St-Germain-en-Laye opens

1825	1830	1835	1840	1845

1830 Revolution in Paris and advent of constitutional monarchy

1831 Victor Hugo's *Notre-Dame de Paris* published. Cholera epidemic hits Paris

1840 Reburial of Napoleon at Les Invalides

Napoleon's tomb

The Grand Transformation

In 1848 Paris saw a second revolution which brought down the recently restored monarchy. In the uncertainties that followed, Napoleon's nephew assumed power in the same way as his uncle before him – by a *coup d'état*. He proclaimed himself Napoleon III in 1851. Under his rule Paris was transformed into the most magnificent city in Europe. He entrusted the task of modernization to Baron Haussmann. Haussmann demolished the crowded, unsanitary streets of the medieval city and created a well-ordered capital within a geometrical grid of avenues and boulevards. Neighbouring districts such as Auteuil were annexed, creating the suburbs.

Lamppost outside the Opéra

EXTENT OF THE CITY

▨	1859	☐	Today

Arc de Triomphe

Boulevard des Italiens
This tree-lined avenue, painted by Edmond Georges Grandjean (1889), was one of the most fashionable of the new boulevards.

Twelve avenues
formed a star (*étoile*).

AVE DE FRIED.

AVE HOCHE

AVE DE WAGRAM

AVE MAC – MAHON

AVE CARNOT

PLA

Laying the Sewers
This engraving from 1861 shows the early work for laying the sewer system (see p190) from La Villette to Les Halles. Most was the work of the engineer Belgrand.

Circular Hoarding
Distinctive hoardings advertised opera and theatre performances.

Grand mansions
were built around the Arc de Triomphe between 1860 and 1868.

TIMELINE

1851 Napoleon III declares the Second Empire

1852 Haussmann begins massive town-planning schemes

Viewing the exhibits at the World Exhibition

1855 World Exhibition

1850	1852	1854	1856	1858

20 centimes stamp showing Napoleon III

1857 The poet, Baudelaire, prosecuted for obscenity for *The Flowers of Evil*

PLACE DE L'ETOILE

The new scheme for the centre of Paris included redesigning the area at one end of the Champs-Elysées (Elysian Fields). Haussmann created a star of 12 broad avenues around the new Arc de Triomphe. (The inset map shows the area as it was in 1790.)

Fields

Avenue des Champs-Elysées

Site of Arc de Triomphe

Drinking Fountain

In 1840, fifty fountains were erected in poor areas of Paris through the generosity of the English francophile, Richard Wallace.

Bois de Boulogne
Given to the city in 1852 by Napoleon III, this park became a popular place for walking and riding (see pp254–5).

BARON HAUSSMANN

Lawyer by training and civil servant by profession, Georges-Eugène Haussmann (1809–91) was appointed Prefect of the Seine by Napoleon III. For 17 years he was in charge of urban planning. With the best architects and engineers of the day, he planned a new city, improved the water supply and sewerage, and created beautiful parks.

Some avenues were named after French generals.

1861 Garnier designs new Opera House	**1863** The nudity in Manet's *Le Déjeuner sur l'Herbe* causes a scandal and is rejected by the Academy *(see pp144–5)*		**1867** World Exhibition		**1870** Napoleon's wife, Eugénie, flees Paris at threat of war
1862	**1864**		**1866**	**1868**	
	1863 Credit Lyonnais bank established				
1862 Victor Hugo's epic novel of Paris's poor, *Les Misérables*, published			**1868** Press censorship relaxed	**1870** Start of Franco-Prussian War	

The Belle Epoque

Art Nouveau pendant

The Franco-Prussian War culminated in the terrible Siege of Paris. When peace came in 1871, it fell to the new government, the Third Republic, to bring about economic recovery. From about 1890 life was transformed: the motor-car, aeroplane, cinema, telephone and gramophone all contributed to the enjoyment of life and the *Belle Epoque* (beautiful age) was born. Paris became a glittering city where the new style, *Art Nouveau*, decorated buildings and objects. The paintings of the Impressionists, such as Renoir, reflected the *joie de vivre* of the times, while later those of Matisse, Braque and Picasso heralded the modern movement in art.

EXTENT OF THE CITY

▨ 1895   ☐ Today

The interior was arranged as tiers of galleries around a central grand staircase.

Cabaret Poster
Toulouse-Lautrec's posters immortalized the singers and dancers of the cafés and cabaret clubs of Montmartre, where artists and writers congregated in the 1890s.

Electricity illuminated the window displays.

Windows facing on to the Boulevard Haussmann displayed the goods on offer.

Art Nouveau Cash Till
Even ordinary objects like this cash till were beautified by the new style.

Central Hall of the Grand Palais
The Grand Palais (p208) was built to house two huge exhibitions of French painting and sculpture at the World Exhibition of 1889.

TIMELINE

1871 Third Republic established	**1874** Monet paints first Impressionist picture: *Impression: Soleil levant*	*Louis Pasteur*	**1889** Eiffel Tower built	
1870	**1875**	**1880**	**1885**	**1890**

Zoo animals were shot to feed the hungry (see p226)

1870 Siege of Paris

1885 Louis Pasteur discovers rabies vaccine

Entrance ticket to the exhibition

TICKET D'ENTRÉE

1891 First metro station opens

1889 Great Exhibition

Citroën 5CV
France led the world in the early development of the motor-car. By 1900 the Citroën began to be seen on the streets of Paris, and long-distance motor racing was popular.

The glass dome could be seen from all parts of the store.

Moulin Rouge (1890)
The old, redundant windmills of Montmartre became nightclubs, like the world-famous Moulin Rouge (red windmill) (see p228).

WHERE TO SEE THE BELLE EPOQUE

Art Nouveau can be seen in monumental buildings like the Grand Palais and Petit Palais (p208), while the Galeries Lafayette (p321) and the Pharamond restaurant (p303) have beautiful Belle Epoque interiors. The Musée d'Orsay (pp144–7) has many objects from this period.

The entrance to the metro at Porte Dauphine was the work of leading Art Nouveau designer Hector Guimard (p226).

GALERIES LAFAYETTE (1906)
This beautiful department store, with its dome a riot of coloured glass and wrought ironwork, was a sign of the new prosperity.

The Naughty Nineties
The Lumière brothers captured the daring negligée fashions of the 1890s in the first moving images of the cinematograph.

The doorway of No. 29 Avenue Rapp (p191), in the Eiffel Tower quarter, is a fine example of Art Nouveau.

Captain Dreyfus was publicly humiliated for selling secrets to the Prussians. He was later found innocent.

1894–1906 Dreyfus affair

1907 Picasso paints *Les Demoiselles d'Avignon*

1913 Proust publishes first volume of *Remembrance of Things Past*

1895	1900	1905	1910

1898 Pierre and Marie Curie discover radium

1909 Blériot flies across the English Channel

1911 Diaghilev brings the Russian ballet to Paris

1895 Lumière brothers introduce cinematography

Avant-Garde Paris

Office chair by Le Corbusier

From the 1920s to the 1940s, Paris became a mecca for artists, musicians, writers and film-makers. The city was alive with new movements such as Cubism and Surrealism represented by Cézanne, Picasso, Braque, Man Ray and Duchamp. Many new trends came from the USA, as writers and musicians including Ernest Hemingway, Gertrude Stein and Sidney Bechet took up residence in Paris. In architecture, the geometric shapes created by Le Corbusier changed the face of the modern building.

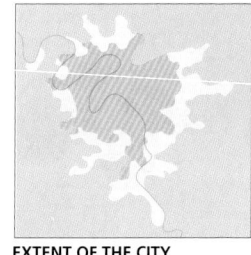

EXTENT OF THE CITY

| 1940 | Today |

Napoleon by Abel Gance
Paris has always been a city for film-makers. In 1927 Abel Gance made an innovative movie about Napoleon, using triple screens and wide-angle lenses.

Occupied Paris
Paris was under occupation for most of World War II. The Eiffel Tower was a favourite spot for German soldiers.

Josephine Baker
Arriving in Paris in 1925, the outlandish dancer catapulted to fame in "La Revue Nègre" wearing nothing but feathers.

Stilts supported the concrete shell.

Living space was made into a picture gallery.

LA ROCHE VILLA BY LE CORBUSIER
Made from concrete and steel, with straight lines, horizontal windows and a flat roof, this house (1923) epitomized the new style.

Sidney Bechet
In the 1930s and 1940s the jazz clubs of Paris resounded to the swing music of black musicians such as the saxophonist Sidney Bechet.

TIMELINE

1919 Treaty of Versailles signed in the Hall of Mirrors

1924 Olympic Games held in Paris

1924 André Breton publishes Surrealist Manifesto

1925 Art Deco style first seen at the Exposition des Arts Décoratifs

1914	1916	1918	1920	1922	1924	1926

1914–18 World War I. Paris is under threat of German attack, saved by the Battle of the Marne. A shell hits St-Gervais–St-Protais.

World War I soldier in uniform

1920 Interment of the Unknown Soldier

An eternal flame for the Unknown Soldier burns under the Arc de Triomphe

Fashion in the 1940s
After World War II, the classic look for men and women was reminiscent of military uniforms.

The roof was designed as a garden terrace.

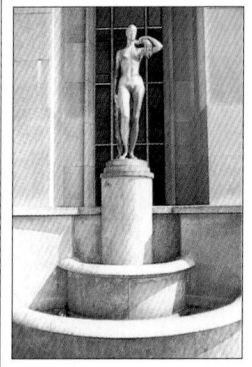

The old Trocadéro was changed to the Palais de Chaillot *(see p200)* for the World Exhibition.

WHERE TO SEE AVANT-GARDE PARIS

La Roche Villa is now part of the Fondation Le Corbusier *(p254)* and can be visited in the Paris suburb of Auteuil. Hemingway's haunt, the bar-brasserie La Closerie des Lilas in Montparnasse *(p179)*, has retained much of its period decor. For fashion don't miss the Musée Galliera *(p203)*.

Airmail Poster
Airmail routes developed during the 1930s, especially to French North Africa.

The bedroom was above the dining room.

The kitchen was built at the back with a sloping glass roof.

The garage was built into the ground floor.

Windows were arranged in a horizontal strip.

Claudine in Paris by Colette
The Claudine series of novels, written by Colette Willy, known simply as "Colette", were extremely popular in the 1930s.

1931 Colonial Exhibition

A visitor to the exhibition in colonial dress

1937 Picasso paints Guernica in protest at the Spanish Civil War

1940 World War II: Paris bombed and occupied by Nazis

| 1930 | 1932 | 1934 | 1936 | 1938 | 1940 | 1942 |

1934 Riots and strikes in response to the Depression

1937 Palais de Chaillot built

Symbol of Free French super-imposed on the victory sign

Aug 1944 Liberation of Paris

The Modern City

In 1962 a programme of renovation was started in Paris, with run-down districts like the Marais being restored. This work was continued by François Mitterrand's *Grand Travaux* (great works) scheme. Access was improved to historical monuments and art collections, such as the Grand Louvre *(see pp122–9)* and the Musée d'Orsay *(pp144–7)*. The scheme was responsible for several monuments to the modern age, including the Opéra National de Paris Bastille *(p98)*, the Cité des Sciences *(pp236–9)* and the Bibliothèque Nationale at Quai de la Gare *(p246)*. With these, and the boldly modern Défense, Grande Arche and Stade de France, Paris prepared herself for the 21st century.

Late President, François Mitterrand

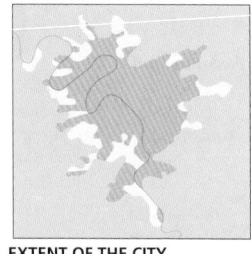

EXTENT OF THE CITY

1959	Today

Christo's Pont Neuf
To create a work of art, the Bulgarian-born artist Christo wrapped Paris's oldest bridge, the Pont Neuf, in fabric in 1985.

La Grande Arche is taller and wider than Notre-Dame and runs in an axis linking the Arc de Triomphe and the Louvre Pyramid.

Simone de Beauvoir
Influential philosopher and life-long companion of J-P Sartre, de Beauvoir fought for the liberation of women in the 1950s.

Shopping centre

Citroën Goddess (1956)
With its ultra-modern lines, this became Paris's most prestigious car.

TIMELINE

1945	1950	1955	1960	1965	1970	1975

1950 Construction of UNESCO, and the Musée de Radio-France

1962 André Malraux, Minister of Culture, begins renovation programme of run-down districts and monuments

Ducting at the Pompidou Centre

1977 Pompidou Centre opens. Jacques Chirac is installed as first elected Mayor of Paris since 1871

1958 Establishment of Fifth Republic with de Gaulle as President

1964 Reorganization of the Ile de France

1968 Student riots and workers strikes in the Latin Quarter

1969 Les Halles market transfers to Rungis

1973 Construction of Montparnasse Tower and the Périphérique (ring road)

President de Gaulle

Marne La Vallée
Like a gigantic loud speaker, this residential complex is in one of Paris's dormitory towns near Disneyland Resort Paris.

Chanel Designs
Paris is the centre of the fashion world with important shows each year.

The Pompidou Centre
The nation's collection of modern art is housed here in this popular building (see pp110–13).

The Fiat Tower is one of Europe's tallest buildings.

Opéra National de Paris Bastille (1989)
It marks the bicentenary of the fall of the Bastille.

STUDENTS AT THE BARRICADES

In May 1968 Paris saw a revolution of a kind. The Latin Quarter was taken over by students and workers. What began as a protest against the war in Vietnam spread to other issues and became an expression of discontent with the Government. President de Gaulle rode out the storm but his prestige was severely damaged.

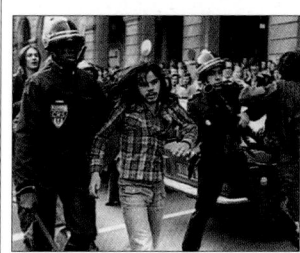

Rioting students clash with police

The Défense Palace, housing the centre for industry, is the oldest tower.

LA DEFENSE
This huge business centre was started on the edge of Paris in 1958. Today 30,000 people commute here from Paris's surrounding areas.

1985 Christo wraps Pont Neuf

Participant of the bi-centenary wearing the French national colours

Victorious French football team holding aloft the World Cup trophy in Paris

80	1985	1990	1995	2000	2005	2010

30 Thousands et Pope John-al on his cial visit

1994 Eurostar inaugurated: Paris to London in 3 hrs

1989 Bicentenary celebrations to mark the French Revolution

1998 France hosts – and wins – the 1998 football World Cup tournament

1999 December hurricanes hit Paris: Versailles loses 10,000 trees

2002 The Euro replaces the Franc as exclusive legal tender

PARIS AT A GLANCE

There are nearly 300 places of interest described in the *Area by Area* section of this book. A broad range of sights is covered: from the ancient Conciergerie and its grisly associations with the guillotine *(see p81)*, to the modern opera house, the Opéra de la Bastille *(see p98)*; from No. 51 Rue de Montmorency *(see p114)*, the oldest houses in Paris, to the elegant Musée Picasso *(see pp100–1)*. To help make the most of your stay, the following 20 pages are a time-saving guide to the best Paris has to offer. Museums and galleries, historic churches, spacious parks, gardens and squares all have a section. There are also guides to Paris's famous personalities. Each sight has a cross reference to its own full entry. Below are the top tourist attractions to start you off.

PARIS'S TOP TOURIST ATTRACTIONS

La Défense
See p255.

Sainte-Chapelle
See pp88–9.

Palace of Versailles
See pp248–53.

Pompidou Centre
See pp110–13.

Musée d'Orsay
See pp144–7.

Musée du Louvre
See pp122–9.

Jardin du Luxembourg
See p172.

Eiffel Tower
See pp194–5.

Bois de Boulogne
See pp254–5.

Notre-Dame
See pp82–5.

Arc de Triomphe
See pp210–11.

◁ The Dôme Church, adjoining the Hôtel des Invalides

Remarkable Parisians

By virtue of its strategic position on the Seine, Paris has always been the economic, political and artistic hub of France. Over the centuries, many prominent and influential figures from other parts of the country and abroad have come to the city to absorb her unique spirit. In return they have left their mark: artists have brought new movements, politicians new schools of thought, musicians and film-makers new trends, and architects a new environment.

Actress Catherine Deneuve

ARTISTS

Sacré-Coeur by Utrillo (1934)

In the early 18th-century, Jean-Antoine Watteau (1684–1721) took the inspiration for his paintings from the Paris theatre. Half a century later, Jean-Honoré Fragonard (1732–1806), popular painter of the Rococo, lived and died here, financially ruined by the Revolution. Later, Paris became the cradle of Impressionism. Its founders Claude Monet (1840–1926), Pierre-Auguste Renoir (1841–1919) and Alfred Sisley (1839–99) met in a Paris studio. In 1907, Pablo Picasso

(1881–1973) painted the seminal work *Les Demoiselles d'Avignon* at the Bateau-Lavoir, *(see p228)* where Georges Braque (1882–1963), Amedeo Modigliani (1884–1920) and Marc Chagall (1887–1985) also lived. Henri de Toulouse-Lautrec (1864–1901) drank and painted in Montmartre. So did Salvador Dalí (1904–89) who frequented the Café Cyrano, centre of the Surrealists. The Paris School eventually moved to Montparnasse, home to sculptors Auguste Rodin (1840–1917), Constantin Brancusi (1876–1957) and Ossip Zadkine (1890–1967).

POLITICAL LEADERS

Hugh Capet, Count of Paris, became King of France in 987. His palace was on the Ile de la Cité. Louis XIV, XV and XVI lived at Versailles *(see pp248–53)* but Napoleon *(see pp32–3)* preferred the Tuileries. Cardinal Richelieu (1585–1642), the power behind Louis XIII, created the Académie Française and the Palais-Royal *(see p120)*. Today the President lives in the Palais de l'Elysée *(p209)*.

FILMS AND FILM-MAKERS

Paris has always been at the heart of French cinema. The prewar and immediate post-war classics were usually made on the sets of the Boulogne and Joinville studios, where whole areas of the city were reconstructed, such as the Canal St-Martin for Marcel Carné's *Hôtel du Nord*. Jean-Luc Godard and other New Wave directors preferred to shoot outdoors. Godard's *A Bout de Souffle* (1960) with Jean-Paul Belmondo and Jean Seberg was filmed in and around the Champs-Elysées.

Simone Signoret (1921– 1985) and Yves Montand (1921–1991), the most celebrated couple of French cinema, were long associated with the Ile de la Cité. Actresses, such as Catherine Deneuve (b.1943) and Isabelle Adjani (b.1955), live in the city to be near their couturiers.

MUSICIANS

Jean-Philippe Rameau (1683–1764), organist and pioneer of harmony, is associated with St-Eustache *(see p114)*. Hector Berlioz (1803–69) had his *Te Deum* first performed there in 1855, and Franz Liszt (1811–86) his *Messe Solemnelle* in 1866. A great dynasty of organists, the Couperins, gave recitals in St-Gervais–St-Protais *(see p99)*.

The stage of the Opéra *(see p217)* has seen many talents, but audiences have not always been appreciative. Richard Wagner (1813–83) had his *Tannhäuser* hooted down. George Bizet's *Carmen*

Portrait of Cardinal Richelieu by Philippe de Champaigne (about 1635)

(1838–75) was booed, as was *Peléas et Mélisande* by Claude Debussy (1862–1918).

Soprano Maria Callas (1923–77) gave triumphal performances here. The composer and conductor Pierre Boulez (b.1925) has devoted his talent to experimental music at IRCAM near the Pompidou Centre *(see p346)*, which he helped to found.

The diminutive *chanteuse* Edith Piaf (1915–63), known for her nostalgic love-songs, began singing in the streets of Paris and then went on to tour the world. There is now a museum devoted to her life and work *(see pp234–5)*.

The Grand Trianon at Versailles, built by Louis Le Vau in 1668

Sainte-Chapelle. Louis Le Vau (1612–70) and Jules Hardouin-Mansart (1646–1708) designed Versailles *(see pp248–53)*. Jacques-Ange Gabriel (1698–1782) built the Petit Trianon *(see p249)* and Place de la Concorde *(see p131)*. Haussmann (1809–91) gave the city its boulevards *(see pp34–5)*. Gustave Eiffel (1832–1923) built his tower in 1889. A century later, I M Pei added the Louvre's glass pyramid *(see p129)*, Jean Nouvel created the Institut du Monde Arabe *(see p164)* and Dominique Perrault the new Bibliothèque Nationale de France *(see p246)*. The 21st century already has several new landmarks underway.

Renée Jeanmaire as Carmen (1948)

ARCHITECTS

Gothic, Classical, Baroque and Modernist – all co-exist in Paris. The most brilliant medieval architect was Pierre de Montreuil, who built Notre-Dame and

WRITERS

French has been dubbed "the language of Molière", after playwright Jean-Baptiste Poquelin, alias Molière, (1622–73), who helped create the Comédie-Française, now situated near his home in Rue Richelieu. On the Left Bank, the Odéon Théâtre de l'Europe was home to playwright Jean Racine (1639–99). It is near the statue of Denis Diderot (1713–84), who published his

L'Encyclopédie between 1751 and 1776. Marcel Proust (1871–1922), author of the 13-volume *Remembrance of Things Past*, lived on the Boulevard Haussmann. To the existentialists, the district of St-Germain was the only place to be *(see pp142–3)*. Here Sylvia Beach welcomed James Joyce (1882–1941) to her bookshop on the Rue de l'Odéon. Ernest Hemingway (1899–1961) and F Scott Fitzgerald (1896–1940) wrote novels in Montparnasse.

Proust by J-E Blanche (about 1910)

SCIENTISTS

Paris has a Quartier Pasteur, a Boulevard Pasteur, a Pasteur metro and the world-famous Institut Pasteur *(see p247)*, all in honour of Louis Pasteur (1822–95), the great French chemist and biologist. His apartment and laboratory are faithfully preserved. The Institut Pasteur is today home to Professor Luc Montagnier, who first isolated the AIDS virus in 1983. Discoverers of radium, Pierre (1859–1906) and Marie Curie (1867–1934), also worked in Paris. The Curies have been the subject of a long-running play in Paris, *Les Palmes de M. Schutz*.

EXILED IN PARIS

The Duke and Duchess of Windsor married in France after his abdication in 1936 as King Edward VIII. The city granted them a rent-free mansion in the Bois de Boulogne. Other famous exiles have included Chou En-Lai (1898–1976), Ho Chi Minh (1890–1969), Vladimir Ilyich Lenin (1870–1924), Oscar Wilde (1854–1900) and ballet dancer Rudolf Nureyev (1938–93).

The Duke and Duchess of Windsor

Paris's Best: Churches

The Catholic Church has been the bastion of Parisian society through time. Many of the city's churches are worth visiting. Architectural styles vary and the interiors are often spectacular. Most churches are open during the day and many have services at regular intervals. Paris's tradition of church music is still alive. You can spend an evening enjoying the interiors while listening to an organ recital or classical concert *(see p346).* A more detailed overview of Paris churches is on pages 48–9.

Early crucifix in St-Gervais-St-Protais

La Madeleine
Built in the style of a Greco-Roman temple, this church is known for its fine sculptures.

Chaillot Quarter

Champs-Elysées

Tuileries Qu

Invalides and Eiffel Tower Quarter

St-Germ des-I

Dôme Church
This memorial to the military engineer Vauban lies in the Dôme Church, where Napoleon's remains were buried in 1840.

Montparnasse

Sainte-Chapelle
With its fine stained glass, this chapel is a medieval jewel.

Panthéon
The Neo-Classical Sainte-Geneviève, now the Panthéon, was inspired by Wren's St Paul's Cathedral in London.

0 kilometres

0 miles   0.5

Montmartre

Sacré-Coeur
Above the altar in this massive basilica, the chancel vault is decorated with a vast mosaic of Christ by Luc-Olivier Merson.

St-Eustache
With its mixture of Gothic and Renaissance styles, this is one of the finest churches in Paris.

St-Paul–St-Louis
This Christ figure is one of the many rich furnishings in this Jesuit church, built in 1641 for Cardinal Richelieu.

Beaubourg and Les Halles

The Marais

Ile de la Cité

Ile St-Louis

Latin Quarter

Notre-Dame
The great cathedral was left to rot after the Revolution, until Victor Hugo led a restoration campaign.

Luxembourg Quarter

Jardin des Plantes Quarter

St-Séverin
The west door leads to one of the finest medieval churches in the city.

Mosquée de Paris
The minaret of this 1920s mosque is 33 m (100 ft) tall.

Exploring Paris's Churches

Some of Paris's finest architecture is reflected in the churches. The great era of church building was the medieval period but examples survive from all ages. During the Revolution *(see pp30–31)* churches were used as grain or weapons stores but were later restored to their former glory. Many churches have superb interiors with fine paintings and sculptures.

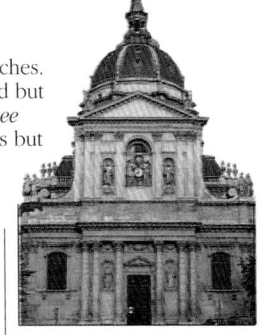

Facade of Eglise de la Sorbonne

MEDIEVAL

Tower of St-Germain-des-Prés

Both the pointed arch and the rose window were born in a suburb north of Paris at the Basilica of St-Denis, where most of the French kings and queens are buried. This was the first Gothic building, and it was from here that the Gothic style spread. The finest Gothic church in Paris is the city cathedral, **Notre-Dame**, tallest and most impressive of the early French cathedrals. Begun in 1163 by Bishop Maurice de Sully, it was completed in the next century by architects Jean de Chelles and Pierre de

Montreuil, who added the transepts with their fine translucent rose windows. Montreuil's masterpiece is Louis IX's medieval palace chapel, **Sainte-Chapelle**, with its two-tier structure. It was built to house Christ's Crown of Thorns. Other surviving churches in Paris are **St-Germain-des-Prés**, the oldest surviving abbey church in Paris (1050); the tiny, rustic Romanesque **St-Julien-le-Pauvre**; and the Flamboyant Gothic **St-Séverin**, **St-Germain l'Auxerrois** and **St-Merry**.

RENAISSANCE

The effect of the Italian Renaissance swept through Paris in the 16th century. It led to a unique architectural style in which fine Classical detail and immense Gothic proportions resulted in an impure, but attractive, cocktail known as "French Renaissance". The best example in Paris is **St-Etienne-du-Mont**, whose interior has the feel of a wide and light basilica. Another is **St-Eustache**, the massive market church in Les Halles, and the nave of **St-Gervais–St-Protais** with its stained glass and carved choir stalls.

St-Gervais–St-Protais

BAROQUE AND CLASSICAL

Churches and convents flourished in Paris during the 17th century, as the city expanded under Louis XIII and his son Louis XIV. The Italian Baroque style was first seen on the majestic front of **St-Gervais–St-Protais**, built by Salomon de Brosse in 1616. The style was toned down to suit French tastes and the rational temperament of the Age of Enlightenment *(see pp28–9)*. The result was a harmonious and monumental Classicism in the form of columns and domes. One example is the **Eglise de la Sorbonne**, completed by Jacques Lemercier in 1642 for Cardinal Richelieu. Grander and more richly decorated, with a painted dome, is the church built by François Mansart to honour the birth of the Sun King at the **Val-de-Grâce** convent. The true gem of the period is Jules Hardouin-Mansart's **Dôme Church**, with its enormous gilded

TOWERS, DOMES AND SPIRES

Paris's many churches have dominated her skyline since early Christian times. The Gothic Tour St-Jacques, the only element still extant from a long-gone church, reflects the medieval love of the defensive tower. St-Etienne-du-Mont, with its pointed gable and rounded pediment, shows the transition from Gothic to Renaissance. The dome, a much-used feature of the French Baroque, was used to perfection in the Val-de-Grâce, while St-Sulpice with its severe arrangement of towers and portico is typically Neo-Classical. With its ornate spires, Ste-Clotilde is a Gothic Revival church. Modern landmarks include the mosque, with its minaret.

Tour St-Jacques

St-Etienn-du-Mont

Gothic   Renaissance

dome. Jesuit extravagance can be seen in **St-Paul–St-Louis** built in the style of Il Gesú in Rome. In contrast are Libéral Bruand's chapels, the **Salpêtrière** and **St-Louis-des-Invalides** with their severe geometry and unadorned simplicity. Other fine Classical churches are **St-Joseph-des-Carmes** and the 18th-century bankers' church, **St-Roch**, with its Baroque Marian chapel.

NEO-CLASSICAL

Interior of the Panthéon

An obsession with all things Greek and Roman swept France in the mid-18th century and well into the 19th century. The excavations at Pompeii (1738) and the influence of the Italian architect Andrea Palladio produced a generation of architects fascinated by the column, geometry and engineering. The best example of such churches is Jacques-Germain Soufflot's Sainte-Geneviève, now the **Panthéon**. Begun in 1773, its colonnaded dome was also inspired by Christopher Wren's St Paul's in London. The dome is supported by four pillars, built by Guillaume Rondelet, linking four great arches. The first colonnaded facade was Giovanni Niccolo Servandoni's **St-Sulpice**. Construction of this church began in 1733 and consisted of a two-storey portico, topped by a triangular pediment. **La Madeleine**, Napoleon's grand temple to his victorious army, was constructed on the ground plan of a Greco-Roman temple.

SECOND EMPIRE AND MODERN

Franz Christian Gau's **Sainte-Clotilde** of the 1840s is the first and best example in Paris of the Gothic Revival or *style religieux*. Showy churches were built in the new districts created by Haussmann in the Second Empire *(pp34–5)*. One of the most lovely is Victor Baltard's St-Augustin, at the intersection of the Boulevard Malesherbes and the Boulevard de la Madeleine. Here historic detail combines with modern iron columns and girders in a soaring interior space. The great basilica of the late 19th century, **Sacré-Coeur**, was built as a gesture of religious defiance. **St-Jean l'Evangéliste** by Anatole de Baudot is an interesting modern church combining the Art Nouveau style with Islamic arches. The modern gem of Islamic architecture, the **Mosquée de Paris**, is an attractive 1920s building in the Hispanic-Moorish style. It has a grand patio, inspired by the Alhambra, woodwork in cedar and eucalyptus, and a fountain.

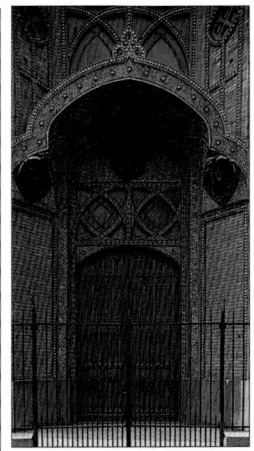

The arches of St-Jean L'Evangéliste, reminiscent of Islamic architecture

FINDING THE CHURCHES

Dôme Church *pp188–9*
Eglise de la Sorbonne *p153*
La Madeleine *p216*
Mosquée de Paris *pp166–7*
Notre-Dame *pp82–5*
Panthéon *pp158–9*
Sacré-Coeur *pp226–7*
Sainte-Chapelle *pp88–9*
Sainte-Clotilde *p187*
Salpêtrière *p167*
St-Etienne-du-Mont *p153*
St-Eustache *p114*
St-Germain-des-Prés *p138*
St-Germain l'Auxerrois *p115*
St-Gervais–St-Protais *p99*
St-Jean l'Evangéliste *p228*
St-Joseph-des-Carmes *p173*
St-Julien-le-Pauvre *p152*
St-Louis-des-Invalides *p186*
St-Merry *p108*
St-Paul–St-Louis *p99*
St-Roch *p121*
St-Séverin *p152*
St-Sulpice *p172*
Tour St-Jacques *p115*
Val-de-Grâce *p173*

Val-de-Grâce

Baroque and Classical

St-Sulpice

Neo-Classical

Sainte-Clotilde

Second Empire

Mosquée de Paris

Modern

Paris's Best: Gardens, Parks and Squares

Few cities can boast the infinite variety of styles found in Parisian gardens, parks and squares today. They date from many different periods and have been central to Parisian life for the past 300 years. The Bois de Boulogne and the Bois de Vincennes enclose the city with their lush, green open spaces, while elegant squares and landscaped gardens, such as the Jardin du Luxembourg, brighten the inner city and provide a retreat for those craving a few moments peace from the bustling city.

Parc Monceau
This English-style park features many follies, grottoes, magnificent trees and rare plants.

Champs-Elysées

Opéra Qu

Chaillot Quarter

Tui Qu

R I V E R S E I N E

Invalides and Eiffel Tower Quarter

St-Germai des-Prés

Luxeml Quar

Montparnasse

Bois de Boulogne
The Bagatelle gardens, set in this wooded park, have an amazing array of flowers including the spectacular rose garden.

Esplanade des Invalides
From this huge square, lined with lime trees, are some brilliant views over the quays.

Jardin des Tuileries
These gardens are renowned for ornamental ponds, terraces and the collection of bronze figure by Aristide Maillol.

Parc des Buttes-Chaumont
Once a scraggy hilltop, this park was transformed to provide open spaces for the growing city. It is now beautifully landscaped with huge cliffs revealing caves.

```
0 kilometres          1
0 miles            0.5
```

Square du Vert-Galant
The square, named after Henri IV's nickname, forms the west point of the Ile de la Cité.

Beaubourg and Les Halles

The Marais

Place des Vosges
Considered one of the most beautiful squares in the world, it was finished in 1612 and is the oldest square in Paris.

Ile de la Cité

Ile St-Louis

Jardin des Plantes
The botanical garden has a vast collection of plants and flowers from around the world.

Latin Quarter

Jardin des Plantes Quarter

Jardin du Luxembourg
This park is a favourite with Parisians wanting to escape the bustle of the Latin Quarter.

Bois de Vincennes
The flower garden in this charming park is the perfect place to relax.

Exploring Gardens, Parks and Squares

Paris is dotted with many areas of parkland, intimate gardens and attractive tree-lined squares. Each is a reminder of the French capital's illustrious past. Many squares were formed during Napoleon III's transformation of the city, creating a pleasant environment for Parisians to live in (*see pp34–5*). This aim has been preserved right up to the present day. Paris's parks and gardens have their own character: some are ideal for a stroll, others for romance, while some provide space for sporting activities such as a game of *boules*.

Engraving of the Jardin du Palais Royal (1645)

HISTORIC GARDENS

The oldest public gardens in Paris were made for queens of France – the **Jardin des Tuileries** for Catherine de Médicis in the 16th century, and the **Jardin du Luxembourg** for Marie de Médicis in the 17th century. The Tuileries form the beginning of the axis running from the Arc de Triomphe du Carrousel through the Arc de Triomphe (*pp210–11*) to La Défense (*p255*). These gardens retain the formality devised by landscape architect André Le Nôtre, originally for the **Palace of Versailles**. Many of the Jardin des Tuileries's original sculptures survive, as well as modern pieces, notably the bronze nudes by Aristide Maillol (1861–1944).

The Jardin du Luxembourg also has the traditional formal plan – straight paths, clipped lawns, Classical sculpture and a superb 17th-century fountain. It is shadier and more intimate than the Tuileries, with lots of seats, pony rides and puppet shows to amuse the children.

The **Jardins des Champs-Elysées**, also by Le Nôtre, were reshaped in the English style during the 19th century. The gardens have Belle Epoque pavilions, three theatres (L'Espace Pierre Cardin, Théâtre Marigny and the Théâtre du Rond Point), smart restaurants – and the ghost of the novelist Marcel Proust, who once played here as a child.

A haven of peace in a busy district is the **Jardin du Palais**

Royal built by Cardinal Richelieu in the 17th century. An elegant arcade encloses the garden. The 19th-century **Parc Monceau**, in the English picturesque style, has follies and grottoes. The flat **Jardins des Invalides** and the landscaped **Champ-de-Mars** were the grounds of the Hôtel des Invalides and the Ecole Militaire. They were the site of the Paris Universal Exhibition, whose reminder is the Eiffel Tower (*pp194–5*).

An attractive public garden is attached to the lovely Hôtel Biron, home of the **Musée Rodin**. The 17th-century botanical garden **Jardin des Plantes** is famous for its ancient trees, flowers, alpine garden, hothouses and small zoo.

19TH-CENTURY PARKS AND SQUARES

Aquatic Garden, Bois de Vincennes

The great 19th-century parks and squares owe much to Napoleon III's long exile in London before he came to power. The unregimented planting and rolling lawns of Hyde Park and the leafy squares of Mayfair inspired him to bring trees, fresh air

FOLLIES AND ROTUNDAS

Dramatic features of Paris's parks and gardens are the many follies and rotundas. Every age of garden design has produced these ornaments. The huge Gloriette de Buffon in the Jardin des Plantes was erected as a memorial to the great naturalist (*p166*). It is the oldest metal structure in Paris. The pyramid in the Parc Monceau, the oriental temple in the Bois de Boulogne, and the recently restored 19th-century temple of love in the Bois de Vincennes reflect a more sentimental age. In contrast are the stark, painted-concrete follies that grace the Parc de la Villette.

Egyptian pyramid

Parc Monceau

Relaxing in Jardin du Luxembourg

and park benches to what was then Europe's most congested and dirty capital. Under his direction, landscape gardener Adolphe Alphand turned two woods at opposite ends of the city, the **Bois de Boulogne** (known as the "Bois") and the **Bois de Vincennes**, into English-style parks with duck ponds, lakes and flower gardens. He also added a racecourse to the "Bois". Today it is traversed by traffic and by prostitutes at night. Its most attractive feature is the Bagatelle rose garden.

Far more pleasant are the two smaller Alphand parks, **Parc Montsouris** in the south and the **Parc des Buttes-Chaumont** in the northeast. The "Buttes" (hills), a favourite with the Surrealists, was a quarry transformed into two craggy mini-mountains with overhanging vegetation, suspended bridge, temple of love and a lake below.

Part of the town-planning schemes for the old city included squares and avenues with fountains, sculptures, benches and greenery. One of the best is the **Square du Vert-Galant** on the Ile de la Cité. The Avenue de l'Observatoire in the **Jardin du Luxembourg** is rich in sculptures made by Jean-Baptiste Carpeaux.

Fountains and sculpture in the Jardins du Trocadéro

MODERN PARKS AND GARDENS

The shady **Jardins du Trocadéro** sloping down to the river from the Palais de Chaillot were planted after the 1937 Universal Exhibition. Here is the largest fountain in Paris and fine views of the river and the Eiffel Tower.

More recent Paris gardens eschew formality in favour of wilder planting, multiple levels, maze-like paths, children's gardens and modern sculpture. Typical are the **Parc André-Citroën**, the **Parc de la Villette** and the Jardins Atlantique, next to the Gare Montparnasse.

Pleasant strolls may be taken in Paris's waterside gardens: in the modern sculpture park behind Notre-Dame, at the Bassin de l'Arsenal at the Bastille, and along the quays of the Seine between the Louvre and the Place de la Concorde, or on the elegantly residential Ile

Parc Montsouris

St-Louis. The planted walkway above the **Viaduc des Arts** is a peaceful way to observe eastern Paris.

FINDING THE GARDENS, PARKS AND SQUARES

Bois de Boulogne (Bagatelle rose garden) pp254–5
Bois de Vincennes p235
Champ-de-Mars p191
Forum des Halles p109
Jardin du Luxembourg p172
Jardin du Palais Royal p121
Jardin des Plantes p167
Jardin des Tuileries p130
Jardins des Champs-Elysées p207
Jardins des Invalides pp184–5
Jardins du Trocadéro p201
Musée Rodin p187
Palace of Versailles pp248–9
Parc André-Citroën p247
Parc des Buttes-Chaumont p234 & pp268–9
Parc Monceau p232 & pp258–9
Parc Montsouris p246
Parc de la Villette pp236–7
Square du Vert-Galant p87
Viaduc des Arts pp270–71

Gloriette de Buffon

Jardin des Plantes

Oriental temple

Bois de Boulogne

Temple of love

Bois de Vincennes

Modern folly

Parc de la Villette

Paris's Best: Museums and Galleries

Some of the oldest, the newest, and certainly some of the finest museums and galleries are to be found in Paris – many are superb works of art in their own right. They house some of the greatest and strangest collections in the world. Some of the buildings complement their themes, such as the Roman baths and Gothic mansion which form the Musée de Cluny, or the Pompidou Centre, a modern masterpiece. Elsewhere there is pleasing contrast, such as the Picassos in their gracious 17th-century museum, and the Musée d'Orsay housed in its grand old railway station. Together they make an unrivalled feast for visitors.

Musée des Arts Décoratifs
Decorative and ornamental art like this Paris bathroom by Jeanne Lanvin is displayed here.

Chaillot Quarter

Champs-Élysées

S E I N E

Invalides and Eiffel Tower Quarter

Petit Palais
A collection of works by the 19th-century sculptor Jean-Baptiste Carpeaux is housed here, including The Fisherman and Shell.

Musée du Quai Branly
This wooden sculpture from Papua New Guinea is one of 3,500 artefacts housed in this striking anthropological museum.

Montparn

Musée Rodin
The museum brings together works bequeathed to the nation by sculptor Auguste Rodin, like the magnificent Gates of Hell *doors.*

Musée d'Orsay
Carpeaux's Four Quarters of the World *(1867–72) can be found among this collection of 19th-century art.*

Musée du Louvre
The museum boasts one of the world's great collections of paintings and sculpture, from the ancient civilizations to the 19th century. This Babylonian monument, the Code of Hammurabi, *is the oldest set of laws in existence.*

Pompidou Centre
Paris's modern art collection from 1905 to the present day is housed here. The centre also has art libraries and an industrial design centre.

a Quarter

uileries Quarter

rmain-Prés

Beaubourg and Les Halles

The Marais

Ile de la Cité

Ile St-Louis

Latin Quarter

Luxembourg Quarter

Jardin des Plantes Quarter

Musée Picasso
Sculptor and Model *(1931) is one of many paintings on display in Picasso's private collection, "inherited" in lieu of tax by the French government after his death in 1973.*

Musée Carnavalet
The museum is devoted to the history of Paris. Its historic buildings surround attractive garden courtyards.

Musée de Cluny
The remains of the old Gallo-Roman baths are part of this fine museum of ancient and medieval art.

| 0 kilometres | 1 |
| 0 miles | 0.5 |

Exploring Paris's Museums and Galleries

Paris holds great treasures in its museums and art galleries. The major national art collection is to be found at the **Musée du Louvre**, which began collecting 400 years ago and is still growing. Other important museums, such as the **Musée d'Orsay**, the **Musée Picasso** and the **Pompidou Centre**, have their own treasures, but there are scores of smaller, specialized museums, each with its own interest.

Dante and Virgil in the Underworld (1822) by Delacroix, Musée du Louvre

GREEK, ROMAN AND MEDIEVAL ART

Golden altar in the Musée de Cluny

Sculpture from Greek and Roman times is well represented in the **Musée du Louvre**, which also has fine medieval sculptures. The major medieval collection is at the **Musée de Cluny**, a superb 15th-century mansion. Among the highlights are the Unicorn Tapestries, the Kings' Heads from Notre-Dame and the golden altar from Basel Cathedral. Adjoining the Cluny are the 3rd-century Roman baths. Remains of houses from Roman and medieval Paris can be seen in the **Crypte Archéologique** near Notre-Dame cathedral.

OLD MASTERS

The *Mona Lisa* was one of the **Musée du Louvre's** first paintings, acquired 400 years ago. It also has other fine Leonardos. They are to be found along with superb Titians, Raphaels and other Italian masters. Other works include Rembrandt's *Pilgrims at Emmäus*, Watteau's *Gilles* and **Fragonard's** *The Bathers*. The **Musée Cognacq-Jay** has a small, but exquisite, collection of paintings and drawings by 18th-century French painters. The **Musée Jacquemart-André** has works by such masters as Mantegna, Uccello, Canaletto, Rembrandt and Chardin.

IMPRESSIONIST AND POST-IMPRESSIONIST ART

Installed in a converted 19th-century railway station, the **Musée d'Orsay** boasts the world's largest collection of art from the period 1848–1904. Admired for its fine Impressionist and Post-Impressionist collections, it also devotes a lot of space to the earlier Realists and the formerly reviled 19th-century academic and "Salon" masters. There are superb selections of Degas, Manet, Courbet, Monet, Renoir, Millet, Cézanne, Bonnard and Vuillard, and some fine Gauguins, Van Goghs and Seurats, but these have to contend with poor lighting and an intrusive stone decor.

A great ensemble of late Monets is to be found at the **Musée Marmottan-Claude Monet** and another at the **Musée de l'Orangerie**, including Monet's last great waterlily murals (1920–25). Here also is a good collection of Cézannes and late Renoirs.

Three artists' studios and homes are now museums of their life and work. The **Musée Rodin**, in an attractive 18th-century mansion and garden, offers a complete survey of the master's sculptures, drawings and paintings. The **Musée Delacroix**, set in a garden near St-Germain-des-Prés, has sketches, prints and oils by the Romantic artist. The **Musée Gustave Moreau**, in an oppressive 19th-century town house, has an extraordinary collection of intricately painted canvases of legendary *femmes fatales* and dying youths. The **Petit Palais** has an interesting collection of 19th-century paintings with four major Courbets, including *The Sleep*.

Dead Poet in Musée Gustave Moreau

MODERN AND CONTEMPORARY ART

As the international centre of the avant-garde from 1900 to 1940, Paris has a great concentration of modern painting and sculpture. The Pompidou Centre houses the **Musée National d'Art Moderne**, covering from 1905 to the present. It has a good selection of Fauvist and Cubist works, particularly by Matisse, Rouault, Braque, Delaunay, and Leger, as well as works by the 1960s' *Nouveaux Réalistes*.

The **Musée d'Art Moderne de la Ville de Paris**, in the elegant 1930s Palais de Tokyo also has an excellent collection, including Delaunays, Bonnards and Fauvist paintings. The highlight is Matisse's 1932 mural, *The Dance*.

Penelope by Bourdelle

The **Musée Picasso** (closed for refurbishment from July 2008–2010/2011), in a lovely 17th-century mansion, has the world's largest Picasso collection. It also has his own personal collection of the work of his contemporaries. Picasso, Matisse, Modigliani, Utrillo and late Derains make up the collection of 1920s art dealer Paul Guillaume on display at the **Musée de l'Orangerie**. For modern sculpture, the small **Musée Zadkine** has Cubist work by a minor school whose leading light was Ossip Zadkine. The **Musée Antoine Bourdelle** and the **Musée Maillol** house work by these two sculptors.

FURNITURE, DECORATIVE ARTS AND OBJETS D'ART

Pride of place after painting must go to furniture and the decorative arts, contained in a plethora of museums. Fine ensembles of French furnishings and decoration are in the **Louvre** (medieval to Napoleonic) and at the **Palace** of Versailles (17th–18th century). Furniture and *objets d'art* from the Middle Ages to the present century are arranged in period rooms at the **Musée des Arts Décoratifs**. The **Musée d'Orsay** has a large collection of 19th-century furniture, notably Art Nouveau. Louis XV (1715–74) and Louis XVI (1774–93) furniture and decoration can be found in the **Musée Nissim de Camondo**, a mansion from 1910 facing the Parc Monceau. Other notable collections are the **Musée Cognacq-Jay**; the **Musée Carnavalet** (18th-century); the **Musée Jacquemart-André** (French furniture and earthenware); the **Musée Marmottan-Claude Monet** (Empire) and **Musée d'Art Moderne de la Ville de Paris** (Art Deco).

Cabinet from Musée des Arts Décoratifs

Jeweller's shop in the Carnavalet

SPECIALIST MUSEUMS

Devotees of antique sporting guns, muskets and hounds of the chase should make for the attractive Marais **Hôtel Guénégaud** (Musée de la Chasse et de la Nature). This museum also has some fine 18th-century animal paintings by Jean-Baptiste Oudry and Alexandre-François Desportes, as well as others by Rubens and Brueghel. **The Musée de la Contrefaçon** gives a fascinating insight into the world of counterfeit with examples from every luxury trade, including perfume, wines and spirits, and clothing. Numismatists will find an extensive coin and medallion collection housed in luxurious surroundings at the 18th-century Paris Mint at the **Musée de la Monnaie**. French coins are no longer minted here, but the old Mint still makes medals which are on sale. Stamps are on show at the **Musée de la Poste**. The history of postal services is also covered, as are all aspects of philately old and new, with temporary shows on current philatelic design. Visitors can discover how radio programmes are made at the **Musée de Radio-France**, which charts the history of communications from 1793 (when the first Chappe telegraph was sent) to the present day and internet broadcasting. The collection of radio and television equipment includes some 2,000 objects.

FASHION AND COSTUME

The two rival fashion museums in Paris are the **Musée Galliera** at the Palais Galliera and the more recent **Musée de la Mode** within the **Musée des Arts Décoratifs**. Neither displays a permanent collection, but both hold regular shows devoted to the great Paris couturiers, such as Saint Laurent and Givenchy. They also display fashion accessories and – more rarely but always fascinatingly – historical costumes.

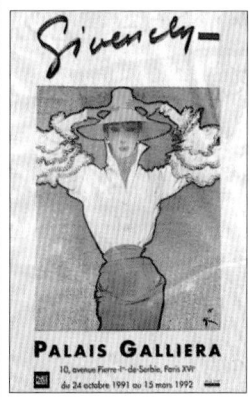

Poster for the Musée Galliera

ASIAN, AFRICAN AND OCEANIAN ART

The major collection of Asian art in France is housed at the **Musée National des Arts Asiatiques Guimet**, covering China, Tibet, Japan, Korea, Indochina, Indonesia, India and Central Asia. It includes Chinese bronzes and lacquerware and some of the best Khmer art outside Cambodia. The **Musée Cernuschi** has a smaller but well-chosen Chinese collection, noted for its ancient bronzes and reliefs. France's premier showcase for African, Asian, American tribal and Oceanian arts and cultures is the **Musée du Quai Branly**, which displays more than 300,000 objects in truly breathtaking surroundings. The **Musée Dapper** also houses African art and is part of an important ethnographic research centre, housed in an elegant 1910 *hôtel particulier* with an "African" garden. Its collection of tribal masks is particularly dazzling.

Sri Lankan theatrical mask

HISTORY AND SOCIAL HISTORY

Café in Musée de Montmartre

Covering the entire history of the city of Paris, the **Musée Carnavalet** is housed in two historic Marais *hôtels*. It has period interiors, paintings of the city and old shop signs, a fascinating section covering events and artefacts from the French Revolution, and even Marcel Proust's bedroom. Also in the Marais, the **Musée d'Art et d'Histoire du Judaïsme** explores the culture of French Jewry. The **Musée de l'Armée**, in the Hôtel des Invalides, recounts French military history, and the Musée de l'Histoire de France, in the Rococo **Hôtel de Soubise**, has historical documents from the national archives on display. Famous *tableaux vivants* and characters, both current and historical, await the visitor at the **Grévin** wax museum. The intriguing **Musée de Montmartre**, overlooking Paris's last surviving vineyard, holds exhibitions on the history of Montmartre.

ARCHITECTURE AND DESIGN

The **Cité de l'Architecture et du Patrimoine** (see p200) charts the history of French architecture with scale models of its most iconic buildings. Superb scale models of fortresses built for Louis XIV and later are on display at the **Musée des Plans-Reliefs**. The work of the celebrated Franco-Swiss architect forms the basis of the **Fondation Le Corbusier**. The showpiece is his 1920s villa for his friend, art collector Raoul La Roche. Some of his furniture is also on display.

THE FRENCH IMPRESSIONISTS

Impression: Sunrise by Monet

Impressionism, the great art revolution of the 19th century, began in Paris in the 1860s, when young painters, influenced in part by the new art of photography, started to break with the academic values of the past. They aimed to capture the "impression" of what the eye sees at a given moment and used brushwork designed to capture the fleeting effects of light falling on a scene. Their favourite subjects were landscapes and scenes from contemporary urban life.

The movement had no founder, though Edouard Manet (1832–83) and the radical Realist painter Gustave Courbet (1819–77) both inspired many of the younger artists. Paintings of scenes of everyday life by Manet and Courbet often offended the academicians who legislated artistic taste. In 1863 Manet's *Le Déjeuner sur l'Herbe (see p144)* was exhibited at the Salon des Refusés, an exhibition set up for paintings rejected by the official Paris Salon of that year. The first time the term "Impressionist" was used to describe this new artistic movement was at another unofficial exhibition, in 1874. The name came from a painting by Claude Monet, *Impression: Sunrise*, a view of Le Havre in the mist from 1872. Monet was almost exclusively a landscape artist, influenced by the works of the English

Monet's sketchbooks

Harvesting (1876) by Pissarro

The living room of La Roche Villa by Le Corbusier (1923)

SCIENCE AND TECHNOLOGY

In the Jardin des Plantes the **Muséum National d'Histoire Naturelle** has sections on palaeontology, minerology, entomology, anatomy and botany, plus a zoo and a botanical garden. In the Palais de Chaillot, the **Musée de l'Homme** is a museum of anthropology and prehistory

with regular temporary exhibitions. Next door, the **Musée de la Marine** covers French naval history from the 17th century onwards, with fine 18th-century models of ships and sculpted figure-heads. The **Musée des Arts et Métiers** displays the world of science and industry, invention and manufacturing. The **Palais de la Découverte** covers the history of science and has a good planetarium, somewhat overshadowed by the spectacular one at the **Cité des Sciences** in the Parc de la Villette. This museum is on several levels, with a spherical movie screen, the Géode.

Gabrielle (1910) by Renoir

artists, Constable and Turner. He always liked to paint out of doors and encouraged others to follow his example.

At the 1874 exhibition, a critic wrote that one should stand well back to see these "impressions" – the further back the better – and that members of the establishment should retreat altogether. Other exhibitors at the show were Pierre-Auguste Renoir, Edgar Degas, Camille Pissarro, Alfred Sisley and Paul Cézanne.

There were seven more Impressionist shows up to 1886. By then the power of the Salon had waned and the whole direction of art had changed. From then on, new movements were defined in terms of their relation to Impressionism. The leading Neo-Impressionist was Georges Seurat, who used thousands of minute dots of colour to build up his paintings. It took later generations to fully

appreciate the work of the Impressionists. Cézanne was rejected all his life, Degas sold only one painting to a museum, and Sisley died unknown. Of the great artists whose genius is now universally recognized, only Renoir and Monet were ever acclaimed in their lifetimes.

Profile of a Model (1887) by Seurat

FINDING THE MUSEUMS

Cité de l'Architecture et du Patrimoine *p200*
Cité des Sciences *pp238–9*
Crypte Archéologique *p81*
Fondation Le Corbusier *p254*
Grévin *p218*
Hôtel Guénégaud *p103*
Hôtel de Soubise *p103*
Musée Antoine Bourdelle *p178*
Musée de l'Armée *p186*
Musée d'Art et d'Histoire du Judaïsme *p103*
Musée d'Art Moderne de la Ville de Paris *p203*
Musée des Arts Décoratifs *p130*
Musée des Arts et Métiers *p103*
Musée Carnavalet *pp96–7*
Musée Cernuschi *p233*
Musée de Cluny *p154–7*
Musée Cognacq-Jay *p94*
Musée de la Contrefaçon *p202*
Musée Dapper *p202*
Musée Delacroix *p138*
Musée Galliera *p203*
Musée Guimet *p203*
Musée Gustave Moreau *p233*
Musée de l'Homme *p201*
Musée Jacquemart-André *p209*
Musée du Louvre *pp122–9*
Musée Maillol *p187*
Musée de la Marine *p201*
Musée Marmottan-Claude Monet *p254*
Musée de la Monnaie de Paris *p141*
Musée de Montmartre *p224*
Musée National d'Art Moderne *pp110–13*
Musée Nissim de Camondo *p232*
Musée de l'Orangerie *p131*
Musée d'Orsay *pp144–7*
Musée Picasso *pp100–1*
Musée des Plans-Reliefs *p186*
Musée de la Poste *pp178–9*
Musée du Quai Branly *pp192–3*
Musée de Radio-France *p202*
Musée Rodin *p187*
Musée Zadkine *p178*
Muséum National d'Histoire Naturelle *p167*
Palais de la Découverte *p208*
Petit Palais *p208*
Pompidou Centre *pp110–13*

Artists in Paris

The city first attracted artists during the reign of Louis XIV (1643–1715), and Paris became the most sophisticated artistic centre in Europe; the magnetism has persisted. During the 18th century, all major French artists lived and worked in Paris. In the the latter half of the 19th century and early part of the 20th century, Paris was the European centre of modern and progressive art, and movements such as Impressionism and Post-Impressionism were founded and blossomed in the city.

Monet's palette

BAROQUE ARTISTS

Champaigne, Philippe de (1602–74)
Coysevox, Antoine (1640–1720)
Girardon, François (1628–1715)
Le Brun, Charles (1619–90)
Le Sueur, Eustache (1616–55)
Poussin, Nicolas (1594–1665)
Rigaud, Hyacinthe (1659–1743)
Vignon, Claude (1593–1670)
Vouet, Simon (1590–1649)

ROCOCO ARTISTS

Boucher, François (1703–70)
Chardin, Jean-Baptiste-Siméon (1699–1779)
Falconet, Etienne-Maurice (1716–91)
Fragonard, Jean-Honoré (1732–1806)
Greuze, Jean-Baptiste (1725–1805)
Houdon, Jean-Antoine (1741–1828)
Oudry, Jean-Baptiste (1686–1755)
Pigalle, Jean-Baptiste (1714–85)
Watteau, Jean-Antoine (1684–1721)

Boucher's Diana Bathing *(1742), typical of the Rococo style (Louvre)*

1600	1650	1700	1750
BAROQUE		ROCOCO	NEO-CLASSICISM
1600	1650	1700	1750

1627 Vouet returns from Italy and is made court painter by Louis XIII. Vouet revived a dismal period in the fortunes of French painting

1667 First Salon, France's official art exhibition; originally held annually, later every two years

1793 Louvre opens as fi... natio... public galle...

Philippe de Champaigne's Last Supper *(about 1652). His style slowly became more Classical in his later years (Louvre)*

1648 Foundation of the Académie Royale de Peinture et de Sculpture, which had a virtual monopoly on art teaching

Vouet's The Presentation in the Temple *(1641) with typically Baroque contrasts of light and shade (Louvre)*

David's The Oath of the Horatii *(1784), in the Neo-Classical style (Louvre)*

NEO-CLASSICAL ARTISTS

David, Jacques-Louis (1748–1825)
Gros, Antoine Jean (1771–1835)
Ingres, Jean-Auguste-Dominique (1780–1867)
Vigée-Lebrun, Elizabeth (1755–1842)

ROMANTIC AND REALIST ARTISTS

Courbet, Gustave (1819–77)
Daumier, Honoré (1808–79)
Delacroix, Eugène (1798–1863)
Géricault, Théodore (1791–1824)
Rude, Francois (1784–1855)

Courbet's The Burial at Ornans *(1850) which showed Courbet to be the foremost exponent of Realism (Musée d'Orsay)*

Rude's Departure of the Volunteers in 1792 (1836), a tribute to the French Revolution (see p211)

MODERN ARTISTS

Arp, Jean (1887–1966)
Balthus (1908–2001)
Brancusi, Constantin (1876–1957)
Braque, Georges (1882–1963)
Buffet, Bernard (1928–1999)
Chagall, Marc (1887–1985)
Delaunay, Robert (1885–1941)
Derain, André (1880–1954)
Dubuffet, Jean (1901–85)
Duchamp, Marcel (1887–1968)
Epstein, Jacob (1880–1959)
Ernst, Max (1891–1976)
Giacometti, Alberto (1901–66)
Gris, Juan (1887–1927)
Léger, Fernand (1881–1955)
Matisse, Henri (1869–1954)
Miró, Joan (1893–1983)
Modigliani, Amedeo (1884–1920)
Mondrian, Piet (1872–1944)
Picasso, Pablo (1881–1973)
Rouault, Georges (1871–1958)
Saint Phalle, Niki de (1930–2002)
Soutine, Chaim (1893–1943)
Stael, Nicolas de (1914–55)
Tinguely, Jean (1925–91)
Utrillo, Maurice (1883–1955)
Zadkine, Ossip (1890–1967)

Giacometti's Standing Woman II (1959), one of his many tall, thin bronze figures (see p112)

1904 Picasso settles in Paris

1886 Van Gogh moves to Paris

1874 First Impressionist exhibition

1905 Birth of Fauvism, the first of the "isms" in modern art

1850	1900	1950
ROMANTICISM/REALISM	IMPRESSIONISM MODERNISM	
1850	1900	1950

1863 Manet's *Le Déjeuner sur l'Herbe* causes a scandalous sensation at the Salon des Refusés, both for "poor moral taste", and for its broad brushstrokes. The artist's *Olympia* was thought just as outrageous, but it was not exhibited until 1865 *(see p144)*

1938 International Surrealist exhibition in Paris

1977 Pompidou Centre opens

Monet's Impression: Sunrise *(1872), which led to the name Impressionism*

Delacroix's Liberty Leading the People *(1830) romantically celebrates victory in war (Louvre)*

1819 Géricault paints *The Raft of the Medusa*, one of the greatest works of French Romanticism (see p124)

IMPRESSIONIST AND POST-IMPRESSIONIST ARTISTS

Bonnard, Pierre (1867–1947)
Carpeaux, Jean-Baptiste (1827–75)
Cézanne, Paul (1839–1906)
Degas, Edgar (1834–1917)
Gauguin, Paul (1848–1903)
Manet, Edouard (1832–83)
Monet, Claude (1840–1926)
Pissarro, Camille (1830–1903)
Renoir, Pierre-Auguste (1841–1919)
Rodin, Auguste (1840–1917)
Rousseau, Henri (1844–1910)
Seurat, Georges (1859–91)
Sisley, Alfred (1839–99)
Toulouse-Lautrec, Henri de (1864–1901)
Van Gogh, Vincent (1853–90)
Vuillard, Edouard (1868–1940)
Whistler, James Abbott McNeill (1834–1903)

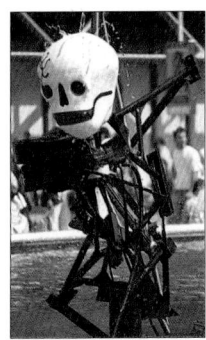

Tinguely and Saint Phalle's Fontaine Igor Stravinsky (1980), a modern kinetic sculpture (Pompidou Centre)

PARIS THROUGH THE YEAR

Paris's pulling power is strongest in spring – the season for chestnuts in blossom and tables under trees. From June Paris is slowly turned over to tourists; the city almost comes to a standstill for the French Tennis Open, and the major race tracks stage the big summer races. Next comes the 14 July Bastille Day parade down the Champs-Elysées; towards the end of the month the Tour de France usually ends here.

The end of July also sees the end of Paris' three-month Jazz Festival, after which most Parisians abandon the city to visitors until *la rentrée,* the return to school and work in September. Dates of events listed on the following pages may vary. For details consult the listings magazines, or contact Paris Infos Mairie *(see p357).* The Office du Tourisme *(see p367)* also produces an annual calendar of events.

SPRING

A good many of the city's annual 20 million visitors arrive in the spring. It is the season for fairs and concerts, when the marathon street race is held and the outdoor temperature is pleasant. Spring is also the time when hoteliers offer weekend packages, often with tickets for jazz concerts and with museum passes included.

French Tennis Open, Stade Roland Garros

MARCH

Spring flower shows
at Parc Floral (Bois de Vincennes, *p235*) and Bagatelle Gardens (Bois de Boulogne, *pp254–5).*
Banlieues Bleues Festival
(mid-Feb–early Apr),
Paris suburbs. Jazz, blues, soul and funk.
Salon International d'Agriculture *(1st week),* Paris-Expo, Porte de Versailles. Vast farming fair.
Jumping International de Paris *(3rd week),* Palais Omnisports de Paris-Bercy.

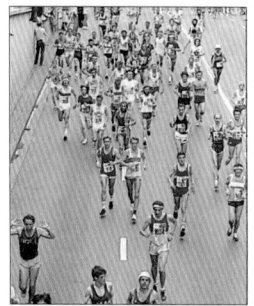
Paris International Marathon

(pp358–9). International show jumping.
Foire du Trône *(late Mar–May),* Bois de Vincennes *(p235).* Large funfair.
Chemin de la Croix *(Good Friday).* Beautiful Stations of the Cross procession, from Montmartre to Sacré Coeur.

APRIL

Six Nations Trophy *(early Apr),* Stade de France *(p358).* International rugby.
Shakespeare Garden Festival *(until Oct),* Bois de Boulogne *(pp254–5).* Classic plays performed outdoors.
Paris International Marathon *(April),* from Place de la Concorde to Avenue Foch.
Foire de Paris *(end Apr–1st week May),* Paris Expo, Porte de Versailles. Food, wine, homes and gardens and tourism show.

MAY

Carré Rive Gauche *(one week, mid-month).* Exhibits

at antiques dealers near the Grand Louvre *(p135).*
Football Cup Final *(2nd week),* Stade de France.
Grandes Eaux Musicales *(Apr–Oct: Sundays; Jul–Sep: Saturdays),* Versailles *(p248).* Open-air concerts.

Spring colour, Jardin du Luxembourg

French Tennis Open *(last week May–1st week Jun),* Stade Roland Garros *(p358).* Parisian society meets sport!
Le Printemps des Rues *(3rd w/end).* Concerts and free street theatre in Bastille/République area.

AVERAGE DAILY HOURS OF SUNSHINE

Hours: 10, 8, 6, 4, 2, 0

Jan Feb Mar Apr May Jun Jul Aug Sep Oct Nov Dec

Sunshine Hours
The northerly position of Paris gives it long and light summer evenings, but in winter the daylight recedes with few truly bright days.

SUMMER

Summer begins with the French Tennis Open, and there are many events and festivities until July. Thereafter the French begin thinking of their own annual holiday, but there are big celebrations on Bastille Day (14 July) with military displays for the president and his guests.

Final lap of the Champs-Elysées during the Tour de France

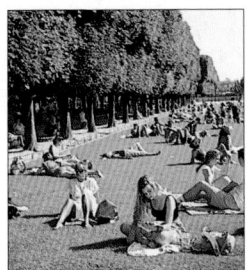

Jardin du Luxembourg in summer

JUNE

Festival St-Denis, Basilique St-Denis. Concerts with emphasis on large-scale choral works (p346).
Fête du Cinéma, films shown all over Paris for €2 nominal entry fee (p354).

Fête de la Musique (21 Jun), all over Paris. Nightlong summer solstice musical celebrations.
Flower show, Bois de Boulogne (pp254–5). Rose season in the Bagatelle Gardens.
Gay Pride (end Jun). Lively parade around the Bastille.
Paris Jazz Festival (May–Jul), Parc Floral de Paris. Jazz musicians come to play in Paris (pp349–50).
Paris Air and Space Technology Show (mid-Jun), Le Bourget Airport.
Prix de Diane-Hermès (2nd Sun), Chantilly. French equivalent of the British Ascot high society horse-racing event.

JULY

Festival du cinéma en plein air (mid-Jul–Aug), Parc de la Villette (pp236-7).
Paris Quartier d'Eté (mid-Jul–mid-Aug). Dance, music, theatre, ballet.
Tour de France (late Jul). The last stage of the world's greatest cycle race comes to a climax in the Champs-Elysées.
Fêtes de Nuit (Jul–mid-Sep: Saturdays), Versailles. Son et lumiere with music, dance and theatre (p249).
Paris-Plage (mid-Jul–mid-Aug). Sand and palm trees are deposited on the Right Bank of the Seine to create a temporary beach.

March past of troops on Bastille Day (14 July)

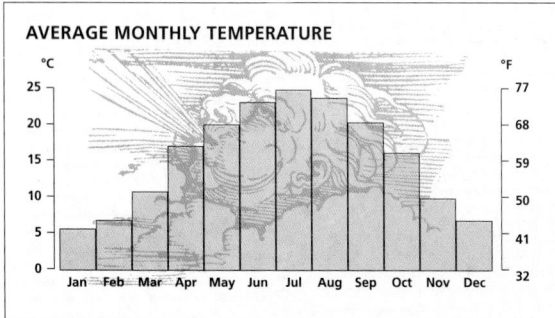

AVERAGE MONTHLY TEMPERATURE

Temperature
The chart shows the average minimum and maximum temperatures for each month. It is hottest in July and August and coolest between December and February, though Paris is rarely freezing cold. Temperatures are pleasant in the spring and autumn.

AUTUMN

September sees the start of the social season, with gala performances of new films, and parties in big houses on the Ile St-Louis. Paris is the world's largest congress centre and there is a rush of shows in September, ranging from children's clothes and gifts to leisure and music. The pace barely slackens in October and November when Parisians begin to indulge their great love for the cinema. French and Hollywood stars frequently make appearances at premieres staged on the Champs-Elysées.

SEPTEMBER

Festival d'Automne à Paris *(mid-Sep–end Dec)*, throughout Paris. Music, dance, theatre *(pp346–7)*.
La Villette Jazz Festival *(mid-Sep)*. Jazz artists come blow their horns with gusto throughout the Cité de la Musique *(p236)*.

The Prix de l'Arc de Triomphe (October)

OCTOBER

Nuit Blanche *(one Sat in Oct)*. Museums stay open all night.
Prix de l'Arc de Triomphe *(1st week)*, Longchamp. An international field competes for the richest prize in European horse-racing.
Salon de l'Automobile *(1st fortnight, alternate years)*, Paris-Expo, Porte de Versailles. Commercial motor show, alternated annually with a motorcycle show.
Journées du Patrimoine *(usually 3rd week)*. Historic buildings, monuments and museums are open free to the public for two days, following an all-night party to kick off proceedings.

Foire Internationale d'Art Contemporain (FIAC) *(last week)*, Paris-Expo, Porte de Versailles. Paris's biggest international modern and contemporary art fair.

Jazz fusion guitarist Al di Meola playing in Paris

NOVEMBER

BNP Paribas Masters *(usually Nov)*, Palais Omnisports de Paris-Bercy *(pp358–9)*.
Festival d'Art Sacré *(Nov–24 Dec)*, at St-Sulpice, St-Eustache and St-Germain-des-Prés churches. Religious art festival.
Mois de la Photo *(Oct–Nov)*. Numerous photography shows.
Beaujolais Nouveau *(3rd Thursday Nov)*. Bars and cafés are crowded on this day, in a race to taste the new vintage.

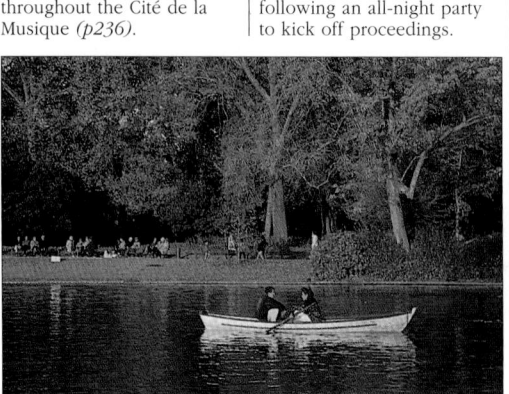

Autumn in the Bois de Vincennes

AVERAGE MONTHLY RAINFALL

Jan, Feb, Mar, Apr, May, Jun, Jul, Aug, Sep, Oct, Nov, Dec

Rainfall
August is the wettest month in Paris as well as the hottest. In August and September you risk getting caught in storms. Sudden showers, sometimes with hail, can occur between January and April – notoriously in March. There is occasional snow in winter.

WINTER

Paris rarely sees snow; winter days tend to be invigorating rather than chilly. There are jazz and dance festivals, candlelit Christmas church services and much celebrating in the streets over the New Year. After New Year, the streets seem to become slightly less congested and on bright days the riverside quays are used as the rendezvous point of strollers and lovers.

Snow in the Tuileries, a rare occurrence

DECEMBER

Christmas illuminations *(until Jan)* in the Grands Boulevards, Opéra, Ave Montaigne, Champs-Elysées and the Rue du Faubourg St-Honoré.
Crèche *(early Dec–early Jan)*, under a canopy in Place de l'Hôtel de Ville, Marais *(p102)*. Lifesize Christmas crib from a different country each year.

January fashion show

Horse & Pony Show *(1st fortnight)*, Paris-Expo, Porte de Versailles.
Paris International Boat Show *(1st fortnight)*, Paris-Expo, Porte de Versailles.

JANUARY

Fête des Rois (Epiphany). *(6 Jan)*. The *boulangeries* are full of *galettes des rois*.
Prix d'Amérique *(mid-Jan)*. Europe's most famous trotting race, Hippodrome de Vincennes.
Fashion shows, summer collections. (*See* Haute Couture *p324*)

FEBRUARY

Carnaval *(weekend before Mardi Gras)*, Quartier de St-Fargeau. **Floraisons** *(all month)*, Parc Floral de Paris, Bois de Vincennes *(p235)* and Parc de Bagatelle, Bois de Boulogne *(pp254–5)*. Say farewell to winter with these colourful displays of crocuses and snowdrops.

PUBLIC HOLIDAYS
New Year's Day (1 Jan)
Easter Monday varies
Labour Day (1 May)
VE Day (8 May)
Ascension Day (6th Thu after Easter)
Bastille Day (14 Jul)
Assumption (15 Aug)
All Saints' Day (1 Nov)
Remembrance Day (11 Nov)
Christmas (25 Dec)

Eiffel Tower Christmas decorations

A RIVER VIEW OF PARIS

Sculpture on the Pont Alexandre III

The remarkable French music-hall star Mistinguett described the Seine as a "pretty blonde with laughing eyes". The river most certainly has a beguiling quality, but the relationship that exists between it and the city of Paris is far more than one of flirtation.

No other European city defines itself by its river in the same way as Paris. The Seine is the essential point of reference to the city: distances are measured from it, street numbers determined by it, and it divides the capital into two distinct areas, with the Right Bank on the north side of the river and the Left Bank on the south side. These are as well defined as any of the supposedly official boundaries. The city is also divided historically, with the east more closely linked to the city's ancient roots and the west more closely linked to the 19th and 20th centuries.

Practically every building of note in Paris is either along the river or within a stone's throw. The quays are lined by fine bourgeois apartments, magnificent town houses, great museums and striking monuments.

Above all, the river is very much alive. For centuries fleets of small boats used it, but motorized land traffic stifled this once-bustling scene. Today, the river is busy with commercial barges and massive *bateaux mouches* pleasure boats cruising sightseers up and down the river.

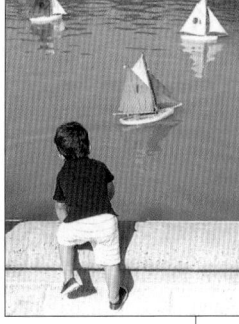

The octagonal lake, in the Jardin de Luxembourg, is a favourite spot for children to sail their toy boats. The Seine is host to larger craft, including many pleasure cruisers.

This map shows the sections of the river depicted on the following pages.

see pp68–9

CHAMPS-ELYSEES

OPERA QUARTER

see pp70–71

CHAILLOT QUARTER

TUILERIES QUARTER

BEAUBOURG AND LES HALLES

THE MARAIS

INVALIDES AND EIFFEL TOWER QUARTER

Seine

ST-GERMAIN-DES-PRES

ILE DE LA CITE

ILE ST-LOUIS

LATIN QUARTER

LUXEMBOURG QUARTER

JARDIN DES PLANTES QUARTER

MONTPARNASSE

Les Bouquinistes, the bookstalls on the river banks, are treasure troves of second-hand books and prints, which passers-by can casually examine.

0 kilometres 2

0 miles 1

KEY

▨ Illustrated area

◁ Pont Alexandre III, encrusted with exuberant statuary

From Pont de Grenelle to Pont de la Concorde

The soaring monuments and grand exhibition halls along this stretch of the river are remnants of the Napoleonic era and the Industrial Revolution with its great exhibitions. The exhilarating self-confidence of the Eiffel Tower, the Petit Palais and the Grand Palais is matched by more recent buildings, such as the Palais de Chaillot, the Maison de Radio-France and the skyscrapers of the Left Bank.

Palais de Chaillot
The curved wings and arching fountains make this a spectacular setting for three museums (p198).

Palais de Tokyo
Figures by Bourdelle adorn this museum (p201).

The Statue of Liberty was given to the city in 1885. It faces west, towards the original Liberty in New York.

Trocadéro M

Bateaux Parisiens
Tour Eiffel
Vedettes de Paris
Ile de France

Passe
Deb

Pont
d'Iéna

M Passy

Maison de Radio-France
Studios and a radio museum are housed in this imposing circular building (p200).

Pont de
Bir-Hakeim

RER Champ de Mars

RER Prés. Kennedy
Radio France

M Bir-Hakeim

Eiffel Tower
The tower is the symbol of Paris (pp192–3).

The Pont Bir-Hakeim
has a dynamic statue by Wederkinch rising at its north end.

Pont de Grenelle

KEY

M	Metro station
RER	RER station
Ⓞ	Batobus stop
🚢	River trip boarding point

Grand Palais
Major exhibitions and a science museum are based here (p206).

Petit Palais
Now the Paris museum of fine arts, this was first designed as a companion to the Grand Palais (p206).

Champs-Elysées Clemenceau Ⓜ

Alma Ⓜ Marceau

Pont de l'Alma

Pont des Invalides

Pont Alexandre III

Pont de la Concorde

RER **Pont de l'Alma**

Ⓜ RER **Invalides**

🚢 **Bateaux Mouches**

The Zouave is a statue of a soldier on a central pier of the bridge. It is used to measure the level of the Seine when it is in flood.

The Liberty Flame, commemorating French Resistance fighters, is also an unofficial memorial to Diana, Princess of Wales.

Pont Alexandre III
Flamboyant statuary decorates Paris's most ornate bridge (p206).

Dôme Church
The majestic gilded dome (pp188–9) is here seen from Pont Alexandre III.

Assemblée Nationale Palais-Bourbon
Louis XIV's daughter once owned this palace, which is now used by the Chambre des Députés as the national forum for political debate (p190).

From Pont de la Concorde to Pont de Sully

The historic heart of Paris lies on the banks and islands of the east river. At its centre is the Ile de la Cité, a natural stepping stone across the Seine and the cultural core of medieval Paris. Today it is still vital to Parisian life.

Jardin des Tuileries
These are in the formal style (p130).

Musée du Louvre
Before becoming the world's greatest museum and home to the Mona Lisa, this was Europe's largest royal palace (pp122–9).

Pont de la Concorde

Assemblée Nationale

Passerelle Solférino

Quai d'Orsay

Pont Royal

Pont du Carrousel

Passerelle des Arts

Musée de l'Orangerie
An important collection of 19th-century paintings is on display here (p131).

The Passerelle des Arts
is a steel reconstruction of Paris's first cast-iron bridge (1804), and was inaugurated in 1984.

Bâteaux Vedettes du Pont Neuf

Musée d'Orsay
Paris's most important collection of Impressionist art is housed in this converted railway station (pp144–7).

Hôtel des Monnaies
Built in 1768–85, this former Mint has a fine coin collection in its old milling halls (p141).

Ile de la Cité

The medieval identity of this small island was almost completely erased in the 19th century by Baron Haussmann's grand scheme. Sainte-Chapelle and parts of the Conciergerie are the only buildings of the period that remain today (pp76–89).

Conciergerie

During the Revolution this building, with its distinctive towers, became notorious as a prison (p81).

The Tour de l'Horloge, a 14th-century clock tower, features the first public clock in Paris. Germain Pilon's fine carvings continue to adorn the clock face.

Ile St-Louis

This has been a desirable address since the 17th century (p87).

St-Gervais–St-Protais
The oldest organ in Paris, dating from the early 17th century, is in this church (p99).

Pont
euf
M

euf

Châtelet
Hôtel de Ville
M

Pont au
Change
Pont Notre
Dame
Cité
M
Pont d'Arcole

RER M
St-Michel

Petit Pont

Pont au
Double

Pont Louis
Philippe

Pont St Louis

M Pont Marie

Pont Marie

Pont de
Archeveché

Pont de la
Tournelle

Pont de Sully

M

Sully Morland

Notre-Dame
This towering cathedral surveys the river (pp82–5).

Bâteaux Parisiens

How to Take a River or Canal Trip

River Seine cruises on a variety of pleasure boats operate along the main sightseeing reaches of the river, taking in many of the city's famous monuments. The Batobus river service operates as a shuttle or bus service, allowing you to get on and off anywhere along the route. The main city canal trips operate along the old industrial St-Martin canal in the east of the city.

Pleasure-cruise boats passing under the Pont Alexandre III

Types of Boats

Bateaux mouches, *the largest of the pleasure-cruise boats, are a spectacular sight with their passenger areas enclosed in glass for excellent all round viewing. At night floodlights are used to pick out river bank buildings. A more luxurious version of these is used on the Bateaux Parisien cruises. The* vedettes *are smaller and more intimate boats, with viewing through glass walls. The* Canauxrama *canal boats are flat-bottomed.*

SEINE CRUISES AND SHUTTLE SERVICES

The Seine cruises and shuttle services information below includes the location of boarding points, the nearest metro and RER stations, and the nearest bus routes. Lunch and dinner cruises must be booked in advance, and passengers must board them 30 minutes before departure.

Vedettes de Paris Seine Cruise

Passengers are carried in comfort and style on a cruise encompassing all major sights along the river. The boarding point is:

Port de Suffren Map 10 D3. **Tel** 01 44 18 19 50. Ⓜ *Bir Hakeim.* 🚇 *Champs de Mars.* 🚌 *22, 30, 32, 44, 63, 69, 72, 82, 87.*

Departures *10am–10pm (11am–6pm Nov–Feb) daily (every 30 min).* **Duration** *1 hr.* **Dinner cruise** *8pm Sat (phone to reserve).* **Duration** *2 hr 30 min.* www.vedettesdeparis. com

Paris Ports Cruise

An educational journey along the city's little-known urban ports (commentary in French). The boarding point is:

Port de la Rapée Map 18 D1. **Tel** 01 44 18 19 50. Ⓜ *Quai de la Rapée.* **Departures** *3pm first Sun of month Mar–Oct (exc Jul, Aug).* **Duration** *1 hr 30 min.* www.vedettesdeparis.com

Bateaux Parisiens Tour Eiffel Cruise

This company has a fleet of seven boats with a carrying capacity of 1,255 passengers. A commentary is provided in 13 languages. The boarding point is:

Port de la Bourdonnais Map 10 D2. **Tel** 01 46 99 43 13. Ⓜ *Trocadéro, Bir Hakeim.* 🚇 *Champs de Mars.* 🚌 *42, 82.* **Departures** *10am–11pm (10pm Oct–Mar) daily (every 30 min).*

Duration *1 hr.* **Lunch cruise** *12.15pm daily.* **Duration** *2 hr 15 min.* **Dinner cruise** *7.45pm.* **Duration** *3 hr. Formal dress required.* www. bateauxparisiens.com

Bateaux Parisiens Notre-Dame Cruise

This trip follows the same route as the Tour Eiffel Cruise, but in the opposite direction. The boarding point is:

Quai de Montebello Map 13 B4. **Tel** 01 46 99 43 13. Ⓜ *Maubert–Mutualite, St-Michel.* 🚇 *St-Michel.* 🚌 *24, 27, 47.* **Departures** *24 Mar–6 Apr, 18 Sep–5 Nov: 5 daily (1.30–6.10pm); 7–28 Apr: 7 daily (2–10pm); 29 Apr–2 Jun: 9 daily (11am–10pm); 3 Jun–26 Aug: 10 daily (11am–11pm); 27 Aug–17 Sep: 9 daily (11am–10pm).* **Duration** *1 hr.*

Boarding Points

The boarding points for the river cruises and the Batobus services are easy to find

along the river. Here you can buy tickets, and there are amenities such as snack-bars. Major cruise companies also have foreign exchange booths. There is limited parking around the points, but none near the Pont Neuf.

River boarding point

BATOBUS CRUISES

Shuttle service. 1–2 day passes available. **Tel** 08 25 05 01 01. **Departures** daily. Early Feb–mid-Mar, mid-Nov–20 Dec: 10.30am–4.30pm; 21 Dec–early Jan: 10.30am–5pm; mid-Mar–May, early Sep–11 Nov: 10am–7pm; Jun–early Sep: 10am–9.30pm. Board at: **Eiffel Tower: Map** 10 D3. Ⓜ Bir Hakeim. **Champs-Elysées: Map** 11 B1. Ⓜ Champs-Elysées-Clemenceau. **Musée d'Orsay: Map** 12 D2. Ⓜ Solferino. **Louvre: Map** 12 E2. Ⓜ Louvre. **St-Germain-des-Prés: Map** 12 E3. Ⓜ St-Germain-de-Prés. **Notre-Dame: Map** 13 B4. Ⓜ Cité. **Hôtel de Ville: Map** 13 B4. Ⓜ Hôtel de Ville. **www**.batobus.com

BATEAUX-MOUCHES

Bateaux Mouches Cruise

This well-known pleasure boat company's fleet of 11 boats carries between 600 and 1,400 passengers at a time. The boarding point is:

Pont de l'Alma Map 10 F1. **Tel** 01 42 25 96 10. Ⓜ Alma-Marceau. Ⓡ Pont de l'Alma. 🚌 28, 42, 49, 63, 72, 80, 83, 92. **Departures** Apr–Sep: 10am–11pm daily (every 30 min); Oct–Mar: 11am–9pm (every 45 min). **Duration** 1 hr 15 min. **Lunch cruise** 1pm Sat, Sun and bank hols (embark from 12.15pm). **Duration** 1 hr 45 min. Under-12s half price. **Dinner cruise** 8.30pm daily (embark from 7.30pm). **Duration** 2 hr 15 min. Jacket and tie required. **www**.bateaux-mouches.fr

Vedettes du Pont Neuf

Bateaux Vedettes Pont Neuf Cruise

This company runs a fleet of six 80-passenger boats. The boats are of an older style, for a quainter cruise. The boarding point is:

Square du Vert-Galant (Pont Neuf). **Map** 12 F3. **Tel** 01 46 33 98 38. Ⓜ Pont Neuf. Ⓡ Châtelet. 🚌 24, 27, 58, 67, 70, 72, 74, 75. **Departures** Mar–Oct: 10am, 11.15am, noon; 1.30–10.30pm daily (every 30 min); Nov–Feb: 10.30am, 11.15am, noon, 2–6.30pm (every 45 min), 8pm, 10pm Mon–Thu; 10.30am, 11.15am, noon, 2–6.30pm, 8pm, 9–10.30pm (every 30 min) Fri–Sun. **Duration** 1 hr. Snacks available on board. **www**.vedettesdupontneuf.com

CANAL TRIPS

The Canauxrama company operates boat cruises along the city's Canal St-Martin and along the banks of the river Marne. The St-Martin journey passes along the tree-lined canal, which has nine locks, two swing bridges and eight romantic footbridges. The Bords de Marne cruise travels well into the suburbs, as far as Bry-sur-Marne. The **Paris Canal Company** (01 42 40 96 97; **www**.pariscanal.com) also has a St-Martin canal trip, from Parc de la Villette and extending beyond the canal, passing into the River Seine and as far as the Musée d'Orsay.

CANAUXRAMA

Canal St-Martin

The Canauxrama company offers many different trips along this canal, but it has two 125-passenger boats that operate regularly between the Bassin de la Villette and the Port de l'Arsenal. The boarding points are: **Bassin de la Villette. Map** 8 E1. Ⓜ Jaurès. **Port de l'Arsenal. Map** 14 E4. Ⓜ Bastille. **Tel** 01 42 39 15 00. **Departures** Apr–Nov, times may vary so phone to check and to make a reservation: Bassin de la Villette 9.45am and 2.45pm; Port de l'Arsenal 9.45am and 2.30pm daily. On weekday mornings there are concessions for students, pensioners and children under 12. Children under six travel free. Concert cruises are available on chartered trips on the Canal St-Martin and the Seine. **Duration** 2 hr 30 min. **www**.canauxrama.fr

Bords de Marne Croisière

This all-day cruise extends westwards out of Paris down the river Marne. The trip includes a commentary, stories and dancing. The boarding point is: **Port de l'Arsenal. Map** 14 E4. Ⓜ Bastille. **Tel** 01 42 39 15 00. **Departures** 8.30am all-year-round. Reservations necessary. **Duration** 8 hr.

Canal-cruise boat in the Bassin de la Villette

PARIS AREA BY AREA

DE LA CITE AND ILE ST-LOUIS 76–89

THE MARAIS 90–103

BEAUBOURG AND LES HALLES 104–115

TUILERIES QUARTER 116–133

ST-GERMAIN-DES-PRES 134–147

LATIN QUARTER 148–159

JARDIN DES PLANTES QUARTER 160–167

LUXEMBOURG QUARTER 168–173

MONTPARNASSE 174–181

INVALIDES AND
EIFFEL TOWER QUARTER 182–195

CHAILLOT QUARTER 196–203

CHAMPS-ELYSEES 204–211

OPERA QUARTER 212–219

MONTMARTRE 220–229

FURTHER AFIELD 230–255

EIGHT GUIDED WALKS 256–273

ILE DE LA CITE AND ILE ST-LOUIS

The history of the Ile de la Cité is the history of Paris. This island on the Seine was no more than a primitive village when the conquering Julius Caesar arrived in 53 BC. Ancient kings later made it the centre of political power and in medieval times it became the home of church and law. It no longer has such power, except to draw armies of tourists to the imposing Palais de Justice and to its Gothic masterpiece, Notre-Dame.

The medieval huddles of tiny houses and narrow streets that so characterized the island at one time

The motto of the city of Paris

were swept away by the spacious thoroughfares built in the 19th century.

But there are still small areas of charm and relief, among them the colourful bird and flower market, the romantic Square du Vert-Galant and the ancient Place Dauphine.

At the eastern end of the island the St-Louis bridge connects it to the smaller Ile St-Louis. This former swampy pastureland was transformed into an elegant 17th-century residential area, with picturesque, tree-lined quays. More recently, rich artists, doctors, actresses and heiresses have lived here.

SIGHTS AT A GLANCE

Historic Buildings
Hôtel Dieu ❻
Conciergerie ❽
Palais de Justice ❿
Hôtel de Lauzun ⓰

Bridges
Pont Neuf ⓬

Monuments
Paris Mémorial
de la Déportation ❹

Markets
Marché aux Fleurs and Marché
aux Oiseaux ❼

Squares and Gardens
Square Jean XXIII ❸
Place Dauphine ⓫
Square du Vert-Galant ⓭

Museums and Galleries
Musée de Notre-Dame de
Paris ❷
Crypte Archéologique ❺

Société Historique et Littéraire
Polonaise ⓮

Churches and Cathedrals
Notre-Dame pp82–5 ❶
Sainte-Chapelle pp88–9 ❾
St-Louis-en-l'Ile ⓯

0 metres		400
0 yards		400

GETTING THERE
This area is served by the metro stations at Cité and St-Michel on the Left Bank. The bus routes 21, 38, 47, 85 and 96 cross the Ile de la Cité, and 67, 86 and 87 cross the Ile St-Louis.

SEE ALSO

• *Street Finder,* map 12–13

• *St-Louis Walk* pp262–3

• *Where to Stay* p284

• *Restaurants* p300

KEY

　　Street-by-Street map

M Metro station

◁ **View of the Conciergerie and the Pont au Change, previous page St-Sulpice church and rooftops**

Street-by-Street: Ile de la Cité

The origins of Paris are here on the Ile de la Cité, the boat-shaped island on the Seine first inhabited over 2,000 years ago by Celtic tribes. One tribe, the Parisii, eventually gave its name to the city. The island offered a convenient river crossing on the route between northern and southern Gaul and was easily defended. In later centuries the settlement was expanded by the Romans, the Franks and the Capetian kings to form the nucleus of today's city.

There is no older place in Paris, and remains of the first buildings can still be seen today in the archaeological crypt under the square in front of Notre-Dame, the great medieval cathedral and place of pilgrimage for millions of visitors each year. At the other end of the island is another Gothic masterpiece, Sainte-Chapelle – a miracle of light.

★ Conciergerie
A grisly ante-chamber to the guillotine, this prison was much used in the Revolution ❽

The Cour du Mai
is the impressive main courtyard of the Palais de Justice.

Metro Cité

★ Sainte-Chapelle
A jewel of Gothic architecture and one of the most magical sights of Paris, Sainte-Chapelle is noted for the magnificence of its stained glass ❾

To Pont Neuf

The Quai des Orfèvres
owes its name to the goldsmiths *(orfèvres)* who frequented the area from medieval times onwards.

The Préfecture de Police
is the headquarters of the police and was the scene of intense battles during World War II.

Palais de Justice
With its ancient towers lining the quays, the old royal palace is today a massive complex of law courts. Its history extends back over 16 centuries ❿

0 metres		100
0 yards		100

The Statue of Charlemagne
commemorates the King of the Franks, who was crowned emperor in 800. He united all the Christian peoples of the West.

★ Marché aux Fleurs et Oiseaux
The flower and bird market is a colourful, lively island sight. Paris was once famous for its flower markets but this is now one of the last **7**

LOCATOR MAP
See Central Paris Map pp14–15

Hôtel Dieu
Once an orphanage, this is now a city hospital **6**

★ Crypte Archéologique
Deep under the square, there are remains of houses from 2,000 years ago **5**

CRYPTE DU PARVIS

STAR SIGHTS

★ Notre-Dame

★ Sainte-Chapelle

★ Conciergerie

★ Marché aux Fleurs et Oiseaux

★ Crypte Archéologique

KEY

━ ━ ━ Suggested route

The Rue Chanoinesse has had many famous residents, such as the 17th-century playwright Racine.

Musée Notre-Dame
Many exhibits tracing the cathedral's history are in this museum **2**

Point Zéro
is a mark from which all distances are measured in France.

The Square Jean XXIII
is a peaceful square close to the river **3**

★ Notre-Dame
This cathedral is a superb example of French medieval architecture **1**

To Latin Quarter

Notre-Dame from
the Left Bank

Notre-Dame ❶

See pp82–5.

Musée de Notre-Dame de Paris ❷

10 Rue du Cloître-Notre-Dame 75004.
Map 13 B4. **Tel** 01 43 25 42 92. M
Cité. RER St-Michel. ◯ 2.30pm–6pm
Wed, Sat, Sun (last adm: 5.40pm).

Founded in 1951, this museum has exhibits and documents that commemorate and illustrate the great events in Notre-Dame's history. The displays include Gallo-Roman objects, old engravings, works of art and the city of Paris's oldest extant Christian relic, a fine 4th-century glass cup.

A Gallo-Roman coin

Square Jean XXIII ❸

Rue du Cloître-Notre-Dame 75004.
Map 13 B4. M Cité.

Notre-Dame's St Stephen's door (porte St-Etienne) opens on to this pleasant garden square, dedicated to Pope John XXIII. The garden runs alongside the river and is an excellent place for enjoying the sculptures, rose windows and flying buttresses of the east end of the cathedral.

From the 17th century, the square was occupied by the archbishop's palace, which was ransacked by rioters in 1831 and later demolished. A square was conceived to replace the Prefect of Paris, Rambuteau. The Gothic-style fountain of the Virgin standing in the centre of the square has been there since 1845.

Paris Mémorial de la Déportation ❹

Sq de l'Ile de France 75004. **Map** 13 B4.
Tel 01 46 33 87 56. M Cité. RER St-Michel. ◯ 10am–6pm Tue–Sun.

The simple, modern memorial to the 200,000 French men, women and children deported to Nazi concentration camps in World War II (often via Drancy, just a few miles to the north of Paris) is covered with a roll-call of names of the camps to which they were deported. Earth from these camps has been used to form small tombs and the interior walls are decorated with poetry. At the far end is the tomb dedicated to the Unknown Deportee.

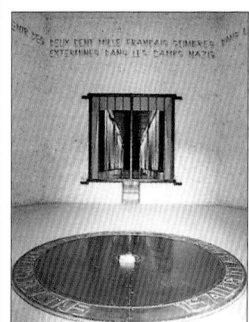

Inside the Paris Mémorial de la Déportation

The Square Jean XXIII behind Notre-Dame

Gallo-Roman ruins in the Crypte Archéologique

Crypte Archéologique ❺

Pl du Parvis Notre-Dame 75004.
Map 13 A4. *Tel* 01 55 42 50 10.
Ⓜ Cité. ◻ Tue–Sun 10am–6pm (last adm: 30 min before closing). ◐ 1 May, 8 May, 1 & 11 Nov, 25 Dec, 1 Jan. 💳 free for children under 12. 🏛

Situated on the main square (the *parvis*) in front of Notre-Dame and stretching 120 m (393 ft) underground, this crypt exhibits the remains of foundations and walls that pre-date the cathedral by several hundred years. There are traces of a sophisticated underground heating system in a house from Lutèce, the settlement of the Parisii, the Celtic tribe who inhabited the island 2,000 years ago, giving their name to the present city.

Hôtel Dieu ❻

1 Pl du Parvis Notre-Dame 75004.
Map 13 A4. ◐ to the public for visits. Ⓜ Cité.

On the north side of the place du Parvis Notre-Dame is the Hôtel Dieu, the hospital serving central Paris. It was built on the site of an

Hôtel Dieu, central Paris's hospital

orphanage between 1866 and 1878. The original Hôtel Dieu, built in the 12th century and stretching across the island to both banks of the river, was demolished in the 19th century to make way for one of Baron Haussmann's urban-planning schemes.

It was here in 1944 that the Paris police courageously resisted the Germans; the battle is commemorated by a monument in Cour de 19-Août.

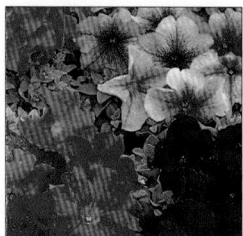

Paris's main flower market

Marché aux Fleurs and Marché aux Oiseaux ❼

Pl Louis-Lépine 75004.
Map 13 A3. Ⓜ Cité.
◻ 8am–7.30pm daily.

The year-round flower market adds colour and scent to an area otherwise dominated by administrative buildings. It is the most famous and unfortunately one of the last remaining flower markets in the city of Paris, offering a wide range of specialist varieties such as orchids. Each Sunday it makes way for the cacophony of the caged bird market.

Conciergerie ❽

1 Quai de l'Horloge 75001.**Map** 13 A3. 🎫 01 53 40 60 93. Ⓜ Cité. ◻ 9.30am–6pm daily (until 5pm Nov–end Feb) (last adm: 30 min before closing). ◐ 1 Jan, 1 May, 25 Dec. 💳 (combined ticket with Ste-Chapelle, pp88–9, available.) 📷 phone to check. 🖥 www.monum.fr

Occupying the north part of the old Capetian palace, the Conciergerie was under the administration of the palace "concierge", the keeper of the King's mansion. When the King moved to the Marais (in 1417), the palace remained the seat of royal administration and law; and the Conciergerie became a prison, with the "concierge" as its chief gaoler. Henry IV's assassin, Ravaillac, was imprisoned and tortured here.

During the Revolution it housed over 4,000 prisoners, including Marie-Antoinette, who was held in a tiny cell and Charlotte Corday, who stabbed Revolutionary leader Marat as he lay in his bath. Ironically, the Revolutionary judges Danton and Robespierre also became "tenants" before being sent to the guillotine.

The Conciergerie has a superb four-aisled Gothic Salle des Gens d'Armes (Hall of the Men-at-Arms), where guards of the royal household once lived. The building, renovated in the 19th century, retains the 11th-century torture chamber, the Bonbec Tower and the 14th-century public clock tower on the Tour de l'Horloge (Palais de Justice). It is the city's oldest and is still operating.

A portrait of Marie-Antoinette in the Conciergerie, awaiting her execution at the guillotine

Notre-Dame ❶

No other building is so associated with the history of Paris as Notre-Dame. It stands majestically on the Ile de la Cité, cradle of the city. Pope Alexander III laid the first stone in 1163, marking the start of 170 years of toil by armies of Gothic architects and medieval crafts-men. Ever since, a procession of the famous has passed through the three main doors below the massive towers.

The cathedral is a Gothic masterpiece, standing on the site of a Roman temple. At the time it was finished, in about 1330, it was 130 m (430 ft) long and featured flying buttresses, a large transept, a deep choir and 69-m (228-ft) high towers.

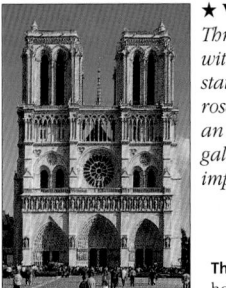

★ West Front
Three main doors with superb statuary, a central rose window and an openwork gallery are important details.

The south tower houses the cathedral's famous Emmanuel bell.

★ Galerie des Chimères
The cathedral's legendary gargoyles (chimères) hide behind a large upper gallery between the towers.

★ West Rose Window
This window depicts the Virgin in a medallion of rich reds and blues.

STAR FEATURES

★ West Front and Portals

★ Flying Buttresses

★ Rose Windows

★ Galerie des Chimères

The Kings' Gallery features 28 Kings of Judah gazing down on the crowds.

Portal of the Virgin
The Virgin surrounded by saints and kings is a fine composition of 13th-century statues.

★ Flying Buttresses
Jean Ravy's spectacular flying buttresses at the east end of the cathedral have a span of 15 m (50 ft).

The spire, designed by Viollet-le-Duc, soars to a height of 90 m (295 ft).

VISITORS' CHECKLIST

Pl du Parvis-Notre-Dame. **Map** 13 B4. 01 42 34 56 10. Cité. 21, 38, 85, 96 to Ile de la Cité. Notre-Dame. Pl du Parvis. 7.45am–6.45pm daily. 8, 9am (not Jul, Aug), noon, 6.15pm Mon– Fri; 6.30pm Sat; 8.30, 10, 11.30am, 12.45, 6.30pm Sun. Towers 10am– 5.30pm (summer: 9.30am– 7.30pm; to 11pm Sat, S www.cathedraledepari

★ South Rose Window
This south facade window, with its central depiction of Christ, is an impressive 13m (43 ft) high.

The transept was built at the start of Philippe-Auguste's reign, in the 13th century.

The treasury houses the cathedral's religious treasures, including Christ's purported Crown of Thorns.

TIMELINE

1163 Foundation stone laid by Pope Alexander III	**1572** Marguerite de Valois marries Henri of Navarre (later Henri IV)	**1793** Revolutionaries loot the cathedral and rename it Temple of Reason		**1944** Liberation of Paris Thanksgiving ceremony
1150	**1550**	**1750**		**1950**
	1708 Choir remodelled by Louis XIV, fulfilling his father's promise to honour the Virgin	**1795–1802** Cathedral closed		**1970** State funeral of General de Gaulle
		1804 Napoleon crowns himself Emperor of France	*Napoleon I*	

A Guided Tour of Notre-Dame

Notre-Dame's interior grandeur is instantly apparent on seeing the high-vaulted central nave. This is bisected by a huge transept, at either end of which are medieval rose windows, 13 m (43 ft) in diameter. Works by major sculptors adorn the cathedral. Among them are Jean Ravy's old choir screen carvings, Nicolas Coustou's *Pietà* and Antoine Coysevox's Louis XIV statue. In this majestic setting kings and emperors were crowned and royal Crusaders were blessed. But Notre-Dame was also the scene of turmoil. Revolutionaries ransacked it, banished religion, changed it into a temple to the Cult of Reason, and then used it as a wine store. Napoleon restored religion in 1804 and architect Viollet-le-Duc later restored the buildings, replacing missing statues, as well as raising the spire and fixing the gargoyles.

A jewelled chalice of Notre-Dame

⑨ **North Rose Window**
This 13th-century stained-glass window depicts the Virgin encircled by figures from the Old Testament.

⑩ **View and Gargoyles**
The 387 steps up the north tower lead to sights of the famous gargoyles and magnificent views of Paris.

Stairs to the tower

Entrance

① **View of Interior**
From the main entrance, the view takes in the high-vaulted central nave looking down towards the huge transept, the choir and the high altar.

KEY

━ ━ ━ Suggested route

② **Le Brun's "May" Paintings**
These religious paintings by Charles Le Brun hang in the side chapels. In the 17th and 18th centuries, the Paris guilds presented a painting to the cathedral on May Day each year.

⑧ Carved Choir Stalls

Noted for their early 18th-century carved woodwork, the choir stalls were commissioned by Louis XIV, whose statue stands behind the high altar. Among the details carved in bas-relief on the back of the high stalls are scenes from the life of the Virgin.

⑦ Louis XIII Statue

After many years of childless marriage, Louis XIII pledged to erect a high altar and to redecorate the east chancel to honour the Virgin if an heir was born to him. The future Louis XIV was born in 1638, but it took 60 years before the promises were made good. One of the surviving features from that time is the carved choir stalls.

Entrance to Treasury

Entrance to Sacristy

⑥ Pietà

Behind the high altar is Nicolas Coustou's Pietà, standing on a gilded base sculptured by François Girardon.

⑤ Chancel Screen

A 14th-century high stone screen enclosed the chancel and provided canons at prayer with peace and solitude from noisy congregations. Some of it has survived to screen the first three north and south bays.

③ South Rose Window

Located at the south end of the transept, this window retains some of its original 13th-century stained glass. The window depicts Christ in the centre, surrounded by virgins, saints and the 12 Apostles.

④ Statue of the Virgin and Child

Against the southeast pillar of the transept stands the 14th-century statue of the Virgin and Child. It was brought to the cathedral from the chapel of St Aignan, and is known as Notre-Dame de Paris (Our Lady of Paris).

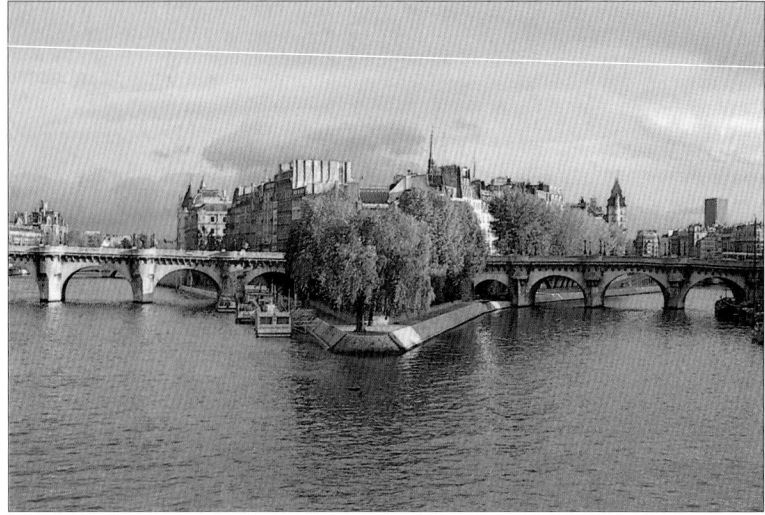

The Pont Neuf, extending to the north and south of the Ile de la Cité

Sainte-Chapelle ❾

See pp88–9.

A Sainte-Chapelle decoration of angels with the Crown of Thorns

Palais de Justice ❿

4 Blvd du Palais (entrance by the Cour de Mai) 75001. **Map** 13 A3.
Tel *01 44 32 50 00.* Ⓜ *Cité.*
⬤ *9am–6.30pm Mon–Fri.*
🚫 ▣ 🚻

This huge block of buildings making up the law courts stretches the entire width of the Ile de la Cité. It is a splendid sight with its old towers lining the quays. The site has been occupied since Roman times and was the seat of royal power until Charles V moved the court to the Marais in the 14th century. In April 1793 the Revolutionary Tribunal began dispensing justice from the Première Chambre (gilded chamber). Today the site embodies Napoleon's great legacy – the French judicial system.

Place Dauphine ⓫

75001 (enter by Rue Henri-Robert). **Map** 12 F3. Ⓜ *Pont Neuf, Cité.*

East of Pont Neuf is this ancient square, laid out in 1607 by Henri IV and named after the Dauphin, the future Louis XIII. No. 14 is one of the few buildings to have avoided any subsequent restoration. This haven of 17th-century charm is popular with *pétanque* (boules) players and employees of the adjoining Palais de Justice.

Pont Neuf ⓬

75001. **Map** 12 F3. Ⓜ *Pont Neuf, Cité.*

Despite its name (New Bridge), this bridge is the oldest in Paris and has been immortalized by major literary and artistic figures since it was built. The first stone was laid by Henri III in 1578, but it was Henri IV who inaugurated it and gave it its name in 1607. The bridge has 12 arches and spans 275 m (912 ft). The first stone bridge to be built without houses, it heralded a new era in the relationship between the Cité and the river and has been popular ever since. Fittingly, Henri IV's statue stands in the central section.

A sculptured relief on the Palais de Justice

Henri IV in Square du Vert-Galant

Square du Vert-Galant ⓭

75001. **Map** 12 F3. Ⓜ Pont Neuf, Cité.

One of the magical spots of Paris, this square bears the nickname of Henri IV. This amorous and colourful monarch did much to beautify Paris in the early 17th century, and his popularity has lasted to this day. From here there are splendid views of the Louvre and the Right Bank of the river, where Henri was assassinated in 1610. This is also the point from which the Vedettes du Pont Neuf pleasure boats depart *(see pp72–3)*.

Société Historique et Littéraire Polonaise ⓮

6 Quai d'Orléans 75004. **Map** 13 C4. **Tel** 01 55 42 83 83. Ⓜ Pont Marie. ◗ 2.15–5.15pm Thu, 9am–noon Sat. ▨ ☑ every 45 min Thu, on the hour Sat; phone to book.

The Polish Romantic poet Adam Mickiewicz, who lived in Paris in the 19th century, was a major force in Polish cultural and political life, devoting his writing to helping his countrymen who were oppressed at home and abroad. His life is the focal point of the museum, which was founded in 1903 by the poet's son. Part of the famous

Polish library has moved to 74 rue Lauriston, but the archives remain. They form the finest Polish collection outside Poland: paintings, books, maps, emigration archive and Frédéric Chopin memorabilia, including his death mask.

St-Louis-en-l'Ile ⓯

19 bis Rue St-Louis-en-l'Ile 75004. **Map** 13 C4. **Tel** 01 46 34 11 60. Ⓜ Pont Marie. ◗ 9am–noon, 3pm–7pm Tue–Sun. ◗ public hols. **Concerts.**

The construction of this church was begun in 1664 from plans by the royal architect Louis Le Vau, who lived on the island. It was completed and consecrated in 1726. Among its outstanding exterior features are the 1741 iron clock at the entrance and the pierced iron spire.

The interior, in the Baroque style, is richly decorated with gilding and marble. There is a statue of St Louis holding a crusader's sword. A plaque in the north aisle, given in 1926, bears the inscription "in grateful memory of St Louis in whose honour the City of St Louis, Missouri, USA is named". The church is also twinned with Carthage cathedral in Tunisia, where St Louis is buried.

A bust of Adam Mickiewicz

The interior of St-Louis-en-l'Ile

Hôtel de Lauzun ⓰

17 Quai d'Anjou 75004. **Map** 13 C4. Ⓜ Pont Marie. ◗ Tue, Thu for conferences. Call 01 43 54 27 14 for details.

This splendid mansion was built by Louis Le Vau in the mid-1650s for Charles Gruyn des Bordes, an arms dealer. It was sold in 1682 to the French military commander Duc de Lauzun, who was a favourite of Louis XIV. It later became a focus for Paris's Bohemian literary and artistic life. It now belongs to the city of Paris and, for those lucky enough to see inside, offers an unsurpassed insight into wealthy lifestyles in the 17th century. Charles Le Brun worked on the decoration of its magnificent panelling and painted ceilings before moving on to Versailles.

The poet Charles Baudelaire (1821–67) lived on the third floor and wrote the major part of his controversial masterpiece *Les Fleurs du Mal* here in a room packed with antiques and bric-a-brac. The celebrated French Romantic poet, traveller and critic, Théophile Gautier (1811–72), had apartments here in 1848. Meetings of the Club des Haschischines (the Hashish-Eaters' Club) took place on the premises.

Other famous residents were the Austrian poet Rainer Maria Rilke, the English artist Walter Sickert and the German composer Richard Wagner. Nowadays it is used for public receptions by the mayor of Paris.

Sainte-Chapelle **9**

Ethereal and magical, Sainte-Chapelle has been hailed as one of the greatest architectural master-pieces of the Western world. In the Middle Ages the devout likened this church to "a gateway to heaven". Today no visitor can fail to be transported by the blaze of light created by the 15 magnificent stained-glass windows, separated by the narrowest of columns that soar 15 m (50 ft) to the star-studded, vaulted roof. The windows portray over 1,000 religious scenes in a kaleidoscope of red, gold, green, blue and mauve. The chapel was built in 1248 by Louis IX to house Christ's purported Crown of Thorns (now housed in the Notre-Dame treasury).

The spire
rises 75 m (245 ft) into the air. It was erected in 1853 after four previous spires burned down.

The Crown of Thorns
decorates the pinnacle as a symbol of the first relic bought by Louis IX.

★ Rose Window
Best seen at sunset, the religious story of the Apocalypse is told in 86 panels of stained glass. The window was a gift from Charles VIII in 1485.

STAR FEATURES

★ Rose Window

★ Window of Christ's Passion

★ Apostle Statues

★ Window of the Relics

Main Portal
The two-tier structure of the portal, the lower half of which is shown here, echoes that of the chapel.

ST LOUIS' RELICS

Louis IX was extremely devout, and was canonized in 1297, not long after his death. In 1239 he acquired the Crown of Thorns from the Emperor of Constantinople and, in 1241, a fragment of Christ's Cross. He built this chapel as a shrine to house them. Louis paid nearly three times more for the relics than for the construction of Sainte-Chapelle. The Crown of Thorns is now kept at Notre-Dame.

VISITORS' CHECKLIST

4 Blvd du Palais. **Map** 13 A3. 01 53 40 60 80. Cité. 21, 27, 38, 85, 96 to Ile de la Cité. St-Michel. Notre-Dame. Palais de Justice. daily. Mar–Oct: 9.30am–6pm; Nov–Feb: 9am–5pm. Last adm 30 mins before closing. 1 Jan, 1 May, 1 Nov, 11 Nov, 25 Dec. (combined ticket with Conciergerie, p81, is available.)

The angel once revolved so that its cross could be seen from anywhere in Paris.

UPPER CHAPEL WINDOWS

Upper Chapel
The windows are a pictorial Bible, showing scenes from the Old and New Testaments.

1 Genesis
2 Exodus
3 Numbers
4 Deuteronomy: Joshua
5 Judges
6 *left* Isaiah *right* Rod of Jesse
7 *left* St John the Evangelist *right* Childhood of Christ
8 Christ's Passion
9 *left* St John the Baptist *right* Story of Daniel
10 Ezekiel
11 *left* Jeremiah *right* Tobiah
12 Judith and Job
13 Esther
14 Book of Kings
15 Story of the Relics
16 Rose Window: The Apocalypse

★ Window of Christ's Passion
The Last Supper is shown here in one of the most beautiful windows in the upper chapel.

★ Apostle Statues
These magnificent examples of medieval stone carving adorn the 12 pillars of the upper chapel.

★ Window of the Relics
This shows the journey of the True Cross and the nails of the Crucifixion to Sainte-Chapelle.

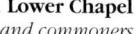

Lower Chapel
Servants and commoners worshipped here, while the chapel above was reserved for the use of the king and the royal family.

THE MARAIS

A place of royal residence in the 17th century, the Marais was all but abandoned during the Revolution, later descending into an architectural wasteland. Sensitive restoration brought the area to life again; some of Paris's most popular museums are now housed in its elegant mansions, while the main streets and narrow passageways bustle with smart boutiques, galleries and restaurants. Many traders have been driven out by high prices, but enough artisans, bakers and small cafés survive, as does the ethnic mix of Jews, former Algerian settlers, Asians and others. Today, the Marais is also the centre of the Parisian gay scene.

SIGHTS AT A GLANCE

Historic Buildings and Streets
Hôtel de Lamoignon ❷
Rue des Francs-Bourgeois ❸
Rue des Rosiers ❽
Hôtel de Ville ❿
Hôtel de Rohan ㉒

Churches
St-Paul–St-Louis ⓯
St-Gervais–St-Protais ⓲
Cloître des Billettes ⓴
Notre-Dame-des-Blancs-Manteaux ㉑

Museums and Galleries
Musée Carnavalet pp96–7 ❶
Musée Cognacq-Jay ❹
Maison de Victor Hugo ❻
Hôtel de Sully ❼
Hôtel de Coulanges ❾
Hôtel Libéral Bruand ❿
Musée Picasso pp100–1 ⓫
Hôtel de Sens ⓰
Hôtel de Soubise ㉓
Hôtel Guénégaud (Musée de la Chasse et de la Nature) ㉔
Musée des Arts et Métiers ㉕
Musée d'Art et d'Histoire du Judaïsme ㉗

Monuments and Statues
Colonne de Juillet ⓭
Mémorial de la Shoah ⓱

Opera Houses
Opéra National de Paris Bastille ⓬

Squares
Place des Vosges ❺
Place de la Bastille ⓮
Square du Temple ㉖

KEY
- ▦ Street-by-Street map
- Ⓜ Metro station
- ⬛ Batobus boarding point

| 0 metres | 400 |
| 0 yards | 400 |

GETTING THERE
The metro stations in the area include Bastille, and Hôtel de Ville. Bus route 29 travels along Rue des Francs-Bourgeois, passing by the Rue de Sévigné, where the Musée Carnavalet is located, and by the Place des Vosges.

SEE ALSO
- *Street Finder,* map 13–14
- *Where to Stay* p284
- *Restaurants* p301

◁ **Lunchtime at a Marais park café**

Street by Street: The Marais

Once an area of marshland as its name suggests (*marais* means swamp), the Marais grew steadily in importance from the 14th century, by virtue of its proximity to the Louvre, the preferred residence of Charles V. Its heyday was in the 17th century, when it became the fashionable area for the monied classes. They built many grand and sumptuous mansions (*hôtels*) that still dot the Marais today. Many of these *hôtels* have recently been restored and turned into museums. Once again fashionable with the monied classes, designer boutiques, trendy restaurants and cafés now line the streets.

To the Pompidou Centre

Rue des Francs-Bourgeois
This ancient street is lined with important museums ❸

Hôtel Libéral Bruand
Named after the architect who built it for his own use, this mansion is now used for temporary art exhibitions ❿

Rue des Rosiers
The smell of hot pastrami and borscht wafts from restaurants and shops in the heart of the Jewish area ❽

Musée Cognacq-Jay
An exquisite collection of 18th-century paintings and furniture is shown in perfect period setting ❹

STAR SIGHTS

★ Musée Picasso

★ Musée Carnavalet

★ Place des Vosges

KEY

- - - Suggested route

| 0 metres | 100 |
| 0 yards | 100 |

Hôtel de Lamoignon
Behind the ornate doorway of this fine mansion is Paris's historical library ❷

★ Musée Picasso
The palatial home of a 17th-century salt-tax collector is the setting for the largest collection of Picassos in the world, the result of a family bequest to the state ⓫

LOCATOR MAP
See Central Paris Map pp14–15

The Hôtel le Peletier de St-Fargeau adjoins the Hôtel Carnavalet to form a museum of Paris history.

★ Musée Carnavalet
The statue of Louis XIV in Roman dress by Coysevox is in the courtyard of the Hôtel Carnavalet ❶.

Maison de Victor Hugo
Author of Les Misérables, *Victor Hugo lived at No. 6 Place des Vosges, where his house is now a museum of his life and work* ❻

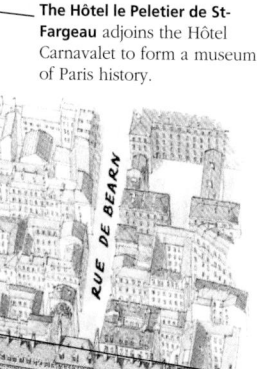

To Metro Sully Morland

★ Place des Vosges
Once the site of jousting and tournaments, the historic Place des Vosges, in the very heart of the Marais, is a square of perfect symmetry ❺

Hôtel de Sully
This Renaissance hôtel was built for a notorious gambler ❼

Musée Carnavalet ❶

See pp96–7.

Hôtel de Lamoignon ❷

24 Rue Pavée 75004. **Map** 14 D3.
Tel *01 44 59 29 40.* Ⓜ *St-Paul.*
◯ *1–6pm Mon–Fri, 9.30am–6pm Sat.* ⬤ *public hols & 1–15 Aug.* ▯

The imposing Hôtel de Lamoignon is home to the historical library of the city of Paris. This mansion was built in 1585 for Diane de France, also known as the Duchesse d'Angoulême, daughter of Henri II. The building is noted for six high Corinthian pilasters topped by a triangular pediment and flourishes of dogs' heads, bows, arrows and quivers – recalling Diane's passion for hunting. The collection includes documents from the French Revolution and 80,000 prints covering the history of Paris.

Rue des Francs-Bourgeois ❸

75003, 75004. **Map** 14 D3.
Ⓜ *Rambuteau, Chemin-Vert.*

This street is an important thoroughfare in the heart of the Marais, linking the Rue des Archives and the Place

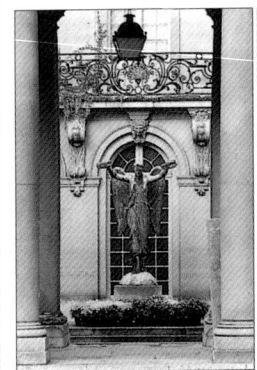

Courtyard of the Musée Carnavalet

des Vosges, with the imposing Hôtel de Soubise at one end and the Musée Carnavalet at the other. The street got its name from the *francs* (free from taxes) – almshouses built for the poor in 1334 at Nos. 34 and 36. These were later closed because of illegal financial activities, although the state kept its pawnshop nearby, still there today.

Musée Cognacq-Jay ❹

Hôtel Donon, 8 Rue Elzévir 75004.
Map 14 D3. ***Tel*** *01 40 27 07 21.*
Ⓜ *St-Paul.* ◯ *10am–6pm Tue–Sun.*
⬤ *public hols.* ☑ *pre-book.* ▯
www.cognacq-jay.paris.fr

This fine small collection of French 18th-century works of art and furniture was formed by Ernest Cognacq and his wife, Louise Jay, founder of the Art Deco La Samaritaine, Paris's largest department store *(see p115)*. The private collection was bequeathed to the city and is now housed in the heart of the Marais at the Hôtel Donon – an elegant building dating from 1575 with an 18th-century extension and facade.

Place des Vosges ❺

75003, 75004. **Map** 14 D3.
Ⓜ *Bastille, St-Paul.*

This square is considered among the most beautiful in the world by Parisians and visitors alike *(see pp24–5)*. Its impressive symmetry – 36 houses, nine on each side, of brick and stone, with deep slate roofs and dormer windows over arcades – is still intact after 400 years. It has been the scene of many historic events over the centuries. A three-day tournament was held here to celebrate the marriage of Louis XIII to Anne of Austria in 1615. The famous literary hostess, Madame de Sévigné, was born here in 1626; Cardinal Richelieu, pillar of the monarchy, stayed here in 1615; and Victor Hugo, the writer, lived here for 16 years.

A 19th-century engraving of the Place des Vosges

Maison de Victor Hugo ⑥

6 Pl des Vosges 75004. **Map** 14 D3.
Tel 01 42 72 10 16. Ⓜ️ Bastille.
◯ 10am–6pm Tue–Sun.
⬤ public hols. 🖼️ ☑ **Library**.
www.musee-hugo.paris.fr

The French poet, dramatist and novelist lived on the second floor of the former Hôtel Rohan-Guéménée from 1832 to 1848. It was here that he wrote most of *Les Misérables* and completed many other famous works. On display are some reconstructions of the rooms in which he lived, pen-and-ink drawings, books and mementos from the crucially important periods in his life, from his childhood to his exile between 1852 and 1870. Temporary exhibitions on Hugo take place regularly.

Marble bust of Victor Hugo by Auguste Rodin

Hôtel de Sully ⑦

62 Rue St-Antoine 75004. **Map** 14 D4. *Tel* 01 42 74 47 75. Ⓜ️ St-Paul. ◯ noon–7pm Tue–Fri; 10am–7pm Sat, Sun. ⬤ 1 Jan, 1 May, 1 & 11 Nov, 25 Dec. 🖼️ ☑ **www**.jeudepaume.org

This fine 17th-century mansion on one of Paris's oldest streets has been extensively restored, using old engravings and drawings as reference. It was built in 1624 for a notorious gambler, Petit Thomas, who lost his whole fortune in one night. The Duc de Sully, Henri IV's chief minister, purchased the house in 1634 and added some of the interior decoration as well as the Petit Sully orangery in the gardens. The Hôtel de Sully has now joined forces with the Tuileries' Jeu de Paume museum (*see p131*), showcasing contemporary works on photography, film and the moving arts.

Late-Renaissance facade of the Hôtel de Sully

Rue des Rosiers ⑧

75004. **Map** 13 C3. Ⓜ️ St-Paul.

The Jewish quarter in and around this street is one of the most colourful areas of Paris. The street's name refers to the rosebushes within the old city wall. Jews first settled here in the 13th century, with a second significant wave of immigration occurring in the 19th century from Russia, Poland and central Europe. Sephardic Jews arrived from Algeria, Tunisia, Morocco and Egypt in the 1950s and 1960s. Some 165 students were rounded up and deported from the old Jewish Boys' school nearby at 10 rue de Hospitalières-St-Gervais. *N'Oubliez pas* (Lest we forget) is engraved on the wall. Today this area contains synagogues, bakeries and kosher restaurants (*see p333*).

Orthodox Jews in the Marais

Hôtel de Coulanges ⑨

35 rue des Francs Bourgeois, 75004. **Map** 13 C3. *Tel* 01 44 61 85 85. Ⓜ️ St-Paul. ◯ 1.30pm–7pm Mon–Fri. ⬤ public hols. **www**.paris-europe.com

This hôtel is a magnificent example of the architecture of the early 18th century. The right wing of the building, separating the courtyard from the garden, dates from the early 17th century. The hôtel was given in 1640 to Phillipe II de Coulanges, the King's counsellor. Renamed the "Petit hôtel Le Tellier" in 1662 by its new owner Le Tellier, this is where the children of Louis XIV and Madame de Montespan were raised in secrecy. It is home to the Maison de L'Europe, with exhibitions on themes relating to Europe.

Musée Carnavalet ❶

Carnavalet entrance

Devoted to the history of Paris, this vast museum occupies two adjoining mansions, with entire decorated rooms with panelling, furniture and *objets d'art;* many works of art such as paintings and sculptures of prominent personalities; and engravings showing Paris being built. The main building is the Hôtel Carnavalet, built as a town house in 1548 and transformed in the mid-17th century by François Mansart. The neighbouring 17th-century mansion, Hôtel Le Peletier, features superb early 20th-century interiors, and the newly-restored Orangery is devoted to Prehistory and Gallo-Roman Paris.

Marie Antoinette in Mourning *(1793) Alexandre Kucharski painted her at the Temple prison after the execution of Louis XVI.*

Memorabilia in this room is dedicated to 18th-century philosophers, in particular Jean-Jacques Rousseau and Voltaire.

★ **Charles Le Brun Ceiling**
Magnificent works by the 17th-century artist decorate the former study and great hall from the Hôtel de la Rivière.

★ **Mme de Sévigné's Gallery**
The gallery includes this portrait of Mme de Sévigné, the celebrated letter-writer, whose beloved home this was for the 20 years up to her death.

STAR EXHIBITS

- ★ Charles Le Brun Ceiling
- ★ Mme de Sévigné's Gallery
- ★ Hôtel d'Uzès Reception Room
- ★ Ballroom of the Hôtel de Wendel

★ **Hôtel d'Uzès Reception Room**
The room was created in 1761 by Claude Nicolas Ledoux. The gold-and-white panelling is from a Rue Montmartre mansion.

Entr the m

Convention Room
Georges Danton's portrait is among the memorabilia of the Revolution.

Second floor

First floor

Hôtel Le Peletier

VISITORS' CHECKLIST

23 Rue de Sévigné 75003. **Map** 14 D3. **Tel** 01 44 59 58 58. M St-Paul. 29, 69, 76, 96 to St-Paul, Pl des Vosges. P Hôtel de Ville, Rue St-Antoine. 10am–6pm Tue–Sun (last adm: 5.30pm). Rooms open in rotas; phone to check). public hols. phone for times. www.carnavalet.paris.fr

Fouquet Jewellery Boutique *(1900)*
The Art Nouveau decor of this shop from Rue Royale is by A Moucha.

★ Ballroom of the Hôtel de Wendel
The early 20th-century ballroom interior has been reconstructed. This immense mural depicts the retinue of the Queen of Sheba and is by the Catalan designer and painter José María Sert y Badia.

Louis XV Room
This delightful room contains art from the Bouvier collection and panelling from the Hôtel de Broglie.

KEY TO FLOOR PLAN

- Prehistory to Gallo-Roman
- Medieval Paris
- Renaissance Paris
- 17th-century Paris
- Louis XV's Paris
- Louis XVI's Paris
- Revolutionary Paris
- 19th Century
- 20th Century
- Temporary exhibitions
- Non-exhibition space

GALLERY GUIDE
The collection is mainly arranged chronologically. It covers the history of Paris up to 1789. The Renaissance is on the ground floor, and the exhibits covering the 17th century to the Revolution are on the first floor. In the Hôtel le Peletier the ground floor covers the First–Second Empires, with the new Prehistory–Gallo-Roman departments in the Orangery; from the Second Empire to the present day is on the first floor, and the second floor is devoted to the Revolution.

Hôtel Libéral Bruand ❿

1 Rue de la Perle 75003.**Map** 14 D3. **Tel** 01 42 77 96 74. Ⓜ St-Paul, Chemin-Vert. **Museum** ⃝ for temporary exhibitions; phone to check. ⬤ Aug & public hols. 🎫

This small private house, built by the architect Libéral Bruand for himself in 1685, is far removed, with its elegant Italianate touches, from his most famous work, the gilded Hôtel des Invalides (see p187).
   The building is usually closed to the public but contains an art gallery that hosts temporary art exhibitions from time to time.

Musée Picasso ⓫

See pp100–1.

Opéra National de Paris Bastille ⓬

120 Rue de Lyon 75012. **Map** 4 E4. 🎟 08 92 89 90 90. Ⓜ Bastille. ⃝ phone for details. ⬤ certain public hols. 🎫 ♿ ⓒ compulsory. See **Entertainment** pp332–5. **www**.operadeparis.fr

The controversial "people's opera" was officially opened on 14 July 1989 to coincide with the bicentennial celebrations of the fall

The "genius of liberty" on top of the Colonne de Juillet

of the Bastille. Carlos Ott's imposing building is a notable break with 19th-century opera-house design, epitomized by Garnier's opulent Opéra in the heart of the city (see pp216–17). It is a massive, modern, curved, glass building. The main auditorium seats an audience of 2,700; its design is functional and modern with black upholstered seats contrasting with the granite of the walls and the impressive glass ceiling. With its five moveable stages, this opera house is certainly a masterpiece of technological wizardry.

Colonne de Juillet ⓭

Pl de la Bastille 75004. **Map** 14 E4. Ⓜ Bastille. ⬤ to the public.

Topped by the statue of the "genius of liberty", this column of hollow bronze reaches 51.5 m (170 ft) into the sky. It is a memorial to those who died in the street battles of July 1830 that led to the overthrow of the monarch (see pp32–3). The crypt contains the remains of 504 victims of the violent fighting and others who died in the 1848 revolution.

Place de la Bastille ⓮

75004. **Map** 14 E4. Ⓜ Bastille.

Nothing is now left of the prison stormed by the revolutionary mob on 14 July 1789 (see pp30–31) – an event celebrated annually by the French at home and abroad – although the stones were used for the Pont de la Concorde. A line of paving stones from Nos. 5 to 49 Blvd Henri IV traces the former towers and fortifications. Until recently, the large, traffic-clogged square which marks the site, was the border between central Paris and the eastern working-class areas (faubourgs). Gentrification, however, is well underway, with a new marina, the Port de Plaisance de l'Arsenal, and attractive cafés and shops.

The glass facade of the Bastille Opéra

St-Paul–St-Louis ⑮

99 Rue St-Antoine 75004. **Map** 14 D4. **Tel** 01 42 72 30 32. Ⓜ St-Paul. ⏲ 8am–8pm daily. **Concerts**

A Jesuit church, St-Paul–St-Louis was an important symbol of the influence which the Jesuits held from 1627, when Louis XIII laid the first stone, to 1762 when they were expelled from France. The Gesù church in Rome served as the model for the nave, while the 60-m high (180-ft) dome was the forerunner of those of the Invalides and the Sorbonne. Most of the church's treasures were removed during periods of turmoil, but Delacroix's masterpiece, *Christ in the Garden of Olives*, can still be seen. The church stands on one of the main streets of the Marais, but can also be approached by the ancient Passage St-Paul.

Christ in the Garden of Olives by Delacroix in St-Paul–St-Louis

him to die of rage in 1594 on hearing that the Protestant Henri IV had entered Paris. Marguerite de Valois, lodged here by her ex-husband, Henri IV, led a life of breathtaking debauchery and scandal. This culminated in the beheading of an ex-lover, who had dared to assassinate her current favourite.

Hôtel de Sens ⑯

1 Rue du Figuier 75004. **Map** 13 C4. **Tel** 01 42 78 14 60. Ⓜ Pont-Marie. ⏲ 1.30–7pm Tue–Sat. ● public hols. 📷 for exhibitions. 📷 by appointment only.

This is one of the few medieval buildings left in Paris. It now houses the Forney fine arts library. In the 16th century, at the time of the Catholic League, it was turned into a fortified mansion and occupied by the Bourbons, the Guises and Cardinal de Pellevé, whose religious fervour led

The memorial to the unknown Jewish martyr, dedicated in 1956

Mémorial de la Shoah ⑰

17 Rue Geoffroy-l'Asnier 75004. 75004. **Map** 13 C4. **Tel** 01 42 77 44 72. Ⓜ Pont-Marie. ⏲ 10am–6pm Sun–Fri (10am–10pm Thu). 📷 ♿ 🅿 www.memorialdelashoah.org

The eternal flame burning in the crypt here is the simple memorial to the unknown Jewish martyr of the Holocaust. Its striking feature is a large cylinder that bears the names of the concentration camps where Jewish victims of the Holocaust died. In 2005 a stone wall, engraved with the names of 76,000 Jews – 11,000 of them children – who were deported from France to the Nazi death camps, was also erected here.

St-Gervais–St-Protais ⑱

Pl St-Gervais 75004. **Map** 13 B3. **Tel** 01 48 87 32 02. Ⓜ Hôtel de Ville. ⏲ 5.30am–10pm daily.

Named after Gervase and Protase, two Roman soldiers who were martyred by Nero, this remarkable church dates from the 6th century. It has the oldest Classical facade in Paris, which is formed of a three-tiered arrangement of columns: Doric, Ionic and Corinthian. Behind its facade lies a beautiful Gothic church renowned for its association with religious music. It was for the church's fine organ that François Couperin (1668–1733) composed his two masses. The church currently has a Roman Catholic monastic community whose liturgy attracts people from all over the world.

The Hôtel de Sens, now home to a fine arts library

The facade of St-Gervais–St-Protais with its Classical columns

Musée Picasso ⑪

On the death of the Spanish-born artist Pablo Picasso (1881–1973), who lived most of his life in France, the French State inherited many of his works in lieu of death duties. It used them to establish the Musée Picasso, which opened in 1985. The museum is housed in a large 17th-century mansion, the Hôtel Salé, in the Marais. The original character of the Hôtel, which was built in 1656 for Aubert de Fontenay, a salt-tax collector (*salé* means "salty"), has been preserved. The breadth of the collection reflects Picasso's artistic development, including his Blue, Pink and Cubist periods. The museum will close for refurbishment from July 2008 to 2010/2011.

★ Self-Portrait
Poverty, loneliness and the onset of winter all made the end of 1901, when this picture was painted, a particularly difficult time for Picasso.

Violin and Sheet Music
This collage (1912) is from the artist's Synthetic Cubist period.

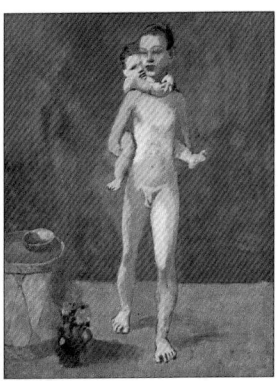

★ The Two Brothers
During the summer of 1906 Picasso returned to Catalonia in Spain, where he painted this picture.

★ The Kiss *(1969)*
Picasso married Jacqueline Roque in 1961, and at around the same time he returned to the familiar themes of the couple and of the artist and model.

GALLERY GUIDE

The collection is mainly presented in chronological order, starting on the first floor with the Blue and Pink periods, Cubist and Neo-Classical works. Exhibitions change regularly – not all paintings are on show at any one time. On the ground floor there is a sculpture garden and works from the late 1920s to late 1930s, and from the mid-1950s to 1973.

Basement

KEY TO FLOORPLAN

☐	Paintings
☐	Illustrations
☐	Sculpture garden
☐	Ceramics
☐	Non-exhibition space

Woman with a Mantilla *(1949)*
Picasso extended his range when he began working in ceramics in 1948.

Painter with Palette and Easel *(1928)*
This Post-Cubist portrait in oils was painted at a time when Picasso's work was verging on Surrealism.

VISITORS' CHECKLIST

Hôtel Salé, 5 Rue de Thorigny.
Map 14 D2. ☎ 01 42 71 25 21. Ⓜ St-Sébastien Froissart, St-Paul. 🚌 29, 69, 75, 96 to St-Paul, Bastille, Pl des Vosges. RER Châtelet-Les-Halles. Ⓟ Rue St-Antoine, Bastille. ⬜ Apr–Sep: 9.30am–6pm Wed–Mon; Oct–Mar: 9.30am–5.30pm Wed–Mon. ⬤ 1 Jan, 25 Dec. 🎦 📷 ♿ 🛍 groups by appointment only. ⬜ 🏠
www.musee-picasso.fr

First floor

★ **Two Women Running on the Beach** *(1922)*
In 1924 this was used for the stage curtain design for Diaghilev's ballet The Blue Train. *It proved to be his last major design work for any theatre.*

Woman Reading *(1932)*
Purples and yellows were often used by Picasso when painting his model Marie-Thérèse Walter.

Ground floor

trance

Entrance

STAR PAINTINGS

★ Self-Portrait

★ The Two Brothers

★ Two Women Running on the Beach

★ The Kiss

PICASSO AND SPAIN

After 1934, Picasso never returned to his homeland due to his rejection of Franco's regime. However, throughout his life in France he used Spanish themes in his art, such as the bull (often in the form of a minotaur) and the guitar, which he associated with his Andalusian childhood.

The town hall (Hôtel de Ville), overlooking a delightful square

Hôtel de Ville ⑲

Pl de l'Hôtel de Ville 75004. **Map** 13 B3. **Tel** *01 42 76 40 40.* Ⓜ *Hôtel-de-Ville.* ⃝ *groups: by arrangement.* ⬤ *public hols, official functions.* ♿ ☑

Home of the city council, the town hall is a 19th-century reconstruction of the 17th-century town hall that was burned down in 1871. It is highly ornate, with elaborate stonework, turrets and statues overlooking a pedestrianized square which is a delight to stroll in, especially at night when the fountains are illuminated.

The square was once the main site for hangings, burnings and other executions. It was here that Ravaillac, Henri IV's assassin, was quartered alive, his body ripped to pieces by four strong horses.

Inside the Hôtel de Ville, a notable feature is the long Salle des Fêtes (ballroom), with adjoining salons devoted to science, literature and the arts. The impressive staircase, the decorated coffered ceilings with their chandeliers and the numerous statues and caryatids all add to the air of ceremony and pomp – a fitting power base for mayors of the city to hold elaborate banquets and receptions for foreign dignitaries in the building's grand halls. It is also the official residence of the Mayor of Paris, although many holders of this office choose to live elsewhere.

Cloître des Billettes ⑳

26 Rue des Archives 75004. **Map** *13 B3.* **Tel** *01 42 72 37 08.* Ⓜ *Hôtel-de-Ville.* ⃝ **Cloister** *11am–7pm daily;* **church** *6.30–8pm Thu, 9.30am–4pm Sun.*

This is the only remaining medieval cloister in Paris. It was built in 1427 for the Brothers of Charity, or *Billettes*, and three of its four original galleries are still standing. The adjoining church is a simple Classical building which replaced the monastic original in 1756.

The oldest cloister in Paris

Notre-Dame-des-Blancs-Manteaux ㉑

12 Rue des Blancs-Manteaux 75004. **Map** *13 C3.* **Tel** *01 42 72 09 37.* Ⓜ *Rambuteau.* ⃝ *10am–noon, 3pm–7pm daily.* **Concerts.** www.notre-dame-des-blancs-manteaux.org

This church, built in 1685, takes its name from the white habits worn by the Augustinian friars who founded a convent on the site in 1258.

It has a magnificent 18th-century Rococo Flemish pulpit, and its famous organ is best appreciated at one of its concerts of religious music.

Hôtel de Rohan ㉒

87 Rue Vieille-du-Temple 75003. **Map** *13 C2.* **Tel** *01 40 27 60 09.* Ⓜ *Rambuteau.* ⃝ *for temporary exhibitions only.*

Although not resembling it in appearance, the Hôtel de Rohan forms a pair with the Hôtel de Soubise. It was built by the same architect, Delamair, for Armand de Rohan-Soubise, a cardinal and Bishop of Strasbourg. The *hôtel* has been home to a part of the national archives since 1927. In the courtyard over the doorway of the stables is the 18th-century sculpture *Horses of Apollo* by Robert Le Lorrain.

Horses of Apollo by Le Lorrain

Hôtel de Soubise ㉓

60 Rue des Francs-Bourgeois 75003.
Map 13 C2. **Tel** 01 40 27 64 19.
Ⓜ *Rambuteau.* ◯ *accessible for research only 9am–4.45pm Mon–Sat; phone for appointment.*

The Hôtel de Soubise

This imposing mansion, built from 1705 to 1709 for the Princesse de Rohan, is one of two main buildings housing the national archives. (The other is the Hôtel de Rohan). The Hôtel de Soubise displays a majestic courtyard and a magnificent interior decoration dating from 1735 to 1740 by some of the most gifted painters of the day: Carl Van Loo, Jean Restout, Charles Natoire and François Boucher.

Natoire's *rocaille* work on the Princess's bedroom, the Oval Salon, forms part of the museum of French history – which is unfortunately only accessible to academics and researchers. Other exhibits include Napoleon's will, in which he asks for his remains to be returned to France.

Hôtel Guénégaud ㉔

60 Rue des Archives 75003.
Map 13 C2. **Tel** 01 53 01 92 40.
Ⓜ *Hôtel de Ville.* ◯ *11am–6pm Tue–Sun.* ◯ *public hols.* 🖼 🎞 📷
www.chassenature.org

The celebrated architect François Mansart built this superb mansion in the mid-17th century for Henri de Guénégaud des Brosses, who was Secretary of State and Keeper of the Seals. One wing

now contains the Musée de la Chasse et de la Nature (Hunting Museum) inaugurated by André Malraux in 1967 and reopened after renovation in 2006. The exhibits include a fine collection of hunting weapons from the 16th to the 19th centuries, many from Germany and Central Europe. There are also drawings and paintings by Oudry, Rubens, Rembrandt, Monet and several other artists.

Musée des Arts et Métiers ㉕

60 Rue Réaumur 75003. **Map** 13 B1-C1. **Tel** 01 53 01 82 00. Ⓜ *Arts et Métiers.* ◯ *10am–6pm Tue–Sun (to 9.30pm Thu).* ◯ *public hols.* 🖼 🎞 ♿ 🖥 🖐 **www**.arts-et-metiers.net

Housed within the old Abbey of Saint-Martin-des-Champs, the Arts and Crafts museum was founded in 1794 and closed down two centuries later for interior restructuring and renovation. It reopened in 2000 as a high-quality museum of science and industry displaying 5,000 items (it has 75,000 other items in store available to academics and researchers). The theme is man's ingenuity and the world of invention and manufacturing, covering such topics as textiles, photography and machines. Among the most entertaining displays are ones of musical clocks, mechanical music instruments and automata (mechanical figures), one of which, the "Joueuse de Tympanon", is said to represent Marie-Antoinette.

Square du Temple ㉖

75003. **Map** 13 C1. Ⓜ *Temple.*

A quiet and pleasant square today, this was once a fortified centre of the medieval Knights Templars. A state within a state, the area contained a palace, a church and shops behind high walls and a drawbridge, making it a haven for those who were seeking to escape from royal jurisdiction. Louis XVI and Marie-Antoinette were held here after their arrest in 1792 *(see pp30–31)*. The king left from here for his execution on the guillotine.

Musée d'Art et d'Histoire du Judaïsme ㉗

Hôtel de St-Aignan, 71 rue du Temple 75003. **Map** 13 B2. **Tel** 01 53 01 86 60. Ⓜ *Rambuteau.* ◯ *11am–6pm Mon–Fri, 10am–6pm Sun (last admission at 5.15pm).* ◯ *Jewish hols.* 🖼 ♿ 🎞 🖐 🖥 **www**.mahj.org

Housed in an elegant Marais mansion, the museum unites collections formerly scattered around the city, and commemorates the culture of French Jewry from medieval times to the present. There has been a sizeable Jewish community in France since Roman times, and some of the world's greatest Jewish scholars were French. Much exquisite craftsmanship is displayed, with elaborate silverware and Torah covers. There are also historical documents, photographs, paintings and cartoons.

"Being a Jew in Paris in 1939", a display in the Jewish Museum

BEAUBOURG AND LES HALLES

This Right Bank area is dominated by the modernistic Forum des Halles and the Pompidou Centre. These two spectacular undertakings are thriving public areas of contact for shoppers, art lovers, students and tourists. Literally millions flow between the two squares. The Halles is for street fashion, with most of the shops underground, and the clientele strolling under the concrete and glass bubbles is young. The surrounding streets, coloured by popular cheap shops and bars, are undergoing refurbishment to combat their seedy image, and there are still enough specialist food shops, butchers and small markets to recall what Les Halles must have been like in its prime as the city's thriving market. All roads round Les Halles lead to the Beaubourg area and the Pompidou Centre, an avant-garde assembly of vast pipes, ducts and cables, renovated in the 1990s to cope with its 20,000 daily visitors. The adjoining streets, such as Rue St-Martin and Rue Beaubourg, house small contemporary art galleries in crooked, gabled buildings.

Fountain in the Place Igor Stravinsky

SIGHTS AT A GLANCE

Historic Buildings and Streets
No. 51 Rue de Montmorency ⑪
Tour de Jean Sans Peur ⑫
Bourse du Commerce ⑭
Tour St-Jacques ⑰

Churches
St-Merry ②
St-Eustache ⑬
St-Germain l'Auxerrois ⑮

Museums and Galleries
Pompidou Centre pp110–13 ①
Galerie Marian Goodman ④
Forum des Images ⑧
Musée de la Poupée ⑩

Modern Architecture
Le Défenseur du Temps ⑤
Forum des Halles ⑨

Cafés
Café Beaubourg ⑥
Bistrot d'Eustache ⑦

Fountains
Fontaine des Innocents ③

Shops
La Samaritaine ⑯

KEY

▦	Street-by-Street map
Ⓜ	Metro station
RER	RER station

0 metres   400
0 yards   400

GETTING THERE

Among the metro stations serving the area are Rambuteau, Hôtel de Ville, Châtelet and Les Halles, as well as Châtelet-Les-Halles on the RER. The 47 bus route goes along Rue Beaubourg past the Pompidou Centre and along Boulevard Sebastopol.

SEE ALSO

• *Street Finder*, map 13

• *Where to Stay* p285

• *Restaurants* pp302–3

◁ St-Eustache and sculptured head, *l'Ecoute*, by Henri de Miller

Street-by-Street: Beaubourg and Les Halles

When Emile Zola described Les Halles as the "belly of Paris" he was referring to the meat, vegetable and fruit market that had thrived here since 1183. Traffic congestion in the 1960s forced the market to move to the suburbs and Baltard's giant umbrella-like market pavilions were pulled down, despite howls of protest, and replaced by a shopping and leisure complex, the Forum. The conversion worked: today, Les Halles and the Pompidou Centre, which lies in the Beaubourg quarter and has been Paris's main tourist attraction ever since it opened in 1977, draw the most mixed crowds in Paris.

Bistrot d'Eustache
This lively café is a favourite venue for enthusiasts of both classic and modern jazz ⑦

★ Forum des Halles
Beneath the shops, restaurants, cinemas and swimming pool is the world's busiest underground station ⑨

Forum des Images
Visitors watch videos in the Salle de Consultation ⑧

To Metro Châtelet

Rue de la Ferronnerie was where, in 1610, the religious fanatic Ravaillac assassinated Henri IV while his carriage was caught in the traffic.

★ Fontaine des Innocents
This is the last Renaissance fountain left in Paris. It was designed by the sculptor and architect Jean Goujon ③

IRCAM is an underground research centre dedicated to pioneering new ways of making music.

STAR SIGHTS

- ★ Forum des Halles
- ★ Fontaine des Innocents
- ★ Le Défenseur du Temps
- ★ Pompidou Centre

KEY

– – – Suggested route

★ **Le Défenseur du Temps**
The passage of time is defended from attack by dragons on this mechanized clock ❺

The Rue Quincampoix is lined by 18th-century *hôtels* that have been beautifully restored and totally refurbished.

LOCATOR MAP
See Central Paris Map pp14–15

★ **Pompidou Centre**
Paris's museum of modern art is housed here, along with extensive art libraries and an industrial design centre ❶

Metro Rambuteau

Place Igor Stravinsky is dominated by the first contemporary Parisian fountain, created by Niki de Saint Phalle and Jean Tinguely.

St-Merry
The pulpit of this beautiful church was designed by the Stodtz brothers in the mid-18th century and is supported by a pair of carved palm trees, one on either side ❷

metres   100
yards   100

Pompidou Centre ❶

See pp110–13.

A Nativity scene from the stained-glass windows in St-Merry

St-Merry ❷

76 Rue de la Verrerie 75004. **Map** 13 B3. *Tel* 01 42 71 93 93. Ⓜ Hôtel-de-Ville. ☐ 3–7pm daily. 🎵 1st & 3rd Sun, pm. **Concerts.**

The site of this church dates back to the 7th century. St Médéric, the abbot of St-Martin d'Autun, was buried here at the beginning of the 8th century. The saint's name, which was eventually corrupted to Merry, was given to a chapel built nearby. The building of the church – in the Flamboyant Gothic style – was not completed until 1552. The west front is particularly rich in decoration, and the northwest turret contains the oldest bell in Paris, dating from 1331. It was the wealthy parish church of the Lombard moneylenders, who gave their name to the nearby Rue des Lombards.

Fontaine des Innocents ❸

Sq des Innocents 75001. **Map** 13 A2. Ⓜ Les Halles. 🚉 Châtelet-Les-Halles.

This carefully-restored Renaissance fountain stands in the Square des Innocents, the area's main crossroads.

Erected in 1549 on the Rue St-Denis, it was moved to its present location in the 18th century, when the square was constructed on the site of a former graveyard. It is popular with the city's youth as a meeting place, and the fountain is one of the landmarks of Les Halles.

Decoration on the Fontaine des Innocents

Galerie Marian Goodman ❹

79 rue du Temple 75003. **Map** 13 C2. *Tel* 01 48 04 70 52. Ⓜ *Rambuteau.* 🚉 *Châtelet-Les-Halles.* ☐ *11am–7pm Tue–Sat.* **www**.mariangoodman.com

One of many art spaces in the area, this cutting edge gallery is the sister of Marian Goodman Gallery, New York which has played an important role in presenting European artists to American audiences since the 1970s. Many important contemporary artists, from the continent and the US, have been exhibited in the Paris gallery, including Gerhard Richter, Jeff Wall, Pierre Huyghe, Chantal Akerman and Cristina Iglesias.

Housed in a beautiful 17th-century mansion, the contemporary works on display and the Manhattan-style interior contrast in an appealing, if strikingly anachronistic way with the period façade.

Le Défenseur du Temps ❺

Rue Bernard-de-Clairvaux 75003. **Map** 13 B2. Ⓜ Rambuteau.

The modern Quartier de l'Horloge (Clock Quarter) is the location of Paris's newest public clock, "The Defender of Time" by Jacques Monastier. An impressive brass-and-steel mechanical sculpture, it stands 4 m (13 ft) high and weighs 1 tonne.

The defender battles against the elements: air, earth and water, which come in the shape of savage beasts. They attack him at the approach of EymJ6aXpRg each hour, to the accompanying sound of earthquakes, hurricanes and rough seas. Although an intriguing sight when static, unfortunately, the clock is due to be renovated and is currently not

Café Beaubourg ❻

100 Rue St-Martin, 75004. **Map** 13 B2. *Tel* 01 48 87 63 96. Ⓜ Les Halles. 🚉 Châtelet-Les-Halles. ☐ 8am–1am Mon–Wed, Sun; 8am–2am Thu–Sat.

Opened by Gilbert Costes in 1987, this stylish café was designed and decorated by one of France's star architects, Christian de Portzamparc, who created the impressive Cité de la Musique in the Parc de la Villette *(see p236).* Its vast terrace is lined with comfortable red and black wicker chairs. The spacious and coolly elegant interior is decorated with rows of books, which soften its severely Art Deco ambience. The café is a favourite meeting point for art dealers from the surrounding galleries and Pompidou Centre staff. It serves light meals and brunch. If the crush gets too much around Les Halles, the Café Beaubourg is the ideal place to soothe the nerves.

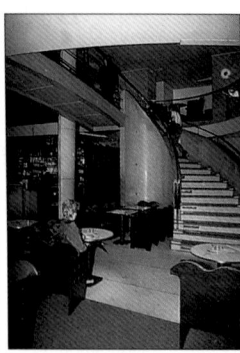

Interior of the Café Beaubourg

Bistrot d'Eustache ❼

37 Rue Berger, 75001. **Map** 13 A2. *Tel*
01 40 26 23 20. Ⓜ *Les Halles.* RER
Châtelet-Les-Halles. ◯ *9am–2am Tue–
Sun.* **Live jazz, blues/bossanova:**
phone or check website. **www.**
bistrot-eustache.com

This compact café, decorated
with old wood panelling and
attractive mirrors, retains a
feeling of Paris as it was in
the 1930s and 1940s – a period
when jazz venues flourished
throughout the city. It is
always packed for live music
shows, when musicians
squeeze into a handkerchief-
sized space to play racy
guitar-led gypsy jazz. The
café serves a variety of traditional French food, at all
times throughout the day.

Terrace of the Bistrot d'Eustache

Forum des Images ❽

2 Grande Galerie, Forum des Halles
75001. **Map** 13 A2. *Tel 01 53 01
96 96.* Ⓜ *Les Halles.* RER *Châtelet-
Les-Halles.* ◯ *1–9pm Tue–Sun.*
◯ *public hols.* ♿ ♿ ▣
www.forumdesimages.net

At the forum you can choose
from thousands of cinema,
television, and amateur films.
Many feature the city of Paris.
There is footage on the
history of Paris since 1895
including a remarkable news-
reel of General de Gaulle
avoiding sniper fire during the
Liberation of Paris in 1944.
There are countless movies
such as Truffaut's *Baisers Volés*.
Admission includes two hours'

viewing of your chosen film in
the Salle de Consultation
(see p106) and entry to two
auditoriums showing films
linked by a theme. In the
evening, the forum also hosts
"Cours de Cinéma", when
classic films are analysed.

François Truffaut's *Baisers Volés*

Forum des Halles ❾

75001. **Map** 13 A2. Ⓜ *Les Halles.*
RER *Châtelet-Les-Halles.*

The present Forum des
Halles, known simply as Les
Halles, was built in 1979,
amid much controversy, on
the site of the famous old
fruit and vegetable market.
Emile Zola named the area *Le
Ventre de Paris* (The Belly of
Paris). The present complex

occupies 7 ha (750,000 sq ft),
above and below ground. The
underground levels 2 and 3
are occupied by a varied array
of shops, from chic boutiques
to megastores, a multi-screen
cinema, swimming pool as
well as the fantastic Forum
des Images *(see p109)* film
archive centre. Beneath this is
a metro station and major
urban railway (RER) hub,
connecting central Paris with
its suburbs. Above ground
there are well-tended gardens,
pergolas and mini-pavilions.
Sadly, the area has recently
become rather seedy, and is
not recommended at night.
However, Les Halles is about
to be revamped under the
direction of architect David
Mangin, and a major and
much-needed remodelling
project will hopefully
transform the area as well as
bring back a food market. The
project is scheduled to begin
sometime in 2008 and is
expected to last for around six
years. Remember to explore
the surrounding streets,
including the trendy rue
Montorgueil to the north.

Pygmalion by Julio
Silva in the
Forum des
Halles

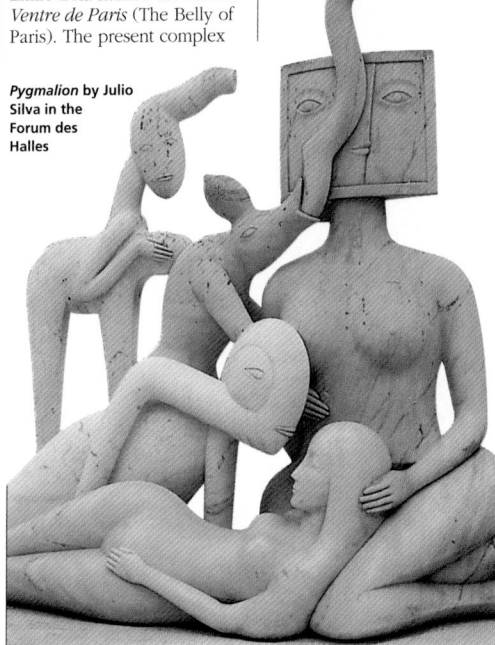

Pompidou Centre ●

The Pompidou is like a building turned inside out: escalators, lifts, air and water ducts and even the massive steel struts that are the building's skeleton have all been placed on the outside. This allowed the architects, Richard Rogers, Renzo Piano and Gianfranco Franchini, to create an uncluttered and flexible space within it for the Musée National d'Art Moderne and for the Pompidou's other activities. Among the schools represented in the museum are Fauvism, Cubism and Surrealism. Outside in the piazza, large crowds gather to watch the street performers. The Pompidou also houses temporary exhibitions that thrust it into the heart of Paris's art scene.

The escalator that rises step by step up the facade overlooking the piazza runs through a glass conduit. From the top there is a spectacular view over Paris that includes Montmartre, La Défense and the Eiffel Tower.

KEY

| ☐ Exhibition space |
| ☐ Non-exhibition space |

GALLERY GUIDE

The permanent collections are on Levels 5 & 4: works from 1905 to 1960 are on the former, with the latter reserved for contemporary art from 1960s onwards. Levels 1 & 6 are for major exhibitions, while Levels 1, 2 & 3 house an information library. The lower levels make up "The Forum", the focal public area, which include a performance centre for dance, theatre and music, a cinema and children's workshop.

Portrait of the Journalist Sylvia von Harden *(1926) The surgical precision of Dix's style makes this a harsh caricature.*

Le Cheval Majeur *This bronze horse (1914–16) by Duchamp-Villon is one of the finest examples of Cubist sculpture.*

To Russia, the Asses and the Others *(1911)*
Throughout his life Chagall drew inspiration from the small Russian town of Vitebsk, where he was born.

VISITORS' CHECKLIST

Pl Georges Pompidou. **Map** 13 B2. *Tel 01 44 78 12 33.* Ⓜ *Rambuteau, Châtelet, Hôtel de Ville.* 🚌 *21, 29, 38, 47, 58, 69, 70, 72, 74, 75, 76, 81, 85, 96.* RER *Châtelet-Les-Halles.* ◯ *MNAM & temp exhibs: 11am–10pm Wed–Mon; Library: noon–10pm Wed–Mon (from 11am Sat, Sun & pub hols); Atelier Brancusi: 2–6pm Wed–Mon.* Ø 🚫 🕮 🗸 🍴 🖵 🖵 **www.centrepompidou.fr**

Basin and Sculpture Terrace

Sorrow of the King *(1952)*
Towards the end of his life, Matisse produced a number of collages using gouache-painted paper cut-outs.

Le Duo *(1937)*
Georges Braque, like Picasso, developed the Cubist technique of representing different views of a subject in a single picture.

Basin and Sculpture Terrace

COLOUR-CODING

The coloured pipes that are the most striking feature at the back of the Pompidou, on the rue du Renard, moved one critic to compare the building to an oil refinery. Far from being merely decorative, the colours serve to distinguish the pipes' various functions: air-conditioning ducts are blue, water pipes green and electricity lines are painted yellow. The areas through which people move vertically (such as escalators) are red. The white funnels are ventilation shafts for the underground areas, and structural beams are clad in stainless steel. The architects' idea was to help the public understand the way the dynamics of a building function.

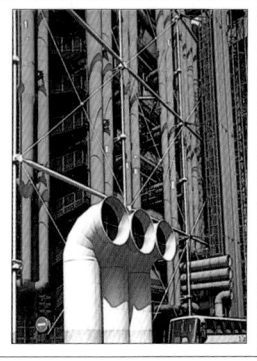

Exploring the Pompidou's Modern Art Collection

With a collection of over 50,000 works of art from more than 42,000 artists, the Pompidou encompasses all of the fine arts. In recent years, classic disciplines – painting, sculpture, drawing and photography – have been integrated with other media such as cinema, architecture, design, and visual and sound archives. The collections now represent a complete, chronological overview of modern and contemporary creation.

The Two Barges (1906) by André Derain

FROM 1905–60

The "historical" collections bring together the great artistic movements of the first half of the 20th century, from Fauvism to Abstract Expressionism to the changing currents of the 1950s. The rich collection of Cubist sculptures, of which the *Cheval Majeur* by Duchamp-Villon (1914–1916) is a fine example, is displayed, as well as examples of the great masters of the 20th century. Matisse, Picasso, Braque, Duchamp, Kandinsky, Léger, Miró, Giacometti and Dubuffet command large areas at the heart of the collection. Towards the end of his life, Matisse made several collages from cut-up large sheets of gouache-painted paper. Among others, the museum possesses *Jazz* (1943–7). With *Homme à la Guitare* (Man with a Guitar), Braque demonstrates his command of the Cubist technique which he pioneered along with Picasso. Considered as one of the first, if not the first, Abstract painter,

Kandinsky transformed works inspired by nature into constructions of colour and form. The museum has a large collection of the Russian painter's works, of which the Impressions (*Impressions V, Parc*, 1911) mark the end of his Expressionist period before his plunge into Abstract art with *Improvisations XIV* or *Avec l'Arc Noir* (With the Black Arc) both dating from 1912 compositions.

The collection also shows the groups and the movements on which the history of modern art is based, or by which it has been affected, including Dada, Abstract Art and Informal. A pioneer of Informal art, Jean Fautrier is represented in the collections with *Otages* (Hostages), a commemoration of the suffering of the resistance fighters.

At the heart of this chronological progression, some newly opened spaces are a revelation. One set shows non-figurative art from "Groupe Espace and the Magazine"; a collaboration between painters, sculptors, architects and engineers. Another room recreates the atmosphere of André Breton's workshop in which the works of his Surrealist friends are also shown. Silent pauses have also been allowed for: the room reserved for Miró has vast, moody canvasses such as *La Sieste* that give visitors reason to meditate on the explosion and revolutions of modern art.

With the Black Arc (1912)
by Vassily Kandinsky

BRANCUSI'S STUDIO

The Atelier Brancusi, on the rue Rambuteau side of the piazza, is a reconstruction of the workshop of the Romanian-born artist Constantin Brancusi (1876-1957), who lived and worked in Paris from 1904. He bequeathed his entire collection of works to the French state on condition that his workshop be rebuilt as it was on the day he died. The collection includes sculptures and plinths, photographs and a selection of his tools. Also featured are some of his more personal items such as documents, pieces of furniture and his book collection.

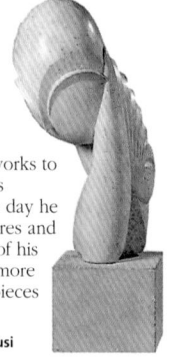

Miss Pogany (1919–20) by Constantin Brancusi

The Good-bye Door (1980) by Joan Mitchell

ART SINCE 1960

The recently rehung contemporary art section occupies the fourth floor of the Pompidou Centre and consists of approximately 500 works. Jean-Michel Alberola's exceptional mural, *Vous avez le bonjour de Marcel* welcomes visitors and sets the tone for the contemporary collection.

The collection starts with works by leading French artists of the second half of the twentieth century: artist and sculptor Louise Bourgeois whose work is strongly influenced by the surrealists, abstract expressionism and minimalism, Pierre Soulages, Jean-Pierre Raynaud, François Morellet and Bertrand Lavier.

Yayoï Kusama's recently restored masterpiece *My Flower Bed*, made of mattress springs and stuffed gloves, is also on display.

The display is organized around a central aisle from which the rooms holding the museum's collections lead off. The central aisle is dotted with sculptures including works by Toni Grand, John Chamberlain and Xavier Veilhan. This hall is however dedicated principally to painting with works by Gerhard Richter, Brice Marden,

Mobile on Two Planes (1955) by Alexander Calder

Jean-Michel Basquiat, Philip Guston, Bernard Piffaretti and Katharina Grosse.

Room three is an hommage to artist, philosopher and art critic Pontus Hulten, chosen by President Georges Pompidou to plan and run the new national museum of modern art that was to be one of the four departments of the Pompidou Centre.

Homogenous Infiltration (1966) by Joseph Beuys

Pontus Hulten was director of the Musée National d'Art Moderne from 1973 to 1981, and was responsible for making it the open and cross-disciplinary museum that its founder had intended. Works by Jean Tinguely, Andy Warhol and Niki de Saint Phalle are to be found in this room.

Since the Pompidou Centre's rehang in 2007, certain areas have been designated to bring together different disciplines around a theme such as minimalist painting or conceptual art and no longer around a school or movement. Other rooms are however artist specific with rooms dedicated to New Realist Martial Raysse, Robert Filliou, Christian Botanski, Sarkis, Joseph Beuys and Marcel Broodthaers. These rooms explore installation and photography as well as painting.

In its new arrangement the fourth floor allows different aspects of the museum's collections to be discovered, often reflecting a preference for the more ironic and conceptual forms. Joseph Beuys's *Plight* (1985), for example, consists of a grand piano and wall to ceiling covered with about 7 tonnes of thick felt.

With regards to design and architecture, inflatable structures are explored in an unprecedented way with acidically coloured inflatable pieces on display.

A room is dedicated to French designer Philippe Starck's work with items from the sixties through to the present day on display.

Another room focuses on leading young international architects and designers of the moment, along with a space dedicated to Japanese artists, including Shigeru Ban, the architect behind the construction of the Pompidou Centre's sister gallery in Metz (due to open in 2009).

Lastly, there is a "global" room bringing together major contemporary pieces by African, Chinese, Japanese, and American artists. *Denkifuku*, a dress made from light-bulbs, is a key work by Atsuko Tanaka of Japan.

The museum gallery allows temporary exhibitions to be mounted from works held in reserve. A graphic arts exhibition room and a video area complete the arrangement. A screening room gives access to the museum's entire collection of videos of a wide range of modern artists.

Le Rhinocéros (1999) by Xavier Veilhan

Musée de la Poupée ⑩

Impasse Berthaud 75003. **Map** 13 B2. **Tel** 01 42 72 73 11. Ⓜ Rambuteau. ◯ 10am–6pm Tue–Sun. 🎫 🎥 for groups, by appt. **www**.museedelapoupeeparis.com

An impressive collection of hand-made dolls, from the mid-19th century to the present day, are on show in this charming museum. Thirty-six of the displays contain French dolls with porcelain heads ranging from 1850 to 1950. Another 24 display windows are devoted to themed exhibitions of dolls from around the world.

Father and son, Guido and Samy Odin, who own the museum, are at your service if your doll needs medical care. The museum shop stocks everything you need to preserve and maintain these unique works of art. The Odins also offer comprehensive classes on doll-making for both adults and children.

A 19th-century French doll with porcelain head

No. 51 Rue de Montmorency ⑪

75003. **Map** 13 B1. Ⓜ Réaumur-Sébastopol. ◯ to the public.

This house is considered to be the oldest in Paris. No. 51 was built in 1407 by Nicolas Flamel, a book-keeper and alchemist. His house was always open to the poor, from whom he asked nothing more than that they should pray for those who were dead. Today, the house is a French restaurant.

The interior of St-Eustache in the 1830s

Tour de Jean Sans Peur ⑫

20 Rue Etienne-Marcel 75002. **Map** 13 A1. **Tel** 01 40 26 20 28. Ⓜ Etienne-Marcel. ◯ early Nov–end Mar: 1.30–6pm Wed, Sat, Sun; Apr–early Nov: 1.30pm–6pm Wed–Sun. 🎫 🎥 **www**.tourjeansanspeur.com

After the Duc d'Orléans was assassinated on his orders in 1408, the Duc de Bourgogne feared reprisals. To protect himself, he had this 27-m (88-ft) tower built on to his home, the Hôtel de Bourgogne, and moved his bedroom up to the fourth floor (reached by a flight of 140 steps).

No. 51 Rue de Montmorency, the oldest house in Paris

St-Eustache ⑬

Pl du Jour 75001. **Map** 13 A1. **Tel** 01 40 26 47 99. Ⓜ Les Halles. 🚇 Châtelet-Les-Halles. ◯ 9.30am–7pm Mon–Fri; 10am–7pm Sat; 9am–7.15pm Sun. 🅿 ✝ 12.30pm, 6pm Mon–Fri; Sat; 9.30am, 11am, 6pm Sun. **Organ recitals 5.30pm Sun.**

With its gothic plan and Renaissance decoration, St-Eustache is one of the most beautiful churches in Paris. Its interior plan is modelled on Notre-Dame, with five naves and side and radial chapels. The 105 years (1532–1637) it took to complete the church saw the flowering of the Renaissance style, which is evident in the arches, pillars and columns. The stained-glass windows in the chancel are created from cartoons by Philippe de Champaigne.

The church has associations with many famous figures: Molière was buried here; the Marquise de Pompadour, official mistress of Louis XV, was baptized here, as was Cardinal Richelieu.

Entrance to the Bourse du Commerce, the old corn exchange

Bourse du Commerce ⓮

2 Rue de Viarmes 75001.
Map 12 F2. **Tel** 01 55 65 55 65.
Ⓜ Les Halles. 🅡🅔🅡 Châtelet-Les-Halles. ◯ 9am–1pm, 2–5pm Mon–Fri. 🗨 groups by appt. ♿

Compared by Victor Hugo to a jockey's cap without a peak, the old corn exchange building was constructed in the 18th century and remodelled in 1889. Today its huge, domed hall is filled with the hustle and bustle of the commodities market for coffee and sugar. It houses a World Trade Centre and the offices of the Chambre de Commerce et d'Industrie de Paris.

St-Germain l'Auxerrois ⓯

2 Pl du Louvre 75001.
Map 12 F2. **Tel** 01 42 60 13 96.
Ⓜ Louvre, Pont-Neuf.
◯ 8am–7pm daily.
Musical Hour 4–5pm Sun.

After the Valois Court decamped to the Louvre from the Ile de la Cité in the 14th century, this became the favoured church of kings, who attended mass here.
　Its many historical associations include the horrific St Bartholomew's Day Massacre on 24 August 1572, the eve of the royal wedding of Henri of Navarre and Marguerite de Valois.

Thousands of Huguenots who had been lured to Paris for the wedding were murdered as the church bell tolled. Later, after the Revolution, the church was used as a barn. Despite many restorations, it is a jewel of Gothic architecture.

La Samaritaine ⓰

19 Rue de la Monnaie 75001.
Map 12 F2. **Tel** 01 40 41 20 20.
Ⓜ Pont-Neuf. ◯ for renovation.
🍴 🖥 🅟 See **Shopping** p313.

Currently closed due to renovation, this fashionable department store was founded in 1900 by Ernest Cognacq. Built in 1926 with a framework of iron and wide expanses of glass, La Samaritaine is an outstanding example of the Art Deco style. The interior has a fine Art Nouveau ironwork staircase and hanging galleries under a large dome.
　Cognacq was also a collector of 18th-century art, and his collection is now on display in the Musée Cognacq-Jay in the Marais quarter *(see p94)*.

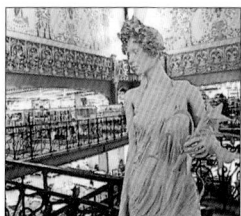

The stylish Art Deco interior of La Samaritaine

The Tour St-Jacques with its ornate decoration

Tour St-Jacques ⓱

Square de la Tour St-Jacques 75004. **Map** 13 A3. Ⓜ Châtelet.
◯ for renovation.

This imposing late Gothic tower, dating from 1523, is all that remains of an ancient church that was a rendezvous for pilgrims setting out on long journeys. The church was destroyed after the Revolution. Earlier, Blaise Pascal, the 17th-century mathematician, physicist, philosopher and writer, used the tower for barometrical experiments. There is a memorial statue to him on the ground floor of the tower. Queen Victoria passed by on her state visit in 1854, giving her name to the nearby Avenue Victoria.

The St Bartholomew's Day Massacre (c. 1572–84) by François Dubois

TUILERIES QUARTER

The Tuileries area is bounded by the vast expanse of the Concorde square at one end and the Grand Louvre at the other. This was a place for kings and palaces. The Sun King (Louis XIV) lives on in the Place des Victoires, which was designed solely to show off his statue. In Place Vendôme, royal glitter has been replaced by the precious stones of Cartier, Boucheron and Chaumet, and the fine cut of Arab, German and Japanese bankers, not to mention the chic ladies visiting the luxurious Ritz. The area is crossed by two of Paris's most magnificent shopping streets – the long Rue de Rivoli, with its arcades, expensive boutiques, bookshops and luxury hotels, and the Rue St-Honoré, another extensive street, bringing together the richest and humblest in people and commerce.

Ornate lamppost on Place de la Concorde

SIGHTS AT A GLANCE

Historic Buildings
Palais Royal ❸
Banque de France ❷⓿

Museums and Galleries
Musée du Louvre pp122–9 ❶
Musée de la Mode et du Textile ❾
Musée de la Publicité ❿
Musée des Arts Décoratifs ⓫
Galerie Nationale du Jeu de Paume ⓯
Musée de l'Orangerie ⓰
Village Royal ⓲

Monuments and Fountains
Fontaine Molière ❻
Arc de Triomphe du Carrousel ⓬

Squares, Parks and Gardens
Jardin du Palais Royal ❺
Place des Pyramides ❽
Jardin des Tuileries ⓮
Place de la Concorde ⓱
Place Vendôme ⓳
Place des Victoires ❷❶

Theatres
Comédie Française ❹

Shops
Louvre des Antiquaires ❷
Rue de Rivoli ⓭

Churches
St-Roch ❼

GETTING THERE
This area is well served by the metro system, with stations at Tuileries, Pyramides, Palais Royal and Louvre. There are frequent buses through the area. Routes 24, 27, 72 and 95 travel along the quayside passing the Jardin des Tuileries and the Musée du Louvre.

KEY

	Street-by-Street map
M	Metro station
i	Tourist information

SEE ALSO

• *Street Finder*, map 6, 11–12

• *Where to Stay* pp285–6

• *Restaurants* pp303–04

◁ **View of the Place de la Concorde and the Obelisk**

Street by Street: Tuileries Quarter

Elegant squares, formal gardens, street arcades and courtyards give this part of Paris its special character. Monuments to monarchy and the arts coexist with contemporary luxury: sumptuous hotels, world-famous restaurants, fashion emporiums and jewellers of international renown. Sandblasting and washing have given a new glow to the facades of the Louvre and the Palais Royal square, where Cardinal Richelieu's creation, the royal palace, is now occupied by government offices. From here the Ministry of Culture surveys the cleaning and restoration of the city's great buildings. The other former royal palace, the Louvre, is now one of the great museums of the world.

St-Roch
The papal statue stands in this remarkably long 17th-century church, unusually set on a north-south axis. St-Roch is a treasure house of religious art **7**

Metro Pyramides

The Paris Convention and Visitors' Bureau

The Normandy is an elegant hotel in the Belle Epoque style, a form of graceful living that prevailed in Paris at the turn of the 20th century.

★ Jardin des Tuileries
Pony rides are a popular attraction in these formal gardens, which were designed by the royal gardener André Le Nôtre in the 17th century **14**

Place des Pyramides
Frémiet's gilded statue of Joan of Arc is the focus of pilgrimage for royalists **8**

To the Quai du Louvre

Musée de la Mode et du Textile
The haute couture collections that are kept in this museum have given the Louvre a new role **9**

Musée des Arts Décoratifs
A highlight of the museum's displays of art and design is the Art Nouveau collection **11**

Fontaine Molière
Louis Visconti's fountain is of the famous playwright, who lived nearby 6

★ Jardin du Palais Royal
The garden is a city haven, bordered by arcades with restaurants and art galleries alongside specialist shops 5

LOCATOR MAP
See Central Paris Map pp14–15

Le Grand Véfour's 18th-century decor makes it one of the most beautiful restaurants in Paris. Napoleon Bonaparte and Victor Hugo were two of the many famous people who dined here. *(See p304.)*

RUE DE RICHELIEU

RUE DE MONTPENSIER

RUE DE VALOIS

★ Palais Royal
In the 18th century this former royal palace was a setting for brilliant gatherings, debauchery and gambling. Today modern sculptures grace the square 3

Comédie Française
France's national theatre is the setting for the works of great dramatists, such as Molière 4

PL DU PALAIS ROYAL

Metro Palais Royal

M

Louvre des Antiquaires
Three floors of a former department store house this chic art and antiques supermarket for the rich collector 2

★ Musée du Louvre
Home to French kings for almost four centuries, the Louvre is now a museum with one of the world's great art collections 1

STAR SIGHTS

★ Jardin des Tuileries

★ Jardin du Palais Royal

★ Palais Royal

★ Musée du Louvre

KEY

– – – Suggested route

0 metres   100

0 yards   100

The five-arched Pont Royal linking the Louvre with the Left Bank

Musée du Louvre ❶

See pp122–9.

Louvre des Antiquaires ❷

2 Pl du Palais Royal 75001. **Map** 12 E2.
Tel *01 42 97 27 27.* ◯ *11am–7pm
Tue–Sun (Jul & Aug: Tue–Sat).* ● *1 Jan,
25 Dec.* 🍴 🖥 *See* **Shopping**
pp336–7. **www**.louvre-antiquaires.com

One of the shops in the Louvre des Antiquaires market

A large department store –
the Grands Magasins du
Louvre – was converted at the
end of the 1970s into this
three-floor collection of art
galleries and antique shops.
Few bargains are found here,
but the 250 shops of this chic
market provide clues about
what *nouveaux riches*
collectors are seeking.

Palais Royal ❸

Pl du Palais Royal 75001. **Map** 12 E1.
Ⓜ *Palais Royal.* **Buildings not open**
to public.

This former royal palace has
had a turbulent history.
Starting out in the early 17th
century as Richelieu's Palais
Cardinale, it passed to the

Crown on his death and
became the childhood home
of Louis XIV. Under the
control of the 18th-century
royal dukes of Orléans it was
the scene of brilliant gatherings, interspersed with
periods of debauchery and
gambling. The cardinal's
theatre, where Molière had
performed, burned down in
1763, but was replaced by the
Comédie Française. After the
Revolution, the palace
became a gambling house. It
was reclaimed in 1815 by the
future King Louis-Philippe,
one of whose librarians was
Alexandre Dumas. The
building narrowly escaped the
flames of the 1871 uprising.
　After being restored again,
between 1872 and 1876, the
palace reverted to the state,
and it now houses both the
Council of State, the supreme
legal body for administrative
matters, and its more recent
"partner", the Constitutional
Council. Another wing of the
palace is occupied by the
Ministry of Culture.

Comédie Française ❹

1 Place Colette 75001. **Map** 12 E1. 🎭
0825 101 680. Ⓜ *Palais Royal.* ◯
for performances. 🎫 *9.30am, 10am,
10.30am Sat, Sun (01 44 58 13 16).* 🖥
🎫 *See* **Entertainment** *pp342–4.*

A stone plaque to Pierre Corneille

Overlooking two charming,
if traffic-choked, squares
named after the writers
Colette and André Malraux,
sits France's national theatre.
The company has its roots
partly in Molière's 17th-
century players. In the foyer is
the armchair in which Molière
collapsed, dying, on stage in
1673 (ironically while he was
performing *Le Malade
Imaginaire – The Hypochon-
driac*). Since the company's
founding in 1680 by Louis
XIV, the theatre has enjoyed
state patronage as a centre of
national culture, and it has
been based in the present
building since 1799. The
repertoire includes works of
Corneille, Racine, Molière and
Shakespeare, as well as those
of modern playwrights.

Daniel Buren's stone columns (1980s) in the Palais Royal courtyard

Jardin du Palais Royal ❺

Pl du Palais Royal 75001. **Map** 12 F1.
Ⓜ *Palais Royal.*

The present garden is about a third smaller than the original one, laid out by the royal gardener for Cardinal Richelieu in the 1630s. This is due to the construction, between 1781 and 1784, of 60 uniform houses bordering three sides of the square. Today restaurants, art galleries and specialist shops line the square, which maintains a strong literary history – Jean Cocteau, Colette and Jean Marais are among its famous recent residents.

Statue in the Jardin du Palais Royal

Fontaine Molière ❻

Rue de Richelieu 75001. **Map** 12 F1.
Ⓜ *Palais Royal.*

France's most famous playwright lived near here, in a house on the site of No. 40 Rue de Richelieu. The 19th-century fountain is by Louis Visconti, who also designed Napoleon's tomb at Les Invalides *(see pp188–9).*

St-Roch ❼

296 Rue St-Honoré 75001. **Map** 12 E1.
Tel *01 42 44 13 20.* Ⓜ *Tuileries.*
⬭ *8am–7pm daily.* ⬤ *non-religious public hols.* ✚ *Daily, times vary.*
Concerts. 📷

This huge church was designed by Lemercier, architect of the Louvre, and its foundation stone was laid by

Vien's *St Denis Preaching to the Gauls* (1767) in St-Roch

Louis XIV in 1653. Jules Hardouin-Mansart added the large Lady Chapel with its richly decorated dome and ceiling in the 18th century and two further chapels extended the church to 126 m (413 ft), just short of Notre-Dame. It is a treasure house of religious art, much of it from now-vanished churches and monasteries. It also contains the tombs of the playwright Pierre Corneille, the royal gardener André Le Nôtre and the philosopher Denis Diderot. The facades reveal marks of Napoleon's attack, in 1795, on royalist troops who were defending the church steps.

Place des Pyramides ❽

75001. **Map** 12 E1. Ⓜ *Tuileries, Pyramides.*

Joan of Arc, wounded nearby fighting the English in 1429, is commemorated by a 19th-century equestrian statue by the sculptor Emmanuel Frémiet. The statue is a rallying point for royalists.

Musée de la Mode et du Textile ❾

107 Rue de Rivoli 75001. **Map** 12 E1.
Tel *01 44 55 57 50.* Ⓜ *Palais Royal, Tuileries.* ⬭ *11am–6pm Tue–Fri (until 9pm Thu); 10am–6pm Sat, Sun.* 🎫
🏠 www.lesartsdecoratifs.fr

Set in the Louvre's Pavillon de Marsan, this museum promotes one of the city's oldest and most famous industries – fashion.
    It houses an impressive collection of *haute couture* costumes and accessories and has become an important venue for temporary exhibitions of costumes.

Schiaparelli jacket in the museum

Musée du Louvre ❶

The Musée du Louvre, containing one of the most important art collections in the world, has a history extending back to medieval times. First constructed as a fortress in 1190 by King Philippe-Auguste to protect Paris against Viking raids, it lost its imposing keep in the reign of François I, who replaced it with a Renaissance-style building. Thereafter, four centuries of French kings and emperors improved and enlarged it. One of the more recent additions is a glass pyramid in the main courtyard from which all the galleries are reached.

The east facade, facing St-Germain l'Auxerroi

The Jardin du Carrousel, now part of the Jardin des Tuileries, was once the grand approach to the Tuileries Palace which was burned down in 1871 by the Communards.

Pavillon des Sessions

The Carrousel du Louvre underground visitors complex, with galleries, cloakrooms, shops, lavatories, parking and an information desk, lies beneath the Arc de Triomphe du Carrousel.

Denon Wing

The inverted glass pyramid brings light to the subterranean complex, echoing the museum's main entrance in the Cour Napoléon.

BUILDING THE LOUVRE

Over many centuries the Louvre was enlarged by a succession of French rulers, shown below with their dates.

MAJOR ALTERATIONS

- ▢ Reign of François I (1515–47)
- ▢ Catherine de' Médici (about 1560)
- ▇ Reign of Henri IV (1589–1610)
- ▢ Reign of Louis XIII (1610–43)
- ▢ Reign of Louis XIV (1643–1715)
- ▢ Reign of Napoleon I (1804–15)
- ▢ Reign of Napoleon III (1852–70)
- ▇ I M Pei (1989) (architect)

★ **Arc de Triomphe du Carrousel**
This triumphal arch was built to celebrate Napoleon's victories in 1805.

STAR FEATURES

- ★ Arc de Triomphe du Carrousel
- ★ Medieval Moats
- ★ Perrault Colonnade
- ★ Pyramid Entrance

Pavillon Richelieu
This imposing 19th-century pavilion is part of the Richelieu Wing, once home to the Ministry of Finance but now converted into magnificent galleries.

VISITORS' CHECKLIST

Map 12 E2. Automatic ticket booths are located in the Carrousel du Louvre (99 Rue de Rivoli). 01 40 20 50 50. *Palais Royal, Musée du Louvre.* 21, 24, 27, 39, 48, 68, 69, 72, 81, 95. *Châtelet-Les-Halles.* *Louvre.* *Carrousel du Louvre (entrance via Ave du General Lemonnier); Pl du Louvre, Rue St-Honoré.* 9am–6pm Wed–Mon (to 10pm Wed, Fri). 1 Jan, 1 May, 8 May, 25 Dec. (free 1st Sun of each month). partial (01 40 20 59 90). phone 01 40 20 52 09. *Lectures, films, concerts* (01 40 20 55 55). **www**.louvre.fr

Cour Marly is the glass-roofed courtyard that now houses the Marly Horses *(see p125).*

Richelieu Wing

★ Pyramid Entrance
The popular new main entrance, designed by the architect I M Pei, was opened in 1989.

Cour Puget

Cour Khorsabad

Sully Wing

Cour Carrée

★ Perrault's Colonnade
The east facade with its majestic rows of columns was built by Claude Perrault, who worked on the Louvre with Louis Le Vau in the mid-17th century.

The Salle des Caryatides
takes its name from the statues of women created by Jean Goujon in 1550 to support the upper gallery.

Cour Napoléon

The Louvre of Charles V
In about 1360, Charles V transformed Philippe-Auguste's robust old fortress into a royal residence.

★ Medieval Moats
The base of the twin towers and the drawbridge support of Philippe-Auguste's fortress can be seen in the excavated area.

The Louvre's Collection

The Louvre's treasures can be traced back to the collection of François I (1515–47), who purchased many Italian paintings including the *Mona Lisa (La Gioconda)*. In Louis XIV's reign (1643–1715) there were a mere 200 works, but donations and purchases augmented the collection. The Louvre was first opened to the public in 1793 after the Revolution, and has been continually enriched ever since.

The Lacemaker
In this exquisite picture from about 1665, Jan Vermeer gives us a glimpse into everyday domestic life in Holland. The painting came to the Louvre in 1870.

The Raft of the Medusa *(1819)*
Théodore Géricault derived his inspiration for this gigantic and moving work from the shipwreck of a French frigate in 1816. The painting shows the moment when the few survivors sight a sail on the horizon.

Cour Marly

Richelieu Wing

Main entrance

GALLERY GUIDE
The main entrance is beneath the glass pyramid. From here corridors radiate out to the museum's wings. The works are displayed on four floors: the painting and sculpture collections are arranged by country of origin. There are separate departments for Oriental, Egyptian, Greek, Etruscan and Roman anti-quities, objets d'art and prints and drawings.

Underground
visitors' complex

Pavillon
des Sessions

Denon Wing

KEY TO FLOORPLAN

☐	Painting
☐	Objets d'art
☐	Sculpture
☐	Antiquities
☐	Non-exhibition space

★ **Venus de Milo**
Found in 1820 on the island of Milos in Greece, this ideal of feminine beauty was made in the Hellenistic Age at the end of the 2nd century BC.

★ Mona Lisa
Leonardo da Vinci painted this small portrait of a Florentine noblewoman, known as La Gioconda, *in about 1504. It was soon regarded as the prototype of the Renaissance portrait. The sitter's engaging smile has prompted endless commentary ever since. The painting has its own wall in the Salle des Etats (Denon Wing).*

Second floor

★ Marly Horses
Since the 19th century, these wild horses by Guillaume Coustou have stood near the Place de la Concorde. Replicas have replaced them – the originals are now in a glass-covered courtyard in the Louvre.

First floor

Cour Puget

Cour Khorsabad

Cour Napoléon

Sully Wing

Cour Carrée

Ground floor

STAR EXHIBITS

★ Mona Lisa by Leonardo da Vinci

★ Venus de Milo

★ Marly Horses by Guillaume Coustou

The Dying Slave
Michelangelo sculpted this work between 1513 and 1520 as part of a group of statues for the base of the tomb of Pope Julius II in Rome.

Exploring the Louvre's Collections

It is important not to underestimate the size of these vast collections and useful to set a few viewing priorities before starting. The collection of European paintings (1400–1850) is comprehensive and 40 per cent of the works are by French artists, while the selection of sculptures is less complete. The museum's antiquities – Oriental, Egyptian, Greek, Etruscan and Roman – are of world renown and offer the visitor an unrivalled range of objects. The *objets d'art* on display are very varied and include furniture and jewellery.

The Fortune Teller (about 1594) by Caravaggio

EUROPEAN PAINTING: 1200 TO 1850

Painting from northern Europe (Flemish, Dutch, German and English) is well covered. One of the earliest Flemish works is Jan van Eyck's *Madonna of Chancellor Rolin* (about 1435) which shows the Chancellor of Burgundy kneeling in prayer before the Virgin and Child.

Portrait of Erasmus (1523) by Hans Holbein

Hieronymus Bosch's *Ship of Fools* (1500) is a fine, satirical account of the futility of human existence. In the Dutch collection, Van Dyck's portrait *King Charles out Hunting* (1635) shows Charles I of England in all his refined elegance. Jacob Jordaens, best known for scenes of gluttony and lust, reveals unusual sensitivity in his *Four Evangelists*. The saucy smile of the *Gipsy Girl* (1628) displays Frans Hals' effortless virtuosity, in sharp contrast to Vermeer's highly-finished *Lacemaker*. Rembrandt's *Self-portraits, Disciples at Emmaus* (1648) and *Bathsheba* (1654) are fine examples of his genius.

There is relatively little German painting, but the three major German painters of the 15th and 16th centuries are represented by important works. There is a *Self-portrait* by Albrecht Dürer as a young artist of 22 (1493), a *Venus* by Lucas Cranach (1529) and a portrait of the great humanist scholar Erasmus by Hans Holbein. Works by English artists include Thomas

Gainsborough's *Conversation in a Park* (about 1746), Sir Joshua Reynolds' *Master Hare* (1788) and several landscapes by J M W Turner.

Many of the master works in the Spanish collection depict the tragic side of life: El Greco's *Christ on the Cross Adored by Donors* (1576) and Francisco de Zurbarán's *Lying-in-State of St Bonaventura* (about 1629) with its dark-faced corpse are two of the Louvre's prize pieces. The subject of José de Ribera's *Club-Footed Boy* (1642) is a poor mute, who carries a scrap of paper requesting alms. In a lighter vein, there are several portraits by Goya from the 19th century.

The museum's collection of Italian paintings is large, covering the period 1200 to 1800. The father figures of the early Renaissance, Cimabue and Giotto, are here, as is Fra Angelico, with his *Coronation of the Virgin* (1435), and Pisanello, with his delightful *Portrait of Ginevra d'Este* (about 1435). There is also a fine portrait in profile of Sigismondo Malatesta by Piero della Francesca (about 1450) and an action-packed battle scene by Paolo Uccello. Several paintings by Leonardo da Vinci, for instance the *Virgin with the Infant Jesus and St Anne*, are as enchanting as his *Mona Lisa*.

The Louvre's fine collection of French painting ranges from the 14th century to 1848. Paintings after this date are housed in the Musée d'Orsay (*see pp144–7*). An outstanding

Gilles or Pierrot (about 1717) by Jean-Antoine Watteau

LEONARDO DA VINCI IN FRANCE

Leonardo, artist, engineer and scientist, was born in 1452 and became a leading figure in the Italian Renaissance. François I met Leonardo in 1515 and invited him to live and work in France. The painter brought the *Mona Lisa* with him. Already in poor health, he died three years later in the arms of the king.

Self-portrait (early 16th century)

early work is Enguerrand Quarton's *Villeneuve-les-Avignon Pietà* (1455). Another early painting shows *Gabrielle d'Estrée*, mistress of Henri IV, in her bathtub. From the 16th and 17th centuries there are several splendid works by Georges de la Tour with the dramatic torch-light effect so typical of his work.

That great 18th-century painter of melancholy, Jean Watteau, is represented, as is J H Fragonard, master of the Rococo. His delightfully frivolous subjects are evident in *The Bathers* from 1770. In stark contrast is the Classicism of Nicolas Poussin and the history painting of J L David. Most of J D Ingres' work is in the Musée d'Orsay, but the Louvre kept the erotic *Turkish Bath* of 1862.

EUROPEAN SCULPTURE: 1100 TO 1850

Early Flemish and German sculpture in the collection has many masterpieces such as Tilman Riemenschneider's *Virgin of the Annunciation* from the end of the 15th century and an unusual life-size, nude figure of the penitent Mary Magdalen by Gregor Erhart (early 16th century). An ornate gilded-wood altarpiece of the same period exemplifies Flemish church art. Another important work of Flemish sculpture is Adrian de Vries's long-limbed *Mercury and Psyche* from 1593, which was originally made for the court of Rudolph II in Prague.

The French section opens with early Romanesque works, such as the figure of Christ by a 12th-century Burgundian sculptor and a head of St Peter. With its eight black-hooded mourners, the tomb of Philippe Pot (a high-ranking official in Burgundy) is one of the more unusual pieces. Diane de Poitiers, mistress of Henri II, had a large figure of her namesake Diana, goddess of the hunt, installed in the courtyard of her castle west of Paris. It is now in the Louvre. The works of Pierre Puget (1620–94), the great sculptor from Marseilles, have been assembled inside a glass-covered courtyard, Cour Puget. They include a figure of Milo of Crotona, the Greek athlete who got his hands caught in the cleft of a tree stump and was eaten by a lion. The wild horses of Marly now stand in the glass-roofed Cour Marly, surrounded by other masterpieces of French sculpture, including Houdon's early 19th-century busts of Diderot and Voltaire, and two equestrian pieces by Coysevox.

The Italian sculpture collection includes pre-Renaissance work by Duccio and Donatello, and later masterpieces such as Michelangelo's *Slaves* and Cellini's Fontainebleau *Nymph*.

Tomb of Philippe Pot (late 15th century) by Antoine le Moiturier

ORIENTAL, EGYPTIAN, GREEK, ETRUSCAN AND ROMAN ANTIQUITIES

The range of antiquities in the Louvre is impressive. There are objects from the Neolithic period (about 6000 BC) to the fall of the Roman Empire. Important works of Mesopotamian art include the seated figure of Ebih-il, from 2400 BC, and several portraits of Gudea, Prince of Lagash, from about 2255 BC. A black basalt block bearing the code of the Babylonian King Hammurabi, from about 1700 BC, is one of the world's oldest legal documents.

The warlike Assyrians are represented by delicate carvings and a spectacular reconstruction of part of Sargon II's (722–705 BC) palace with its huge, winged bulls. A fine example of Persian art is the enamelled brickwork depicting the king of Persia's personal guard of archers (5th century BC). It decorated his palace at Susa.

Most Egyptian art was made for the dead, who were provided with the things that they needed for the after-life. It often included vivid images of daily life in ancient Egypt. One example is the tiny funeral chapel built for a high official in about 2500 BC. It is covered with exquisite carvings: men in sailing ships, catching fish, tending cattle and fowl.

It is also possible to gain insights into family life in ancient Egypt through a number of life-like funeral portraits, like the squatting scribe, and several sculptures of married couples. The earliest sculpture dates from 2500 BC, the latest from 1400 BC.

From the New Kingdom (1555–1080 BC) a special crypt dedicated to the god Osiris contains some colossal sarcophagi, and a large number of mummified animals.

Some smaller objects of considerable charm include a 29-cm (11-inch) headless body of a woman, sensually outlined by the transparent veil of her dress and thought to be Queen Nefertiti (about 1365–1349 BC).

The department of Greek, Roman and Etruscan antiquities contains a vast array of fragments, among them some exceptional pieces. There is a large, geometric head from the Cyclades (2700 BC) and an elegant, swan-necked bowl, quite modern in its unadorned simplicity. It is hammered out of a single gold sheet and dates from about 2500 BC. The Archaic Greek period, from the 7th to the 5th century BC, is represented by the *Auxerre Goddess*, one of the earliest-known pieces of Greek sculpture, and the *Hera of Samos* from the Ionian Islands. From the height of the Classical Greek period (about the 5th century BC)

Winged Bull with Human Head from 8th century BC, found in Khorsabad, Assyria

Winged Victory of Samothrace (Greece, late 3rd–early 2nd century BC)

there are several fine male torsos and heads such as the *Laborde Head*. This head has been identified as part of the sculpture that once decorated the west pediment of the Parthenon in Athens.

The two most famous Greek statues in the Louvre, the *Winged Victory of Samothrace* and the *Venus de Milo (see p 124)*, belong to the Hellenistic period (late 3rd to 2nd century BC) when more natural-looking human forms were beginning to be produced.

The undisputed star of the Etruscan collection is the terracotta *Sarcophagus of the Cenestian Couple*, who appear

Etruscan sarcophagus (6th century BC)

as though they are attending an eternal banquet.

The sculptures in the Roman section demonstrate the great debt owed to the art of ancient Greece. There are many fine pieces: a bust of Agrippa, a basalt head of Livia, the wife of Augustus, and a splendid, powerful bronze head of Emperor Hadrian from the 2nd century AD. This has the look of a true portrait, unlike so many Imperial heads which are uninspired and impersonal.

Squatting Scribe (Egyptian, about 2500 BC)

OBJETS D'ART

The term *objets d'art* (art objects) covers a vast range of "decorative art" objects: jewellery, furniture, clocks, watches, sundials, tapestries, miniatures, silver and glassware, cutlery, small French and Italian bronzes, Byzantine and Parisian carved ivory, Limoges enamels, porcelain, French and Italian stoneware, rugs, snuffboxes, scientific instruments and armour. The Louvre has well over 8,000 items, from many ages and regions.

Many of these precious objects were in the Abbey of St-Denis, where the kings of France were crowned. Long before the Revolution, a regular flow of visitors had made it something of a museum. After the Revolution all the objects were removed and presented to the nation. Much was lost or stolen during the move but what remains is still outstanding.

The treasures include a serpentine stone plate from the 1st century AD with a 9th-century border of gold and precious stones. (The plate itself is inlaid with eight golden dolphins.) There is also a porphyry vase which Suger, Abbot of St-Denis, had mounted in gold in the shape of an eagle, and the golden sceptre made for King Charles V in about 1380.

The French crown jewels include the coronation crowns of Louis XV and Napoleon, sceptres, swords and other accessories of the coronation ceremonies. On view is also the Regent, one of the purest diamonds in the world. It was bought in 1717 and worn by Louis XV at his coronation in 1722.

One whole room is taken up with a series of tapestries called the *Hunts of Maximilian,* which were originally executed for Emperor Charles V

The Eagle of Suger (mid-12th century)

in 1530 after drawings by Bernard Van Orley.

The large collection of French furniture ranges from the 16th to the 19th centuries and is assembled by period, or in rooms devoted to donations by distinguished collectors such as Isaac de Camondo. On display are important pieces by exceptionally prominent furniture-makers such as André-Charles Boulle, cabinet-maker to Louis XIV, who worked at the Louvre in the late 17th to mid-18th centuries. He is noted for his technique of inlaying copper and tortoiseshell. From a later date, the curious inlaid steel and bronze writing desk, created by Adam Weisweiler for Queen Marie-Antoinette in 1784, is one of the more unusual pieces in the museum's collection.

THE GLASS PYRAMID

Plans for the modernization and expansion of the Louvre were first conceived in 1981. They included the transfer of the Ministry of Finance from the Richelieu wing of the Louvre to new offices elsewhere, and a new main entrance to the museum. A Chinese-American architect, I M Pei, was chosen to design the changes. He designed the pyramid as both the focal point and new entrance to the Louvre. Made out of glass, it enables the visitor to see the historic buildings that surround it while allowing light down into the underground visitors' reception area.

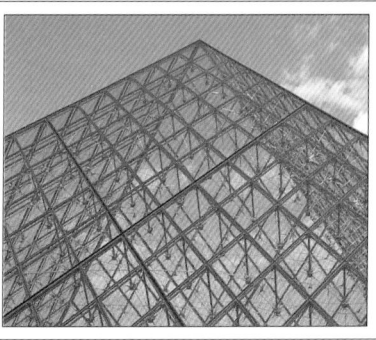

Musée de la Publicité ⓾

Palais du Louvre, 107 rue de Rivoli
75001. **Map** 12 E2. **Tel** 01 44 55 57
50. Ⓜ *Palais Royal, Tuileries.*
🕐 *11am–6pm Tue–Fri (until 9pm
Thu); 10am–6pm Sat–Sun.* 🖶
www.lesartsdecoratifs.fr

The Museum of Advertising
brings together over 40,000
historic posters dating from
the 18th century to 1949, plus
around 45,000 more recent
posters, and different varieties
of modern multimedia advertising. There is also a good
reference library.

Musée des Arts Décoratifs ⓫

Palais du Louvre, 107 Rue de Rivoli
75001. **Map** 12 E2. **Tel** 01 44 55 57
50. Ⓜ *Palais Royal, Tuileries.* 🕐
*11am–6pm Tue–Fri (until 9pm Thu);
11am–9pm Wed; 10am–6pm Sat &
Sun.* **Library** 🖶 *publ hols.* 🖶 ♿
www.lesartsdecoratifs.fr

With five floors and over
100 rooms, this museum
offers an eclectic display of
decorative and ornamental
art and design from the
Middle Ages to the present.
Among the highlights are
the Art Nouveau and Art
Deco rooms, jewellery
and Gallé glass. The doll
collection is remarkable.
   The Galerie des Bijoux is
particularly interesting, with
a magnificent collection of
more than 1,300 pieces,
from medieval brooches
to contemporary Cartier.
   The restaurant offers
breathtaking views over
the Tuileries Gardens.

Lemot's Restoration group of statues with the gilded figure of Victory

Arc de Triomphe du Carrousel ⓬

Pl du Carrousel 75001. **Map** 12 E2.
Ⓜ *Palais Royal.*

Built by Napoleon in 1806–
1808 as an entrance to the
former Palais des Tuileries, its
marble columns are topped by
soldiers of the Grande Armée.
They replaced the Horses of St
Mark's which he was forced to
return in 1815, after Waterloo.

Arcades along the Rue de Rivoli

Rue de Rivoli ⓭

75001. **Map** 11 C1 & 13 A2.
Ⓜ *Louvre, Palais Royal, Tuileries,
Concorde.*

The long arcades with their
shops, topped by Neo-
Classical apartments, date back
to the early 18th century,
though they were only finished in the 1850s. Commissioned
by Napoleon after his victory
at Rivoli, in 1797, the street
completed the link between
the Louvre and the Champs-
Elysées, and became an
important artery as well as an
elegant centre for commerce.
The Tuileries walls were
replaced by railings and the
whole area opened up.
   Today along the Rue de
Rivoli there are makers of
expensive men's shirts and
bookshops towards the Place
de la Concorde, and popular
department stores near the
Châtelet and Hôtel de Ville.
Angélina's, at No. 226, is
said to serve the best hot
chocolate in Paris (*see p318*).

Jardin des Tuileries ⓮

75001. **Map** 12 D1.
Tel 01 40 20 90 43.
Ⓜ *Tuileries, Concorde.*
🕐 *7.30am–7pm (or sunset).*

These formal gardens were
once the gardens of the old
Palais des Tuileries. They are
an integral part of the
landscaped area running
parallel to the Seine from the
Louvre to the Champs-Elysées
and the Arc de Triomphe.
   The gardens were laid out
in the 17th century by André
Le Nôtre, royal gardener to
Louis XIV. Restoration has
created a new garden as well
as filling the entire gardens
with striking modern and
contemporary sculpture.

**A 17th-century engraving of the
Jardin des Tuileries by G Perelle**

Galerie Nationale du Jeu de Paume ⑮

Jardin des Tuileries, Pl de la Concorde 75008. **Map** 11 C1. **Tel** 01 47 03 12 50. Ⓜ *Concorde*. ◯ *noon–7pm Tue–Sun (to 9pm Tue, from 10am Sat, Sun)*. ⬤ *1 Jan, 1 May, 25 Dec.* 🖼 🚫 ♿ 📷 📧 🎫 📱 **www**.jeudepaume.org

Monet's water lilies, on display in the Musée de l'Orangerie

The Jeu de Paume – or *réal* tennis court – was built by Napoleon III in 1851. When *réal* (royal) tennis was replaced in popularity by lawn tennis, the court was used to exhibit art. Eventually an Impressionist museum was founded here. In 1986, the collection moved to the Musée d'Orsay *(see pp144–7)*. The Jeu de Paume now houses the Centre National de la Photographie, and shows exhibitions of contemporary art. Its sister site is the Hôtel de Sully *(see p95)*.

Entrance to the Jeu de Paume

Musée de l'Orangerie ⑯

Jardin des Tuileries, Pl de la Concorde 75008. **Map** 11 C1. **Tel** 01 44 77 80 07. Ⓜ *Concorde*. ◯ *9am–12.30pm Wed–Mon (groups only); 12.30–7pm Wed–Mon (to 9pm Fri; individual visitors).* 🖼 📷 ♿ 🎫 *by appt.* 📱 **www**.musee-orangerie.fr

Claude Monet's crowning work, the water lily series, or *Nymphéas*, can be found here. The series was painted in his garden at Giverny, near Paris, and presented to the public in 1927. This superb work is complemented well by the outstanding Walter-Guillaume collection of artists of the Ecole de Paris, from the late Impressionist era to the inter-war period. This is a remark-

able concentration of masterpieces, including a room of dramatic works by Soutine and some 14 works by Cézanne – still lifes, portraits *(Madame Cézanne)* and landscapes, such as *Dans le Parc du Château Noir*.

Renoir is represented by 27 canvases, including *Les Fillettes au Piano (Young Girls at the Piano)*. There are early Picassos, works by Henri Rousseau – notably *La Carriole du Père Junier (Old Junier's Cart)* – Matisse and a portrait of Paul Guillaume by Modigliani. All are bathed in the natural light which flows through the window.

Place de la Concorde ⑰

75008. **Map** 11 C1. Ⓜ *Concorde*.

This is one of Europe's most magnificent and historic squares, covering more than 8 ha (20 acres) in the middle of Paris. Starting out as Place Louis XV, for displaying a statue of the king, it was built in the mid-18th century by architect Jacques-Ange Gabriel, who chose to make it an open octagon with only the north side containing mansions.

The 3,200-year-old obelisk from Luxor

In the square's next incarnation, as the Place de la Révolution, the statue was replaced by the guillotine. The death toll in the square in two and a half years was 1,119, including Louis XVI, Marie-Antoinette (who died in view of the small, secret apartment she kept at No. 2 Rue Royale) and the revolutionary leaders Danton and Robespierre.

Renamed Concorde (originally by chastened Revolutionaries) in a spirit of reconciliation, the grandeur of the square was enhanced in the 19th century by the 3,200-year-old Luxor obelisk, two fountains and eight statues personifying French cities. It has become the culminating point of triumphal parades down the Champs-Elysées each 14 July, most notably on the memorable Bastille Day of 1989 when the Revolution's bicentenary was celebrated by a million people, and many world leaders.

Colonnaded entrance to the Village Royale

Village Royal ⑱

75008. **Map** 5 C5. **M** *Madeleine.* *Galerie Royale* ◻ *10am–7pm Tue–Sat.* ◐ *public hols.*

This delightful enclave of 18th-century town houses sits discreetly between the Rue Royale and the Rue Boissy d'Anglas. The Galerie Royale is the former home of the Duchess d'Abrantès. It was converted in 1994 by architect Laurent Bourgois who has combined both classical and modern elements in superb style. The village was formerly the home of glassworkers and silversmiths, and for a while examples of

antique glass and silverware were on display. Nowadays, chic shoppers flock in droves to the designer boutiques that are here, such as Chanel, Dior and Eric Bompard Cashmere, or they stop by for a coffee break in the up-market café, Le Village.

Place Vendôme ⑲

75001. **Map** 6 D5 **M** *Tuileries.*

Perhaps the best example of 18th-century elegance in the city, the architect Jules Hardouin-Mansart's royal square was begun in 1698. The original plan was to house academies and embassies behind the arcaded facades. However, bankers moved in and created opulent homes. Miraculously the square has remained virtually intact, and is home to jewellers and bankers. Among the famous, Frédéric Chopin died here in 1848 at No. 12 and César Ritz established his famous hotel at the turn of the 20th century at No. 15.

Banque de France ⑳

39 Rue Croix des Petits Champs 75001. **Map** 12 F1. **M** *Palais Royal.* ◻ *for details phone 01 42 92 42 92.*

Founded by Napoleon in 1800, France's central bank is housed in a building intended for quite different purposes. The 17th-century architect François Mansart designed this mansion for Louis XIII's wealthy Secretary of State,

Napoleon's statue in Place Vendôme

FORMAL GARDENS IN PARIS

The South Parterre at Versailles *(see pp248–9)*

For the past 300 years the main formal gardens in Paris have been open to the public and are a firm fixture in the city's life. The Jardin des Tuileries *(see p130)* will soon be undergoing extensive renovation and replanting; the Jardin du Luxembourg *(see p172)*, the private garden of the French Senate, is still beloved of Left Bankers; and the Jardin du Palais Royal *(see p121)* is enjoyed by those who seek peace and privacy.

French landscaping was raised to an art form in the 17th century, thanks to Louis XIV's talented landscaper André Le Nôtre, who created the gardens of Versailles *(see pp248–9)*. He achieved a brilliant marriage between the traditional Italian Renaissance garden and the French love of rational design.

The role of the French garden architect was not to tend nature but to transform it, pruning and planting to

The long Galerie Dorée in the Banque de France

Louis de la Vrillière, with the sumptuous 50-m (164-ft) long Galerie Dorée specially created for hanging his great collection of historical paintings. The house was later sold to the Comte de Toulouse, son of Louis XIV and Madame de Montespan. The building was extensively reconstructed in the 19th century after the ravages of the Revolution. The bank's most famous modern alumnus is Jacques Delors, president of the European Commission 1985–1994.

Place des Victoires ㉑

75002. **Map** 12 F1. **M** *Palais Royal.*

This circle of elegant mansions was built in 1685 solely to offset the statue of Louis XIV by Desjardins, which was placed in the middle, with torches burning day and night. The proportions of the buildings and even the arrangement of the surrounding streets were all designed by the architect and courtier Jules Hardouin-Mansart to display the statue to its best advantage.

Unfortunately, the 1792 mobs were less sycophantic and tore down the statue. A replacement, of a different style, was erected in 1822, to the detriment of the whole system of proportions of buildings to statue. Yet the square retains much of the original design, and today it is the address of major names in the fashion business, most notably Thierry Mugler and Kenzo.

Louis XIV on Place des Victoires

A Bagatelle garden with floral colour (see p255)

create leafy sculptures out of trees, bushes and hedges. Complicated geometrical designs that were created in beds and paths were interspersed with pebbles and carefully thought-out splashes of floral colour. Symmetry and harmony were the landscaper's passwords, a sense of grandeur and magnificence his ultimate goal.

In the 17th century, as now, French formal gardens served two purposes: as a setting or backdrop for a château or palace, and for enjoyment. The best view of a formal garden was from the first floor of the château, from which the combination of boxwood hedges, flowers and gravel came together in an intricate, abstract pattern, a blossoming tapestry which complemented the château's interior. Paths of trees drew the eye into infinity, reminding the onlooker of how much land belonged to his host, and therefore establishing his undoubted wealth. So, early on the formal garden became a status symbol, and it still is. This is obvious in both private gardens and in grand public projects. Napoleon Bonaparte completed his vista from the Jardin des Tuileries with a triumphal arch. The late President Mitterrand applied the principle in building his Grand Arche de la Défense (*see pp40–41, 255*) along the same axis as the Tuileries and Arc de Triomphe.

But formal gardens were also made to be enjoyed. People in the 17th century believed that walking in the fresh air kept them in good health. What more perfect spot than a formal garden bedecked with statues and fountains for additional entertainment. The old and infirm could be pushed around in sedan chairs and people could meet one another around a boxwood hedge or on a stone bench under the marbly gaze of the goddess Diana.

ST-GERMAIN-DES-PRES

This Left Bank area is fuller and livelier, its streets and cafés more crowded than when it was at the forefront of the city's intellectual life in the 1950s. The leading figures of the time have now gone, and the rebellious disciples have retreated to their bourgeois backgrounds. But the new philosophers are there, the radical young thinkers who emerged from the 1960s upheavals, and the area still has its major publishing

Musée d'Orsay clock

houses, whose executives entertain treasured writers and agents at the celebrated cafés. But they now share the area with the smart set, those who patronize Yves St-Laurent's opulent premises and the elegant Rue Jacob's smart interior designers. On the south side of Boulevard St-Germain the streets are quiet and quaint, with lots of good restaurants, and at the Odéon end there are brassy cafés and a profusion of cinemas.

SIGHTS AT A GLANCE

Historic Buildings and Streets

Palais Abbatial ❷
Boulevard St-Germain ❼
Rue du Dragon ❽
Rue de l'Odéon ❿
Cour de Rohan ⓬
Cour du Commerce St-André ⓭
Institut de France ⓯
Ecole Nationale Supérieure des Beaux-Arts ⓰
Ecole Nationale d'Administration ⓱
Quai Voltaire ⓲

Churches

St-Germain-des-Prés ❶

Museums and Galleries

Musée Eugène Delacroix ❸
Musée de la Monnaie de Paris ⓮
Musée d'Orsay pp144–7 ⓳
Musée Nationale de la Légion d'Honneur ⓴

Theatres

Odéon Théâtre de L'Europe ⓫

Cafés and Restaurants

Les Deux Magots ❹
Café de Flore ❺
Brasserie Lipp ❻
Le Procope ❾

GETTING THERE

Metro stations St-Germain-des-Prés and Odéon and the RER station at Musée d'Orsay serve the area. Bus route 63 travels down Boulevard St-Germain, and 48 and 95 go along Rue Bonaparte. Routes 58 and 70 pass along Rue Mazarine.

0 metres 400
0 yards 400

KEY

- ▥ Street-by-Street map
- Ⓜ Metro station
- ▣ Batobus boarding point
- RER RER station

SEE ALSO

- *Street Finder*, map 11–12
- *Where to Stay* pp286–7
- *Restaurants* pp304–06

◁ **Les Deux Magots café beside the church of St-Germain-des-Prés**

Street-by-Street: St-Germain-des-Prés

After World War II, St-Germain-des-Prés became synonymous with intellectual life centred around bars and cafés. Philosophers, writers, actors and musicians mingled in the cellar nightspots and brasseries, where existentialist philosophy co-existed with American jazz. The area is now smarter than in the heyday of Jean-Paul Sartre and Simone de Beauvoir, the haunting singer Juliette Greco and the New Wave film-makers.

Organ grinder in St-Germain

The writers are still around, enjoying the pleasures of sitting in Les Deux Magots, Café de Flore and other haunts. The 17th-century buildings have survived, but signs of change are evident in the plethora of affluent shops dealing in antiques, books and fashion.

Les Deux Magots
The café is famous for the patronage of celebrities such as Hemingway ❹

Café de Flore
In the 1950s, French intellectuals wrestled with new philosophical ideas in the Art Deco interior of the café ❺

R U E D U D R A G O N

R U E D U S A B O T

R U E D E R E N N E S

R U E B O N A P A R T E

R U E B O N A P A R T E

B L V D

Ⓜ

Metro St-Germain-des-Prés

R U E D U F O U R

Brasserie Lipp
Colourful ceramics decorate this famous brasserie frequented by politicians ❻

★ **St-Germain-des-Prés**
Descartes and the king of Poland are among the notables buried here in Paris's oldest church ❶

★ **Boulevard St-Germain**
Café terraces, boutiques, cinemas, restaurants and bookshops characterize the central section of the Left Bank's main street ❼

Picasso's sculpture *Homage to Apollinaire is a tribute to the artist's friend, the poet Guillaume Apollinaire. It was erected in 1959, near the Café de Flore, where the poet held court.*

LOCATOR MAP
See Central Paris Map pp14–15

★ **Musée Delacroix**
Here, Delacroix created the splendid mural, Jacob Wrestling, *for St-Sulpice (see p172)* ❸

Rue de Fürstenberg is a tiny square with old-fashioned street lamps and shady trees. It is often used as a film setting.

STAR SIGHTS

★ St-Germain-des-Prés

★ Boulevard St-Germain

★ Musée Delacroix

KEY

--- --- Suggested route

| 0 metres | 100 |
| 0 yards | 100 |

Rue de Buci was for centuries an important Left Bank street and the site of some Real Tennis courts. It now holds a lively market every day.

Palais Abbatial
This was the residence of abbots from 1586 till the 1789 Revolution ❷

Metro Odéon

Metro Mabillon

Marché St-Germain is an old covered food market which was opened in 1818, taking over the site of a former fairground. *(See p334.)*

Danton's statue *(1889), by Auguste Paris, is a tribute to the Revolutionary leader.*

St-Germain-des-Prés ❶

3 Pl St-Germain-des-Prés 75006.
Map 12 E4. **Tel** 01 55 42 81 33. Ⓜ
St-Germain-des-Prés. ◯ 8am–7pm
daily. **Concerts** 8pm Tue, Thu. ✞
12.15pm, 7pm Mon–Fri; 12.15pm;
7pm Sun. ▣ ▢

This is the oldest church in
Paris, originating in 542 when
King Childebert built a basilica
to house holy relics. This
became an immensely
powerful Benedictine abbey,
which was suppressed during
the Revolution, when most of
the buildings were destroyed
by a fire in 1794. One of the
Revolution's most horrific
episodes took place in a
nearby monastery
when 318 priests
were hacked to
death by the mob
on 3 September
1792. The present
church dates from
about the 11th
century and was
heavily restored
in the 19th
century. One of
the three original
towers survives,
housing one of
the oldest belfries
in France. The
interior is an
interesting mix of
architectural styles,
with some 6th-
century marble
columns, Gothic
vaulting and Romanesque
arches. Famous tombs include
those of René Descartes, the
poet Nicolas Boileau and John
Casimir, king of Poland, who
later became abbot of St-
Germain-des-Prés in 1669.

Our Lady of Consolation statue in St-Germain-des-Prés

Palais Abbatial ❷

1–5 Rue de l'Abbaye 75006.
Map 12 E4. Ⓜ St-Germain-des-Prés.
Not open to the public.

This brick and stone palace
was built in 1586 for Charles
of Bourbon who was
cardinal-abbot of St-Germain
and, very briefly, king of
France. Ten more abbots
lived here until the Revolution, when the building was

An ironwork detail from the facade of the Palais Abbatial

sold. James Pradier, the 19th-
century sculptor who was
famous for his female figures,
established a studio here. The
palace is now noted for its
mixture of building materials
and its vertical windows.

Musée Eugène Delacroix ❸

6 Rue de Fürstenberg 75006.
Map 12 E4. **Tel** 01 44 41 86 50.
Ⓜ St-Germain-des-Prés. ◯ 9.30am–
5pm Wed–Mon (last adm: 4.30pm).
▨ ▢ **www**.musee-delacroix.fr

Eugène Delacroix

The leading non-conformist
Romantic painter, Eugène
Delacroix, known for his
passionate and highly-
coloured canvases, lived and
worked here from 1857 to his
death in 1863. Here he
painted *The Entombment
of Christ* and *The Way to
Calvary* (which now hang in
the museum). He also created
superb murals for the Chapel
of the Holy Angels in the
nearby St-Sulpice church,
which is part of the reason
why he moved to this area.

The first-floor apartment and
garden studio now form a
national museum, where
regular exhibitions of
Delacroix's work are held.
The apartment has a portrait
of George Sand, self-portraits,
studies for future works and
artistic memorabilia.
  The charm of Delacroix's
garden is reflected in the tiny
Fürstenberg square. With its
pair of rare catalpa trees and
old-fashioned street lamps,
the square is one of Paris's
most romantic corners.

Les Deux Magots ❹

6 Pl St-Germain-des-Prés 75006.
Map 12 E4. **Tel** 01 45 48 55 25.
Ⓜ St-Germain-des-Prés.
◯ 7.30am–1am daily.
◉ for one week in Jan.
www.lesdeuxmagots.com

The café still trades on its
reputation as the meeting place
of the city's literary and
intellectual elite. This derives
from the patronage of
Surrealist artists and writers
including Ernest Hemingway
in the 1920s and 1930s, and
existentialist philosophers and
writers in the 1950s.
  The present clientele is
more likely to be publishers
or people-watchers than the
new Hemingway. The café's
name comes from the two
wooden statues of Chinese
commercial agents *(magots)*
that adorn one of the pillars.
This is a good place for
enjoying an old-fashioned hot
chocolate and watching the
world go by.

The interior of Les Deux Magots

Facade of the Café de Flore, former meeting-place of existentialists

Café de Flore ❺

172 Blvd St-Germain 75006.
Map *12 D4.* **Tel** *01 45 48 55 26.*
Ⓜ *St-Germain-des-Prés.* ◯ *7.30am–1.30am daily.* ♿ *restricted.*
www.cafe-de-flore.com

The classic Art Deco interior of this café, all-red seating, mahogany and mirrors, has changed little since the war. Like its rival Les Deux Magots, Café de Flore has hosted most of the French intellectuals during the post-war years. Jean-Paul Sartre and Simone de Beauvoir developed their philosophy of existentialism here.

A waiter at the Brasserie Lipp

Brasserie Lipp ❻

151 Blvd St-Germain 75006.
Map *12 E4.* **Tel** *01 45 48 72 93.*
Ⓜ *St-Germain-des-Prés.*
◯ *11.45am–2am daily. (See p305.)*
www.brasserie-lipp.fr

Third of the famous cafés around St-Germain-des-Prés, Brasserie Lipp combines Alsatian beer, sauerkraut and sausages (it was founded by a refugee from Alsace) with excellent coffee to produce a Left Bank fixture popular with French politicians and fashion gurus as well as visitors. Originally opened in the late 19th century, it is regarded by many as the quintessential Parisian brasserie, although the experience is more atmospheric than culinary these days. The interior is bright with ceramic tiles of parrots and cranes.

Boulevard St-Germain ❼

75006, 75007. **Map** *11 C2 & 13 C5.* Ⓜ *Solférino, Rue du Bac, St-Germain-des-Prés, Mabillon, Odéon.*

The left bank's most celebrated thoroughfare, over 3 km (2 miles) long, curves across three districts from the Ile St-Louis to the Pont de la Concorde. The architecture is homogeneous because the boulevard was another of Baron Haussmann's bold strokes of 19th-century urban planning, but it encompasses a wide range of different lifestyles as well as a number of religious and cultural institutions. From the east (the low street numbers) the boulevard passes the late François Mitterrand's private town residence in the Rue de Bièvre, as well as the Maubert-Mutualité market square, the Musée de Cluny and the Sorbonne university, before crossing the lively Boulevard St-Michel.

It continues past the Ecole de Médecine and the Place de l'Odéon to St-Germain-des-Prés, with its historic church and café terraces. Fashion boutiques, cinemas, restaurants and bookshops give this central portion its distinctive character. It is also here that one is most likely to see a celebrity. The area is active from midday to the early morning hours.

Continuing further, beyond this section the boulevard becomes more exclusively residential and then distinctly political with the Ministry of Defence and the National Assembly buildings.

Rue du Dragon ❽

75006. **Map** *12 D4.*
Ⓜ *St-Germain-des-Prés.*

This short street, between the Boulevard St-Germain and the Carrefour de la Croix Rouge, dates back to the Middle Ages and still has houses from the 17th and 18th centuries. Notice their large doors, tall windows and ironwork balconies. A group of Flemish painters lived at No. 37 before the Revolution. The novelist Victor Hugo rented a garret at No. 30 when he was a 19-year-old bachelor.

A plaque at No. 30 Rue du Dragon commemorating Victor Hugo's house

Le Procope ⑨

13 Rue de l'Ancienne-Comédie
75006. **Map** 12 F4. **Tel** 01 40 46 79
00. Ⓜ Odéon. ◯ noon–1am daily.
See **The History of Paris** pp26–7.
www.procope.com

The rear facade of Le Procope restaurant

Founded in 1686 by the
Sicilian Francesco Procopio
dei Coltelli, this claims to be
the world's first coffee house.
It quickly became popular
with the city's political and
literary elite and with actors
from the Comédie-Française.

Its patrons have included
the philosopher Voltaire –
who supposedly drank 40 cups
of his favourite mixture of
coffee and chocolate every
day – and the young Napoleon,
who would leave his hat as
security while he went search-
ing for the money to pay the
bill. Now a restaurant, in 1989
Le Procope was revamped in
the style of the 18th century.

Odéon Théâtre de l'Europe, former
home of the Comédie-Française

Rue de l'Odéon ⑩

75006. **Map** 12 F5. Ⓜ Odéon.

Sylvia Beach's bookshop
Shakespeare & Company
(see pp331–2) stood at No. 12
from 1921 to 1940. She
befriended many struggling
American and British writers,
such as Ezra Pound, T S Eliot,
Scott Fitzgerald and Ernest
Hemingway. It was largely
due to her support – as
secretary, editor, agent and
banker – that James Joyce's
Ulysses was first published in
English. Adrianne Monnier's
French equivalent at No. 7
opposite, Les Amis des Livres,
was frequented by André
Gide and Paul Valéry.

Opened in 1779 to improve
access to the Odéon theatre,
this was the first street in
Paris to have pavements with
gutters and it still has many
attractive houses and shops,
most of them dating from the
18th century.

Odéon Théâtre de l'Europe ⑪

1 Pl Paul-Claudel 75006. **Map** 12
F5. **Tel** 01 44 85 40 40. Ⓜ Odéon,
Luxembourg. ◯ for performances
only. See **Entertainment** pp342–4.
www.theatre-odeon.fr

This Neo-Classical theatre
was built in 1779 by Marie-
Josephe Peyre and Charles
de Wailly in the grounds of
the former Hôtel de Condé.
The site had been purchased
by the king and given to the
city to house the Comédie
Française. The premiere of
The Marriage of Figaro, by
Beaumarchais, took place
here in 1784. With the arrival
of a new company in 1797
the name of the theatre was
changed to Odéon. In 1807 the
theatre was consumed by fire.
It was rebuilt later the same
year by the architect Jean-
François Chalgrin.

Following World War II, the
theatre specialized in 20th-
century drama and was the
best attended in Paris. The
auditorium is particularly
impressive, not least for its
ceiling, painted by André
Masson in 1965.

A young Hemingway in the 1920s

Cour de Rohan ⑫

75006. **Map** 12 F4. Ⓜ Odéon.
Access from the Rue du Jardinet
until 8pm; 8pm–8am access from
the Blvd St-Germain.

The unusual middle courtyard in
the Cour de Rohan

This picturesque series
of three courtyards was
originally part of the 15th-
century pied-à-terre of the
archbishops of Rouen
(corrupted to "Rohan"). The
middle courtyard is the most
unusual. Its three-legged
wrought-iron mounting block,
known as a pas-de-mule, was
used at one time by elderly
women and overweight
prelates to mount their mules.
It is probably the last
mounting block left in Paris.
Overlooking the yard is the
facade of a fine Renaissance
building, dating from the
beginning of the 17th century.
One of its important former
residents was Henri II's
mistress, Diane de Poitiers.

The third courtyard opens
on to the tiny Rue du
Jardinet, where the composer
Saint-Saëns was born in 1835.

Cour du Commerce St-André ⓭

75006. **Map** 12 F4. Ⓜ *Odéon.*

No. 9 has a particularly grisly past, because it was here that Dr Guillotin is supposed to have perfected his "philanthropic decapitating machine". In fact, although the idea was Guillotin's, it was Dr Louis, a Parisian surgeon, who was responsible for putting the "humane" plan into action. When the guillotine was first used for execution in 1792 it was known as a *Louisette*.

A print of a Revolutionary mob at a guillotine execution

Musée de la Monnaie de Paris ⓮

11 Quai de Conti 75006.
Map 12 F3. **Tel** *01 40 46 56 66.*
Ⓜ *Pont-Neuf, Odéon.* ◻ *11am–5.30pm Tue–Fri, noon–5.30pm Sat–Sun.* 🖼 🔲 🔲 *Films.*
www.monnaiedeparis.fr

When Louis XV decided to rehouse the Mint in the late 18th century, he hit upon the idea of launching a design competition for the new

building. The present Hôtel des Monnaies is the result of this competition. It was completed in 1777, and the architect, Jacques Antoine, lived here until his death.

Coins were minted in the mansion until 1973, when the process was moved to Pessac in the Gironde. The minting and milling halls now contain the coin and medallion museum. The extensive collection is displayed in vertical glass stands so that both sides of the coins are visible, and everything is presented in the context of the history of the day. The final room of the museum shows a production cycle with late 19th-century and early 20th-century tools and machines on display.

Instead of minting coins, the building's workshops are now devoted to the creation of medallions, a selection of which are on sale in the museum shop.

Institut de France ⓯

23 Quai de Conti 75006.
Map 12 E3. **Tel** *01 44 41 44 41.*
Ⓜ *Pont-Neuf, St-Germain-des-Prés.* ◻ *Sat & Sun by appointment only.*
🖼 🔲 **www.**institut-de-france.fr

Now home to the illustrious Académie Française, this Baroque building was built as a palace in 1688 and was given over to the Institut de France in 1805. Its distinctive cupola was designed by the palace's architect, Louis Le Vau, to harmonize with the Palais du Louvre.

The Académie Française is the most famous of the five academies within the institute. It was founded in 1635 by

A sign to the former Mint, which is now a museum

Cardinal Richelieu and charged with the compilation of an official dictionary of the French language. From the beginning, membership has been limited to 40, who are entrusted with working on the dictionary.

Ecole Nationale Supérieure des Beaux-Arts ⓰

13 Quai Malaquais 75006. **Map** 12 E3.
Tel *01 47 03 50 00.* Ⓜ *St-Germain-des-Prés.* ◻ *Mon pm to groups by appt only (phone 01 47 03 50 74 to arrange).* 🔲 *Library.* **www.**ensba.fr

The main French school of fine arts occupies an enviable position at the corner of the Rue Bonaparte and the riverside Quai Malaquais. The school is housed in several buildings, the most imposing being the 19th-century Palais des Etudes.

A host of budding French and foreign painters and architects have crossed the large courtyard to study in the ateliers of the school. Young American architects, in particular, have studied there over the past century.

The facade of the Ecole Nationale Supérieure des Beaux-Arts

THE CELEBRATED CAFES OF PARIS

One of the most enduring images of Paris is the café scene. For the visitor it is the romantic vision of great artists, writers or eminent intellectuals consorting in one of the Left Bank's celebrated cafés. For the Parisian the café is one of life's constants, an everyday experience, providing people with a place to tryst, drink and meet friends, or to conclude business deals, or to simply watch the world go by.

The first café anywhere can be traced back to 1686, when the café Le Procope (see p140) was opened. In the following century cafés became a vital part of Paris's social life. And with the widening of the city's streets, particularly during the 19th century and the building of Haussmann's Grands Boulevards, the cafés spread out on to the pavements, evoking Emile Zola's comment as to the "great silent crowds watching the street live".

The nature of a café was sometimes determined by the interests of its patrons. Some were the gathering places for those interested in playing chess, dominoes or billiards. Literary gents gathered in Le Procope during Molière's time in the 17th century. In the 19th century, First Empire Imperial guards officers were drawn to the Café d'Orsay and Second Empire financiers gathered in the cafés along the Rue de la Chaussée d'Antin. The smart set patronized the Café de Paris and Café Tortini, and theatre-goers met at the cafés around the Opéra, including the Café de la Paix (see p215).

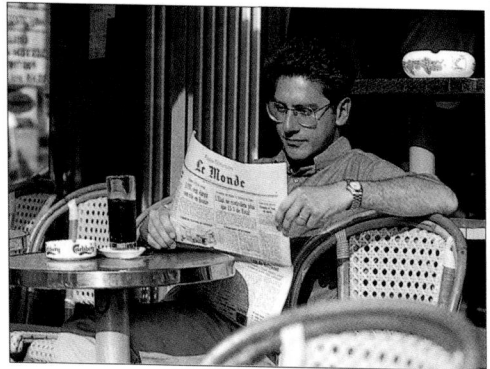

Newspaper reading is still a typical café pastime

Ecole Nationale d'Administration ⑰

13 Rue de l'Université 75007. **Map** 12 D3. **Tel** 01 49 26 45 45. Ⓜ Rue du Bac. ◉ to the public.

This fine 18th-century mansion was originally built as two houses in 1643 by Briçonnet. In 1713 they were replaced by a hôtel, built by Thomas Gobert for the widow of Denis Feydeau de Brou. It was passed on to her son, Paul-Espirit Feydeau de Brou, until his death in 1767. The hôtel then became the residence of the Venetian ambassador. It was occupied by Belzunce in 1787 and became a munitions depot during the Revolution until the restoration of the monarchy in 1815.

Until recently it housed the Ecole Nationale d'Administration (now in Strasbourg), where a high percentage of the elite in politics, economics and science were once students.

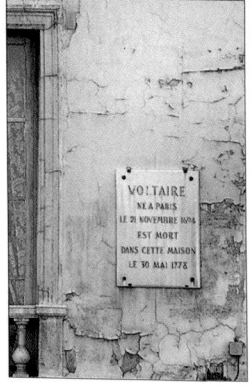

Plaque marking the house in Quai Voltaire where Voltaire died

Quai Voltaire ⑱

75006 and 75007. **Map** 12 D3. Ⓜ Rue du Bac.

Formerly part of the Quai Malaquais, then later known as the Quai des Théatins, the Quai Voltaire is now home to some of the most important antiques dealers in Paris. It is also noted for its attractive 18th-century houses and for the famous people who lived in many of them, making it an especially interesting and pleasant street to walk along.

The 18th-century Swedish ambassador Count Tessin lived at No. 1, as did the sculptor James Pradier, famed for his statues and for his wife, who swam naked across the Seine. Louise de Kéroualle, spy for Louis XIV and created Duchess of Portsmouth by the infatuated Charles II of England, lived at Nos. 3–5.

Famous past residents of No. 19 included the composers Richard Wagner and Jean Sibelius, the novelist Charles Baudelaire and the exiled Irish writer and wit Oscar Wilde.

The French philosopher Voltaire died at No. 27, the Hôtel de la Villette. St-Sulpice, the local church, refused to accept his corpse (on the grounds of his atheism) and his body was rushed into the country to avoid a pauper's grave.

Entertainment in the Claude Alain café in the Rue de Seine during the 1950s

The most famous cafés are on the Left Bank, in St-Germain and Montparnasse, where the literati of old used to gather and where the glitterati of today love to be seen. Before World War I, Montparnasse was haunted by hordes of Russian revolutionaries, most eminently Lenin and Trotsky, who whiled away their days in the cafés, grappling with the problems of Russia and the world over a *petit café*. Cultural life flourished in the 1920s, when Surrealists, like Salvador Dalí and Jean Cocteau, dominated café life, and later when American writers led by Ernest Hemingway and Scott Fitzgerald talked, drank and worked in various cafés, among them La Coupole *(see p178)*, Le Sélect and La Closerie des Lilas *(see p179)*.

After the end of World War II, the cultural scene shifted northwards to St-Germain. Existentialism had become the dominant creed and Jean-Paul Sartre its tiny charismatic leader. Sartre and his intellectual peers and followers, among them the writers Simone de Beauvoir and Albert Camus, the poet Boris Vian and the enigmatic singer Juliette Greco, gathered to work and discuss their ideas in Les Deux Magots *(see p138)* and the nearby rival Café de Flore *(see p139)*. The traditional habitué of these cafés is still to be seen, albeit mixing with the international jet-set and with self-publicizing intellectuals hunched over their notebooks.

Works by one of St-Germain's elite, Albert Camus (1913–60)

Musée d'Orsay ⑲

See pp144–7.

Musée Nationale de la Légion d'Honneur ⑳

2 Rue de Bellechasse (2 Rue de la Légion d'Honneur) 75007. **Map** 11 C2. **Tel** 01 40 62 84 25. Ⓜ Solférino. ▣ Musée d'Orsay. ○ 1–6pm Wed–Sun. ● public hols. **www**. legiondhonneur.fr

Next to the Musée d'Orsay is the truly massive Hôtel de Salm. It was one of the last

Napoleon III's Great Cross of the Legion of Honour

great mansions to be built in the area (1782). The first owner was a German count, Prince de Salm-Kyrbourg, who was guillotined in 1794.

Today the building contains a museum where one can learn all about the Legion of Honour, a decoration launched by Napoleon I. Those awarded the honour

The Musée d'Orsay, converted from a railway station into a museum

wear a small red rosette in their buttonhole. The impressive displays of medals and insignia are complemented by paintings. In one of the rooms, Napoleon's Legion of Honour is on display with his sword and breastplate.

The museum also covers decorations from most parts of the world, among them the British Victoria Cross and the American Purple Heart.

Musée d'Orsay **⑲**

In 1986, 47 years after it had closed as a mainline railway station, Victor Laloux's superb late 19th-century building was reopened as the Musée d'Orsay. Commissioned by the Orléans railway company to be its Paris terminus, it avoided demolition in the 1970s following the outcry over the destruction of Baltard's pavilions at Les Halles food market. During the conversion much of the original architecture was retained. The museum, which has undergone extensive renovation, was set up to present each of the arts of the period from 1848 to 1914 in the context of the contemporary society and all the forms of creative activity happening at the time.

The Museum, from the Right Bank
Victor Laloux designed the building for the Universal Exhibition in 1900.

Chair by Charles Rennie Mackintosh
The style developed by Mackintosh was an attempt to express ideas in a framework of vertical and horizontal forms, as in this tearoom chair (1900).

★ **The Gates of Hell** *(1880–1917)*
Rodin included figures that he had already created, such as The Thinker *and* The Kiss, *in this famous gateway.*

★ **Le Déjeuner sur l'Herbe** *(1863)*
Manet's painting, first exhibited in Napoleon III's Salon des Refusés, is presently on display in the first area of the upper level.

KEY TO FLOORPLAN

- ☐ Architecture & Decorative Arts
- ☐ Sculpture
- ☐ Painting before 1870
- ☐ Impressionism
- ☐ Neo-Impressionism
- ☐ Naturalism and Symbolism
- ☐ Art Nouveau
- ☐ Temporary exhibitions
- ☐ Non-exhibition space

GALLERY GUIDE

The collection occupies three levels. On the ground floor there are works from the mid to late 19th century. The middle level features Art Nouveau decorative art and a range of paintings and sculptures from the second half of the 19th century to the early 20th century. The upper level has an outstanding collection of Impressionist and Neo-Impressionist art.

The Dance *(1867–8)*
Carpeaux's sculpture caused a scandal when first exhibited.

★ Dancing at the Moulin de la Galette
To capture the dappled light filtering through the trees, Renoir painted this colourful picture (1876) out in the open in Montmartre.

Upper level

★ La Belle Angèle
This portrait (1889) by Paul Gauguin shows the sitter in traditional Breton costume.

Middle level

The Tiger Hunt by Eugène Delacroix
Painted in 1854 for a dealer named Weill, this was described by Baudelaire as profound, sensual and terrible.

Ground floor

Entrance

Shop

STAR EXHIBITS

★ The Gates of Hell by Rodin

★ Le Déjeuner sur l'Herbe by Manet

★ Dancing at the Moulin de la Galette by Renoir

★ La Belle Angèle by Gauguin

Exploring the Musée d'Orsay

Many of the exhibits now in the Musée d'Orsay originally came from the Louvre, and the superb collection of Impressionist art that was housed in the cramped Jeu de Paume until it closed in 1986 has been rehung here. In addition to the main exhibition, there are displays that explain the social, political and technological context in which the art was created, including exhibits on the history of cinematography.

Ceiling design (1911) by the artist and designer Maurice Denis

ART NOUVEAU

The Belgian architect and designer Victor Horta was among the first to give free rein to the sinuous line that gave Art Nouveau its French sobriquet of *Style Nouille* (noodle style). Taking its name from a gallery of modern design that opened in Paris in 1895, Art Nouveau flourished throughout Europe until World War I.

In Vienna, Otto Wagner, Koloman Moser and Josef Hoffmann combined high craft with the new design, while the School of Glasgow, under the impetus of Charles Rennie Mackintosh, developed a more rectilinear approach which anticipated the work of Frank Lloyd Wright in the United States.

René Lalique introduced the aesthetics of Art Nouveau into jewellery and glassware, while Hector Guimard, inspired by Horta, is most famous today for his once-ubiquitous Art Nouveau entrances to the Paris metro.

One exhibit not to be missed is the carved wooden bookcase by Rupert Carabin (1890), with its proliferation of allegorical seated female nudes, bronze palm fronds and severed bearded heads.

SCULPTURE

The museum's central aisle overflows with an oddly-assorted selection of sculptures. These illustrate the eclectic mood around the middle of the 19th century when the Classicism of Eugène Guillaume's *Cenotaph of the Gracchi* (1848–53) co-existed with the Romanticism of François Rude. Rude created the relief on the Arc de Triomphe (1836), often referred to as *La Marseillaise (see p211)*.

There is a wonderful series of 36 busts of members of parliament (1832) – bloated, ugly, unscrupulous and self-important – by the satirist Honoré Daumier, and work by the vital but short-lived genius Jean-Baptiste Carpeaux, whose first major bronze, *Count Ugolino* (1862), was a character from Dante. In 1868 he produced his Dionysian delight, *The Dance*, which caused a storm of protest: it was "an insult to public morals". This contrasts with the derivative and mannered work of such sculptors as Alexandre Falguière and Hyppolyte Moulin.

Edgar Degas' famous *Young Dancer of Fourteen* (1881) was displayed during his lifetime, but the many bronzes on show were made from wax sculptures found in his

studio after his death. In contrast, the sculpture of Auguste Rodin was very much in the public eye, and his sensuous and forceful work makes him pre-eminent among 19th-century sculptors. The museum contains many of his works, including the original plaster of *Balzac* (1897). Rodin's talented companion, Camille Claudel, who spent much of her life in an asylum, is represented by a grim allegory of mortality, *Maturity* (1899–1903).

The turn of the 20th century is marked by the work of Emile-Antoine Bourdelle and Aristide Maillol.

PAINTING BEFORE 1870

The surprising diversity of styles in 19th-century painting is emphasized by the close juxtaposition on the ground floor of all paintings prior to 1870 – the crucial year in which Impressionism first made a name for itself. The raging colour and almost Expressionistic vigour of Eugène Delacroix's *Lion Hunt* (1854) stands next to Jean-Dominique Ingres' cool Classical *The Spring* (1820–56). As a reminder of the academic manner that dominated the century up to that point, the uninspired waxwork style of Thomas Couture's monumental *The Romans in the Age of Decadence* (1847) dominates the central aisle. In a class of their own are Edouard Manet's provocative *Olympia* and *Le Déjeuner sur l'Herbe* (1863), while works painted around the same time by his friends, Claude Monet, Pierre-Auguste Renoir, Frédéric Bazille and Alfred Sisley, give a glimpse of the Impressionists before the Impressionist movement began.

Young Dancer of Fourteen (1881) by Edgar Degas

Olympia (1863) by Edouard Manet

IMPRESSIONISM

Rouen Cathedral caught at various moments of the day (1892–3) is one of the many works on show by Claude Monet, the leading figure of the Impressionist movement. Pierre-Auguste Renoir's plump nudes and his young people *Dancing at the Moulin de la Galette* (1876) were painted at the high point of his Impressionist period. Other artists on display include Camille Pissarro, Alfred Sisley and Mary Cassatt.

Edgar Degas, Paul Cézanne and Vincent Van Gogh are included here although their techniques differed from those of the Impressionists. Degas often favoured crisp Realism, though he was quite capable of using the sketchy manner of the Impressionists, as, for instance, in *L'Absinthe* (1876). Cézanne was more concerned with substance than light, as can be seen in his *Apples and*

Blue Waterlilies (1919) by Claude Monet

Oranges (1895–1900). Van Gogh was momentarily influenced by the movement but then went his own way, illustrated here by works from the collection of Dr Gachet.

Breton Peasant Women (1894) by Paul Gauguin

NEO-IMPRESSIONISM

Although labelled Neo-Impressionism, the work of Georges Seurat (which includes *The Circus* from 1891) was quite unrelated to the older movement. He, along with Maximilien Luce and Paul Signac, painted by applying small dots of colour that blended together when viewed from a distance. *Jane Avril Dancing* (1892) is just one of many pictures by Henri de Toulouse-Lautrec on display. The work Paul Gauguin did at Pont-Aven in Brittany is shown next to that of younger artists who

knew him at the time, such as Emile Bernard and the Nabis group. There are also a number of paintings from his Tahitian period.

The Nabis (which included Pierre Bonnard) tended to treat the canvas as a flat surface out of which a sense of depth emerged as the viewer gazed upon it.

The dream-like visions of Odilon Redon are in the Symbolist vein, while the naïve art of Henri (Douanier) Rousseau is represented by *War* (1894) and *The Snake Charmer* (1907).

NATURALISM AND SYMBOLISM

Three large rooms are devoted to paintings that filled the Salons from 1880 to 1900. The work of the Naturalists was sanctioned by the Third Republic and widely reproduced at the time. Fernand Cormon's figure of *Cain* was highly acclaimed when it first appeared in the 1880 Salon. Jules Bastien-Lepage's interest lay in illustrating peasant life, and in 1877 he painted *Haymaking*, which established him as one of the leading Naturalists. His fairly free handling of paint was influenced by what he had learned from Manet and his friends. More sombrely (and effectively) naturalistic is Lionel Walden's view of *The Docks of Cardiff* (1894).

Symbolism developed as a reaction against Realism and Impressionism and tended to be dominated by images of dreams and thoughts. This resulted in a wide variety of subjects and modes of expression. There is the over-sweet vision of levitating harpists, *Serenity* by Henri Martin (1899), Edward Burne-Jones' monumental work *Wheel of Fortune* (1883) and Jean Delville's *School of Plato* (1898). One of the most evocative paintings in this section is Winslow Homer's lyrical *Summer Night* (1890).

LATIN QUARTER

15th-century stained glass in Musée de Cluny

Student book shops, cafés, cinemas and jazz clubs fill this ancient, riverside quarter between the Seine and the Luxembourg Gardens. Famous institutes of learning abound, among them the two most prestigious *lycées*, Henri IV and Louis le Grand, through which passes a large percentage of the future French elite.

As the leaders of the 1968 revolt *(see pp40–41)* disappeared into the mainstream of French life, so the Boulevard St-Michel, the area's spine, turned increasingly to commerce, not demonstrations. Today, there are cheap shops and fast-food outlets, and the maze of narrow, cobbled streets off the boulevard are full of inexpensive ethnic shops, quirky boutiques and avant-garde theatres and cinemas. But the area's 800 years of history are difficult to efface. The Sorbonne retains much of its old character and the eastern half of the area has streets dating back to the 13th century. And the Rue St-Jacques still remains the long Roman road stretching out of the city, and the forerunner of all the city's streets.

A young musician playing music under the Pont St-Michel is part of the Latin Quarter's long tradition as a focus for the young from all walks of life.

SIGHTS AT A GLANCE

Historic Buildings and Streets
Boulevard St-Michel ❷
La Sorbonne ❼
Collège de France ❽

Museums and Galleries
Musée National du Moyen Age pp154–7 ❶
Musée de la Préfecture de Police ❻

Churches and Temples
St-Séverin ❸
St-Julien-le-Pauvre ❹

Squares
Place Maubert ❺

Chapelle de la Sorbonne ❾
St-Etienne-du-Mont ❿
Panthéon pp158–9 ⓫

GETTING THERE

Metro stations in the area include those at St-Michel and Cluny La Sorbonne. The Balabus and routes 24 and 87 travel along Blvd St-Germain, and 38 travels along Blvd St- Michel, passing the Sorbonne and the Musée National du Moyen Age.

KEY

▨	Street-by-Street map
Ⓜ	Metro station
⬚	Batobus boarding point
RER	RER station

SEE ALSO

- *Street Finder*, map 12, 13, 17
- *Where to Stay* p287
- *Restaurants* p306

◁ **A peaceful spot along a Latin Quarter quay**

Street-by-Street: Latin Quarter

Since the Middle Ages this riverside quarter has been dominated by the Sorbonne, and acquired its name from the early Latin-speaking students. It dates back to the Roman town across from the Ile de la Cité; at that time the Rue St-Jacques was one of the main roads out of Paris. The area is generally associated with artists, intellectuals and the bohemian way of life; it also has a history of political unrest. In 1871, the Place St-Michel became the centre of the Paris Commune, and in May 1968 it was the site of the student uprisings. Today the eastern half has become sufficiently chic, however, to contain the homes of some of the Establishment.

Place St-Michel contains a fountain by Davioud. The bronze statue by Duret shows St Michael killing the dragon.

Metro St-Michel

Little Athens is a lively place in the evening, especially at the weekend, when the Greek restaurants situated in the picturesque streets around St-Séverin are at their busiest.

Metro Cluny La Sorbonne

★ **Boulevard St-Michel**
The northern end of the Boul'Mich, as it is affectionately known, is a lively mélange of cafés, book and clothes shops, with nightclubs and experimental cinemas nearby ❷

★ **Musée National du Moyen Age**
One of the finest collections of medieval art in the world is kept here in a superb late 15th-century building ❶

No. 22 Rue St-Séverin is the narrowest house in Paris and used to be the residence of Abbé Prévost, author of *Manon Lescaut.*

★ St-Séverin
Begun in the 13th century, this beautiful church took three centuries to build and is a fine example of the flamboyant Gothic style ❸

Rue du Chat qui Pêche is a narrow pedestrianized street which has changed little in its 200-year history.

LOCATOR MAP
See Central Paris Map pp14–15

Shakespeare & Co *(see pp331-2)* at No.37 Rue de la Bûcherie is a delightful, if chaotic, bookshop. Any books purchased here are stamped with *Shakespeare & Co Kilomètre Zéro Paris*.

★ St-Julien-le-Pauvre
Rebuilt in the 17th century, this church was used to store animal feed during the Revolution ❹

Rue du Fouarre used to host lectures in the Middle Ages. The students sat on straw *(fouarre)* in the street.

Ⓜ Metro Maubert Mutualité

Rue Galande was home to the rich and chic in the 17th century, but subsequently became notorious for its taverns.

STAR SIGHTS

- ★ Boulevard St-Michel
- ★ Musée National du Moyen Age
- ★ St-Séverin
- ★ St-Julien-le-Pauvre

KEY

– – – Suggested route

| 0 metres | 100 |
| 0 yards | 100 |

Musée National du Moyen Age ❶

See pp154–7.

Boulevard St-Michel ❷

75005 & 75006. **Map** 12 F5 & 16 F2.
Ⓜ St-Michel, Cluny-La Sorbonne.
ⓇⒺⓇ Luxembourg.

Cut through the area in 1869, the boulevard initially gained fame from its many literary cafés, but nowadays many have been replaced by clothes shops. Nos. 60–64 house the Ecole Nationale Supérieure des Mines, one of France's leading engineering schools (see p173). In the Place St-Michel, marble plaques commemorate the many students who died here in 1944 fighting the Nazis.

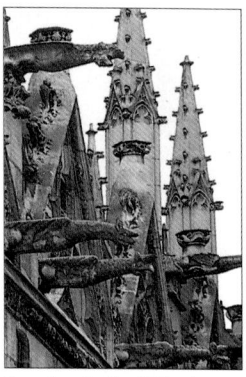

Gargoyles adorning St-Séverin

St-Séverin ❸

1 Rue-des-Prêtres-St-Séverin 75005.
Map 13 A4. **Tel** 01 42 34 93 50.
Ⓜ St-Michel. ⃝ 11am–7.30pm daily.
◉ **Concerts.**

One of the most beautiful churches in Paris, St-Séverin is a perfect example of the Flamboyant Gothic style. It is named after a 6th-century hermit who lived in the area and persuaded the future St Cloud, grandson of King Clovis, to take holy orders. Construction finished in the early 16th century and included a remarkable double ambulatory circling the chancel. In 1684 the Grande

Inside St-Julien-le-Pauvre

Mademoiselle, cousin to Louis XIV, adopted St-Séverin after breaking with her parish church of St-Sulpice and had the chancel modernized.

The burial ground here, which is now a garden, was the site of the first operation for gall stones in 1474. An archer who had been condemned to death was offered his freedom by Louis XI if he consented to the operation and lived. (It was a success, and the archer went free.) In the garden stands the church's medieval gable-roofed charnel house.

St-Julien-le-Pauvre ❹

1 Rue St-Julien-le-Pauvre 75005.
Map 13 A4. **Tel** 01 43 54 52 16.
Ⓜ St-Michel. ⃝ 9.30am–1.30pm, 3pm–6pm daily. **Concerts.**
See **Entertainment** p336.

At least three saints can claim to be patron of this church, but the most likely is St Julian the Hospitalier. The church, together with St-Germain-des-Prés, is one of the oldest in Paris, dating from between 1165 and 1220. The university held its official meetings in the church until 1524, when a student protest created so much damage that university meetings were barred from the church by parliament. Since 1889 it has belonged to the Melchite sect of the Greek Orthodox Church, and it is now the setting for chamber and religious music concerts.

Place Maubert ❺

75005. **Map** 13 A5.
Ⓜ Maubert-Mutualité.

From the 12th to the middle of the 13th century, "La Maub" was one of Paris's scholastic centres, with lectures given in the open air. After the scholars moved to the new colleges of the Montagne St-Geneviève, the square became a place of torture and execution, including that of the philosopher Etienne Dolet, who was burnt at the stake in 1546.

So many Protestants were burnt here in the 16th century that it became a place of pilgrimage for the followers of the new faith. Its dark reputation has been replaced by respectability and a notable street market.

Musée de la Préfecture de Police ❻

4 Rue de la Montagne Ste-Geneviève 75005. **Map** 13 A5.
Tel 01 44 41 52 50. Ⓜ Maubert-Mutualité. ⃝ 9am–5pm Mon–Fri; 10am–5pm Sat (last adm: 4.30pm). ◉ public hols.

Weapons in the police museum

A darker side to Paris's history is illustrated in this small, rather old-fashioned museum. Created in 1909, the collection traces the development of the police in Paris from the Middle Ages to the 20th century. Curiosities on show include arrest warrants for figures such as the famous revolutionary Danton, and a rather sobering display of weapons and tools used by famous criminals. There is also a section on the part the police played in the Resistance and subsequent liberation of Paris.

La Sorbonne ❼

47 Rue des Ecoles 75005.
Map 13 A5. **Tel** *01 40 46 22 11.*
Ⓜ *Cluny-La Sorbonne, Maubert-Mutualité.* ⬜ *9am–5pm Mon–Fri.*
⬤ *public hols.* 🎫 *only, by appt: write to Service des Visites.*

The Sorbonne, seat of the University of Paris, was established in 1253 by Robert de Sorbon, confessor to Louis IX, for 16 poor students to study theology. From these modest beginnings the college soon became the centre of scholastic theology. In 1469 the rector had three printing machines brought over from Mainz, thereby founding the first printing house in France. The college's opposition to liberal 18th-century philosophy led to its suppression during the Revolution. It was re-established by Napoleon in 1806. The buildings built by Richelieu in the early 17th century were replaced by the ones seen today, with the exception of the chapel.

Statues outside the college

Collège de France ❽

11 Pl Marcelin-Berthelot 75005.
Map 13 A5. **Tel** *01 44 27 12 11.*
Ⓜ *Maubert-Mutualité.* ⬜ *Oct–Jun: 9am–6pm Mon–Fri.*

One of Paris's great institutes of research and learning, the college was established in 1530 by François I. Guided by the great humanist Guillaume Budé, the king aimed to counteract the intolerance and dogmatism of the Sorbonne. A statue of Budé stands in the west courtyard, and the unbiased approach to learning is reflected in the inscription on the entrance to the old college: *docet omnia* (all are taught here). Lectures are free and open to the public.

Chapelle de la Sorbonne ❾

Pl de la Sorbonne 75005.
Map 13 A5. **Tel** *01 40 46 22 11.*
Ⓜ *Cluny-La Sorbonne, Maubert-Mutualité.* ⒭⒠⒭ *Luxembourg.*
⬜ *for temporary exhibitions only.*
🎫

Designed by Lemercier and built between 1635 and 1642, this chapel is, in effect, a monument to Richelieu, with his coat of arms on the dome supports and his white marble tomb, carved by Girardon in 1694, in the chancel. The chapel's attractive lateral facade looks on to the main courtyard of the Sorbonne.

Eglise de la Sorbonne clock

St-Etienne-du-Mont ❿

Pl Ste-Geneviève 75005. **Map** 17 A1.
Tel *01 43 54 11 79.* Ⓜ *Cardinal Lemoine.* ⬜ *8.45am–7.30pm Tue–Fri, noon–7.30pm Mon; w/e closed midday.* ⬤ *Mon in Jul–Aug.* 📷 🎫

This remarkable church houses not only the shrine of Sainte Geneviève, patron saint of Paris, but also the remains of the great literary figures Racine and Pascal. Some parts are in the Gothic style and others date from the Renaissance, including a magnificent rood screen. The stained glass windows are also of note.

16th-century belfry tower

ST-ETIENNE-DU-MONT

Medieval window

Rood screen

Panthéon ⓫

See pp158–9.

Musée National du Moyen Age ❶

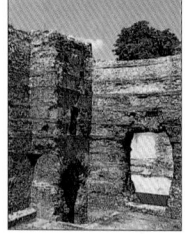

Head of St John the Baptist

Previously known as the Musée de Cluny, its original owner was Pierre de Chalus, Abbot of Cluny, who bought the ruins in 1330. Surrounded by imaginatively recreated medieval gardens, the museum is a unique combination of Gallo-Roman ruins, ncorporated into a medieval mansion, and one of the world's finest collections of medieval art.

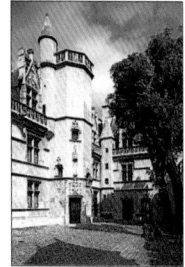

Medieval Mansion
The museum building, completed in 1500, was erected by Jacques d'Amboise, Abbot of Cluny.

Medieval chapel

★ Lady with the Unicorn
This outstanding series of six tapestries is a fine example of the millefleurs *style, which was developed in the 15th and early 16th centuries. The style is noted for its graceful depiction of plants, animals and people.*

★ Golden Rose of Basel *(1330)*
The goldsmith Minucchio da Siena made this rose for the Avignon Pope John XXII.

Caldarium (hot bath room)

Gallo-Roman Baths
Built in AD 200, the baths lasted for about 100 years before being sacked by the barbarians.

STAR EXHIBITS

★ Lady with the Unicorn

★ Golden Rose of Basel

★ Gallery of the Kings

Gallo-Roman Frigidarium
The arches of this cold bath room, dating from the 1st and 2nd centuries, were once decorated with pairs of carved ship prows, the symbol of the association of Paris boatmen (nautes).

Books of Hours
The museum possesses two Books of Hours from the first half of the 15th century. The illuminated pages include scenes showing the Labours of the Months, accompanied by the relevant sign of the zodiac.

VISITORS' CHECKLIST

6 Pl Paul-Painlevé. **Map** 13 A5.
🛈 *01 53 73 78 16/00.* Ⓜ
*Cluny-La-Sorbonne, St-Michel,
Odéon.* 🚌 *63, 86, 87, 21, 27, 85,
38 to Rue Soufflot, Rue des Ecoles.*
ⓇⒺⓇ *St-Michel, Cluny-La Sorbonne.*
🅿 *Blvd St-Germain, Pl Edmond
Rostand.* ⬜ *9.15am–5.45pm
Wed–Mon.* ⬤ *1 Jan, 1 May, 25
Dec.* 🖼 📷 ✅ 🅱 **Concerts.
Medieval poetry readings.**
www.musee-moyenage.fr

★ Gallery of the Kings
In 1977, 21 of the 28 stone heads of the Kings of Judah (carved around 1220 during the reign of Philippe Auguste) were unearthed during excavations in the Rue de la Chaussée-d'Antin behind the Opéra.

Octagonal tower

Entrance

Courtyard

Courtyard entrance

KEY TO THE BUILDING

🟦 Gallo-Roman ruins

🟦 Medieval mansion

🟦 19th- and 20th-century section

GALLERY GUIDE
The collection is spread throughout the two floors of the building. It is mainly medieval and covers a wide range of items, including illuminated manuscripts, tapestries, textiles, precious metals, alabaster, ceramics, sculpture and church furnishings. A number of Gallo-Roman artefacts are displayed around the sides of the frigidarium, *and the small circular room nearby contains some capitals.*

TIMELINE

200	1450	1750	1800	1850
c. 200 Public baths built	**1747** Octagonal tower used as observatory		**1789** Seized in the Revolution and sold by the State	**1833** Acquired by Alexandre du Sommerard, collector of medieval artefacts
1500 Building of mansion by Jacques d'Amboise completed				**1844** Opened as a museum
c. 300 Baths sacked and burned by barbarians			**1819** Baths excavated on the orders of Louis XVIII	
1600 Hôtel becomes residence of papal nuncios		*Louis XVIII at his desk*	**1842** House and collection bought by State	

Exploring the Cluny's Collection

Alexandre du Sommerard took over the Hôtel de Cluny in 1833 and installed his art collection with great sensitivity to the surroundings and a strong sense of the dramatic. After his death the Hôtel and its contents were sold to the State and turned into a museum.

The Grape Harvest tapestry

TAPESTRIES

The museum's tapestries are remarkable for their quality, age and state of preservation. The images present a surprising mixture of the naive with more complex notions. One of the earliest, *The Offering of the Heart* (early 15th century), shows a man who is literally proffering his heart to a seated medieval beauty. More everyday scenes are shown in the magnificent series *The Noble Life* (about 1500). Upstairs is the mysterious *Lady with the Unicorn* series.

CARVINGS

The diverse techniques of medieval European woodcarvers are well represented. From the Nottingham workshops in England, there are wood as well as alabaster works which were widely used as altarpieces all over Europe. Among the smaller works of this genre are *The School,* which is touchingly realistic and dates from the early 16th century.

Upstairs there are some fine Flemish and south German woodcarvings. The multicoloured figure of St John is typical. Two notable altarpieces on display are the intricately carved and painted *Lamentation of Christ* (about 1485) from the Duchy of Clèves, and the Averbode altarpiece, which was made in 1523 in Antwerp, and depicts three scenes including the Last Supper. Not to be missed is a beautiful full-length figure of Mary Magdalene.

STAINED GLASS

Most of the Cluny's glass from the 12th and 13th centuries is French. The oldest examples were originally installed in the Basilique St-Denis in 1144. There are also three fragments from the Troyes Cathedral, destroyed by fire, two of which illustrate the life of St Nicholas while the third depicts that of Christ.

Numerous panels came to the Cluny from Sainte-Chapelle *(see pp88–9),* during its mid-19th-century restoration, and were never returned, including five scenes from the story of Samson dating from 1248.

The technique of contrasting coloured glass with surrounding grisaille (grey-and-white panels) developed in the latter half of the 13th century. Four panels from the royal château at Rouen illustrate this.

Stained-glass scenes from Brittany (1400)

The School woodcarving (English, early 16th century)

Head of a queen from St-Denis from before 1120

SCULPTURE

The highlight here is the Gallery of the Kings, a display of heads and decapitated figures from Notre-Dame. There is also an very graceful statue of Adam, sculpted in the 1260s.

In the vaulted room opposite are displays of fine Romanesque sculpture retrieved from French churches. Among the earliest are the 12 capitals from the nave of St-Germain- des-Prés, from the early 11th century. Retrieved from the portal of St-Denis is a boldly sculpted head of a queen (c.1140) which, though badly mutilated, is still compelling.

Other Romanesque and early Gothic capitals include six finely sculpted works from Catalonia and four of the museum's most famous statues, early 13th-century apostles made for Sainte-Chapelle.

EVERYDAY OBJECTS

Household goods show another side to medieval life, and this large collection is grouped in a sensitive way to illustrate their use – from wallhangings and caskets to kitchenware and clothing. Children's toys bring a very human aspect to the display, while travel cases and religious emblems evoke journeys of exploration and pilgrimage.

PRECIOUS METALWORK

The Cluny has a fine collection of jewellery, coins, metal and enamelwork from Gallic times to the Middle Ages. The showcase of Gallic jewellery includes gold torques, bracelets and rings, all of a simple design. In between these is one of the Cluny's most precious exhibits, the Golden Rose of Basel, a delicately wrought piece from 1330 and the oldest known of its kind.

The earliest enamelwork on display is the late Roman and Byzantine *cloisonné* pieces, culminating in the remarkable Limoges enamels, which flourished in the late 12th century. There are also two exceptional altarpieces, the Golden Altar of Basel and the Stavelot altarpiece.

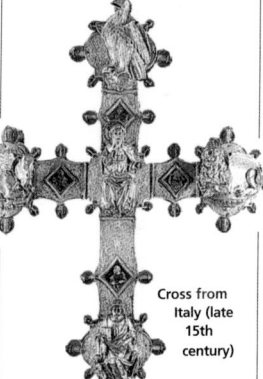

Cross from Italy (late 15th century)

The Pillar of the Nautes

GALLO-ROMAN RUINS

One of the main reasons for visiting the Musée de Cluny is to see the scale and layout of its earliest function, the Gallo-Roman baths. The vaulted *frigidarium* (cold bath room) was the largest of its kind in France. Here there is another of the Cluny's highlights, the recently restored Pillar of the Nautes (boatmen), unearthed during excavations beneath Notre-Dame in 1711. Composed of five carved stone blocks representing Gallic and Roman divinities, its crowning element is presumed to depict the Seine's boatmen. There are also the ruins of the *caldarium* and *tepidarium* (hot and tepid baths), and visitors can tour the underground vaults.

LADY WITH THE UNICORN TAPESTRIES

This series of six tapestries was woven in the late 15th century in the southern Netherlands. It is valued for its fresh harmonious colours and the poetic elegance of the central figure. Allegories of the senses are illustrated in the first five: sight (gazing into a mirror), hearing (playing a portable organ), taste (sampling sweets), smell (sniffing carnations) and touch (the lady holding the unicorn's horn).

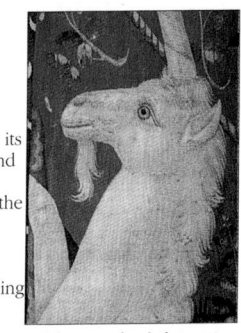

Unicorn on the sixth tapestry

The enigmatic sixth tapestry (showing jewels being placed in a box) includes the words "to my only desire" and is now thought to represent the principle of free choice.

Panthéon ⓫

When Louis XV recovered from desperate illness in 1744, he was so grateful to be alive that he conceived a magnificent church to honour Sainte Geneviève. The design was entrusted to the French architect Jacques-Germain Soufflot, who planned the church in Neo-Classical style. Work began in 1764 and was completed in 1790, ten years after Soufflot's death, under the control of Guillaume Rondelet. But with the Revolution underway the church was soon turned into a pantheon – a location for the tombs of France's good and great. Napoleon returned it to the Church in 1806, but it was secularized and then desecularized once more before finally being made a civic building in 1885.

The Facade
Inspired by the Rome Pantheon, the temple portico has 22 Corinthian columns.

The arches of the dome show a renewed interest in the lightness of Gothic architecture and were designed by Rondelet. They link four pillars supporting the dome, which weighs 10,000 tonnes and is 83 m (272 ft) high.

Pediment Relief
David d'Angers' pediment bas-relief depicts the mother country (France) granting laurels to her great men.

The Panthéon Interior
The interior has four aisles arranged in the shape of a Greek cross, from the centre of which the great dome rises.

Entrance

STAR FEATURES

★ Iron-Framed Dome

★ Frescoes of Sainte Geneviève

★ Crypt

★ **Frescoes of Sainte Geneviève**
Murals along the south wall of the nave depict the life of Sainte Geneviève. They are by Pierre Puvis de Chavannes, the 19th-century fresco painter.

The dome lantern allows only a little light to filter into the church's centre. Intense light was thought inappropriate for the place where France's heroes rested.

VISITORS' CHECKLIST

Pl du Panthéon. **Map** 17 A1. **Tel** 01 44 32 18 00. M Jussieu, Cardinal-Lemoine. 84 to Panthéon; 21, 27, 38, 82, 84, 85, 89 to Gare du Luxembourg. RER Luxembourg. P Pl Edmond Rostand. Apr–Sep: 10am–6.30pm daily; Oct–Mar: 10am–6pm daily. 1 Jan, 1 May, 25 Dec.

★ Iron-Framed Dome
The tall dome, with its stone cupolas and three layers of shells, was inspired by St Paul's in London and the Dôme Church (see pp188–9).

The dome galleries afford a magnificent panoramic view of France's capital.

Colonnade
The colonnade encircling the dome is both decorative and part of an ingenious supporting system.

Monument to Diderot
This is Alphonse Terroir's statue (1925) to the political writer Denis Diderot.

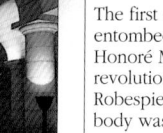

★ Crypt
Covering the entire area under the building, the crypt divides into galleries flanked by Doric columns. Many French notables rest here.

THE PANTHEON'S ENSHRINED

The first of France's great men to be entombed was the popular orator Honoré Mirabeau. (Later, under the revolutionary leadership of Maximilien Robespierre, he fell from grace and his body was removed.) Voltaire followed. A statue of Voltaire by Jean-Antoine Houdon stands in front of his tomb. In the 1970s the remains of the wartime Resistance leader Jean Moulin were reburied here. Pierre and Marie Curie's remains were transferred here in 1995, and Malraux's followed in 1996. Others here include Jean-Jacques Rousseau, Victor Hugo and Emile Zola.

JARDIN DES PLANTES QUARTER

This area, traditionally, has been one of the most tranquil corners of Paris. It takes its character from the 17th-century botanical gardens where the kings of the *ancien régime* grew medicinal herbs and where the National Natural History Institute stands today. The many hospitals in the area, notably Paris's largest, Pitié-Salpêtrière, add to the atmosphere. A colourful market takes over much of Rue Mouffetard every day, and the streets off Mouffetard are redolent of life in medieval times.

SIGHTS AT A GLANCE

Museums and Galleries
Musée de la Sculpture en Plein Air ❷
Collection des Minéraux de l'Université ❹
Muséum National d'Histoire Naturelle ❿
La Manufacture des Gobelins ⓭

Modern Architecture
Institut du Monde Arabe ❶

Churches and Temples
St-Médard ❽
Mosquée de Paris ❾

Squares, Parks and Gardens
Ménagerie ❸
Place de la Contrescarpe ❻
Jardin des Plantes ⓫

Historic Buildings and Streets
Arènes de Lutèce ❺
Rue Mouffetard ❼
Groupe Hospitalier Pitié-Salpêtrière ⓬

GETTING THERE

There are metro stations at Cardinal Lemoine, Gare d'Austerlitz, St-Marcel, Gobelins and Place d'Italie, and RER and SNCF stations at Gare d'Austerlitz. The bus route 47 travels down Rue Monge and 89 passes around the gardens.

SEE ALSO

• *Street Finder,* map 17–18
• *Restaurants* p307

KEY

▨	Street-by-Street map
Ⓜ	Metro station
RER	RER station
Ⓡ	SNCF (train) station

0 metres   400
0 yards   400

◁ **Market scene on the Rue Mouffetard**

Street-by-Street: Jardin des Plantes Quarter

Two physicians to Louis XIII, Jean Hérouard and Guy de la Brosse, obtained permission to establish the royal medicinal herb garden in the sparsely populated St-Victor suburb in 1626. The herb garden and gardens of various religious houses gave the region a rural character. In the 19th century the population and thus the area expanded and it became more built up, until it gradually assumed the character it has today: a well-to-do residential patchwork of 19th- and early 20th-century buildings interspersed with much older and some more recent buildings.

Metro Cardinal Lemoine

Place de la Contrescarpe
This village-like square filled with restaurants and cafés buzzes with student life after dusk ❻

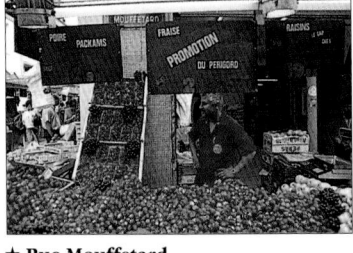

★ **Rue Mouffetard**
Locals flock to the daily open-air market here which is one of the oldest Paris street markets. A hoard of louis d'or *gold coins from the 18th century was found at No. 53 during its demolition in 1938* ❼

Pot de Fer fountain is one of 14 that Marie de Médicis had built on the Left Bank in 1624 as a source of water for her palace in the Jardin du Luxembourg. The fountain was rebuilt in 1671.

Metro Monge

Passage des Postes is an ancient alley which was opened in 1830. Its entrance is in the Rue Mouffetard.

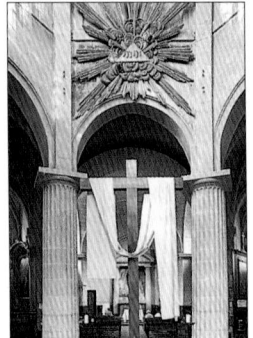

St-Médard
This church was started in the mid-15th century and completed by 1655. In 1784 the choir was made Classical in style, and the nave's 16th-century windows were replaced with contemporary stained glass ❽

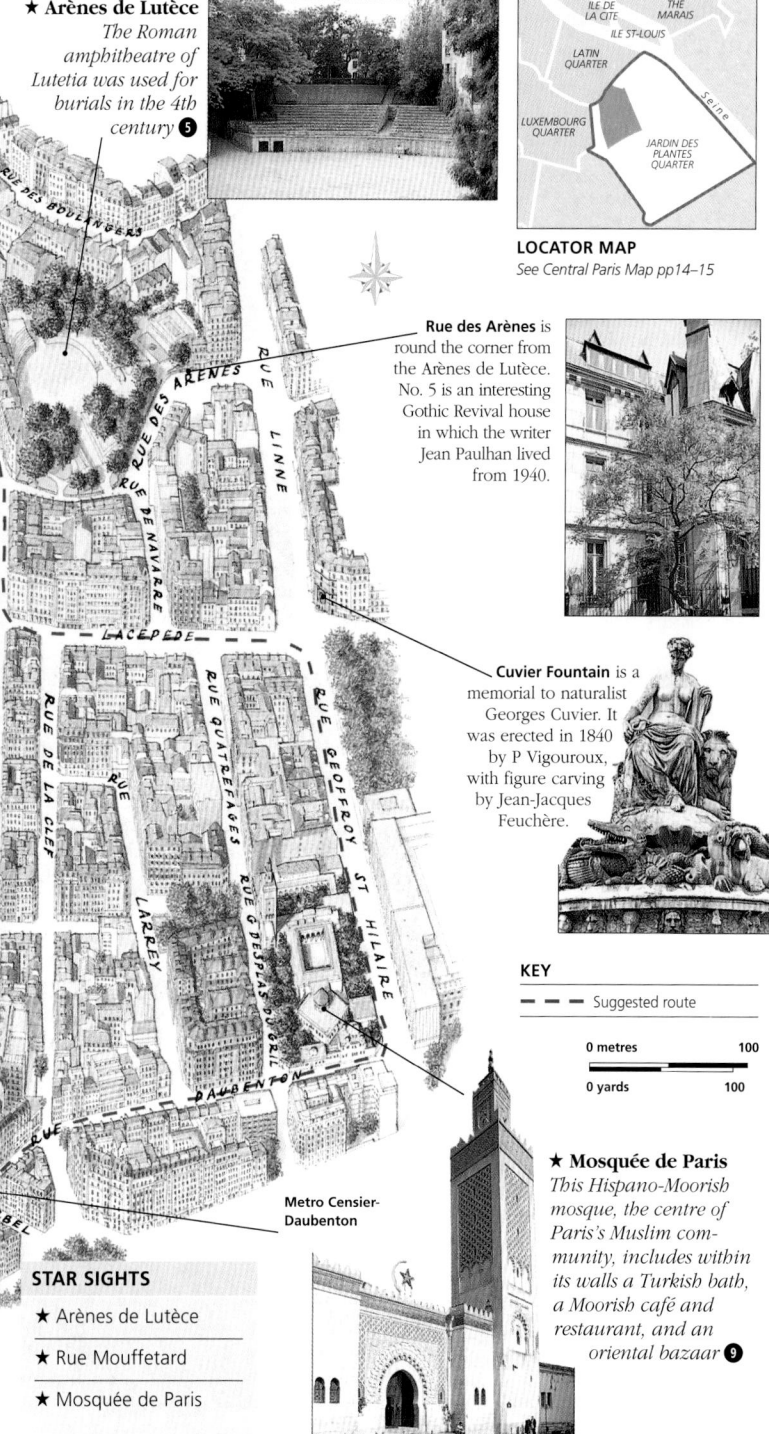

★ Arènes de Lutèce
The Roman amphitheatre of Lutetia was used for burials in the 4th century ⑤

LOCATOR MAP
See Central Paris Map pp14–15

ILE DE LA CITÉ
THE MARAIS
ILE ST-LOUIS
LATIN QUARTER
LUXEMBOURG QUARTER
JARDIN DES PLANTES QUARTER
Seine

Rue des Arènes is round the corner from the Arènes de Lutèce. No. 5 is an interesting Gothic Revival house in which the writer Jean Paulhan lived from 1940.

Cuvier Fountain is a memorial to naturalist Georges Cuvier. It was erected in 1840 by P Vigouroux, with figure carving by Jean-Jacques Feuchère.

KEY

– – – Suggested route

0 metres   100
0 yards   100

Metro Censier-Daubenton

★ Mosquée de Paris
This Hispano-Moorish mosque, the centre of Paris's Muslim community, includes within its walls a Turkish bath, a Moorish café and restaurant, and an oriental bazaar ⑨

STAR SIGHTS

★ Arènes de Lutèce

★ Rue Mouffetard

★ Mosquée de Paris

Institut du Monde Arabe ❶

1 Rue des Fossées St-Bernard 75005.
Map 13 C5. **Tel** 01 40 51 38 38.
Ⓜ Jussieu, Cardinal-Lemoine.
⬤ **Museum & temp exhibs:** 10am–6pm Tue–Sun. **Library:** 1pm–8pm Tue–Sat. 📷 ♿ ✔ **Lectures.**
🍴 💻 www.imarabe.org

This cultural institute was founded in 1980 by France and 20 Arab countries with the intention of fostering cultural links between the Islamic world and the West. It is housed in a magnificent modern building designed by the French architect Jean Nouvel (also responsible for the Musée du Quai Branly, *see p192–3*), that combines modern materials with the spirit of traditional Arab architecture. The white marble book tower, which can be seen through the glass of the west wall, spirals upwards

bringing to mind the minaret of a mosque. The emphasis that is traditionally placed on interior space in Arab architecture has been used here to create an enclosed courtyard reached by a narrow gap splitting the building in two.

From floors four to seven, there is a fascinating display of Islamic works of art from the 9th to the 19th centuries, including glassware, ceramics, sculpture, carpets and astrolabes. There is also a library and media archive.

Musée de la Sculpture en Plein Air ❷

75004/75005. **Map** 13 C5. Ⓜ Gare d'Austerlitz, Sully-Morland.

Butting up to the left hand corner of the Institut du Monde Arabe, the Pont de Sully links the Ile St Louis with both banks of the Seine. Opened in 1877 and built of cast iron, the Pont de Sully is not an especially beautiful structure. Despite this, it is well worth pausing for a moment on the bridge for a fabulous view of Notre-Dame rising dramatically behind the wonderfully graceful Pont de la Tournelle.

Running along the river from the Pont de Sully as far as the Pont d'Austerlitz is the peaceful Quai St-Bernard. Not always so sedate, Quai St-Bernard was famous during the 17th century as a spot for nude bathing, until scandalized public opinion made it illegal. The grassy slopes adjoining the quai make a perfect spot to enjoy a picnic. Opened in 1975, they are known as the Jardin

Tino Rossi in honour of the celebrated Corsican singer. The garden has a display of open-air sculpture known as the Musée de la Sculpture en Plein Air. Vandalism and other problems have unfortunately necessitated the removal of some of the exhibits.

Ménagerie ❸

57 Rue Cuvier 75005.
Map 17 C1. **Tel** 01 40 79 30 00 or 01 40 79 37 94.
Ⓜ Jussieu, Austerlitz.
⬤ 9am–5.30pm daily. 📷 🍴 💻

France's oldest public zoo is situated in the lovely sur-roundings of the Jardin des Plantes. It was set up during the Revolution to house survivors from the Royal menagerie at Versailles – all four of them. The state then rounded up animals from circuses and exotic creatures were sent from abroad. Unfortunately, during the Prussian siege of Paris (1870–71), most of them were slaughtered to feed the hungry citizens *(see p226)*. Today the zoo

specializes in small mammals, insects, birds, primates and reptiles, and it is a great favourite with children as it is possible for them to get quite close to the animals. The lion house contains panthers from China and other attractions include a large monkey house, a large waterfowl aviary and wild sheep and goats.

The displays in the vivarium (enclosures of live animals in natural habitat) are changed at regular intervals and there is a permanent exhibition of micro-arthropods (also known as creepy-crawlies!).

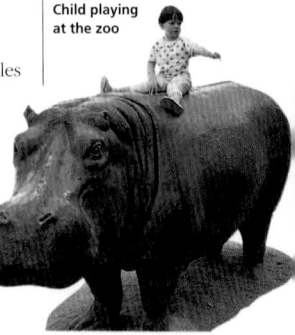

Child playing at the zoo

Light Screens

The south elevation is made up of 1,600 high-tech metal screens which filter the light entering the building. Their design is based on moucharabiyahs *(carved wooden screens found on the outsides of buildings from Morocco to Southeast Asia).*

Each screen contains 21 irises which are controlled electronically, opening and closing in response to the amount of sunlight falling on photosensitive screens.

The central iris is made up of interlocking metal blades which move to adjust the size of the central opening.

The peripheral irises are linked to one another and to the central iris. They open and close in unison forming a delicate pattern of light and shade inside the institute.

Collection des Minéraux de l'Université ❹

Paris VI-Jussieu, 4 Pl Jussieu 75005. **Map** 17 B1. **Tel** 01 44 27 52 88. Ⓜ Jussieu. ◯ 1pm–6pm Wed–Mon. ● 1 Jan, Easter, 1 May, 14 Jul, 1 Nov, 25 Dec. ⓟ 🗓 🎫 groups Tue pm. ♿

This fascinating small museum is housed in the main **Topaz** university building, named after the distinguished scientists. The collection comprises cut and uncut gemstones and rock crystal from all over the world, shown to maximum advantage through the expert use of specialized lighting.

Arènes de Lutèce ❺

Rue de Navarre 75005. **Map** 17 B1. Ⓜ Jussieu. See p21.

The remains of this vast Roman arena (Lutetia was the Roman name for Paris) date from the late 2nd century. Its destruction began towards the end of the 3rd century at the hands of the Barbarians, and later, parts of it were used to build the walls of the Ile de la Cité. The arena was then gradually buried and its exact location preserved only in old documents and the local name Clos des Arènes. It was rediscovered in 1869 during the construction of the Rue Monge and the allocation of building plots nearby.

Action towards its restoration began with the campaigning of Victor Hugo (among others) in the 19th century but work did not get really underway until 1918.

With a seating capacity of 15,000, arranged in 35 tiers, the original arena was used both for theatrical performances and as an amphitheatre for the more gruesome spectacle of gladiator fights. This type of combined use was peculiar to Gaul (France), and the arena is similar to the other French ones in Nîmes and Arles.

The public park at the Arènes de Lutèce

BUFFON AND THE JARDIN DES PLANTES

At the age of 32 Georges Louis Leclerc, Comte de Buffon (1707–88), became the curator of the Jardin des Plantes at a time when the study of natural history was at the forefront of contemporary thought – Charles Darwin's *The Origin of Species* was to be published 120 years later. Buffon masterminded the reorganization of the Jardin, propelling it to a pre-eminent position within the scientific world. He was elected to the Académie Française in 1752 following the publication of his two main works, *Natural History* and *The Epoques of Nature*. He died in his house in the Jardin.

Illustration of a primate from Buffon's *Natural History*

Place de la Contrescarpe **❻**

75005. **Map** 17 A1. **Ⓜ** *Place Monge.*

At one time this site lay outside the city walls. It gets its name from the backfilling of the moat that ran along Philippe-Auguste's wall. The present square was laid out in 1852. At No. 1 there is a memorial plaque to the old "pine-cone club" immortalized in the writings of Rabelais; here a group of writers known as *La Pléiade* (named after the constellation of The Pleiades) used to meet in the 16th century.

The area has always been used for meetings and festivals. Today it is extremely lively at weekends, and on Bastille Day *(see p65)* a delightful ball is held here.

Part of the medieval city wall

Cheese in the Mouffetard market

Rue Mouffetard **❼**

75005. **Map** 17 B2. **Ⓜ** *Censier-Daubenton, Place Monge.* **❑** *Market Place Maubert: 7am–2.30pm Tue, Thu, Sat (to 3pm Sat); Place Monge: 7am–2.30pm Wed, Fri, Sun (to 3pm Sun). See **Shops and Markets** p339.*

A major thoroughfare since Roman times, when it linked Lutetia (Paris) and Rome, this street is one of the oldest in the city. In the 17th and 18th centuries it was known as the Grande Rue du Faubourg St-Marcel, and many of its buildings date from that time. Some of the small shops still have ancient painted signs, and some houses have mansard roofs. No. 125 has an attractive, restored Louis XIII facade, and the entire front of No. 134 has beautiful decoration of wild beasts, flowers and plants.

The area is known for its open-air markets, especially those in Place Maubert, Place Monge, and Rue Daubenton, a side street where a lively African market takes place.

St-Médard **❽**

141 Rue Mouffetard 75005. **Map** 17 B2. **Tel** *01 44 08 87 00.* **Ⓜ** *Censier-Daubenton.* **❑** *8am–noon, 2.30–7pm Tue–Sat; 4–7pm Sun.* **⊙** **❑**

The origins of this charming church go back to the 9th century. St Médard, counsellor to the Merovingian kings, was known for his custom of giving a wreath of white roses to young girls noted for their virtue. The churchyard, now a garden, became notorious in the 18th century as the centre of the cult of the Convulsionnaires, whose hysterical fits were brought on by the contemplation of miracle cures. The interior has many fine paintings, including the 17th-century *St Joseph Walking with the Christ Child* by Francisco de Zurbarán.

Mosquée de Paris **❾**

2 bis Pl du Puits de l'Ermite 75005. **Map** 17 C2. **Tel** *01 45 35 97 33; 01 43 31 38 20 (tearoom); 01 43 31 18 14 (Turkish baths).* **Ⓜ** *Place Monge.* **❑** *9am–noon, 2pm–6pm Sat–Thu.* **●** *Muslim hols.* **⊙** **❑** **❑** **❑** *Library.* www.mosquee-de-paris.com

Built in the 1920s in the Hispano-Moorish style, this group of buildings is the spiritual centre for Paris's Muslim community and the home of the Grand Imam. The complex comprises religious, educational and commercial sections; at its heart is a mosque. Each of the mosque's

Decoration inside the mosque

domes is decorated differently, and the minaret stands nearly 33 m (100 ft) high. Inside is a grand patio with mosaics on the walls and tracery on the arches.

Once used only by scholars, the mosque's place in Parisian life has grown over the years. The Turkish baths can be enjoyed by both men and women, but on alternate days. There is also a tearoom serving Moorish specialities.

Muséum National d'Histoire Naturelle ⑩

2 Rue Buffon 75005. **Map** 17 C2. **Tel** 01 40 79 54 79. Ⓜ *Jussieu, Austerlitz.* ◯ *10am–6pm Wed–Mon.* ● *1 May.* 🎦 & *restricted.* ▢ 🛈 *Library.* **www**.mnhn.fr

Skull of the reptile dimetrodon

The highlight of the museum is the Grande Galerie de l'Evolution. There are also four other departments: palaeontology, featuring skeletons, casts of various animals and an exhibition showing the evolution of the vertebrate skeleton; palaeobotany, devoted to plant fossils; mineralogy, including gemstones; and entomology, with some of the oldest fossilized insects on earth. The bookshop is in the house that was occupied by the naturalist Buffon, from 1772 until his death in 1788.

Jardin des Plantes ⑪

57 Rue Cuvier 75005. **Map** 17 C1. **Tel** 01 40 79 56 01. Ⓜ *Jussieu, Austerlitz.* ◯ *8am–6.45pm (to 5pm winter) daily.*

The botanical gardens were established in 1626, when Jean Hérouard and Guy de la Brosse, Louis XIII's physicians, obtained permission to found a royal medicinal herb garden here and then a school of botany, natural history and pharmacy. The garden was opened to the public in 1640 and flourished under Buffon's direction. Now one of Paris's great parks, it includes a natural history museum, botanical school and zoo.

As well as beautiful vistas and walkways flanked by ancient trees and punctuated with statues, the park has a remarkable alpine garden with plants from Corsica, Morocco, the Alps and the Himalayas and an unrivalled display of herbaceous and wild plants. It also has the first Cedar of Lebanon to be planted in France, originally from Britain's Kew Gardens.

Groupe Hospitalier Pitié-Salpêtrière ⑫

47 Blvd de l'Hôpital 75013. **Map** 18 D3. Ⓜ *St-Marcel, Austerlitz.* Ⓡ *Gare d'Austerlitz.* ◯ **Chapel** *8.30am–6.30pm daily.* ✝ *3.30pm daily.* 🎦 &

The vast Salpêtrière Hospital stands on the site of an old gunpowder factory and derives its name from the saltpetre used in the making of explosives. It was founded by Louis XIV in 1656 to help sick or socially-disadvantaged women and children and later became renowned for its pioneering humane treatment of the insane. It was here that Princess Diana died in 1997, following an automobile accident in a Paris underpass.

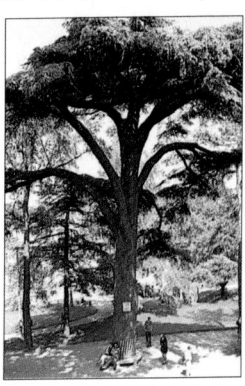

The Cedar of Lebanon in the Jardin

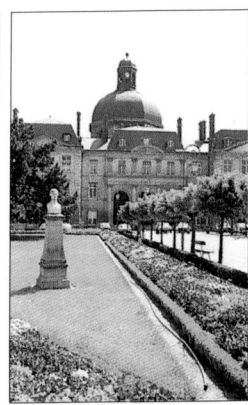

Outside the Hôpital Salpêtrière

La Manufacture des Gobelins ⑬

42 Ave des Gobelins 75013. **Map** 17 B3. **Tel** 01 44 08 52 00. Ⓜ *Gobelins.* ◯ **guided tours only** *2.15pm and 2.30pm Tue–Thu (arrive 15 mins earlier). Groups by appt.* 🎦 ● *public hols.*

Versailles tapestry by Le Brun

Originally a dyeing workshop set up in about 1440 by the Gobelin brothers, the building became a tapestry factory early in the 17th century. Louis XIV took it over in 1662 and gathered together the greatest craftsmen of the day – carpet weavers, cabinet makers and silversmiths – to furnish his new palace at Versailles *(see pp248–53).* Working under the direction of court painter Charles Le Brun, 250 Flemish weavers laid the foundations for the factory's international reputation. Today weavers continue to work in the traditional way but with modern designs, including those of Picasso and Matisse.

LUXEMBOURG QUARTER

Many a Parisian dreams of living in the vicinity of the Luxembourg Gardens, a quieter, greener and somehow more reflective place than its neighbouring areas. Luxembourg is one of the most captivating places in the capital. Its charm is in its old gateways and streets, its bookshops, and in the sumptuous yet intimate gardens. Though writers of the eminence of Paul Verlaine and André Gide no longer stroll in its groves, the paths, lawns and avenues are still full of charm, drawing to them the numerous students from the nearby *grandes écoles* and *lycées*. And on warm days old men meet under the chestnut trees to play chess or the traditional game of *boules*.

To the west the buildings are public and official, and on the east the houses are shaded by the tall chestnut trees of the Boulevard St-Michel.

Sailing boats are hired by children and adults to sail in the *grand bassin* (ornamental pond) in the Luxembourg Gardens.

SIGHTS AT A GLANCE

Museums
Musée du Service de Santé des Armées ❿
Ecole Nationale Supérieure des Mines ⓫

Historic Buildings
Palais du Luxembourg ❸
Institut Catholique de Paris ❻

Churches
St-Sulpice ❷
St-Joseph-des-Carmes ❼
Val-de-Grâce ❾

Squares and Gardens
Place St-Sulpice ❶
Jardin du Luxembourg ❺

Fountains
Fontaine de Médicis ❹
Fontaine de l'Observatoire ❽

GETTING THERE

The area is served by the metro, with stations at Mabillon and St-Sulpice, and by the RER, with a station at Luxembourg. Several bus routes pass through the area. Route 38 travels along Boulevard St-Michel on the east side of the Gardens and 58 and 89 pass along the Rue de Rennes on the north side. Route 82 passes along the southern end.

SEE ALSO

• **Street Finder,** map 12, 16
• **Where to Stay** p288

KEY

Street-by-Street map
M Metro station
RER RER station

0 metres 400
0 yards 400

◁ Playing chess in the Jardin du Luxembourg

Street-by-Street: Luxembourg Quarter

Situated only a few steps from the bustle of St-Germain-des-Prés, this graceful and historic area offers a peaceful haven in the heart of a modern city. The Jardin du Luxembourg and Palais du Luxembourg dominate the vicinity. The gardens became fully open to the public in the 19th century under the ownership of the Comte de Provence (later Louis XVIII), when for a small fee visitors could come in and feast on fruit from the orchard. Today the gardens, palace and old houses on the streets to the north remain unspoilt and attract many visitors.

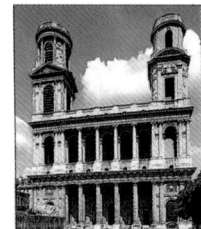

★ St-Sulpice
This Classical church was built over 134 years to Daniel Gittard's plans. It has a facade by the Italian architect Giovanni Servandoni ❷

To St-Germain-des-Prés

Place St-Sulpice
The Fontaine des Quatre Points Cardinaux depicts four church leaders at the cardinal points of the compass. Point also means "never": the leaders were never made cardinals ❶

RUE HENRI DE JOUVENEL
RUE FÉROU
RUE SERVANDONI
RUE DE VAUGIRARD

The Monument to Delacroix (1890) by Jules Dalou is situated near the private gardens of the French Senate. Beneath the bust of the leading Romantic painter Eugène Delacroix are the allegorical figures of Art, Time and Glory.

STAR SIGHTS

★ St-Sulpice

★ Jardin du Luxembourg

★ Palais du Luxembourg

★ Fontaine de Médicis

★ Jardin du Luxembourg
Many fine statues were erected in the Luxembourg gardens in the 19th century during the reign of Louis-Philippe ❺

The Rue de Tournon is full of elegant architecture, boutiques and old bookshops. At No. 12 is the Grand Hôtel d'Entragues, reconstructed by Neveu in the 18th century during Louis XVI's reign.

LOCATOR MAP
See Central Paris Map pp14–15

KEY

– – – Suggested route

| 0 metres | 100 |
| 0 yards | 100 |

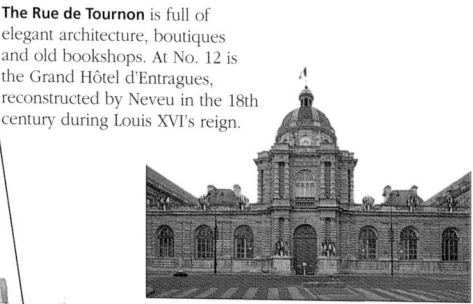

★ **Palais du Luxembourg**
In 1794, during the Revolution, the painter Jacques-Louis David was imprisoned here and made sketches for the Intervention of the Sabine Women ❸

★ **Fontaine de Médicis**
The 17th-century fountain is in the style of an Italian grotto and is thought to have been designed by Salomon de Brosse ❹

Sainte Geneviève, the patron saint of Paris, was a wealthy 5th-century Gallo-Roman land-owner. When Paris was invaded by the Huns in AD 451, she prayed with women friends that the city would be spared – their prayers were answered. This statue by Michel-Louis Victor (1845) pays homage to her.

RUE DE TOURNON

RUE DE MEDICIS

The Octagonal Lake (Grand Bassin), attributed to Jean-François Chalgrin, is surrounded by formal terraces where visitors to the gardens often sunbathe.

Place St-Sulpice ❶

75006. **Map** 12 E4. Ⓜ *St-Sulpice.*

This large square, which is dominated on the east side by the enormous church from which it takes its name, was built in the last half of the 18th century.

Two main features of the square are the Fountain of the Four Bishops by Joachim Visconti (1844) and the pink-flowering chestnut trees. There is also the Café de la Mairie, a rendezvous of writers and students, which is often featured in French films.

Stained-glass window of St-Sulpice

St-Sulpice ❷

Pl St-Sulpice 75006. **Map** 12 E5. *Tel* 01 42 34 59 98. Ⓜ *St-Sulpice.* ☐ 7.30am–7.30pm daily. ✠ frequent. ◉

It took more than a century, from 1646, for this huge and imposing church to be built. The result is a simple two-storey west front with two tiers of elegant columns. The overall harmony of the building is marred only by the towers, one at each end, which do not match.

Large arched windows fill the vast interior with light. By the front door are two huge shells given to François I by the Venetian Republic – they rest on rock-like bases sculpted by Jean-Baptiste Pigalle.

In the side chapel to the right of the main door are three magnificent murals by Eugène Delacroix: *Jacob Wrestling with the Angel (see p137)*, *Heliodorus Driven from the Temple* and *St-Michael Killing the Dragon*. If you are lucky you can catch an organ recital.

Palais du Luxembourg ❸

15 Rue de Vaugirard 75006. **Map** 12 E5. *Tel* 01 42 34 20 60 (groups); 01 44 54 19 49 (individuals). Ⓜ Odéon. Ⓡ *Luxembourg.* ✎ one Sat each mth. ◙ www.senat.fr

Now the home of the French Senate, this palace was designed by Salomon de Brosse in the style of the Pitti Palace in Florence to remind Marie de Médicis, widow of Henri IV, of her native town. By the time it was finished (1631), Marie had been banished, but it remained a royal palace until the Revolution. Since then the palace has been used as a prison, and in World War II it was the head-quarters of the Luftwaffe, with air-raid shelters built under its gardens. The Musée du Lux-embourg, in the east gallery, hosts renowned art exhibitions.

Figures on the Fontaine de Médicis

Fontaine de Médicis ❹

15 Rue de Vaugirard 75006. **Map** 12 F5. Ⓡ *Luxembourg.*

Built in 1624 for Marie de Médicis by an unknown architect, this vigorous Baroque fountain stands at the end of a long pond filled with goldfish and shaded by trees. The mythological figures were added much later by Auguste Ottin (1866).

Jardin du Luxembourg ❺

Blvd St-Michel 75006. **Map** 12 E5. *Tel* 01 42 34 23 89. Ⓡ *Luxembourg.* ☐ dawn–dusk daily. ▣

A green oasis covering 25 ha (60 acres) in the heart of the Left Bank, this is the most popular park in the whole of Paris. The layout of the gardens is centred around the Luxem-bourg Palace and is dominated by a splendid octagonal pool – usually full of toy sailing boats.

Apart from the aesthetic attraction of its formal terraces and broad avenues, statues of various queens of France are also dotted throughout the park, as well as an impressive figure of Saint Genevieve, the patron of Paris, and, by way of contrast, a Cyclops.

The park also includes an open-air café, a puppet theatre, numerous tennis courts, a bandstand and a bee-keeping school.

Sculptures on Palais du Luxembourg

Institut Catholique de Paris ⑥

21 Rue d'Assas 75006.
Map 12 D5. **Tel** 01 44 39 52 00.
Ⓜ St-Placide, Rennes. **Musée Biblique** ☐ 4–6pm Sat or by appt.
Tel 01 45 48 09 15.
www.icp.fr

Founded in 1875, this is one of the most distinguished teaching institutions in France with some 23,000 students. It also houses a small museum: the Musée Biblique which displays objects excavated in the Holy Land. They give an interesting insight into daily life in Palestine throughout the ages.

Courtyard statue at the Institut Catholique

St-Joseph-des-Carmes ⑦

70 Rue de Vaugirard 75006.
Map 12 D5. **Tel** 01 44 39 52 00.
Ⓜ St-Placide. ☐ 7am–7pm Mon–Sat; 9am–7pm Sun.
🚪 Easter Mon, Pentecost.
♿ restricted. 🎦 3pm Sat.

Completed in 1620, this church was built as the chapel for a Carmelite convent but was used as a prison during the Revolution. In 1792 more than a hundred priests met a grisly end in the church's courtyard as part of the September Massacres *(see pp30–31)*. Their remains are now in the crypt.

Facade of St-Joseph-des-Carmes

Carpeaux's fountain sculpture

Fontaine de l'Observatoire ⑧

Pl Ernest Denis, in Ave de l'Observatoire. **Map** 16 E2.
🚇 Port Royal.

Situated at the southern tip of the Jardin du Luxembourg, this is one of the liveliest fountains in Paris. Made of bronze, it has four women holding aloft a globe representing four continents – the fifth, Oceania, was left out for reasons of symmetry. There are some subsidiary figures, including dolphins, horses and a turtle. The sculpture was erected in 1873 by Jean-Baptiste Carpeaux.

Val-de-Grâce ⑨

1 Pl Alphonse-Laveran. **Map** 16 F2. **Tel** 01 40 51 51 92. Ⓜ Gobelins.
🚇 Port Royal. ☐ noon–6pm Tue, Wed, Sat & Sun. 🎦 (except for nave).
✝ frequent, pm. 🎦 by appt.

One of the most beautiful churches in France, it was built for Anne of Austria (wife of Louis XIII) in thanks for the birth of her son. Young Louis XIV himself laid the first stone in 1645. The design is in the style of the great architect François Mansart.

The church is noted for its beautiful imposing lead-and-gilt dome, which stands at an impressive 41 m (135 ft) and is 19 m (62 ft) in diameter. In the cupola is Pierre Mignard's enormous fresco, with over 200 triple-life-size figures.

The six huge, twisted marble columns that frame the altar are similar to those made by Bernini for St Peter's in Rome.

Henrietta of France (wife of Charles I) is buried at this site, along with 26 members of the French royal family.

Today the church is part of a military hospital complex.

Musée du Service de Santé des Armées ⑩

1 Pl Alphonse-Laveran 75005. **Map** 16 F2. **Tel** 01 40 51 51 92. 🚇 Port Royal. ☐ noon–6pm Tue, Wed, Sat & Sun. 🎦 🎦 phone to arrange.

Founded during World War I and run by the army medical corps, this museum is also known as the Musée du Val-de-Grâce. It is in the west wing of the Val-de-Grâce church, where it became a military hospital in 1795.

The exhibits cover the history of medicine with some appropriately gruesome memorabilia such as artificial limbs and various surgical instruments. There are even reconstructions of military hospital trains.

Ecole Nationale Supérieure des Mines ⑪

60 Blvd St-Michel. **Map** 16 F1.
Tel 01 40 51 91 39. 🚇 Luxembourg.
☐ 1.30–6pm Tue–Fri; 10am–12.30pm, 2–5pm Sat. 🎦 📷 🎦

Louis XIV set up the School of Mines in 1783 to train mining engineers. Today, it is one of the most prestigious *grandes écoles* – schools that provide the élite for the civil service and professions. It also houses the national collection of minerals – the Musée de Minéralogie.

MONTPARNASSE

In the first three decades of the 20th century, Montparnasse was a thriving artistic and literary centre. Many modern painters and sculptors, new novelists and poets, the great and the young were drawn to this area. Its ateliers, conviviality and renowned Bohemian lifestyle made it a magnet for genius, some of it French, much of it foreign. The great epoch ended with World War II, and change continued with the destruction

of many ateliers and the construction of the soaring Tour Montparnasse, Paris's tallest office tower, which heralded the more modern *quartier*. But the area has not lost its appeal. The great cafés remain very much in business and attract a lively international crowd. Small café-theatres have opened and the area springs to life at the weekends with cinema crowds.

Monument to Charles Augustin Ste-Beauve in the Cimetière du Montparnasse

SIGHTS AT A GLANCE

Historic Buildings and Streets
Rue Campagne-Première **3**
Catacombes **10**
Observatoire de Paris **11**

Cafés and Restaurants
La Coupole **1**
La Closerie des Lilas **12**

Museums and Galleries
Musée Zadkine **2**
Musée Antoine Bourdelle **6**
Musée de la Poste **7**

Musée du Montparnasse **8
Fondation Cartier **9**

Modern Architecture
Tour Montparnasse **5**

Cemeteries
Cimetière du Montparnasse pp180–81 **4**

GETTING THERE

This area is well served by the metro system and SNCF trains. Bus routes through the area include route 38, 68 and 95 which travels along Boulevard Raspail, passing the north-eastern side of the Cimetière du Montparnasse.

0 metres   400
0 yards   400

KEY

	Street-by-Street map
M	Metro station
R	SNCF (train) station
RER	RER station

SEE ALSO

• *Street Finder*, map 15–16
• *Where to Stay* p288
• *Restaurants* pp307–308

◁ **View of Tour Montparnasse from the Cimetière du Montparnasse**

Street-by-Street: Montparnasse

Renowned for its mix of art and high living, Montparnasse continues to live up to its name: Mount Parnassus was the mountain dedicated by the ancient Greeks to Apollo, god of poetry, music and beauty. That mix was especially potent in the 1920s and 1930s, when such artists and writers as Picasso, Hemingway, Cocteau, Giacometti, Matisse and Modigliani were to be seen in the local bars, cafés and cabarets.

★ La Coupole
This traditional brasserie-style café, with its large enclosed terrace, opened in 1927 and became a famous meeting place for artists and writers ❶

★ Tour Montparnasse
Europe's second-tallest tower block rests on 56 piles that extend 62 m (203 ft) below the surface ❺

Metro Edgar Quinet

★ Cimetière du Montparnasse
This fine sculpture, The Separation of a Couple *by de Max, stands in the smallest of the city's major cemeteries* ❹

The Théâtre Montparnasse at No. 31, with its fully-restored original 1880s decor.

RUE DU DEPART

RUE D'ODESSA

RUE DU MONTPARNASSE

RUE DE LA GAÎTÉ

BLVD

BLVD EDGAR QUI

To Metro Gaîté

STAR SIGHTS

★ La Coupole

★ Tour Montparnasse

★ Rue Campagne-Première

★ Cimetière du Montparnasse

Rue Bréa has a variety of shops, including two restaurants and even a nightclub, all within 90 m (300 ft). A small square and two cinemas lie just across the street.

LOCATOR MAP
See Central Paris Map pp14–15

No. 14, Rue de la Grande Chaumière offers tuition in painting and sculpture.

The statue of Balzac by Auguste Rodin was erected in 1939, and stands 3 m (10 ft) tall.

Metro Vavin

★ **Rue Campagne-Première**
The block of artists' studios at No. 31 was built in 1911, and the facade was decorated by the ceramicist Paul Bigot

❸

RUE BRÉA

RUE J. CHAPLAIN

RUE NOTRE DAME DES CHAMPS

RUE DE LA GDE-CHAUMIERE

TPARNASSE

BLVD RASPAIL

SQ DELAMBRE

RUE HUYGHENS

RUE LEOPOLD ROBERT

0 metres   100
0 yards   100

Metro Raspail

KEY

– – – Suggested route

The interior of La Coupole

La Coupole ❶

102 Blvd du Montparnasse 75014.
Map 16 D2. **Tel** 01 43 20 14 20. Ⓜ
Vavin, Montparnasse. ◯ 8am–1am
Mon–Thu, 8.30am–1.30am Fri–Sun.
See **Restaurants and Cafés** p307.
www.flobrasseries.com

Established in 1927, this historic café-restaurant and dance hall underwent a face-lift in the 1980s. Its red velvet seats and famous columns, decorated by various artists, have survived. Among its clientele have been Jean-Paul Sartre, Josephine Baker and Roman Polanski.

The museum's Les Trois Belles (1950) by Ossip Zadkine

Musée Zadkine ❷

100 bis Rue d'Assas 75116.
Map 16 E1. **Tel** 01 55 42 77 20.
Ⓜ Notre-Dame-des-Champs.
◯ 10am–6pm Tue–Sun.
⬤ public hols. 📷 🎥 by appt.
♿ limited. **www**.zadkine.paris.fr

The Russian-born sculptor Ossip Zadkine lived here

from 1928 until his death in 1967. The small house, studio and daffodil-filled garden contain his works. Here he produced his great commemorative sculpture, *Ville Détruite*, commissioned by Rotterdam after World War II, and two monuments to Vincent Van Gogh, one for Holland and one for Auverssur-Oise, where Van Gogh died. The museum's works span the development of Zadkine's style, from his Cubist beginnings to Expressionism and Abstractionism.

Rue Campagne-Première ❸

75014. **Map** 16 E2. Ⓜ Raspail.

This street has some interesting Art Deco buildings and a long artistic tradition. Modigliani, ravaged by opium and tuberculosis, lived at No. 3 during his last years. Between the wars many artists resided here, including Picasso, Joan Miró and Kandinsky.

Cimetière du Montparnasse ❹

See pp180–1.

Tour Montparnasse ❺

Pl Raoul Dautry 75014. **Map** 15 C2.
Ⓜ Montparnasse-Bienvenüe. **Tel** 01
45 38 52 56. ◯ Apr–Sep: 9.30am–
11.30pm daily; Oct–Mar: 9.30am–
10.30pm daily (to 11pm Fri, Sat).
🎥 🍴 💻 📷

This was Europe's largest office block when it was built in 1973 as the focal point of a new business sector. It stands 210 m (690 ft) high, is made of curved steel and smoked glass, and totally dominates the area's skyline. The views from the 59th floor are spectacular (up to 40 km on a clear day). The tower also boasts Europe's fastest lift (56 floors in 38 seconds).

The Archer (1909) by Antoine Bourdelle

Musée Antoine Bourdelle ❻

18 Rue Antoine Bourdelle 75015.
Map 15 B1. **Tel** 01 49 54 73 73.
Ⓜ Montparnasse-Bienvenüe.
◯ 10am–6pm Tue–Sun.
⬤ public hols. 📷 ♿ limited.
www.bourdelle.paris.fr

The prolific sculptor, Antoine Bourdelle, lived and worked in the studio here from 1884 until his death in 1929. The house, studio and garden are now a museum devoted to his life and work. Among the 900 sculptures on display are the original plaster casts of his monumental works planned for wide public squares. They are housed in the Great Hall in an extension and include the group of sculptures for the relief decoration of the Théâtre des Champs-Elysées.

Musée de la Poste ❼

34 Blvd de Vaugirard 75015.
Map 15 B2. 📞 01 42 79 23 00.
Ⓜ Montparnasse-Bienvenüe. ◯
10am–6pm Mon–Sat.
⬤ public hols. 📷 📱
♿ **Library**. **www**.
museedelaposte.fr

Every conceivable aspect of the history of the French postal service and methods of transportation is covered in this well laid out collection. There is even a room devoted to

A view of the tower

mail delivery in times of war – carrier pigeons were used during the Franco-Prussian War with postmarks stamped on their wings. Postage stamp art is displayed in the gallery.

A Miró-designed postage stamp

Musée du Montparnasse **8**

21 Ave du Maine 75015. **Map** 15 C1. **Tel** 01 42 22 91 96. Ⓜ Montparnasse-Bienvenüe, Falguière. ◯ 12.30–7pm Tue–Sun. 🖼 www. museedumontparnasse.net

During World War I, this was a canteen for needy artists which, by its status as a private club, was not subject to curfew, and so the likes of Picasso, Braque, Modigliani and Léger could eat for 65 centimes and then party until late at night. This symbolic place is now a museum that recalls, through paintings and photos, how at the Vavin crossroads Western art took radical new directions.

Fondation Cartier **9**

261 Blvd Raspail 75014. **Map** 16 E3. **Tel** 01 42 18 56 50. Ⓜ Raspail. ◯ 11am–8pm Tue–Sun (until 10pm Thu). ● 1 Jan, 25 Dec. 🖼 ♿ 🎥 www.fondation.cartier.fr

This foundation for contemporary art is housed in a building designed by architect Jean Nouvel. He has created an air of transparency and light, as well as incorporating a cedar of Lebanon planted in 1823 by François-René de Chateaubriand. The structure complements the nature of the exhibitions of progressive art, which showcase personal, group or thematic displays, often including works by young unknowns.

Catacombes **10**

1 Ave du Colonel Henri Rol-Tanguy 75014. **Map** 16 E3. **Tel** 01 43 22 47 63. Ⓜ Denfert-Rochereau. ◯ 10am–5pm Tue–Sun (last adm: 4pm). ● public hols. 🖼 📷 🎥 www.catacombes.paris.fr

In 1786 a monumental project began here: the removal of the millions of skulls and bones from the unsanitary city cemetery in Les Halles to the ancient quarries formed by excavations at the base of the three "mountains": Montparnasse, Montrouge and Montsouris. It took 15 months to transport the bones and rotting corpses across the city in huge carts to their new resting place; the transportation was carried out at night.

Just before the Revolution, the Comte d'Artois (later Charles X) threw wild parties in the catacombs, and during World War II the French Resistance set up its headquarters here. Above the door outside are the words "Stop! This is the empire of death."

Observatoire de Paris **11**

61 Ave de l'Observatoire 75014. **Map** 16 E3. **Tel** 01 40 51 21 70. Ⓜ Denfert-Rochereau. **Visits** (2 hrs) apply 2 mths ahead: 1st Sat of mth: 2.30pm; groups by appt. ● Aug. 🖼 🎥 www.obspm.fr

In 1667 Louis XIV was persuaded by his scientists and astronomers that France needed a royal observatory. Building began on 21 June,

the day of the summer solstice, and took five years to reach completion.

Astronomical research undertaken here included the calculation of the exact dimensions of the solar system in 1672, calculations of the dimensions of longitude, the mapping of the moon in 1679 and the discovery of the planet Neptune in 1846.

The facade of the Observatoire

La Closerie des Lilas **12**

171 Blvd du Montparnasse 75014. **Map** 16 E2. **Tel** 01 40 51 34 50. Ⓜ Vavin. 🚇 Port Royal. ◯ Bar: 11–2am, brasserie: noon–1am daily.

Lenin, Trotsky, Hemingway and Scott Fitzgerald all frequented the numerous bars and cafés of Montparnasse, but the Closerie was their favourite. Much of Hemingway's novel *The Sun Also Rises* takes place here. Hemingway wrote it on the terrace in just six weeks. Today the terrace is ringed with trees and the whole place is more elegant in appearance, but much of the original decor remains (*see pp38–9*).

Skulls and bones stored in the catacombs

Cimetière du Montparnasse ❹

The Montparnasse Cemetery was
planned by Napoleon outside the city
walls to replace the numerous, congested small cemeteries within the old
city, viewed as a health hazard at the
turn of the 19th century. It was opened
in 1824 and became the resting place of
many illustrious Parisians, particularly
Left Bank personalities. Like all French
cemeteries it is divided into rigidly
aligned paths forming blocks or
divisions. The Rue Emile Richard cuts it
into two parts, the Grand Cimetière
and the Petit Cimetière.

★ **Charles Baudelaire Cenotaph**
*This is a monument to
the great poet and critic
(1821–67), author of*
The Flowers of Evil.

Samuel Beckett, the great
Irish playwright renowned
for *Waiting for Godot*,
spent most of his life in
Paris. He died in 1989.

The Pétain tomb contains the
family of the marshal who
collaborated with the Germans
during World War II. Pétain
himself is buried on Ile d'Yeu,
where he was imprisoned.

Guy de Maupassant was a
19th-century novelist.

Alfred Dreyfus was a Jewish
army officer whose unjust trial
for treason in 1894 provoked a
political and social scandal.

Frédéric Auguste Bartholdi was the
sculptor of the Statue of Liberty (1886)
in New York.

André Citroën, an engineer and
industrialist who died in 1935, founded
the famous French car firm.

★ **Charles Pigeon Family Tomb**
*This wonderfully
pompous Belle Epoque
tomb depicts the French
industrialist and inventor
in bed with his wife.*

Charles-Augustin Sainte-Beuve was a critic
of the French Romantic
generation, and is
generally described as
the "father of modern
criticism".

STAR FEATURES

★ Charles Baudelaire
Cenotaph

★ Charles Pigeon Family
Tomb

★ Jean-Paul Sartre and
Simone de Beauvoir

★ Serge Gainsbourg

The Kiss by Brancusi
*This is the famous
Primitivo-Cubist
sculpture (a
response to Rodin's
Kiss) by the great
Romanian artist,
who died in 1957
and is buried just
off the Rue Emile
Richard.*

Camille Saint-Saëns, the
pianist, organist and
composer who died in
1921, was one of
France's great post-
Romantic musicians.

Serge Gainsbourg
The French singer, composer and pop icon of the 1970s and 1980s is best known for his wistful and irreverent songs. He was married to the actress Jane Birkin.

VISITORS' CHECKLIST

3 Blvd Edgar Quinet. **Map** 16 D3.
Tel 01 44 10 86 50. Ⓜ Edgar
Quinet. 🚌 38, 83, 91 to Port
Royal. 🚆 Port Royal. 🅿 Rue
Campagne-Première, Blvd St-
Jacques. ◯ Mid-Mar–early Nov:
8am–6pm daily (from 8.30am Sat,
from 9am Sun); early Nov–mid-
Mar closes 5.30pm. **Adm free**.
📷 ♿

The Tower is all that remains of a 17th-century windmill. It was part of the old property of the Brothers of Charity on which the cemetery was built.

Génie du Sommeil Eternel
Horace Daillion's wistful bronze angel of Eternal Sleep (1902) is the cemetery's centrepiece.

Tristen Tzara, the Romanian writer, was leader of the literary and artistic Dada movement in Paris in the 1920s.

Henri Laurens
The French sculptor (1885–1954) was a leading figure in the Cubist movement.

Man Ray was an American photographer who immortalized the Montparnasse artistic and café scene in the 1920s and 1930s.

Charles Baudelaire, the 19th-century poet, is buried here in his detested stepfather's family tomb, along with his beloved mother.

Chaïm Soutine, a poor Jewish Lithuanian, was a Montparnasse Bohemian painter of the 1920s. He was a friend of the Italian artist Modigliani.

Jean Seberg
The Hollywood actress, chosen by François Truffaut as the star for his film A bout de souffle, *was the epitome of American blonde beauty, youth and candour.*

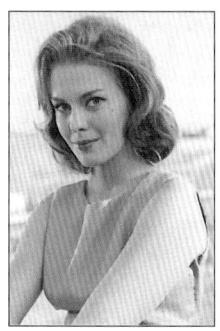

JEAN PAUL SARTRE
1905 - 1980
SIMONE DE BEAUVOIR
1908 - 1986

★ Jean-Paul Sartre and Simone de Beauvoir
The famous existentialist couple, undisputed leaders of the post-war literary scene, lie here close to their Left Bank haunts.

INVALIDES AND EIFFEL TOWER QUARTER

Musée de l'Armée cannon

Everything in the area of Invalides is on a monumental scale. Starting from the sprawling 18th-century buildings of the Ecole Militaire on the corner of the Avenue de la Motte Picquet, the Parc du Champ de Mars stretches down to the Eiffel Tower and the Seine. The avenues around the Tower are lined with luxurious buildings, some in the Art Nouveau style, and numerous embassies. The area was already highly prized between the World Wars when the noted actor Sacha Guitry lived there. Even earlier, in the 18th century, wealthy residents of the Marais moved to this part of the city, building the aristocratic town houses that line the Rue de Varenne and Rue de Grenelle.

SIGHTS AT A GLANCE

Historic Buildings and Streets
Hôtel des Invalides ❻
Hôtel Matignon ❽
Assemblée Nationale Palais-Bourbon ⓫
Rue Cler ⓬
Les Egouts ⓭
Champ-de-Mars ⓯
No. 29 Avenue Rapp ⓱
Ecole Militaire ⓳

Museums and Galleries
Musée de l'Ordre de la Libération ❸
Musée de l'Armée ❹
Musées des Plans-Reliefs ❺

Musée Rodin ❼
Musée Maillol ❾
Musée du Quai Branly ⓮

Churches and Temples
Dôme Church pp188–9 ❶
St-Louis-des-Invalides ❷
Sainte-Clotilde ❿

Monuments and Fountains
Eiffel Tower pp194–5 ⓰

Modern Architecture
Village Suisse ⓲
UNESCO ⓴

GETTING THERE
The metro system serves this area well, with stations at Invalides, Solférino, Sèvres Babylone, Varenne, Latour Maubourg and Ecole Militaire. There are also several bus routes through the area. Route 69 passes along Rue St-Dominique heading east and along Rue de Grenelle on the way back. Route 82 travels along the Avenue de Suffren and 28 along Avenue de la Motte Picquet.

0 metres 400
0 yards 400

SEE ALSO
• **Street Finder**, map 9–10, 11
• **Where to Stay** pp288–9
• **Restaurants** pp308–09

KEY

	Street-by-Street map
M	Metro station
RER	RER station
	Batobus boarding point
	Tourist information

◁ View of the Eiffel Tower

Street-by-Street: Invalides

The imposing Hôtel des Invalides, from which the area takes its name, was built from 1671 to 1676 by Louis XIV for his wounded and homeless veterans and as a monument to his own glory. At its centre lies the glittering golden roof of the Sun King's Dôme Church, which marks the final resting place of Napoleon Bonaparte. The emperor's body was brought here from St Helena in 1840, 19 years after he died, and placed inside the majestic red sarcophagus, designed by Joachim Visconti, that lies at the centre of the Dôme's circular glass-topped crypt. Just to the east of the Hôtel on the corner of the Boulevard des Invalides, the superb Musée Rodin offers artistic relief from the pomp and circumstance of the surrounding area.

Mounted military policeman

Metro La Tour Maubourg

The facade of the Hôtel is 196 m (645 ft) long and is topped by dormer windows, each decorated in the shape of a different trophy. A head of Hercules sits above the central entrance.

★ Musée de l'Armée
This vast museum covers military history from the Stone Age to World War II. It contains the third-largest collection of armoury in the world ❹

STAR SIGHTS

- ★ Dôme Church and Napoleon's Tomb
- ★ St-Louis-des-Invalides
- ★ Musée de l'Armée
- ★ Musée Rodin

Musée de l'Ordre de la Libération
The Order was set up to honour feats of heroism during World War II ❸

AVE DE TOURVILLE

Musées d Plans-Reli
This museum conta military models of forts a towns, as well as a disp on model-making

KEY

– – – Suggested route

| 0 metres | 100 |
| 0 yards | 100 |

General de Gaulle's Liberation Order and compass

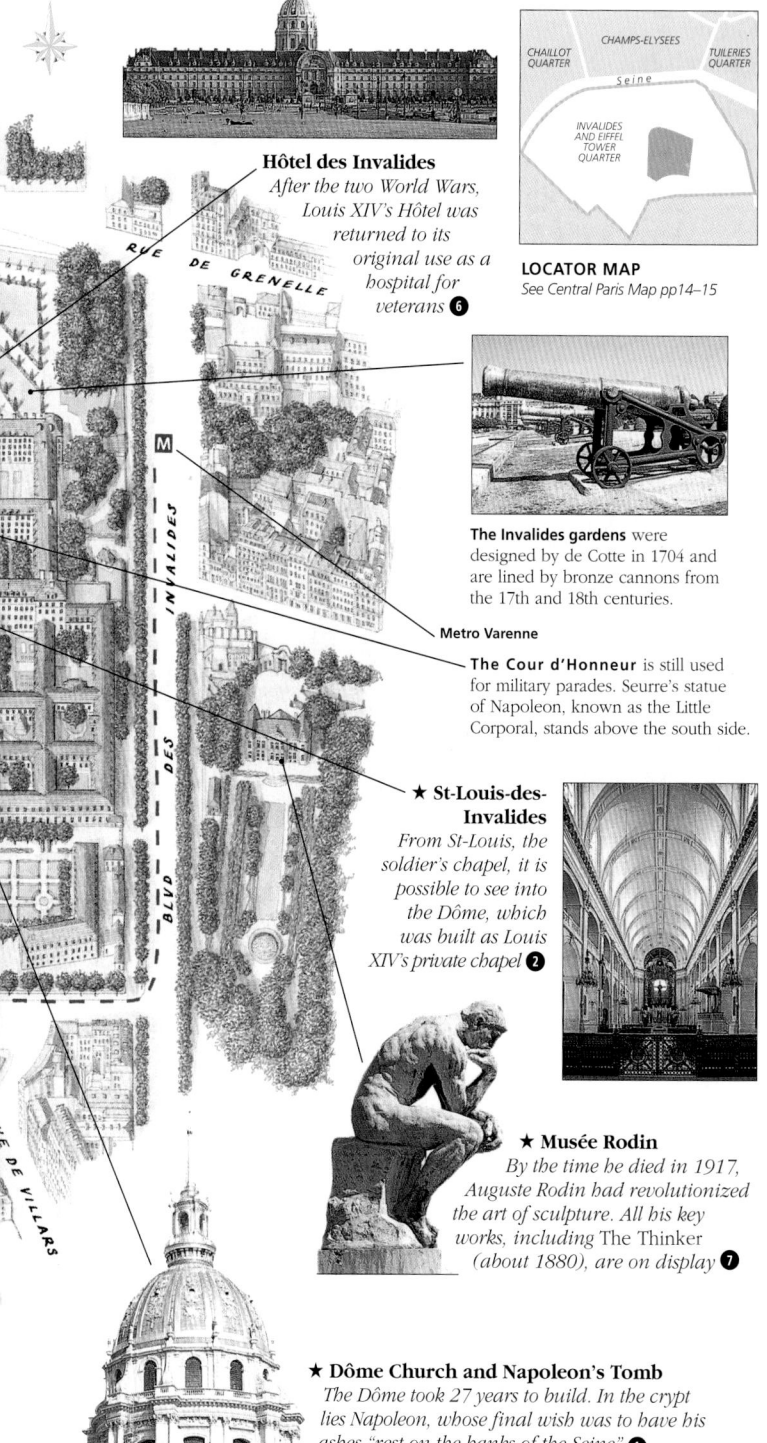

Hôtel des Invalides
After the two World Wars, Louis XIV's Hôtel was returned to its original use as a hospital for veterans 6

LOCATOR MAP
See Central Paris Map pp14–15

The Invalides gardens were designed by de Cotte in 1704 and are lined by bronze cannons from the 17th and 18th centuries.

Metro Varenne

The Cour d'Honneur is still used for military parades. Seurre's statue of Napoleon, known as the Little Corporal, stands above the south side.

★ St-Louis-des-Invalides
From St-Louis, the soldier's chapel, it is possible to see into the Dôme, which was built as Louis XIV's private chapel 2

★ Musée Rodin
By the time he died in 1917, Auguste Rodin had revolutionized the art of sculpture. All his key works, including The Thinker (about 1880), are on display 7

★ Dôme Church and Napoleon's Tomb
The Dôme took 27 years to build. In the crypt lies Napoleon, whose final wish was to have his ashes "rest on the banks of the Seine" 1

Dôme Church ❶

See pp188–9.

St-Louis-des-Invalides ❷

Hôtel des Invalides 75007. **Map** 11 A3. Ⓜ *Varenne, La Tour-Maubourg.* **Tel** *01 44 42 37 65.* ☐ *Apr–Sep: 10am–5.30pm daily; Oct–Mar: 10am–4.30pm daily.*

Also known as the "soldiers' church", this is the chapel of the Hôtel des Invalides. It was built from 1679 to 1708 by Jules Hardouin-Mansart from the original designs by Libéral Bruand, architect of the Hôtel des Invalides. The imposing, but stark, interior is decorated with banners seized in battle.

The fine 17th-century organ was built by Alexandre Thierry. The first performance of Berlioz's *Requiem* was given on it in 1837, with an orchestra accompanied by a battery of outside artillery.

Musée de l'Ordre de la Libération ❸

51 bis Blvd de La Tour-Maubourg 75007. **Map** 11 A4. **Tel** *01 47 05 04 10.* Ⓜ *La Tour-Maubourg.* ☐ *10am–6pm (to 5pm in winter) daily.* ● *1st Mon of mth, some pub hols.* 📷 🔲 (*groups should apply 1 mth before*).

This museum is devoted to the wartime Free French and their leader, General Charles

The altar of St-Louis-des-Invalides

The facade of the Musée de l'Ordre de la Libération

de Gaulle. The Order of Liberation was created by de Gaulle at Brazzaville in 1940. It is France's highest honour and was eventually bestowed on those who made an outstanding contribution to the final victory in World War II. The *companions* who received the honour were French civilians and members of the armed forces, plus some overseas leaders, including King George VI, Winston Churchill and General Dwight Eisenhower.

Cannons at the Musée de l'Armée

Musée de l'Armée ❹

Hôtel des Invalides 75007. **Map** 11 A3. **Tel** *01 44 42 38 77.* Ⓜ *La Tour-Maubourg, Varenne.* Ⓡ *Invalides.* ☐ *10am–6pm (to 5pm winter) daily (last adm: 45 mins before closing time).* ● *1st Mon of month (unless a bank hol), 1 Jan, 1 May, 1 Nov, 25 Dec.* 📷 (*ticket includes entry to the Musée de l'Ordre de la Libération and the Musée des Plans-Reliefs.*) *Some sections may close during 2008 renovations.* 📷 ♿ *ground floor only.* 🔲 📷 **Film.** **www.** invalides.org

This is one of the most comprehensive museums of military history in the world, with exhibits ranging from the Stone Age to the final days of World War II. The third-largest collection of armoury in the world is housed here. The whole place is being revamped, so some sections may be closed at the time of your visit.

Situated in the northeast refectory, the Ancient Armoury

department is worth visiting for the collection on display as much as for the 17th-century murals adorning the walls. Visible for the first time in 200 years after extensive restoration, the murals by Joseph Parrocel celebrate Louis XIV's military conquests.

In the Cour de Valeur is an educational display on the life of Charles de Gaulle.

Napoleon's mementoes are temporarily on display in an adjacent chapel in the Dôme church, but their permanent home will be in the Departement Moderne from 2008.

Musées des Plans-Reliefs ❺

Hôtel des Invalides 75007. **Map** 11 B3. **Tel** *01 45 51 95 05.* Ⓜ *La Tour-Maubourg, Varenne.* Ⓡ *Invalides.* ☐ *10am–6pm (5pm in winter) daily.* ● *1st Mon of mth, 1 Jan, 1 May, 1 & 11 Nov, 25 Dec.* 📷 📷 🔲

A map of Alessandria, Italy (1813)

The detailed models of French forts and fortified towns, some dating back to Louis XIV's reign, were considered top secret until the 1950s, when they were put on public display. The oldest model is that of Perpignan, dating to 1686. It shows the fortifications drawn up by the legendary 17th-century military architect Vauban, who built the defences around several French towns, including Briançon.

Hôtel des Invalides ⓺

75007. **Map** 11 A3. **Tel** 01 44 42 37 72. Ⓜ La Tour-Maubourg, Varenne. ⏰ 10am–6pm daily (5pm winter). 🌐 1 Jan, 1 May, 1 Nov, 25 Dec. www. invalides.org

The Invalides main entrance

Founded by Louis XIV, this was the first military hospital and home for French war veterans and disabled soldiers who had hitherto been reduced to begging. The decree for building this vast complex was signed in 1670, and construction, following the designs of Libéral Bruand, was finished five years later.

Today the harmonious Classical facade is one of the most impressive sights in Paris, with its four storeys, cannon in the forecourt, garden and tree-lined esplanade stretching to the Seine. The south side leads to St-Louis-des-Invalides, the soldiers' church, which backs on to the magnificent Dôme church of Jules Hardouin-Mansart. The dome was regilded in 1989 and now glitters anew.

Musée Rodin ⓻

77 Rue de Varenne 75007. **Map** 11 B3. **Tel** 01 44 18 61 10. Ⓜ Varenne. ⏰ Apr–Sep: 9.30am–5.45pm Tue–Sun; Oct–Mar: 9.30am–4.45pm (gdn 1 hr later) Tue–Sun. 🌐 1 Jan, 1 May, 25 Dec. 📷 ⬤ ♿ restricted. ▢ 🛈 🔲 occas. www.musee-rodin.fr

Auguste Rodin, widely regarded as the greatest 19th-century French sculptor, lived and worked in the Hôtel

Biron, an elegant 18th-century mansion, from 1908 until his death in 1917. In return for a state-owned flat and studio, Rodin left his work to the nation, and it is now exhibited here. Some of his most celebrated sculptures are on display in the garden: *The Burghers of Calais, The Thinker, The Gates of Hell* and *Balzac*. The garden has a stunning array of 2,000 rose bushes.

The indoor exhibits are arranged in chronological order, spanning the whole of Rodin's career, with highlights such as *The Kiss* and *Eve*.

Hôtel Matignon ⓼

57 Rue de Varenne 75007. **Map** 11 C4. Ⓜ Solférino, Rue du Bac. ⬤ to the public.

One of the most beautiful mansions in the Faubourg area, this was built by Jean Courtonne in 1721 and has been substantially remodelled since. Former owners include Talleyrand, the statesman and diplomat who held legendary parties and receptions here, and several members of the nobility. It has been the official residence of the French Prime Minister since 1958 and has the largest private garden in Paris.

Rodin's *The Kiss* (1886) at the Musée Rodin

Musée Maillol ⓽

61 Rue de Grenelle 75007. **Map** 11 C4. **Tel** 01 42 22 59 58. Ⓜ Sèvres-Babylone, Rue du Bac. ⏰ 11am–6pm Wed–Mon (last adm: 5.15pm). ⬤ pub hols. ♿ ▢ 🛈 www.museemaillol.com

Once the home of novelist Alfred de Musset, this museum was created by Dina Vierny, former model of Aristide Maillol. All aspects of the artist's work are here: drawings, engravings, paintings, sculpture and decorative objects. Also displayed is Vierny's private collection, in which naïve art sits alongside works by Matisse, Dufy, Picasso and Rodin.

Large allegorical figures of the city of Paris and the four seasons decorate Bouchardon's fountain in front of the house.

Sculptured figures at Ste-Clotilde

Sainte-Clotilde ⓾

12 Rue de Martignac 75007. **Map** 11 B3. 🎵 01 44 18 62 60. Ⓜ Solférino, Varenne, Invalides. ⏰ 9am–7pm daily. ⬤ non-religious public hols. 🛈 🔲

Designed by the German-born architect François-Christian Gau and the first of its kind to be built in Paris, this Neo-Gothic church was inspired by the mid-19th-century enthusiasm for the Middle Ages, made fashionable by such writers as Victor Hugo. The church is noted for its imposing twin towers, visible from across the Seine. The interior decoration includes sculpted stations of the cross by James Pradier and stained-glass windows with scenes relating to the patron saint of the church. The composer César Franck was the church organist here for 32 years.

Dôme Church ❶

Jules Hardouin-Mansart was asked in 1676 by the Sun King, Louis XIV, to build the Dôme Church among the existing buildings of the Invalides military refuge. A soldiers' church had already been built, but the Dôme was to be reserved for the exclusive use of the Sun King and for the location of royal tombs. The resulting masterpiece complements the surrounding buildings and is one of the greatest examples of 17th-century French architecture.

After Louis XIV's death, plans to bury the royal family in the church were abandoned, and it became a monument to Bourbon glory. In 1840 Louis-Philippe decided to install Napoleon's remains in the crypt, and the addition of the tombs of Vauban, Marshal Foch and other figures of military prominence have since turned this church into a French military memorial.

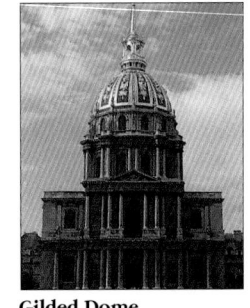

Gilded Dome
The cupola was first gilded in 1715.

① Tomb of Joseph Bonaparte
The sarcophagus of Napoleon's older brother, the King of Naples and later of Spain, is in the side chapel to the right as visitors enter.

Main entrance

② Memorial to Vauban
Commissioned by Napoleon I in 1808, this contains an urn with Sébastien le Prestre de Vauban's heart. He was Louis XIV's great military architect and engineer who died in 1707. His long military career culminated in his appointment as Marshal of France in 1703. He revolutionized siege warfare when he introduced his ricochet-batteries. His reclining figure by Antoine Etex lies on top of the memorial, mourned by Science and War.

VAUBAN

⑥ Glass Gallery
Access to the glass-topped crypt containing Napoleon's tomb is by the curved stairs in front of the altar. The glass partition behind the altar separates the Dôme from the older Invalides chapel beyond.

VISITORS' CHECKLIST

Hôtel National des Invalides, 129 Rue de Grenelle. **Map** 11 A3. *Tel 01 44 42 38 77.* Ⓜ *La Tour-Maubourg, Varenne.* 🚌 *28, 49, 63, 69, 80, 82, 83, 87, 92, 93 to Les Invalides.* Ⓡ *Invalides.* Ⓞ *Tour Eiffel.* Ⓟ *Rue de Constantine.* Ⓞ *10am–5pm daily (Apr–Sep: to 6).* ● *1st Mon of mth, 1 Jan, 1 May, 17 Jun, 1 Nov, 25 Dec.* 🎫 📷 ♿ *restricted.* 📢 *groups Tel 01 44 42 37 72.* 📺 📖

KEY

▬ ▬ ▬ Tour route

⑤ St Jérôme's Chapel
Passing across the centre of the church, the side chapel to the right of the main entrance contains the tomb of Napoleon's younger brother, Jérôme, King of Westphalia.

Stairs to crypt

④ Dôme Ceiling
Looking upwards, Charles de la Fosse's circular painting (1692) on the ceiling shows the Glory of Paradise, *with Saint Louis presenting his sword to Christ.*

③ Tomb of Marshal Foch
Ferdinand Foch's imposing bronze tomb was built by Paul Landowski in 1937.

NAPOLEON'S RETURN

King Louis-Philippe decided to bring the Emperor Napoleon's body back from St Helena *(see pp32–3)* as a gesture of reconciliation to the Republican and Bonapartist parties contesting his regime. The Dôme Church, with its historical and military associations, was an obvious choice for Napoleon's final resting place. His body was encased in six coffins and finally placed in the crypt in 1861, in the culmination of a grand ceremony which was attended by Napoleon III.

Neo-Classical facade of the Assemblée Nationale Palais-Bourbon

Assemblée Nationale Palais-Bourbon ⓫

126 Rue de l'Université 75007. **Map** 11 B2. *Tel* 01 40 63 60 00. M *Assemblée-Nationale.* RER *Invalides.* ◯ *to group visits only. Call the above number for more information.* www.assemblee-nationale.fr

Built in 1722 for the Duchesse de Bourbon, daughter of Louis XIV, the Palais-Bourbon was confiscated during the Revolution. It has been home to the lower house of the French Parliament since 1830.

During World War II, the palace became the Nazi administration's seat of government. The public can enter to watch parliament in action. The grand neo-

Classical facade with its fine columns was added in 1806, partly to mirror the facade of La Madeleine church facing it across the Seine. The adjacent Hôtel de Lassay, built by the Prince de Condé, is now the residence of the president of the National Assembly.

Rue Cler ⓬

75007. **Map** 10 F3. M *Ecole-Militaire, La Tour-Maubourg.* **Market** ◯ *Tue–Sat. See Shops and Markets p338.*

This is the street market of the seventh arrondissement, the richest in Paris, for here live the bulk of senior civil servants, captains of industry and many diplomats. The market area occupies a pedestrian precinct stretching

south from the Rue de Grenelle. It is colourful, but very much an exclusive market, with the best-dressed shoppers in town. As one would expect, the produce is excellent, the pâtisserie and cheese shops in particular.

Les Egouts ⓭

Opposite 93 Quai d'Orsay 75007. **Map** 10 F2. ⓕ 01 53 68 27 81. M *Alma-Marceau.* RER *Pont de l'Alma.* ◯ *11am–5pm (4pm in winter) Sat–Wed.* 2 wks Jan.

One of Baron Haussmann's finest achievements, the majority of Paris's sewers *(égouts)* date from the Second Empire *(see pp32–3)*. If laid end to end the 2,100 km (1,300 miles) of sewers would stretch from Paris to Istanbul. In the 20th century the sewers became a popular tourist attraction. All tours have been limited to a small area around the Quai d'Orsay entrance and are on foot. A sewer museum has been established here where visitors can discover the mysteries of underground Paris.

Musée du Quai Branly ⓮

See pp192–3.

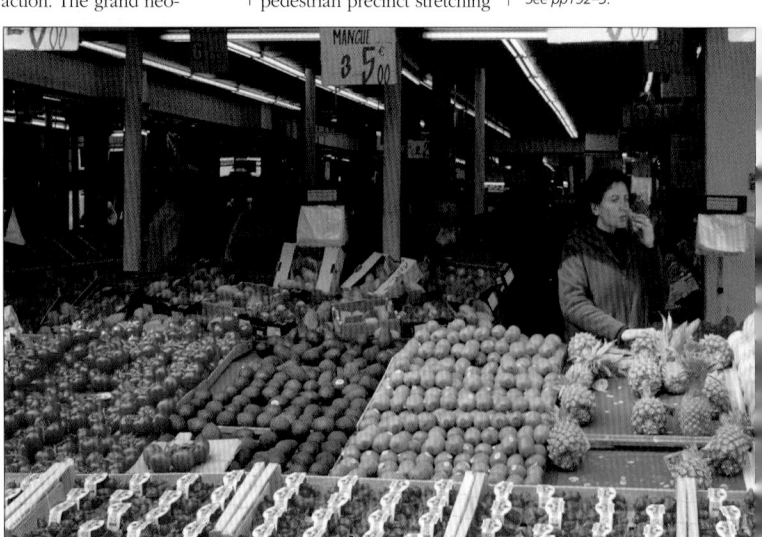

The fruit and vegetable market in the Rue Cler

Doorway at No. 29 Avenue Rapp

Champ-de-Mars ⑮

75007. **Map** 10 E3. **M** *Ecole-Militaire.*
RER *Champ-de-Mars–Tour-Eiffel.*

The gardens stretching from the Eiffel Tower to the Ecole Militaire were originally a parade ground for the officer cadets of the Ecole Militaire. The area has since been used for horse-racing, balloon ascents and the mass celebrations for 14 July, the anniversary of the Revolution.

A Paris balloon ascent

The first ceremony was held in 1790 in the presence of a glum, captive Louis XVI. Vast exhibitions were held here in the late 19th century, including the 1889 World Fair for which the Eiffel Tower was erected. *Le Mur de la Paix*, Jean-Michel Wilmotte's monument to world peace, stands at one end.

Eiffel Tower ⑯

See pp194–5.

No. 29 Avenue Rapp ⑰

75007. **Map** 10 E2. **M** *Pont-de-l'Alma.*

A prime example of Art Nouveau architecture is No. 29 and it won its designer, Jules Lavirotte, first prize at the Concours des Facades de la Ville de Paris in 1901. Its ceramics and brickwork decorated with animal and flower motifs intermingling with female figures. These are superimposed on a multi-coloured sandstone base to produce a facade that is deliberately erotic, and was certainly subversive in its day. Also worth visiting is Lavirotte's building, complete with watchtower, which can be found in the Square Rapp.

Village Suisse ⑱

38-78 Ave de Suffren 75015.
Map 10 E4. **M** *Dupleix.*
◯ *10.30am–7pm Thu–Mon.*

The Swiss government built a mock-Alpine village for the 1900 Universal Exhibition held in the Champ-de-Mars nearby. It was later used as a centre for dealing in secondhand goods. In the 1950s and 1960s antique dealers moved in, and everything became more fashionable and expensive. The village was renovated in the late 1960s.

Ecole Militaire ⑲

1 Pl Joffre 75007. **Map** 10 F4.
M *Ecole-Militaire.* **Visits** by special permission only – contact the Commandant in writing. ◎

The Royal Military Academy of Louis XV was founded in 1751 to educate 500 sons of impoverished officers. It was designed by architect Jacques-Ange Gabriel, and one of the features is the central pavilion. This is a magnificent example of the French Classical style, with eight Corinthian pillars and a quadrangular dome. The interior is decorated in Louis XVI style; of main interest are the chapel and a superb Gabriel-designed wrought-iron banister on the main staircase.

An early cadet at the academy was Napoleon, whose passing-out report stated that "he could go far if the circumstances are right".

A 1751 engraving showing the planning of the Ecole Militaire

UNESCO ⑳

7 Pl de Fontenoy 75007. **Map** 10 F5.
Tel 01 45 68 10 00. ☎ 01 45 68 10 60 (in English). **M** *Ségur, Cambronne.* ◯ *guided visits 3pm Tue (English) & 3pm Wed (French).* ⬤ *public hols & during conference sessions.* ◎ ♿ 🎬 📖 📷 *Exhibitions, films.* **www**.unesco.org

This is the headquarters of the United Nations Educational, Scientific and Cultural Organization (UNESCO). The organization's stated aim is to contribute to international peace and security through education, science and culture.

UNESCO is a trove of modern art, notably a huge mural by Picasso, ceramics by Joan Miró and sculptures by Henry Moore.

Moore's *Reclining Figure* at UNESCO (erected 1958)

Musée du Quai Branly ⑭

Widely regarded as former President Jacques Chirac's legacy to Paris's cultural scene, Quai Branly has proved a major tourist pull since it opened in 2006. The stylish Jean Nouvel building displays 3,500 exhibits from the French state's vast non-western art collection, one of the world's most prolific. Outside, the grounds offer visitors breathing space among paths, pools and almost 200 trees. In summer, the museum's 500-seat auditorium opens onto an outdoor theatre for music and dance.

Interior
Subdued natural light creates intimacy, while an undulating open-plan design reflects the diversity and convergence of different cultures.

Brass pendant (India, 19–20th century)
Topped by three heads, this pendant is associated with headhunting, a tradition once practised by Naga warriors.

Musical instrument tower

Collection of slit drums (Vanuatu, mid-20th century)
Used for dance and transmitting messages, these vertical drums produce different sounds depending on the thickness of the slit cut into them.

Ramp to main collection

Ticket desks entra

STAR EXHIBITS

★ Androgynous statue

★ Museum architecture

Sculpted hook (Papua New Guinea, early 20th century)
Tribal men would hang ritual offerings on the hook protruding from this sculpted female figure.

Head Trophy (Nigeria, 20th century)
Ekoi tribes transformed their enemies' heads into war trophies, decorating them with wooden horns and antelope skins.

Mezzanine level

Different-sized display boxes jut out of the building façade, lending it a unique shape.

★ Androgynous statue (Mali, 10–11th century)
This 1.91 m (6.3 ft) wooden statue combines a regal male head with the breasts of a fertile woman. The bracelets worn around the wrist total seven, the number of perfect union.

Main collection level

Ramp from entrance level

GALLERY GUIDE

Tickets are bought outside the main building. Once inside, visitors take a 180-metre (590-ft) ramp that spirals up around a large glass tower displaying the museum's reserve of musical instruments. This leads to the main collection level, where a suggested route passes through four colour-coded zones of Oceania, Asia, Africa and the Americas. There are stairs from the main collection level to the three mezzanine galleries, one of which is for multimedia resources.

Giant headdress (Bolivia)
Worn for the Macheteros warrior dance, this colourful headdress weighs almost 10 kg (22 lb).

KEY

- [ ] Asia
- [ ] Africa
- [ ] The Americas
- [ ] Oceania
- [ ] Temporary exhibition space
- [ ] Multimedia gallery
- [ ] Musical instrument tower
- [ ] Non-exhibition space

★ Museum architecture
Set on pillars above the verdant museum gardens, architect Jean Nouvel's elegant building resembles the elongated shadow of the nearby Eiffel Tower. An exterior glass wall and thickets of trees help shield the museum from the outside world.

Eiffel Tower 16

Eiffel Tower from the Trocadéro

Originally built to impress visitors to the Universal Exhibition of 1889, the Eiffel Tower (Tour Eiffel) was meant to be a temporary addition to the Paris skyline. Designed by the engineer Gustave Eiffel, it was fiercely decried by 19th-century aesthetes. The author Guy de Maupassant lunched there to avoid seeing it. The world's tallest building until 1931, when New York's Empire State Building was completed, the tower is now the symbol of Paris. Since its recent renovation and installation of new lighting it has never looked better.

Ironwork Pattern
According to Eiffel, the complex pattern of pig-iron girders came from the need to stabilize the tower in strong winds. But Eiffel's design quickly won admirers for its pleasing symmetry.

Lift Engine Room
Eiffel emphasized safety over speed when choosing the lifts for the tower.

STAR FEATURES

★ Cineiffel

★ Hydraulic Lift Mechanism

★ Viewing Gallery

★ Eiffel Bust

★ Cineiffel
This small museum tells the history of the tower through a short film. It includes footage of famous personalities who have visited the tower, including Charlie Chaplin, Josephine Baker and Adolf Hitler.

THE DARING AND THE DELUDED

The tower has inspired many crazy stunts. It has been climbed by mountaineers, cycled down by a journalist, and used by trapeze artists and as a launch pad by parachutists. In 1912 an Austrian tailor, Franz Reichelt, attempted to fly from the parapet with only a modified cape for wings. He plunged to his death in front of a large crowd. According to the autopsy, he died of a heart attack before even touching the ground.

Birdman Reichelt

★ Hydraulic Lift Mechanism
Still in working order, this part of the original 1900 mechanism was automated in 1986.

The third level, 276 m (905 ft) above the ground, can hold 800 people at a time.

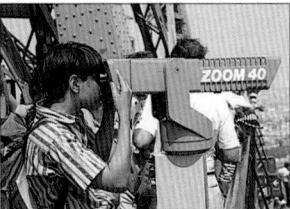

★ **Viewing Gallery**
*On a clear day it is possible to see
for 72 km (45 miles), including a
distant view of Chartres Cathedral.*

Double-Decker Lifts
*During the tourist season, the
limited capacity of the lifts means
that it can take up to a couple of
hours to reach the top. Queuing for
the lifts requires patience and a
good head for heights.*

THE TOWER IN FIGURES

• the top (including the antennae) is 324 m (1,063 ft) high
• the top can move in a curve of 18 cm (7 in) under the effect of heat
• 1,665 steps to the third level
• 2.5 million rivets hold the tower together
• never sways more than 7 cm (2.5 in)
• 10,100 tonnes in weight
• 60 tonnes of paint are used every seven years

A workman building the tower

The second level is at 115 m (376 ft), separated from the first level by 359 steps, or a few minutes in the lift.

Le Jules Verne Restaurant is one of the best restaurants in Paris, offering superb food and panoramic views (see p309).

The first level, at 57 m (187 ft) high, can be reached by lift or by 360 steps. There is a post office here.

★ **Eiffel Bust**
*Eiffel's (1832–1923)
achievement was
crowned with the Légion
d'Honneur in 1889.
Another honour was the
bust by Antoine
Bourdelle, placed
beneath the tower
in 1929.*

Gilded bronze statues by a number of sculptors decorating the central square of the Palais de Chaillot

Porte Dauphine

Avenue Foch RER 11

BLVD FLANDRIN
RUE DE LA FAISANDE
RUE DE LA

AVE F

Avenue Henri Martin RER

AVE HENRI MARTI

RUE

M La

RUE D

RER
Boulainvilliers La Muette

RUE DES

RUE DE BOULAINVILLIE

CHAILLOT QUARTER

The village of Chaillot was absorbed into Paris in the 19th century and transformed into an area rich in grand Second Empire avenues *(see pp34–5)* and opulent mansions. Some of the avenues converge on the Place du Trocadéro, renowned for its elegant cafés, which leads on to the Avenue du Président Wilson, with

Sculptures at the base of the Chaillot pool

a greater concentration of museums than any other street in Paris. Many of the area's private mansions are occupied by embassies, including the imposing Vatican embassy, and by major company headquarters. To the west is the territory of the *haute bourgeoisie*, one of Paris's most exclusive, if staid, residential neighbourhoods.

SIGHTS AT A GLANCE

Museums and Galleries
Cité de l'Architecture et du Patrimoine ❸
Musée de l'Homme ❹
Musée de la Marine ❺
Musée du Vin ❼
Maison de Balzac ❽
Musée de Radio-France ❾
Musée de la Contrefaçon ⓫
Musée Arménien ⓬
Musée Dapper ⓭
Musée du Cristal de Baccarat ⓮
Musée National des Arts Asiatiques Guimet ⓯
Musée Galliera ⓰
Musée d'Art Moderne de la Ville de Paris ⓱

Gardens
Jardins du Trocadéro ❻

Aquariums
Aquarium du Trocadéro ❷

Modern Architecture
Palais de Chaillot ❶

Cemeteries
Cimetière de Passy ❿

GETTING THERE
This area is served by the metro and RER system, with metro stations at Passy, Trocadéro and Iéna, and RER stations at Avenue Foch and Avenue Henri Martin. Bus routes include the No. 63, which travels along Avenue Georges Mandel and Avenue du Président Wilson.

| 0 metres | 400 |
| 0 yards | 400 |

SEE ALSO
• *Street Finder*, map 3, 9–10
• *Where to Stay* pp289–290
• *Restaurants* pp309–310

KEY
▨ Street-by-Street map
Ⓜ Metro station
Ⓡ RER station

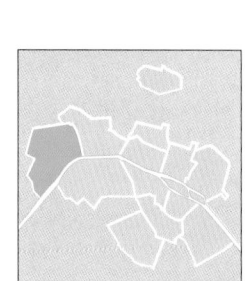

Street-by-Street: Chaillot

The Chaillot hill, with its superb position overlooking the Seine, was the site chosen by Napoleon for "the biggest and most extraordinary" palace that was to be built for his son – but by the time of his downfall only a few ramparts had been completed. Today, the monumental Palais de Chaillot, with its two massive curved wings, stands on the site. From the terrace in front of the Palais there is a magnificent view over the Trocadéro gardens and the Seine to the Eiffel Tower.

The statue of Marshal Ferdinand Foch, who led the Allies to victory in 1918, was unveiled on 11 November 1951. It was built by Robert Wlérick and Raymond Martin to commemorate the centenary of Foch's birth and the 33rd anniversary of the 1918 Armistice.

Metro Trocadéro

The Place du Trocadéro was created for the Universal Exhibition of 1878. Initially it was known as the Place du Roi-de-Rome, in honour of Napoleon's son.

★ **Musée de la Marine**
While concentrating on France's maritime history, this museum also has exhibits of navigational instruments ❺

★ **Palais de Chaillot**
This Neo-Classical building was constructed for the World Fair of 1937. It replaced the Palais du Trocadéro, which was built in 1878 ❶

Musée de l'Homme
The Vénus de Lespugue, *dating from around 25,000 BC, is one of the many artifacts housed in this museum* ❹

The Théâtre National de Chaillot,
beneath the terrace, includes a multi-purpose cultural centre and a modern 1,200-seat theatre. *(See pp342–4.)*

Jardins du Trocadéro
The present layout of the gardens was created by R Lardat after the World Fair of 1937 **6**

LOCATOR MAP
See Central Paris Map pp14–15

Aquarium du Trocadéro
Built to blend in with the Chaillot hillside, this innovative aquarium also has a cinema complex **2**

Cité de l'Architecture et du Patrimoine
This vast complex houses an Architecture Museum, a school, library and archive, and various heritage organizations **3**

The Trocadéro fountains are operated in sequence, culminating in the massive water cannons in the centre firing towards the Eiffel Tower. They are illuminated at night.

The Pont d'Iéna was built by Napoleon to celebrate his victory in 1806 over the Prussians at Jena (Iéna) in Prussia. It was widened in 1937 to complement the building of the Palais de Chaillot.

KEY

– – – Suggested route

0 metres 100

0 yards 100

STAR SIGHTS

★ Palais de Chaillot

★ Musée de la Marine

Trocadéro fountains in front of the Palais de Chaillot

Palais de Chaillot ❶

17 Pl du Trocadéro 75016.
Map 9 C2. Ⓜ *Trocadéro.*
🔳 🔳 🔳

The Palais, with its huge, curved colonnaded wings each culminating in an immense pavilion, was designed in Neo-Classical style for the 1937 Paris Exhibition by Léon Azéma, Louis-Hippolyte Boileau and Jacques Carlu. It is adorned with sculptures and bas-reliefs. On the walls of the pavilions there are gold inscriptions by the poet and essayist Paul Valéry.

The *parvis* or square, situated between the two pavilions is decorated with large bronze sculptures and ornamental pools. On the terrace in front of the *parvis* stand two bronzes, *Apollo* by Henri Bouchard and *Hercules*

by Albert Pommier. Stairways lead from the terrace to the Théâtre National de Chaillot *(see pp342–3)*, which, since World War II, has enjoyed huge fame for its avant-garde productions.

Aquarium du Trocadéro ❷

Ave Albert de Mun 75016.
Map 9 C2. *Tel 01 40 69 23 23.*
Ⓜ *Trocadéro.* 🔳 *10am–8pm daily.*
🔳 ♿ **CinéAqua** 2 ave des
Nations Unies 75016. 🔳 *10am–8pm daily.* **www.cineaqua.com**

Originally built in 1878 for the Universal Exhibition, this is now a state-of-the-art aquarium and is home to over 500 species of sea creatures, including seahorses, clownfish, stonefish and some spectacular sharks and rays. The building is located in a

former quarry and has been designed to blend in entirely with the Chaillot hillside. There is also a futuristic cinema complex, CinéAqua, which combines aquariums with film technology.

Church model from Bagneux, Cité de l'Architecture et du Patrimoine

Cité de l'Architecture et du Patrimoine ❸

Palais de Chaillot, Pl du Trocadéro 75016. **Map** 9 C2. *Tel 01 58 51 52 00.* Ⓜ *Trocadéro.* 🔳 *noon–8pm Mon, Wed–Fri, 11am–7pm Sat–Sun.*
🔳 📷 🔳 🔳 **www.citechaillot.fr**

In the east wing of the Palais de Chaillot, this museum charts the development of French architecture through the ages. Among the unmissable displays is the Galerie des Moulages, which covers the period between the Middle Ages and the Renaissance. Here you will find three-dimensional models of great French cathedrals, such as Chartres. Also worth a look is the Galerie Moderne et Contemporaine, with a reconstruction of a Le Corbusier-designed apartment.

Shark basin, one of the 43 tanks at the Aquarium du Trocadéro

Musée de l'Homme ❹

Palais de Chaillot, 17 Pl du Trocadéro 75016. **Map** 9 C2. *Tel* 01 44 05 72 72. Ⓜ Trocadéro. ◯ 9.45am–5.15pm Mon, Wed–Fri; 10am–6.30pm Sat, Sun. ● public hols. *Exhibitions, films.* www.mnhn.fr

Situated in the west wing of the Chaillot palace, this museum traces the process of human evolution, from prehistoric times to the present, through a series of anthropological exhibits from around the world.

The museum is currently undergoing extensive renovations that will ultimately lead to its housing one of the most comprehensive prehistoric collections in the world. Until then visitors can enjoy a series of temporary exhibitions.

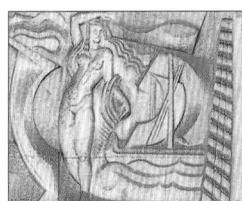
Gabon mask at Musée de l'Homme

Musée de la Marine ❺

Palais de Chaillot, 17 Pl du Trocadéro 75016 **Map** 9 C2. *Tel* 01 53 65 69 69. Ⓜ Trocadéro. ◯ 10am–6pm Wed–Mon. ● 1 Jan, 1 May, 25 Dec. *Films, videos.* www.musee-marine.fr

French maritime history from the days of the royal wooden warships to today's aircraft carriers and nuclear submarines is told through wonderfully exact scale models (most of them two centuries old), mementos of naval heroes, paintings and navigational instruments. The museum was set up by Charles X in

1827, and was then moved to the Chaillot palace in 1943. Exhibits include Napoleon's barge, models of the fleet he assembled at Boulogne-sur-Mer in 1805 for his planned invasion of Britain, and displays on underwater exploration and fishing vessels.

Jardins du Trocadéro ❻

75016. **Map** 10 D2. Ⓜ Trocadéro.

These lovely gardens cover 10 ha (25 acres). Their centrepiece is a long rectangular ornamental pool, bordered by stone and bronze-gilt statues, which look spectacular at night when the fountains are illuminated. The statues include *Man* by P Traverse and *Woman* by G Braque, *Bull* by P Jouve and *Horse* by G Guyot. On either side of the pool, the slopes of the Chaillot hill gently lead down to the Seine and the Pont d'Iéna. There is a freshwater aquarium in the northeast corner of the gardens, which are richly laid out with trees, walkways, small streams and bridges.

Musée du Vin ❼

Rue des Eaux, 5 Sq Charles Dickens 75016. **Map** 9 C3. *Tel* 01 45 25 63 26. Ⓜ Passy. ◯ 10am–6pm Tue–Sun. ● 24 Dec–1 Jan. *groups only.* lunchtime only. www.museeduvinparis.com

Waxwork figures and cardboard cut-outs graphically illustrate the history of winemaking in these atmospheric vaulted medieval cellars, which were once used by the monks of Passy. The exhibits include a collection of old wine bottles, glasses and corkscrews, as well as an array of scientific instruments that were used in the wine-making and bottling processes. There is also an excellent restaurant, wine for sale and tours which include a wine-tasting session.

Bridge in the Trocadéro gardens

Maison de Balzac ❽

47 Rue Raynouard 75016. **Map** 9 B3. *Tel* 01 55 74 41 80. Ⓜ Passy, La Muette. ◯ 10am–6pm Tue–Sun (last adm: 5.30pm). ● public hols. www.balzac.paris.fr

The novelist Honoré de Balzac lived here from 1840 to 1847 under a false name, Monsieur de Brugnol, to avoid his numerous creditors. During this time he wrote many of his most famous novels, among them *La Cousine Bette* (1846).

The house now contains a reference library, with some of his original works, and a museum with memorabilia from his life. Many of the rooms have drawings and paintings portraying Balzac's family and close friends. The Madame Hanska room is devoted to the memory of the Russian woman who corresponded with Balzac for 18 years and was his wife for the five months before his death in 1850.

The house has a back entrance leading into the Rue Berton, which was used to evade unwelcome callers. Rue Berton, with its ivy-covered walls, has retained much of its old, country-like charm.

Plaque marking Balzac's house

Relief outside the Maritime Museum

Radio (1955) in radio museum

Musée de Radio-France ⑨

116 Ave du Président-Kennedy 75016. **Map** 9 B4.
Tel 01 56 40 15 16. Ⓜ Ranelagh.
☐ for tours only, Mon–Sat.
● public hols. 🖼 🚫 ♿
📷 10–11am, 2.30–4pm Mon–Fri.
www.radiofrance.fr

Radio-France House is an impressive building designed by Henri Bernard in 1963 as the headquarters of the state-run Radio-France. The largest single structure in France, it is made up of three incomplete concentric circular constructions with a rectangular tower. The building covers an area of 2 ha (5 acres).

Here, in the 70-odd studios and main public auditorium, French radio programmes are produced. The museum traces the history of communications from the 18th century to the present.

Cimetière de Passy ⑩

2 Rue du Commandant-Shloesing 75016. **Map** 9 C2. **Tel** 01 47 27 51 42. Ⓜ Trocadéro. ☐ 8am–6pm Mon–Fri; 8.30am–6pm Sat; 9am–6pm Sun.

Located in the elegant 16th arrondissement, this small cemetery, which opened in 1820, is packed with the graves of eminent Parisians. There are more famous people here than in any other cemetery in Paris, such as the composers Claude Debussy and Gabriel Fauré and painter Edouard Manet, as well as many politicians and aristocrats.

Musée de la Contrefaçon ⑪

16 Rue de la Faisanderie 75016.
Map 3 A5. **Tel** 01 56 26 14 00.
Ⓜ Porte Dauphine. ☐ 2–5.30pm Tue–Sun. ● public hols. 🖼 🚫
www.unifab.com

French cognac and perfume producers, and the luxury trade in general, have been plagued for years by counterfeiters operating around the world. This museum was set up by the manufacturers' union and illustrates the history of this type of fraud, which has been going on since Roman times. Among the impressive display of forgeries are copies of Louis Vuitton luggage, Cartier watches and fake wine.

Musée Arménien ⑫

59 Ave Foch 75016. **Map** 3 B5.
Tel 01 45 56 15 88. Ⓜ Porte Dauphine. ● for renovation until further notice. **www**.paris.fr

The ground floor of No. 59 Avenue Foch houses the Armenian museum, founded after World War II. Despite its small size the collection has many fascinating treasures, including church plates, exquisite miniatures, carpets and contemporary paintings. Although closed until further notice, there are occasional exhibitions.

Armenian crown (19th century)

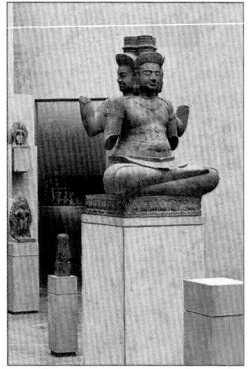
Khmer art in the Musée National des Arts Asiatiques Guimet

Musée Dapper ⑬

35 bis Rue Paul-Valéry, 75116.
Tel 01 45 00 91 75. Ⓜ Victor-Hugo.
☐ 11am-7pm Wed–Mon. 🖼 🔲

Not just a museum, but a world-class ethnographic research centre called the Dapper Foundation, this is France's premier showcase of African art and culture. Located in an attractive building with an "African" garden, it is a treasure house of vibrant colour and powerful, evocative work from the black nations. The emphasis is on pre-colonial folk arts, with sculpture, carvings, and tribal work, but there is later art too. The highlight is tribal masks, with a dazzling array of richly carved religious, ritual and funerary masks, as well as theatrical ones used for comic, magical or symbolic performances, some dating back to the 12th century.

Debussy's grave in the Cimetière de Passy, in the shadow of the Eiffel Tower

Musée du Cristal de Baccarat ⓮

11 Place des Etats-Unis 75016.
Map 4 D5. **Tel** 01 40 22 11 00.
Ⓜ Boissière. ◯ 10am–6.30pm
Mon–Sat. ● public hols. 🖼 📷
🎫 🏛 **www**.baccarat.fr

The Musée du Cristal, also known as the Galerie-Musée Baccarat, has on display over 1,200 articles made by the Baccarat company, which was founded in 1764 in Lorraine. These include services created for the royal and imperial courts of Europe and the finest pieces created in the workshops.

Musée National des Arts Asiatiques Guimet ⓯

6 Pl d'Iéna 75116. **Map** 10 D1. **Tel**
01 56 52 53 00. Ⓜ Iéna. ◯ 10am–
6pm Wed–Mon (last adm: 5.30pm).
🖼 🚫 ♿ 🍴 🛍 🏛 Panthéon
Bouddhique (additional galleries) at
19 Ave d'Iéna **Tel** 01 40 73 88 11.
www.museeguimet.fr

The Musée Guimet has the finest collection of Khmer (Cambodian) art in the West. It was originally set up in Lyon in 1879 by the industrialist and orientalist Emile Guimet.
  Moved to Paris in 1884, it meticulously represents every artistic tradition from Afghani-

Gabriel Forestier's sculpted doors, Musée d'Art Moderne

stan to India, to China and Japan, to Korea and Vietnam and the rest of southeast Asia. With over 45,000 artworks, the museum is acclaimed for some especially unusual collections, including the Cambodian Angkor Wat sculptures and 1600 displays of Himalayan Art. Other highlights include Chinese bronzes and lacquerware, and many statues of Buddha.

Musée Galliera ⓰

10 Ave Pierre 1er de Serbie 75116.
Map 10 E1. **Tel** 01 56 52 86 00.
Ⓜ Iéna, Alma Marceau. ◯ for
exhibitions only, 10am–6pm
Tue–Sun (from 2pm on some public
hols). 🖼 **Children's room**.
www.galliera.paris.fr

Devoted to the evolution of fashion, this museum is housed in the Renaissance-style palace built for the Duchesse

Maria de Ferrari Galliera in 1892. The collection comprises more than 100,000 outfits, from the 18th century to the present day. Some, from more recent times, have been donated by such fashionable women as Baronne Hélène de Rothschild and Princess Grace of Monaco. The various garments are displayed in rotation twice per year.

Musée d'Art Moderne de la Ville de Paris ⓱

Palais de Tokyo, 11 Ave du Président-
Wilson 75016. **Map** 10 E1. **Tel** 01 53
67 40 00. Ⓜ Iéna, Alma Marceau.
◯ 10am–6pm Tue–Sun (to 10pm
Wed). 🖼 temporary exhibitions. ♿
🎫 📖 🖼 **Films**. **www**.mam.paris.fr

This large, lively museum is the municipality's own ren-owned collection of modern art, covering all major 20th century trends (the 21st century will be included). The museum occupies the vast east wing of the Palais de Tokyo, built for the 1937 World Fair. One of the highlights is Raoul Dufy's gigantic mural *La Fée Electricité*. Also notable are the Cubists, Amadeo Modigliani, Georges Rouault and The Fauves, especially Henri Matisse, whose *La Danse* is here in both versions.

Garden and rear facade of the Musée Galliera

CHAMPS-ELYSEES

Two great streets dominate this area – the Avenue des Champs-Elysées and the Rue St-Honoré. The former is the capital's most famous thoroughfare. Its breadth is spectacular. The pavements are wide and their cafés, cinemas and shops attract throngs of people, who come to eat and shop, but also to see and to be seen. Rond Point des Champs-Elysées is the pretty end, with shady chestnut trees and pavements colourfully bordered by flower beds. Luxury and political power are nearby. Five-star hotels, fine restaurants and upmarket shops line the nearby streets and avenues. And along Rue St-Honoré are the impressive, heavily guarded Palais de l'Elysée, the sumptuous town mansions of business chiefs, and the many embassies and consulates.

Ornate lamp-post on Pont Alexandre III

SIGHTS AT A GLANCE

Historic Buildings and Streets
Palais de l'Elysée ❺
Avenue Montaigne ❻
Avenue des Champs-Elysées ❽
Place Charles de Gaulle
(l'Etoile) ❾

Monuments
Arc de Triomphe pp210–11 ❿

Bridges
Pont Alexandre III ❶

Museums and Galleries
Grand Palais ❷
Palais de la Découverte ❸
Petit Palais ❹
Musée Jacquemart-André ❼

GETTING THERE
There is a metro station at Champs-Elysées Clemenceau and both a metro and RER station at Etoile. Among the bus routes, 42 and 73 pass down the Avenue des Champs-Elysées.

KEY
▨	Street-by-Street map
Ⓜ	Metro station
RER	RER station

SEE ALSO
• *Street Finder*, map 3–4, 5, 11
• *Where to Stay* pp290–91
• *Restaurants* pp310–11

0 metres   400
0 yards   400

◁ **View of the Arc de Triomphe at night**

Street-by-Street: Champs-Elysées

The formal gardens that line the Champs-Elysées from the Place de la Concorde to the Rond-Point have changed little since they were laid out by the architect Jacques Hittorff in 1838. They were used as the setting for the World Fair of 1855, which included the Palais de l'Industrie, Paris's response to London's Crystal Palace. The Palais was later replaced by the Grand Palais and Petit Palais, which were created as a showpiece of the Third Republic for the Universal Exhibition of 1900. They sit on either side of an impressive vista that stretches from the Place Clémenceau across the elegant curve of the Pont Alexandre III to the Invalides.

The Théâtre du Rond-Point was the home of the Renaud-Barrault Company. There are plaques on the back door of the theatre representing Napoleon's campaigns.

Metro Franklin D Roosevelt M

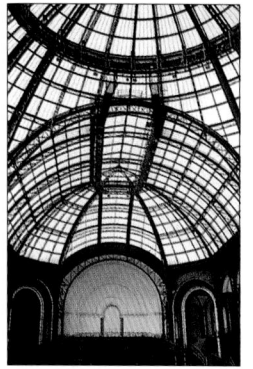

Avenue Montaigne
Christian Dior and other haute couture houses are based in this chic avenue **6**

★ Grand Palais
Designed by Charles Girault, this grand 19th-century building is still used for major exhibitions **2**

The Lasserre restaurant is decorated in the style of a luxurious ocean liner from the 1930s.

RUE JEAN GOUJON

RUE FRANÇOIS PREMIER

ROOSEVELT

FRANKLIN

AVE

AVE G¹ EISENHOWER

PL DU CANADA

COURS

PONT DES INVALIDES

STAR SIGHTS

★ Avenue des Champs-Elysées

★ Grand Palais

★ Petit Palais

★ Pont Alexandre III

Palais de la Découverte
Outside this museum of scientific discoveries is a pair of equestrian statues **3**

KEY

– – – Suggested route

0 metres   100

0 yards   100

★ **Avenue des Champs-Elysées**
This was the setting for the victory parades following the two World Wars, and for the bicentennial parade in 1989 ⑧

LOCATOR MAP
See Central Paris Map pp14–15

CHAMPS-ELYSEES

CHAILLOT QUARTER

Seine

INVALIDES AND EIFFEL TOWER QUARTER

Metro Champs-Elysées-Clemenceau

The Jardins des Champs-Elysées, with their fountains, flowerbeds, paths and pleasure pavilions, became very popular towards the end of the 19th century. Fashion-able Parisians, including Marcel Proust, often came here.

To the Place de la Concorde

★ **Petit Palais**
Lit by natural light, this palace is as much a work of art as the 19th-century items it contains, such as sculptures and Impressionist paintings ④

To the Invalides

★ **Pont Alexandre III**
The bridge's four columns help to anchor the piers that absorb the immense forces generated by such a large single-span structure ①

Pont Alexandre III ❶

75008. **Map** 11 A1. Ⓜ *Champs-Elysées-Clemenceau.*

This is Paris's prettiest bridge with its exuberant Art Nouveau decoration of lamps, cherubs, nymphs and winged horses at either end. It was built between 1896 and 1900, in time for the Universal Exhibition and it was named after Tsar Alexander III (father of Nicholas II) who laid the foundation stone in October 1896.

The style of the bridge reflects that of the Grand Palais, to which it leads on the Right Bank. The construction of the bridge is a marvel of 19th-century engineering, consisting of a 6-m (18-ft) high single-span steel arch across the Seine. The design was subject to strict controls that prevented the bridge from obscuring the view of the Champs-Elysées or the Invalides. So today you can still enjoy magnificent views from here.

Pont Alexandre III

Grand Palais ❷

Porte A, Ave Général Eisenhower 75008. **Map** 11 A1. 📞 *01 44 13 17 17.* Ⓜ *Champs-Elysées-Clemenceau.* ◯ *for temporary exhibitions (usually 10am–8pm Thu–Mon, 10am–10pm Wed, but phone to check).* ◯ *1 May, 25 Dec.* 🎟 📷 ♿ 🎧 *usually 3pm Mon, Fri, Sat, 7pm Wed but call to check.* 📞 ▯ 🎧 **www**.rmn.fr

Built at the same time as the Petit Palais and the Pont Alexandre III, the exterior of this massive palace combines an imposing Classical stone

facade with a riot of Art Nouveau ironwork. It has a splendid glass roof, and Récipon's colossal bronze statues of flying horses and chariots at its four corners. The enormous glass roof (15,000 sq metres/160,000 sq ft) has recently been restored to its former glory. The metal structure supporting the glass weighs 8,500 tonnes, some 500 tonnes more than the Eiffel Tower.

Temporary exhibitions are held in the Galeries Nationales du Grand Palais. The basement houses a major police station.

Palais de la Découverte

Palais de la Découverte ❸

Ave Franklin D Roosevelt 75008. **Map** 11 A1. 📞 *01 56 43 20 21.* Ⓜ *Franklin D Roosevelt.* ◯ *9.30am–6pm Tue–Sat; 10am–7pm Sun.* ◯ *1 Jan, 1 May, 14 Jul, 15 Aug, 25 Dec.* 🎟 📷 *by permission.* ▯ ▯ **www**.palais-decouverte.fr

Opened in a wing of the Grand Palais for the World Fair of 1937, this museum of scientific discoveries was an immediate success and continues to be popular. The displays, including a planetarium, help to explain the basics of all the sciences.

Entrance to the Petit Palais

Petit Palais ❹

Ave Winston Churchill 75008. **Map** 11 B1. **Tel** *01 53 43 40 00.* Ⓜ *Champs-Elysées-Clemenceau.* ◯ *10am–6pm Tue–Sun (to 8pm Tue during exhibitions).* ◯ *public hols.* 🎟 📷 🎧 *for exhibitions.* ▯ **www**.petitpalais-paris.fr

Built for the Universal Exhibition in 1900, to stage a major display of French art, this jewel of a building now houses the Musée des Beaux-Arts de la Ville de Paris. Arranged around a pretty semi-circular courtyard and garden, the palace is similar in style to the Grand Palais, and has Ionic columns, a grand porch and a dome which echoes that of the Invalides.

The Cours de la Reine wing, nearest the river, is used for temporary exhibitions, while the Champs-Elysées side of the palace houses the permanent collections. These are divided into sections: Greek and Roman; medieval and Renaissance ivories and sculptures; Renaissance clocks and jewellery; and 17th-, 18th-and 19th-century art and furniture. There are also many works by the Impressionists.

GRAND PALAIS

Iron supports

Exhibition space

Palais de l'Elysée ⑤

55 Rue du Faubourg-St-Honoré 75008. **Map** 5 B5. Ⓜ St-Philippe-du-Roule. **Not open** to the public.

Set amid splendid English-style gardens, the Elysée Palace was built in 1718 for the Comte d'Evreux and has been the official residence of the President of the Republic since 1873. From 1805 to 1808 it was occupied by Napoleon's sister, Caroline, and her husband, Murat. Two charming rooms have been preserved from this period: the Salon Murat and the Salon d'Argent. General de Gaulle used to give press conferences in the Hall of Mirrors. Today, the President's modernized apartments can be found on the first floor opposite the Rue de l'Elysée.

Elysée guard

Avenue Montaigne ⑥

75008. **Map** 10 F1. Ⓜ Franklin D Roosevelt.

In the 19th century this avenue was famous for its dance halls and its Winter Garden, where Parisians went to hear Adolphe Sax play his newly-invented saxophone. Today it is still one of Paris's most fashionable streets, bustling with restaurants, cafés, hotels and designer boutiques.

Inside the Musée Jacquemart-André

Musée Jacquemart-André ⑦

158 Blvd Haussmann 75008. **Map** 5 A4. **Tel** 01 45 62 11 59. Ⓜ Miromesnil, St-Philippe-du-Roule. ◯ 10am–6pm daily. 📷 🚫 🛈 🍴 🛍 **www**.musee-jacquemart-andre.com

This museum is known for its fine collection of Italian Renaissance and French 18th-century works of art, as well as its beautiful frescoes by Tiepolo. Highlights include works by Mantegna, Uccello's masterpiece *St George and the Dragon* (about 1435), paintings by Boucher and Fragonard and 18th-century tapestries and furniture.

Avenue des Champs-Elysées ⑧

75008. **Map** 5 A5. Ⓜ Franklin D Roosevelt, George V.

Paris's most famous and popular thoroughfare had its beginnings in about 1667, when the landscape garden designer, André Le Nôtre, extended the royal view from the Tuileries by creating a tree-lined avenue which eventually became known as the Champs-Elysées (Elysian Fields). It has been the "triumphal way" (as the French call it) ever since the home-coming of Napoleon's body from St Helena in 1840. With the addition of cafés and restaurants in the second half of the 19th century, the Champs-Elysées became the place in which to be seen.

Place Charles de Gaulle (l'Etoile) ⑨

75008. **Map** 4 D4. Ⓜ Charles de Gaulle-Etoile.

Known as the Place de l'Etoile until the death of Charles de Gaulle in 1969, the area is still referred to simply as l'Etoile, the star. The present *place* was laid out in accordance with Baron Haussmann's plans of 1854 (*see pp34–5*). For motorists, it is the ultimate challenge.

Arc de Triomphe from the west

Arc de Triomphe ⑩

See pp210–11.

Glass cupola

Quadriga (chariot and four horses) by Récipon

Arc de Triomphe ❿

The east facade of the Arc de Triomphe

After his greatest victory, the Battle of Austerlitz in 1805, Napoleon promised his men, "You shall go home beneath triumphal arches." The first stone of what was to become the world's most famous triumphal arch was laid the following year. But disruptions to architect Jean Chalgrin's plans and the demise of Napoleonic power delayed the completion of this monumental building until 1836. Standing 50 m (164 ft) high, the Arc is now the customary starting point for victory celebrations and parades.

Thirty shields just below the Arc's roof each bear the name of a victorious Napoleonic battle fought in either Europe or Africa.

East facade

The frieze was executed by Rude, Brun, Jacquet, Laitié, Caillouette and Seurre the Elder. This east facade shows the departure of the French armies for new campaigns. The west side shows their return.

The Battle of Aboukir, a bas-relief by Seurre the Elder, depicts a scene of Napoleon's victory over the Turkish army in 1799.

Triumph of Napoleon
J P Cortot's high-relief celebrates the Treaty of Vienna peace agreement of 1810.

STAR FEATURES

★ Departure of the Volunteers in 1792

★ Tomb of the Unknown Soldier

★ Tomb of the Unknown Soldier
An unknown French soldier from World War I is buried here.

TIMELINE

1806 Napoleon commissions Chalgrin to build triumphal Arc

1836 Louis-Philippe completes the Arc

1885 Victor Hugo's body lies in state under the Arc

1944 Liberation of Paris. De Gaulle leads the crowd from the Arc

1800	1850	1900	1950

1840 Napoleon's cortège passes under the Arc

1815 Downfall of Napoleon. Work on Arc ceases

1919 Victory parade of Allied armies through the Arc

NAPOLEON'S NUPTIAL PARADE

Napoleon divorced Josephine in 1809 because she was unable to bear him children. A diplomatic marriage was arranged in 1810 with Marie-Louise, daughter of the Austrian emperor. Napoleon was determined to impress his bride by going through the Arc on their way to the wedding at the Louvre, but work had barely been started. So Chalgrin built a full-scale mock-up of the arch on the site for the couple to pass beneath.

VISITORS' CHECKLIST

Pl Charles de Gaulle. **Map** 4 D4. **Tel** 01 55 37 73 77. Ⓜ REER Charles de Gaulle-Etoile. 22, 30, 31, 73, 92 to Pl C de Gaulle. Ⓟ off Pl C de Gaulle. **Museum** ◯ Apr–Sep: 10am–11pm daily; Oct–Mar: 10am–10.30pm daily (last adm: 30 mins earlier). ◯ 1 Jan, 1 May, 8 May, 14 Jul, 11 Nov, 25 Dec. www.monum.fr

The viewing platform affords one of the best views in Paris, overlooking the grand Champs-Elysées on one side. Beyond the other side is La Défense.

General Marceau's Funeral
Marceau defeated the Austrians in 1795, only to be killed the following year, still fighting them.

The Battle of Austerlitz by Gechter shows Napoleon's army breaking up the ice on the Satschan lake in order to drown thousands of enemy troops.

Officers of the Imperial Army are listed on the walls of the smaller arches.

Entrance to museum

★ **Departure of the Volunteers in 1792**
François Rude's work shows citizens leaving to defend the nation.

Place Charles de Gaulle
Twelve avenues radiate from the Arc at the centre. Some bear the names of important French military leaders, such as Avenues Marceau and Foch.
(See pp34–5.)

OPERA QUARTER

The Opéra quarter bustles with bankers and stockbrokers, newspapermen and shoppers, theatre-goers and sightseers. Much of its 19th-century grandeur survives in the Grands Boulevards of Baron Haussmann's urban design. These are still a favourite with thousands of Parisian and foreign promenaders, drawn by the profusion of shops and department stores, which range from the exclusively expensive to the popular.

Much more of the area's older character is found in the many *passages*, delightful narrow shopping arcades with steel and glass roofs. Fashion's bad boy, Jean-Paul Gaultier, has a shop in the smartest

Les Coulisses de l'Opéra (1889) by J Beraud

one, Galerie Vivienne. But more authentically old-style Parisian are the Passage des Panoramas and the Passage Jouffroy, the Passage Verdeau, with its old cameras and comics, and the tiny Passage des Princes. Two of Paris's finest food shops are in the area. Fauchon and Hédiard are noted for mouthwatering mustards, jams, pâtés and sauces. The area still has a reputation as a press centre, although *Le Monde* has moved out, and a history of cinema and theatre – the Lumière brothers held the world's first public film show here in 1895, and the Opéra National de Paris Garnier is famed for its ballet and opera.

SIGHTS AT A GLANCE

Historic Buildings and Streets
Place de la Madeleine ❷
Les Grands Boulevards ❸
Palais de la Bourse ❾
Avenue de l'Opéra ⓬

Churches
La Madeleine ❶

Opera Houses
Opéra National de Paris Garnier ❹

Museums and Galleries
Musée de l'Opéra ❺
Grévin ❼
Cabinet des Médailles et des Antiques ❿
Bibliothèque Nationale ⓫

Shops
Drouot (Hôtel des Ventes) ❻
Les Passages ❽

GETTING THERE

This area is served by the metro and RER systems. Metro lines 3, 7 and 8 serve the station at the Opéra, line 14 stops at Madeleine and the RER Line A stops at Auber. Among the bus routes passing through the area, 42 and 52 travel along Boulevard Madeleine, and 21, 27, 29 and 95 along Avenue de l'Opéra.

0 metres   400
0 yards   400

KEY

Street-by-Street map

M Metro station

RER RER station

SEE ALSO

- *Street Finder*, map 5–6
- *Where to Stay* p291
- *Restaurants* pp311–12

◁ Jean-Baptiste Carpeaux's *La Danse* outside the Opéra National de Paris Garnier

Street-by-Street: Opéra Quarter

It has been said that if you sit for long enough at the Café de la Paix (opposite the Opéra National de Paris Garnier) the whole world will pass by. During the day, the area is a mixture of commerce – France's top three banks are based here – and tourism. A profusion of shops, ranging from the chic, exclusive and expensive to the popular department stores, draw the crowds. In the evening, the theatres and cinemas attract a totally different crowd, and the cafés along the Boulevard des Capucines throb with life.

Statue by Gumery on the Opéra

Place de la Madeleine
On the north side of the square, the windows of the Fauchon shop are filled with food from around the world ❷

KEY

– – – Suggested route

```
0 metres    100
0 yards     100
```

RUE TRONCHET

RUE VIGNON

RUE GODOT DE MAUROY

RUE CAUMARTIN

PL DE LA MADELEINE

BLVD

Ⓜ **Metro Madeleine**

BLVD DE LA MADELEINE

STAR SIGHTS

★ La Madeleine

★ Boulevard des Capucines

★ Opéra National de Paris Garnier

★ **La Madeleine**
The final design of this church, which is dedicated to Mary Magdalene, differs from this original model, now in the Musée Carnavalet (see pp96–7) ❶

★ **Opéra National de Paris Garnier**
With a mixture of styles ranging from Classical to Baroque, this building from 1875 has come to symbolize the opulence of the Second Empire ❹

LOCATOR MAP
See Central Paris Map pp14–15

Metro Chaussée d'Antin Ⓜ

Musée de l'Opéra
Famous artists' work is often shown in temporary exhibition rooms ❺

The Place de l'Opéra
was designed by Baron Haussmann and is one of Paris's busiest intersections.

Metro Opéra Ⓜ

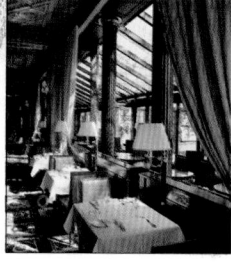

The Café de la Paix maintains its old-fashioned ways and still has its 19th-century decor, designed by Garnier. Their vanilla slices are legendary. *(See p319.)*

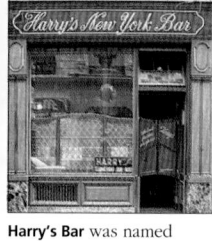

Harry's Bar was named after Harry MacElhone, a bartender who bought the bar in 1913. Past regulars have included F Scott Fitzgerald and Ernest Hemingway.

★ **Boulevard des Capucines**
At No. 14 a plaque tells of the world's first public screening of a movie, by the Lumière brothers in 1895; it took place in the Salon Indien, a room in the Grand Café ❸

Charles Marochetti's *Mary Magdalene Ascending to Heaven* (1837) behind the high altar of La Madeleine

La Madeleine ❶

Pl de la Madeleine 75008.
Map 5 C5. **Tel** 01 44 51 69 00.
Ⓜ Madeleine. ◯ 7am–7pm daily.
🚌 frequent. **Concerts.** 📷 🚻
See **Entertainment** pp346–7.

This church, which is
dedicated to Mary
Magdalene, is one of
the best-known build-
ings in Paris because
of its prominent locat-
ion and great size. It
stands at one end of
the curve of the Grands
Boulevards and is the
architectural counter-
point of the Palais-
Bourbon (home of the
Assemblée Nationale,
the French parliament)
across the river. It was
started in 1764 but not
consecrated until 1845. There
were proposals to convert it
into a parliament, a stock
exchange or a public library
for the nation.
   Napoleon decided to build
a temple dedicated to military
glory and he commissioned
Pierre Vignon to design it,
after the battle of Jena (Iéna)
in 1806. A colonnade of 20 m
high (64 ft) Corinthian
columns encircles the
building and supports a
sculptured frieze. The bas-
reliefs on the bronze doors
are by Henri de Triqueti and
show the Ten Commandments.

The inside is decorated with
marble and gilt, and has some
fine sculpture, notably François
Rude's *Baptism of Christ*.

Place de la Madeleine ❷

75008. **Map** 5 C5. Ⓜ
Madeleine. **Flower market**
◯ 8am–7.30pm Tue–Sun.

Fauchon tin

The place de la
Madeleine was
created at the same
time as the Madeleine
church. It is a food
lover's paradise, with
many shops special-
izing in luxuries such
as truffles, champagne,
caviar and handmade
chocolates. Fauchon, the
millionaires' supermarket, is
situated at No. 26 and stocks
more than 20,000 items *(see
pp333–5)*. The large house at
No. 9 is where Marcel Proust
spent his childhood. To the
east of La Madeleine is a small
flower market *(see p338)* and
some excellently preserved
19th-century public toilets.

**OPERA NATIONAL DE
PARIS GARNIER**

Scenery backdrop
operated by pulley

Backstage area   Stag

Les Grands Boulevards ❸

75002 & 75009. **Map** 6 D5–7C5.
Ⓜ *Madeleine, Opéra, Richelieu-Drouot, Grands Boulevards.*

Eight broad boulevards – Madeleine, Capucines, Italiens, Montmartre, Poissonnière, Bonne Nouvelle, St-Denis and St-Martin – run from around La Madeleine to the Place de la République. They were constructed in the 17th century to turn obsolete city fortifications into fashionable promenades – *boulevard* came from the Middle Dutch *bulwerc*, which means bulwark or rampart. The boulevards became so famous in the 19th century that the name *boulevardier* was coined for one who cuts a figure on the boulevards.

Around the Madeleine church and the Opéra it is still possible to gain an impression of what the Grands Boulevards looked like in their heyday, lined with cafés and chic shops. Elsewhere, most of the cafés and restaurants have long since gone, and the old facades are now hidden by neon

advertising. However, the Grands Boulevards and the nearby department stores on the Boulevard Haussmann still attract large crowds.

Boulevard des Italiens

Opéra National de Paris Garnier ❹

Pl de l'Opéra 75009. **Map** 6 E4.
01 40 01 22 63. Ⓜ *Opéra.*
10am–6pm daily (5pm winter).
public hols. See ***Entertainment*** pp345–7. **www**.operadeparis.fr

Sometimes compared to a giant wedding cake, this sumptuous building was designed by Charles Garnier for Napoleon III; construction started in 1862. Its unique appearance is due to a mixture of materials (including stone, marble and bronze) and styles, ranging from Classical to Baroque, with a multitude of

columns, friezes and sculptures on the exterior. The building was not completed until 1875; work was interrupted by the Prussian War and 1871 uprising.

In 1858 Orsini had attempted to assassinate the emperor outside the old opera house. This prompted Garnier to include a pavilion on the east side of the new building, with a curved ramp leading up to it so that the sovereign could safely step out of his carriage into the suite of rooms adjoining the royal box.

The functions performed by each part of the building are reflected in the structure. Behind the flat-topped foyer, the cupola sits above the auditorium, while the triangular pediment that rises up behind the cupola marks the front of the stage. Underneath the building is a small lake, which provided inspiration for the phantom's hiding place in Paul Leroux's *Phantom of the Opera.*

Both the interior and the exterior have been recently refurbished. Don't miss the magnificent Grand Staircase, made of white marble with a balustrade of red and green marble, and the Grand Foyer, with its domed ceiling covered with mosaics. The five-tiered auditorium is a riot of red velvet, plaster cherubs and gold leaf, which contrast with the false ceiling painted by Marc Chagall in 1964.

Most operas are performed in the new Opéra Nationale de Paris Bastille *(see p98),* but the ballet remains here.

Statue by Millet

Copper-green roofed cupola

Emperor's pavilion

Grand Foyer with mosaic ceiling

Auditorium with seating for about 2,000

Grand Staircase

Sign outside the Grévin waxwork museum

Musée de l'Opéra **❺**

Pl de l'Opéra 75009. **Map** 6 E5. **Tel** 01 40 01 24 93. **M** Opéra. ◯ 10am–5pm daily. ● 1 Jan, 1 May. 🖼 ☑ 01 41 10 08 10. ☐

The entrance to this small, charming museum was originally the emperor's private entrance to the Opéra. The museum relates the history of opera through a large collection of musical scores, manuscripts, photographs and artists' memorabilia, such as the Russian dancer Vaslav Nijinsky's ballet slippers and tarot cards. Other exhibits include models of stage sets and busts of major composers. The museum also houses a superb library, containing books and manuscripts on theatre, dance and music, as well as more memorabilia.

Drouot (Hôtel des Ventes) **❻**

9 Rue Drouot 75009. **Map** 6 F4. **Tel** 01 48 00 20 20. **M** Richelieu Drouot. ◯ 11am–6pm Mon–Sat. 🖼 ☑ ☐ See **Shops and Markets** pp336–7. **www**.drouot.fr

This is the leading French auction house (Hôtel des Ventes) and it takes its name from the Comte de Drouot who was Napoleon's aide-de-camp. There has been an auction house on the site since 1858, and in 1860 Napoleon III visited the Hôtel and purchased a couple of earthenware pots. It has been known as the Nouveau Drouot ever since the 1970s, when the existing building was demolished and replaced with today's rather dull structure.

Although overshadowed internationally by Christie's and Sotheby's, auctions at the Nouveau Drouot nevertheless provide a lively spectacle and involve a fascinating range of rare objects. Its presence in the area has attracted many antique and stamp shops.

Grévin **❼**

10 Blvd Montmartre 75009. **Map** 6 F4. **Tel** 01 47 70 85 05. **M** Grands Boulevards ◯ 10am–6:30pm Mon–Fri, 10am–7pm Sat & Sun. (last admission 1 hour before closing). 🖼 ☐ **www**.grevin.fr

This waxwork museum was founded in 1882 and is now a Paris landmark, on a par with Madame Tussauds in London.

It contains tableaux of vivid historical scenes (such as Louis XIV at Versailles and the arrest of Louis XVI), distorting mirrors and the Cabinet Fantastique, which includes regular conjuring shows given by a live magician. Famous figures from the worlds of art, sport and politics are also on show, with new celebrities replacing faded and forgotten stars.

Galerie Vivienne

Les Passages **❽**

75002. **Map** 6 F5. **M** Bourse.

The early 19th-century Parisian shopping arcades (known as passages or galeries) are located between the Boulevard Montmartre and the Rue St-Marc (the extensive Passage des Panoramas). Other arcades are found between the Rue du Quatre Septembre and the Rue des Petits Champs.

At the time of their construction, the Passages represented a new traffic-free area for commerce, workshops and apartments. They fell into disuse, but were dramatically revamped in the 1970s and now house an eclectic mixture of small shops selling anything from designer jewellery to rare books. They have high, vaulted roofs of iron and glass. Many have seen better days but one of the most charming is the Galerie Vivienne (off the Rue Vivienne or the Rue des Petits Champs) with its mosaic floor and excellent tearoom.

Model of a set for Les Huguenots (1875) in the Musée de l'Opéra

The colonnaded Neo-Classical facade of the Palais de la Bourse

Palais de la Bourse ❾

(Bourse des Valeurs) 4 Pl de la Bourse 75002. **Map** 6 F5. **Tel** 01 49 27 55 54 (tours). Ⓜ Bourse. ⬜ by appt only. 🚫 📷 📹 compulsory (01 49 27 55 50). **Films.**

This neo-classical temple of commerce was commissioned by Napoleon and was home to the French Stock Exchange from 1826 to 1987. Today the French stock market is located at 29 Rue Cambon (not open to visits). The hectic floor trading of the Palais de la Bourse has been considerably reduced and is limited to the Matif (the futures market) and the Monep (the traded options market).

Sainte-Chapelle cameo in the Cabinet des Médailles

Cabinet des Médailles et des Antiques ❿

58 Rue de Richelieu 75002. **Map** 6 F5. **Tel** 01 53 79 83 30. Ⓜ Bourse. ⬜ 1–5.45pm Mon–Sat (to 4.45pm Sat); noon–6pm Sun. ⬤ public hols. 🚫 📷 www.bnf.fr

This valuable collection of coins, medals, jewels and Classical objects is part of the Bibliothèque Nationale. Exhibits include the Berthouville Treasure (1st-century Gallo-Roman silverware) and the Grand Camée (cameo) from Sainte-Chapelle.

Bibliothèque Nationale ⓫

58 Rue de Richelieu 75002. **Map** 6 F5. **Tel** 01 53 79 59 59. Ⓜ Bourse. ⬜ 9am–6pm Mon–Fri, 9am–5pm Sat. www.bnf.fr

The Bibliotheque Nationale (National Library) originated with the manuscript collections of medieval kings, to which a copy of every French book printed since 1537, has, by law, been added. The collection, which includes two Gutenberg bibles, is partially housed in this complex, created in the 17th century by Cardinal Mazarin. Despite the recent removal of the printed books, periodicals and CD-Roms to the newly-built Bibliothèque Nationale de France (see p246) at Tolbiac, the rue Richelieu buildings still contain a huge variety of items, including original manuscripts by Victor Hugo and Marcel Proust, among others. The library also has the richest collection of engravings and photographs in the world, and departments for maps and plans, theatrical arts, and musical scores. Sadly, the 19th-century reading room is not open to the public.

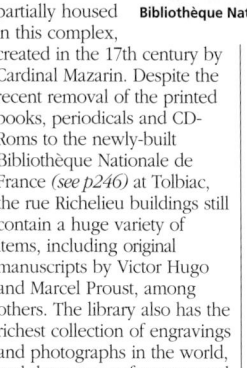

Bibliothèque Nationale

Avenue de l'Opéra ⓬

75001 & 75002. **Map** 6 E5. Ⓜ Opéra, Pyramides.

This broad avenue is a notable example of Baron Haussmann's dramatic modernization of Paris in the 1860s and 1870s (see pp34–5). Much of the medieval city (including a mound from which Joan of Arc began her crusade against the English) was cleared to make way for the wide thoroughfares of today. The Avenue de l'Opéra, running from the Louvre to the Opéra de Paris Garnier, was completed in 1876. The uniformity of the five-storey buildings that line it contrast with those found in nearby streets, which date from the 17th and 18th centuries. Nearby, in the Place Gaillon, is the Café and Restaurant Drouant where the prestigious Goncourt Prize for literature is decided. The avenue is dominated by travel and luxury shops. At No. 27 there is the National Centre for the Visual Arts, which has a false entrance.

Avenue de l'Opéra

MONTMARTRE

Montmartre and art are insep-arable. By the end of the 19th century the area was a mecca for artists, writers, poets and their disciples, who gathered to sample the bor-dellos, cabarets, revues and other exotica which made Montmartre's reputation as a place of depravity in the eyes of the city's more sober up-standing citizens. Many of the artists and writers have long since left the area and the lively night life no longer has the same charm.

But the hill of Montmartre (the Butte) still has its physical charms and the village atmosphere remains

Street theatre in Montmartre

remarkably intact. Mobs of eager tourists ascend the hill, most of them gathering in the most spa-cious parts, particularly where quick portrait artists and sou-venir sellers thrive, as in the old village square, the Place du Tertre. Elsewhere there are tiny, exquisite squares, winding streets, small ter-races, long stairways, plus the Butte's famous vineyard where the few grapes are harvested in an atmosphere of revel-ry in early autumn. And there are spectacular views of the city from various points, most especially from the monumental Sacré-Coeur.

SIGHTS AT A GLANCE

Historic Buildings and Streets
Bateau-Lavoir ⓫
Moulin de la Galette ⓮
Avenue Junot ⓯

Churches
Sacré-Coeur pp224–5 ❶
St-Pierre de Montmartre ❷
Chapelle du Martyre ❽
St-Jean l'Evangéliste de Montmartre ❿

Museums and Galleries
Espace Dalí Montmartre ❹
Musée de Montmartre ❺
La Halle Saint Pierre ❼

Squares
Place du Tertre ❸
Place des Abbesses ❾

Cemeteries
Cimetière de Montmartre ⓭

Theatres and Nightclubs
Au Lapin Agile ❻
Moulin Rouge ⓬

GETTING THERE
This area is served by several metro stations, including Abbesses and Pigalle. The Montmartrobus leaves Pigalle for the village area and bus route 80 passes Montmartre's cemetery. Route 85 passes along Rue de Clignancourt.

KEY

▢	Street-by-Street map
Ⓜ	Metro station
ⓘ	Tourist information

SEE ALSO
- *Street Finder*, map 2, 6, 7
- *Montmartre Walk* pp266–7
- *Where to Stay* p291
- *Restaurants* p312

0 metres   400
0 yards   400

◁ **The narrow Rue St-Rustique winding up the hill to Sacré-Coeur**

Street-by-Street: Montmartre

The steep butte (hill) of Montmartre has been associated with artists for 200 years. Théodore Géricault and Camille Corot came here at the start of the 19th century, and in the 20th century Maurice Utrillo immortalized the streets in his works. Today street painters thrive on a lively tourist trade as travellers flock to this picturesque district which in places still preserves the atmosphere of prewar Paris. The name of the area is ascribed to local martyrs tortured in Paris around AD 250, hence *mons martyrium*.

Streetside painter

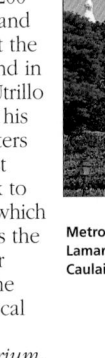

Montmartre vineyard is the last surviving vineyard in Paris. On the first Saturday in October the start of the grape harvest is celebrated.

Metro Lamarck Caulaincourt

RUE SAIVTE ST
RUE DE L'ABREUVOIR
RUE DES
RUE
RUE ST-
RUE
NORVIN
RUE LEPIC
PL. J-B CLEMENT
RUE POULBOT
RUE DE LA MIRE
RAVIGNAN
PL E GOUDEAU
RUE
RUE
RUE
RUE DES TROIS FRERES

★ Au Lapin Agile
Literary meetings have been held in this rustic nightclub ("The Agile Rabbit") since 1910 ❻

A La Mère Catherine was a favourite eating place of Russian Cossacks in 1814. They would bang on the table and shout *"Bistro!"* (Russian for "quick") – hence the bistro was named.

Espace Dalí Montmartre
The exhibition pays homage to the eclectic artist Dalí. Some of the works are on public display for the first time in France ❹

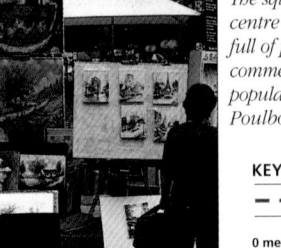

★ Place du Tertre
The square is the tourist centre of Montmartre and is full of portraitists. No. 3 commemorates local children, as popularized in the artist Poulbot's drawings ❸

STAR SIGHTS

★ Au Lapin Agile

★ Place du Tertre

★ Musée de Montmartre

★ Sacré-Coeur

KEY

– – – Suggested route

| 0 metres | 100 |
| 0 yards | 100 |

★ Musée de Montmartre
The museum includes the work of artists who lived in the area: this Portrait of a Woman (1918) is by the Italian painter and sculptor Amedeo Modigliani ❺

LOCATOR MAP
See Central Paris Map pp14–15

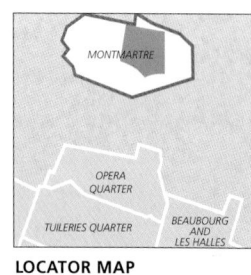

★ Sacré-Coeur
This Romano-Byzantine church, started in the 1870s and completed in 1914, has many treasures, such as this figure of Christ by Eugène Benet (1911) ❶

St-Pierre de Montmartre
This church became the Temple of Reason during the Revolution ❷

The funiculaire, or cable railway, at the end of the Rue Foyatier takes you to the foot of the basilica of the Sacré-Coeur. Metro tickets are valid on it.

Square Willette lies below the forecourt of the Sacré-Coeur. It is laid out on the side of the hill in a series of descending terraces with lawns, shrubs, trees and flowerbeds.

To metro Anvers

La Halle Saint Pierre
The museum hosts exhibitions of Art Brut and Naive Art. This oil painting, L'Opéra de Paris (1986), is by L Milinkov ❼

Montmartre streetside paintings

Sacré-Coeur **①**

See pp226–7.

St-Pierre de Montmartre **②**

2 Rue du Mont-Cenis 75018. **Map** 6
F1. **Tel** 01 46 06 57 63. M
Abbesses. ◯ 8.45am–7pm daily. ✚
frequent. 🎥 ♿ **Concerts**. www.
sacre-coeur-montmartre.com

Situated in the shadow of
Sacré-Coeur, St-Pierre de
Montmartre is one of the
oldest churches in Paris. It is
all that remains of the great
Benedictine Abbey of
Montmartre, founded in 1133
by Louis VI and his wife,
Adelaide of Savoy, who, as its
first abbess, is buried here.

Inside are four marble
columns supposedly from
a Roman temple which
originally stood on the site.
The vaulted choir dates from
the 12th century, the nave
was remodelled in
the 15th century
and the west front
in the 18th. During
the Revolution the
abbess was
guillotined, and
the church fell into
disuse. It was
reconsecrated in
1908. Gothic-style
stained-glass
windows replace
those destroyed by
a bomb in World
War II. The church
also has a tiny
cemetery, which is open to
the public only on 1 November.

Place du Tertre **③**

75018. **Map** 6 F1. M Abbesses.

Tertre means "hillock", or
mound, and this picturesque
square is the highest point in
Paris at some 130 m (430 ft).
It was once the site of the
abbey gallows but is associated with artists, who began
exhibiting paintings here in
the 19th century. It is lined
with colourful restaurants –
La Mère Catherine dates back
to 1793. The house at No. 21
was formerly the home of the
irreverent "Free Commune",
founded in 1920 to perpetuate
the Bohemian spirit of the
area. It is now the site of
the Old Montmartre infor-
mation office.

The Spanish artist Salvador Dalí

Espace Dalí Montmartre **④**

11 Rue Poulbot 75018.
Map 6 F1. **Tel** 01 42
64 40 10. M Abbesses.
◯ 10am–6pm daily.
🎥 📷 groups by appt.
www.daliparis.com

A permanent exhi-
bition of 330 works
of the painter and
sculptor Salvador
Dalí is on display
here at the heart of
Montmartre. Inside,
the vast, dark
setting reflects the
dramatic character of this
20th-century genius as

Doors to St-Pierre church

moving lights grace first one,
then another, of his Surrealist
works. This in turn is
counterpointed with the
rhythm of Dalí's recorded
voice. There is an art gallery
as well as a library housed
in this original museum.

Musée de Montmartre **⑤**

12 Rue Cortot 75018. **Map** 2 F5.
Tel 01 49 25 89 37. M Abbesses,
Anvers, Blanche, Lamarck-Caulaincourt.
◯ 10am–6pm Tue–Sun. 🎥 📷 ♿
www.museedemontmartre.fr

During the 17th century this
charming home belonged to
the actor Roze de Rosimond
(Claude de la Rose), a member
of Molière's theatre company
who, like his mentor Molière,
died during a performance of
Molière's play *Le Malade
Imaginaire*. From 1875 the
big white house, undoubtedly
the finest in Montmartre,
provided living and studio
space for numerous artists,
including Maurice Utrillo and
his mother, Suzanne Valadon,
a former acrobat and model
who became a talented
painter, as well as Raoul Dufy
and Pierre-Auguste Renoir.

The museum recounts the
history of Montmartre from
the days of the abbesses to
the present, through artefacts,
documents, drawings and
photographs. It is particularly
rich in memorabilia of
Bohemian life, and even has
a reconstruction of the Café
de l'Abreuvoir, Utrillo's
favourite watering hole.

Café de l'Abreuvoir reconstructed

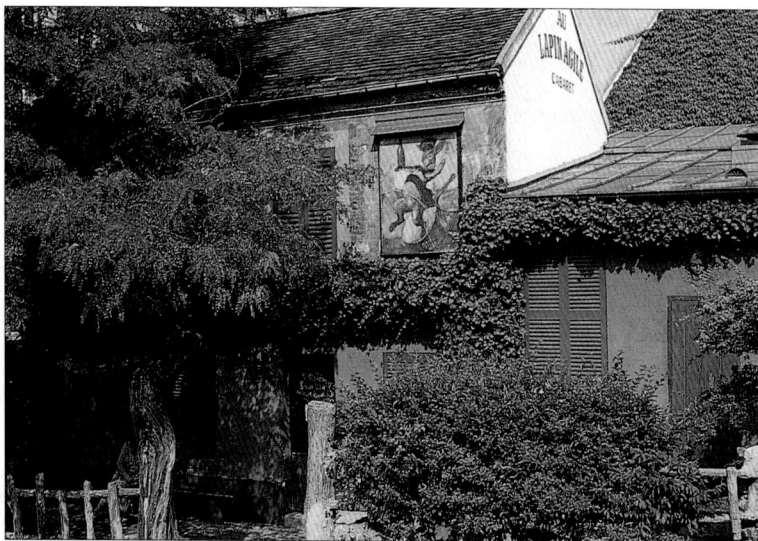

The deceptively rustic exterior of Au Lapin Agile, one of the best-known nightspots in Paris

Au Lapin Agile 6

22 Rue des Saules 75018. **Map** 2 F5. **Tel** 01 46 06 85 87. Lamarck-Caulaincourt. ◯ 9pm–2am Tue–Sun. See **Entertainment** pp342–3. **www**.au-lapin-agile.com

The former Cabaret des Assassins derived its current name from a sign painted by the humorist André Gill. His picture of a rabbit escaping from a pot (Le Lapin à Gill) became known as the nimble rabbit (Lapin Agile). The club enjoyed popularity with intellectuals and artists at the start of the 20th century. Here in 1911 the novelist Roland Dorgelès' hatred for modern art, as practised by Picasso and the other painters at the "Bateau-Lavoir" (No. 13 Place Emile-Goudeau), led him to play an illuminating practical joke on one of the customers, Guillaume Apollinaire, who was a poet, art critic and passionate champion of Cubism. He tied a paintbrush to the tail of the café-owner's donkey, and the resulting daub was shown at a Salon des Indépendents exhibition under the enlightening title Sunset over the Adriatic.

In 1903 the premises were bought by the cabaret entrepreneur Aristide Bruand (painted in a series of posters by Toulouse-Lautrec). Today it manages to retain much of its original atmosphere.

Halle Saint Pierre 7

Halle St-Pierre, 2 Rue Ronsard 75018. **Map** 7 A1. **Tel** 01 42 58 72 89. Anvers. ◯ 10am–6pm daily. **www**.hallesaintpierre.org

In 1945 the French painter Jean Dubuffet developed the concept of Art Brut (Outsider or Marginal Art) to describe works created outside the boundaries of "official" culture, often by insane asylum inmates or the mentally handicapped. The Halle Saint Pierre, at the foot of the Butte, is a museum and gallery devoted to these "raw"

Art Brut at Halle Saint Pierre

art forms. It also hosts avant-garde theatre and musical productions, holds regular literary evenings and debates and runs children's workshops. The permanent collection includes a compilation of Naive art (works by self-taught artists) collected by the publisher Max Fourny in the 1970s. There is also a specialised bookshop and café.

Chapelle du Martyre 8

9 Rue Yvonne-Le-Tac 75018. **Map** 6 F1. Pigalle. ◯ 10am–noon, 3pm–5pm Fri–Wed.

This 19th-century chapel stands on the site of a medieval convent's chapel, which was said to mark the place where the early Christian martyr and first bishop of Paris, Saint Denis, was beheaded by the Romans in AD 250. It remained a major pilgrimage site throughout the Middle Ages. In the crypt of the original chapel in 1534 Ignatius de Loyola, founder of the Society of Jesus (the mighty Jesuit order designed to save the Catholic Church from the onslaught of the Protestant Reformation), took his Jesuit vows with six companions.

Sacré-Coeur ❶

South-east rose window (1960)

At the outbreak of the Franco Prussian War in 1870, two Catholic businessmen made a private religious vow. It was to build a church dedicated to the Sacred Heart of Christ should France be spared the impending Prussian onslaught. The two men, Alexandre Legentil and Hubert Rohault de Fleury, lived to see Paris saved from invasion despite the war and a lengthy siege – and the start of what is the Sacré-Coeur basilica. The project was taken up by Archbishop Guibert of Paris. Work began in 1875 to Paul Abadie's designs. They were inspired by the Romano-Byzantine church of St-Front in Périgueux. The basilica was completed in 1914, but the German invasion forestalled its consecration until 1919, when France was victorious.

The Facade
The best view of the domed and turreted Sacré-Coeur is from the gardens below.

The belltower (1895) is 83 m (252 ft) high and contains one of the heaviest bells in the world. The bell itself weighs 18.5 tonnes and the clapper 850 kg (1,900 lb).

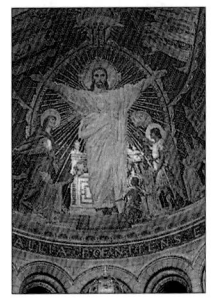

★ **Great Mosaic of Christ**
The colossal mosaic (1912–22) dominating the chancel vault was designed by Luc Olivier Merson and Marcel Magne.

Virgin Mary and Child (1896)
This Renaissance-style silver statue is one of two in the ambulatory by P Brunet.

THE SIEGE OF PARIS

Prussia invaded France in 1870. During the four-month siege of Paris, instigated by the Prusso-German statesman Otto von Bismarck, Parisians became so hungry that they ate all the animals in the city.

★ **Crypt Vaults**
A chapel in the basilica's crypt contains Legentil's heart in a stone urn.

STAR FEATURES

★ Great Mosaic of Christ

★ Bronze Doors

★ Ovoid Dome

★ Crypt Vaults

VISITORS' CHECKLIST

Place du Parvis de Notre Dame 75018. **Map** 6 F1.
Tel 01 53 41 89 00.
Ⓜ Abbesses (then take the funiculaire to the steps of the Sacré-Coeur), Anvers, Barbès-Rochechouart, Lamarck-Caulaincourt.
🚌 30, 54, 80, 85.
Ⓟ Blvd de Clichy, Rue Custine.
Basilica ⏰ 6am–8.30pm daily.
Dome and crypt ⏰ 9am–6pm daily. 🎟 **for crypt and dome**.
✝ 7am, 11.15am, 6.30pm, 10pm Mon–Thu; 3pm Fri; 10pm Sat; 11am, 6pm, 10pm Sun.
🚫 ♿ restricted. 🚻
www.sacre-coeur-montmartre.com

★ **Ovoid Dome**
This is the second-highest point in Paris, after the Eiffel Tower.

Spiral staircase

The inner structure supporting the dome is made from stone.

The stained-glass gallery affords a view of the whole of the interior.

Statue of Christ
The basilica's most important statue is symbolically placed above the two bronze saints.

Equestrian Statues
The statue of Joan of Arc is one of a pair by H Lefebvre. The other is of Saint Louis.

★ **Bronze Doors**
Relief sculptures on the doors in the portico entrance illustrate scenes from the life of Christ, such as the Last Supper.

Main entrance

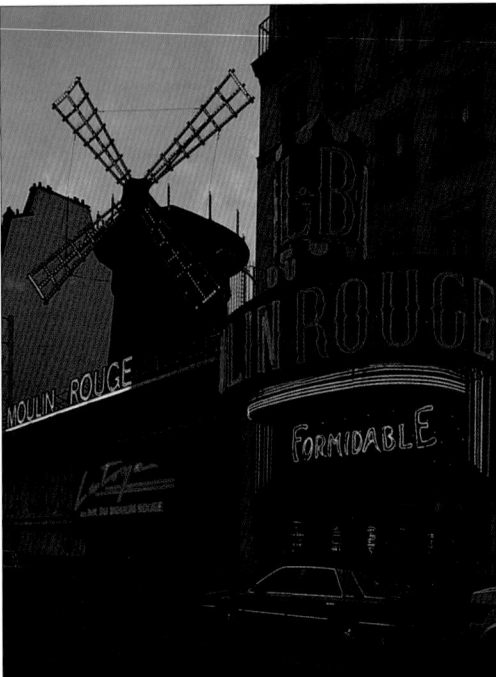

The famous silhouette of the Moulin Rouge nightclub

Place des Abbesses **⑨**

75018. **Map** 6 F1. **M** Abbesses.

This is one of Paris's most picturesque squares. It is sandwiched between the rather dubious attractions of the Place Pigalle with its strip clubs and the Place du Tertre which is mobbed with hundreds of tourists. Be sure not to miss the Abbesses metro station with its unusual green wrought-iron arches

Entrance to the Abbesses metro

and amber lights. Designed by the architect Hector Guimard, it is one of the few original Art Nouveau stations.

St-Jean l'Evangéliste de Montmartre **⑩**

19 Rue des Abbesses 75018. **Map** 6 F1. **Tel** 01 46 06 43 96. **M** Abbesses. 🚪 9am–noon, 3pm–7pm Mon–Sat; 2pm–7pm Sun. 🕆 frequent. 📷 ✔ once a month.

Designed by Anatole de Baudot and completed in 1904, this church was the first to be built from reinforced concrete. The flower motifs on the interior are typical of Art Nouveau, while its interlocking arches suggest Islamic architecture. The red-brick facing has earned it the nickname St-Jean-des-Briques.

Detail of St-Jean l'Evangéliste facade

Bateau-Lavoir **⑪**

13 Pl Emile-Goudeau 75018. **Map** 6 F1. **M** Abbesses. ⬤ to public.

This artistic and literary mecca was an old piano factory. Its name comes from its resemblance to the laundry boats that used to travel along the River Seine. Between 1890 and 1920 it was home to some of the most talented artists and poets of the day. They lived in squalid conditions with only one tap and took it in turns to sleep in the beds. The artists Picasso, Van Dongen, Marie Laurencin, Juan Gris and Modigliani were just a few of the residents. It was here that Picasso painted *Les Demoiselles d'Avignon* in 1907, usually regarded as the painting that inspired Cubism. The shabby building burned down in 1970, but a concrete replica has been built – with studio space for up-and-coming artists.

Moulin Rouge **⑫**

82 Blvd de Clichy 75018. **Map** 6 E1. **Tel** 01 53 09 82 82. **M** Blanche. 🚪 Dinner: 7pm; shows: 9pm and 11pm daily. 🎞 See **Entertainment** pp343–4. **www**.moulinrouge.com

Built in 1885, the Moulin Rouge was turned into a dance hall as early as 1900. The cancan originated in Montparnasse, in the polka gardens of the Rue de la Grande-Chaumière, but it will always be associated with the Moulin Rouge where the wild and colourful dance shows were immortalized in the posters and drawings of Henri de Toulouse-Lautrec. The high-kicking routines of famous Dorriss dancers such as Yvette Guilbert and Jane Avril continue today in a glittering, Las Vegas-style revue that includes computerized lights and displays of magic.

Vaslav Nijinsky lies in Montmartre

Cimetière de Montmartre ⑬

20 Ave Rachel 75018. **Map** 2 D5. **Tel** 01 53 42 36 30. Ⓜ *Place de Clichy, Blanche.* ◯ *8am–5.30pm daily (opens 8.30am Sat, 9am Sun; closes 6pm daily in summer).* ♿

This has been the resting place for many artistic luminaries since the beginning of the 19th century. The composers Hector Berlioz and Jacques Offenbach (who wrote the famous cancan tune) are buried here, alongside many other celebrities such as La Goulue (stage name of Louise Weber, the high-kicking *danceuse* who was the cancan's first star performer and Toulouse-Lautrec's model), the painter Edgar Degas, writer Alexandre Dumas *fils*, German poet Heinrich Heine, Russian dancer Vaslav Nijinsky, and film director François Truffaut. It's an evocative, atmospheric

place, conveying some of the heated energy and artistic creativity of Montmartre a century ago.

Nearby, close to Square Roland Dorgelès, there is another, smaller, often overlooked Montmartre cemetery – **Cimetière St-Vincent.** Here lie more of the great artistic names of the district, including the Swiss composer Arthur Honegger and the writer Marcel Aymé. Most notable of all at St-Vincent is the grave of the great French painter Maurice Utrillo, the quintessential Montmartre artist, many of whose works are now some of the most enduring images of the area.

Moulin de la Galette ⑭

T-junction at Rue Tholoze and Rue Lepic 75018. **Map** 2 E5. **Tel** 01 46 06 84 77. Ⓜ *Lamarck-Caulaincourt.*

Once more than 30 windmills dotted the Montmartre skyline and were used for grinding wheat and pressing grapes. Now only two remain: the Moulin du Radet, which stands further along the Rue Lepic, and the rebuilt Moulin de la Galette, now converted into a decent restaurant. The latter was built in 1622 and is also known as the Blute-fin; one of its mill owners, Debray, was supposedly crucified on the windmill's sails during the 1814 Siege of Paris. He had been trying to repulse the invading Cossacks. At the end

of the 19th century the mill became a famous dance hall and provided inspiration for many artists, notably Pierre-Auguste Renoir and Vincent Van Gogh.

The steep Rue Lepic is a busy shopping area with a good market *(see p339)*. The Impressionist painter Armand Guillaumin once lived on the first floor of No. 54, and Van Gogh inhabited its third floor.

Moulin de la Galette

Avenue Junot ⑮

75018. **Map** 2 E5. Ⓜ *Lamarck-Caulaincourt.*

Opened in 1910, this broad, peaceful street includes many painters' studios and family houses. No. 13 has mosaics designed by its former resident illustrator Francisque Poulbot, famous for his drawings of urchins. He is credited with having invented a bar billiards game. At No. 15 is Maison Tristan Tzara, named after its previous owner, the Romanian Dadaist poet. Its eccentric design by the Austrian architect Adolf Loos aimed to complement the poet's character. No. 23 bis is the Villa Léandre, a group of perfect Art Deco houses.

Just off the Avenue Junot up the steps of the Allée des Brouillards is an 18th-century architectural folly, the Château des Brouillards. In the 19th century it was the home of the French symbolist writer Gérard de Nerval, who committed suicide in 1855.

Sacré-Coeur, Montmartre, **by Maurice Utrillo**

FURTHER AFIELD

Many of the great châteaux outside Paris originally built as country retreats for the aristocracy and post-revolutionary bourgeoisie are now preserved as museums. Versailles is one of the finest, but if your tastes are Modernist, there's also Le Corbusier architecture to see. There are two theme parks – Disneyland Resort Paris and Parc de la Villette – to amuse adults and children alike, and excellent parks to relax in when the bustle of the city gets too much.

SIGHTS AT A GLANCE

Museums and Galleries
Musée Nissim de Camondo ❸
Musée Cernuschi ❹
Musée Gustave Moreau ❺
Musée Edith Piaf ⓬
Musée Marmottan-Claude Monet ㉙
Musée des Années 30 ㉛
Palais de la Porte Dorée ⓰

Churches
St-Alexandre-Nevsky Cathedral ❶
Basilique Saint-Denis ❼
Notre-Dame du Travail ㉓

Historic Buildings and Streets
Bercy ⓲
Bibliothèque Nationale de France ⓳
13th Arrondissement ⓴
Cité Universitaire ㉒
Institut Pasteur ㉔
Versailles pp248–53 ㉖
Rue de la Fontaine ㉗
Fondation Le Corbusier ㉘
La Défense ㉜
Château de Malmaison ㉝

Markets
Marché aux Puces de St-Ouen ❻
Portes St-Denis et St-Martin ❽
Marché d'Aligre ⓯

Parks, Gardens and Canals
Parc Monceau ❷
Canal St-Martin ❾
Parc des Buttes-Chaumont ❿
Château et Bois de Vincennes ⓱
Parc Montsouris ㉑
Parc André Citroën ㉕
Bois de Boulogne ㉚

Cemeteries
Cimetière du Père Lachaise pp240–41 ⓭

Theme Parks
Parc de la Villette pp236–9 ⓫
Disneyland Resort Paris pp242–5 ⓮

GREATER PARIS

KEY

▨ Main sightseeing areas

═ Major roads

0 kilometres   5

0 miles   3

SIGHTS OUTSIDE THE CENTRE

◁ **A landscaped island in the Bois de Boulogne**

North of the City

St-Alexandre-Nevsky Cathedral

St-Alexandre-Nevsky Cathedral ❶

12 Rue Daru 75008. **Map** 4 F3.
Tel 01 42 27 37 34. Ⓜ Courcelles.
⬜ 3pm–5pm Tue, Fri, Sun.
✝ 6pm Sat, 10.30am Sun. ✗ ⬜

This imposing Russian Orthodox cathedral with its five golden-copper domes signals the presence of a large Russian community in Paris. Designed by members of the St Petersburg Fine Arts Academy and financed jointly by Tzar Alexander II and the local Russian community, the cathedral was completed in 1861. Inside, a wall of icons divides the church in two. The Greek-cross plan and the rich interior mosaics and frescoes are Neo-Byzantine in style,

while the exterior and gilt domes are traditional Russian Orthodox in design.

The Russian population in the city increased dramatically following the Bolshevik Revolution of 1917, when thousands of Russians fled to Paris for safety. The Rue Daru, in which the cathedral stands, and the surrounding area form "Little Russia", with its Russian schools and the many dance academies, and delightful tea shops and bookshops where visitors can browse.

Parc Monceau ❷

Blvd de Courcelles 75017. **Map** 5 A3.
Tel 01 42 27 08 64. Ⓜ Monceau.
⬜ 7am–8pm daily (to 10pm summer).
See **Eight Guided Walks** pp258–9.

This green haven dates back to 1778 when the Duc de Chartres (later Duc d'Orléans) commissioned the painter-writer and amateur landscape designer Louis Carmontelle to create a magnificent garden. Also a theatre designer, Carmontelle created a "garden of dreams", an exotic landscape full of architectural follies in imitation of English and German fashion of the time. In 1783 the Scottish landscape gardener Thomas Blaikie laid out an area of the garden in English style. The park was the scene of the first recorded parachute landing, made by André-Jacques Garnerin on 22 October 1797. Over the years

the park changed hands and in 1852 it was acquired by the state and half the land sold off for property development. The remaining 9 ha (22 acres) were made into public gardens. These were restored and new buildings erected by Adolphe Alphand, architect of the Bois de Boulogne and the Bois de Vincennes.

Today the park remains one of the most chic in the capital but has unfortunately lost many of its early features. A *naumachia* basin flanked by Corinthian columns remains. This is an ornamental version of a Roman pool used for simulating naval battles. There are also a Renaissance arcade, pyramids, a river and the Pavillon de Chartres, a charming rotunda designed by Nicolas Ledoux which was once used as a tollhouse. Just south of here is a huge red pagoda, which now houses a gallery devoted to Asian art.

Musée Nissim de Camondo ❸

63 Rue de Monceau 75008.
Map 5 A3. ☎ 01 53 89 06 40. Ⓜ Monceau, Villiers. ⬜ 10am–5.30pm Wed–Sun (last adm: 4.30pm).
⬤ public hols. ✗ ⬜ 11am Sun (01 44 55 59 26; Oct–May). ⬤
www.lesartsdecoratifs.fr

Comte Moïse de Camondo, a leading Jewish financier, commissioned this mansion in 1914 to be designed in the style of the Petit Trianon, at Versailles (*see pp248–9*), to house a rare collection of 18th-century furniture, tapestries, paintings and other precious objects. The museum has been faithfully and lovingly restored to recreate an aristocratic town house of the Louis XV and XVI eras. In the museum there are Savonnerie carpets, Beauvais tapestries and the Buffon service

Colonnade beside the *naumachia* basin in Parc Monceau

(Sèvres porcelain). The very latest gadgets, for the period, are now displayed in the restored kitchen and service quarters, equipped with the utmost efficiency, taste and forethought by their owner.

Musée Nissim de Camondo

Musée Cernuschi ❹

7 Ave Vélasquez 75008. **Map** 5 A3. *Tel 01 53 96 21 50.* Ⓜ *Villiers, Monceau.* ◻ *10am–6pm Tue–Sun.* ◕ *public hols.* ⓪ ⑫ ⓓ **www**.cernuschi.paris.fr

This mansion near Parc Monceau contains an intriguing private collection of late East Asian art which was amassed by the Milanese-born politician and banker Enrico Cernuschi (1821–96). The original bequest of 5,000 lacquered, ceramic, bronze and ivory items has been augmented by donations and acquisitions over the years. The wide-ranging collection, now about ten thousand items, includes a 5th-century seated Bodhisattva (Buddhist divine being) from Yunkang; *La Tigresse* (a 12th-century BC bronze vase); and *Horses and Grooms*, an 8th-century T'ang painting on silk attributed to the era's greatest horse painter, court artist Han Kan.

Bodhisattva in the Musée Cernuschi

Musée Gustave Moreau ❺

14 Rue de la Rochefoucauld 75009. **Map** 6 E3. *Tel 01 48 74 38 50.* Ⓜ *Trinité.* ◻ *10am–12.45pm, 2–5.15pm Wed–Mon.* ● *1 Jan, 1 May, 25 Dec.* ⓐ ⓞ ⓓ **www**.musee-moreau.fr

The symbolist painter Gustave Moreau (1825–98), known for his vivid, imaginative works depicting biblical and mythological fantasies, left to the French state a vast collection of more than 1,000 oils, watercolours and some 7,000 drawings in his town house. One of Moreau's best-known and most outstanding works, *Jupiter and Semele*, can be seen here. There is also a superb collection of his unfinished sketches.

Marché aux Puces du St-Ouen, a large antique market

Marché aux Puces de St-Ouen ❻

Rue des Rosiers, St-Ouen 75018. **Map** 2 F2. Ⓜ *Porte-de-Clignancourt.* ◻ *9am–6pm Sat–Mon. See* **Markets** *p335.* **www**.lespuces.com

This is the oldest and largest of the Paris flea markets, covering 6 ha (15 acres). In the 19th century, rag merchants and tramps would gather outside the city limits and offer their wares for sale. By the 1920s there was a proper market here, where masterpieces could sometimes be purchased cheaply

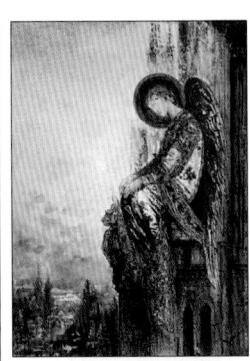

***Angel Traveller* by Gustave Moreau, in the Musée Gustave Moreau**

from the then-unknowing sellers. Today it is divided into specialist markets. Known especially for its profusion of furniture and ornaments from the Second Empire (1852–70), few bargains are to be found these days, yet some 150,000 bargain-hunters, tourists and dealers still flock here to browse among more than 2,000 stalls *(see p339).*

Basilique Saint-Denis ❼

2 Rue de Strasbourg, 93200 St-Denis. *Tel 01 48 09 83 54.* Ⓜ *St-Denis-Basilique.* Ⓡ *St-Denis.* ◻ *Apr–Sep: 10am–6.15pm Mon–Sat, noon–6.15pm Sun; Oct–Mar: 10am–5.15pm Mon–Sat, noon–5.15pm Sun (last adm: 15 mins before closing).* ✝ *8.30am, 10am Sun.* ⓐ ⓞ ⓒ ⓓ

Constructed between 1137 and 1281, the Basilica is on the site of the tomb of St Denis, the first bishop of Paris, who was beheaded in Montmartre in AD 250. The building was the original influence for Gothic art. From Merovingian times it was a burial place for rulers of France. During the Revolution many tombs were desecrated and scattered, but the best were stored, and now represent a collection of funerary art. Memorials include those of Dagobert (died 638), Henri II (died 1559) and Catherine de' Medici (died 1589), and Louis XVI and Marie-Antoinette (died 1793).

Western arch of the Porte St-Denis, once the entrance to the city

Portes St-Denis et St-Martin **8**

Blvds St-Denis & St-Martin 75010.
Map 7 B5. **M** St-Martin, Strasbourg-St-Denis.

These gates give access to the two ancient and important north–south thoroughfares whose names they bear. They once marked the entrance to the city. The Porte St-Denis is 23 m (76 ft) high and was built in 1672 by François Blondel. It is decorated with figures by Louis XIV's sculptor, François Girardon. They commemorate victories of the king's armies in Flanders and the Rhine that year. Porte St-Martin is 17 m (56 ft) tall and was built in 1674 by Pierre Bullet. It celebrates Besançon's capture and the defeat of the Triple Alliance of Spain, Holland and Germany.

Boats berthed at Port de l'Arsenal

East of the City

Canal St-Martin **9**

Map 8 E2. **M** Jaurès, J Bonsergent, Goncourt. See pp260–61.

The 5-kilometre (3-mile) canal, opened in 1825, provides a short-cut for river traffic between loops of the Seine. It has long been loved by novelists, film directors and tourists alike. It is dotted with barges and pleasure boats that leave from the Port de l'Arsenal. At the north end of the canal is the Bassin de la Villette waterway and the elegant Neo-Classical Rotonde de la Villette, spectacularly floodlit at night.

Parc des Buttes-Chaumont **10**

Rue Manin 75019 (main access from Rue Armand Carrel). **M** Botzaris, Buttes-Chaumont. ◯ 7am–8.15pm daily (1 Jun–15 Aug: to 10.15pm; May, 16 Aug–30 Sep: to 9.15pm) . **11** See pp268–9.

For many this is the most pleasant and unexpected park in Paris. The panoramic hilly site was converted in the 1860s by Baron Haussmann from a rubbish dump and quarry with a gallows below.

Haussmann worked with the landscape architect/designer Adolphe Alphand, who organized a vast programme to furnish the new pavement-lined avenues with benches and lampposts. Others involved in the creation of this park were the engineer Darcel and the landscape gardener Barillet-Deschamps. They created a lake, made an island with real and artificial rocks, gave it a Roman-style temple and added a waterfall, streams, footbridges leading to the island and beaches. Today visitors will also find boating facilities and donkey rides.

Parc de la Villette **11**

See pp234–9.

Musée Edith Piaf **12**

5 Rue Crespin du Gast 75011. *Tel* 01 43 55 52 72. **M** Ménilmontant. ◯ 1–6pm Mon–Wed, 10am–noon Thu (last adm: 30 mins before closing time), by appointment only. ● public hols. 🎦 🚫 🎦 🛗

Edith Piaf – "the little sparrow" (1915–63)

Born Edith Gassion in the working-class east end of Paris in 1915, Edith Piaf took her stage name from her nickname meaning "the little sparrow". She started her career as a torch singer in local cafés and bars before becoming an international star in the late 1930s.

She never lived at the address of this museum, which was founded in 1967 by an association of fans, Les Amis d'Edith Piaf. Since then, they have collected a host of

memorabilia and squeezed it
into this small apartment.
It contains many photographs
and portraits, lithographs by
Charles Kiffer, intimate letters,
clothes and books – gifts
from Piaf's parents-in-law or
bequests from other singers.
Records by the singer, who
died in 1963 and lies in Père
Lachaise cemetery *(see
pp240–41)*, are played in the
museum on request (visits are
by appointment only).

Cimetière du Père Lachaise ⑬

See pp240–41.

Disneyland Paris ⑭

See pp242–5.

Marché d'Aligre ⑮

Place d'Aligre 75012. **Map** 14 F5. Ⓜ
Ledru-Rollin. ⬜ 9am–1pm, 4–
7.30pm Tue–Fri; 9am–1pm, 3.30–
7.30pm Sat; 9am–1.30pm Sun.

On Sunday mornings this
lively market offers one of
the most colourful sights in
Paris. French, Arab and
African traders hawk fruit,
vegetables, flowers and
clothing on the streets, while
the adjoining covered market,
the Beauveau St-Antoine,
offers meats, cheeses, pâtés
and many intriguing
international delicacies.
  Aligre is where old and new
Paris meet. Here the established
community of this old artisan

Exterior relief on Palais de la Porte Dorée

The imposing Château de Vincennes

quarter coexists with a more
recently established group of
up-and-coming young people,
lured here by the recent
transformation of the nearby
Bastille area *(see p98)*.

Palais de la Porte Dorée ⑯

293 Ave Daumesnil 75012. **Tel** 01 53
59 58 60. Ⓜ Porte Dorée. ⬜ 10am–
6pm Wed–Mon. 🅿 🅰 restricted.
🖥 www.palais-portedoree.org

This museum and aquarium
is housed in a beautiful Art
Deco building that was
designed especially for the
1931 Colonial Exhibition. The
impressive facade has a vast
frieze by A Janniot, depicting
the contributions of France's
overseas territories.
  Formerly the home of
the Musée National des
Arts d'Afrique et d'Océanie
(whose collection has now
been moved to the Musée
du Quai Branly, *see pp192–3*),
the Palais de la Porte Dorée
now houses the Cité
Nationale de l'Histoire de
l'Immigration. This acts as
both a museum and a cultural
centre, with regular live
performances and films on
the subject of immigration.
  The magnificent 1930s
Hall d'Honneur and the
Salle des Fêtes (ballroom)
are also open to the public.
In the basement there is a
magnificent tropical aquarium
filled with colourful fish, as
well as terrariums containing
tortoises and crocodiles.

Château et Bois de Vincennes ⑰

Ⓜ Château de Vincennes. ⓇⒺⓇ
Vincennes. **Château** Ave de Paris
94300 Vincennes. **Tel** 01 48 08 31
20. ⬜ 10am–noon, 1–5pm (to 6pm
May–Aug) daily (various options are
available for guided visits. Call for
details). ⬤ public hols. 📷 📷 📷
compulsory in keep & chapel. 🅿
Bois de Vincennes ⬜ dawn to
dusk daily. **www**.chateau-vincennes.fr

The Château de Vincennes,
enclosed by a defensive wall
and a moat, was once a royal
residence. It was here that
Henry V of England died
painfully of dysentery in 1422.
His body was boiled in the
Château's kitchen to prepare
it for shipping back to
England. Abandoned when
Versailles was completed, the
château was converted into
an arsenal by Napoleon.
  The 14th-century keep and
donjon (the tallest in Europe)
is a fine example of medieval
military architecture and
houses the Château's museum.
The Gothic chapel was finished
around 1550, with beautiful
stone rose windows and a
magnificent single aisle. Two
17th-century pavilions house
a museum of army insignia.
  Once a royal hunting
ground, the forest of
Vincennes was given to the
City of Paris by Napoleon III
in 1860. Baron Haussman's
landscape architect added
ornamental lakes and
cascades. Among its main
attractions is the largest
funfair in France (from Palm
Sunday to end of May).

Parc de la Villette ⓫

The old slaughterhouses and livestock market of Paris have been transformed into this Bernard Tschumi-designed urban park. Its vast facilities stretch across 55 ha (136 acres) of a previously run-down part of the city. The plan is to revive the tradition of parks for meetings and activities and to stimulate interest in the arts and sciences. Work began in 1984, and the park has grown to include a science museum, a concert hall, an exhibition pavilion, a spherical cinema, a circus and a music centre. Linking them all is the park itself, with its *folies*, walkways, gardens and playgrounds. In the summer the park holds an open-air film festival.

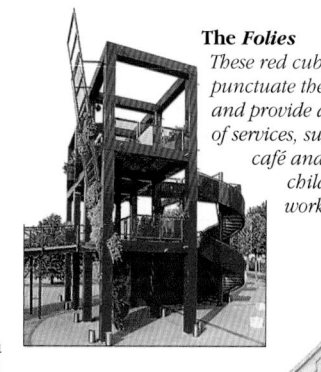

The *Folies*
These red cubes punctuate the park and provide a variety of services, such as a café and a children's workshop.

Children's Playground
A dragon slide, sand pits and colourful play equipment in a maze-like setting make the playground a paradise for young children.

★ Grande Halle
The old cattle hall has been transformed into a flexible exhibition space with mobile floors and auditorium.

Entrance

STAR BUILDINGS

★ Cité des Sciences et de l'Industrie

★ Grande Halle

★ Cité de la Musique

★ Zénith Theatre

★ Cité de la Musique
This quirky but elegant all-white complex holds the music conservatory, a concert hall, library, studios and a museum.

Maison de la Villette regularly holds shows and exhibitions.

Entrance

★ **Cité des Sciences et de l'Industrie**
This huge science museum boasts the latest in futurist equipment and has dazzling hands-on displays (see pp236–9).

La Géode
The cinema's gigantic 180° movie screen combines visual and sound effects to create fantastic experiences, such as the sense of travelling in space.

★ **Zénith Theatre**
This vast polyester tent was built as a venue for pop concerts with a capacity to seat more than 6,000 spectators.

Musicians from Guadeloupe performing outside the Museum

L'Argonaute
The exhibit consists of a 1950s submarine and a nearby navigation museum.

LE MUSEE DE LA MUSIQUE

This museum brings together a collection of over 4,500 instruments, objects, tools and works of art covering the history of music since the Renaissance. The permanent collection of over 900 items is displayed chronologically and can be traced using infrared audio headphones.

Cité des Sciences et de l'Industrie

This hugely popular science and technology museum occupies the largest of the old Villette slaughterhouses, which now form part of a massive urban park. Architect Adrien Fainsilber has created an imaginative interplay of light, vegetation and water in the high-tech, five-storey building, which soars 40 m (133 ft) high, stretching over 3 ha (7 acres). At the museum's heart is the Explora exhibit, a fascinating guide to the worlds of science and technology. Visitors can take part in computerized games on space, the earth and ocean, computers and sound. On other levels there are a children's science city, cinemas, a science newsroom, a library and shops.

A young visitor at La Villette

Planetarium
In this 260-seat auditorium, you can watch eclipses and fly over Martian landscapes, thanks to their "Allsky" video system.

Le Nautile
This full-scale model of the Nautile, France's technologically advanced exploration submarine, represents one of the most sophisticated machines in the world.

★ **Ariane**
Rocket displays explain how astronauts are sent into space, and include an example of the European rocket Ariane.

400-seat auditorium

Hemispheric screen

Main lobby

LA GÉODE
This giant entertainment sphere houses a huge hemispherical cinema screen, 1,000 sq m (11,000 sq ft), showing IMAX films on nature, travel and space.

The moat was designed by Fainsilber so that natural light could penetrate into the lower levels of the building.

The main hall is vast, with a soaring network of shafts, bridges, escalators and balconies, and has a cathedral-like atmosphere.

STAR EXHIBITS

- ★ Children's City
- ★ Ariane
- ★ La Géode

VISITORS' CHECKLIST

30 av Corentin-Cariou 75019.
01 40 05 80 00. M Porte
de la Villette. 75, 151, PC2,
PC3. 10am–6pm Tue–Sat
(7pm Sun). Shows, films, videos,
library, conference centre.
www.cite-sciences.fr

Cupolas
*The two glazed domes,
17 m (56 ft) in diameter,
filter the flow of natural
light into the main hall.*

The greenhouse is a
square hothouse, 32 m
(105 ft) high and wide,
linking the park to the
building.

Mirage Aircraft
*A full-size model of the
French-built jet fighter is one
of the exhibits illustrating
advances in technology.*

To La Géode

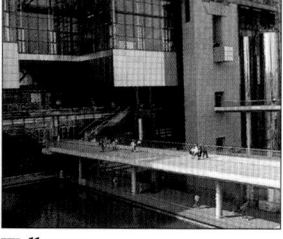

Walkways
*The walkways cross the
encircling moat to link the
various floors of the museum
to the Géode and the park.*

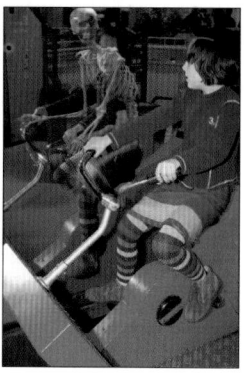

★ Children's City
*In this lively, extensive
area children can
experiment and play
with machines that
show how scientific
principles work.*

Cimetière du Père Lachaise ⑬

Paris's most prestigious cemetery is set on a wooded hill overlooking the city. The land was once owned by Père de la Chaise, Louis XIV's confessor, but it was bought by order of Napoleon in 1803 to create a new cemetery. The cemetery became so popular with the Paris bourgeoisie that it was expanded six times during the century. Here were buried celebrities such as the writer Honoré de Balzac and the composer Frédéric Chopin, and more recently, the singer Jim Morrison and the actor Yves Montand. Famous graves and striking funerary sculpture make this a pleasant place for a leisurely, nostalgic stroll.

The Columbarium was built at the end of the 19th century. The American dancer Isadora Duncan is one of the many celebrities whose ashes are housed here.

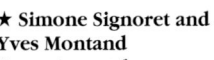

Marcel Proust
Proust brilliantly chronicled the Belle Epoque in his novel Remembrance of Things Past.

★ **Simone Signoret and Yves Montand**
France's most famous post-war cinema couple were renowned for their left-wing views and long turbulent relationship.

Allan Kardec was the founder of a 19th-century spiritual cult, which still has a strong following. His tomb is forever covered in pilgrims' flowers.

Sarah Bernhardt
The great French tragedienne, who died in 1923 aged 78, was famous for her portrayal of Racine heroines.

Monument aux Morts
by Paul Albert Bartholomé is one of the best monumental sculptures in the cemetery. It dominates the central avenue.

STAR FEATURES

★ Oscar Wilde

★ Jim Morrison

★ Edith Piaf

★ Simone Signoret and Yves Montand

Entrance

Frédéric Chopin, the great Polish composer, belonged to the French Romantic generation.

Théodore Géricault
The French Romantic painter's masterpiece, The Raft of Medusa *(see p124), is depicted on his tomb.*

★ Oscar Wilde
*The Irish dramatist, aesthete
and great wit was cast away
from virtuous Britain to die
of drink and dissipation in
Paris in 1900. Jacob Epstein
sculpted the monument.*

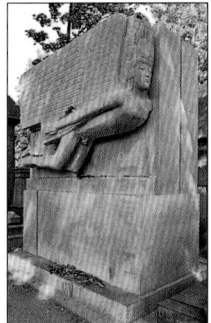

The remains of Molière, the
great 17th-century actor and
dramatist, were transferred
here in 1817 to add historic
glamour to the new cemetery.

VISITORS' CHECKLIST

16 Rue du Repos. *Tel* 01 55
25 82 10. **M** Père Lachaise,
Alexandre Dumas. **🚌** 60, 69, 26
to Pl Gambetta. **P** Pl Gambetta.
🕐 8am–5.30pm daily (from
8.30am Sat, 9am Sun; mid-Mar–
early Nov: to 6pm). **◙ ✓ ℹ**

Mur des Fédérés is the wall against
which the last Communard rebels
were shot by government forces in
1871. It is now a place of pilgrimage
for left-wing sympathizers.

★ Edith Piaf
*Known as "the
little sparrow" because
of her size, Piaf was
the 20th century's
greatest French
popular singer. In
her tragic voice
she sang of the
sorrows and love
woes of the Paris
working class.*

Victor Noir
*The life-size statue of this 19th-century
journalist shot by Pierre Bonaparte, a cousin
of Napoleon III, is said to have fertility powers.*

George Rodenbach, the 19th-century poet, is
depicted as rising out of his tomb with a rose in
the hand of his outstretched arm.

Elizabeth Demidoff, a Russian
princess who died in 1818, is
honoured by a three-storey
Classical temple by Quaglia.

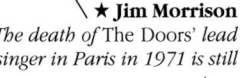

★ Jim Morrison
*The death of The Doors' lead
singer in Paris in 1971 is still
a mystery.*

François Raspail
*The tomb of this much-imprisoned
partisan of the 1830 and 1840
revolutions is in the form of a prison.*

Disneyland Resort Paris ⑭

Disneyland Resort Paris is built on a massive scale – the 2,000-ha (5,000-acre) site encompasses two theme parks; seven hotels (several with swimming pools), a shopping, dining and entertainment village; a seasonal ice skating rink; lakes; two convention centres; and a golf course. One stop down the line from their very own train station lies Val d'Europe, a huge new shopping mall with more than 180 shopping outlets, including 60 discount stores, and a Sea World centre.

Unbeatable for complete escapism, combined with vibrant excitement and sheer energy, the Parks offer extreme rides and gentle experiences, all accompanied by phenomenal visual effects.

The Queen of Hearts' Castle, in Alice's Curious Labyrinth

THE PARKS

Disneyland Resort Paris consists of Disneyland Park and Walt Disney Studios Park. Disneyland Park is based on the Magic Kingdom of California and has more than 40 rides or attractions. The newest is Walt Disney Studios Park, where interactive exhibits and live shows bring alive the wizardry of the movie and television industry. Find out more at: www.disneylandparis. com or call 08 705 03 03 03 (UK), 0825 30 60 30 (France).

GETTING THERE

By Car
Disneyland Resort Paris lies 32 km (20 miles) to the east of Paris, and has its own link (exit 14) from the A4 westbound from Paris and eastbound A4, from Strasbourg. Simply follow the signs to Marne la Vallée (Val d'Europe) until you see the Disneyland signs. (The Davy Crockett Ranch is exit 13.)

By Air
Both Orly and Charles de Gaulle Airports have a shuttle bus which runs every 30 minutes (45 in the low season). No booking is necessary. The fare is about 13€ per person.

By Train
The Paris RER runs directly to the parks, as does the TGV which has connections throughout Europe.

PARKING

There is space for over 12,000 vehicles, and an efficient moving sidewalk conveys you to the exit. Parking costs 8€ per day for cars, and 10€ for campers and coaches. Parking at Disneyland Resort Paris hotels is free to guests, and the Disneyland and New York hotels offer valet parking.

OPENING HOURS

The Parks tend to open at 9am in high season and 10am otherwise. Disneyland Park closes at 11pm in high season and 8pm in low season. The Walt Disney Studios Park closes at 8pm in high season and 6pm in low season. Special events, such as Hallowe'en, can mean extended hours.

WHEN TO VISIT

The busiest times are Christmas and New Year, mid-February to early April and July to early September, and mid-October. Busiest days are Saturday–Monday; Tuesday and Wednesday are quietest.

LENGTH OF VISIT

To experience everything Disneyland Resort Paris has to offer you really need to spend three or four days at the resort. Although it is possible to tour the Parks in one day each, to enjoy them at less than breakneck pace you need at least two days for Disneyland Park alone, and if you want to include Buffalo Bill's Wild West show or visit some of the

EATING AND DRINKING

There's no need to leave the park to eat during the day. **Au Chalet de la Marionnette** (Fantasyland) is excellent for kids (and almost deserted at 3pm) as is the **Cowboy Cookout Barbecue** (Frontierland), which tends to be rather more crowded. **Colonel Hathi's Pizza Outpost** (Adventureland) is worth a visit just to see the authentic colonial gear, whilst **Café Hyperion – Videopolis** (Discoveryland) offers good food plus excellent entertainment, but service is very slow.

You pay a premium for full-service restaurants but the experience of eating in **Blue Lagoon Restaurant** (Adventureland) is one you will remember. You dine on the "shore" of a Caribbean Pirate hideaway while the boats from Pirates of the Caribbean glide past. **Walt's**, on Main Street, USA, is also a good but pricey restaurant offering American fare. If you're lucky, they'll seat you so that you can watch the afternoon Main Street parade in comfort from an upstairs window.

In Disney Village **Annette's Diner** is staffed by rollerskating waitresses against a background of '50s records. **Planet Hollywood** is another good option, and the **Rainforest Cafe** provides an interestingly animated meal. Bavarian specialities are on the menu in **King Ludwig's Castle**, while a giant **McDonald's** serves the usual fare. The hotel restaurants are more expensive the nearer they are located to the park.

sney Village,
ushed to
under four
i up on a daily
, which is only
y on the RER,
but most guests from further
afield will stay in hotels.
Disney offer several packages
for those who wish to stay on
site. These include passes for
the Parks, and accommodation
with continental breakfast
included. All-inclusive
packages can also be booked.

TICKETS

If you book a package, tickets
will be included in the price.
Tickets for both Parks can be
bought from any Disney Store
before you leave home, or at
the Park upon arrival – though
this means queuing at a ticket
booth. One-, 2- or 3-day tickets
are available, and prices vary
according to season. The
Hopper ticket allows entry to
both Parks on the same day.
The Paris transport system
RATP also sells tickets that
combine travel on the RER
and entry to the Parks.

GETTING AROUND

Disney provides an efficient
transport system between the
Parks and the hotels (ex-
cluding Davy Crockett Ranch)
with buses on the half hour.
In summer, a fleet of little
open-top buses drives slowly
around Lake Disney, ferrying
guests between the three
lakeside hotels and Disney
Village. If you're staying at
any of the on-site hotels it's
only a short walk (20 minutes
at most) to the Park gates.

**Sleeping Beauty Castle,
the centrepiece of the Park**

WHICH HOTEL?

There are six hotels on site, and one in woodland 2 km
(3 miles) away. The best hotels are the closest to the Parks.

Hotel Santa Fe: basic, small and reasonably inexpensive. The
only hotel offering parking immediately outside your room.
Hotel Cheyenne: a Wild West theme hotel, about 17
minutes' walk from the park. Small rooms (with bunks for
the kids), a Native American village play area. Inexpensive
and a great experience. Kids love this hotel.
Sequoia Lodge: a lakeside "hunter's lodge", moderately
priced with more than 1,000 rooms. Ask for a room in the
main building. Rooms at the front have great views.
Newport Bay Club: a huge, nautically-themed, hotel on the
lakeside. Moderately priced, this massive hotel has a huge
convention centre, magnificent swimming pool and three
floors offering extra services for a supplement.
Hotel New York: expensive and business-oriented; not a lot
for the kids. This hotel also has a large convention centre,
and there's an ice-skating rink from October to March.
Disneyland Hotel: the jewel in the crown. Expensive, but
right at the entrance to the Disneyland Park. Full of
delightful touches, such as grandfather clocks and ever-
present Disney characters. The Castle Club is a 50-room
hotel-within-a-hotel. If you can afford it, a week of decadent fawning and unrestrained hedonism can be yours!
Davy Crockett Ranch: log cabins sleeping 4–6 are grouped
around a woodland trail, as well as traditional camping
facilities. Some excellent facilities: the pool ranks as one
of the best in Disneyland Resort Paris.

MONEY

Credit cards are accepted
everywhere within the resort.
ATMs and commission-free
foreign exchange are
available immediately inside
the Park entrances and at
reception in all the hotels.

DISABLED TRAVELLERS

City Hall (immediately
within Disneyland Park) has
a brochure outlining the
facilities for the disabled, and
a Disabled Guest Guide can
be pre-ordered (free) from the
Disneyland Resort Paris
website. The complex is
designed very much with the
disabled in mind, but note that
cast members are not allowed
to assist with lifting people or
moving wheelchairs.

STAYING IN A DISNEY HOTEL

The on-site hotels offer rooms
at a wide range of prices,
with the rule of thumb being
that those closest to the Parks
are the most expensive.
Advantages include virtually

**The runaway mine-train track of
Big Thunder Mountain**

no travelling to reach the
Parks, and "early bird" entry
to the parks on selected dates
(usually at peak times).
    If you stay at a Disney hotel
you will be given a hotel ID
card. This unprepossessing
little item is very important.
As well as being used to
charge anything you buy
back to your hotel room (and
have it delivered there), it
also allows you entry to the
Disneyland hotel grounds
early in the morning while
they're still shut to day
trippers (the grounds also act
as an entrance to the Park).
    For children (of any age),
one of the most exciting
bonuses of staying in an on-
site hotel is the chance to
dine with Disney characters.

Exploring Disneyland Resort Paris

The resort is comprised of two large entertainment areas, Disneyland Park and the Walt Disney Studios Park. The former celebrates lands from a past strongly coloured by Hollywood folklore, and the latter highlights the ingenuity of the production processes involved in cinema, animation and television.
The resort offers a plethora of attractions and themed parades chosen from the "Wonderful World Of Disney".

DISNEYLAND PARK

MAIN STREET, USA

Main Street represents a fantasy small-town America, right down to the traffic, which includes horse-drawn rail cars, a paddy wagon and other vintage transport in a system that runs between Town Square and Central Plaza. The Victorian facades offer a wealth of detail, and hide several interesting stores. The Emporium is the place for gifts. Further along, you can snack at Casey's Corner or succumb to the aromas from Cookie Kitchen or the Cable Car Bake Shop. Either side of the shops are the Discovery and Liberty Arcades, offering a covered route to the Central Plaza and hosting displays and cute small stalls.

At night, thousands of lights set Main Street's paving aglow. Disney's Fantillusion, a fantasy of music, live action and illuminated floats, begins at Town Square. From Main Street you can ride a 19th-century "steam" engine. Do note that boarding elsewhere than Main Street is not always possible before noon.

FRONTIERLAND

This homage to America's Wild West hosts some of the Park's most popular attractions. Big Thunder Mountain, a rollercoaster ride, is circled by two paddle-steamers that take a musical cruise around America's finest natural monuments. Phantom Manor is a ghost ride, and at the outdoor Chaparral Theatre you can see some amazing stage performances.

Pocahontas Indian Village and Critter Corral are both popular with younger children.

ADVENTURELAND

Enjoy the wild rides and Audio-Animatronics™ of Adventureland. Indiana Jones™ and the Temple of Peril hurtles you through a derelict mine. The ride has torches, steep drops and tight 360° loops.

Pirates of the Caribbean is a great boat ride through underground prisons and past 16th-century fighting galleons. La Cabane des Robinson, based on Jonathan Wyss's *Swiss Family Robinson*, starts with a shaky climb up a 27-m (88-ft) Banyan Tree. From here you explore the rest of the island, including the caves of Ben Gunn from *Treasure Island* and the awe-inspiring suspension bridge near Spyglass Hill. The children's playground, Pirates' Beach, is also well worth a visit.

FANTASYLAND

The buildings here are mod–elled on those in animated movies. Many attractions are for younger children, such as Snow White and the Seven Dwarfs, and Pinocchio's Fantastic Journey. The very young will love Dumbo the Flying Elephant. Peter Pan's Flight is a triumph of imag–ination and technology, flying you high over the streets of London. A popular diversion is Alice's Curious Labyrinth.

Hourly, there's a musical parade of clockwork figures at "it's a small world". Aboard a boat, you meander through lands of animated models to the strains of the eponymous

song. Le Pays des Contes des Fées (Storybook Land) is another boat ride. Next, hop aboard Casey Jr for a train ride circling the boats.

DISCOVERYLAND

Science fiction and the future are the themes here. The multi-loop ride Space Mountain draws crowds from the outset, but at the end of the day you can often walk straight on. Les Mystères du Nautilus takes you right into the submarine from *20,000 Leagues Under the Sea*. Autopia, where you can drive a real, petrol-engined car, is a magnet for youngsters. Orbitron features spaceships and soon gets crowded, but is worth experiencing. Star Tours makes you a passenger in a star shuttle on a breathtaking journey of narrow escapes.

The best shows are in Videopolis, a cavernous café showing cartoons between shows. Honey, I Shrunk the Audience is a masterpiece of total sensory stimulation.

WALT DISNEY STUDIOS PARK

FRONT LOT

Inside the giant studio gates, the central feature of Front Lot is a fountain in the shape of Mickey Mouse as he appears in *The Sorceror's Apprentice*. It's also hard to miss 'Earful Tower', a massive studio icon based on the water tower at the Disney Studios in California. Disney Studio 1 houses a film set boulevard, complete with facades that front a street and represent stylised locations such as the 1930's-style Club Swankedero, the Liki Tiki tropical bar and the ultra cool rat-packesque Hep Cat Club.

ANIMATION COURTYARD

Celebrating the key art that facilitated Disney's great success, the courtyard is made up of three areas. A huge *Sorcerer's Apprentice* hat marks the entrance to the Art of Disney Animation, an interactive attraction tracing the entire history of moving imagery. Animagique is a show that brings together some of the greatest moments from the Disney corpus. In Flying Carpets over Agrabah, the genie from *Aladdin* invites spectators to participate in an astonishing magic carpet ride all around a magical set whose amazing centrepiece is a giant genie's bottle. Participants even get to be the stars of a film directed by the magical man himself.

PRODUCTION COURTYARD

Here the emphasis is on the production process. At the Walt Disney Television Studios you can see behind the scenes of television production, while Ciné–Magique is a must for film buffs, as it covers the history of both American and European cinema. The Studio Tram Tour gives you a tour of the studio premises, including a visit to Catastrophe Canyon, where you can enjoy the fun of a spectacular film shoot.

BACKLOT

This area concentrates its focus on the topics of special effects, film music recording and crazy dare-devil stunts. Armageddon Special Effects presents a tour of film trickery, while Rock 'n' Roller Coaster is a high-speed attraction (in fact, it is the fastest ride in any Disney theme park) that combines a once-in-a-lifetime ride set against a pulsating musical soundtrack provided by rock legends Aerosmith.

RIDES AND ATTRACTIONS

This chart is designed to help you make the best use of your time at Disneyland Paris, decide on which rides and tours are best for you, and choose when to visit them.

	Queues	Height / Age Restriction	Best Time to Ride or Visit	Fastpass	Scary Rating	May Cause Motion Sickness	Rating Overall
Phantom Manor	▶		Any		❷		★
Rivers of the Far West	○		Any		❶		▼
Big Thunder Mountain	●	1.2m	FT	✔	❷		★
Pocahontas Indian Village	○		Any		❶		▼
Indiana Jones & the Temple of Peril	●	1.4m	LT	✔	❸	✔	★
Adventure Isle	○		Any		❶		▼
La Cabane des Robinson	○		Any		❶		▼
Pirates of the Caribbean	○		Any		❶		★
Peter Pan's Flight	●		FT	✔	❶		◆
Snow White & the Seven Dwarfs	●		>11		❶		◆
Pinocchio's Fantastic Journey	●		>11		❶		▼
Dumbo the Flying Elephant	●		FT		❶		▼
Mad Hatter's Teacups	▶		>12		❶		▼
Alice's Curious Labyrinth	○		Any		❶		▼
"It's a Small World"	○		Any		❶		◆
Casey Jr – Le Petit Train du Cirque	○		>11		❶		◆
Le Pays des Contes des Fees	○		Any		❶		◆
Star Tours	○	1.3m	Any	✔	❶		★
Space Mountain	●	1.4m	LT	✔	❸	✔	★
Honey, I Shrunk the Audience	○		Any		❶		★
Autopia	●		FT		❶		▼
Orbitron	●	1.2m	FT		❶		▼
Disney Studio 1	▶		Any		❶		◆
Art of Disney Animation	▶		Any		❶		▼
Animagique	●		Any		❶		◆
Flying Carpets Over Agrabah	●	1.2m	FT		❶	✔	◆
Walt Disney Television Studios	●		Any		❶		◆
CinéMagique	▶		Any		❶		◆
Studio Tram Tour	●		FT		❶		★
Armageddon Special Effects	●		Any		❶		▼
Rock 'n' Roller Coaster	●	1.2m	Any		❸	✔	★

Short - ○   Medium - ▶   Long - ●   Anytime - Any   Before 11- >11   First thing -FT   Last thing- LT
Not Scary - ❶   Slightly - ❷   Very - ❸   Quite good - ▼   Very good - ◆   Outstanding - ★

Bercy ⑱

75012. **Map** 18 F3. Ⓜ *Bercy, Cour St-Emilion.* ▣ *Port de Bercy (01 43 43 40 30).*

This former wine-trading quarter east of the city centre, with its once-grim ware-houses, pavilions and slum housing, has been transformed into a modern district. An automatic metro line (Line 14) links it to the heart of the city.

The centrepiece of Bercy is the Palais Omnisports de Paris-Bercy, now the city centre's principal venue. The vast pyramidal structure has become a contemporary land-mark. Many sports events are held here, as well as classical operas and rock concerts *(see pp345 and 349).*

Other architecturally adventurous buildings dominate Bercy, notably Chemetov's building for the Ministry of Finance, and Frank Gehry's American Center (which houses the Maison du Cinema and the Cinémathèque Française).

At the foot of these struc-tures, the imaginatively designed 70-ha (173-acre) Parc de Bercy provides a welcome green space for this part of the city. The park's attractions for children include a traditional carousel.

Former wine stores and cellars along Cours St Emilion have been restored as bars, restaurants and shops, and one of the warehouses now contains the Musée des Arts Forains (Fairground Museum). There is also a multiscreen

Bibliothèque Nationale de France

cinema. Nearby, the Viaduc des Arts houses artists' workshops, boutiques and restaurants.

The Marina de Bercy is the starting and finishing point for some cruises along the Seine.

Bibliothèque Nationale de France ⑲

Quai François-Mauriac 75013. **Map** 18 F4. ⬛ *01 53 79 59 59.* Ⓜ *Biblio-thèque F Mitterrand, Quai de la Gare.* ◯ *9am–7pm daily (from 2pm Mon, from 1pm Sun).* ◯ *pub hols & 2 wks mid-Sep.* ▦ ⬛ ⬛ ⬛ www.bnf.fr

Dominique Perrault's 1996 landmark national library is the most striking of all the *Grands Projets* with which President Mitterrand revitalized this eastern part of the city. Four towers house 12,000,000 volumes, with reference and research libraries in the central podium. Resources include 50,000 digitized illustrations, sound archives and CD-ROMs.

South of the City

13th Arrondissement ⑳

Zac Paris Rive Gauche, 75013. Ⓜ *Bibliotheque F Mitterrand.* **Map** 18 F5

Following a ten-year project called the Zac Paris Rive Gauche, the 13th arrondisse-ment has become an area of startling urban regeneration. The once-disused area of land between Gare d'Austerlitz and Ivry-sur-Seine has now been revived to house a new uni-versity that will have some 30,000 students. The area also boasts the MK2 Bibliothèque, a vast cinema complex which, with its 14 screens, cafés and exhibition areas, is already attracting keen film-goers.

Connected to Bercy by a bridge, the area also offers new housing, schools and business opportunities.

Parc Montsouris ㉑

Blvd Jourdan 75014. **Tel** *01 45 88 28 60.* Ⓜ *Porte d'Orléans.* ⬛ *Cité Universitaire.* ◯ *8am–5.30pm Mon–Fri; 9am–dusk weekends. Times may vary. Call ahead to confirm.* ▣

This English-style park was laid out by the landscape architect Adophe Alphand between 1865 and 1878. It has a restaurant, lawns, slopes and a lake that is home to many species of birds. The park is the second largest in central Paris and is also home to a meteorological weather station.

Bercy's striking American Center, designed by Frank Gehry

Cité Universitaire ㉒

17–21 Blvd Jourdan 75014.
📞 01 44 16 64 00. 🚇 Cité
Universitaire. **www**.ciup.fr

This is an international city in miniature for more than 5,000 foreign students attending the University of Paris. Created in the 1920s, it now contains 37 houses and, fascinatingly, each is in an architectural style linked to different countries. The Swiss House and the Franco-Brazilian House were designed by the Modernist architect Le Corbusier. The International House, donated by John D Rockefeller in 1936, has a library, restaurant, swimming pool and theatre. The student community makes this a lively and stimulating area of the city to visit.

Japan House at Cité Universitaire

Notre-Dame du Travail ㉓

59 Rue Vercingetorix 75014. **Map** 15
B3. **Tel** 01 44 10 72 92. 🚇 Pernety.
🕙 10am–noon, 2pm–5pm daily.
✝ 9am, 7pm Mon–Fri, 6pm Sat,
9am, 11am Sun.

This church dates from 1901 and is made of an unusual mix of materials: stone, rubble and bricks over a riveted steel and iron framework. It was the creation of Father Soulange-Boudin, a priest who organized cooperatives and sought to reconcile labour and capitalism. Local parishioners

The Sebastopol Bell in Notre-Dame du Travail

raised the money for its construction, but lack of funds meant that many features, such as the bell towers, were never built. On the façade hangs the Sebastopol Bell, a trophy from the Crimean War given to the people of the Plaisance district by Napoleon III. The Art Nouveau interior has been completely restored, and features paintings of patron saints.

Institut Pasteur ㉔

25–28 Rue du Docteur Roux 75015.
Map 15 A2. **Tel** 01 45 68 82 83. 🚇
Pasteur. 🕙 2pm–5.30pm Mon–Fri
(last adm: 4.45pm). 🔴 Aug, public
hols. 🎟 📷 **Films, videos**. 📹
compulsory. 🖥 **www**.pasteur.fr

The Institut Pasteur is France's leading medical research centre and was founded by the world-renowned scientist Louis Pasteur in 1888–9. He discovered the process of milk pasteurization as well as vaccines against rabies and anthrax. The centre houses a museum which includes a reconstruction of Pasteur's apartment and laboratory. It was designed by his grand-children (also scientists) and is faithful to the original down to the last detail. Pasteur's tomb is in a basement crypt built in the style of a small Byzantine chapel. The tomb of Dr Emile Roux, the inventor of the

Louis Pasteur

treatment of diphtheria by serum injection, lies in the garden. The institute has laboratories for pure and applied research, lecture theatres, a reference section, and a hospital founded to apply Pasteur's theories.

There is also a library – the institute's original building from 1888 – where research into AIDS is carried out, led by pioneering Professor Luc Montagnier who discovered the HIV virus in 1983.

Garden in the Parc André Citroën

Parc André Citroën ㉕

Rue Balard 75015. **Tel** 01 56 56 11
56. 🚇 Javel, Balard. 🕙 8am–dusk
Mon–Fri (9am Sat, Sun & public hols).

Opened in 1992, this park is the third large-scale vista on the Seine, along with Les Invalides and the Champ-de-Mars. Designed by both landscapers and architects, it is a fascinating blend of styles, ranging from wildflower meadow in the north to the sophisticated mono-chrome mineral and sculpture gardens of the southern section. Numerous modern water sculptures dot the park, and huge glasshouses nurture a range of environments. During the summer, there is a tethered hot-air balloon from which groups of visitors can enjoy great views over the city.

Versailles ㉖

See pp248–53.

The Palace and Gardens of Versailles ㉖

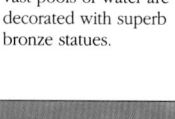

Visitors passing through the rich interior of this colossal palace, or strolling in its vast gardens, will understand why it was the glory of the Sun King's reign. Starting in 1668 with his father's modest hunting lodge, Louis XIV built the largest palace in Europe, housing 20,000 people at a time. Architects Louis Le Vau and Jules Hardouin-

Garden statue of a flautist

Mansart designed the buildings, Charles Le Brun did the interiors, and André Le Nôtre, the great landscaper, redesigned the gardens. The gardens are formally styled into regular patterns of paths and groves, hedges and flowerbeds, pools of water and fountains.

★ **Formal Gardens**
Geometric paths and shrubberies are features of the formal gardens.

The Orangery was built beneath the Parterre du Midi to house exotic plants in winter.

The South Parterre's shrubbery and ornate flowerbeds overlook the Swiss pond.

★ **The Château**
Louis XIV made the château into the centre of political power in France (see pp250–53).

The Water Parterre's vast pools of water are decorated with superb bronze statues.

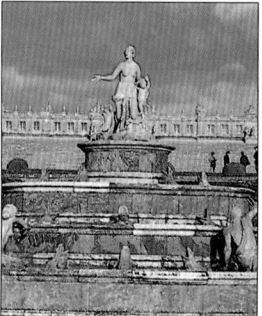

Fountain of Latona
Marble basins rise to Balthazar Marsy's statue of the goddess Latona.

Dragon Fountain
The fountain's centrepiece is a winged monster.

The King's Garden with Mirror Pool are a 19th-century English garden and pool created by Louis XVIII.

Colonnade
Mansart designed this circle of marble arches in 1685.

VISITORS' CHECKLIST

Versailles. *Tel* 01 30 83 78 00.
01 30 83 77 77. 171 to Versailles. Versailles Rive Gauche. **Château** Nov–Mar: 9am–5.30pm Tue–Sun; Apr–Oct: 9am–6.30pm Tue–Sun.
Grand Trianon & Petit Trianon
Apr–Oct: noon–6.30pm daily; Nov–Mar: noon–5.30 daily. Les Grandes Eaux Musicales (Apr–Sep); Les Fêtes de Nuit (Aug–Sep); Les Grandes Eaux Nocturnes (Sat during summer). www.chateauversailles.fr

The Grand Canal was the setting for Louis XIV's many boating parties.

Petit Trianon
Built in 1762 as a retreat for Louis XV, this small château became a favourite of Marie-Antoinette.

Fountain of Neptune
Groups of sculptures spray spectacular jets of water in Le Nôtre and Mansart's 17th-century fountain.

★ Grand Trianon
Louis XIV built this small palace of stone and pink marble in 1687 to escape the rigours of court life, and to enjoy the company of his mistress, Madame de Maintenon.

STAR SIGHTS

★ The Château

★ Formal Gardens

★ Grand Trianon

The Main Palace Buildings of Versailles

Gold crest from the Petit Trianon

The present palace grew as a series of envelopes enfolding the original hunting lodge, whose low brick front is still visible in the centre. In the 1660s, Louis Le Vau built the first envelope, a series of wings which expanded into an enlarged courtyard. It was decorated with marble busts, antique trophies and gilded roofs. On the garden side, columns were added to the west facade and a great terrace was created on the first floor. Mansart took over in 1678 and added the two immense north and south wings and filled Le Vau's terrace to form the Hall of Mirrors. He designed the chapel, which was finished in 1710. The Opera House (*L'Opéra*) was added by Louis XV in 1770.

South Wing
The wing's original apartments for great nobles were replaced by Louis-Philippe's museum of French history.

The Royal Courtyard
was separated from the Ministers' Courtyard by elaborate grillwork during Louis XIV's reign. It was accessible only to royal carriages.

Louis XIV's statue, erected by Louis Philippe in 1837, stands where a gilded gateway once marked the beginning of the Royal Courtyard.

STAR SIGHTS

★ Marble Courtyard

★ L'Opéra

★ Chapelle Royale

Ministers' Courtyard

Main Gate
Mansart's original gateway grille, surmounted by the royal arms, is the entrance to the Ministers' Courtyard.

TIMELINE

1650	1700	1750	1800	1850

1667 Grand Canal begun

Louis XV

1722 12-year-old Louis XV occupies Versailles

1793 Louis XVI and Marie-Antoinette executed

1833 Louis-Philippe turns the château into a museum

1668 Construction of new château by Le Vau

1671 Interior decoration by Le Brun begun

1715 Death of Louis XIV. Versailles abandoned by court

1789 King and queen forced to leave Versailles for Paris

1682 Louis XIV and Marie-Thérèse move to Versailles

1919 Treaty of Versailles signed on 28 June

1661 Louis XIV enlarges château

1774 Louis XVI and Marie-Antoinette live at Versailles

The Clock
Hercules and Mars flank the clock overlooking the Marble Courtyard.

★ Marble Courtyard
The courtyard is decorated with marble paving, urns, busts and a gilded balcony.

North Wing
The chapel, Opéra and picture galleries occupy this wing, which originally housed royal apartments.

★ L'Opéra
Built for the 1770 marriage of the future Louis XVI and Marie-Antoinette, the Opéra is usually closed to the public.

★ Chapelle Royale
Mansart's last great work, this two-storey Baroque chapel, was Louis XIV's last addition to Versailles.

Inside the Château of Versailles

The sumptuous main apartments are on the first floor of the vast château complex. Around the Marble Courtyard are the private apartments of the king and the queen. On the garden side are the state apartments where official court life took place. These were richly decorated by Charles Le Brun with coloured marbles, stone and wood carvings, murals, velvet, silver and gilded furniture. Beginning with the Salon d'Hercule, each state room is dedicated to an Olympian deity. The climax is the Hall of Mirrors, where 17 great mirrors face tall arched windows.

★ Queen's Bedroom
In this room the queens of France gave birth to the royal children in full public view.

STAR SIGHTS

★ Chapelle Royale

★ Salon de Vénus

★ Hall of Mirrors

★ Queen's Bedroom

KEY

☐	South wing
☐	Coronation room
☐	Madame de Maintenon's apartments
☐	Queen's apartments and private suite
☐	State apartments
☐	King's apartments and private suite
☐	North wing
☐	Non-exhibition space

Entrance

Louis XVI's library features Neo-Classical panelling and the king's terrestrial globe.

The Salon du Sacre is adorned with huge paintings of Napoleon by Jacques-Louis David.

Entrance

★ Salon de Vénus
A Louis XIV statue stands amidst the rich marble decor of this room.

★ Chapelle Royale
The chapel's first floor was reserved for the royal family and the ground floor for the court. The interior is richly decorated in white marble, gilding and Baroque murals.

★ Hall of Mirrors
*Great state occasions were held in
this multi-mirrored room stretching
70 m (233 ft) along the west façade.
The Treaty of Versailles was ratified
here in 1919, ending World War I.*

Oeil-de-Boeuf

The King's Bedroom
is where Louis XIV died
in 1715, aged 77.

Salon de la Guerre
*The room's theme of war is
dramatically reinforced by
Antoine Coysevox's
stuccoed relief of Louis
XIV riding to victory.*

**The Cabinet du
Conseil** is where
the king received
his ministers and
his family.

Salon d'Apollon
*Designed by Le Brun and
dedicated to the god Apollo,
this was Louis XIV's throne
room. A copy of Hyacinthe
Rigaud's famous portrait of
the king (1701) hangs here.*

Salon d'Hercule

**Stairs to ground floor
reception area**

PURSUIT OF THE QUEEN

On 6 October 1789, a Parisian mob invaded the palace
seeking the despised Marie-Antoinette. The queen, roused
in alarm from her bed, fled towards the king's rooms
through the anteroom known as the Oeil-de-Boeuf. As the
mob tried to break into the room, the queen beat on the
door of the
king's bedroom.
Once admitted
she was safe, at
least until
morning, when
she and the king
were removed
to Paris by the
cheering and
triumphant mob.

West of the City

An Art Nouveau window in the Rue la Fontaine

Rue la Fontaine ㉗

75016. **Map** 9 A4. Ⓜ *Jasmin, Michel-Ange Auteuil.*

The Rue la Fontaine and surrounding streets act as a showcase for some of the most exciting architecture of the early 20th century. At No. 14 stands the Castel Béranger, a stunning apartment block made from cheap building materials to keep costs low, yet featuring stained glass, convoluted ironwork, balconies and mosaics. It established the reputation of Art Nouveau architect Hector Guimard, who went on to design the entrances for the Paris metro. Several more examples of his work can be seen further along the street, such as the Hôtel Mezzara at No. 60.

Fondation Le Corbusier ㉘

8–10 Square du Docteur Blanche 75016. **Tel** 01 42 88 41 53. Ⓜ *Jasmin.* ◯ *1.30–6pm Mon; 10am–12.30pm, 1.30–6pm Tue–Fri (to 5pm Fri); 10am–5pm Sat (Villa La Roche only).* ● *pub hols, Aug, 24 Dec–2 Jan.* ▦ ◙ **Films, videos.** ▯ See **History of Paris** pp38–9. **www.**fondationlecorbusier.asso.fr

In a quiet corner of Auteuil are the villas La Roche *(see p265)* and Jeanneret, the first two Parisian houses built by the 20th-century architect Charles-Edouard Jeanneret, known as Le Corbusier. Built in the 1920s, they show his revolutionary use of white concrete in Cubist forms. Rooms flow into each other allowing maximum light, and the houses stand on stilts with windows along their entire length.

Villa La Roche was owned by the art patron Raoul La Roche. Today both villas serve as a fascinating documentation centre on Le Corbusier.

Musée Marmottan-Claude Monet ㉙

2 Rue Louis Boilly 75016. ◪ 01 40 50 65 84. Ⓜ *Muette.* ◯ *10am–6pm Tue–Sun (last adm: 5.30pm).* ● *1 Jan, 1 May, 25 Dec.* ▦ & ▯ **www.**marmottan.com

The museum was created in the 19th-century mansion of the art historian Paul Marmottan in 1932, when he bequeathed his house and his Renaissance, Consular and First Empire collections of paintings and furniture to the Institut de France. The focus of the museum changed after the bequest by Michel Monet of 65 paintings by his father, the Impressionist Claude Monet. Some of his most famous paintings are here, including *Impression – Sunrise*, a beautiful painting of Rouen Cathedral and several *Water Lilies*.

Part of Monet's personal art collection also passed to the museum, including paintings by Camille Pissarro and the Impressionists Pierre Auguste Renoir and Alfred Sisley. The museum also displays medieval illuminated manuscripts.

La Barque (1887) by Claude Monet, in the Musée Marmottan

Bois de Boulogne ㉚

75016. Ⓜ *Porte Maillot, Porte Dauphine, Porte d'Auteuil, Sablons.* ◯ *24 hrs daily.* ▦ *to specialist gardens and museum.* &
Shakespeare garden ◯ *8am–dusk daily (from 9am Sat, Sun & pub hols).* ▮ **Open-air theatre Tel** 01 40 19 95 33/01. ◯ *May–Sep.*
Bagatelle & Rose gardens Tel 01 40 67 97 00. ◯ *9.30am. Closing times vary from 4.30pm to 8pm according to season.*
Jardin d'Acclimatation Tel 01 40 67 90 82. ◯ *10am–7pm daily (Oct–May: 6pm).* ▣ ▯▮
Musée en Herbe Tel 01 40 67 97 66. ◯ *10am–6pm Mon–Fri, 2pm–6pm Sat.* ▦ &

Between the western edges of Paris and the River Seine this 865-ha (2,137-acre) park offers greenery for strolling, boating, picnicking or spending a day at the races.

Villa La Roche, home of the Fondation Le Corbusier

Kiosque de l'Empereur, on an island in the Grand Lac, Bois de Boulogne

The Bois de Boulogne is all that remains of the vast Forêt du Rouvre. In the mid-19th century Napoleon III had it redesigned and landscaped by Haussmann along the lines of London's Hyde Park.

There are many beautiful areas within the Bois. The Pré Catelan is a self-contained park with the widest beech tree in Paris, and the charming Bagatelle gardens feature architectural follies and an 18th-century villa famous for its rose garden, where an international rose competition is held in June. The villa was built in 64 days as a bet between the Comte d'Artois and Marie-Antoinette. The Bois has a reputation as a seedy area after dark so is best avoided at night.

Musée des Années 30 🕦

28 Ave André Morizet, Boulogne-Billancourt 92100. *Tel* 01 55 18 46 42. M *Marcel Sembat.* ◯ 11am–5.45pm Tue–Sun. & 🖼 ▢ ▯ **www**.annees30.com

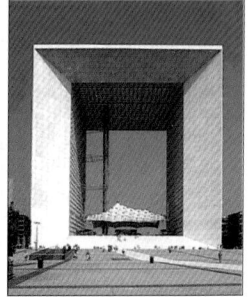

La Grande Arche in La Défense

Inaugurated in 1998, this museum of the 1930s forms part of an arts complex, the Espace Landowski, named after Paul Landowski, a sculptor who lived in Boulogne-Billancourt from 1905 until his death in 1961, and his musician brother, Marcel. Several of Paul's works are on show in the museum. The complex also includes a library, a gallery of video directors and a cinema, and will soon have a multimedia centre with artists' studios.

Through paintings, drawings, sculpture and artifacts, the museum gives a vivid impression of the aesthetic mood of the era. The museum also organizes temporary thematic exhibitions relating to the period. Themed tours of the architectural and industrial heritage of Boulogne-Billancourt are also run.

La Défense 🕦

La Grande Arche. *Tel* 01 49 07 27 27. 🖭 *La Défense.* ◯ 10am–7pm daily (Apr–Sep: to 8pm). 🖼 ▢ ▯ See *History of Paris* pp38–9. **www**.grandearche.com

This skyscraper business city on the western edge of Paris is the largest new office development in Europe and covers 80 ha (198 acres). It was launched in the 1960s

to create a new home for leading French and multi-national companies. Since then, a major artistic scheme has transformed many of the squares into fascinating open-air museums.

In 1989 La Grande Arche was added to the complex, an enormous hollow cube large enough to contain Notre-Dame cathedral. This was designed by Danish architect Otto von Spreckelsen as part of major construction works, or *Grands Travaux*, which were initiated by (and are now a memorial to) the late President François Mitterrand.

The arch now houses an exhibition gallery and a conference centre, and commands a superb view over the city of Paris.

Château de Malmaison 🕄

Ave du Château 92500 Rueil-Malmaison. *Tel* 01 41 29 05 55. 🖭 *La Défense then bus 258.* ◯ 10am–5pm Wed–Mon; closing times vary; phone for details. 🌑 12.30–1.30pm for lunch, Oct–Mar. 🖼 🖥 ▯ See *History of Paris* pp32–3. **www**.chateau-malmaison.fr

This 17th-century château was bought in 1799 by Josephine de Beauharnais, wife of Napoleon I. A magnificent veranda, Classical statues and a small theatre were added. After his campaigns, Napoleon and his entourage would come

The Empress Josephine's bed in the Château de Malmaison

here to relax. The Château became Josephine's main residence after their divorce. Today, it is an important Napoleonic museum, together with the nearby Château de Bois-Préau.

Furniture, portraits, artefacts and mementos of the imperial family are displayed in rooms reconstructed in the style of the First Empire.

Part of the original grounds still exists, including Josephine's famous rose garden.

EIGHT GUIDED WALKS

Paris is a city for walking. It is more compact and easier to get around than many other great capitals. Most of its great sights are within walking distance of one another and they are close to the heart of the city, the Ile de la Cité.

There are 14 classic tourist areas described in the *Area by Area* section of this book, each with a short walk marked on its *Street-by-Street* map, taking you past many of the most interesting sights. Yet Paris offers a wealth of lesser-known but equally remarkable areas, whose special history, architecture and local customs reveal other facets of the city.

The eight walks around the following neighbourhoods take in the main sights and also introduce visitors to their subtle details, such as street markets, quirky churches, canals, gardens, old village streets and bridges. And the literary, artistic and historical associations allow the past and present to blend into the changing and vibrant life of the modern city.

Parc Monceau statue

Auteuil is renowned for its luxury modern residential architecture, Monceau for its sumptuous Second Empire mansions and St-Louis for its *ancien régime* town houses and narrow streets. The old-fashioned charm of the iron footbridges survives along Canal St-Martin, and steep village streets that were once home to famous artists still enrich Montmartre. A tranquil village atmosphere also pervades two lesser-known hilltop districts – Buttes-Chaumont, with one of Paris's loveliest parks, and Butte-aux-Cailles, whose quaint, cobbled alleyways belie its association with the ill-fated Paris Commune of 1871, while the once working-class area of Faubourg St-Antoine has been given a new lease of life as an artisans' quarter with a pleasure-boat harbour.

All the walk areas are readily accessible by public transport and the nearest metro stations and bus routes are listed in the *Tips for Walkers* boxes. For each walk there are suggestions on convenient resting points, such as cafés and squares, along the route.

Montmartre
(pp266–7)

Parc Monceau
(pp258–9)

Buttes-Chaumont
(pp268–9)

Canal St-Martin
(pp260–61)

OPERA QUARTER

CHAMPS-ELYSEES

CHAILLOT QUARTER

TUILERIES QUARTER

BEAUBOURG AND LES HALLES

THE MARAIS

Faubourg St-Antoine
(pp270–71)

INVALIDES AND EIFFEL TOWER QUARTER

Seine

ST-GERMAIN-DES-PRES

ILE DE LA CITE

Ile St-Louis
(pp262–3)

Auteuil
(pp264–5)

LATIN QUARTER

LUXEMBOURG QUARTER

MONTPARNASSE

JARDIN DES PLANTES QUARTER

Buttes-aux-Cailles
(pp272–3)

0 kilometres 2

0 miles 1

KEY

··· Walk route

◁ **Bridge over the Canal St-Martin**

A 90-Minute Walk around Parc Monceau

This leisurely walk passes through the exquisite late-18th-century Parc Monceau, the centrepiece of a smart Second Empire district. It then follows a route along surrounding streets, where groups of opulent mansions stunningly convey the magnificence in which some Parisians live, before ending at Place St-Augustin. For details on Monceau sights, see pages 232–33.

Ruysdaël gate

Parc Monceau to Avenue Velasquez

The walk starts at the Monceau metro station ① on the Boulevard de Courcelles. Enter the park where Nicolas Ledoux's 18th-century tollhouse ② stands. On either side are sumptuously gilded 19th-century wrought-iron gates which support ornate lampposts.

Parc Monceau's tollhouse ②

Take the second path on the left past the monument to Guy de Maupassant (1897). This is only one of a series of six Belle Epoque monuments of prominent French writers and musicians which are picturesquely scattered throughout the park. Most of them feature a solemn bust of a great man who is accompanied by a swooning muse.

Straight ahead is the most important remaining folly, a moss-covered Corinthian colonnade ④ running around the edge of a charming tiny lake with the requisite island in the centre. Walk around the colonnade and under a 16th-century arch ⑤ transplanted from the old Paris Hôtel de Ville *(see p102)*, which burned down in 1871.

Turn left on the Allée de la Comtesse de Ségur and go into Avenue Velasquez, a wide tree-lined street with 19th-century Neo-Classical mansions. At No. 7 is the splendid Cernuschi museum ⑥, which houses a collection of Far Eastern art.

Colonnade in Parc Monceau ④

Avenue Velasquez to Avenue Van Dyck

Re-enter the park and turn left into the second small winding path, which is bordered by an 18th-century mossy pyramid ⑦, antique tombs, a stone arcade, an obelisk and a small Chinese stone pagoda. The romantically melancholy tone of these false ruins suits the spirit of the late 18th century.

Turn right on the first path past the pyramid and walk back to the central avenue. Straight ahead a Renaissance bridge fords the little stream running from the lake. Turn left and walk past the

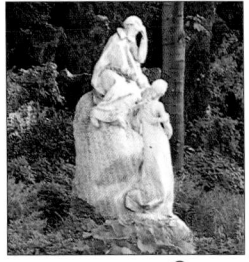

Ambroise Thomas statue ⑧

monument (1902) to the musician Ambroise Thomas ⑧. Immediately behind there is a lovely artificial mountain with cascade. Turn left on the next avenue and walk to the monument (1897) to the composer Charles Gounod ⑨ on the left. From here follow the first winding path to the right towards the Avenue Van Dyck exit. Ahead to the right, in the corner of the park, is the Chopin monument ⑩ (1906), and looking along the Allée de la Comtesse de Ségur, the monument to the 19th-century French poet Alfred de Musset.

Avenue Van Dyck to Rue de Monceau

Leave the park and pass into Avenue Van Dyck. No. 5 on the right is an impressive Parc Monceau mansion ⑪, a Neo-Baroque structure built by chocolate manufacturer Emile Menier; No. 6 is in the French Renaissance style that came back into favour in the 1860s. Straight ahead, beyond the ornate grille, there is a fine view of Avenue Hoche and in the distance the Arc de Triomphe. Walk past the gate

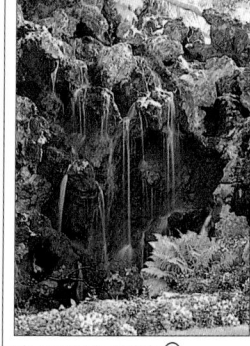

The mountain cascade ⑧

and turn left into Rue de Courcelles and left again into Rue Murillo, bordered by more elaborate town houses in 18th-century and French Renaissance styles ⑫. At the crossing of Rue Rembrandt, on the left, is another gate into the park and on the right a massive apartment building from 1900 (No. 7) and an elegant French Renaissance house with an elaborately carved wooden front door (No. 1). At the corner of the Rue Rembrandt and the Rue de Courcelles is the oddest of all the neighbourhood buildings, a striking five-storey red Chinese pagoda ⑬. It is an exclusive emporium of Chinese art.

Turn left on to the Rue de Monceau, walk past Avenue Ruysdaël and continue to the Musée Nissim de Camondo at No. 63 Rue de Monceau ⑭. Some nearby buildings worth having a look at are Nos. 52, 60 and 61 ⑮.

Boulevard Malesherbes

At the junction of Rue de Monceau and Boulevard Malesherbes turn right. This long boulevard with dignified six-storey apartment buildings is typical of the great avenues cut through Paris by Baron Haussmann, Prefect of the Seine during the Second Empire (see pp34–5). They

greatly pleased the Industrial Age bourgeoisie, but horrified sensitive souls and writers who compared them with the buildings of New York.

No. 75 is the posh marble front of Benneton, the most fashionable Paris card and stationery engraver ⑯. On the left, approaching the Boulevard Haussmann, looms the greatest 19th-century Paris church, St-Augustin ⑰, built by Victor-Louis Baltard. Enter the church through the back door on Rue de la Bien-faisance. Walk through the church and leave by the main door. On the left is the massive stone building of the French Officers' club, the Cercle Militaire ⑱. Straight ahead is a bronze statue of Joan of Arc ⑲. Continue on to Place St-Augustin to St-Augustin metro station.

Joan of Arc statue ⑲

KEY

••• Walk route

🔆 Good viewing point

Ⓜ Metro station

| 0 metres | 250 |
| 0 yards | 250 |

Chinese pagoda emporium ⑬

TIPS FOR WALKERS

Starting point: Blvd de Courcelles.
Length: 3 km (2 miles).
Getting there: The nearest metro is Monceau, reached by bus No. 30; No. 84 goes to metro Courcelles and No. 94 stops between Monceau & Villiers metros.
St Augustin church: Open 8.30am–7pm daily (closed 12.30–3.30pm public hols).
Stopping-off points: Near the Renaissance bridge in the Parc Monceau there is a kiosk serving coffee and sandwiches. There are two cafés at Place de Rio de Janeiro and several brasseries around Place St-Augustin. The Square M Pagnol is a pleasant place to relax and take in the beauty of the park at the end of the walk.

A 90-Minute Walk along the Canal St-Martin

The walk along the quays on either side of the Canal St-Martin is an experience of Paris very different from that of smarter districts. Here, the older surviving landmarks of the neighbourhood – the factories, warehouses, dwellings, taverns and cafés – hint at life in a thriving 19th-century industrial, working-class world. But there are also the softer charms of the old iron footbridges, the tree-lined quays, the inevitable fishermen, the river barges, and the still waters of the broad canal basins. A walk along the canal, which connects the Bassin de la Villette with the Seine, will evoke images of the Pernod-drinking, working-class Paris of Jean Gabin and Edith Piaf.

The 18th-century Barrière de la Villette ②

Bassin de la Villette looking north ③

Place de Stalingrad to Avenue Jean-Jaurès

From the Stalingrad metro station ①, follow Boulevard de la Villette to the new square in front of the Barrière de la Villette ②. This is one of the few remaining 18th-century tollhouses in Paris, designed by the celebrated Neo-Classical architect

Nicolas Ledoux in the 1780s. The fountains, square and terraces were designed in the 1980s to provide an attractive setting and fine views of the Bassin de la Villette ③ to the north.

Walk towards Avenue Jean-Jaurès. On the left is the first lock ④ leading down to the canal, as well as the art-house cinema chain MK2's landmark complexes, which are linked together by a boat.

TIPS FOR WALKERS

Starting point: *Place de Stalingrad.*
Length: *3.5 km (2 miles).*
Getting there: *The nearest metro is Stalingrad: bus No.54 stops there, and No.26 at metro Jaurès.*
Hôpital St-Louis: *Chapel open 2–5pm Fri–Sun; the courtyard is open daily.*
Stopping-off points: *Ethnic food shops and restaurants abound in the lively Rue du Faubourg du Temple and nearby streets. The Quai de Valmy also has plenty of modish restaurants and bars (Le Point Ephémère, La 25e Image, Chez Prune), and is lined with benches to rest on, and there is a shady public garden on Boulevard Jules Ferry.*

View from Rue E Varlin bridge ⑦

KEY

••• Walk route

☆ Good viewing point

Ⓜ Metro station

| 0 metres | 500 |
| 0 yards | 500 |

Courtyard garden of Hôpital St-Louis ⑭

good view of the towering buildings of a social housing estate ⑧. Nearby is the French Communist Party headquarters ⑨ on Place du Colonel Fabien, with its curving glazed tower.

Return to the Quai de Jemmapes, where at No. 134 ⑩ stands one of the few surviving brick-and-iron industrial buildings that used to line the canal in the 19th century. At No. 126 ⑪ is another notable modern building, a residence for the aged, with monumental concrete arches and glazed bay windows. Further along, at No. 112 ⑫, is an Art Deco apartment building with bay windows, decorative iron balconies and tiles. On the ground floor there is a typical 1930s proletarian café. Here the canal curves gracefully into the third lock, spanned by a charming transparent iron footbridge ⑬.

Hôpital St-Louis to Rue Léon-Jouhaux

Turn left into Rue Bichat, which leads to the remarkable 17th-century Hôpital St-Louis ⑭. Enter through the hospital's old main gate with its high-pitched roof and massive stone arch. Pass into the courtyard. The hospital was founded in 1607 by Henri IV, the first Bourbon king, to care for the victims of the plague. Leave the courtyard from the central gate on the wing on your left. Here you pass by the 17th-century hospital chapel ⑮ and out into the Rue de la Grange aux Belles.

Turn left and walk back to the canal. At the junction of Rue de la Grange Batelière and the Quai de Jemmapes stood, until 1627, the notorious Montfaucon gallows ⑯, one of the chief public execution spots of medieval Paris. Turn into the Quai de Jemmapes. At No. 101 ⑰ is the original front of the Hôtel du Nord, made famous in the eponymous 1930s film. In front is another iron footbridge and a draw-bridge ⑱ for traffic, providing a charming setting with views of the canal on either side. Cross over and continue down the Quai de Valmy until the last footbridge ⑲ at the corner of the Rue Léon-Jouhaux. From here the canal can be seen disappearing under the surface of Paris, to continue its journey through a great stone arch.

Entrance to Hôpital St-Louis ⑭

Square Frédéric Lemaître to Place de la République

Walk along Square Frédéric Lemaître ⑳ to the start of Boulevard Jules Ferry, which has a public garden stretching down its centre. The garden was built over the canal in the 1860s. At its head stands a charmingly nostalgic statue of a flower girl of the 1830s, *La Grisette* ㉑. On the left is a busy working-class street, Rue du Faubourg du Temple ㉒, with flourishing ethnic shops and restaurants. Follow the street to the right and on to the metro station in the Place de la République.

Shop, Rue du Faubourg du Temple ㉒

Iron footbridges over the canal ⑤

Quai de Valmy to Rue Bichat

Cross over to the Quai de Jemmapes, which runs the length of the east side of the canal and down to the first bridge on Rue Louis Blanc ⑤. Cross the bridge to the Quai de Valmy. From the corner there is a glimpse of the oblique granite and glass front of the new Paris Industrial Tribunal ⑥ on the Rue Louis Blanc.

Continue along Quai de Valmy. At Rue E Varlin cross the bridge ⑦, from where there is an attractive view of the second canal lock, lock-keeper's house, public gardens and old lampposts. At the other side of the bridge and slightly to the left, go along the pedestrianized Rue Haendel, which provides a

A 90-Minute Walk around the Ile St-Louis

The walk around this charming tiny island passes along the enchanting, picturesque tree-lined quays from Pont Louis-Philippe to Quai d'Anjou, taking in the sumptuous 17th-century *hôtels* that infuse the area with such a powerful sense of period. It then penetrates into the heart of the island along the main street, Rue St-Louis-en-l'Ile, enlivened by chic restaurants, cafés, art galleries and boutiques, before returning to the north side of the island and back to Pont Marie. For more information on the main sights, see pages 77 and 87.

Left Bank view of the Ile St-Louis

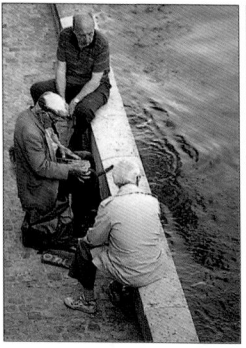

Fishing on a St-Louis quayside

Metro Pont Marie to Rue Jean-du-Bellay

From the Pont Marie metro station ① walk down Quai des Celestins and Quai de l'Hôtel de Ville, lined with traditional bookstands, from where there is a good view of Ile St-Louis. Turn left at Pont Louis-Philippe ② and, having crossed it, take the steps down to the lower quay immediately to the right. Walk around the tree-shaded west point of the island ③, then up the other

side to the Pont St-Louis ④. Opposite the bridge, on the corner of Rue Jean-du-Bellay, is Le Flore en l'Ile ⑤, the smartest café-cum-tea salon on the island.

Quai d'Orléans

From the corner of the Quai d'Orléans and the Rue Jean-du-Bellay there are fine views of the Panthéon's dome and Notre-Dame. Along the quay, Nos. 18–20, the Hôtel Rolland, has unusual Hispano-Moorish windows. No. 12 ⑥ is one of several stately 17th-century houses with handsme wrought-iron balconies. At No. 6 the former Polish library,

SQUARE JEAN XXIII

SQUARE DE L'ILE DE FRANCE

Pont de l'Archevéché

KEY

••• Walk route

☀ Good viewing point

Ⓜ Metro station

0 metres	250
0 yards	250

founded in 1838, now houses the Société Historique et Littéraire Polonaise, focusing on the life of Polish poet Adam Mickiewicz ⑦; it also contains some Chopin scores and autographs by George Sand and Victor Hugo. On the right, the Pont de la Tournelle ⑧ links the island to the Left Bank.

Seine barge passing a St-Louis quay

Quai de Béthune to Pont Marie

Continue beyond the bridge and into Quai de Béthune, where the Nobel-laureate Marie Curie lived at No. 36 ⑨, and where beautiful wrought-iron balconies gracefully decorate Nos. 34 and 30. The Hôtel Richelieu ⑩ at No. 18 is one of the island's most beautiful houses.

St-Louis church door ⑰

It features a fine garden where it has retained its original Classical blind arcades.

If you turn left down Rue Bretonvilliers there is an imposing 17th-century house ⑪, with a high-pitched roof resting on a great Classical arch spanning the street. Back on the Quai de Béthune, proceed to the Pont de Sully ⑫, a late 19th-century bridge joining the river banks. Ahead is the charming 19th-century Square Barye ⑬, a shady public garden at the east point of the island, from where there are fine river views. From here travel towards the Quai d'Anjou as far as the corner of Rue St-Louis-en-l'Ile to see the most famous house on

Gargoyle at No. 51 Rue St-Louis-en-l'Ile ⑳

small, chic, bistro-style restaurants with pleasantly old-fashioned decors. No. 31 is the original Berthillon shop ⑱, No. 60 an art gallery ⑲ with an original 19th-century window front, and at No. 51 is one of the few 18th-century *hôtels* on the island, Hôtel Chernizot ⑳, with a superb Rococo balcony which rests on leering gargoyles.

Turn right into Rue Jean-du-Bellay and along to Pont Louis-Philippe. Turn right again into the Quai de Bourbon, which is lined by one of the island's finest rows of *hôtels*, the most notable being Hôtel Jassaud at No. 19 ㉑. Continue to the 17th-century Pont Marie ㉒ and cross it to the Pont Marie metro on the other side.

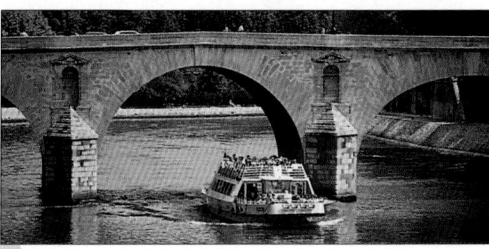

The 17th-century Pont Marie ㉒

the island, the Hôtel Lambert ⑭ *(see pp26–7)*. Continue into the Quai d'Anjou where Hôtel de Lauzun ⑮ at No. 17 has a severe Classical front and a beautiful gilded balcony and drain-pipes. Now turn left into Rue Poulletier and note the convent of the Daughters of Charity ⑯ at No. 5 bis. Further on, at the corner of Rue Poulletier and Rue St-Louis-en-l'Ile, is the island church, St-Louis ⑰, with its unusual tower, projecting clock and carved main door.

Proceed along Rue St-Louis-en-l'Ile, which abounds in

Windows of the Hôtel Rolland

TIPS FOR WALKERS

Starting point: *Pont Marie metro.*
Length: *2.6 km (1.6 miles).*
Getting there: *The walk starts from the Pont Marie metro. However, bus route 67 takes you to Rue du Pont Louis-Philippe and also crosses the island along Rue des Deux Ponts and Blvd Pont de Sully; routes 86 and 87 also cross the island along Blvd Pont de Sully.*
Stopping-off points: *There are cafés, such as Flore en l'Ile and the Berthillon shops for ice cream (see p317). Restaurants on the Rue St-Louis-en-l'Ile include Auberge de la Reine Blanche (No. 30) and Le Fin Gourmet (No. 42), as well as a pâtisserie and a cheese shop. Good resting-points are the tree-shaded quays and Square Barye to the eastern end of the island.*

A 90-Minute Walk in Auteuil

Part of the fascination of the walk around this bastion of bourgeois life in westernmost Paris lies in the contrasting nature of the area's streets. The old village provincialism of Rue d'Auteuil, where the walk begins, leads on to the masterpieces of luxurious modern architecture along Rue La Fontaine and Rue du Docteur Blanche. The walk ends at the Jasmin metro station. For more on the sights of Auteuil, see page 254.

Rue d'Auteuil

The walk begins at Place d'Auteuil ①, a leafy village square with a striking Guimard-designed metro station entrance, an 18th-century funerary obelisk, and the 19th-century Neo-Romanesque Notre Dame d'Auteuil. Walk down Rue d'Auteuil, the main street of the old village, and take in the sense of a past provincial world. The Auberge du Mouton Blanc brasserie at No. 40 ② now occupies the premises of the area's oldest tavern, favoured by Molière and his actors in the 1600s. The house at Nos. 45–47 ③ was the residence of American presidents John Adams and his son John Quincy Adams. Move on to the pleasantly shaded Place Jean Lorrain ④, the site of the local market. Here there is a Wallace drinking fountain,

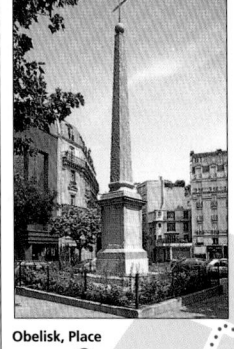
Obelisk, Place d'Auteuil ①

donated by the English millionaire, Richard Wallace in the 19th century. On the right, down Rue Donizetti, is the Villa Montmorency ⑤, a private enclave of luxury villas, built on the former country estate of the Comtesse de Boufflers.

Rue La Fontaine

Continue the walk along Rue La Fontaine, renowned for its many Hector Guimard buildings. Marcel Proust was born at No.96. Henri Sauvage's ensemble of artists' studios at No. 65 ⑥ is one of the most original Art Deco buildings in Paris. No. 60 is a Guimard Art Nouveau house ⑦ with elegant cast-iron balconies. Further along there is a small Neo-Gothic chapel at No. 40 ⑧ and Art Nouveau apartment buildings at Nos. 19 and 21 ⑨. No. 14 is Guimard's most spectacular building, the Castel Béranger ⑩, with a superb iron gate.

Wallace fountain ④

TIPS FOR WALKERS

Starting point: Place d'Auteuil.
Length: 3 km (2 miles).
Getting there: The nearest metro station to the starting point is Eglise d'Auteuil, and buses that take you there are Nos. 22, 52 and 62.
Stopping-off points: Along Rue d'Auteuil is the inexpensive trendy brasserie, L'Auberge du Mouton Blanc, with 1930s decor. No. 40 Rue La Fontaine is a tiny 1900 Art Nouveau café with old tiled floors and original zinc-covered bar. Place Jean Lorrain is a pleasantly shaded square where walkers can rest, and on Rue La Fontaine there is a small park in front of the Neo-Gothic chapel at No. 40. Further on at Place Rodin there is a pleasant public garden.

A map showing the walk route with labels: RUE DU DOCTEUR BLANCHE ⑯, RUE DE L'YV, RUE RAFFET ⑰ ⑱, RUE DE LA SOURCE, Villa Montmorency, AVENUE, RUE POUSSIN, RUE LA FONT ⑤, RUE D'AUTEUIL, PLACE J LORRAIN ④, RUE ② D'AUT, RUE MICHEL ANGE, Michel Ange Auteuil Ⓜ③, RUE BOILEAU

Doorway of No. 28 Rue d'Auteuil.

KEY

••• Walk route

Good viewing point

Ⓜ Metro station

0 metres   250
0 yards   250

Rue de l'Assomption to Rue Mallet-Stevens

At the corner of Rue de l'Assomption there is a view of the massive Maison de Radio-France ⑪ built in 1963 to house French radio and television (see p202). It was one of the first modern postwar buildings in the city. Turn left into Rue de l'Assomption and walk to the fine 1920s apartment building at No. 18 ⑫. Turn left into Rue du Général Dubail and follow the street to Place Rodin, where the great sculptor's bronze

Shuttered bay window at No. 3 Square Jasmin ⑲

nude, *The Age of Bronze* (1877) ⑬, occupies the centre of the roundabout.

Take the Avenue Théodore Rousseau back to Rue de l'Assomption and turn left

were altered dramatically by the addition of an extra three storeys in the 1960s.

Continue on Rue du Docteur Blanche until coming to Villa du Docteur Blanche on the left. At the end of this small cul de sac is the most celebrated modern house in Auteuil, Le Corbusier's Villa Roche ⑰. Together with the adjoining Villa Jeanneret, it is now part of the Corbusier Foundation (see pp38–9). Built for an art collector in 1924 using the new technique of reinforced concrete, the house, with its geometric forms and lack of ornamentation, is a model of early Modernism.

No. 18 Rue de l'Assomption, detail ⑫

Rue du Docteur Blanche to Rue Jasmin

Walk back to Rue du Docteur Blanche and turn right into Rue Henri Heine. No. 18 bis ⑱ is a very elegant Neo-Classical 1920s apartment building offering a good contrast to one of Guimard's last creations from 1926 next door – an Art Nouveau facade much tamer than that at Castel Béranger but still employing brick, and with projecting bay windows and a terraced roof. Turn left on Rue Jasmin. In the second cul de sac on the left there is another Guimard house at No. 3 Square Jasmin ⑲. Towards the end of Rue Jasmin is the metro station.

towards Avenue Mozart. Cut through in the 1880s, this is the principal artery of the 16th arrondissement, linking north and south and lined with typical bourgeois apartment buildings of the late 19th century. Cross the avenue and continue to the Avenue des Chalets where there is a typical collection of weekend villas ⑭ recalling the quieter suburban Auteuil of the mid-19th century. Further along Rue de l'Assomption, Notre-Dame de l'Assomption ⑮ is a Neo-Renaissance 19th-century church. Turn left into Rue du Docteur Blanche. At No. 9 and down the adjoining Rue Mallet-Stevens ⑯ there is a row of celebrated modern houses in the International Modern style by the architect Robert Mallet-Stevens. In this expensive, once avant-garde enclave lived architects, designers, artists and their modern-minded clients. The original proportions, however,

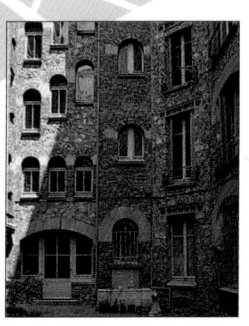

Courtyard of No. 14 Rue La Fontaine

The Age of Bronze ⑬

A 90-Minute Walk in Montmartre

The walk begins at the base of the sand-stone *butte* (hill), where old theatres and dance halls, once frequented and depicted by painters from Renoir to Picasso, have now been taken over by rock clubs. It continues steeply uphill to the original village, along streets which still retain the atmosphere caught by artists like Van Gogh, before winding downhill to end at Place Blanche. For more on the main sights of Montmartre and the Sacré-Coeur, see pages 220–29.

Montmartre seen from a distance

Place Pigalle to Rue Ravignan

The walk starts at the lively Place Pigalle ① and follows Rue Frochot to the Rue Victor Massé. At the corner is the ornate entrance to an exclusive private street bordered by late 19th-century chalets ②. Opposite, at No. 27 Rue Victor Massé, is an ornate mid-19th-century apartment building, and No. 25 is where Vincent Van Gogh and his brother Theo lived in 1886 ③. The famous Chat Noir ④, Montmartre's most renowned artistic cabaret in the 1890s, flourished at No. 12. At the end of the street begins the wide tree-lined Avenue Trudaine. Take Rue Lallier on the left to Boulevard de Rochechouart. Continue east. No. 84 is the first address of the Chat Noir and No. 82 was the Grand Trianon ⑤, Paris's oldest-surviving cinema, from the early 1890s. It is now

Entrance gate to Avenue Frochot

TIPS FOR WALKERS

Starting point: *Place Pigalle.*
Length: *2.3 km (1.4 miles). The walk goes up some very steep streets to the top; if you do not feel like the climb, consider taking the Montmartrobus, which covers most of the walk and starts at Place Pigalle.*
Getting there: *The nearest metro is Pigalle; buses that take you there are Nos. 30, 54 and 67.*
Stopping-off points: *There are many cafés and shops in Rue Lepic and the Rue des Abbesses. Le Saint Jean (16 Pl des Abbesses) remains a locals' haunt and serves well-priced brasserie food. For shade and a rest, Place Jean-Baptiste Clément and Square S Buisson at Avenue Junot are charming public squares.*

a theatre. Further along, No. 74 is the original front of Montmartre's first great cancan dance hall, the Elysée-Montmartre ⑥. Today it is a nightclub and concert hall.

Turn left on to Rue du Steinkerque, which leads to Sacré-Coeur gardens, and then left into Rue d'Orsel, which leads to the leafy square, Place Charles Dullin, where the small early 19th-century Théâtre de l'Atelier ⑦ stands. Continue up the hill on Rue des Trois Frères and turn left on Rue Yvonne le Tac, which leads to Place des Abbesses ⑧. This is one of the most pleasant and liveliest squares in the area. It has conserved its entire canopied Art Nouveau metro entrance by Hector Guimard. Opposite is St-Jean l'Evangéliste ⑨, an

Rue André Antoine ⑩

unusual brick and mosaic Art Nouveau church. To the right of the church a flight of steep steps leads to the tiny Rue André Antoine, where the Pointillist painter Georges Seurat lived at No. 39 ⑩. Continue along Rue des Abbesses and turn right at Rue Ravignan.

Rue Ravignan

From here there is a sweeping view of Paris. Climb the steps straight ahead to the deeply shaded Place Emile Goudeau ⑪. To the left, at No. 13, is the original entrance to the Bateau-Lavoir, the most important cluster of artists'

St-Jean l'Evangéliste, detail ⑨

studios in Montmartre. Here Picasso lived and worked in the early 1900s. Further up, at the corner of Rue Orchampt and Rue Ravignan, there is a row of picturesque 19th-century artists' studios ⑫.

Rue Ravignan to Rue Lepic

Continue up the hill along the small public garden, Place Jean-Baptiste Clément ⑬. At the top, cross Rue Norvins. Opposite is an old Monmartois restaurant, Auberge de la Bonne Franquette ⑭, which used to be a favourite gathering place for 19th-century artists. Continue along the narrow Rue St-Rustique, from where Sacré-Coeur can be seen. At the end and to the right is Place du Tertre ⑮, the main village square. From here go north on Rue du Mont Cenis and turn left to Rue Cortot. Erik Satie, the eccentric composer, lived in No. 6 ⑯, and at No. 12 is the Musée de Montmartre ⑰. Turn right on Rue des Saules and walk past the very pretty Montmartre vineyard ⑱ to the Au Lapin Agile ⑲ at the corner

of Rue St-Vincent. Go back down Rue des Saules and right on Rue de l'Abreuvoir, an attractive street of late 19th-century villas and gardens. Continue into l'Allée des Brouillards, a leafy pedestrian alley. No. 6 ⑳ was Renoir's last house in Montmartre. Take the steps down into the Rue Simon Dereure and immediately turn left into a small park, which can be crossed to reach Avenue Junot. Here, No. 15 ㉑ was the house of Dadaist Tristan Tzara in the early 1920s. Continue up Avenue Junot, turn right on Rue Girardon and right again on Rue Lepic.

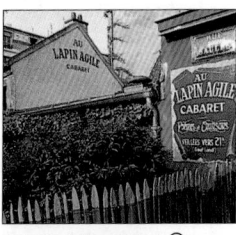

Au Lapin Agile nightclub ⑲

Rue Lepic to Place Blanche

At the corner is one of the area's few surviving windmills, the Moulin du Radet ㉒. Continue along Rue Lepic: to the right at the top of a slope is another windmill survivor, the Moulin de la Galette ㉓, now a restaurant. Turn left on Rue de l'Armée d'Orient, with its picturesque artists' studios ㉔, and left again into Rue Lepic. Van Gogh lived at No. 54 ㉕ in June 1886. Continue to Place Blanche, and on Boulevard de Clichy to the right is one of the area's great landmarks, the Moulin Rouge ㉖.

RUE SAINT VINCENT

⑰ ⑯
⑮

Artist selling his work at Place du Tertre ⑮

PLACE C DULLIN
⑦
⑤ ⑥
RUE DANCOURT
DE ROCHECHOUART
Anvers Ⓜ
RUE BOCHART DE SARON

KEY

••• Walk route

✿ Good viewing point

Ⓜ Metro station

0 metres	250
0 yards	250

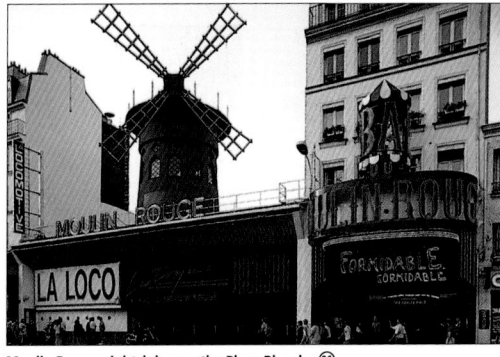

Moulin Rouge nightclub near the Place Blanche ㉖

A 90-Minute Walk in Buttes-Chaumont

This area in the east of the city is little known to many visitors, yet it contains one of Paris's biggest and most beautiful parks and some fascinating architecture. The walk is quite strenuous with many steps, and takes in a charming micro-village, the Butte Bergeyre, which is perched high above the city and has rare houses in contrasting styles. After descending from the village, the walk continues in Buttes-Chaumont park, a vast hill complete with a lake with a huge island and folly, rocky outcrops and a wonderful variety of trees and plants.

a small garden ⑩. This is owned by the city but tended by local residents who can often be found working here.

Head back down the Rue Georges Lardennois to the Rue Michel Tagrine and take the ivy-draped steps back down to the main road ⑪. Continue straight and then turn right onto the Avenue Mathurin-Moreau, noting the fine Art Deco building ⑫ at 42 with its glittering gold-coloured tile detail. At the end of the road, cross the Rue Manin to the entrance to the park.

View across city towards Sacré-Coeur ⑧

The Butte Bergeyre

From the metro Buttes-Chaumont ① take the Rue Botzaris, turning right onto the Avenue Simon Bolivar until you reach the stairs at 54 ②, which lead up into the Butte Bergeyre. At the top of the stairs pause to absorb the enchanting atmosphere of this micro-village of five little streets. Construction started in the 1920s but there are also some modern buildings. Carry on into the Rue Barrelet de Ricou ③ to admire the ivy-covered house at 13 ④, then continue to the end of the road to take a left into the Rue Philippe Hecht ⑤ where the chalet-style house at 7 ⑥ is an interesting contrast to the creeper-covered Art Deco gem at 13 ⑦. At the end of the street take a left up to the corner of the Rue Georges Lardennois and the Rue Rémy-de-Gourmont for a wonderful view across the city ⑧ of Montmartre with its wedding-cake Sacré-Coeur on top. Be sure to admire the tiny patch of grapevines ⑨ in the residents' garden below. Close to this mini-vineyard is

Some of the lovely mature trees in the park

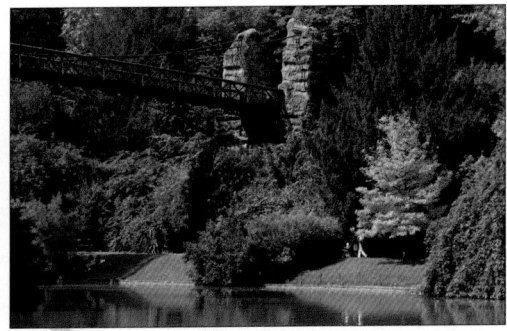

The suspension bridge, for the best view of the park ⑯

PARC DES BUTTES CHAUMONT

RUE DE CRIMEE

RUE BOTZARIS

UE DE LA CASCADE

MANIN

㉓ Ⓜ Botzaris

Clifftop folly, the park's summit ㉒

The Buttes-Chaumont Park

Commissioned by Napoleon III and Baron Haussman in 1864, the park covers 25 ha (61 acres) and took four years to complete. It was built by the engineer Adolphe Alphand and the architect Gabriel Davioud. Today, the hilly park is popular with joggers as it provides a fierce work-out. It is packed with mature trees including planes, poplars, ash, maples, chestnuts, sequoias and beautiful magnolias. At the entrance to the park

there is a man-made rock structure ⑬ with steps carved out of the façade; climb them to the top. Go on along a tree-lined path to join the Avenue du General Puebla Liniers and follow this until reaching the Carrefour de la Colonne ⑭ where there is a red brick mansion house. With your back to this go ahead to a little bridge lined with terracotta tiles. Take the bridge ⑮ then branch left down the steps within man-made rock to an impressive 63-m (206-ft) long bridge ⑯. Towering over the lake, this provides wonderful views of the park. Cross the bridge and follow the path down to the lake. The lake ⑰ is encircled by weeping willows and benches for breaks to admire the 50-m (164-ft) high man-made island ⑱. Follow the lake round until you hear rushing water. One of the park's most impressive features is the 32-m (105-ft) high waterfall ⑲ hidden inside a grotto. Walk right up to the waterfall looking up to see a patch of sky and some glorious man-made stalactites. Take a stepping-stone to the other

side of the cave and then exit and rejoin the path round the lake, heading left. Ascend the few steps, then veer to the left and up the hill ⑳. Bear left over the terracotta-tiled bridge. Take the right branch of steps and head up to the top of the cliff. Cross a tiny bridge ㉑ and turn left up some steps to the folly ㉒, a copy of the Temple of Sibyl near Rome. This is the highest point in the park providing views across the city all the way to the Sacré-Coeur. Now take the path on the right back to the Carrefour de la Colonne. Turn left and continue along the Avenue de la Cascade all the way to the exit ㉓. From here you can take the metro from station Botzaris.

KEY

• • • Walk route

Good viewing point

Ⓜ Metro station

0 metres	200
0 yards	200

Man-made waterfall, inside the grotto ⑲

A 90-Minute Walk in Faubourg St-Antoine

In the east of the city a few steps away from the bustle of the Bastille lies the Faubourg St-Antoine district, traditionally a working-class neighbourhood full of furniture designers, carpenters and artisans and this legacy can still be seen today. From the Place de la Bastille, the walk takes in Paris's pleasure-boat port, the artisan area around the Viaduc des Arts – a former viaduct with arts and crafts studios nestling in the arches – and onto the Promenade Plantée for a fascinating tree-filled stroll.

Les Grandes Marches, Place de la Bastille

The Port de Plaisance, with many pleasure boats ④

Port de Plaisance

Tucked away near the traffic of Place de La Bastille ① lies an area of tranquillity that's of interest to boat-lovers and landlubbers alike. The Port de Plaisance and Paris-Arsenal garden ② was inaugurated in 1983 to provide a harbour for pleasure craft. Linking the Seine to the Canal St-Martin, the harbour was previously where commercial barges loaded and unloaded cargo. Today, it's a pretty spot full of yachts, dinghies and Parisians out for a stroll. The cobbled stones on the quayside and old-fashioned lamp-posts add to the port's atmosphere. The lawns are perfect for a picnic and the children's play areas, while small, are well stocked with rocking chairs, slides and climbing apparatus ③. Continue to the end of the marina to the lock ④. Cross over the lock bridge, observing the pedestrian crossing sign, and head down on the other quayside turning back towards the Place de La Bastille. Just before the grey

steel bridge ⑤, take the stairs up and then the bridge over to the Boulevard de la Bastille ⑥. Cross the Boulevard and take a right and then left onto the Rue Jules César ⑦ all the way to the end of the street, turn left and then cross the Rue de Lyon turning right onto the Avenue Daumesnil and the start of the Viaduc des Arts ⑧.

Viaduc des Arts

In 1859 the Paris Viaduct was built to take a railway line that linked the Faubourg St-Antoine district with the suburbs. In 1994 the restored and revamped Viaduc des Arts opened with 50 shops and studios nestling in the bridge's rose stone archways.

In keeping with the tradition of the area, the ateliers are all linked to the arts, and some of the city's master craftsmen call the arches home. The superb

Place de la Bastille with the impressive Opéra de Paris Bastille ①

window displays at the first studio "Fleur d'Art Guillet" ⑨ give a hint of the quality of craftsmanship to come. Guillet specializes in providing silk flowers for Paris's top theatre and fashion houses. The "Ateliers du Temps Passé" ⑩ at 5 is a restorer of paintings, while Lorenove at 11 restores period glass. Number 13 is the base for hot interior designer Cherif, and the whimsical "Au Bonheur des Dames" ⑪ at 17 provides all sorts of materials for embroidery fans. For refreshment, stop at the Viaduc Café at 43 ⑫, which dishes up simple meals and hearty salads to the area's hip creatives. The SEMAEST

One of the arts and crafts shop fronts under the Viaduc des Arts ⑧

gallery space at 55/57 ⑬ hosts temporary exhibitions. Moving on past the metal furniture-maker Baguès at 73, the antique lace restorers Marie Lavande at 83, the Atelier Le Tallec 93/95, which specializes in hand-painted porcelain, it is clear that the spirit of the old artisans' area is alive and well. For those of a musical bent, Allain Cadinot repairs and sells Boehm flutes at 99, while Roger Lanne is a violin- and cello-maker at 103. With the coppersmith at 111, the terracotta tile specialist at 113 and the frame-maker at 117, you are close to the end of the viaduct, where the last atelier Jean-

Vincennes woods. For a longer walk, turn right here and go through tunnels to the city's edge and the woods. Or turn left and head back towards the Bastille. This narrow walkway offers wonderful views of the rooftops, and you can also see into some apartments. With bamboo, roses, lavender and maples, the walkway is a delight. At the end ⑰, take the steps down to the Rue de Lyon ⑱ leading to the Bastille metro, pausing only to admire the splendid Opéra de Paris Bastille ⑲ (see p98).

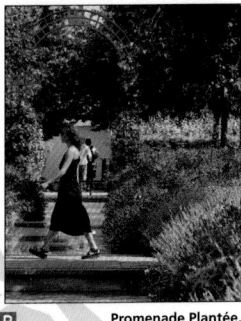

Promenade Plantée, a lovely rooftop walkway ⑯

TIPS FOR WALKERS

Starting point: *Bastille Metro*
Length: *2.6 km (1.6 miles).*
Getting there: *Bastille Metro is served by lines 1, 8 and 5. Bus Nos. 29, 65, 69, 76, 86, 87, 91 and more. Get out at "Place de la Bastille" stop.*
Stopping off points: *The area is full of great cafés, bars and restaurants. Les Grandes Marches (Place de la Bastille) is a chic place for lunch, dinner or just coffee before you start or afterwards. Nearby Rue de Lappe is lined with some fun bars. During the walk, take a break at the Viaduc Café (43 Viaduc des Arts).*

Charles Brosseau-Licences ⑮ perhaps sums up the street's diversity specializing in making hats, scent and cutlery.

Promenade Plantée

Turn left, follow the signs and take the steps up to the Promenade Plantée ⑯, a walkway on top of the viaduct. It is 4.5km (2.8 miles) long and goes all the way to the

KEY

••• Walk route

••• Detour route

⚹ Good viewing point

Ⓜ Metro station

A 90-Minute Walk in Butte-aux-Cailles

This walk takes place in and around the Butte-aux-Cailles, a lovely "village" set on a hill that is all quiet streets, leafy squares and buzzy local bistros. The area made history in 1783 when the first manned balloon flight touched down here. In the 1800s it was home to many workers from the small factories in the area and was one of the first areas to fight during the Paris Commune. However, it only really developed after 1910 and the architecture reflects the social ideals of the day – that individual houses and green spaces aid health.

de la Butte-aux-Cailles ⑪. Head up the street to the Place de la Commune de Paris ⑫, which today looks unremarkable yet was the site of a major battle in May 1871. Continue up the Rue de la Butte-aux-Cailles. Les Abeilles at 21 ⑬ is a curious store dedicated to bee-keeping and a delight for honey lovers. Pancakes in the old-fashioned crêperie Des Crêpes et des Cailles at 13 may satisfy if you are just peckish, but further down at 20 is the area's best-known restaurant Les Temps de Cerises ⑭. Fittingly, as it's only a few minutes' walk from the Place de la

Quiet, cobbled streets typify the Butte-aux-Cailles ⑪

Buttes-aux-Cailles

Take the "Auguste Blanqui" exit out of the Place d'Italie metro station ①, noting the Guimard decoration. Follow the bustling Rue Bobillot until you reach the Rue Paulin-Méry ② and take your first steps into the peace of the Butte-aux-Cailles. The contrast is surprising as you walk the quiet, narrow, cobbled streets with their old-fashioned street lamps. Note the lovely lilac painted shutters on 5 ③ and the trees in the small garden in front of the house opposite. Continue straight ahead, cross over the Rue du Moulin-des-Prés and turn left into the Rue Gérard past the red brick terraces and plant-decked villas ④. Keep on into the Rue Samson and then turn right onto the Rue Jonas and left onto the Rue des Cinq Diamants ⑤. The charming theatre at 10 performs well-reviewed shows, while at 43 ⑥ Hansel et Gretel is a quaint old sweet shop with a few tables and chairs. Those

13e Arrt RUE DE LA BUTTE AUX CAILLES

Road sign in the Butte aux Cailles area

interested in history may appreciate the Association des Amis de la Commune de Paris at 46 ⑦, which sells T-shirts, books and pamphlets on that bloody episode in Parisian history. Turn right into the Passage Barrault, a cobbled alleyway with ivy-covered walls and a countryside feel ⑧. At the end of the passage, turn left onto the Rue Barrault and continue up the street until the right turn into the Rue Daviel. At 10 Rue Daviel the row of cottages known as "Little Alsace" ⑨ because of their chalet style are, in fact, one of the first public housing schemes in Paris. Opposite, walk down the Villa Daviel ⑩, a tiny street of terraces with small front gardens overflowing with greenery. Retrace your steps back up to the Rue Barrault, turn left and then right onto the artery of the area, the Rue

Corvisart Ⓜ

RUE DE TOLBIAC

Theatre, Rue des Cinq-Diamants ⑤

Le Temps des Cerises, full of bohemian atmosphere ⑭

TIPS FOR WALKERS

Starting point: Place de l'Italie metro.
Length: 2.6 km (1.6 miles).
Getting there: Start from the Place D'Italie metro via lines 5, 6 and 7. Or take buses Nos 27, 47, 57, 67 and 83 and get off at the stop "Place d'Italie".
Stopping-off Points: The Rue de la Butte-aux-Cailles is full of great cafés and restaurants. Les Temps des Cerises (No. 18) is very atmospheric, while Tandem (No. 10) is devoted to fusion cuisine. On Rue des Cinq Diamants, Chez Gladines (No. 30) is a great bet for a good lunch, while Les Cailloux (No. 58) is a chic option.

Commune, it's run as a co-operative and is also the unofficial neighbourhood HQ. At the end of the road is the Place Paul Verlaine ⑮. On the other side of the square is the red brick Art Nouveau swimming pool ⑯. Built in 1924, it houses one indoor pool and two lovely outdoor swimming areas. Take the steps in front of the building to find the modern fountain on the Place ⑰.

Crêpes from Des Crêpes et des Cailles

This is supplied by a local well 580 m (1,902 ft) deep, dating from 1863, and was refurbished in 2000. You may see locals queuing to fill plastic bottles here. Exit the square, take a right and then another right past the chic restaurant Chez Nathalie with its flowery terrace, which is always packed in summer, into the Rue Vandrezanne, continuing down this pedestrianized street into the passage Vandrezanne, a steep cobbled alleyway with antiquated lampposts ⑱. Cross over the Rue Moulinet and take the Rue Moulin des Prés until you come to the Rue Tolbiac. Cross this busy road then take a right stepping back into another time at the Square des Peupliers ⑲. Built in 1926, each house is different, reflecting the ideals of the time. All have pretty little gardens, most have lovely Art Nouveau porches and the ornate gilded lamp posts are

very special. Leave the Square des Peupliers and take a right back onto the Rue du Moulin-des-Prés. Head down the street, noting the interesting rough stone houses ⑳, straight past an unusual purple Art Nouveau-style house at 104 ㉑. Take a right onto the Rue Damesme, turn right into the Rue du Docteur Leray and then right again onto Rue Dieulafoy ㉒. Here are several unique, colourful cottages. At the end of the row, take a right onto the Rue Henri Pape, a left onto the Rue Damesme, walk up to the Rue Tolbiac and back out into modern, busy, Paris. Turn right and walk up to the metro Tolbiac ㉓.

KEY

••• Walk route

Ⓜ Metro station

0 metres   200
0 yards   200

Square des Peupliers, with its unique houses ⑲

TRAVELLERS' NEEDS

WHERE TO STAY 276–291

RESTAURANTS, CAFES AND BARS 292–319

SHOPS AND MARKETS 320–339

ENTERTAINMENT IN PARIS 340–359

CHILDREN'S PARIS 360–363

WHERE TO STAY

Paris has more guest rooms than almost any other city in Europe. Its hotels vary from magnificent luxurious places like the Ritz (the French call them *palaces*) and exclusive establishments like L'Hôtel, where Oscar Wilde died beyond his means, to much simpler hotels in charming older parts of Paris. It is worth noting that *hôtel* does not always mean "hotel". It can also mean a town hall *(hôtel de ville)*, hospital

We have inspected hotels in all price brackets and have selected a broad range, all of which are good value for money. The listings on pp284–91 are organized by area, as in the sightseeing section of the guide, and according to hotel price. Other types of accommodation such as bed and breakfast rooms, self-catering apartments and hostels *(see pp278–9)* are also well worth considering, especially for visitors who are on a tight budget.

WHERE TO LOOK

Hotels in Paris tend to cluster by type in particular areas, with the river separating the business and leisure districts. Luxury hotels tend to be on the north side and *hôtels de charme* on the south side.

In the fashionable districts near the Champs-Elysées and the Opéra Garnier lie many of the grandest hotels in Paris, including the Royal Monceau, the Bristol, the Four Seasons George V, the Meurice and the Plaza Athénée. Several less well known but elegant hotels can be found in the residential and ambassadorial quarter near the Palais de Chaillot.

To the east, still on the Right Bank, in the regenerated Marais, a number of the old mansions and palaces have been converted into exceptionally attractive small hotels at reasonable prices. The nearby areas around Les

Halles and the Rue St-Denis, however, attract prostitutes and drug addicts. Just south of the Marais across the Seine, the Ile St-Louis and Ile de la Cité have several charming hotels.

The Left Bank covers some of the most popular tourist areas and has an excellent range of small hotels of great character. The atmosphere subtly changes from the much upgraded Latin Quarter and the chic and arty areas north and south of Boulevard St-Germain, to the rather tatty Boulevard itself and the staid institutional area towards Les Invalides and the Eiffel Tower. The hotels tend to reflect this.

Further from the centre, Montparnasse has several large business hotels in high-rise blocks, and the Porte de Versailles area to the south is usually packed with trade fair participants. The station areas around Gare du Nord and Gare de Lyon offer a number

Hôtel de Crillon *(see pp282, 285)*

of basic hotels (choose carefully). Montmartre has one or two pleasant hotels if you don't mind the hilly location, but beware of hotels allegedly in Montmartre but actually in the red-light, sex-show district of Pigalle. If you are looking for a hotel in person, the best times for inspecting are late morning or mid-afternoon. If the hotels are fully booked, try again after 6pm, when unclaimed provisional bookings become free. Don't rely on the impression of a hotel given by reception: ask to see the room offered. (For airport hotels *see p379.)*

HOTEL PRICES

Hotel prices aren't always cheaper in low season (mid-November to March or July and August) because fashion shows and other major events throughout the year can pack rooms, raising prices.

The Hôtel du Louvre *(see p285)*, between the Louvre and the Palais Royal

◁ River view of Notre-Dame

However, in the older hotels differences in the size and position of rooms can have a marked effect on cost.

Twin rooms are slightly more expensive than doubles; single occupancy rates as high or nearly as high as for two people sharing (tariffs are nearly always quoted per room, not per person). Single rooms are rare and many are extremely poky or poorly equipped. Rooms without a bath tend to be about 20% cheaper than those with. You might find a half-board arrangement unnecessary with such a wide choice of good restaurants around.

It is always worth asking for a discount: you may get a corporate rate, for instance. In some hotels special deals are offered for students, families or senior citizens. Discounts are often available when booking online or when booking a package trip.

HIDDEN EXTRAS

By law, tax and service must be included in the price quoted or displayed at the reception desk or in the rooms. Tips are unnecessary other than for exceptional service – if the concierge books you a show, for instance, or if the maid does some washing for you. However, before you make a reservation you should always establish whether breakfast is included in the price or not. Beware of extras such as drinks or snacks from

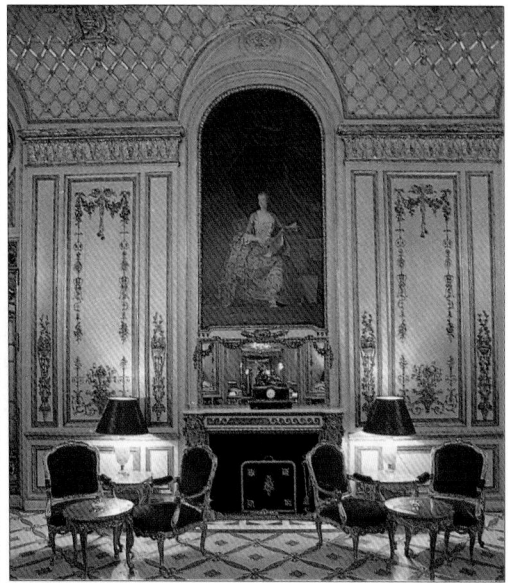

The Hôtel Meurice *(see p285)* in the Tuileries Quarter

a mini-bar, which will probably be pricy, as will laundry services, garage parking and telephone calls from your room – especially telephone calls made through the switchboard.

Exchange rates in hotels invariably tend to be lower than in a bank, so make sure you have enough cash to pay your bill unless you are paying by credit card or using travellers' cheques.

HOTEL GRADINGS

French hotels are classified by the tourist authorities into five broad categories: one to four stars, plus a four-star deluxe rating. Some very simple places are unclassified. Star ratings indicate something about the level of facilities you can expect (for example, any hotel with more than three stars should have a lift). But the French rating system is no reliable guide to friendliness, cleanliness or tastefulness of the decor.

FACILITIES

Few Parisian hotels below a four-star rating have a restaurant, although there is nearly always a breakfast room. Quite a few hotel restaurants close in August. Many of the older hotels also lack a public lounge area. More modern or expensive hotels have correspondingly better facilities and generally some kind of bar. Inexpensive hotels may not have a lift – significant when you are dragging suitcases upstairs. Usually only the more expensive hotels have parking facilities. For exceptions to this rule, see the listings on pages 284–91. If you are driving you may prefer to stay in one of the peripheral motel-style chain hotels *(see pp279–80)*.

All but the very simplest of city hotels will have a telephone in the bedroom; many also have television. Business facilities (fax and internet) are now available in the grander hotels. Double beds *(grands lits)* are common, but you must specify whether or not you want one.

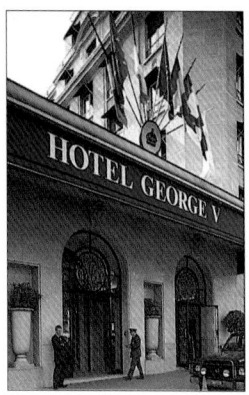

Four Seasons George V *(see p290)*

Statue in the Hôtel Relais Christine *(see pp283, 287)*

The Plaza Athénée *(see p291)* in Champs-Elysées

WHAT TO EXPECT

Many hotel beds still stick to the time-honoured French bolster, a sausage-shaped headrest that can be uncomfortable if you are unused to it. If you prefer pillows, ask for *oreillers*. If you want to make sure you get a toilet, specify a *WC*, and if you want a bath, ask for a *bain*. Otherwise, a *cabinet de toilette* is just a basin and bidet, and *eau courante* means simply a basin with hot and cold running water. A duplex room is a suite on two floors.

The traditional French hotel breakfast of fresh coffee, croissants, jam and orange juice is in Paris gradually changing into an elaborate buffet breakfast with cold meats and cheeses. Some of the luxury hotels are now such popular venues for breakfast that it is worth reserving a place in the breakfast area if you don't want to eat in your room. A pleasant alternative is to head for the nearest café, where French workers are enjoying breakfast over a newspaper.

Check-out time is usually noon and if you stay longer you will pay for an extra day.

SPECIAL BREAKS

Because Paris is such a popular destination with leisure as well as business travellers, weekend packages are often available via travel agents or the Internet. Providing there are no major events taking place, you can reduce costs by visiting in low season and negotiating a discount, or by seeking out an all-inclusive package.

TRAVELLING WITH CHILDREN

Families with young children will often find they can share a room at no or very little extra cost, and some operators offer packages with this in mind. Few hotels refuse to accept children, though facilities specifically for children are not universal. Some hotels will arrange baby-sitting.

DISABLED TRAVELLERS

Our information about wheelchair access to hotels was gathered by questionnaire and therefore relies on the hotels' own assessment of their suitability. Not many are well geared for use by disabled visitors. The **Association des Paralysés de France** and the **Groupement pour l'Insertion des Personnes Handicapées Physiques (GIHP)** have pertinent information *(For addresses see p367.)*

SELF-CATERING

A scheme called **Résidence Internationale de Paris** provides apartments in specially-run self-catering blocks. Some hotel-type facilities are available, but you pay extra for them. Prices vary from around 90€ a night for a small studio to over 300€ a night for an apartment for several people. Either contact

The quiet Hôtel des Grands Hommes (see p287)

Paris-Séjour-Réservation or get in touch with each *résidence* directly. The **Office du Tourisme et des Congrès de Paris** also provides a full list of *résidences*.

Self-catering accommodation is an increasingly popular alternative for staying in Paris. The better known agencies include **Allo Logement Temporaire, At Home In Paris, ASLOM, Paris Appartements Services** and **France Appartements. Good Morning Paris** and **France-Lodge** also arrange self-catering apartments, as well as being B&B agencies *(see* Directory *p280).* All provide furnished apartments for stays from one week to six months, sometimes in the apartment of a Parisian who is abroad. Prices are comparable to the Résidence Internationale de Paris, sometimes slightly cheaper for the larger apartments.

STAYING IN PRIVATE HOMES

Bed and breakfast, that typically-British phenomenon, is known as *chambre d'hôte* or *café-couette* ("coffee and a quilt"). B&B accommodation is available at moderate prices, between 35€ and 75€ for a double room per night. **Alcôve & Agapes** offers rooms in some enviable districts of Paris, all within walking distance of a metro station. It is worth enquiring about suites and rooms with a private lounge, kitchen or terrace. All homes are routinely inspected.

France-Lodge is a good-value agency specialising in long-stay room rentals and apartments. A registration fee of 15€ a year is payable but rentals are generally cheaper than with other agencies.

Good Morning Paris provides guest rooms and tourist information. A two-night minimum stay is required when booking *(for details see* Directory *p280).*

CHAIN HOTELS

A mushroom crop of motel-style establishments on the outskirts of Paris now take large numbers of both business and leisure visitors.

The Hôtel Atala terrace (see *p290*)

The garden of the Relais Christine (see *p287*)

The very cheapest chains such as Formule 1, Première Class and Fast Hotel, really have nothing except price to recommend them. Further up the ladder are **Campanile, Ibis** and **Choice Hotels**. These places are practical, relatively inexpensive and useful if you have a car, but lack any real

The Hôtel Prince de Galles Sheraton (see *p291*)

Parisian atmosphere or character. Many are in charmless locations on busy roads and may suffer from traffic noise. The newer motels of these chains are better equipped and more smartly decorated than the older ones. Several chains (**Sofitel, Novotel** and **Mercure**) are especially geared to business travellers, providing better facilities at higher prices; indeed some of the more central ones are positively luxurious. Reductions can make these hotels good value at

weekends. Many of the hotels have restaurants attached. Most of the chains produce their own brochures, often with useful maps detailing the motel's precise location *(see* Directory *p280).*

HOSTELS AND DORMITORY ACCOMMODATION

There are several hostel networks in Paris. **Maisons Internationales de la Jeunesse et des Etudiants (MIJE)** provides dormitory accommodation for the 18–30s in three splendid mansions in the Marais. There is no advance booking (except for groups) – call at the central offices on the day.

The **Bureau Voyage Jeunesse (BVJ)** has two 'hotels' with double rooms and dormitory accommodation (23–28€ and 25€ respectively), with breakfast and nearly private bathrooms. Bookings cannot be made more than a fortnight in advance.

La Maison de l'UCRIF (Union des Centres de Rencontres Internationales de France) has nine centres around Paris with individual, shared and dormitory rooms. No age limit is imposed. Cultural and sporting activities are available at some centres.

Fédération Unie des Auberges de Jeunesse (FUAJ) is a member of the International Youth Hostels Federation. There is no age limit at their two Paris hostels. *(For addresses see* Directory *p280.)*

DIRECTORY

OFFICE DU TOURISME

25 Rue des Pyramides 75001.
Tel 08 92 68 30 00.
See also p367. English tourist hotline 118 247.
www.parisinfo.com

AGENCIES

Ely 12 12
182 Rue du Faubourg St-Honoré 75008.
Tel 01 43 59 12 12.
www.ely1212.com

Paris-Séjour-Réservation
90 Ave des Champs-Elysées 75008.
Tel 01 53 89 10 50.
www.psrparis.com

SELF-CATERING

Allo Logement Temporaire
64 Rue du Temple 75003.
Tel 01 42 72 00 06.
www.allo-logement-temporaire.asso.fr

ASLOM
75–77 Ave Parmentier 75011.
Tel 01 43 49 67 79.
www.aslom.com

At Home in Paris
16 Rue Médéric 75017.
Tel 01 42 12 40 40.
Fax 01 42 12 40 48.
www.athomeinparis.fr

France Appartements
97 Ave des Champs-Elysées 75008.
Tel 01 56 89 31 00.
www.rentapart.com

Paris Appartements Services
20 Rue Bachaumont 75002.
Tel 01 40 28 01 28.
www.paris-apts.com

RESIDENCES DE TOURISME

Les Citadines
Tel 0825 333 332.
www.citadines.com

Pierre et Vacances
Tel 0892 70 21 80.
www.pierre-vacances.fr

Résidence Internationale de Paris
44 Rue Louis Lumière 75020.
Tel 01 40 31 45 45.
www.residence-inter-paris.com

Résidence du Roy
8 Rue François-1er 75008.
Tel 01 42 89 59 59.
www.hroy.com

BED & BREAKFAST

Alcôve & Agapes
8bis Rue Coysevox 75018.
Tel 01 44 85 06 05.
Fax 01 44 85 06 14.
www.bed-and-breakfast-in-paris.com

France-Lodge
2 Rue Meissonier 75017.
Tel 01 56 33 85 85.
Fax 01 56 33 85 89.
www.apartments-in-paris.com

Good Morning Paris
43 Rue Lacépède, 75005.
Tel 01 47 07 28 29.
Fax 01 47 07 44 45.
www.goodmorningparis.fr

CHAIN HOTELS

Campanile
Tel 0825 003 003
(central reservations).
www.campanile.fr

Choice Hotels
Tel 08 00 12 12 12
(central reservations).
www.choicehotels.com

Hilton
18 Ave de Suffren 75015.
Tel 01 44 38 56 00.
www.hilton.com

Holiday Inn République
10 Pl de la République 75011.
Tel 0800 910 617.
www.holiday-inn.com

Holiday Inn St-Germain-des-Prés
Tel 0800 911 617 or
01 49 54 87 00.
www.holiday-inn.com

Ibis
Tel 0892 686 686
(central reservations).
www.ibishotel.com

Mercure Paris Austerlitz
6 Blvd Vincent Auriol 75013. *Tel* 01 45 82 48 00. **www**.mercure.com

Mercure Paris Bercy
77 Rue de Bercy 75012.
Tel 01 53 46 50 50.
www.mercure.com

Mercure Paris Montparnasse
20 Rue de la Gaîté 75014.
Tel 01 43 35 28 28.
www.mercure.com

Mercure Paris Porte de Versailles
69 Blvd Victor 75015.
Tel 01 44 19 03 03.
www.mercure.com

Mercure Paris Tour-Eiffel
64 Blvd de Grenelle 75015.
Tel 01 45 78 90 00.
www.mercure.com

Méridien Montparnasse
19 Rue du Commandant René Mouchotte 75014.
Tel 01 44 36 44 36.
www.lemeridien.fr

Novotel Paris Bercy
85 Rue de Bercy 75012.
Tel 01 43 42 30 00.
www.novotel.com

Novotel Paris Les Halles
8 Pl Marguerite de Navarre 75001.
Tel 01 42 21 31 31.
www.novotel.com

Novotel Tour Eiffel
61 Quai de Grenelle 75015.
Tel 01 40 58 20 00.
www.novotel.com

Paris Rive Gauche Hotel and Conference Centre
17 Blvd St-Jacques 75014.
Tel 01 40 78 79 80.
www.sofitel.com

Royal Garden St-Honoré
218 Rue du Faubourg St-Honoré 75008.
Tel 01 49 53 03 03.
www.gtshparis.com

Hotel Sofitel Scribe
1 Rue Scribe 75009.
Tel 01 44 71 24 24.
www.sofitel.com

Sofitel Paris La Défense Centre
34 Cours Michelet, 92060.
Tel 01 47 76 44 43.
www.sofitel.com

Sofitel Le Faubourg
15 Rue Boissy d'Anglas 75008. *Tel* 01 44 94 14 14. **www**.sofitel.com

Warwick Champs-Elysées
5 Rue de Berri 75008.
Tel 01 45 63 14 11.

HOSTELS

BVJ
20 Rue Jean-Jacques Rousseau 75001.
Tel 01 53 00 90 90.
Fax 01 53 00 90 91.

FUAJ – Centre National
27 Rue Pajol 75018.
Tel 01 44 89 87 27.
Fax 01 44 89 87 10.
www.fuaj.org

La Maison de l'UCRIF
27 Rue de Turbigo 75002.
Tel 01 40 26 57 64.
Fax 01 40 26 58 20.
www.ethic-etapes.fr

MIJE
Head Office: 11 Rue du Fauconnier 75004.
Tel 01 42 74 23 45.
Fax 01 42 74 08 93.
www.mije.com

CAMPING

Camping du Bois de Boulogne/Ile de France
Allée du Bord de l'Eau 75016. *Tel* 01 45 24 30 00. *Fax* 01 42 24 42 95.
www.campingparis.fr

Camping International de Jablines
Jablines-Annet 77450.
Tel 01 60 26 09 37.
Fax 01 60 26 43 33.
www.camping-jablines.com

FFCC
78 Rue de Rivoli 75004.
Tel 01 42 72 84 08.
Fax 01 42 72 70 21.
www.ffcc.fr

CAMPING

The only campsite in Paris itself is the **Camping du Bois de Boulogne/Ile de France** (around 12€–35€ per night). This well-equipped site next to the Seine is open all year round but is usually fully booked during the summer. Pitches for tents, caravans as well as rental of mobile homes are available. There are many other campsites in the surrounding region, some close to an RER line. The **Camping International de Jablines** (around 20€–25€ per night) is conveniently located just 9km (5.5 miles) from Disneyland Paris and a 25-minute RER train ride from central Paris. Details of other sites can be obtained from the Paris tourist office or from a booklet produced by the **Fédération Française de Camping-Caravaning (FFCC)** (see Directory p280).

HOW TO BOOK

The busiest tourist seasons are May, June, September and October, but special events such as fashion shows, trade fairs or major exhibitions can fill most rooms in Paris throughout the year. Disneyland Resort Paris has further increased the pressure to find accommodation, as many visitors choose to stay in the capital and commute to the park on the RER. July and August are quieter, as many Parisians are on their annual holiday.

If you have decided on a hotel, it is vital to book ahead by at least a month as Paris is a popular destination. The hotels in the listings are among the best in their category and will fill particularly fast. Make a reservation six weeks in advance between May and October. The best way is to book directly with the hotel. If you make your initial inquiry by telephone, ring during the day if possible – you are more likely to find staff authorized to take bookings. You should send confirmation of your reservation (websites or email addresses are provided where

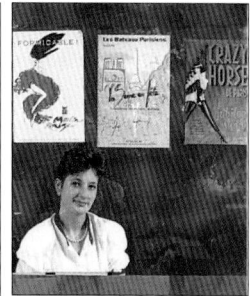

Tourist information desk, Charles de Gaulle airport

available); credit card details are often required to guarantee your booking.

If you prefer to use an agency, **Ely 12 12** and **Paris-Séjour-Réservation** can book hotels and other kinds of accommodation, sometimes even a barge along the Seine.

If you aren't too fussy about where you stay, or if all the hotels are reportedly full, you can book via the **Office du Tourisme et des Congrès de Paris**, which offers an on-the-spot booking service for a reasonable fee.

DEPOSITS

If you make a reservation by telephone you will be asked for either your credit card number (from which any cancellation fee may be deducted) or a deposit (*arrhes*). These *arrhes* can be as much as the price of a night's stay, but usually cost only about 15% of this. Pay your deposit by credit card or by sending an international money order. You can sometimes send an ordinary cheque for an amount equivalent to the deposit as evidence of your intention to keep the booking. Usually the hotel will simply keep your foreign cheque as security until you arrive, then return it to you and give you one total bill when you leave. But do check with the hotel before sending an ordinary cheque. It's also quite acceptable in France to specify your choice of room when you book.

Try to arrive at your hotel by 6pm on the day you have booked, or at least telephone

to say you will be late, otherwise you may well lose the room. A hotel that breaks a confirmed, prepaid booking is breaking a contract, and the client is entitled to compensation of at least twice any deposit paid. Alternatively, the hotel must offer you equivalent or better accommodation elsewhere. If you have any problems, consult the Office du Tourisme.

TOURIST INFORMATION DESKS

You can book hotels at all airport information desks but only in person and for the same day. The Gare de Lyon and the Tour Eiffel (seasonal) information desks provide a similar booking arrangement for all forms of accommodation. Many Paris information desks also keep a complete list of city hotels and some book entertainment, excursions etc (see Practical Information p367).

Paris's Best: Hotels

Paris is famous for its hotels. It excels in all categories from the glittering opulent *palaces* (the top luxury hotels) to the *hôtels de charme*, full of character and romantic appeal, to the simpler good-value family hotels in quiet back streets. As a centre of culture and fashion, the city has long been a mecca for the rich and famous, great and good from all walks of life. Not surprisingly, therefore, it can boast some of the most magnificent hotels in the world and has more than a thousand hotels in the inner city alone. Whatever the price level, however, the hotels in our listings *(see pp284–91)* all show that inimitable style and taste that Parisians bring to everything they do. These are a selection of the very best.

Bristol
In the chic heart of Paris, this epitomizes luxury. (See p290.)

Champs-Elysées

Chaillot Quarter

R I V E R   S   E

Invalides and Eiffel Tower Quarter

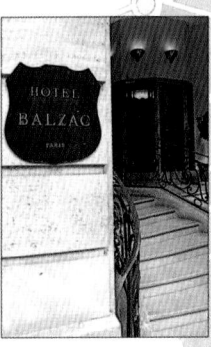

Balzac
Small but stylish, this hotel exudes period charm. The restaurant, Pierre Gagnaire, is highly rated. (See p290.)

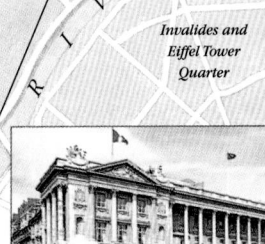

Hôtel de Crillon
One of the great palace *hotels, this was built for Louis XV.* (See p285.)

Plaza Athénée
In the heart of haute couture *Paris, this is the favourite haunt of the fashion world. Magnificent decor and a superb restaurant are the main attractions.* (See p291.)

Duc de St-Simon
Bedrooms overlook a leafy garden in this comfortable and peaceful hôtel de charme *situated in an 18th-century mansion south of the Seine.* (See p289.)

Le Grand Hôtel Intercontinental
Built for Napoleon III in 1862, this historic hotel has been patronized by the rich and famous from Mata Hari to Winston Churchill.
(See p291.)

L'Hôtel
Best known as the last home of Oscar Wilde, this stylish hotel boasts rooms both impressive and slightly bizarre. One room was furnished and occupied by the music hall star Mistinguett.
(See p287.)

Opéra Quarter

es Quarter

Beaubourg and Les Halles

rmain-des-Prés

The Marais

Ile de la Cité

Ile St-Louis

Luxembourg Quarter

Latin Quarter

Jardin des Plantes Quarter

Relais Christine
An oasis of calm in the hub of the city, this charming hotel offers tradition- al comforts such as a welcoming open fire in the drawing room.
(See p287.)

Hôtel du Jeu de Paume
This cleverly converted hotel was once a court for playing real tennis – jeu de paume.
(See p284.)

| 0 kilometres | 1 |
| 0 miles | 0.5 |

Hotel de l'Abbaye
A pleasant garden and courtyard and attractive rooms are features of this small secluded hotel near the Jardins du Luxembourg.
(See p286.)

Lutétia
This was decorated by top designer Sonia Rykiel. (See p287.)

Choosing a Hotel

The hotels listed in the following pages have been selected for their facilities, good value and location. The list covers all the areas and price categories with additional information to help you choose a hotel that best meets your needs. Hotels within the same category are listed alphabetically.

PRICE CATEGORIES
For a standard double room per night including breakfast and necessary charges:
€ under 90 euros
€€ 90–140 euros
€€€ 140–180 euros
€€€€ 180–260 euros
€€€€€ over 260 euros

ILE DE LA CITÉ AND ILE ST-LOUIS

Hôtel des Deux-Iles   €€€
59 Rue St-Louis-en-l'Ile, 75004 **Tel** *01 43 26 13 35* **Fax** *01 43 29 60 25* **Rooms** *17*   **Map** *13 C4*

Its a privilege to be able to stay on the Ile St-Louis, and this converted 17th-century mansion offers an affordable way to do so. Here the atmosphere is peaceful, the small bedrooms are attractive and the lounge has a real fire. **www.deuxiles-paris-hotel.com**

Hôtel du Jeu de Paume   €€€€
54 Rue St-Louis-en-l'Ile, 75004 **Tel** *01 43 26 14 18* **Fax** *01 40 46 02 76* **Rooms** *30*   **Map** *13 C4*

Standing on the site of a former real tennis court, the hotel has been skilfully converted into a warm, elegant place to stay. Features include a glass-walled lift, wooden beams, old terracotta paving, a sauna and several charming duplex rooms. **www.hoteljeudepaume.com**

THE MARAIS

Hôtel de la Bretonnerie   €€
22 Rue Ste-Croix de la Bretonnerie, 75004 **Tel** *01 48 87 77 63* **Fax** *01 42 77 26 78* **Rooms** *29*   **Map** *13 C3*

Carved stone walls and an arched dining room in the basement are some of the charming features of Hôtel de la Bretonnerie, housed in a 17th-century mansion. One of the most comfortable hotels in the area, it has spacious bedrooms with wooden beams and antique furniture. Service is warm and friendly. **www.bretonnerie.com**

Hôtel du Septième Art   €€
20 Rue St-Paul, 75004 **Tel** *01 44 54 85 00* **Fax** *01 42 77 69 10* **Rooms** *23*   **Map** *14 D4*

A film buff's dream, this charming little spot is stuffed full with mementos of the movies. The rooms are clean and all have a cinematic touch, from advertising posters to mini-statuettes of Marilyn Monroe. Staff are very friendly too. An ideal place to retire after a long day of sightseeing. **www.paris-hotel-7art.com**

Hôtel du Bourg Tibourg   €€€
19 Rue du Bourg Tibourg, 75004 **Tel** *01 42 78 47 39* **Fax** *01 40 29 07 00* **Rooms** *30*   **Map** *13C*

This stylish spot was decorated by top interior designer Jacques Garcia and is extremely popular with fashionable visitors to Paris. Rooms are opulent and all bathrooms are fully clad in black marble. The beautiful interior courtyard is a pleasant surprise. **www.hotelbourgtibourg.com**

St-Merry   €€€
78 Rue de la Verrerie, 75004 **Tel** *01 42 78 14 15* **Fax** *01 40 29 06 82* **Rooms** *12*   **Map** *13 B3*

A historic hotel which was the presbytery of the adjoining church in the 17th century and later became a bordello, is today a simply lovely place to stay. Furnished in Gothic style, note the flying buttresses crossing room 9. **www.hotelmarais.com**

St-Paul-le-Marais   €€€
8 Rue de Sévigné, 75004 **Tel** *01 48 04 97 27* **Fax** *01 48 87 37 04* **Rooms** *28*   **Map** *14 D3*

Close to the historic Place des Vosges, this hotel has wooden beams and old stone, although the furnishings are simple and modern. Ask for bedrooms facing the courtyard to avoid the noise of traffic coming from the Rue de Sévigné. **www.hotel-paris-marais.com**

Pavillon de la Reine   €€€€€
28 Pl des Vosges, 75003 **Tel** *01 40 29 19 19* **Fax** *01 40 29 19 20* **Rooms** *56*   **Map** *14 D3*

Set back from the marvellous Place des Vosges, the Pavillon de la Reine is the best hotel in the Marais. Incredibly romantic, the courtyard is a haven of peace and the bedrooms are sumptuous and furnished with excellent reproduction antiques. **www.pavillon-de-la-reine.com**

Key to Symbols *see back cover flap*

BEAUBOURG AND LES HALLES

Hôtel Roubaix

6 Rue Greneta, 75003 **Tel** *01 42 72 89 91* **Fax** *01 42 72 58 79* **Rooms** *53* €

Map *13B*

Hôtel Roubaix is pleasantly old-fashioned and inexpensive in an area with few good places to stay. The owners are exceptionally friendly and the rooms are clean, if a little shabby. The hotel is popular with return guests, so be sure to book a room in advance.

TUILERIES QUARTER

Hôtel St-Honoré

85 Rue St-Honoré, 75001 **Tel** *01 42 36 20 38* **Fax** *01 42 21 44 08* **Rooms** *29* €

Map *12 F2*

Close to Concorde, Tuileries, Louvre and Palais-Royal, the St-Honoré has an attractive green façade. The rooms, recently renovated and equipped with all modern amenities, are extremely well kept. Very good value for money considering the excellent location. A few rooms have been designed for families. **www.parishotel.com**

Brighton

218 Rue de Rivoli, 75001 **Tel** *01 47 03 61 61* **Fax** *01 42 60 41 78* **Rooms** *65* €€€

Map *12 D1*

A real insiders' location, the Brighton provides a much-sought after Rivoli address without the sky-high prices. The bedrooms have beautiful, high ceilings and large windows that look out either on to the Jardin des Tuileries or on to the courtyard. **www.esprit-de-france.com**

Hotel and Spa Saint James Albany

202 Rue de Rivoli, 75001 **Tel** *01 44 58 43 21* **Fax** *01 44 58 43 11* **Rooms** *195* €€€€€

Map *12 E1*

This quiet and tidy hotel is currently undergoing a much needed renovation to do away with its aura of faded grandeur. It is perfectly situated in the heart of Paris, opposite the Tuileries gardens, and boasts a charming spa and swimming pool area. **www.clarionsaintjames.com**

Hôtel Costes

239 Rue St Honoré, 75001 **Tel** *01 42 44 50 00* **Fax** *01 42 44 50 01* **Rooms** *82* €€€€€

Map *12 D1*

One of the most fashionable places to stay in Paris, the Costes is a favourite with models and film stars. A sumptuous affair, it is designed to resemble a Second Empire palace. The balcony rooms are the most in demand. In summer, eat in the Italianate courtyard. **www.hotel costes.com**

Hôtel de Crillon

10 Pl de la Concorde, 75008 **Tel** *01 44 71 15 00* **Fax** *01 44 71 15 02* **Rooms** *147* €€€€€

Map *11 C1*

With its magnificent location on the glittering Place de la Concorde, the Crillon offers unsurpassed elegance. The hotel has a fine Royal Suite and terrace, a sublime dining room and a fashionable bar designed by Sonia Rykiel. **www.crillon.com**

Hôtel du Louvre

Pl André Malraux, 75001 **Tel** *01 44 58 38 38* **Fax** *01 44 58 38 01* **Rooms** *177* €€€€€

Map *12 E1*

The first luxury hotel in France was built in 1855 by order of Napoleon III. The lavish rooms have spectacular views: the Pissarro Suite is where the artist painted his view of Place du Théâtre Français, while if you book room 551 you can admire the opera house from your bath! **www.hotel dulouvre.com**

Hôtel Regina

2 Pl des Pyramides, 75001 **Tel** *01 42 60 31 10* **Fax** *01 40 15 95 16* **Rooms** *120* €€€€€

Map *12 E1*

Surprisingly, the Regina is not known to many tourists, even though it is popular with the media. The wood detail in the lounge is stunning Art Nouveau and many films have been shot here. Some of the rooms have superb views. **www.regina-hotel.com**

Meurice

228 Rue de Rivoli, 75001 **Tel** *01 44 58 10 10* **Fax** *01 44 58 10 15* **Rooms** *160* €€€€€

Map *12 D1*

The Meurice is a perfect example of successful restoration, with excellent replicas of the original plasterwork and furnishings. The staff here are unstintingly helpful and the hotel offers personalised shopping and art buying tours. There is also a top spa. **www.meuricehotel.com**

Ritz Paris

15 Pl Vendôme, 75001 **Tel** *01 43 16 30 30* **Fax** *01 43 16 45 38* **Rooms** *162* €€€€€

Map *6 D5*

A legendary address, the Ritz still lives up to its reputation, combining elegance and decadence. The Louis XVI furniture and chandeliers are all originals, and the floral arrangements are works of art. The Hemingway Bar is home to the glitterati. **www.ritzparis.com**

The Westin Paris
🖼 🕕 🏛 📺 🗐   €€€€€

3 Rue de Castiglione, 75001 **Tel** *01 44 77 11 11* **Fax** *01 44 77 14 60* **Rooms** *438*   **Map** *12 D1*

This elegant late 19th-century hotel is situated between the Jardin des Tuileries and the Place Vendôme. It was designed by Charles Garnier, architect of the Paris Opéra. Bedrooms are quiet – the best overlook one of the courtyards. **www.westin.com**

ST-GERMAIN-DES-PRÈS

Grand Hôtel des Balcons
🖼   €€

3 Rue Casimir Delavigne, 75006 **Tel** *01 46 34 78 50* **Fax** *01 46 34 06 27* **Rooms** *50*   **Map** *12 F5*

Embellished with Art Nouveau features, this hotel has a beautiful hall with stained-glass windows and striking 19th-century-style lamps and wood panelling. Most guestrooms, quiet and well-decorated, enjoy a balcony. High-speed Internet access with Wi-Fi available. **www.balcons.com**

Hôtel du Globe
€€

15 Rue des Quatre-Vents, 75006 **Tel** *01 43 26 35 50* **Fax** *01 46 33 62 69* **Rooms** *14*   **Map** *12 F4*

A 17th-century building right by the Jardin du Luxembourg, with excellent accommodation. Antique furniture and colourful fabrics liven up the guestrooms. Breakfast is brought to your room. Extremely popular, so book in advance. **www.globe-paris-hotel.com**

Hôtel de Lille
🖼 🗐   €€

40 Rue de Lille, 75007 **Tel** *01 42 61 29 09* **Fax** *01 42 61 53 97* **Rooms** *20*   **Map** *12 D2*

The jewel-like Hôtel de Lille is situated near the Orsay and Louvre museums in the heart of Faubourg St-Germain. The modern, standard bedrooms are small and the bar is minute. Breakfast is served in the charming arched basement. **www.hotel-paris-lille.com**

Hôtel du Quai Voltaire
🖼   €€

19 Quai Voltaire, 75007 **Tel** *01 42 61 50 91* **Fax** *01 42 61 62 26* **Rooms** *33*   **Map** *12 D2*

Overlooking the river, this hotel was once the favourite of Blondin, Baudelaire and Pissarro, and has featured in several films. Bedrooms on the quay are better avoided, as they suffer from traffic noise. Higher floors are quieter, though, and the views are superb. **www.quaivoltaire.fr**

Hôtel des Marronniers
🖼 🗐   €€€

21 Rue Jacob, 75006 **Tel** *01 43 25 30 60* **Fax** *01 40 46 83 56* **Rooms** *37*   **Map** *12 E3*

Situated between a courtyard and a garden, this hotel provides perfect peace. The decor is homely, with lots of textured fabrics, and bedrooms on the fourth floor, garden side, provide very special views over the Parisian rooftops and the St-Germain-des-Prés church steeple. **www.paris-hotel-marronniers.com**

Hôtel des Sts-Pères
🖼 🗐   €€€

65 Rue des Sts-Pères, 75006 **Tel** *01 45 44 50 00* **Fax** *01 45 44 90 83* **Rooms** *39*   **Map** *12 E3*

The hotel occupies one of the old aristocratic mansions of St-Germain-des-Prés. The lounge bar is very popular with authors from the publishing houses nearby. The bedrooms are quiet and roomy – the best has an outstanding ceiling fresco. **www.paris-hotel-saints-peres.com**

Hôtel Lenox
🖼 🗐   €€€

9 Rue de l'Université, 75007 **Tel** *01 42 96 10 95* **Fax** *01 42 61 52 83* **Rooms** *34*   **Map** *12 D3*

The charm of the Lenox lies in its simplicity and literary history – T.S. Elliot, Ezra Pound and James Joyce all lived here. The staff are extremely friendly and the cocktail bar is lovely. The rooms are impeccably decorated. The hotel enjoys a great location in the heart of St-Germain-des-Prés. **www.lenoxsaintgermain.com**

Hôtel de Fleurie
🖼 🗐   €€€€

32/34 Rue Grégoire de Tours, 75006 **Tel** *01 53 73 70 00* **Fax** *01 53 73 70 20* **Rooms** *29*   **Map** *12 F4*

The statue-filled façade is enough to make one want to stay in this welcoming, family-run hotel. Inside, the woodwork and white stone create the same light feel, as do the bedrooms, all of which are beautifully decorated, with well-equipped bathrooms. **www.hotel-de-fleurie.tm.fr**

Hôtel de l'Abbaye St-Germain
🖼 🗐   €€€€

10 Rue Cassette, 75006 **Tel** *01 45 44 38 11* **Fax** *01 45 48 07 86* **Rooms** *44*   **Map** *12 D5*

A 17th-century abbey, just steps from the Jardin du Luxembourg, this charming hotel has been a preferred hideout for artists and writers. Its finely furnished guestrooms and apartments have been tastefully done up and provided with modern facilities. **www.hotel-abbaye.com**

Hôtel d'Angleterre
🖼   €€€€

44 Rue Jacob, 75006 **Tel** *01 42 60 34 72* **Fax** *01 42 60 16 93* **Rooms** *27*   **Map** *12 E3*

Once the British Embassy, the Hôtel d'Angleterre has retained many of the original features, including the fine old staircase (listed), the exquisite garden and the salon mantelpiece. Bedrooms are individually decorated, many have exposed beams and wonderful four-poster beds. **www.hotel-dangleterre.com**

Key to Price Guide *see p284* **Key to Symbols** *see back cover flap*

L'Hôtel

🖥 🔢 📶 📧   €€€€€

13 Rue des Beaux-Arts, 75006 **Tel** *01 44 41 99 00* **Fax** *01 43 25 64 81* **Rooms** *20*

Map *12 E3*

A riot of exuberance and opulence, this Jacques Garcia-designed hotel is gloriously decadent. Each room is different; the hotel's most famous one is the Oscar Wilde suite, where the author died and which boasts period furnishings. There's also a beautiful spa. **www.l-hotel.com**

Lutétia

🖥 🅿 🔢 📶 📧   €€€€€

45 Blvd Raspail, 75006 **Tel** *01 49 54 46 46* **Fax** *01 49 54 46 00* **Rooms** *230*

Map *12 D4*

The Lutétia is a mainstay of glamour on the south side of the river. The building is partly Art Nouveau and partly Art Deco, and has been restored throughout. Publishers and chic shoppers are regular customers in the restaurant. Convenient location. **www.lutetia-paris.com**

Montalembert

🖥 🔢 🏃 📧   €€€€€

3 Rue de Montalembert, 75007 **Tel** *01 45 49 68 68* **Fax** *01 45 49 69 49* **Rooms** *56*

Map *12 D3*

Situated in the heart of the publishing district, this fashionable hotel combines modernity and timeless elegance. The bedrooms boast fine wood and designer fabrics with excellent quality linen sheets, towels and bathrobes. The eighth-floor suites have good views. Wi-Fi facilities are provided. **www.montalembert.com**

Relais Christine

🖥 🅿 📶 📧   €€€€€

3 Rue Christine, 75006 **Tel** *01 40 51 60 80* **Fax** *01 40 51 60 81* **Rooms** *51*

Map *12 F4*

Always full, the Relais Christine is the epitome of the *hôtel de charme*. It is part of the cloister of a 16th-century abbey and is a romantic haven of peace. The bedrooms are bright and spacious, especially the duplex rooms. Wi-Fi is available, as are spa and sauna facilities. **www.relais-christine.com**

LATIN QUARTER

Esmeralda

€

4 Rue St-Julien-le-Pauvre, 75005 **Tel** *01 43 54 19 20* **Fax** *01 40 51 00 68* **Rooms** *19*

Map *13 A4*

The much-loved bohemian Esmeralda lies in the heart of the Latin Quarter. With old stone walls and beamed ceilings, its charm has seduced the likes of Terence Stamp and Serge Gainsbourg. The best rooms overlook Notre-Dame. No breakfast provided.

Hôtel des Grandes Ecoles

🖥 🅿   €€

75 Rue Cardinal Lemoine, 75005 **Tel** *01 43 26 79 23* **Fax** *01 43 25 28 15* **Rooms** *51*

Map *13 B5*

This hotel is a cluster of three small houses around a beautiful garden, where you can breakfast in good weather. The rooms are all comfortable and furnished with traditional 18th-century-style floral wallpaper, some open onto the courtyard. Internet access available. **www.hotel-grandes-ecoles.com**

Hôtel des Grands Degrés de Notre Dame

🔢   €€

10 Rue des Grands Degrés, 75005 **Tel** *01 55 42 88 88* **Fax** *01 40 46 95 34* **Rooms** *10*

Map *13 B4*

An exceptionally friendly place to stay. The staff are genuinely welcoming and the wood-panelling and oak beams around the building make it even more special. Lovely, very clean bedrooms with Internet access available. The Bar Restaurant and Tea Room serves great food at a low price. **www.lesdegreshotel.com**

Hôtel des Grands Hommes

🖥 🏃 📧   €€€

17 Pl du Panthéon, 75005 **Tel** *01 46 34 19 60* **Fax** *01 43 26 67 32* **Rooms** *31*

Map *17 A1*

Teachers at the Sorbonne frequent this quiet family hotel close to the Jardin du Luxembourg. It boasts a great view of the Panthéon from the attic rooms on the upper floor. The bedrooms are comfortable. Wi-Fi services available. **www.hoteldesgrandshommes.com**

Hôtel de Notre-Dame

🖥 📧   €€€

19 Rue Maître Albert, 75005 **Tel** *01 43 26 79 00* **Fax** *01 46 33 50 11* **Rooms** *34*

Map *13 B5*

The picturesque Hôtel de Notre-Dame overlooks Notre-Dame cathedral and the Seine on one side and the Panthéon on the other. The furnishings are functional, but some rooms have beams or an old stone wall. The main appeal here is the location. The hotel has its own sauna and Wi-Fi access. **www.hotel-paris-notredame.com**

Hôtel du Panthéon

🖥 📧   €€€

19 Pl du Panthéon, 75005 **Tel** *01 43 54 32 95* **Fax** *01 43 26 64 65* **Rooms** *36*

Map *17 A1*

This hotel is managed by the same family as the Hôtel des Grands Hommes: the welcome is equally warm and the decor similarly Classical. Extra romance and luxury can be found in room 33 with its divine four-poster bed. Wi-Fi available in the reception room only. **www.hoteldupantheon.com**

Hôtel Residence Hotel IV

🖥   €€€€

50 Rue des Bernardins, 75005 **Tel** *01 44 41 31 81* **Fax** *01 46 33 93 22* **Rooms** *13*

Map *13 B5*

Overlooking a pretty park square and with window boxes full of geraniums in season, this hotel is a real jewel. Bedrooms are bright and airy, some of the larger rooms have attached kitchens and there is also a flat for four people available. Wi-Fi services provided. Very quiet for the area. **www.residencehenri4.com**

LUXEMBOURG QUARTER

Hôtel Récamier
€€   Map 12 E4

3 bis Pl St-Sulpice, 75006 **Tel** *01 43 26 04 89* **Fax** *01 46 33 27 73* **Rooms** *30*

Hotel Récamier, which is situated on the quiet Place St-Sulpice, is a family hotel with an air of old-fashioned Parisian charm. The hotel was constructed in 1905 and remains a favourite both with writers and Left Bank tourists. Bedrooms overlooking the square have lovely views.

Aviatic
€€€   Map 12 E5

105 Rue de Vaugirard, 75006 **Tel** *01 53 63 25 50* **Fax** *01 53 63 25 55* **Rooms** *43*

True to its Parisian past and long-standing family hotel tradition, the much-loved Aviatic combines bohemian style with modern comforts. The rooms are individually decorated with charming pieces found at local flea markets and warm, bright textiles. Parking is available for 26 euros per day and picnics on request. **www.aviatic.fr**

MONTPARNASSE

Hôtel Apollon Montparnasse
€€   Map 15 C3

91 Rue Ouest, 75014 **Tel** *01 43 95 62 00* **Fax** *01 43 95 62 10* **Rooms** *33*

Close to the Parc des Expositions of the Porte de Versailles, the Apollon Montparnasse is decorated with Grecian statues, fine furnishings and lots of peach. You can get simple, well-equipped guestrooms. Parking is available for 12 euros per day. The hotel also provides Wi-Fi facilities. **www.apollon-montparnasse.com**

Hôtel Delambre
€€   Map 16 D2

35 Rue Delambre, 75014 **Tel** *01 43 20 66 31* **Fax** *01 45 38 91 76* **Rooms** *30*

Located a few steps away from Montparnasse cemetery, and close to the Jardin du Luxembourg and Latin Quarter, this hotel stylishly mixes modern and classical styles. Guestrooms are simply furnished with all mod cons. **www.hoteldelambre.com**

Ferrandi
€€€   Map 15 C1

92 Rue du Cherche-Midi, 75006 **Tel** *01 42 22 97 40* **Fax** *01 45 44 89 97* **Rooms** *42*

The Rue du Cherche-Midi is well-known to lovers of antiques. The Hôtel Ferrandi is a quiet hotel with a fireplace in the lounge and comfortable bedrooms filled with dark wood and decorated in warm tones. Four-poster beds in some rooms. **www.france-hotel-guide.com**

Ste-Beuve
€€€   Map 16 D1

9 Rue Ste Beuve, 75006 **Tel** *01 45 48 20 07* **Fax** *01 45 48 67 52* **Rooms** *22*

The Ste-Beuve is a small, carefully restored hotel for aesthetes and habitués of the Rive Gauche galleries. There is a fireplace in the hall, the rooms are pleasantly decorated in pastel shades and there are several classic, contemporary paintings. **www.paris-hotel-charme.com**

Villa des Artistes
€€€   Map 16 D2

9 Rue de la Grande Chaumière, 75006 **Tel** *01 43 26 60 86* **Fax** *01 43 54 73 70* **Rooms** *59*

The Villa des Artistes aims to recreate Montparnasse's artistic heyday when Modigliani, Beckett and Fitzgerald were all visitors here. The bedrooms are clean, but the main draw is the large patio garden and fountain, where you can breakfast in peace. **www.villa-artistes.com**

Le Saint-Grégoire
€€€€   Map 11 C5

43 Rue de l'Abbé Grégoire, 75006 **Tel** *01 45 48 23 23* **Fax** *01 45 48 33 95* **Rooms** *20*

Le Saint-Grégoire is a fashionable townhouse hotel with immaculately-decorated bedrooms and 19th-century furnishings. At the centre of the drawing room is a charming fireplace with a real fire. Book a room with a delightful private terrace. Parking costs 13 euros a day. **www.lesaintgregoire.com**

INVALIDES AND EIFFEL TOWER QUARTER

Grand Hôtel Levêque
€€   Map 10 F3

29 Rue Cler, 75007 **Tel** *01 47 05 49 15* **Fax** *01 45 50 49 36* **Rooms** *50*

On a street with a quaint fruit-and-vegetable market, the Levêque lies between the Eiffel Tower and the Invalides. The great location isn't the only attraction – guestrooms are well-kept and the hotel also provides Internet facilities. **www.hotel-leveque.com**

Key to Price Guide *see p284* **Key to Symbols** *see back cover flap*

Hôtel de Varenne

🖼️ 📋 €€

44 Rue de Bourgogne, 75007 **Tel** *01 45 51 45 55* **Fax** *01 45 51 86 63* **Rooms** *24* **Map** *11 B2*

Beyond its severe façade, this hotel conceals a narrow courtyard garden where guests breakfast in the summer. The bedrooms, recently refurbished in elegant Louis XVI or Empire style, are impeccable. The hotel is popular with French government officials. **www.hoteldevarenne.com**

Eiffel Park Hôtel

€€€

17 bis Rue Amélie, 75007 **Tel** *01 45 55 10 01* **Fax** *01 47 05 28 68* **Rooms** *36* **Map** *10 F3*

In the heart of the Champs de Mars, the charming Eiffel Park Hôtel has been entirely renovated. It offers individually designed guestrooms with intricate wallpaper in some and exotic furniture in others. On the top floor is a breakfast terrace. Wi-Fi facilities provided. **www.eiffelpark.com**

Hôtel de Suède St-Germain

🖼️ 📋 €€€

31 Rue Vaneau, 75007 **Tel** *01 47 05 00 08* **Fax** *01 47 05 69 27* **Rooms** *40* **Map** *11 B4*

Located near the Orsay and Rodin museums, the Hôtel de Suède St-Germain offers elegant rooms, decorated in late 18th-century styles in pale colours and the owners' welcome is exceptionally warm. Deluxe rooms offer a view over the park. A lovely little garden to breakfast in completes the picture. **www.hoteldesuede.com**

Hôtel Bourgogne et Montana

🖼️ 📋 €€€€

3 Rue de Bourgogne, 75007 **Tel** *01 45 51 20 22* **Fax** *01 45 56 11 98* **Rooms** *32* **Map** *11 B2*

Situated in front of the Assemblée Nationale, the hotel has an air of sobriety. Features include a mahogany bar, an old lift and a circular hall with pink marble columns. The bedrooms were recently refurbished in an aristocratic style. Extremely stylish. **www.paris-hotel-montana.com**

Duc de St-Simon

🖼️ 📋 €€€€€

14 Rue de St-Simon, 75007 **Tel** *01 44 39 20 20* **Fax** *01 45 48 68 25* **Rooms** *34* **Map** *11 C3*

The Hôtel Duc de St-Simon is justifiably one of the most sought-after hotels on the south side of the Seine. A charming 18th-century mansion furnished with antiques, it lives up to its aristocratic pretensions. **www.hotelducdesaintsimon.com**

CHAILLOT QUARTER

Hameau de Passy

🖼️ €€

48 Rue de Passy, 75016 **Tel** *01 42 88 47 55* **Fax** *01 42 30 83 72* **Rooms** *32* **Map** *9 B3*

In the heart of the residential quarter of Passy, a stone's throw from the Eiffel Tower and the Trocadero, Hameau de Passy lies in a private lane, which is an oasis of greenery. Rooms overlook the garden. Breakfast can be served in your room upon request. **www.hameaudepassy.com**

Hôtel du Bois

€€€

11 Rue du Dôme, 75016 **Tel** *01 45 00 31 96* **Fax** *01 45 00 90 05* **Rooms** *41* **Map** *4 D5*

Two minutes from the Arc de Triomphe and the Champs Elysées, Hôtel du Bois is ideal for haute-couture boutique lovers. Behind a typically Parisian façade, is an interior exuding British charm – Georgian furniture in the lounge, thick patterned carpeting and fine prints in the bedrooms. **www.hoteldubois.com**

Concorde La Fayette

🖼️ 🅿️ 🍴 📺 📋 €€€€€

3 Pl du Général Koenig, 75017 **Tel** *01 40 68 50 68* **Fax** *01 40 68 50 43* **Rooms** *950* **Map** *3 C2*

The formulaic Concorde La Fayette with its fascinating egg-shaped tower is thoroughly high-tech. It has numerous facilities, including a fitness club, a bar on the 33rd floor, restaurants, a shopping gallery, and identical bedrooms with some absolutely splendid views. **www.concorde-lafayette.com**

Hôtel Keppler

🖼️ 📋 €€€€€

12 Rue Keppler, 75016 **Tel** *01 47 20 65 05* **Fax** *01 47 23 02 29* **Rooms** *29* **Map** *4 E5*

Within walking distance from the Champs-Elysées, this four-star hotel is located in a quiet street of the elegant 16th arrondissement. The rooms are spacious with high ceilings and the decor is neo-Art Deco with bold patterns and colours. **www.hotelkeppler.com**

Hotel Square

🖼️ 🅿️ 🍴 📺 📋 €€€€€

3 Rue de Boulainvilliers, 75016 **Tel** *01 44 14 91 90* **Fax** *01 44 14 91 99* **Rooms** *22* **Map** *9 A4*

An exceptional hotel, the curvy granite façade hides 22 rooms and suites furnished with exotic fabrics and woods. The hotel boasts a fashionable restaurant and night club and, most unusually, a small but well-stocked modern art gallery. **www.hotelsquare.com**

Costes K

🖼️ 🅿️ 🍴 🏊 🏋️ 📺 📋 €€€€€

81 Ave Kléber, 75016 **Tel** *01 44 05 75 75* **Fax** *01 44 05 74 74* **Rooms** *83* **Map** *4 D5*

This hotel, not to be confused with the more expensive Hôtel Costes, is situated steps from the Eiffel Tower. A piece of modern art by Spanish architect Ricardo Bofill, who used sycamore, stucco, marble and stainless steel in the construction. Cool Asian interiors for the guestrooms. **www.hotelcostesk.com**

Raphaël
🖼 🅿 🍽 🛗 📋   €€€€€

17 Ave Kléber, 75016 **Tel** *01 53 64 32 00* **Fax** *01 53 64 32 01* **Rooms** *85*   **Map** *4 D4*

The epitome of discreet elegance, film stars come here to be sheltered from the paparazzi. The decor is opulent and the roof terrace bar is the loveliest in Paris and extremely popular with the jet set. There are amazing views of the city and its principal monuments illuminated at night. **www.raphael-hotel.com**

St-James Paris
🖼 🅿 🍽 🛗 📋   €€€€€

43 Ave Bugeaud, 75016 **Tel** *01 44 05 81 81* **Fax** *01 44 05 81 82* **Rooms** *48*   **Map** *3 B5*

The St-James occupies a mansion with a small park near the Avenue Foch and the Bois de Boulogne. Reminiscent of a gentleman's club, guests here become "temporary members" and a token fee is included in the room price. Aristocratic atmosphere. **www.saint-james-paris.com**

Villa Maillot
🖼 🅿 📋   €€€€€

143 Ave de Malakoff, 75016 **Tel** *01 53 64 52 52* **Fax** *01 45 00 60 61* **Rooms** *42*   **Map** *3 C4*

Conveniently situated for Porte Maillot and La Défense, the hotel was once an embassy and remains suitably refined with delightful Art-Deco style furnishings. The rooms have large beds, concealed kitchenettes and marble bathrooms. A new spa area offers massages. **www.lavillamaillot.fr**

CHAMPS-ELYSÉES

Résidence Lord Byron
🖼 📋   €€€

5 Rue Chateaubriand, 75008 **Tel** *01 43 59 89 98* **Fax** *01 42 89 46 04* **Rooms** *31*   **Map** *4 E4*

Close to the Etoile, the Résidence Lord Byron is a discreet, small hotel with a courtyard garden for breakfast. Its bright bedrooms are quiet but small; if you want more space, ask for a salon bedroom or a ground-floor room. **www.escapade-paris.com**

Atala
🖼 🍽 🧑 📋   €€€€

10 Rue Chateaubriand, 75008 **Tel** *01 45 62 01 62* **Fax** *01 42 25 66 38* **Rooms** *48*   **Map** *4 E4*

Situated in a quiet street near the Champs-Elysées, the Atala's rooms overlook a tranquil garden with tall trees. The bedrooms are functional rather than charming, so book a room on the eighth floor with spectacular views of the Eiffel Tower. **www.hotelatala.com**

Balzac
🖼 🍽 📋   €€€€€

6 Rue Balzac, 75008 **Tel** *01 44 35 18 00* **Fax** *01 44 35 18 05* **Rooms** *70*   **Map** *4 F4*

This calm and luxurious hotel in a typically Parisian Belle Epoque building has just been refurbished. Its trendy address is nothing compared to its bar; designed by Philippe Starck in violets and electric blues, it is a favourite destination for fashionable night owls. **www.hotelbalzac.com**

Bristol
🖼 🅿 🍽 🏊 🧑 🛗 📋   €€€€€

112 Rue du Faubourg-St-Honoré, 75008 **Tel** *01 53 43 43 00* **Fax** *01 53 43 43 01* **Rooms** *180*   **Map** *5 A4*

One of Paris's finest hotels, the Bristol's large rooms are sumptuously decorated with antiques and magnificent marble bathrooms. The period dining room, with its Flemish tapestries and glittering crystal chandeliers, has been winning rave reviews. Wonderful swimming pool. **www.lebristolparis.com**

Claridge-Bellman
🖼 📋   €€€€€

37 Rue François 1er, 75008 **Tel** *01 47 23 54 42* **Fax** *01 47 23 08 84* **Rooms** *42*   **Map** *4 F5*

The Claridge-Bellman is a miniature version of the old Claridge Hotel and is managed by its former directors. The hotel has a truly traditional feel. It is quiet, sober and efficiently run, and is furnished throughout with tapestries and antiques. **www.hotel-claridge-bellman.com**

Four Seasons George V
🖼 🅿 🍽 🏊 🧑 🛗 📋   €€€€€

31 Ave George V, 75008 **Tel** *01 49 52 70 00* **Fax** *01 49 52 70 10* **Rooms** *246*   **Map** *4 E5*

This legendary hotel, dotted with salons, old furniture and art, lost a little of its charm when it was renovated. But it gained a stunning restaurant, Le Cinq, which boasts the world's top sommelier and an award-winning chef. Great spa. **www.fourseasons.com/paris**

Hôtel de la Trémoille
🖼 🅿 🍽 🛗 📋   €€€€€

14 Rue de la Trémoille, 75008 **Tel** *01 56 52 14 00* **Fax** *01 40 70 01 08* **Rooms** *93*   **Map** *10 F1*

The Hôtel de la Trémoille is an impressive, yet relaxed, establishment. Rooms are decorated with comfortable antiques and the bathrooms are extremely luxurious. A fashionable restaurant, Senso, by Terence Conran is now a hit with Paris's beautiful people. **www.hotel-tremoille.com**

Hôtel Fouquet's Barrière
🖼 🅿 🍽 📋   €€€€

46 Ave George V, 75008 **Tel** *01 40 69 60 00* **Rooms** *107*   **Map** *4 E5*

Paris's newest palace-hotel is the only hotel that is actually located on the Champs-Elysées. It is equipped with all the state-of-the-art technology you would expect in a modern, luxury establishment. The rooms are ultra stylish and are decorated in mahogany, silk and velvet. **www.fouquets-barriere.com**

Key to Price Guide *see p284* **Key to Symbols** *see back cover flap*

Hôtel Franklin Roosevelt 🖭🗐 €€€€€

18 Rue Clément Marot, 75008 **Tel** *01 53 57 49 50* **Fax** *01 53 57 49 59* **Rooms** *48* **Map** *4 F5*

Chic interior throughout, complete with period furniture, old paintings and a fireplace in the lounge. The bedrooms are generally very large. Cosy atmosphere at the Lord's bar, though the cafés of the Champs-Elysées are also nearby. **www.hroosevelt.com**

Hôtel Vernet 🖭🅿🍴🏊🏃🖭🗐 €€€€€

25 Rue Vernet, 75008 **Tel** *01 44 31 98 00* **Fax** *01 44 31 85 69* **Rooms** *51* **Map** *4 E4*

Gustave Eiffel, architect of the Eiffel Tower, created the dazzling glass roof of the dining room here. The hotel lobby is impressive with Persian rugs, precious woods, antiques and parquet flooring. The large, quiet bedrooms are pleasantly furnished and guests have free use of the Royal Monceau's fitness club. **www.hotelvernet.com**

Plaza Athénée 🖭🅿🍴🏃🖭🗐 €€€€€

25 Ave Montaigne, 75008 **Tel** *01 53 67 66 65* **Fax** *01 53 67 66 66* **Rooms** *188* **Map** *10 F1*

The legendary Plaza Athénée is popular with honeymooners, aristocracy and haute couture shoppers. The restaurant by Alain Ducasse is wonderfully romantic, while Le Bar du Plaza is now the hottest address in Paris for cocktails. The last word in luxury. **www.plaza-athenee-paris.com**

Prince de Galles 🖭🍴🖭🗐 €€€€€

33 Ave George V, 75008 **Tel** *01 53 23 77 77* **Fax** *01 53 23 78 78* **Rooms** *168* **Map** *4 E5*

Less prestigious than its neighbour the Four Seasons George V, the Prince de Galles most definitely has its own identity and charm. The marble and chandelier filled lobby gives way to subdued elegance in the bedrooms. Wi-Fi facilities available. **www.luxurycollection.com/princedegalles**

San Régis 🖭🍴🗐 €€€€€

12 Rue Jean Goujon, 75008 **Tel** *01 44 95 16 16* **Fax** *01 45 61 05 48* **Rooms** *44* **Map** *11 A1*

Since it opened in 1923 the San Régis has been popular with the jet set, who enjoy its quiet but central location. This particularly welcoming, intimate luxury hotel is full of excellent antiques, overstuffed sofas and a distinctly opulent air. **www.hotel-sanregis.fr**

OPÉRA QUARTER

Ambassador 🖭🍴🖭🗐 €€€€€

16 Blvd Haussmann, 75009 **Tel** *01 44 83 40 40* **Fax** *01 42 46 19 84* **Rooms** *300* **Map** *6 E4*

One of the best of Paris's Art Deco hotels, it has been restored to its former glory and has deep carpeting and antique furniture. The ground floor has pink marble columns, Baccarat crystal chandeliers and Aubusson tapestries. The restaurant, 16 Haussmann, is extremely popular with Parisian gourmets. **www.hotelambassador-paris.com**

Edouard VII Hotel 🖭🍴🏃🗐 €€€€€

39 Ave de l'Opéra, 75002 **Tel** *01 42 61 56 90* **Fax** *01 42 61 47 73* **Rooms** *69* **Map** *6 E5*

The only hotel on the impressive Avenue de l'Opéra, the Edouard VII is centrally located between the Louvre and the Opéra Garnier, which makes it perfect for sightseeing. Ask for a room at the front for a breathtaking view over the Opéra House, and book a table at the excellent hotel restaurant, Angl'Opera. **www. edouard7hotel.com**

Le Grand Hôtel Intercontinental 🖭🅿🍴🖭🗐 €€€€€

2 Rue Scribe, 75009 **Tel** *01 40 07 32 32* **Fax** *01 40 07 32 02* **Rooms** *478* **Map** *6 D5*

Directly next to the Opéra Garnier, the hotel is a sumptuous example of good taste. The bedrooms all have pictures with a musical theme reflecting the hotel's location. The renowned restaurant, the Café de La Paix, is an opulent affair in Opéra Quarter. **www.paris.intercontinental.com**

MONTMARTRE

Regyn's Montmartre €

18 Pl des Abbesses, 75018 **Tel** *01 42 54 45 21* **Fax** *01 42 23 76 69* **Rooms** *22* **Map** *6 E1*

Near Sacré-Coeur, this is an impeccably kept hotel. Top-floor guestrooms have views of the Eiffel Tower. Round the corner from here is Tabac des Deux Moulins on 15 Rue le Pic where Amélié worked in the 2001 film *Amélié*. **www.regynsmontmartre.com**

Terrass Hôtel 🖭🍴🗐 €€€€€

12-14 Rue Joseph-de-Maistre, 75018 **Tel** *01 46 06 72 85* **Fax** *01 42 52 29 11* **Rooms** *100* **Map** *6 E1*

Montmartre's most luxurious hotel, the rooms here are comfortably, if unremarkably, furnished. A few bedrooms retain the original Art-Deco woodwork. The big draw is the rooftop restaurant, where in the summer fashionable Parisians take in a world-class view. **www.terrass-hotel.com**

RESTAURANTS, CAFES AND BARS

The French national passion for good cuisine makes eating out one of the greatest pleasures of a visit to Paris. Everywhere in the city you see people eating – in restaurants, bistros, tea salons, cafés and wine bars.

Most restaurants serve French food but there is a range of Chinese, Vietnamese and North African eateries in many areas as well as Italian, Greek, Lebanese and Indian places. The restaurants in the listings *(see pp300–315)* have been selected from the best that Paris can offer across all price ranges. The listings are organized by area, as in the sightseeing section of the guide, and by price. Most places will serve lunch from noon until around 2pm, and the menu often includes fixed-price meals. Parisians usually start to fill restaurants for dinner around 8.30pm and most places serve from around 7.30pm until 11pm. *(See also Light Meals and Snacks pp316–19.)*

WHAT TO EAT

A tremendous range of food is available in Paris, from the rich meat dishes and perfect pâtisserie for which France is most famous to simpler French regional cuisines *(see pp296–7)*. The latter are available in brasseries and bistros – the type usually depends on the birthplace of the chef. At any time of day simple, tasty meals can be had in cafés, wine and beer bars, and brasseries, bistros and cake shops – or pâtisseries – abound.

The best ethnic food comes from France's former colonies: Vietnam and North Africa. North African places are known as *couscous* restaurants and serve filling, somewhat spicy, inexpensive food that varies in quality. Vietnamese restaurants are also good value and provide a light alternative to rich French food. Paris also has some good Japanese restaurants, notably around Rue Monsieur le Prince (6th arrondissement); Rue Ste-Anne (2nd) and Rue de Belleville (19th) have others.

WHERE TO FIND GOOD RESTAURANTS AND CAFES

You can eat well in almost any part of Paris. Wherever you are, as a rule of thumb you will find that the most outstanding restaurants and cafés are those that cater predominantly to a French clientele.

The Left Bank probably has the greatest concentration of restaurants, especially in tourist areas like St-Germain-des-Prés and the Latin Quarter. The quality of food varies, but there are some commendable bistros, outdoor cafés and wine bars – see pages 316–19 for a selection of the best places to go in Paris for light meals and snacks. The Latin Quarter also has a high

Beauvilliers restaurant *(see p312)*

concentration of Greek restaurants centred chiefly around Rue de la Huchette.

In the Marais and Bastille areas, small bistros, tea salons and cafés are plentiful, some new and fashionable. There are also many good, traditional long-established bistros and brasseries.

In the Champs-Elysées and Madeleine area it is difficult to find inexpensive good food. Sadly, this area tends to be overrun with fast food joints and pricy but not very good cafés. There are, however, some very good expensive restaurants here.

Montparnasse still has some great cafés from the 1920s, including Le Sélect and La Rotonde, on the Boulevard du Montparnasse *(see p319)*. Sensitive renovation has recaptured much of their old splendour. This area is also well known for its many pancake restaurants. Rue de Montparnasse, for example,

The prim Mariage Frères shop and tea room *(see p318)*

is lined with *crêperies* serving *galettes*, sweet *crêpes* and Normandy cider.

There are many noteworthy restaurants, bistros and cafés in the Louvre-Rivoli area, competing with tourist-oriented, overpriced cafés. Just to the east, Les Halles is choc-a-bloc with fast food joints and mediocre restaurants but there are few places of note.

Good Japanese food can be found near the Opéra together with some fine brasseries, but otherwise the area around the Opéra and Grands Boulevards is not the best for restaurants. Near the Bourse are a number of reputable restaurants and bistros frequented by stockbrokers.

Montmartre has a predictable number of tourist restaurants, but it also has a few very pleasant small bistros. One expensive and luxurious exception is Beauvilliers *(see p312)*, a Montmartre landmark tucked on the far side of the Butte.

Quiet neighbourhoods in the evening, the Invalides, Eiffel Tower and Palais de Chaillot tend to have less noisy, more serious restaurants than areas with lively nightlife. Prices can be high.

Two Chinatowns, one in the area south of the Place d'Italie, the other in the traditionally working-class, hill-top area of Belleville, have concentrations of ethnic food but few French restaurants of note. There are a number of Vietnamese eating places as well as large, inexpensive Chinese ones, and Belleville is also packed with small North African restaurants.

Tour d'Argent decoration *(see p306)*

Le Grand Véfour in the Palais Royal *(see p304)*

TYPES OF RESTAURANTS AND CAFES

One of the most enjoyable aspects of eating in Paris is the diversity of places to eat. Bistros are small, often moderately priced restaurants with a limited selection of dishes. Those from the Belle Epoque era are particularly beautiful, with zinc bars, mirrors and attractive tiles. The food is generally, but not always, regional and traditional. Many chefs from the smartest restaurants have now also opened bistros and these can be very good value.

Brasseries are generally large bustling eateries, many with an Alsatian character serving carafes of Alsatian wine and platters of sauerkraut and sausage. They have immense menus, and most serve food throughout the day and are open late. Outside you may well see impressive pavement displays of shellfish, with apron-clad oyster shuckers working late into the night.

Cafés open early in the morning, and apart from the large tourist cafés, the majority close by around 10pm. They serve drinks and food all day long from a short menu of salads, sandwiches and eggs. At lunch most also offer a small choice of hot daily

A typical bistro menu

specials. Café prices vary from area to area, in direct proportion to the number of tourists. Smarter cafés, like Café de Flore and Les Deux Magots serve food until late at night. Those cafés specializing in beer almost always include onion tarts, French fries and hearty bowls of steamed mussels on the menu. Brunch is now served in many places at weekends, from around 17€.

Wine bars are informal. They usually have a moderately priced, simple lunch menu and serve wine by the glass. They serve snacks at any time of day – such as marvellous open sandwiches *(tartines)* made with sourdough Poilâne bread topped with cheese, sausage or pâté – until around 10pm, but a few stay open for dinner.

Tea salons open for breakfast or mid-morning until the early evening. Many offer lunch, as well as a selection of sweet pastries for afternoon tea. They are at their best in the middle of the afternoon and offer coffee and hot chocolate as well as fine teas. Some, like Le Loir dans la Théière, are casual with sofas and big tables, while Mariage Frères is more formal. Angélina on the Rue de Rivoli is famous for its hot chocolate, and Ladurée has excellent macaroons. *(For addresses see pp318–19.)*

VEGETARIAN FOOD

Vegetarian restaurants in Paris are few, and non-vegetarian restaurant menus are usually firmly oriented towards meat and fish. However, you can get a good salad almost anywhere and you can often fare well by ordering two courses from the list of *entrées* (first courses). The North African restaurants will serve you *couscous nature* – which doesn't have meat.

Never be timid about asking for a change in a dish. If you see a salad with ham, bacon or *foie gras*, ask the waiter for it without the meat. If you are going to a smart restaurant, telephone ahead and ask the manager if it is possible to prepare a special meal for you. Most restaurants will be happy to oblige.

Organic produce is starting to be used in French cuisine.

HOW MUCH TO PAY

Prices for meals in Paris range from extremely economic to astronomical. You can still enjoy a hearty restaurant or café lunch for 15€, but a typical good bistro, brasserie or restaurant meal in central Paris will average 30€–38€ with wine. (Remember that the better French wines will increase the size of your bill significantly.) More expensive restaurants begin at about 45€ with wine and go up to 200€ for the top places. Many places offer a *formule* or *prix-fixe* (fixed price) menu, especially at

Le Carré des Feuillants *(see p304)*

lunch, and this will almost always offer the best value. Some restaurants feature menus for under 15€ – a few at this price include wine. Coffee usually carries an extra charge.

All French restaurants are obliged by law to display their menu outside. The posted rates include service but a tip for particularly good service will always be appreciated (any amount from one Euro to 5% of the total).

The most widely accepted credit card is Visa. Few restaurants accept American Express, and some bistros do not accept credit cards at all, so it is wise to enquire when you book. Travellers' cheques are not widely accepted either, and cafés require cash.

MAKING RESERVATIONS

It is best to reserve a table in all restaurants, brasseries and bistros. Although you can usually get into a brasserie without a reservation, you may have to wait for a table.

Le Pavillon Montsouris near the Parc Montsouris *(see p315)*

DRESS CODE

Except for some three-star restaurants which can be rather formal, you can dress up or down in Parisian restaurants – within reason. The restaurant listings *(see pp300–319)* indicate which places require formal dress.

READING THE MENU AND ORDERING

Menus in small restaurants and bistros, and even in big brasseries, are often handwritten and can be difficult to decipher, so ask for help if necessary.

The waiter usually takes your choice of *entrée* (first course), then the *plat* (main course). Dessert is ordered after you have finished your main course, unless there are some hot desserts which have to be ordered at the start of

The Angélina restaurant, also known for its tea room *(see p318)*

the meal. The waiter will tell you this, or the dessert section of the menu will be marked *à commander avant le repas*.

The first course generally includes a choice of seasonal salads or vegetables, pâté and small hot or cold vegetable dishes or tarts. Small fish dishes like smoked salmon, grilled sardines, herring, fish salads and tartares are also offered. Brasseries have shellfish such as oysters, which can also be eaten as a main course. (The French tend to eat shellfish only when the month ends in 're'!)

Main dishes usually include a selection of meat, poultry and fish and upmarket restaurants offer game in

Le Train Bleu station restaurant in the Gare de Lyon *(see p315)*

autumn. Most restaurants also offer daily specials *(plats du jour)*. These dishes will incorporate fresh, seasonal produce and are usually good value.

Cheese is eaten either as a dessert or as a pre-dessert course. Some people have a green salad with their cheese. Coffee is served after, not with, dessert. You will need to ask specifically if you want it *au lait* (with milk). Decaffeinated coffee *(décaféiné)* and herbal teas *(tisanes)* are also popular after-dinner beverages.

In most restaurants you will be asked if you would like a drink before ordering food. A typical apéritif is *kir* (white wine with a drop of crème de cassis, a blackcurrant liqueur) or *kir royal* (champagne with crème de cassis). Beer, however, is rarely drunk before a meal in France *(see* What to Drink in Paris *pp298–9).*

Bistros and brasseries usually include the wine list with the menu. The more expensive restaurants have separate wine lists, which are generally brought to the table by the wine waiter after you have seen the meal menu. The wine waiter will be able to advise on choosing the wine if you wish.

SERVICE

As eating is a leisurely pastime in France, although the general standard of service in Paris restaurants is high, it is not always fast. In small restaurants in particular don't expect rapid attention: there may be only one waiter, and dishes are cooked to order.

CHILDREN

Children are usually very welcome, but there may be little room in a busy restaurant for push-chairs or prams. Nor are special facilities like high-chairs or baby seats commonly provided in eating places.

SMOKING

From February 2008, France will join several other countries enforcing strict anti-tobacco laws. It will therefore be against the law to smoke in public places such as bars and restaurants.

WHEELCHAIR ACCESS

Parisian restaurants are generally accommodating, and a word when you book should ensure that you are given a more conveniently situated table when you arrive. It is always worth checking that toilets can also be used by wheelchair users, since access can be restricted.

USING THE LISTINGS

Key to symbols used in the restaurant listings on pp300–315.

🧍 children's portions
♿ wheelchair access
👔 formal dress required
🪑 outside tables
💳 no credit cards accepted
🅿 parking

Price categories for a three-course meal including a half-bottle of house wine, tax and service:

€ under 25 euros
€€ 26–35 euros
€€€ 36–50 euros
€€€€ 51–75 euros
€€€€€ over 75 euros

An elegant Parisian restaurant

The Flavours of Paris

From the glittering temples of haute cuisine to the humblest neighbourhood bistro, Paris is a paradise for food lovers, whether you dine on foie gras and truffles or steak-frites, a seafood platter or a perfumed Moroccan couscous. France is immensely proud of its cuisine, from its classic origins to the most rustic of regional dishes. All are available in the capital and, though the French themselves will debate endlessly about the ideal sauce to complement meat or fish, or the right wine to accompany them, they will always be in total agreement that theirs is the best food in the world.

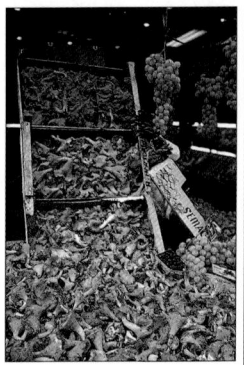

Girolles (chanterelles) on a stall in rue Mouffetard market

the season. Even if you are not shopping for food to cook, the markets are worth browsing and, after an hour or so in the crowded, narrow streets of the rue de Buci or rue Moufettard you will be more than ready for lunch.

The food of the French provinces, once despised for its rusticity, is now celebrated and almost every region is represented in the capital,

from the rich, bourgeois cuisines of Burgundy and Lyon to the celebrated healthy Mediterranean diet of Provence. Paris itself is surrounded by top quality market gardens which supply young peas, carrots and potatoes. Salmon, asparagus, and wild mushrooms come from the Loire; Normandy brings salt-marsh lamb, apples and Camembert.

What all French chefs agree on is the importance of using the finest quality ingredients, and there is no better place to appreciate the quality of French produce than in the markets of Paris. Here, top chefs may be spied early in the morning, alongside local shoppers, seeking inspiration and the prize ingredients of

Comté

Brie de Meaux

Tomme de chevre

Ami du Chambertin

Roquefort

Selection of fine French cheeses in perfect condition

CLASSIC FRENCH CUISINE

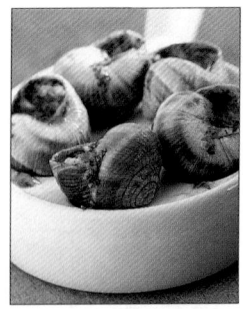

What is usually thought of as classic French cuisine developed in kings' palaces and noble châteaux, with the emphasis on luxury and display, not frugality or health. Dishes are often bathed in rich sauces of butter or cream, enhanced with luxurious ingredients like truffles, foie gras, rare mushrooms and alcohol. Meat is treated with reverence, and you will usually be asked how you want your beef, lamb or duck cooked; the French tend to like their beef rare (*bleu* or *saignant*) and their lamb and duck pink (*rose*). For well-cooked meat, ask for "*bien cuit*" but still expect at least a tinge of pinkness. The most famous country classics include slowly cooked casseroles like *coq au vin* and *boeuf à la bourguignonne*, as well as the bean, sausage and duck baked dish *cassoulet*, from the southwest.

Escargots à la Bourguignonne *are plump Burgundy snails served in their shells with garlic, butter and parsley.*

Salers beef and lentils come from the Auvergne; beef and Bresse chickens from Burgundy; not forgetting Basque ham, Collioure anchovies, lamb from the Pyrenees, or fragrant Provençal melons.

THE NEW STYLE

In recent years, innovative chefs have developed new styles of cooking, reacting against the richness of traditional cookery, and using fresh ingredients, lightly cooked to retain their flavour.

Mouthwatering display in a Parisian patisserie

Sealed jars of whole duck-liver foie gras, a luxury item

Sauces are made of light reductions to enhance, not obscure, the main ingredient of a dish. A wave of invention and originality has resulted in a plethora of unusual ingredients, fresh twists on the classics, and sometimes wonderful new combinations and flavours, such as sea bass with bean purée and red wine sauce, or with fermented grape juice; sole with quince juice and tarragon; tempura of langoustines with cinnamon beurre blanc; rabbit with Indian spices and tomato polenta; and rosemary ice cream or lavender sorbet.

FOREIGN FOOD

Paris can also offer diners an amazing selection of world flavours, especially those of France's former colonies – for example, Moroccan tajines and Cambodian fish with coconut milk. Most fascinating of all is to observe how these cuisines are developing, as young chefs adapt and combine traditional ingredients and culinary styles with those of France.

ON THE MENU

Andouillettes Sausages made of pork intestines

Blanquette de veau Veal stew with eggs and cream

Crottin chaud en salade Goat's cheese on toast with salad

Cuisses de grenouille Frogs' legs in garlic butter

Iles flottantes Meringues floating in creamy sauce

Plateau de fruits de mer Platter of raw and cooked seafood

Ris de veau Veal sweetbreads

Rognons à la moutarde Kidneys in mustard sauce

Salade frisée aux lardons Endive salad with fried bacon

Sole meunière Fried sole with melted butter

Moules marinière *are mussels steamed in a fragrant sauce of white wine, garlic, parsley and sometimes cream.*

Coq au vin *is a male chicken braised with red wine, herbs, garlic, baby onions and button mushrooms.*

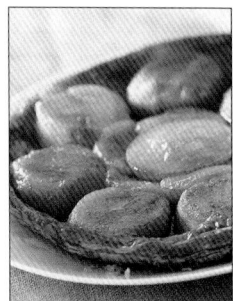

Tarte tatin *is a caramelized upside-down buttery apple tart, created at the hotel Tatin in the Loire Valley.*

What to Drink in Paris

Paris is the best place in France to sample a wide range of the country's many different wines. It's cheapest to order wine by the carafe, normally referred to by size: 25cl (*quart*), 33cl (*fillette*), 50cl (*demi*) or 75cl (*pichet*, equivalent to a bottle). Cafés and wine bars always offer wine by the glass – *un petit blanc* is a small glass of white, a larger glass of red, *un ballon rouge*. House wine is nearly always reliable.

Paris's last vineyard, near Sacré-Coeur (*see p222*)

RED WINE

Some of the world's finest red wines come from the Bordeaux and Burgundy regions, but for everyday drinking choose from the vast range of basic Bordeaux or Côtes du Rhône wines. Or try one of the Beaujolais *crus*, such as Morgon or Fleurie, situated in the southern end of Burgundy, or Beaujolais Villages, which is light enough to serve chilled.

Distinctive bottle shapes for Bordeaux and Burgundy

Bordeaux châteaux include Margaux, which makes some of the world's most elegant red wines.

Burgundy includes some big, strong red wines from the village of Gevrey-Chambertin in the Côte de Nuits.

Beaujolais Nouveau, the fruity first taste of the year's new wine, is released on the third Thursday of November.

The Loire has very good red wines from the area around Chinon. They are usually quite light and very dry.

Southern Rhône is famous for its dark, rich red wines from Châteauneuf-du-Pape, north of Avignon.

Northern Rhône has some dark, spicy red wines, best aged for at least 10 years, from Côte-Rôtie near Vienne.

FINE WINE VINTAGE CHART

	2005	2004	2003	2002	2001	2000	1999	1998	1997
BORDEAUX									
Margaux, St-Julien, Pauillac, St-Estèphe	9	7	8	6	7	8	7	7	7
Graves, Pessac-Léognan (red)	9	7	6	6	7	8	7	8	7
Graves, Pessac-Léognan (white)	9	8	7	6	7	8	8	7	8
St-Emilion, Pomerol	9	7	6	5	8	8	7	7	7
BURGUNDY									
Chablis	9	8	7	8	8	8	8	8	9
Côte de Nuits (red)	9	7	7	6	7	7	7	7	8
Côte de Beaune (white)	9	8	7	8	8	7	7	8	9
LOIRE									
Bourgueil, Chinon	9	7	7	8	7	8	8	7	9
Sancerre (white)	9	8	7	7	8	8	8	7	9
RHONE									
Hermitage (red)	9	7	7	4	7	7	8	8	7
Hermitage (white)	9	7	6	4	8	9	7	8	8
Côte-Rôtie	9	7	6	4	7	8	9	8	7
Châteauneuf-du-Pape	9	7	6	3	7	8	7	8	7

The quality scale from 1 to 10 represents an overall rating for the year and is only a guideline

WHITE WINE

The finest white Bordeaux and Burgundy are best with food, but for everyday drinking try a light dry wine such as Entre-Deux-Mers from Bordeaux, or Anjou Blanc or Sauvignon de Touraine from the Loire. Alsace makes some reliable white wines. Sweet wines such as Sauternes, Barsac or Coteaux du Layon are delicious with *foie gras*.

Alsace Riesling and Burgundy

Alsace wines are usually labelled by grape variety. Gewürztraminer is one of the most distinctive.

Burgundy wines include Chablis, a fresh, full-flavoured dry wine from the northernmost vineyards.

Champagne vineyards east of Paris produce the famous sparkling wine. Billecart-Salmon is a light, pink Champagne.

Loire wines include Pouilly-Fumé, from the east of the region. It is very dry, often with a slightly smoky perfume.

The Loire has the perfect partner to seafood dishes in Muscadet, a dry white wine from the Atlantic Coast.

Sweet Bordeaux are luscious, golden-coloured dessert wines, the most famous being Barsac and Sauternes.

SPARKLING WINE

In France champagne is the first choice for a celebration drink, and styles range from non-vintage to deluxe. Many other wine regions make sparkling wines by the champagne method which tend to be a lot cheaper. Look out for Crémant de Loire, Crémant de Bourgogne, Vouvray Mousseux, Saumur Mousseux and Blanquette de Limoux.

Champagne

APERITIFS AND DIGESTIFS

Kir, white wine mixed with a small amount of blackcurrant liqueur or *crème de cassis*, is the ubiquitous apéritif. Also common is aniseed-flavoured *pastis* which is served with ice and a pitcher of water and can be very refreshing. Vermouths, especially Noilly-Prat, are also common apéritifs. *Digestifs*, or after-dinner drinks, are often ordered with coffee and include *eaux-de-vie*, the strong colourless spirits infused with fruit, and brandies such as Cognac, Armagnac and Calvados.

Kir: white wine with cassis

BEERS

Beer in France is sold either by the bottle or, more cheaply, on tap by the glass – *un demi*. The cheapest is lager-style *bière française*, and the best brands are Meteor and Mutzig, followed by "33", "1664" and Kronenbourg. A maltier beer is Leffe, which comes as *blonde* (lager) or *brune* (darker, more fully flavoured). Pelforth makes very good dark beer and lager. Some bars and cafés specialize in foreign beers, especially from Belgium, and these are very malty and strong; others brew their own beer. (For beer bars see p317.)

OTHER DRINKS

The brightly-coloured drinks consumed in cafés all over Paris are mixtures of flavoured syrups and mineral waters, called *sirops à l'eau*. The emerald-green drinks use mint syrup, the red ones grenadine. Fruit juices and tomato juice are sold in bottles unless you specify *citron pressé* or *orange pressée* (freshly-squeezed lemon or orange), which is served with a pitcher of water and with sugar or sugar syrup for you to dilute and sweeten to taste. If you ask for water, you will be served mineral water, sparkling *(gazeuse)* or still *(naturelle)*; if you don't want to be charged, ask for tap water *(eau de robinet)*.

Fresh lemon juice is served with water and sugar

Choosing a Restaurant

The restaurants listed on the following pages have been selected for their good value or exceptional food. The chart below lists restaurants in Paris by area, and the entries are alphabetical within each price category. Details on snack and sandwich bars are in Light Meals and Snacks on pages 316–19.

PRICE CATEGORIES
For a three-course meal per person, with a half-bottle of house wine, including tax and service.
€ under 25 euros
€€ 26–35 euros
€€€ 36–50 euros
€€€€ 51–75 euros
€€€€€ over 75 euros

ILE DE LA CITÉ AND ÎLE SAINT-LOUIS

Au Rendez-Vous des Camionneurs
€
72 Quai des Orfèvres, 75001 **Tel** *01 43 54 88 74*
Map 12 F3

There aren't many *camionneurs* (lorry drivers) on picturesque Ile de la Cité, but this restaurant can satisfy the biggest appetite. Veal stew in white sauce is the house speciality, along with *foie gras* terrine and puff pastry filled with tomato, basil and mozzarella. Extra charges for evenings.

L'Ane et la Mule
€€
74 Quai des Orfèvres, 75001 **Tel** *01 43 54 16 71*
Map 12 F3

Formerly called Ristorante il Delfino, this is a comfortable and stylish Italian restaurant, complete with fireplace and 17th-century cellar, and well suited to a romantic dinner. Pasta, tiramisu and the Delfino escalope (breaded veal cutlet) deserves its place as house speciality.

La Rose de France
€€€
24 Pl Dauphine, 75001 **Tel** *01 43 54 10 12*
Map 12 F3

Majestic setting, looking onto a 17th-century square. The cooking updates French classics, with specialities like the John Dory with rhubarb, ginger and Basmati rice. More traditional is the duck fillet in ratatouille. A *cuisine du marché* restaurant, La Rose uses the freshest produce from the day's market.

Nos Ancêtres les Gaulois
€€€
39 Rue St-Louis en l'Ile, 75004 **Tel** *01 46 33 66 07*
Map 13 C4

This restaurant has a jolly atmosphere and caters to big appetites. Only one set menu, which includes assorted salads, a buffet of cooked meats, one grilled meat, cheeseboard, fruit, dessert and plenty of wine. Satisfying and entertaining. Children's menu available for 10 euros.

Le Vieux Bistro
€€€€
14 Rue du Cloître du Notre-Dame, 75004 **Tel** *01 43 54 18 95*
Map 13 B4

This authentic bistro is popular with many Paris restaurateurs and entertainers. The slightly rundown decor suits the place and the rendition of favourites like *boeuf bourguignon, gratin dauphinois* (sliced potatoes baked in cream), *tarte tatin* (upside-down apple tart) and profiteroles are good.

THE MARAIS

Galerie 88
€
88 Quai de l'Hotel de Ville, 75004 **Tel** *01 42 72 17 58*
Map 13 B2

The bare-walled decor in this tiny restaurant on the banks of the Seine appeals to students and people on a budget. Prices are low, service is friendly if slow, and you really know you are in Paris. The food is old-fashioned, and includes terrines and a selection of delicious homemade tarts. A few vegetarian dishes too.

Le Baracane
€
38 Rue des Tournelles, 75004 **Tel** *01 42 71 43 33*
Map 14 E3

A tiny restaurant with good quality food at reasonable prices. The fixed-price menu is particularly good value. The Southwestern cuisine includes a delicious rabbit *confit*, braised oxtail, pears poached in Madeira and Cassis (blackcurrant liqueur) and superb homemade chestnut bread.

Le Passage des Carmagnoles
€
18 Passage de la Bonne Graine, 75011 **Tel** *01 47 00 73 30*
Map 14 F4

A short walk from the Place de la Bastille, the proprietor Soizik may personally greet you. Although it calls itself a wine bar (and the selection of wines by the glass and bottle is excellent), it offers a full menu including five styles of *andouillette* (tripe sausage) and a variety of daily specials. Excellent cheeses; desserts include a vast chocolate éclair.

Key to Symbols *see back cover flap*

Aux Vins des Pyrénées 🏃 ♿ 🍴 €€

25 Rue Beautreillis, 75004 **Tel** *01 42 72 64 94*

Map *13 C3*

A very old bistro with a friendly and typically Parisian atmosphere. The day's menu, written up on a blackboard, typically offers a selection of grilled meats. There is an excellent selection of wines by the glass (particularly good value Bordeaux and lesser-known wines from Southwest France). Extra charges for a menu *à la carte*.

Brasserie Bofinger 🏃 €€

3 Rue de la Bastille, 75004 **Tel** *01 42 72 87 82*

Map *14 E4*

Established in 1864, Bofinger claims to be the oldest brasserie in Paris. It is certainly one of the prettiest, with stained glass, leather banquettes, brass decorations and murals by the Alsatian artist Hansi. It serves good shellfish, as well as respectable *choucroute*, and grilled meats.

Chez Jenny 🏃 ♿ 🍴 €€

39 Blvd du Temple, 75003 **Tel** *01 44 54 39 00*

Map *14 D1*

This huge brasserie on the Place de la République has been a bastion of Alsatian cooking since it was founded over 60 years ago. Service by women in Alsatian dress adds to the atmosphere. The *choucroute* (sauerkraut) *spéciale Jenny* makes a hearty meal with a fruit tart or sorbet, served with a fruit liqueur for dessert.

Le Colimaçon 🏃 €€

44 Rue Vieille du Temple, 75004 **Tel** *01 48 87 12 01*

Map *13 C3*

Le Colimaçon (snail) refers to the restaurant's centrepiece: a corkscrew staircase. A listed building dating to 1732, it has period wooden beams in the ceiling. Snails are also on the menu along with frogs' legs in parsley and tomato sauce and *gigot de sept heures*.

Le Potager du Marais €€

22 Rue Rambuteau, 75003 **Tel** *01 42 72 17 79*

Map *13 C3*

Organic vegetarian food gets pride of place in this popular restaurant. The food is delicious, imaginative and comes in generous portions. Specialties include aubergine curry, leek gratin and chocolate mousse. Their wines are organic as well. Advance booking is recommended.

Trésor 🏃 ♿ 🍴 €€

5–7 Rue du Trésor, 75004 **Tel** *01 42 71 35 17*

Map *13 C3*

The decor of the tiny and trendy Trésor is defined by a contemporary elegance, with a touch of kitsch. Lasagne, grilled steak in wine sauce and tiramisu show the blending of French and Italian cooking. A wide selection of wines, whiskeys and cocktails available. Service is not always with a smile, but the dining room opens on to a pleasant terrace.

Auberge Nicolas Flamel 🏃 €€€

51 Rue de Montmorency, 75003 **Tel** *01 42 71 77 78*

Map *13 B1*

Located in Paris's oldest house (1407) and named after the famous alchemist who lived here. The restaurant's specialities include *Tatin de foie gras poêlé* and *Gala au pain d'épices*, while the *tour de force* here is *gigot de sept heures* following a medieval recipe. Comprehensive wine list.

La Guirlande de Julie 🍴 €€€

25 Pl des Vosges, 75003 **Tel** *01 48 87 94 07*

Map *14 D3*

Consummate restaurant professional Claude Terrail of the Tour d'Argent (see p306) has employed a good chef here, and the decor is fresh and appealing. For the best views, ask for a table near the window in the first dining room. In good weather meals are served under the cool vaulted stone arcades.

Le Bar à Huîtres 🅿 🏃 ♿ 🍴 €€€

33 Blvd Beaumarchais, 75003 **Tel** *01 48 87 98 92*

Map *14 E3*

Oysters predominate in Paris's three Bars à Huîtres (the others are in Montparnasse and St-Germain-des-Prés). You can compose your own seafood platter to start, followed by a choice of hot fish dishes, with meat on offer for carnivores. Convenient for the Place de la Bastille and the Marais.

Le Dôme du Marais €€€

53bis Rue des Francs-Bourgeois, 75004 **Tel** *01 42 74 54 17*

Map *14 D3*

Come here for serious French cuisine: sweetbreads, pig's trotters and *tête de veau* are all regulars on the menu. Other, more delicate, features include fillet of sea bream with a spiced crust, and cod cooked in Champagne. Decent service and the remarkable domed building contribute to a truly memorable dining experience. Book ahead.

Le Repaire de Cartouche 🏃 ♿ €€€

8 Blvd des Filles du Calvaire, 75011 **Tel** *01 47 00 25 86*

Map *14 D2*

Like its "sister" establishment, Le Villaret, this restaurant is run by former employees of Astier, to the same excellent standards. It too has a changing seasonal menu, which includes roast pigeon with leeks in a vinegar sauce and rabbit terrine with chocolate. Its decor is reassuringly traditional.

L'Ambroisie 🅿 🏃 ♿ 🍴 🍷 €€€€€

9 Pl des Vosges, 75004 **Tel** *01 42 78 51 45*

Map *14 D3*

Housed in a former jewellery shop restored by Chef Mousieur Pacaud, this is one of only seven Michelin three-star restaurants in Paris. The cuisine includes a mousse of sweet red peppers, *truffle feuilleté* (layered pastry) and langoustines. Reservations are accepted one month in advance.

BASTILLE

Boca Chica
58 Rue de Charonne, 75011 **Tel** *01 43 57 93 13*   **Map** *14 F4*

The upbeat Boca Chica boasts a funky decor, trendy tunes and Spanish fare. Tapas, paella, grilled sardines, pork ribs and *gâteau Basque* are all on the menu. On Mondays, there's a clairvoyance night here, while salsa is featured every Tuesday night.

Barrio Latino
46 Rue du Faubourg St-Antoine, 75012 **Tel** *01 55 78 84 75*   **Map** *14 F4*

Three floors of exuberant and luxurious South American decor in a building designed by Gustave Eiffel. Exotic food includes *guacamole, quesadillas* (grilled cheese-filled tortillas), Brazilian grilled pork and Uruguayan-style scallops on a skewer with salsa. Cheaper lunch. Children are not allowed into the restaurant after 10pm. Discotheque and salsa.

China Club
50 Rue de Charenton, 75012 **Tel** *01 43 43 82 02*   **Map** *14 F5*

Chinese restaurants can be kitsch, but this one is revolutionary in an extremely glamorous way. China Club has a Colonial chic decor as well as superior Asian cuisine. Specialities include five-spice crispy pigeon and sautéed sole with ginger-plum sauce. Jazz and world-music concerts are also regular fixtures.

Blue Elephant
43 Rue de la Roquette, 75011 **Tel** *01 47 00 42 00*   **Map** *14 F3*

An island of refinement in the trendy Bastille area, with a tropical decor of lush plants, gurgling fountains and Thai woodwork. Superbly presented Thai cuisine: *som tam* (green papaya, dried shrimp and lime salad) and cashew nut chicken served in a fresh pineapple. Sunday brunch.

BEAUBOURG AND LES HALLES

Au Crocodile
28 Rue Léopold Bellan, 75002 **Tel** *01 42 36 92 44*   **Map** *13 A1*

The limited menu of this welcoming neighbourhood restaurant is seasonal, with dishes such as marinated sardines, salmon profiteroles and sea trout with basil. The varnished ivory-coloured ash wood decor with abundant flowers creates a refreshing atmosphere.

La Victoire Suprême du Coeur
41 Rue des Bourdonnais, 75001 **Tel** *01 40 41 93 95*   **Map** *13 A2*

Comforting vegetarian fare served in a bright blue and white dining room. Mushrooms are a speciality here, as in mushroom pâté or roast mushrooms with blackberry sauce. Desserts include a famous berry crumble. No alcohol served except cider; try the biodynamic carrot juice.

Le Bistrot Beaubourg
25 Rue Quincampoix, 75004 **Tel** *01 42 77 48 02*   **Map** *13 B2*

This arty but chic establishment serves classic French food. Skate with "black" butter sauce and rib-eye steak with green pepper sauce are typical of their excellent menus, changed daily. Lingering over one's meal is no sin here. Equally pleasurable inside, or outside on the sunny terrace.

Aux Tonneau des Halles
28 Rue Montorgueil, 75001 **Tel** *01 42 33 36 19*   **Map** *13 A1*

A genuine Parisian bistro, Aux Tonneau des Halles is one of the last of its kind, with its real zinc bar, smoky interior and one of the tiniest kitchens in Paris. Service is not quick, but when the food is this good, who cares! The wines are original and good value.

Café Beaubourg
43 Rue Saint-Merri, 75004 **Tel** *01 48 87 63 96*   **Map** *13 B2*

With views of the animated piazza of the Beaubourg museum, Café Beaubourg has an elegant and contemporary decor. Simple and reliable, if slightly overpriced, fare is guaranteed – a variety of tartares, grilled meats and fish. The menu even offers a Thai salad.

Le Grizzli
7 Rue St-Martin, 75004 **Tel** *01 48 87 77 56*   **Map** *13 B3*

A change of ownership has breathed new life into the Grizzli, founded in 1903 when it was one of the last Parisian places to have dancing bears! The owner orders much produce from his native Southwest including local ham, lamb chops, cooked on a sizzling slate, cheeses and wines made by his family.

Key to Price Guide *see p300* **Key to Symbols** *see back cover flap*

Le Louchebem

31 Rue Berger, 75001 **Tel** *01 42 33 12 99*

Map *12 F2*

A former butcher's shop (*louchebem* means "butcher" in old French slang). Meat is what this no-nonsense eatery is all about, with portions designed more for rugby players than ballet dancers. *L'assiette du rôtisseur* is a classic (3-meat roast platter, each with its own sauce), and the *aiguillettes à la ficelle* are still prepared in the traditional manner.

Le Tire-bouchon

22 Rue Tiquetonne, 75002 **Tel** *01 42 21 95 51*

Map *13 A1*

The chef elaborates on various regional classics adding a gourmet touch. *Confit de canard*, prawns in puff pastry with saffron sauce and roast pigeon with morels. One of the popular dishes served at the restaurant is the honey-roasted *Magret de canard au miel*.

Au Pied de Cochon

6 Rue Coquillière, 75001 **Tel** *01 40 13 77 00*

Map *12 F1*

This colourfully restored brasserie was once popular with high society, who came to observe the workers in the old market and to relish the onion soup. Although touristy, this gigantic place is fun, and has a menu with something for everyone (including excellent shellfish). Still one of the best places after a night out.

Joe Allen

30 Rue Pierre Lescot, 75001 **Tel** *01 42 36 70 13*

Map *13 A2*

Known to offer some of the best burgers in Paris, Joe Allen boasts an American menu, with chicken wings, grilled tuna with pesto and cheesecake. Chilled but chic atmosphere, candlelit in the evening. The restaurant serves an excellent brunch on Sunday. Midweek lunchtimes also see some special deals.

Le 404

69 Rue Gravilliers, 75003 **Tel** *01 42 74 57 81*

Map *13 B1*

Magnificently located in the *hôtel particulier* built for Gabrielle d'Estrées (Henri IV's mistress) in 1737, Le 404 is impeccably run by debonair actor Smaïn, who also owns London's Momo restaurant. The food is deeply rooted in his native Morocco: genuine-tasting *couscous*, tajine and vegetarian delicacies. Cheaper lunches.

Le Pharamond

24 Rue de la Grande-Truanderie, 75001 **Tel** *01 40 28 45 18*

Map *13 A1*

Founded in 1870, this bistro is a charming remnant of its age, with tiles and mosaics, handsome woodwork and mirrors. Specialities include *tripes à la mode de Caen* (tripe cooked with onions, leeks, cider and Calvados) and *boeuf en daube* (beef stew). The Normandy cider is strongly recommended.

Saudade

34 Rue des Bourdonnais, 75001 **Tel** *01 42 36 03 65*

Map *13 A2*

This is probably Paris's finest Portuguese restaurant, with all the tiles you expect to see along the Tagus not the Seine. The staple salt cod is prepared in fritters, with tomato and onion or with potatoes and eggs. Roast suckling pig and *cozido* (Portuguese stew) are other dishes. A good selection of wines and ports.

Georges

19 Rue Beaubourg, 75004 **Tel** *01 44 78 47 99*

Map *13 B2*

On the top floor of the Pompidou Centre, the Georges offers stunning views. Light and inspired cuisine, such as cherry tomato and goat's cheese cake, *sole meunière*, lamb with chutney and macaroons. Roasted scallops with lemon butter is a hit. Terrace seating too. Decor is minimalist, with lots of steel and aluminium.

Benoît

20 Rue St-Martin, 75004 **Tel** *01 42 72 25 76*

Map *13 B2*

A gem of a Parisian bistro. The owner has retained the faux-marbre, polished-brass and lace-curtain decor created by his grandfather in 1912. The menu includes *saladiers* (assorted cold salads), house *foie gras, boeuf à la mode* and *cassoulet* (white bean and meat stew). The wine list is outstanding.

TUILERIES QUARTER

Salon de Thé Angélina

226 Rue de Rivoli, 75001 **Tel** *01 42 60 82 00*

Map *11 C1*

The speciality of this smart tearoom is the *Mont Blanc*: a soft, chewy meringue topped with whipped cream and chestnut cream. The hot chocolate is also one of the best in town, and the Belle Epoque setting is the ideal background for a quick lunch or a sticky treat.

Toraya

10 Rue St-Florentin, 75001 **Tel** *01 42 60 13 00*

Map *11 C1*

One of the oldest Japanese pâtisseries in Paris, Toraya offers a slice of Japan to Parisians. Dark wood contrasts with the vivid colours of the leather armchairs. Beautifully crafted Japanese pastries are on the menu: red-bean or green-tea-flavoured macaroons and many authentic, delicate rice dishes.

Il Palazzo at Hôtel Normandy
€€

7 Rue de l'Echelle, 75001 **Tel** 01 42 60 91 20   **Map** 12 E1

This high-class venue offers both French and Italian cuisine. On the menu are such delicacies as roast pigeon flambéed with grappa with a mushroom fricassée and potato pancakes, and scallops with green asparagus and truffle. Note that Il Palazzo is open only for lunch.

La Muscade
€€

36 Rue Montpensier, 75001 **Tel** 01 42 97 51 36   **Map** 12 E1

The epitome of French classicism: a Regency-style dining room nestled at the heart of the Palais Royal gardens. Mediterranean-inspired food such as the orange, glazed tomatoes and veal tagine. Tearoom in the afternoon, with pastries such as fig pastilla (in filo).

Barlotti
€€€€

35 Pl du Marché St-Honoré, 75001 **Tel** 01 44 86 97 97   **Map** 12 D1

From the creators of super-trendy Buddha Bar and Barrio Latino is this flash Italy-themed restaurant with its impressive atrium. Aubergine (eggplant) pasta, prawn risotto and cod satisfy the most delicate palates. Great Sunday brunch. Lunch at Barlotti is a little cheaper than dinner.

Café Marly
€€€€

93 Rue de Rivoli, 75001 **Tel** 01 49 26 06 60   **Map** 12 E2

Wonderful views of the Louvre and inventive French cuisine: carpaccio, caramel and coconut duck, salmon with spinach cream and raspberry macaroons. Beef with Roquefort cream sauce is one of the main draws, while for the raw-fish lovers, there's spiced avocado and tuna tartare.

Le Grand Louvre
€€€€

Le Louvre, 75001 **Tel** 01 40 20 53 41   **Map** 12 F2

It's rare to find such a good restaurant situated under the Louvre's glass pyramid entrance. The menu draws inspiration from Southwest France – stuffed goose neck, foie gras, boeuf en daube (beef stew), prune ice cream with Armagnac – and was originally developed by André Daguin, one of the region's gastronomic stars.

Goumard
€€€€€

9 Rue Duphot, 75001 **Tel** 01 42 60 36 07   **Map** 5 C5

Opened in 1872 and still possessing many original features such as glass chandeliers and inlaid wood panelling. Quality seafood on the menu including bouillabaisse and sea bass with oyster sauce as well as plenty of Champagne (over 150 vintages).

Le Carré des Feuillants
€€€€€

14 Rue Castiglione, 75001 **Tel** 01 42 86 82 82   **Map** 12 D1

In this chic dining room near Place Vendôme, chef Alain Dutournier delights the taste buds with his fine cuisine. The menu changes regularly, but chestnuts, white truffles, oysters and foie gras, all prepared to perfection, feature regularly. The lunch menu is far more affordable than dinner.

Le Grand Véfour
€€€€€

17 Rue de Beaujolais, 75001 **Tel** 01 42 96 56 27   **Map** 12 F1

This 18th-century restaurant is considered by many to be Paris's most attractive. The chef Guy Martin effortlessly maintains his third Michelin star with dishes such as scallops with Beaufort cheese, cabbage ravioli with a truffle cream and endive galette (pancake).

SAINT-GERMAIN-DES-PRÈS

Aux Charpentiers
€

10 Rue Mabillon, 75006 **Tel** 01 43 26 30 05   **Map** 12 E4

There are no surprises at this old-established bistro, popular with students and St-Germain-des-Prés locals. The menu changes daily but you can count on bistro stand-bys such as Marengo veal, boeuf à la mode and homely pastries, served at reasonable prices. Extra charges for dinner.

Chez les Filles
€

64 Rue du Cherche Midi, 75006 **Tel** 01 45 48 61 54   **Map** 11 C5

Moroccan sisters run this charming little tearoom, where afternoons offer an exotic tea break. Tagines, salads and couscous are on the lunch menu, and a Berber brunch is served on Sundays. Features include wrought-iron work and kilims bearing Moroccan accents.

Le Petit Saint-Benoît
€

4 Rue St-Benoît, 75006 **Tel** 01 42 60 27 92   **Map** 12 E3

This is the place for anyone who wants to mix with the locals; the waitresses speak their mind and you might be seated at a table with others. Not much has been done to the decor, but the good-value food is simple and homely. Its cuisine du marché offers six plats du jour, different every day.

Key to Price Guide see p300 **Key to Symbols** see back cover flap

Polidor

41 Rue Monsieur le Prince, 75006 **Tel** *01 43 26 95 34*   🍴🚹🐾   €

          Map *12 F5*

Once frequented by Verlaine and Rimbaud, this is bohemian Paris incarnate. The place has kept its reputation by sticking to traditional cuisine at rock-bottom prices. Grilled steak, *daube de boeuf* and Marengo veal (slow cooked with tomatoes). Various tarts such as chocolate, lemon or apple.

Coffee Parisien

4 Rue Princesse, 75006 **Tel** *01 43 54 18 18*   🚹🐾   €€

          Map *12 E1*

With wooden panelling, punctuated with pictures of American presidents, this is one of the best places for brunch. American classics on the menu include one of the best burgers in Paris (bacon and cheese), eggs Benedict and all sorts of pancakes and sundaes.

L'Arbuci

25 Rue de Buci, 75006 **Tel** *01 44 32 16 00*   🚹🐾🎔   €€

          Map *12 E4*

The Blanc brothers, owners of venerable institutions such as Procope, experiment at this unwaveringly contemporary venue. The menu boasts a great deal of seafood, including shellfish platters; other dishes accommodate foreign spices and vegetables, as exemplified in the lemon grass tuna and pineapple kebabs.

Alcazar

62 Rue Mazarine, 75006 **Tel** *01 53 10 19 99*   🚹🐾   €€€

          Map *12 F4*

A fashionable club in the 1970s, Alcazar was bought by Sir Terence Conran in 1999. He converted it into a new brasserie-bar, and the result is this huge, elegant and thoroughly modern establishment which serves simple but well-made cuisine. Cheaper lunches.

Barroco

23 Rue Mazarine, 75006 **Tel** *01 43 26 40 24*   🚹   €€€

          Map *12 F3*

This restaurant serves traditional Brazilian cuisine: *Feijoada* (black bean casserole), *churrasco* (grilled meat) and Portuguese-style cod. A chic and cosy interior, complete with a library. Brazilian musical groups perform at the Barroco several nights a week.

Bouillon Racine

3 Rue Racine, 75006 **Tel** *01 44 32 15 60*   🅿🚹🐾   €€€

          Map *12 F5*

Stuffed roast suckling pig, liquorice-flavoured lamb and seafood risotto are all served at Bouillon Racine. This was where the *bouillons*, the popular meat-flavoured soups, first made an appearance. Its listed building, dating to 1906, is an Art Nouveau masterpiece.

Brasserie Lipp

151 Blvd St Germain, 75006 **Tel** *01 45 48 53 91*   🅿🚹🐾🎔   €€€

          Map *12 E4*

This is the brasserie that everyone loves to hate. Yet, its clientele, which includes entertainers and politicians, keeps returning for the good food. The dishes include herring in cream and a huge *millefeuille* pastry. Ask to be seated downstairs with the "in" crowd: the first floor is referred to as Siberia.

Rôtisserie d'en Face

2 Rue Christine, 75006 **Tel** *01 43 26 40 98*   🅿🚹   €€€

          Map *12 F4*

Jacques Cagna's rôtisserie is located opposite his eponymous gastronomic restaurant. Perfectly mastered traditional recipes on the menu: veal chop with morel sauce and mashed potato and pan-fried red mullet with capers, lemon and caramelized chicory (endive).

Tan Dinh

60 Rue de Verneuil, 75007 **Tel** *01 45 44 04 84*   🍴🚹🐾   €€€

          Map *12 D3*

The relatively high prices in this Franco-Vietnamese restaurant run by the discreet Vifian family are due to a combination of the good quality cuisine and an outstanding wine list with one of the biggest collections of Pomerols in the city. There are no Oriental lanterns here – the interior decor is sober.

Yugaraj

14 Rue Dauphine, 75006 **Tel** *01 43 26 44 91*   🚹   €€€

          Map *12 F3*

Yugaraj is still considered by many to be the best Indian restaurant in Paris. The chef, proud of his high-quality products, emphasizes dishes from his native northern India, and key spices are brought in directly from the subcontinent. The wine list is perhaps surprisingly good too.

Procope

13 Rue de l'Ancienne Comédie, 75006 **Tel** *01 40 46 79 00*   €€€€

          Map *12 F4*

Opened in 1686, Paris's oldest café welcomed literary and political figures such as Voltaire and Diderot. Nowadays, it's still a hub for the intelligentsia, who sit alongside those curious about this historical monument. *Coq au vin* is the speciality. Shellfish platters, too.

Jacques Cagna

14 Rue des Grands Augustins, 75006 **Tel** *01 43 26 49 39*   🅿🚹🐾🎔   €€€€€

          Map *12 F4*

This elegant 17th-century townhouse showcases chef-owner Jacques Cagna's trinkets and excellent classic-cum-modern cuisine. Try the red mullet salad with *foie gras*, pigeon *confit* with turnips, and a classic Paris-Brest (choux pastry filled with praline-flavoured cream). The wine list is admirable.

Lapérouse

P & T €€€€€

51 Quai des Grands Augustins, 75006 **Tel** *01 43 26 68 04*

Map *12 F4*

This famous establishment from the 19th century was once one of the glories of Paris. Under the impeccable management of owner-chef Alain Hacquard, this is still the case. The series of salons have kept their 1850s decor. The best tables are by the window. Valet parking available.

LATIN QUARTER

Le Grenier de Notre Dame

P ⚥ & 🏠 €

18 Rue de la Bûcherie, 75005 **Tel** *01 43 29 98 29*

Map *13 A4*

Le Grenier de Notre Dame opened in the 1970s and still exudes its original hippie atmosphere. Mostly organic ingredients are used to make the filling meals such as fish gratin, vegetarian casserole or vegetarian escalope in breadcrumbs. The wine list offers a good choice of reasonably priced labels, including Château Chaurignac Bordeaux.

Christophe

€€

8 Rue de Descartes, 75005 **Tel** *01 43 26 72 49*

Map *13 A4*

You must not be put off by the somewhat lacklustre decor, because it is what they present on the plates that makes Christophe's a restaurant not to be missed. The menu includes a wide range of imaginative dishes, such as sautéed langoustines in filo pastry and wonderful *moelleux au chocolat* that oozes onto the plate.

Loubnane

⚥ 🏠 €€

29 Rue Galande, 75005 **Tel** *01 43 26 70 60 or 01 43 54 21 27*

Map *9 A4*

A Lebanese restaurant where specialities include delicious and generous *mezzes*, served under the watchful eye of a patron whose main aim in life actually seems to be the happiness of his customers. Live Lebanese music is often performed in the basement.

La Truffière

€€€

4 Rue Blainville, 75005 **Tel** *01 46 33 29 82*

Map *17 A1*

This classic Latin Quarter address is best in winter, when you can warm up under a medieval vaulted ceiling, in front of a roaring fire. The *prix-fixe* lunch menu is by far the best value for money; but if you like your truffles, then there are plenty of dishes to splash out on.

Le Balzar

⚥ 🏠 €€€

49 Rue des Ecoles, 75005 **Tel** *01 43 54 13 67*

Map *13 A5*

There's a fair choice of brasserie food here but the main attraction is the ambience. It's typically Left Bank: traditionally-dressed waiters weave their way amongst the hustle and bustle providing express service, with archetypal brasserie decor to match: there are large mirrors and comfortable leather seats.

Le Petit Pontoise

⚥ 🏠 €€€

9 Rue Pontoise, 75005 **Tel** *01 43 29 25 20*

Map *13 B5*

Popular neighbourhood venue. Inventive use of herbs and spices: pan-fried quail with honey, dried fruits and nuts and prawns Provençal. A perfect menu will probably be composed of a *Risotto à la Truffe*, followed by a duck *parmentier* and stir-fried *foie gras* and, finally, a hot vanilla *soufflé*. Reservations recommended.

Moissonnier

🍴 ⚥ & €€€

28 Rue des Fossés St-Bernard, 75005 **Tel** *01 43 29 87 65*

Map *13 B5*

This family-run bistro serves favourites which have Lyonnais overtones, such as *saladiers* (assorted salads), *tablier de sapeur* (ox tripe), *quenelles de brochet* (pike dumplings) and chocolate cake. Beaujolais wines are traditionally served in a small bottle known as a *pot*. Ask to be seated downstairs.

Rôtisserie du Beaujolais

& €€€

19 Quai de la Tournelle, 75005 **Tel** *01 43 54 17 47*

Map *13 B5*

Facing the Seine and owned by Claude Terrail of the Tour d'Argent next door, the restaurant has a large rôtisserie for roasting poultry and meats. Many of the meats and cheeses are ordered specially from the best suppliers in Lyon. A Beaujolais is, of course, the wine you should order here.

L'Atelier Maître Albert

P ⚥ & €€€€

1 Rue Maître Albert, 75005 **Tel** *01 56 81 30 01*

Map *13 B5*

The antique fireplace is purely decorative, yet dishes from the rôtisserie are this restaurant's speciality. Traditional fare such as veal kidneys and mouthwatering chocolate cake are the chief attractions. Other specialities include veal, mixed salad *du moment* and chicken livers. Owned by Guy Savoy (*see p311*).

La Tour d'Argent

P ⚥ & T €€€€€

15–17 Quai de la Tournelle, 75005 **Tel** *01 43 54 23 31*

Map *13 B5*

Established in 1582, the Tour appears to be eternal. Patrician owner Claude Terrail has hired young chefs who have rejuvenated the classic menu. The ground-floor bar is also a gastronomic museum; from here take a lift to the luxurious panoramic restaurant. One of the finest wine cellars. Lunch menu is much cheaper than dinner.

JARDIN DES PLANTES QUARTER

Les 5 Saveurs d'Anada
72 Rue du Cardinal Lemoine, 75005 **Tel** *01 43 29 58 54*
€
Map *17 A1*

Les 5 Saveurs d'Anada offers a small menu, featuring high-class macrobiotic, organic and (mostly) vegetarian food. Inventive soups are flavoured with butternut squash or cinnamon; mains include fish bento or seitan (gluten) curry. Good choice of organic wines, plus fruit cocktails.

Marty Restaurant
20 Ave des Gobelins, 75005 **Tel** *01 43 31 39 51*
€€€
Map *17 B3*

Authentic Art Deco interior but the cuisine steals the show. Serves a hearty fare, such as roast duck or rabbit casserole. Insist on seasonal dishes such as gazpacho. Excellent *crème brûlée*. The Marty was established by E Marty in 1913 and is still family-run.

Mavrommatis
42 Rue Daubenton, 75005 **Tel** *01 43 31 17 17*
€€€€
Map *17 B2*

With an elegant decor, this restaurant is manned by the Mavrommatis brothers, one in the kitchen, the other welcomes guests. Its Greek specialities include roast lamb and *moussaka*. The Hellenic excursion continues with Greek yogurt and *baklava* for dessert.

MONTPARNASSE

Aux Petits Chandeliers
62 Rue Daguerre, 75014 **Tel** *01 43 20 25 87*
€
Map *16 D3*

Unpretentious bistro, established in 1962 and still featuring the small chandeliers after which it was named. This was the first restaurant in Paris to serve cuisine from the island of Réunion. On the menu are Creole-style pudding, exotic fruit sorbets and coconut-and-vanilla punch.

La Cerisaie
70 Blvd Edgar Quinet, 75012 **Tel** *01 43 20 98 98*
€€
Map *16 D2*

Somewhat overshadowed by the Montparnasse tower, this bistro serves generous portions of traditional dishes such as mackerel with creamy potato purée and pork with asparagus. The excellent wine list includes many small but talented producers.

La Régalade
49 Ave Jean Moulin, 75014 **Tel** *01 45 45 68 58*
€€
Map *15 C5*

Gourmet fare for a bargain at this traditional bistro. Duck *foie gras* casserole and pan-fried cod with leek vinaigrette are main courses. Grand Marnier soufflé is the chef's speciality dessert. The seasonal menu, based on a *cuisine du marché*, is often renewed, depending on market. Reservations essential.

Natacha
17bis Rue Campagne Première, 75014 **Tel** *01 43 20 79 27*
€€
Map *16 E2*

Long drapes by the entrance and theatre seats bring drama to an otherwise simple interior of the Natacha restaurant. You can get a hint of the exotic on the menu, which includes chicken terrine with pistachios and glazed kumquats and steamed fish with herb dressing. Brunch on Sundays.

Wadja
10 Rue de la Grande-Chaumière, 75006 **Tel** *01 46 33 02 02*
€€€
Map *16 D2*

This is a favourite hangout for local families and arty types on a budget, thanks to its excellent-value *menu du jour*. Game, meat and fish are permanent fixtures, the wine list is suitably eclectic, and the waiters are always ready to advise on the right wine to go with the dishes you have chosen.

Contre-Allée
83 Ave Denfert-Rochereau, 75014 **Tel** *01 43 54 99 86*
€€€
Map *16 E3*

Sylvain Pineau (former chef at Le Crillon) conjures up mouth-watering dishes such as lamb steak in a herb crust with potatoes sautéed in goose fat, and scallops in parsley butter. The decor is minimalist, with lots of dark woods; the service is friendly.

La Cagouille
10–12 Pl Constantin Brancusi, 75014 **Tel** *01 43 22 09 01*
€€€
Map *15 C3*

This large venue, on the stark new Place Brancusi in the rebuilt Montparnasse district, is one of Paris's best fish restaurants. Big fish are served simply with few fancy sauces or adornments. You might also find unusual seasonal delicacies like black bay scallops and *vendangeurs* (tiny red mullet).

La Coupole
€€€
102 Blvd du Montparnasse, 75014 **Tel** *01 43 20 14 20*
Map *16 D2*

This famous brasserie has been popular with the fashionistas, artists and thinkers since its creation in 1927. Under the same ownership as Brasserie Flo, it has a similar menu: shellfish, smoked salmon and good desserts. Lamb curry is a speciality. Open from breakfast to 2am.

Le Parc aux Cerfs
€€€
50 Rue Vavin, 75006 **Tel** *01 43 54 87 83*
Map *16 D1*

Parc aux Cerfs means "deer park". Although the area surrounding this bistro is quite built up, the inner courtyard, perfect for an alfresco dining experience, adds a touch of the outdoors. The menu is good value and the food inventive, with creative twists on traditional French dishes.

INVALIDES AND EIFFEL TOWER QUARTER

Sip Babylone
€
46 Bd Raspail, 75007 **Tel** *01 45 48 87 17*
Map *12 D4*

Close to Le Bon Marché and great for a tasty shopping break, this is more a snack bar than a restaurant. Tea and pastries are served all day long in the elaborate dining room. For lunch, try the cheese platters, bacon and Parmesan salad or a plate of smoked salmon, *taramasalata* and aubergine (eggplant).

Au Sauvignon
€€
80 Rue des Sts-Pères, 75007 **Tel** *01 45 48 49 02*
Map *12 D4*

This restaurant revolves around wine. Walls are plastered with posters of the beverage, and the wine list boasts fine vintages accompanied by savoury snacks such as fine cheese or smoked salmon toast. Sweets include puff pastry with apple, plum or other seasonal fruit. Sunny terrace.

La Billebaude
€€
29 Rue de l'Exposition, 75007 **Tel** *01 45 55 20 96*
Map *10 F3*

This friendly restaurant offers good home-cooking, using the freshest ingredients at reasonable prices. Specialities from Burgundy include excellent home-made foie gras, scallops and rabbit, as well as a perfect pot-roasted calves' liver served with a *confiture d'oignons*.

L'Oeillade
€€
10 Rue de St-Simon, 75007 **Tel** *01 42 22 01 60*
Map *11 C3*

A welcoming restaurant with a good-value and varied set menu featuring deep-fried smelt, *pipérade* (stewed sweet peppers, tomatoes and garlic) with poached egg, *sole meunière*, cod *brandade* (salt cod and garlic purée), roast lamb with cumin and *ile flottante* (meringue in vanilla custard). Extra charges depending on wine.

La Villa Corse
€€€
164 Bd de Grenelle, 75015 **Tel** *01 53 86 70 81*
Map *10 E5*

In a pleasant neighbourhood, La Villa Corse is regarded as one of the city's best, serving fresh and strongly flavoured Corsican-Mediterranean cuisine. The menu features wild boar stew, olive veal, Brocciu cheese and chestnut bread, a speciality from the city of Bonifacio. Good choice of Corsican wines.

Le Troquet
€€€
21 Rue François Bonvin, 75015 **Tel** *01 45 66 89 00*
Map *10 F5*

This is a jewel in an unlikely, quiet residential street with a view of the Eiffel Tower. Locals soak up the friendly atmosphere and devour Basque chef Christian Etchebest's fabulous cooking. Expect unusual dishes such as smoked eel tart with avocado purée and apples.

Le Récamier
€€€€
4 Rue Récamier, 75007 **Tel** *01 45 48 86 58*
Map *12 D4*

A Paris institution, attracting writers, publishers, journalists and political figures, the Récamier is reputed for its classic French character. The menu features Burgundian specialities, such as *boeuf bourguignon*, pike mousse and Grand-Marnier soufflé. Tucked away in a pedestrian street, its terrace is one of the best in Paris.

Thoumieux
€€€€
79 Rue St-Dominique, 75007 **Tel** *01 47 05 49 75*
Map *11 A2*

This bustling traditional French bistro is good value for money. Ingredients are fresh and almost everything is made on the premises, including *foie gras*, duck *rillettes* (similar to pâté), *cassoulet* (white bean and meat stew) and chocolate mousse. Prompt service.

L'Arpège
€€€€€
84 Rue de Varenne, 75007 **Tel** *01 45 51 47 33*
Map *11 B3*

Alain Passard's three-star restaurant near the Musée Rodin is one of the most highly regarded in Paris. It has striking pale-wood decor and sprightly young service as well as good food. Passard's lobster and turnip vinaigrette and duck Louise Passard are classics. Don't miss the apple tart.

Le Jules Verne

□ 冬 ⌂ ▮ €€€€€

2nd platform, Eiffel Tower, 75007 **Tel** *01 45 55 61 44*

Map 10 D3

This is no tourist trap: the Jules Verne on the second platform of the Eiffel Tower is now one of the hardest dinner reservations to obtain in Paris. The sleek, all-black decor suits the monument perfectly and the pretty, flavourful cuisine is very good indeed.

Vin sur Vin

▮ €€€€€

20 Rue de Monttessuy, 75007 **Tel** *01 47 05 14 20*

Map 10 E2

Owner Patrice Vidal is justly proud of his eight-table restaurant. The menu is seasonal and original, the wine list fabulous with interesting wines at reasonable prices. Dishes might include *pot-au-feu de foie gras*, *salade folle* and *cote de veau de Cantal*.

CHAILLOT AND PORTE MAILLOT

Chez Géraud

€€

31 Rue Vital, 75016 **Tel** *01 45 20 33 00*

Map 9 B3

Géraud Rongier, the jovial owner, is a scrupulous observer of *cuisine du marché*, using what's best at the market that day to create dishes like shoulder of lamb cooked on a spit, *sabodet* sausage in red wine sauce, skate with mustard, roast pigeon with port sauce and bitter chocolate cake. The mural was specially created.

Oum El Banine

冬 €€

16 bis Rue Dufrenoy, 75016 **Tel** *01 45 04 91 22*

Map 9 A1

The owner of this small, authentic restaurant in the chic residential quarter learned her art from her mother in Morocco. There is good *harira* soup (a thick, spicy soup), flavourful tagines, *pastilla* (a savoury puff-pastry tart) and *brik* (stuffed pastry triangle). *Couscous* is served with five choices of ragoût.

6 New York

⌂ €€€

6 Ave de New York, 75016 **Tel** *01 40 70 03 30*

Map 10 E1

A trendy restaurant, with an impressive minimalist interior, 6 New York marries pale wood and soft tones of grey. Though known to be a fashionable venue, it serves a surprisingly traditional cuisine, featuring pig's trotters (feet), Niçoise sole and vegetable risotto.

La Plage

冬 & ⌂ €€€

Port de Javel 75015 **Tel** *01 40 59 41 00*

Map 9 B5

A spectacular site facing the Statue of Liberty on the Ile aux Cignes. Thankfully, the cuisine's as good as the view. The huge terrace is the place to be seen at lunchtime, as well as an idyllic spot for a candlelit dinner on a balmy summer's eve. The decor is an attractive mix of wood and pastel tones.

L'Huîtrier

□ 冬 & €€€

16 Rue Saussier Leroy, 75017 **Tel** *01 40 54 83 44*

Map 4 E2

This freshly-decorated restaurant specializes in shellfish, especially oysters which you order by the half-dozen or dozen. It also serves several hot fish dishes and makes a good restorative stop before or after visiting the animated market in the nearby Rue Poncelet.

La Butte Chaillot

冬 & ⌂ €€€€

110 Bis Ave Kléber, 75016 **Tel** *01 47 27 88 88*

Map 4 D5

This is the boutique restaurant of the renowned, not to say deified, chef Guy Savoy. The country bistro cuisine includes snail salad, oysters with a cream mousse, roast breast of veal with rosemary and apple tart. The clientele are smart, so make sure you dress up.

Le Timgad

冬 & ▮ €€€€

21 Rue Brunel, 75017 **Tel** *01 45 74 23 70*

Map 3 C3

This has been Paris's best-known, most elegant Maghrebian restaurant for years, hence the need to reserve in good time. The menu has many different briks, tagines and *couscous* dishes as well as specialities like grilled pigeon, *pastilla* and *méchoui* (whole roast lamb), which needs to be ordered in advance.

Prunier

□ 冬 €€€€

16 Ave Victor Hugo, 75116 **Tel** *01 44 17 35 85*

Map 4 D4

One of the prettiest seafood restaurants, Prunier was founded in 1925. Its dazzling Art-Deco interior features wooden panels in the upstairs dining room. Wonderful seafood including smoked salmon and a variety of caviars. The menu changes with the season. Valet parking available.

Zebra Square

□ 冬 & ⌂ €€€€

3 Pl Clément Ader, 75016 **Tel** *01 44 14 91 91*

Map 9 B4

Part of the Hotel Square complex, a modern building with minimalist decor spiced up by splashes of zebra prints. Equally modern fare: crab cakes, aubergine (eggplant) *carpaccio* and salmon tartare. Brunch on Sundays. Stylish rooms done up in rich, soothing colours. A hit with the fashion and media crowd.

L'Astrance
🅿 ♿   €€€€€
4 Rue de Beethoven, 75016 **Tel** *01 40 50 84 40*   **Map** *9 C3*

The inventive cuisine of L'Astrance's two chefs has made it so popular that you must book at least a month ahead. Dishes include sauté pigeon with a caramelized hazelnut sauce and apple and celery minestrone with roasted spice ice cream. The Menu Surprise is as lovely as the mountain flower this restaurant is named after.

Le Relais du Parc
🏃 🍽   €€€€€
55–57 Ave Raymond Poincaré, 75016 **Tel** *01 47 27 59 59*   **Map** *9 C1*

In this historic townhouse, Alain Ducasse and Joel Robuchon create France's great "classic" dishes. Each culinary region is featured, and dishes include *turbot de Bretagne, chevreuil* (venison) *d'Alsace* and *fois gras de canard des Landes*. The enviable wine list highlights the Bordeaux region. The restaurant has just received a Michelin star.

CHAMPS-ELYSÉES

Ladurée
🏃   €
75 Ave des Champs-Elysées, 75008 **Tel** *01 40 75 08 75*   **Map** *4 F5*

Celebrated as one of the best tearooms in town since 1862, Ladurée hasn't lost any of its class. This elegant tearoom, famous for its Renaissance-style interior, still serves its renowned macaroons, which come in all sorts of inventive flavours: aniseed, caramel, chestnut, lime and basil.

Le Stübli
€
11 Rue Poncelet, 75017 **Tel** *01 42 27 81 86*   **Map** *4 E3*

A little corner of Germany with a patisserie, deli and tearoom. For lunch, try the great classics, such as sauerkraut. Their apple *strudel, linzertorte* and authentic Viennese hot chocolate make for a fine afternoon tea. Lunch is served on the terrace. German beer and wine is available.

L'Ascot
🏃 �C   €€€
66 Rue Pierre Charron, 75008 **Tel** *01 43 59 28 15*   **Map** *4 F5*

The present restaurant is an offshoot of the original Sébillon based in the bourgeois suburb of Neuilly since 1913. The menu specializes in meat-based dishes, and puddings are traditionally French. The decor is stately, with red banquettes and lots of dark woods.

Le Boeuf sur le Toit
🅿 🏃 🍽   €€€
34 Rue du Colisée, 75008 **Tel** *01 53 93 65 55*   **Map** *5 A4*

Highly inspired by the 1930s – *Les Années Folles* – the building (The Ox on the Roof) was formerly a venue hosting cabarets. Exemplifying the classic Paris Art-Deco brasserie, its changing menu can include sole meunière, snails, *foie gras* and *crème brûlée.*

Verre Bouteille
€€€
85 Ave des Ternes, 75017 **Tel** *01 45 74 01 02*   **Map** *3 C2*

Verre Bouteille proves that simple can be tasty. The house speciality is steak tartare, but goat's cheese ravioli, *foie gras* and chocolate cake are also superb. Lunch is much cheaper than dinner. If you liked what you ate here, and feel audacious enough to try the recipe, you can find it on their website: **www.leverrebouteille.com**

Flora Danica
🅿 🏃 ♿ 🚇   €€€
142 Ave des Champs-Elysées, 75008 **Tel** *01 44 13 86 26*   **Map** *4 E4*

On the ground floor of the House of Denmark, this venue is more relaxed and less pricey than Copenhague upstairs. Original Scandinavian cuisine, with just a touch of France. Specialities include grilled salmon and strawberries with mulled wine. Interiors are prettily done in Danish style. Valet parking available.

La Fermette Marbeuf 1900
🏃 ♿ 🚇   €€€€
5 Rue Marbeuf, 75008 **Tel** *01 53 23 08 00*   **Map** *4 F5*

Fabulous Belle Époque mosaics, tiles and ironwork were discovered beneath the formica walls of this Champs-Elysées bistro. La Fermette Marbeuf also serves good brasserie-style food including a commendable set menu with many *appellation contrôlée* wines – a measure of their quality.

L'Avenue
🅿 🏃 ♿ 🚇   €€€€
41 Ave Montaigne, 75008 **Tel** *01 40 70 14 91*   **Map** *10 F1*

Located at the hub of *couture* fashion, L'Avenue attracts an elegant crowd. The unusual Neo-1950s decor is fresh and colourful. Service can get a bit hectic at peak lunch and dinner times, but then this is a brasserie. The cuisine is varied and supper is served until late.

Man Ray
🏃 ♿   €€€€
34 Rue Marbeuf, 75008 **Tel** *01 56 88 36 36*   **Map** *4 F5*

A hip resto-bar filled with golden Buddhas, Chinese lanterns and Oriental artefacts. French-Asian fusion cuisine features citrus and ginger tuna and wok-fried scampi with oyster mushrooms. Great selection of sushi. A live orchestra plays Mozart on occasional Monday evenings.

Key to Price Guide *see p300* **Key to Symbols** *see back cover flap*

Sens
🅿️ €€€€

23 Rue de Pontieux, 75008 **Tel** *01 42 25 95 00* **Map** *5 A5*

This new concept restaurant, clad in soft greys and silvers, makes clever use of lighting to create the urban-chic feel that attracts the trendy crowds. Plastic tree trunk-like pillars prop up the mezzanine and young chef Christophe Fluck serves interesting Mediterranean-influenced dishes.

Guy Savoy
🛗 €€€€€

18 Rue Troyon, 75017 **Tel** *01 43 80 40 61* **Map** *4 D3*

A handsome dining room and professional service further complement the remarkable cuisine of Guy Savoy himself. The three-starred Michelin menu includes oysters in aspic, Bresse chicken with a sherry vinegar glaze, poached or grilled pigeon with lentils, and then an extraordinary dessert.

La Maison Blanche
🅿️🚶♿🛗🛗 €€€€€

15 Ave Montaigne, 75008 **Tel** *01 47 23 55 99* **Map** *10 F1*

The popular Maison Blanche restaurant affixed 15 Avenue Montaigne to its name when it moved here. Although the decor is modern, the restaurant is almost opulently vast. The cuisine, with its Provençale and Southwestern influences, is flavoursome and is the main attraction for its worldly clientele.

Pavillon Ledoyen
🅿️🚶🛗 €€€€€

1 Ave Dutuit, 75008 **Tel** *01 53 05 10 02* **Map** *11 B1*

The refined cuisine at Pavillon Ledoyen mainly features turbot breast and mashed potatoes with truffle *butte* (a sea fish recipe) and *mille-feuilles de Krampouz croustillante avec crème de citron*. Ask for a table in the dining room – a re-creation of a 1950s grill room – or on the terrace.

OPÉRA QUARTER

Chartier
🚶♿ €

7 Rue du Faubourg Montmartre, 75009 **Tel** *01 47 70 86 29* **Map** *6 F4*

Despite its impressive, listed 1900s decor, Chartier still caters to people on a budget, mostly students and tourists, though some of the old habitués still come for the basic cuisine (hard-boiled eggs with mayonnaise, house pâté, roast chicken and pepper steak). No frills, and expect to wait: the waiters are very busy.

Chez Clément
🚶 €€

17 Blvd des Capucines, 75002 **Tel** *01 53 43 82 00* **Map** *6 E5*

Just two minutes' walk from the Opéra, this comfortable bistro (part of a chain) serves its signature dishes of roast meats until well after midnight every day of the year. The dish of the day is always good value and, unusually, is available for both lunch and dinner.

La Vaudeville
🚶🛗 €€

29 Rue Vivienne, 75002 **Tel** *01 40 20 04 62* **Map** *6 F5*

This is one of seven brasseries owned by Paris's reigning brasserie king, Jean-Paul Bucher. Good shellfish, Bucher's famous smoked salmon, many different fish dishes as well as classic brasserie standbys like pig's trotters and *andouillette*. A quick, friendly service and noisy ambience make it lots of fun.

Le Noces de Jeanette
🚶♿ €€

14 Rue Favart, 75002 **Tel** *01 42 96 36 89* **Map** *6 F5*

A typical Parisian bistro, named for the one-act curtain-raising opera performed at the Opéra Comique across the street. An ornate interior belies the cosy atmosphere. The fixed-price menu offers a wide choice of classic dishes. Try the vichyssoise or *terrine de crustacés à la crème d'Oseille*. Menu changes regularly.

Angl'Opéra
🚶🛗 €€€

39 Ave de l'Opéra, 75002 **Tel** *01 42 61 86 25* **Map** *6 E5*

In this chic, informal restaurant, top chef Gilles Choukroun flexes his culinary muscles with his trademark cooking of blending and marrying flavours in ways quite unlike anywhere else in Paris's food circuit. Expect iconoclastic dishes such as *crème brulée* of foie gras.

Le Grand Colbert
€€€

2–4 Rue Vivienne, 75002 **Tel** *01 42 86 87 88* **Map** *6 F5*

Situated in the restored Galérie Colbert owned by the Bibliothèque Nationale, this must be one of the prettiest brasseries in Paris. The menu offers classic brasserie fare – herring fillets with potatoes or cream, snails, onion soup, classic whiting Colbert (in breadcrumbs) and grilled meats.

Les Alchimistes
♿ €€€

16 Rue Favart, 75002 **Tel** *01 42 96 69 86* **Map** *6 F5*

In the shadow of the Opéra Comique, this friendly restaurant offers dishes such as veal parmentier with oyster mushrooms, and warm chocolate tart with white-chocolate ice cream. The decor is a mix of old and new, with red walls and dark furniture.

Willi's Wine Bar

€€€

Map 12 F1

13 Rue des Petits-Champs, 75001 **Tel** *01 42 61 05 09*

Original wine posters cover the walls and over 250 vintages are in the cellar at Willi's Wine Bar. The menu includes onion tart with a salad topped with pine nuts, beef *fricassée* with braised chicory (endive) and rosemary sauce and bitter chocolate terrine.

Café Drouant

€€€€

Map 6 E5

18 Rue Gaillon, 75002 **Tel** *01 42 65 15 16*

Founded in the 19th century, this is one of Paris's most historic restaurants. The café, not to be confused with the more expensive restaurant, is a fashionable spot which serves excellent food until late and has an extremely good value menu at dinner. The interior has a famous shellfish-motif ceiling.

La Fontaine Gaillon

€€€€€

Map 6 E5

1 Rue de la Michodière, 75002 **Tel** *01 47 42 63 22*

In a 17th-century mansion, Fontaine Gaillon is partly owned by legendary film actor, Gérard Depardieu. The menu showcases sautéed John Dory, Merlan Colbert with sorrel purée, *confit de canard* and lamb chops. Comfortable interiors and a good wine list.

Senderens

€€€€€

Map 5 C5

9 Pl de la Madeleine, 75008 **Tel** *01 42 65 22 90*

Super-chef Alain Senderens has just given up the Michelin stars of his Lucas Carton restaurant to open this more informal eatery, on the same spot as its famous predecessor. His legendary creations include *foie gras* with cabbage, spicy duck Apicius and a mango *mille-feuille vanille*. The Belle-Époque decor is stunning and the crowd glamorous.

MONTMARTRE

Au Grain de Folie

€

Map 6 F1

24 Rue la Vieuville, 75018 **Tel** *01 42 58 15 57*

Paris has only a handful of vegetarian restaurants, and Au Grain de Folie has a truly cosy feel. Main courses consist of salads with interesting combinations of vegetables and grains (most of which are organic). The apple crumble is highly recommended.

Musée de la Halle St-Pierre

€

Map 7 A1

2 Rue Ronsard, 75018 **Tel** *01 42 58 72 89*

Formerly a covered market, this venue now hosts a library, the Max Fourny primitive art museum and a restaurant. This is a popular spot for afternoon tea and pastries. At lunch, the menu is more substantial with savoury bites such as quiche, pies and tarts. Children's activities provided.

Le Restaurant

€€

Map 6 E1

32 Rue Véron, 75018 **Tel** *01 42 23 06 22*

Almost invisible from the main road, this place teems with locals every night of the week. Its original distressed-chic decor provides a unique setting, while the kitchen offers French food with a twist. The split-pea soup with giant *gambas* (prawns) is a must, as is the delicious chocolate tart.

Le Wepler

€€€

Map 6 D1

14 Pl de Clichy, 75018 **Tel** *01 45 22 53 29*

Retro-style brasserie open until late into the night. Good for afternoon tea, early evening cocktails and pre- or post-show suppers. Large shellfish platters as well as sauerkraut, *andouillette* and *confit de canard*. An institution, established in 1892.

Beauvilliers

€€€€€

Map 2 E5

52 Rue Lamarck, 75018 **Tel** *01 42 55 05 42*

Montmartre's best and one of the most festive in Paris, this is where effusive chef Edouard Carlier delves into old cookbooks for ideas. Favourites are *escabèche* of red mullet (the fish is cooked and marinated), veal *rognonnade* (part of a loin of veal with the kidney) and a very lemony lemon tart.

FURTHER AFIELD

Beyrouth

€

16 Rue de la Vacquerie, 75011 **Tel** *01 43 79 27 46*

In a residental street near the cemetery of Père Lachaise, this is a wonderful Lebanese restaurant frequented by a mixture of locals, media types (from the TV studio next door) and drama students. The food is as copious and delicious as it is well priced, and the service is friendly.

Key to Price Guide *see p300* **Key to Symbols** *see back cover flap*

Chez Gladines

30 Rue des Cinq Diamantes, 75013 **Tel** *01 45 80 70 10*   **Map** *17 C4*

In the villagey Butte-aux-Cailles quarter, hidden behind the high-rises of Place d'Italie, this is a haven of decent, no-frills food. The place is so popular, it is always busy. Giant salads are among the favourite items on the menu: they are served in massive bowls and are often covered in sautéed potatoes.

Favela Chic

18 Rue Faubourg du Temple, 75011 **Tel** *01 40 21 38 14*   **Map** *8 D5*

Not much of Brazil is missing from this lively haven, run by Jerome and Roseanne. The *caipirinha* (fresh lime, cane-sugar alcohol and lots of crushed ice) has lost none of its buzz, and the *feijoada* tastes just as it does back in Salvador Bahia. The place gets noisy as the evening progresses, so come early.

La Boulangerie

15 Rue des Panoyaux, 75020 **Tel** *01 43 58 45 45*

Set in a converted bakery, this is a real neighbourhood bistro that fills up quickly with locals and regulars. The atmosphere is friendly and the food is excellent value for money. Try the crab ravioli in lobster cream sauce or the tender steaks.

Le Baron Rouge

1 Rue Théophile Roussel, 75012 **Tel** *01 43 43 14 32*   **Map** *14 F5*

Right next to the lively Marché d'Aligre (see p338), Parisians rush here at weekends to sample the divine oysters, brought straight from Cap Ferret on the Atlantic coast. These can be eaten out on the pavement, standing round large wine barrels. Also a good wine bar during the week.

Le Volant

13 Rue Beatrix Dussane, 75015 **Tel** *01 45 75 27 67*   **Map** *10 D5*

The owner of Le Volant (The Steering Wheel) is fanatical about motorcar racing. There's nothing racy, however, about the cooking: it is simple, traditional French cuisine at its best; *boeuf bourguignon*, mouth-watering homemade fruit tarts and the never-to-be-forgotten chocolate mousse.

L'Occitanie

96 Rue Oberkampf, 75011 **Tel** *01 48 06 46 98*   **Map** *14 F1*

As the name indicates, the cuisine here is deeply rooted in the Southwest, as is the welcome from the Occitan-speaking *bon-viveur* owner. *Cassoulet, confit or potage à rouzole* (soup with sausage-meat and herb dumplings) are some of the typical dishes served here. Helpings are generous.

Piston Pélican

15 Rue de Bagnolet, 75020 **Tel** *01 43 70 35 00*

A long bar, wooden benches and a collection of old advertisements adorn this quaint venue. Salads served in hollowed-out bread, salmon tartare with sesame oil and caramel-centred chocolate cake exemplify the menu's twist on classic dishes.

Astier

44 Jean-Pierre Timbaud, 75011 **Tel** *01 43 57 16 35*   **Map** *14 E1*

Quality here is among the best for the price in Paris, and the dining rooms are always full in this hugely popular bistro. The food is very good, including mussel soup with saffron, rabbit in mustard sauce, duck breast with honey, and good cheeses and wines.

Chez Prune

36 Rue Beaurepaire, 75010 **Tel** *01 42 41 30 47*   **Map** *8 D4*

With wonderful views of Canal Saint-Martin, this is a top spot for brunch on Sundays, with a choice of smoked salmon or ham with croissants. Upmarket cuisine for lunch: saffron and lime fish and three-cheese ravioli. Platters of cold meats and cheeses in the evening. Daily food based on *cuisine du marché*.

La Gazzetta

29 Rue de Cotte, 75012 **Tel** *01 43 47 47 05*   **Map** *14 F5*

The young chef at this delightful restaurant is Petter Nilsson and he creates a superb gastronomic harmony with contemporary French dishes, such as venison with polenta, dried figs and dandelion leaves. The food is served in a relaxing neo-Art Deco setting.

La Mère Lachaise

78 Bd de Ménilmontant, 75020 **Tel** *01 47 97 61 60*

This is a friendly bistro with a split personality. A great terrace and two dining rooms – one traditional and the other plastered in aluminium. Uncomplicated food includes asparagus and citrus fruit salad, beef with potato gratin, *charcuterie* and crumble with seasonal fruit.

Le Bistro des Deux Théâtres

18 Rue Blanche, 75009 **Tel** *01 45 26 41 43*   **Map** *6 D3*

If you are on a strict budget this formula restaurant in the theatre district is a real find. The reasonable set menu includes an apéritif, a choice of first and main courses, cheese or dessert and a half bottle of wine. The food is reliably good, including duck *foie gras* and smoked salmon with *blinis* (small savoury pancakes).

Le Clos Morillons   🏃   €€
50 Rue des Morillons, 75015 **Tel** *01 48 28 04 37*

This discreet family-run restaurant's menu evolves constantly. The Far Eastern travels of chef Philippe Delacourcelle are evident in specialities such as cod roasted with cinnamon, pigeon with sesame and monkfish and lobster with ginger. Other dishes are more French. Respectable Loire wines complement the set menu which changes regularly.

Les Allobroges   🏃   €€
71 Rue des Grands-Champs, 75020 **Tel** *01 43 73 40 00*

It's worth the trip out to taste chef Olivier Pateyron's fresh and innovative cooking. Specialities include *Canettes aux épices* (duck with spices) and *Souris d'agneau ail en chemise et purée de poix* (lamb with garlic and bean mash). A complimentary *amuse-bouche*, different every day of the year, is offered.

Les Zygomates   €€
7 Rue Capri, 75012 **Tel** *01 40 19 93 04*

This former butcher's shop is now a popular eatery – surprising, given its out-of-town-centre address. The ceiling is painted tin and the dining room is filled with other interesting touches. Food is plentiful and wonderfully innovative, with dishes such as turkey in a salted rosemary crust or snail and mushroom ravioli.

Ma Pomme/Colimaçon   🏃   €€
107 Rue de Ménilmontant, 75020 **Tel** *01 40 33 10 40*

It is worth the 10-minute walk up steep Rue de Ménilmontant to get to this well-kept secret. Excellent food is served with a smile in a bright-yellow dining room with temporary art collections on the walls. Expect unusual dishes with ingredients such as ostrich and kangaroo.

Pause Café   🏃♿🛗   €€
41 Rue de Charonne, 75011 **Tel** *01 48 06 80 33*   **Map** *14 F4*

Since the shooting of the 1996 film *Chacun Cherche son Chat*, this has been a top spot to be seen. Luckily this has not ruined the friendly ambience nor the fine cuisine: light dishes such as steak tartare, tarts with salads and excellent homemade pastries. The stone and glass interior lends a rustic-elegant charm

Brasserie Flo   P🏃♿🛗   €€€
7 Cour des Petites-Ecuries, 75010 **Tel** *01 47 70 13 59*   **Map** *7 B4*

This authentic Alsatian brasserie is situated in a passageway in a slightly unsavoury neighbourhood. But it is worth the effort to find it: the rich wood and stained-glass decor is unique and very pretty and the straightforward brasserie menu includes good shellfish and *choucroute* (sauerkraut).

Brasserie Julien   P🏃   €€€
16 Rue du Faubourg St-Denis, 75010 **Tel** *01 47 70 12 06*   **Map** *7 B5*

With its superb 1880s decor, Julien is upmarket but reasonable. Under the same ownership as Brasserie Flo, it has the same friendly service and wide dessert variety. The imaginative brasserie cuisine includes hot *foie gras* with lentils, breaded pig's trotter and Julien's version of *cassoulet*.

La Marine   🏃🛗   €€€
55 Quai Valmy, 75010 **Tel** *01 42 39 69 81*   **Map** *8 D5*

For several years now this establishment has been a popular mainstay of the Canal St-Martin district, and as such, is usually packed, so book ahead. The main courses are good and mainly fishy, such as red mullet in puff pastry, fish steak with a creamy nettle sauce, or fish stew. The desserts aren't so highly recommended.

L'Auberge du Bonheur   P🏃♿🛗   €€€
Allée de Longchamps, Bois de Boulogne, 75016 **Tel** *01 42 24 10 17*   **Map** *3 A3*

This is probably the only affordable restaurant in the Bois. In summer you can sit on the gravel terrace under chestnut and plane trees, surrounded by wisteria and bamboo. It's also delightful in cool weather inside the cosy chalet. The simple service complements cuisine that emphasizes grilled meats.

Le Bistro d'à Côté Flaubert   🏃🛗   €€€
10 Rue Gustave Flaubert, 75017 **Tel** *01 42 67 05 81*   **Map** *4 E2*

This was the first and remains the most appealing of star-chef Michel Rostang's boutique bistros. Many Lyonnais dishes are served including lentil salad, *cervelas* or *sabodet* sausage, *andouillette*, and macaroni gratin. Popular with executives at lunch and with the upper layers of the bourgeoisie at night.

Le Chardenoux   🏃♿🛗   €€€
1 Rue Jules Vallès, 75011 **Tel** *01 43 71 49 52*

This classic bistro is one of the prettiest in Paris. Both fish and meat feature on the traditional French menu, with dishes such as roasted cod, preserved duck and fricassée of kidney. The wine list covers all of France's wine regions. The menu changes depending on the market.

Le Clou   🏃♿🛗   €€€
132 Rue Cardinet, 75017 **Tel** *01 42 27 36 78*   **Map** *5 A1*

Traditional bistro, complete with a collection of old advertisements and blackboard menus. Scallops, grilled beef and desserts such as glazed nougat and chocolate cake never leave the menu. The well-priced wine list features a great range of French wines from various regions.

Key to Price Guide *see p300* **Key to Symbols** *see back cover flap*

Le Paprika

28 Ave Trudaine, 75009 **Tel** *01 44 63 02 91*

Map 6 F2

Gourmet Hungarian cuisine and live gypsy music (October–April and June). A dish such as the *csáky bélszin* (beef with morels and *foie gras*) is familiar to the French palate, but desserts such as apple and cinnamon strudel offer a taste of Central Europe.

Le Train Bleu

Pl Louis Armand, 75012 **Tel** *01 43 43 09 06*

Map 18 E1

Train station restaurants were once grand places for a meal. Today this is not usually so, but the Train Bleu (named after the fast train that once took the élite to the Riviera) in the Gare de Lyon is a pleasant exception. Upmarket brasserie cuisine such as hot Lyonnais sausage, with excellent pastries. The Belle Époque decor is a landmark.

Villa Pereire

116 Blvd Pereire, 75017 **Tel** *01 43 80 88 68*

Map 4 E1

The perfect place if you are looking to rub shoulders with the chic locals. The French fushion menu includes delights such as crayfish and vegetable spring rolls in sweet and sour sauce and *confit de canard* with truffle oil and mashed potatoes. It is also open for breakfast.

Le Villaret

13 Rue Ternaux, 75011 **Tel** *01 43 57 89 76*

Map 14 E2

Tucked away on the Oberkampf district's northern fringes, this restaurant is run by the former staff from Astier close by. Well-known for its *cuisine du marché* (using the freshest ingredients from the day's market), carefully chosen and prepared meat and big cheese selection. Packed at weekends.

Why Not

123 Ave de Wagram, 75017 **Tel** *01 42 27 61 50*

Map 4 E2

Monsieur and Mme Faucher take a great interest in their restaurant and guests. The big dining room with large windows is pretty and the terrace a delight in fine weather. The original food includes *mille-feuille* of spinach and sliced raw beef, truffle-stuffed egg, turbot with caviar cream and a good selection of desserts.

Le Chalet des Îles

14 Chemin de Ceinture du Lac Inférieur du Bois de Boulogne, 75116 **Tel** *01 42 88 04 69*

Map 3 A4

Idyllic setting, nestled on an island in the middle of a lake. The country-style interior suits the bucolic environment, but the cuisine showcases a modern approach: pan-fried sole with a Creole-style sauce, coconut and lemon chicken with red rice and chocolate cake with a red berry *coulis*.

Le Pavillon Montsouris

20 Rue Gazan, 75014 **Tel** *01 43 13 29 00*

This restored building once counted Trotsky, Mata Hari and Lenin among its clientele. Today the attractive interior and terrace make fine surroundings for a good value set menu. Specialities include fish tartar, wild boar with bacon and wine sauce, and *crème brulée à la vanille Bourbon*.

L'Oulette

15 Pl Lachambeaudie, 75012 **Tel** *01 40 02 02 12*

L'Oulette's vast new premises may lack intimacy, but Chef Marcel Baudis's cuisine, reflecting his native Quercy, remains excellent. Dishes include duck *foie gras* cooked en terrine and jurançon sauce, lamb from the Pyrenées, and *pain d'épices* (a kind of spiced cake).

Augusta

98 Rue de Tocqueville, 75017 **Tel** *01 47 63 39 97*

Map 5 A1

This reliable restaurant serves excellent fish and a few meat dishes. The *salade augusta* is generously garnished with shellfish and the house speciality *bouillabaise* with potatoes must be one of the best in Paris. An unusual dish is langoustines flavoured with tarragon and saffron.

Au Trou Gascon

40 Rue Taine, 75012 **Tel** *01 43 44 34 26*

This authentic 1900s bistro owned by star-chef Alain Dutournier (of Carré des Feuillants) is one of Paris's most popular places. The delicious Gascon food includes ham from the Chalosse region, great *foie gras*, lamb from the Pyrenees and local poultry. Dutournier's desserts are also worth finding room for.

Dessirier

9 Pl du Maréchal Juin, 75017 **Tel** *01 42 27 82 14*

Map 4 E1

Dedicated to seafood since 1883, this is one of Paris's best-known fish restaurants. Oyster risotto, whole grilled sea bass and langoustine salad feature. A combination of fish brasserie and wet-fish market, it offers a variety of fish-based dishes, depending on the season. Affordable wine list available. Valet parking.

Le Pré Catelan

Route de Suresnes, Bois de Boulogne, 75016 **Tel** *01 44 14 41 14*

This elegant Belle Époque restaurant in the Bois is a delight, either in midsummer when you can dine on the terrace, or in midwinter when the lights inside are magical. The menu is luxurious, with huge langoustines, special Duclair duck with spices and sea urchin soufflé. Divine desserts. There is a cheaper menu at lunchtime.

Light Meals and Snacks

Good food and drink is so much a part of everyday life in Paris that you can eat and drink well without ever going to a restaurant. Whether you want to enjoy a meal or casual drink at a café, wine bar or tearoom, buy a crêpe from a street stand or a quiche or crusty *baguette* sandwich from a bakery, or put together a picnic from cheeses, breads, salads and *pâtés*, informal eating is one of the city's great gastronomic strengths.

Paris is also a wonderful city for drinking. Wine bars in every quarter offer various wines by the glass. Beer bars have astounding selections, and Irish pubs are much-loved spots which serve Guinness in a relaxed, sometimes rowdy atmosphere. Or choose from chic hotel bars or fun late-night bars. *(See also pp298–9.)*

CAFES

Paris is famous for its cafés, and rightly so. You can't walk far in this city without passing one. They range in size from tiny to huge, some with pinball machines, a tobacconist and betting stations, some with elegant Belle Epoque decorations and immaculately attired waiters. Every Parisian has their favourite local café and these establishments function as the heart of any neighbourhood. The life of a café changes throughout the day and it's always fascinating to check out the locals at leisure, sipping their morning espresso, tucking into a hearty lunch or drinking an *apéritif* after work. Most cafés will serve you light food and drink at any time of day.

Breakfast definitely is one of the busiest times and fresh croissants and *pains au chocolat* (chocolate-filled pastries) sell fast. The French often eat these dipped in a bowl or large cup of milky coffee or hot chocolate. Eating breakfast out at a café, or at least grabbing a quick caffeine fix in the morning is a fundamental part of the French lifestyle.

The café lunch usually includes *plats du jour* (daily specials) and, in the smaller cafés, is one of the great Parisian bargains, rarely costing more than 12€ for two courses with wine. The specials are often substantial meat dishes such as *sauté d'agneau* (sautéed lamb) or *blanquette de veau* (veal with a white sauce), with fruit tarts for dessert. For a simpler lunch, salads, sandwiches and omelettes are usually available at any time of day. One of the best places for this kind of food is **Le Bourdonnec Pascal** in St-Germain-des-Prés. **Le Rostand** by the Luxembourg Gardens is also an excellent place to eat as is **Café Constant** *(see p319)* in the Invalides district.

Most museums have reliable cafés, but those at the Pompidou Centre *(see pp110–11)* and the Musée d'Orsay *(see pp144–5)* are especially good. When visiting the Louvre, it is worth waiting till you re-emerge from the galleries and stopping at the upmarket **Café Marly** in front of the glass pyramid for an expensive, yet memorable drink or meal. Should you find yourself in the department store **Galeries Lafayette** *(see p321)*, it's worth going to the café for the fabulous views over Paris.

Cafés in the main tourist and nightlife areas (Boulevard St-Germain, Avenue des Champs-Elysées, Boulevard Montparnasse, the Opéra and Bastille) generally stay open late – some until 2am.

It is important to note that prices change depending on where in the café you choose to enjoy your drink. Standing at the bar with a glass of beer is usually a little cheaper than sitting at one of the tables and heading outside to the terrace will normally cost you more again.

TEA SALONS

Tearooms have become increasingly popular in Paris over the last few years and the selection of teas is normally impressive. Some tea salons also offer light lunches, as well as breakfast and afternoon tea, including **Angélina**, with its Belle Epoque decor. **Mariage Frères** in the Marais is well known for its exhaustive drink list and also sells loose tea and lovely teapots to take home. **Ladurée** on the Champs Elysées is a Parisian institution where well-heeled ladies sip tea and nibble the house speciality macaroons. For another type of tea, visit the mosaic-tiled **Café de la Mosquée**, at Paris's mosque in the Jardin des Plantes area, for sticky pastries and excellent mint tea.

WINE BARS

Most Parisian wine bars are small, convivial neighbourhood places. They open early, many doubling as cafés for breakfast, and offer a small, good-quality lunch menu. It's best to get there early or after 1.30pm if you want to avoid the crowd. Most wine bars are usually closed by 9pm.

Wine bar owners tend to be passionate about wine, most of them buying directly from producers. Young Bordeaux wines and those from the Loire, Rhône and the Jura can be surprisingly good, and wine bar owners usually seek out interesting tipples. The **L'Ecluse** chain specializes in Bordeaux, but for the most part you will find delicious lesser-known wines at very reasonable prices. Serious oenophiles might like to visit wine bars which form part of wine shops so that any interesting vintages tasted can be ordered by the caseload and enjoyed at home. There are several examples of this type of place in Paris – **Juveniles**, **Lavinia** and **Legrand Filles et Fils** in the Opéra district are among the finest. Juveniles is a small shop with a zinc bar run by a Scotsman. The selection is very good, especially for wines from the New World and great food is also served here. Lavinia is Europe's largest wine store, the choice is vast, there are regular tastings and the sleek bar serves many wines by the glass. The climate-controlled fine wines section is also worth a visit. Legrand is an old-fashioned vintner which is extremely popular with Parisian wine buffs. The bar has a lovely selection and knowledgeable staff. The most fashionable wine bar of this type is **Wine and Bubbles** in the Beaubourg and Les Halles district. This is a great place to spend a whole evening.

BEER BARS AND PUBS

Paris has both pubs and beer bars. Whereas pubs are simply for drinking, beer bars also serve a particular style of food and are larger. *Moules-frites* (a generous bowl of steamed mussels served with French fries), *tarte aux poireaux* (leek tart) and *tarte aux oignons* (onion tart) are classic examples of the food they serve. The chief reason for going to a beer bar, however, is for the beer. The lists are often vast: some specialize in Belgian *gueuze* (heavy, malty, very alcoholic beer), others have beers from all around the world.

Some beer bars are open from noon, whereas pubs may open later in the afternoon. Pubs are usually open every day, often until 1 or 2am. The pubs in Paris have a good mix of expatriate and French clients. Some pubs are also micro-breweries serving beer brewed on the premises. The **Frog and Princess** and the **Frog and Rosbif** are good examples of this type of pub, serving several types of home-brewed beer. The bar staff are very friendly and will happily help you choose the pint that's right for you. Aside from traditionally English pubs such as **The Bombardier** in the Latin Quarter, Paris has

dozens of Irish pubs and a few Scottish pubs. The best Irish pubs include **Coolin** and **Corcoran's** in St-Germain-des-Prés, **Kitty O'Sheas** and **Carrs** in the Tuileries district and **O'Sullivans by the Mill** in Montmartre. A Highland fling and good whisky can be found in the **Highlander** in St-Germain-des-Prés and **The Auld Alliance** in the Marais.

BARS

Being such an elegant city, it's no surprise that Paris has more than its share of cocktail and late-night bars too. Some pretty Paris brasseries, such as **La Coupole**, **La Rotonde** and **La Closerie des Lilas**, have long wooden or zinc bars, accomplished bartenders, a glamorous ambience and a sense of distinguished times past. Hotel bars are some of the loveliest places for cocktails in Paris. **The Hemingway Bar** at the Ritz (*see p286*) is the most famous hotel bar in Paris. It is full of nostalgia, small, intimate, lined with heavy wood and has the official Best Bartender in the World, Colin Peter Field. The cocktails here are wonderful and each drink for a lady comes complete with a fresh flower. Other hotel bars of note include the bar at the hotel Four Seasons George V (*see p290*) where the bartenders will shake your martini at your table and present it in an individual silver shaker, the rooftop terrace at the Hôtel Raphaël (*see p289*) and the fashionable bar at the hotel Plaza Athénée (*see p291*).

La Mezzanine de l'Alcazar is one of Paris's most fashionable bars, while **Le Rosebud** and the **China Club** are young and trendy. Other hip bars include **Le Fumoir** next to the Louvre with its long elegant bar and excellent cocktails, **Andy Wahloo** which is tiny with a Moroccan design, **De LaVille** café which is popular as a pre-club destination, **Rhubarb** which has a wonderful martini menu and **The Lizard Lounge**, which attracts a noisy, young crowd. The

Philippe Starck-designed bar and restaurant **Kong**, on top of the Kenzo store near the Pont Neuf, is currently Paris's trendiest place for drinks.

Bars which are less trendy but great for a relaxing drink include the tiny, stone-clad **Stolly's** in the Marais and legendary **Harry's Bar**, which claims to have invented the Bloody Mary.

TAKE-AWAY FOOD

Crêpes are the traditional Parisian street food. Although there are fewer good crêpe stands than there used to be, they still exist. Sandwich bars provide *baguettes* with a wide range of fillings; a Parisien – a type of *baguette* – is normally Emmental cheese with ham. Camembert-filled sandwiches tend to be delicious, but beware the misguidingly named *crudités* (salad) which normally includes tuna and mayonnaise along with the *crudités*. The best fast food in Paris is freshly-baked flat *focaccia* bread sprinkled with savoury flavourings. It is sold fresh from a wood-burning oven and filled with one or more fillings of your choice. You can buy it at **Cosi** in Rue de Seine. Busy tourist areas also have their share of kebab shops, if this is what appeals.

Ice-cream stands open around noon, and stay open late in summer. It's worth queuing for the city's best ice cream at **Maison Berthillon**. Seasoned gourmets come from across the city to queue around the block for a scoop or two of their delicious concoctions. Chocoholics will be delighted with their intense cocoa ice cream, whilst fruit fans can expect sorbets packed with flavour. There are several branches of Berthillon in the city but the Ile St Louis store is recommended: nothing beats strolling along the Seine catching the drips from a divine ice-cream cone. Ice-cream obsessives might also like to head to **Amorino** which makes Italian-style *gelati*. Don't miss the *amaretto gelato* which comes sprinkled with crushed *amaretti* biscuits.

DIRECTORY

ILE DE LA CITÉ AND ILE ST-LOUIS

WINE BARS
Jazz Club de l'Ile Saint-Louis
1 Quai de Bourbon 75004.
Map 13 C4.

TEA SALONS
Le Flore en l'Isle
42 Quai d'Orléans 75004.
Map 13 B4.

ICE-CREAM PARLOURS
Amorino
47 Rue St-Louis-en-l'Ile 75004.
Map 13 C4.

Maison Berthillon
31 Rue St-Louis-en-l'Ile 75004. **Map** 13 C4.

TUILERIES QUARTER

CAFÉS
Café Marly
93 Rue de Rivoli
Cour Napoleon du Louvre 75001.
Map 12 F1.

WINE BARS
La Cloche des Halles
28 Rue Coquillière 75001.
Map 12 E2.

Juveniles
47 Rue de Richelieu 75001.
Map 12 E1.

TEA SALONS
Angélina
226 Rue de Rivoli 75001.
Map 12 D1.

Ladurée
16 Rue Royale 75008.
Map 5 C5.

PUBS
Carr's
1 Rue Mont Thabor 75001.
Map 12 D1.

Kitty O'Sheas
10 Rue des Capucines 75002.
Map 6 D5.

BARS
Bars du Ritz
15 Pl Vendôme 75001.
Map 6 D5.

Le Comptoir
37 Rue Berger 75001.
Map 12 F2.

Le Fumoir
6 Rue de l'Amiral-de-Coligny 75001.
Map 12 F2.

Harry's Bar
5 Rue Daunou 75002.
Map 6 E5.

THE MARAIS

CAFÉS
Au Petit Fer à Cheval
30 Rue Vielle du Temple 75004.
Map 13 C3

L'Etoile Manquante
34 Rue Vielle du Temple 75004.
Map 13 C3.

Ma Bourgogne
19 Pl des Vosges 75004.
Map 14 D3.

Le Trésor
5 Rue du Trésor 75004.
Map 13 C3.

TEA SALONS
Le Loir dans la Théière
3 Rue des Rosiers 75004.
Map 13 C3.

Mariage Frères
30–32 Rue du Bourg-Tibourg 75004.
Map 13 C3.

BEER BARS
Café des Musées
49 Rue de Turenne 75003.
Map 14 D3.

WINE BARS
La Belle Hortense
31 Rue Vielle du Temple 75004.
Map 13 C3.

Le Coude Fou
12 Rue du Bourg-Tibourg 75004.
Map 13 C3.

Le Passage des Carmagnoles
18 Passage de la Bonne-Graine 75011.
Map 14 F4.

PUBS
The Auld Alliance
80 Rue François Miron 75004.
Map 13 C3.

BARS
L'Apparement Café
18 Rue des Coutures St-Gervais 75004.
Map 14 D2.

Chez Richard
37 Rue Vieille du Temple 75004.
Map 13 C3.

China Club
50 Rue de Charenton 75012. **Map** 14 F5.

Le Connetable
55 Rue des Archives 75004. **Map** 13 C2.

Les Etages
35 Rue Vieille du Temple 75004.
Map 13 C3.

The Lizard Lounge
18 Rue du Bourg-Tibourg 75004. **Map** 13 C3.

Les Philosophes
28 Rue Vieille du Temple 75004.
Map 13 C3.

Stolly's
16 Rue Cloche Perce 75004. **Map** 13 C3.

BEAUBOURG AND LES HALLES

CAFÉS
Bistrot d'Eustache
(See p109).

Café Beaubourg
100 Rue St Martin 75004.
Map 13 B2.
(See p108).

WINE BARS
Wine and Bubbles
3 Rue Français 75001.
Map 13 A1.

PUBS
La Taverne des Halles
12 Rue de la Cossonnerie 75001.
Map 13 A2.

Frog and Rosbif
116 Rue Saint-Denis 75002. **Map** 13 B1.

BARS
Andy Wahloo
69 Rue des Gravilliers 75003.
Map 13 B1.

Kong
1 Rue du Pont Neuf 75001. **Map** 13 A2.

ST-GERMAIN-DES-PRÉS

CAFÉS
Le Bourdonnec Pascal
75 Rue de Seine 75006.
Map 12 E4.

Café de Flore
(See p139).

Café de la Mairie
8 Place St-Sulpice 75006.
Map 12 E4.

Les Deux Magots
(See p138).

La Palette
43 Rue de Seine 75006.
Map 12 E4.

SANDWICH BARS
Cosi
54 Rue de Seine 75006.
Map 12 E4.

WINE BARS
Au Sauvignon
80 Rue des Sts-Pères 75007.
Map 12 D4.

Bistro des Augustins
39 Quai des Grands-Augustins 75006.
Map 12 F4.

PUBS
Coolin
15 Rue Clément 75006.
Map 12 E4.

Corcoran's
28 Rue Saint-André des Arts 75006.
Map 12 F4.

Frog and Princess
9 Rue Princesse 75006.
Map 12 E4.

Highlander
8 Rue de Nevers 75006.
Map 12 F3.

The Moosehead
16 Rue des Quatre-Vents 75006.
Map 12 F4.

BARS
Le Bar Dix
10 Rue de l'Odéon 75006.
Map 12 F4.

Birdland
8 Rue Guisarde 75006. **Map** 12 E4.

DIRECTORY

Café Mabillion
164 Blvd St-Germain
75006.
Map 12 E4.

Don Carlos
66 Rue Mazarine 75006.
Map 12 F4.

Fubar
5 Rue St Sulpice 75006.
Map 12 F4.

La Mezzanine de l'Alcazar
62 Rue Mazarine 75006.
Map 12 F4.

Zéro de Conduite
14 Rue Jacob 75006.
Map 12 E3.

LATIN QUARTER

CAFÉS
Panis
21 Quai Montebello
75005.
Map 13 A4.

WINE BARS
Les Pipos
2 Rue de l'Ecole
Polytechnique 75005.
Map 13 A5.

BEER BARS
La Gueuze
19 Rue Soufflot 75005.
Map 12 F5.

PUBS
The Bombardier
2 Place du Panthéon
75005.
Map 17 A1.

BARS
Le Caveau des Oubliettes
52 Rue Galande 75005.
Map 13 A4.

Rhubarb
8 Rue Laplace 75005.
Map 13 A5.

JARDIN DES PLANTES

CAFÉS
Café Egyptien
112 Rue Mouffetard
75005.
Map 17 B2.

TEA SALONS
Café de la Mosquée
39 Rue Geoffroy St-Hilaire
75005.
Map 17 C2.

PUBS
Finnegan's
9 Rue des Boulangers
75005.
Map 17 B1.

ICE-CREAM PARLOURS
Häagen-Dazs
3 Pl de la Contrescarpe
75005.
Map 17 A1.

LUXEMBOURG QUARTER

CAFÉS
Au Petit Suisse
16 Rue de Vaugirard
75006.
Map 21 F5.

Le Rostand
6 Place Edmond
Rostand 75006.
Map 12 F5.

BEER BARS
L'Académie de la Bière
88 Blvd de Port-Royal
75005. **Map** 17 B3.

MONTPARNASSE

CAFÉS
Café de la Place
23 Rue d'Odessa 75014.
Map 15 C2.

La Rotonde
7 Pl 25 Août 1944 75014.
Map 16 D2.

Le Sélect Montparnasse
99 Blvd du Montparnasse
75006.
Map 16 D2.

WINE BARS
Le Rallye Peret
6 Rue Daguerre
75014.
Map 16 D4.

TEA SALONS
Max Poilâne
29 Rue de l'Ouest 75014.
Map 15 C3.

BARS
La Closerie des Lilas
171 Blvd du
Montparnasse 75006.
Map 16 D2.

La Coupole (Café Bar)
102 Blvd du
Montparnasse 75014.
Map 16 D2.
(See p178).

Cubana Café
45 Rue Vavin 75006.
Map 12 F5.

Le Rosebud
11 bis Rue Delambre
75014.
Map 16 D2.

INVALIDES AND EIFFEL TOWER QUARTER

CAFÉS
Café Constant
139 Rue St-Dominique
75007.
Map 11 B2.

PUBS
O'Brien's
77 Rue Saint-Dominique
75007.
Map 10 F3.

BARS
Café Thoumieux
4 Rue de la Comète
75007.
Map 11 A3.

CHAMPS-ELYSÉES

WINE BARS
L'Ecluse
64 Rue François Premier
75008.
Map 4 F5.

Ma Bourgogne
133 Blvd Haussmann
75008.
Map 5 B4.

TEA SALONS
Ladurée
75 Ave des Champs-
Elysées 75008.
Map 4 F5.

BARS
Le Bar du Plaza at the Plaza Athénée
(See p291).

Hôtel Raphaël
(See p289).

Le V at Four Seasons George V
(See p290).

OPÉRA QUARTER

CAFÉS
Café de la Paix
12 Blvd des Capucines
75009. **Map** 6 E5.
(See p213).

WINE BARS
Bistro du Sommelier
97 Blvd Haussmann
75008.
Map 5 C4.

Lavinia
3-5 Blvd de la Madeleine
75001.
Map 6 D5.

Legrand Filles et Fils
1 Rue de la Banque
75002.
Map 12 F1.
Tel 01 42 60 07 12.

MONTMARTRE

CAFÉS
Le Saint Jean
16 Place des Abbesses
75018.
Map 6 F1.

Le Sancerre
35 Rue des Abbesses
75018.
Map 6 E1.

PUBS
O'Sullivans by the Mill
92 Blvd de Clichy
75018.
Map 6 E21.

FURTHER AFIELD

WINE BARS
Le Verre Volé
67 Rue de Lancry 75010.
Map 8 D4.

BARS
L'Autre Café
62 Rue Jean-Pierre
Timbaud 75011.
Map 8 F5.

Café Charbon
109 Rue Oberkampf
75011. **Map** 14 E1.

Chez Prune
36 Rue Beaurepaire
75010. **Map** 8 D4.

Pause Café
41 Rue de Charonne
75011.
Map 14 F4.

SHOPS AND MARKETS

Paris seems to be the very definition of luxury and good living. Beautifully dressed people sip wine by the banks of the Seine against a backdrop of splendid architecture, or hurry down gallery-lined streets carrying parcels from specialist shops. The least expensive way of joining the chic set is to create French style with accessories or costume jewellery.

Alternatively, splash out on the fashion, or the wonderful food and related items from kitchen gadgets to tableware. Remember too that Parisian shops and markets are the ideal place to indulge in the French custom of strolling through the streets, seeing and being seen. For high fashion there's the exquisite *couture* house window displays on Avenue Montaigne or browse around the bookstalls along the Seine. A survey of some of the most famous places to shop follows.

OPENING HOURS

Shops are usually open from 10am to 7pm, Monday to Saturday, but hours can vary. Many department stores stay open late on Thursday, while boutiques may shut for an hour or two at midday. Markets and local neighbourhood shops close on Mondays. Some places shut for the summer, usually in August, but they may leave a note on the door suggesting an open equivalent nearby.

HOW TO PAY

Cash is readily available from the ATMs in most banks, which accept both credit and bank debit cards. Visa and MasterCard are the most widely accepted credit cards.

VAT EXEMPTION

A sales tax (TVA) from 5.5–19.6 per cent is imposed on most goods and services in EU countries. Non-EU residents shopping in France are entitled to a refund of this if they spend a minimum of 175€ in one shop in one day. You must have been resident in France for less than six months and either carry the goods with you out of the country within three months of purchase or get the shop to forward them to you. If shopping in a group, you can usually buy goods together in order to reach the minimum.

Larger shops will generally supply a form (*bordereau de détaxe* or *bordereau de vente*) and help you to fill it in. When you leave France or the EU you present the form to Customs, who either permit you to be reimbursed straight away, or forward your claim to the place where you bought the merchandise; the shop eventually sends you a refund. If you know someone in Paris it may be quicker if they can pick up the refund for you at the

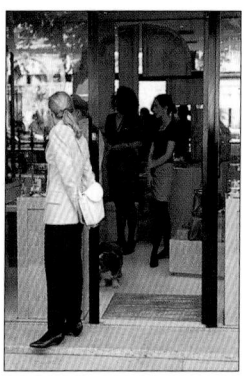

Shopping in Avenue Montaigne

shop. Alternatively at large airports such as Orly and Roissy some banks may have the facilities to refund you on the spot. Though the process involves a lot of paperwork, it can be worth it. There is no refund on food, drink, tobacco, cars and motorbikes. Bicycles, however, can be reimbursed.

SALES

The best sales (*soldes*) are held in January and July, although you can sometimes find sale items before Christmas. If you see goods labelled *Stock*, it means that they are stock items. *Dégriffé* means designer labels marked down, frequently from the previous year's collections. *Fripes* indicates that the clothes are second-hand. The sales tend to occupy prime floor space for the first month and are then relegated to the back of the store.

Au Printemps, the *grande dame* of Parisian department stores

DEPARTMENT STORES

Much of the pleasure of shopping in Paris is derived from going to the small specialist shops. But if time is short, try the *grands magasins* (department stores). Some still operate a ticket system for selling goods. The shop assistant writes up a ticket for goods from their own boutique which you take to one of the cashiers. You then return with your validated ticket to pick up your purchase. This can be time-consuming, so go early in the morning and don't shop on Saturdays. The French don't pay much attention to queues, so be assertive! One peculiarity of a visit is that the security guards may ask to inspect your bags as you leave. These are random checks and should not be taken as an implication of theft.

Kenzo designerwear in the Place des Victoires *(see pp324–5)*

Though department stores have different emphases, all have places to eat. **Au Printemps** is noted for its exciting and innovative household goods section, and large menswear store. The clothes departments for women and children are well-stocked. The lovely domed restaurant in the cupola often hosts chic after-hours parties;

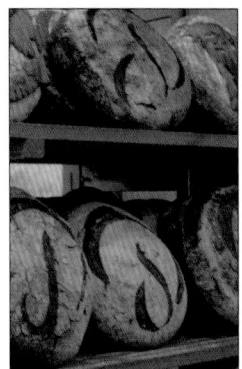

Apolonia Poilâne's bread bearing her trademark "P" *(see pp333–5)*

Snails from the *charcuterie*

these are private, but do visit the restaurant during shopping hours.

BHV (Le Bazar de l'Hôtel de Ville) is a DIY enthusiast's paradise. It also sells a host of other items related to home decor. The Left Bank **Le Bon Marché** was Paris's first department store and today is its most chic. The designer clothing sections are well-sourced, the high-end accessories are excellent and the own-brand linen has a good quality to price ratio. The prepared food sections serve restaurant-quality fare to take away.

Galeries Lafayette is perhaps the best-known department store and has a wide range of clothes available at all price levels. Its first-floor trends section plays host to lots of innovative designers. Having taken over the old Marks & Spencer, Galeries Lafayette also boasts a wonderful food hall, Lafayette Gourmet, which offers a vast array of mouthwatering goodies.

Virgin Megastore is open until late and has an excellent record selection and an impressive book section. **FNAC** sells records, books (foreign editions can be found at Les Halles) and electronic equipment. The branch on the Champs-Elysées specializes in music, videos and DVDs and concert tickets. **FNAC Digitale** sells a wide range of the latest technological equipment.

ADDRESSES

Au Printemps
64 Blvd Haussman 75009.
Map 6 D4. *Tel 01 42 82 50 00.*

BHV
52–64 Rue de Rivoli 75004.
Map 13 B3. *Tel 01 42 74 90 00.*

Le Bon Marché
24 Rue de Sèvres 75007.
Map 11 C5. *Tel 01 44 39 80 00.*

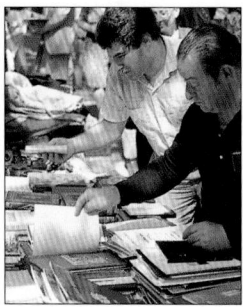

Bookstall, Vanves market *(see p339)*

FNAC
Forum des Halles, 1 Rue Pierre Lescot 75001. **Map** 13 A2.
Tel 0825 020 020.
74 Ave des Champs-Elysées 75008.
Map 4 F5. *Tel 0825 020 020.*

FNAC Digitale
77–81 Blvd St-Germain 75006.
Map 13 A5. *Tel 0825 020 020.*

Galeries Lafayette
40 Blvd Haussmann 75009.
Map 6 E4. *Tel 01 42 82 34 56.*

Virgin Megastore
52–60 Ave des Champs-Elysées 75008. **Map** 4 F5.
Tel 01 42 56 15 96.

Paris's Best: Shops and Markets

Old-fashioned and conservative yet full of surprises, Paris is a treasure trove of quality shops and boutiques. Time-honoured emporia mix with modern precincts in a city that buzzes with life in its inner quarters, not least in the markets. Here you can buy everything from exotic fruit and vegetables to fine china and antiques. Whether you're shopping for handmade shoes, perfectly-cut clothes or traditionally-made cheeses, or simply soaking in the atmosphere, you won't be disappointed.

Place de la Madeleine
Top-class groceries and delicacies are sold on the north side of this square. (See p214.)

THE CENTRE OF PARIS COUTURE

Yves Saint Laurent
Guy Laroche
Nina Ricci
Hermès

RUE DU FAUBOURG
AVE GEORGE V
AVE DES
RUE FRANÇOIS I
ROND POINT
CHAMPS ELYSEES
ST HONORE
COURS ALBERT I   COURS LA REINE
PLACE DE LA CONCORDE
Givenchy   Christian Dior
Chanel

See inset map
Champs-Elysées

R I V E R

Invalides and Eiffel Tower Quarter

Chanel
Coco Chanel (1883–1971) reigned over the fashion world from No. 31 Rue Cambon. The main boutique is in the Avenue Montaigne. (See p325.)

Rue de Rivoli
Inexpensive mementos like this Paris snow shaker can be found in the shops on the Rue de Rivoli. (See p130.)

Marché de la Porte de Vanves
This charming and relaxed market sells old books, linen, postcards, china and musical instruments. (weekends only – see p339.)

Kenzo
The Japanese designer has colourful apparel for men, women and children in his clothes shops. (See p327.)

Cartier
*The early Cartier jewellery designs
with their beautifully-cut stones
are still highly sought after. This
shop in the Rue de la Paix sells all
the Cartier lines. (See p329.)*

Rue de Paradis
*You can buy porcelain and
crystal at reduced prices at
the company showrooms on
this street. Look out for
Porcelainor, Baccarat and
Lumicristal. (See pp330–2.)*

Passage des Panoramas
*This once-prosperous arcade
at Les Galeries has an old
engraving house. (See p216.)*

Opéra Quarter

0 kilometres 1

0 miles 0.5

leries Quarter

Beaubourg and Les
Halles

The Marais

St-Germain-
des-Prés

Ile de la
Cité

Ile St-Louis

Latin Quarter

Rue des Francs-Bourgeois
*Stylish fashion stores such
as A-Poc (see pp324–5)
line this thoroughfare
in the Marais.*

Luxembourg
Quarter

Jardin des Plantes
Quarter

ontparnasse

Rue Mouffetard
*The market sells cheeses and
other quality foods. (See p339.)*

Forum des Halles
*This modern glass arcade
has many shops. (See p109.)*

Clothes and Accessories

For many people Paris is synonymous with fashion and Parisian style is the ultimate in chic. More than anywhere else in the world, women in Paris seem to be in tune with current trends and when a new season arrives appear, as one, to don the look. Though less trend-conscious generally, Parisian men are aware of style and mix and match patterns and colours with élan. Finding the right clothes at the right price means knowing where to shop. For every luxury boutique on the Avenue Montaigne, there are ten young designers' shops waiting to become the next Jean-Paul Gaultier – and hundreds more selling imitations.

HAUTE COUTURE

Paris is the home of *haute couture*. The original *couture* garments, as opposed to the imitations and adaptations, are one-off creations, designed by one of the nine *haute couture* houses listed with the Fédération Française de la Couture. The rules for being classified are fairly strict, and many of the top designers are not included. Astronomical prices put *haute couture* beyond the reach of all but a few immensely deep pockets, but it's still the lifeblood of the fashion industry providing inspiration for the mass market.

The fashion seasons are launched with the *couture* shows in January and July. Most shows are held in the Carrousel du Louvre *(see p123)*. If you want to see a show, you stand a much better chance of getting a seat at the private *couture* shows (the main shows are for buyers and the press). To do this call the press offices of the *haute couture* houses a month in advance. You can only be sure you have a place when you receive the ticket. For the private shows, telephone the fashion house or, if you're in Paris, try going to the boutique and asking if there's a show – and do remember to dress the part.

Most *couture* houses make *prêt-à-porter* clothes as well – ready-to-wear clothes fitted on a standard model. They're still not cheap, but give you an idea of some of the designer elegance and creativity at a fraction of the cost.

WOMEN'S CLOTHES

The highest concentration of *couture* houses is on the Right Bank. Most are on or near the Rue du Faubourg-St-Honoré and the classier Avenue Montaigne: **Christian Dior**, **Pierre Cardin**, **Chanel**, **Christian Lacroix**, **Gianni Versace**, **Givenchy**, **Louis Féraud**, **Nina Ricci** and **Yves Saint Laurent**. This is where you will rub shoulders with the rich and famous.

Hermès has classic country chic. **MaxMara's** Italian elegance is quite popular in France and no one can resist a **Giorgio Armani** suit. **Karl Lagerfeld** has a shop where the latest creations from his own line, Lagerfeld Gallery, are exhibited.

The theatrical **Paco Rabanne** and chic **Prada** have also stuck to the Right Bank, but many other fine fashion houses prefer the Left Bank. Try **Sonia Rykiel** for knitwear, **Junko Shimada** for sporty casuals and **Barbara Bui** for soft, feminine clothes.

Many designers have a Left Bank branch in addition to their Right Bank bastions, and they all have ready-to-wear shops here. For sheer quality there's **Georges Rech**, but don't forget Yves Saint Laurent or **Jil Sander** for their exquisite tailoring. Try Armani's St-Germain temple of fashion, or Prada's affordable boutique, **Miu Miu**, in the Rue de Grenelle. **Onward Kashiyama France** has its cult following for some imaginative clothes, and **Irié** is the place for reasonably-priced clothes

which are trendy but will stand the test of time. Also in the Saint-Germain-des-Près district, the **Comptoir des Cotonniers** stocks excellent basics, **Maje** has everything from boho chic to stylish cuts, and **Vanessa Bruno** is extremely popular for feminine flair. Simple cuts with quirky details can be found at **Zadig et Voltaire**, which has a following amongst French fashionistas.

Ready-to-wear shops blanket Paris, and in the beautiful Place des Victoires they thrive off shoppers visiting the Rue du Faubourg-St-Honoré. The **Victoire** boutique offers one of the best collections of current designer labels with Michael Klein, Helmut Lang and Thierry Mugler among many others. **Kenzo** is here (although a new flagship store now exists near the Pont Neuf), along with fellow Japanese designers **Comme des Garçons**, with its avant-garde, quirky fashion for both sexes, and **Yohji Yamamoto** just down the street, near Ventilo. The nearby Rue Jean-Jacques-Rousseau has now become one of the city's prime shopping stops.

Moving east to the Rue du Jour, **Agnès B** and **Claudie Pierlot's** clothes have timeless elegance. There are also many shops selling inexpensive copies of new designs in the centre. **Martin Margiela** carries excellent quality basics with a twist.

The Marais is a haven for up-and-coming designers and is always busy on Saturdays. One of the best streets is the Rue des Rosiers, which includes Issey Miyake's **Pleats Please**, **L'Eclaireur** and a branch of **Tehen** for clothes. **Nina Jacob** is on the neighbouring Rue des Francs-Bourgeois, and daring designer **Azzedine Alaïa's** shop is just around the corner. **Abou d'Abi Bazar** stocks a range of designers, **A-Poc** is an offshoot of Issey Miyake and has daring designs.

The Bastille area has trendy boutiques, as well as some

DIRECTORY

WOMEN'S CLOTHES

Abou d'Abi Bazar
10 Rue des Francs
Bourgeois 75003.
Map 13 C3.
Tel 01 42 77 96 98.

Agnès B
2–3–6–19 Rue du Jour
75001. **Map** 13 A1.
Tel 01 45 08 56 56.
One of several branches.
www.agnesb.com

A-Poc
47 Rue des Francs-
Bourgeois 75004.
Map 14 D3.
Tel 01 44 54 07 05.

Azzedine Alaïa
7 Rue de Moussy 75004.
Map 13 C3.
Tel 01 42 72 19 19.

Barbara Bui
23 Rue Etienne-Marcel
75001. **Map** 13 A1.
Tel 01 40 26 43 65.
www.barbarabui.com
One of several branches.

Chanel
42 Ave Montaigne 75008.
Map 5 A5.
Tel 01 47 23 47 12.
www.chanel.com
One of several branches.

Christian Dior
30 Ave Montaigne 75008.
Map 10 F1.
Tel 01 40 73 73 73.
www.dior.com

Christian Lacroix
73 Rue du Faubourg-
St-Honoré 75008.
Map 5 B5.
Tel 01 42 68 79 00.
www.christian-
lacroix.com

Claudie Pierlot
1 Rue Montmartre 75001.
Map 13 A1.
Tel 01 42 21 38 38.
www.claudie-pierlot.
com
One of three branches.

Colette
213 Rue St-Honoré
75001.
Map 12 D1.
Tel 01 55 35 33 90.
www.colette.fr

Comme des Garçons
54 Rue du Faubourg
St-Honoré 75008.
Map 4 E3.
Tel 01 53 30 27 27.

Comptoir des Cotonniers
59 Rue Bonaparte 75006.
Map 12 E3.
Tel 01 43 26 07 56.

L'Eclaireur
3 ter Rue des Rosiers
75004. **Map** 13 C3.
Tel 01 48 87 10 22.

Eres
2 Rue Tronchet 75008.
Map 5 C5.
Tel 01 47 42 28 82.
One of two branches.

Gaëlle Barré
17 Rue Keller 75011.
Map 14 F4.
Tel 01 43 14 63 02.

Georges Rech
54 Rue Bonaparte 75006.
Map 12 E3.
Tel 01 43 26 84 11.
www.georges-rech.fr
One of several branches.

Giorgio Armani
50 Rue du Faubourg-St-
Honoré 75008.
Map 4 E3.
Tel 01 42 61 55 09
www.giorgioarmani.com

Givenchy
3 Ave Georges V 75008.
Map 4 E5.
Tel 01 44 31 50 00.
www.givenchy.com

Hennes
15 Rue du Commerce
75015. **Map** 10 E5.
Tel 01 40 57 24 60.
One of several branches.

Hermès
24 Rue du Faubourg-
St-Honoré 75008.
Map 5 C5. **Tel** 01 40 17
47 17. www.hermes.com
One of several branches.

Irié
8 Rue du Pré-aux-Clercs
75007. **Map** 12 D3.
Tel 01 42 61 18 28.

Isabel Marant
16 Rue de Charonne
75011. **Map** 14 F4.
Tel 01 49 29 71 55.

Jay Ahr
9 Rue du 29 Juillet 75001.
Map 12 D1.
Tel 01 42 96 52 23.

Jean-Paul Gaultier
6 Rue Vivienne 75002.
Map 12 F1.
Tel 01 42 86 05 05.
One of several branches.

Jil Sander
52 Ave Montaigne 75008.
Map 10 F1.
Tel 01 44 95 06 70.

Junko Shimada
13 Rue St-Florentin 75008.
Map 11 C1.
Tel 01 42 60 94 12.
One of two branches.

Kenzo
3 Pl des Victoires 75001.
Map 12 F1.
Tel 01 40 39 72 00.
One of several branches.

Kookaï
82 Rue Reaumur 75002.
Map 13 B1.
Tel 01 45 08 93 69.
One of several branches.

La City
141 Rue de Rennes 75006.
Map 16 D1.
Tel 01 45 44 71 18.
One of several branches.

Louis Féraud
90 Rue du Faubourg-St-
Honoré 75008. **Map** 4 E3.
Tel 01 44 71 03 86.

Mac Douglas
9 Rue de Sèvres 75006.
Map 12 D4.
Tel 01 45 48 14 09.
One of several branches.

Maje
42 Rue du Four 75006.
Map 12 E4.
Tel 01 42 22 43 69.

Martin Margiela
23 Rue de Montpensier
75001. **Map** 12 E1.
Tel 01 40 15 07 55.

MaxMara
37 Rue du Four 75006. **Map**
12 D4. **Tel** 01 43 29 91 10.
One of several branches.

Miu Miu
16 Rue de Grenelle 75007.
Map 12 D4.
Tel 01 53 63 20 30.
www.miumiu.com

Morgan
165 Rue de Rennes 75006.
Map 16 D1.
Tel 01 45 48 96 77.
One of several branches.

Nina Jacob
23 Rue des Francs-
Bourgeois 75004.
Map 14 D3.
Tel 01 42 77 41 20.

Nina Ricci
39 Ave Montaigne 75008.
Map 10 F1.
Tel 01 40 88 67 60.
www.ninaricci.fr

Onward Kashiyama France
147 Blvd St-Germain
75006. **Map** 12 E4.
Tel 01 55 42 77 55.

Paco Rabanne
Lobato, 6 Rue Malher
75004. **Map** 13 C3.
Tel 01 48 87 68 14.

Pierre Cardin
27 Ave de Marigny 75008.
Map 5 B5.
Tel 01 42 66 68 98.
www.pierrecardin.com
One of two branches.

Pleats Please
3 bis Rue des Rosiers
75004.
Map 13C3.
Tel 01 40 29 99 66.
One of two branches.

Prada
18 Ave Matignon 75008.
Map 3C5.
Tel 01 56 21 30 70.

Promod
60 Rue Caumartin 75009.
Map 6 D4.
Tel 01 45 26 01 11.
One of several branches.

Ragtime
23 Rue de l'Echaudé
75006. **Map** 12 E4.
Tel 01 56 24 00 36.

Sinéquanone
16 Rue du Four 75006.
Map 12 E4.
Tel 01 56 24 27 74.
One of several branches.

Versace
41 Rue François Premier
75008.
Map 10 F1.
Tel 01 47 42 88 02.
www.versace.com

more established names. Designer **Jean-Paul Gaultier** has a boutique in the Rue du Faubourg St-Antoine. His "senior" and "junior" collections reflect price and attitude. **Isabel Marant's** boutique is renowned for its originality, and **Gaëlle Barré** is a stylist with a fast-growing reputation. The swimsuit store is **Eres**, while for leather, it's **Mac Douglas**.

Young designers' clothes are found at **Colette**, **Stella Cadente** and **Jay Ahr** (where you will find great evening dresses), while **Zucca** now has several boutiques. For fabulous, if somewhat pricey, clothes from the 1920s to the 1950s, try **Ragtime**.

Not all Parisians have pocketbooks that allow them to shop on the Avenue Montaigne, but those on smaller budgets still manage to look chic in clothes from high street stores. There are many large chain stores here which have branches in other European cities. Chain stores tend to stock each store differently, depending on the desires and buying patterns of the local clientele. Because of this it is possible to find quintessentially French fashion in large chains such as **Zara**, particularly at the branches in Passy and near the Opera.

Mighty Swedish retailer **Hennes** has an exciting concept store for young fashion in Paris's 15th arrondissement and stocks designs by Karl Lagerfeld in some of its larger shops. French high street stores are also numerous. Well-known names such as **Kookaï** and **Morgan** stock fresh and funky items. **Sinéquanone** and **LA City**, on the other hand, are rather classic in their designs, while **Promod** is a very cheap store for fun merchandise.

CHILDREN'S CLOTHES

Lots of options for children exist in various styles and many price ranges. Many top designers of adult clothes also have boutiques for children. These include **Kenzo**, **Baby Dior**, **Agnès B**, **Sonia Rykiel** and **Teddy's**. Ready-to-wear shops such as **Jacadi** and **Du Pareil au Même** are serviceable and wide-ranging; and **Tartine et Chocolat's** best-selling garments are overalls. **Bonpoint** stocks adorably chic clothing for mini-Parisians. **Petit Bateau** is coveted as much by grown-ups as it is by children. The inevitable has finally happened – children now have their own concept store in **Bonton**.

For little feet, **Froment-Leroyer** probably offers the best all-round classics. **Six Pieds Trois Pouces** has a vast choice of styles.

MEN'S CLOTHES

Men don't have the luxury of *haute couture* dressing and their choice is limited to ready-to-wear. Still, some men's clothes, mostly by womens-wear designers, can be very expensive.

On the Right Bank, there's **Giorgio Armani**, **Pierre Cardin**, **Kenzo**, **Lanvin** (also good for accessories) and **Yves Saint Laurent**. On the Left Bank, **Michel Axael** and **Jean-Charles de Castelbajac** are known for their ties and **Francesco Smalto's** elegant creations are worn by some of the world's leading movie stars. **Yohji Yamamoto's** clothes are for those who are intent on making a serious fashion statement, while **Gianni Versace** is classic, suave and Italian in style. **APC**, **Paul Smith** and **Ron Orb** garments are rather more contemporary, and **Olivier Strelli**, **Polo by Ralph Lauren** and **Loft Design By** are chic without being overtly trendy, and thus are likely to have a longer shelf-life.

The ultimate in Parisian elegance for men is a suit, custom-made shirt or silk tie from **Charvet**. A trip to the **Place Vendôme** store is a pleasure in itself. Be sure to ask the charming and friendly staff for a tour around their atelier for an insight into how such exquisite creations are crafted. **Madelios** is a great shopping mall for men which mixes designer and high-street brands.

LIFESTYLE STORES

Since **Colette** first burst on to the Parisian shopping scene six years ago, the fad for lifestyle shops has shown no sign of slowing down. Concept stores tend to be high-end affairs crammed with designer labels, some obscure, some household names, all grouped together to kit you out with everything you could possibly need. From fashionable books to shoes, beauty products, household goods, music and furniture via designer mineral water, handbags, trainers and evening gowns, the one-stop shopping experience provides the ultimate in retail therapy.

Spree in Montmartre mixes fashion, art and design so that you can buy a great outfit and some interesting art at the same time, whilst **Surface to Air** is a creative studio cum boutique bringing together cutting edge fashion and art.

VINTAGE AND SECOND-HAND STORES

The vintage craze hit Paris some time back and there are some wonderful shops to plunder for a retro look. The best of the bunch is **Didier Ludot**, where an Aladdin's Cave of chic *haute couture* is elegantly displayed. From vintage Courrèges dresses to excellent condition Chanel suits, this is the place for top of the range retro. The **Depôt-Vente de Buci-Bourbon** is another good place to bargain hunt. A cheaper option and a way to access more recent looks is to head for one of the many second-hand or consignment stores in the city. Chic Parisians discard their outfits with the seasons so it is very easy to pick up some quality items which are normally in top condition from places such as **Réciproque** in Passy or **Alternatives** in the Marais. Sample pieces, sale stock and last season's collection pieces can be found at **Le Mouton à Cinq Pattes**.

DIRECTORY

Sonia Rykiel
175 Blvd St-Germain
75006. **Map** 12 D4.
Tel 01 49 54 60 60.
www.soniarykiel.com
One of several branches.

Stella Cadente
4 Quai des Célestins
75004. **Map** 13 C4.
Tel 01 44 78 05 95.
www.stella-cadente.com
One of two branches.

Vanessa Bruno
25 Rue St-Sulpice 75006.
Map 12 E5.
Tel 01 43 54 41 04.
www.vanessabruno.com

Ventilo
27 bis Rue du Louvre
75002. **Map** 12 F2. *Tel 01
44 76 83 00.* **www**.ventilo
.fr *One of six branches.*

Victoire
2 Rue du Mail 75002.
Map 12 F1.
Tel 01 42 96 46 76.
www.victoire-paris.com
One of several branches.

Yohji Yamamoto
25 Rue du Louvre 75001.
Map 12 F1.
Tel 01 42 21 42 93.

Yves Saint Laurent
38 Rue du Faubourg-St-
Honoré 75008.
Map 5 C5.
Tel 01 42 65 74 59.
www.ysl.com
One of several branches.

Zadig et Voltaire
3 Rue Vieux Colombier
75007. **Map** 12 D4.
Tel 01 45 48 39 37.

Zara
53 Rue Passy 75016.
Map 9 B3. *Tel 01 45 25
07 00.* **www**.zara.fr
One of several branches.

Zucca
8 Rue St-Roch 75001.
Map 12 E1.
Tel 01 44 58 98 88.

CHILDREN'S CLOTHES

Agnès B
(See p325).

Baby Dior
(See p325 Christian Dior).

Bonpoint
320 Rue St-Honoré 75001.
Map 13 A2.
Tel 01 49 27 94 82.
www.bonpoint.com
One of several branches.

Bonton
82 rue de Grenelle 75007.
Map 10 F3. *Tel 01 44 39
09 20.* **www**.bonton.fr

Du Pareil au Même
1 Rue St-Denis 75001.
Map 13 A3. *Tel 01 42 36
07 57.* **www**.dpam.fr

Froment-Leroyer
7 Rue Vavin 75006. **Map**
16 E1. *Tel 01 43 54 33 15.*
www.froment-leroyer.fr
One of several branches.

Jacadi
17 Rue Tronchet 75008.
Map 5 C5. *Tel 01 42 65
84 98.* **www**.jacadi.fr

Kenzo
(See p325).

Petit Bateau
116 Ave des Champs
Elysées 75008. **Map** 4 E4.
Tel 01 40 74 02 03.
www.petit-bateau.com

Six Pieds Trois Pouces
78 Ave de Wagram
75017. **Map** 4 E2.
Tel 01 46 22 81 64.
One of several branches.

Tartine et Chocolat
105 Rue du Faubourg-St-
Honoré 75008. **Map** 5 B5.
Tel 01 45 62 44 04.

Teddy's
38 Rue François-1er
75008. **Map** 10 F1.
Tel 01 47 20 79 79.

MEN'S CLOTHES

APC
45 Rue Madame 75006.
Map 12 E5. *Tel 01 42 22
12 77.* **www**.apc.fr

Celio
26 Rue du Faubourg St-
Antoine 75012. **Map** 14
E4. *Tel 01 43 42 31 68.*

Charvet
28 Place Vendôme 75001.
Map 6 D5.
Tel 01 42 60 30 70.

Francesco Smalto
44 Rue François-1er
75008. **Map** 4 F5.
Tel 01 47 20 96 04.
www.smalto.com

Gianni Versace
41 Rue François
Premier 75008.
Map 10 F1.
Tel 01 47 42 88 02.
www.versace.com

Giorgio Armani
(See p325).

Jean-Charles de Castelbajac
10 Rue de Vauvilliers
75001.
Tel 01 55 34 10 10.
www.jedecastelbajac.com

Kenzo
(See p325).

Lanvin
15 Rue du Faubourg
St-Honoré 75008.
Map 14 F4.
Tel 01 44 71 31 33.
www.lanvin.com
One of several branches.

Loft Design By
175 Blvd Pereire 75017.
Map 3 C3.
Tel 01 46 22 44 20.
One of several branches.

Michel Axael
121 Blvd St-Germain
75006.
Map 12 E4.
Tel 01 43 26 01 96.

Olivier Strelli
7 Blvd Raspail 75007.
Map 12 D4.
Tel 01 45 44 62 21.
www.strelli.be
One of two branches.

Paul Smith
22 Blvd Raspail 75007.
Map 12 D4.
Tel 01 42 84 15 30.

Pierre Cardin
(See p325).

Ron Orb
147 Rue du Temple 75003.
Map 13 B2.
Tel 01 40 28 09 33.

Yohji Yamamoto
47 Rue Etienne
Marcel 75001.
Tel 01 45 08 82 45.

Yves Saint Laurent
12 Pl St-Sulpice 75006.
Map 12 D4.
Tel 01 43 26 84 40.

LIFESTYLE STORES

Colette
(See p325).

Spree
16 Rue de La Vieuville
75018. **Map** 6 F1.
Tel 01 42 23 41 40.

Surface to Air
46 Rue de l'Arbre Sec
75001. **Map** 12 F2.
Tel 01 43 57 97 62.

VINTAGE AND SECOND-HAND STORES

Alternatives
18 Rue du Roi-de-Sicile
75004. **Map** 13 C3.
Tel 01 42 78 31 50.

Depôt-Vente de Buci-Bourbon
6 Rue de Bourbon-le-
Château 75006.
Map 12 E4.
Tel 01 46 34 45 05.

Didier Ludot
19-24 Galerie
Montpensier 75001.
Map 12 E1.
Tel 01 42 96 06 56.

Le Mouton à Cinq Pattes
8 Rue St-Placide
75006.
Map 11 C5.
Tel 01 43 29 73 56.
One of several branches.

Réciproque
95 Rue de la Pompe
75016.
Map 9 A1.
Tel 01 47 04 30 28.

JEWELLERY

Agatha
97 Rue de Rennes 75006.
Map 12 D5.
Tel 01 45 48 81 30.
www.agatha.fr
One of several branches.

JEWELLERY

The *couture* houses probably stock some of the best jewellery and scarves. **Chanel's** jewels are classics and **Christian Lacroix's** are fun. **Boutique YSL** is a great place for accessories.

Among the main expensive Paris jewellery outlets are **Boucheron**, **Mauboussin** and **Poiray**. They are for the serious jewellery buyer. Other top retailers include **Harry Winston** and **Cartier**. **Dinh Van** has some quirky pieces, whilst **Mikimoto** is a must for pearls and **H Stern** has some innovative designs using semi-precious and precious stones. For a range of more unusual jewellery and accessories, try the **Daniel Swarovski Boutique**, which is owned by the Swarovksi crystal family.

Trends and imitations can be found around the Marais, the Bastille and Les Halles, in that order for quality. Those of note include **Scooter**, where chic young Parisians shop, **Métal Pointu's**, which sells great fantasy jewellery, and **Agatha** for copies of Chanel designs and basics.

Imitations in precious metals are available at **Verlor**, a cheap jeweller where one can find copies of pieces by top jewellers using genuine stones. Another reasonably priced Parisian jeweller is **Chaput**, where decent jewellery, especially the pieces made with semi-precious stones, can be found at good prices.

SHOES, BAGS AND BELTS

Fair trade trainers (organic cotton and natural Amazonian rubber) by Veja can be found in **Le Bon Marché**. Go to **Charles Jourdan** for a big selection of shoe colours or to **Sidonie Larizzi** who will make up shoes from one of numerous leather swatches. Current favourites with the fashion set include **Michel Perry**, **Bruno Frisoni** and **Robert Clergerie**. **Christian Louboutin** and **Rodolphe Ménudier** are mainstays for sexy stilettos. **Carel** stocks

smart basics, **Cosmo Paris** sell trendy models and **Jonak** is a must for good imitations of designer footwear. **Bowen** has a selection of traditional men's shoes and **Fenestrier** creates chic versions of classics. **J M Weston** or **Berluti** are the last words in elegance for many Parisian men.

Christian Lacroix makes wonderful handbags and belts. Beautifully made leather goods can also be found at **Longchamp**, **Gucci** and **Hermès**. For ladies handbags, nothing beats **Chanel** or **Dior** at the top end of the scale, although **Goyard** comes close. Mid-range bags from **Furla** are a great compromise, as are the colourful bags from **Karine Dupont**. Fabric bags from **Jamin Puech**, **Vanessa Bruno** or **Hervé Chapelier** are a feature in every chic Parisian closet. For a great range of shoes, boots and bags at reasonable prices, try **Jet-Set**. Cheap, cheerful and very stylish bags can be found at **Lollipops**.

HATS

One of Paris's favourite milliners is **Marie Mercié**. **Anthony Peto** now creates men's hats at her old shop in Rue Tiquetonne. For quirky creations in wool try **Grevi** who sell matching scarves and gloves.

LINGERIE

For a delightful selection of modern lingerie go to **Fifi Chachnil**, whose shop is filled with colourful underwear. **La Boîte à Bas** sells fine French stockings, whereas **Princesse Tam Tam** offers quality items at reasonable prices, whilst divine designer underwear can be found at cult store **Sabbia Rosa**. The ultimate in magnificent Parisian lingerie can be bought off the peg or made to order at **Cadolle**, the store which invented the bra. For a more raunchy number, go to **Yoba**.

SIZE CHART

For Australian sizes follow the British and American conversions.

Children's clothing

French	2–3	4–5	6–7	8–9	10–11	12	14	14+ (years)
British	2–3	4–5	6–7	8–9	10–11	12	14	14+ (years)
American	2–3	4–5	6–6x	7–8	10		12	14 16 (size)

Children's shoes

French	24	25½	27	28	29	30	32	33	34
British	7	8	9	10	11	12	13	1	2
American	7½	8½	9½	10½	11½	12½	13½	1½	2½

Women's dresses coats and skirts

French	34	36	38	40	42	44	46
British	6	8	10	12	14	16	18
American	2	4	6	8	10	12	14

Women's blouses and sweaters

French	81	84	87	90	93	96	99 (cms)
British	31	32	34	36	38	40	42 (inches)
American	6	8	10	12	14	16	18 (size)

Women's shoes

French	36	37	38	39	40	41
British	3	4	5	6	7	8
American	5	6	7	8	9	10

Men's suits

French	44	46	48	50	52	54	56	58
British	34	36	38	40	42	44	46	48
American	34	36	38	40	42	44	46	48

Men's shirts

French	36	38	39	41	42	43	44	45
British	14	15	15½	16	16½	17	17½	18
American	14	15	15½	16	16½	17	17½	18

Men's shoes

French	39	40	41	42	43	44	45	46
British	6	7	7½	8	9	10	11	12
American	7	7½	8	8½	9½	10½	11	11½

DIRECTORY

Boucheron
26 Pl Vendôme 75001.
Map 6 D5.
Tel 01 42 61 58 16.
www.boucheron.com

Boutique YSL
38 Rue du Faubourg-St-
Honoré 75008.
Map 5 C5.
Tel 01 42 65 74 59.

Cartier
13 Rue de la Paix 75002.
Map 6 D5. *Tel 01 42 18
43 83.* www.cartier.fr
One of several branches.

Chanel
(See p325).

Chaput
6 Rue Donizetti 75116.
Tel 01 40 50 11 50.

Christian Lacroix
(See p325).

**Daniel Swarovski
Boutique**
7 Rue Royale 75008.
Map 5 C5. *Tel 01 40 17
07 40.* www.daniel-
swarovski.com

Dinh Van
15 Rue de la Paix 75002.
Map 6 D5. *Tel 01 42 86
02 66.* www.dinhvan.com
One of several branches.

H Stern
3 Rue Castiglione 75001.
Map 12 D1. *Tel 01 42 60
22 27.* www.hstern.net
One of several branches.

Harry Winston
29 Ave Montaigne 75008.
Map 10 F1.
Tel 01 47 20 03 09.
www.harrywinston.com

Mauboussin
20 Pl Vendôme 75001.
Map 6 D5.
Tel 01 44 55 10 00.
www.mauboussin.com

Métal Pointu's
2 Rue du Marché St-
Honoré 75001. **Map** 12
D1. *Tel 01 42 60 01 42.*
www.metalpointus.com

Mikimoto
8 Pl Vendôme 75001.
Map 6 D5.
Tel 01 42 60 33 55.
www.mikimoto.fr

Poiray
1 Rue de la Paix 75002.
Map 6 D5. *Tel 01 42 61
70 58.* www.poiray.com

Scooter
10 Rue de Turbigo 75001.
Map 13 A1.
Tel 01 45 08 89 31.
One of several branches.

Verlor
19 Rue de la Paix 75002.
Map 6 D5.
Tel 01 40 07 08 86.

SHOES, BAGS AND BELTS

Bowen
97 Rue St-Lazare 75009.
Map 6 D3.
Tel 01 53 32 32 40.

Berluti
26 Rue Marbeuf 75008.
Map 4 F5. *Tel 01 53 93
97 97.* www.berluti.com

Bruno Frisoni
34 Rue de Grenelle 75007.
Map 12 D4.
Tel 01 42 84 12 30.

Carel
4 Rue Tronchet 75008.
Map 6 D4.
Tel 01 43 12 37 00.
One of several branches.

Charles Jourdan
22 Rue François-1er 75008.
Tel 01 47 20 81 28.
www.charles-jourdan.com
One of several branches.

Christian Louboutin
38-40 Rue de Grenelle
75007.
Map 10 F3.
Tel 01 42 22 33 07.

Cosmo Paris
25 Rue du Four 75006.
Map 12 E4.
Tel 01 56 24 15 49.

Eden Shoes
8 Rue de Marignan
75008. **Map** 4 F5.
Tel 01 42 25 76 26.

Fenestrier
23 Rue du Cherche-Midi
75006.
Map 12 D5.
Tel 01 42 22 66 02.
www.jfenestrier.com

Furla
8 Rue de Sèvres 75006.
Map 11 C5.
Tel 01 40 49 06 44.
www.furla.com
One of several branches.

Goyard
233 Rue St-Honoré
75001. **Map** 5 C5.
Tel 01 42 60 57 04.
www.goyard.com

Gucci
23 Rue Royale 75001.
Map 5 C5.
Tel 01 44 94 14 70.
www.gucci.com

Hermès
(See p325).

Hervé Chapelier
1 Rue du Vieux-Colombier
75006.
Map 12 D4.
Tel 01 44 07 06 50.

Jamin Puech
61 Rue de Hauteville
75010.
Map 7 B4.
Tel 01 40 22 08 32.

Jet-Set
85 Rue de Passy 75016.
Map 9 B3.
Tel 01 42 88 21 59.
One of two branches.

Jonak
70 Rue de Rennes 75006.
Map 16 D1.
Tel 01 45 48 27 11.

Karine Dupont
16 Rue du Cherche-Midi
75006.
Map 12 D4.
Tel 01 42 84 06 30.

Le Bon Marché
24 Rue de Sevres 75007.
Map 11 C5.
Tel 01 44 39 80 00.

Lollipops
60 Rue Tiquetonne 75002.
Map 13 A1.
Tel 01 42 33 15 72.
www.lollipops.fr

Longchamp
404 Rue St-Honoré 75001.
Map 5 C5.
Tel 01 43 16 00 18.
www.longchamp.com

Michel Perry
42 Rue de Grenelle 75007.
Map 10 F3.
Tel 01 42 84 12 45.

Robert Clergerie
5 Rue du Cherche-Midi
75006. **Map** 12 D1.
Tel 01 42 84 03 14.

Rodolphe Ménudier
14 Rue de Castiglione
75001. **Map** 12 D1.
Tel 01 42 60 86 27.

Vanessa Bruno
(See p327).

HATS

Anthony Peto
56 Rue Tiquetonne 75002.
Map 13 A1.
Tel 01 40 26 60 68.

Grevi
1 Place Alphonse-Deville
75006. **Map** 14 D3.
Tel 01 42 22 02 49.
www.grevi.com

Marie Mercié
23 Rue St-Sulpice 75006.
Map 12 E4.
Tel 01 43 26 45 83.

LINGERIE

La Boîte à Bas
27 Rue Boissy-d'Anglas
75008. **Map** 5 C5.
Tel 01 42 66 26 85.

Cadolle
4 Rue Cambon 75001.
Map 6 D5.
Tel 01 42 60 94 22.

Fifi Chachnil
26 Rue Cambon 75001.
Map 6 D5.
Tel 01 42 60 38 86.
One of several branches.

Princesse Tam Tam
52 Blvd St-Michel 75006.
Map 12 F5.
Tel 01 42 34 99 31.
One of several branches.

Sabbia Rosa
73 Rue des Sts-Pères
75006.
Map 12 D4.
Tel 01 45 48 88 37.

Yoba
11 Rue du Marché St-
Honoré 75001.
Map 12 D1.
Tel 01 40 41 04 06.

Gifts and Souvenirs

Paris has a wealth of stylish gifts and typical souvenirs, from designer accessories and perfume to French delicacies and Eiffel Tower paperweights. Shops on the Rue de Rivoli and around major tourist attractions such as Nôtre Dame or Sacré Coeur offer a range of cheap holiday paraphernalia, or go to some of the souvenir shops such as **Les Drapeaux de France**. Mementos can often be found in museum shops, including reproductions and creations by young designers. Try **Le Musée du Louvre, Musée d'Orsay** or **Musée Carnavalet**.

GIFTS

Au Printemps has excellent own-brand accessories, especially ladies handbags. The luxury floor is ideal for window-shopping or high-end purchases such as Tiffany jewellery or Cartier watches. It also stocks small, reasonably-priced items.

For those looking to take home gastronomic tasters, the famed food hall at **Le Bon Marché**, La Grande Epicerie, offers anything and everything you might need for a gourmet feast or quick snack. **Galeries Lafayette** now boasts the world's biggest lingerie department.

PERFUME AND COSMETICS

Many shops advertise discounted perfume and cosmetics. Some even offer duty-free perfume to shoppers outside the EU, with discounts on the marked prices when you show your passport. They include **Eiffel Shopping** near the Eiffel Tower. The **Sephora** chain has a big selection, or try the department stores for a range of designers' perfumes. In particular, the beauty department at **Au Printemps** is one of Europe's biggest with one of the world's largest perfume selections. It stocks many beauty brands which are hard to find elsewhere.

If you fancy stepping back in time, **Detaille 1905** is the place for you. In this old-fashioned perfumery filled to the brim with fragrant goodies, everything rings true to the early 20th century.

They created their own range of six main fragrances for women and for men, all made from original recipes.

Parfums Caron also has many scents created over 100 years ago, which are unavailable elsewhere, so this is the place to find exclusive presents that you will almost certainly decide to keep for yourself. Beautifully packaged perfumes made from natural essences are available from **Annick Goutal**. **Guerlain** has the ultimate in beauty care, while the elegant shops of **L'Artisan Parfumeur** specialize in exquisitely packaged scents that evoke specific memories. They have also reissued favourites from the past, including perfume made to exactly the same formula as one that was worn at the court of Versailles. **Frédéric Malle** is another big name in top-of-the-range scent. Exclusive perfumes can also be found in the beautiful surroundings of the **Salons du Palais Royal**, an upscale Shiseido store. Serge Lutens, the company's creative director and a renowned parfumier creates exquisite and exotic scents which can only be bought in this store.

Paris is also home to several *haute* cosmetics designers. One of the most renowned is Terry de Gunzberg, whose store **By Terry** stocks fantastic products. Personalize your gift by having a message inscribed on the sleek, silver packaging. Further bespoke beauty products can be found at the **Galerie Noemi**, where lipstick can be mixed up just for you.

HOUSEHOLD GOODS

Though certain items are obviously rather delicate to carry home, it is difficult to ignore some of the world's most elegant tableware, found in Paris's chic shops. If you are wary of loading up your hold-all with breakable pieces, many shops will arrange to ship crockery overseas. Luxury household goods can be found on the Rue Royale, where many of the best shops are located. They sell items such as rustic china and reproduction and modern silverware. **Lalique's** Art Nouveau and Art Deco glass sculptures are collected all over the world. Impeccable silverware including fine photograph frames and even chopsticks comes from **Christofle**.

For significant savings on porcelain and crystal, try **Lumicristal**, which stocks Baccarat, Daum and Limoges crystal, or go to **Baccarat** itself. Baccarat also has a boutique on the Place de la Madeleine. The interior designer **Pierre Frey** has a showroom displaying fabrics which have been made into a fabulous array of cushions, bedspreads and tablecloths. Excellent quality bed linen can also be found at **Yves Delorme**.

La Chaise Longue has a selection of well-designed *objets*, along with fun gift ideas. **Plus Bo** is contemporary, while **Résonances** provide an eclectic array of household cooking items and books. **DOM** and **Why** stock an excellent range of cheap, kitsch home accessories for funky flats. A newly opened interior design store at **Galeries Lafayette** has everything from fancy mops to cutting-edge, three-piece suites. The **Sentou Gallery** is a clutch of stores full of chic pieces for Parisian living. One shop carries interesting tableware, whilst another focuses on practical purchases, with the final store dedicated to high-end furniture.

Kitchen equipment which can't be beaten comes from **E. Dehillerin**. A must-have item in many Parisian homes is a scented candle from **Diptyque**. Figuier is their most popular fragrance. The basement at **BHV** *(see p321)* is full of all sorts of tools and equipment for doing up your house and garden.

BOOKS, MAGAZINES AND NEWSPAPERS

Many English and American publications can be found at large magazine stands or at some of the bookshops listed. If French is no obstacle the weeklies *Pariscope*, *L'Officiel des Spectacles* and *Zurban* have the most comprehensive listings of what's going on around town.

The *International Herald Tribune*, an English-language daily newspaper, is published in Paris and contains good American news coverage. Two periodicals, *Paris Free Voice* and the bi-weekly *France–US Contacts*, are also published in English.

Some of the large department stores have a book section *(see Department Stores p321)*. There is a large branch of **W H Smith** and a useful **Galignani**, or try **Brentano's**. A small, somewhat disorganized, but cosy and convivial bookshop is **Shakespeare & Co**. The American-influenced **Village Voice** has a good literary and intellectual selection of new

books, while **The Abbey Bookshop** does the same for second-hand books. **Tea and Tattered Pages** is a British second-hand bookshop.

French-language bookshops include **La Hune**, specializing in art, design, architecture, photography, fashion and cinema; **Gibert Joseph**, selling general and educational books; and **Le Divan** which has social science, psychology, literature and poetry sections. The **Red Wheelbarrow Bookstore** sells a wide range of French–English bilingual books set in France as well as a great selection of classics translated from French.

FLOWERS

Some Parisian florists such as **Christian Tortu** are very well known, so be sure to buy one of Tortu's signature vases. **Art Nature Harmonie** and **Monceau Fleurs** offer a good selection at reasonable prices; **Mille Feuilles** is the place to go to in the Marais. *(See also Specialist Shops p332.)* Stunning silk flowers can be found at **Hervé Gambs**, whose chic store is brimming over with beautiful artifical blooms.

SPECIALIST SHOPS

For cigars, **A La Civette** is perhaps Paris's most beautiful tobacconist. It is also probably the most devoted to its wares and has humidified

shop windows to keep its merchandise in top condition. Go to **A L'Olivier** in the Rue de Rivoli for a wonderful selection of exotic oils and vinegar. Or, if honey is your favourite condiment, try **La Maison du Miel** where you can buy all sorts of fine honeys, including those made from the flowers of lavender and acacia. You can also buy refreshing beeswax soap and candles here. **Mariage Frères** has become a cult favourite for its 350 varieties of tea; it also sells teapots.

Couture fabrics can be purchased from a range at **Wolff et Descourtis**. For an unusual gift of traditional French card games or tarot cards, go to **Jeux Descartes**.

One of the world's most famous and delightful toyshops is **Au Nain Bleu**, while the name **Cassegrain** is synonymous with high-quality stationery and paper products. **Calligrane** sells a tempting range of high-quality desk accessories and paper products.

Hidden away down an atmospheric passage, **Pep's** repairs all broken umbrellas and parasols in France's only brolly hospital.

However, the ultimate in eccentric shopping can undoubtedly be found at **Deyrolle**, which is Paris's most famous taxidermist, and where you can find just the right gift for the person who truly has everything – well almost.

DIRECTORY

SOUVENIR AND MUSEUM SHOPS

Les Drapeaux de France
1 Place Colette 75001.
Map 12 E2.
Tel 01 40 20 00 11.

Le Musée
Niveau 2, Forum des Halles, Porte Berger 75001.
Map 13 A2.
Tel 01 40 39 97 91.

Musée Carnavalet
(See p97).

Le Musée du Louvre
(See p123).

Musée d'Orsay
(See p145).

GIFTS

Au Printemps
64 Blvd Haussman 75009.
Map 6 D4.
Tel 01 42 82 50 00.

Le Bon Marché
24 Rue de Sèvres 75007.
Map 11 C5.
Tel 01 44 39 80 00.

Galeries Lafayette
40 Blvd Haussmann 75009.
Map 6 E4.
Tel 01 42 82 34 56.
One of two branches.

PERFUME AND COSMETICS

Annick Goutal
16 Rue de Bellechasse 75007.
Map 11 C3.
Tel 01 45 51 36 13.
One of several branches.

L'Artisan Parfumeur
24 Blvd Raspail 75007.
Map 16 D1.
Tel 01 42 22 23 32.
One of several branches.

By Terry
36 Passage Vérot-Dodat 75001.
Map 12 F2.
Tel 01 44 76 00 76.

Detaille 1905
10 Rue St-Lazare 75009.
Map 6 D3.
Tel 01 48 78 68 50.

DIRECTORY

Tel 01 48 78 68 50.

Eiffel Shopping
9 Ave de Suffren 75007.
Map 10 D3.
Tel 01 45 66 55 30.

Frédéric Malle
21 Rue du Mont Thabor
75001. **Map** 12 D1.
Tel 01 42 22 74 10.

Galerie Noemi
92 Ave des Champs
Elysées 75008.
Map 4 F5.
Tel 01 45 62 78 27.

Guerlain
68 Ave des Champs-
Elysées 75008. **Map** 4 F5.
Tel 01 45 62 52 57.
One of several branches.
www.guerlain.com

Parfums Caron
34 Ave Montaigne 75008.
Map 10 F1.
Tel 01 47 23 40 82.

Sephora
70 Ave des Champs-
Elysées 75008.
Map 11 B1. **Tel** 01 53 93
22 50. **www**.sephora.fr
One of several branches.

**Salons du Palais
Royal**
25 Rue de Valois 75001.
Map 12 F1.
Tel 01 49 27 09 09.

HOUSEHOLD
GOODS

Baccarat
11 Pl de la Madeleine
75008. **Map** 5 C5.
Tel 01 42 65 36 26.
www.baccarat.com
(See also p201)

La Chaise Longue
30 Rue Croix-des-Petits-
Champs 75001. **Map** 12
F1. **Tel** 01 42 96 32 14.
One of several branches.

Christofle
24 Rue de la Paix 75002.
Map 6 D5.
Tel 01 42 65 62 43.
www.christofle.com
One of several branches.

Diptyque
34 Bld St Germain 75006.
Map 13 B5.
Tel 01 43 26 45 27.

www.diptyqueparis.com

DOM
21 Rue Ste-Croix de la
Bretonnerie 75004. **Map**
13 B3. **Tel** 01 42 71 08 00.

E. Dehillerin
18 Rue Coquillière 75001.
Map 12 F1.
Tel 01 42 36 53 13.
www.e-dehillerin.com

Lalique
11 Rue Royale 75008.
Map 5 C5. **Tel** 01 53 05 12
12. **www**.cristallalique.fr

Lumicristal
29 Rue de Paradis 75010.
Map 7 B4.
Tel 01 45 23 23 73.

Pierre Frey
47 Rue des Petits Champs
75001. **Map** 5 C5.
Tel 01 44 77 36 00.
www.pierrefrey.com

Plus Bô
8 Rue St-Merri 75004.
Map 13 B3.
Tel 01 42 74 55 10.

Point à la Ligne
67 Ave Victor Hugo
75116. **Map** 3 B5.
Tel 01 45 00 87 01.

Résonances
Carrousel du Louvre,
99 Rue de Rivoli 75001.
Map 11 C1.
Tel 01 42 97 06 00.

Sentou Gallery
18 & 24 Rue Pont
Louis-Philippe 75004.
Map 13 C3.
Tel 01 42 71 00 01.

Why
93 Rue Rambuteau 75001.
Map 13 A2.
Tel 01 40 26 39 56.

Yves Delorme
8 Rue Vavin 75006.
Map 16 D1.
Tel 01 44 07 23 14.

BOOKS, MAGAZINES
AND NEWSPAPERS

Abbey Bookshop
29 Rue de la Parcheminerie
75005. **Map** 13 A4.
Tel 01 46 33 16 24.

Brentano's
37 Ave de l'Opéra 75002.
Map 6 E5. **Tel** 01 42 61

52 50. **www**.brentanos.fr

Le Divan
203 Rue de la Convention
75015. **Map** 12 E3.
Tel 01 53 68 90 68.

Galignani
224 Rue de Rivoli 75001.
Map 13 A2.
Tel 01 42 60 76 07.

Gibert Joseph
26 Blvd St-Michel 75006.
Map 12 F5.
Tel 01 44 41 88 88.

La Hune
170 Blvd St-Germain
75006. **Map** 12 D4.
Tel 01 45 48 35 85.

**The Red
Wheelbarrow
Bookstore**
22 Rue St-Paul 75004.
Map 14 D4. **Tel** 01 48 04
75 08. **www**.
theredwheelbarrow.com

Shakespeare & Co
37 Rue de la Bûcherie
75005. **Map** 13 A4.
Tel 01 43 25 40 93.

**Tea and Tattered
Pages**
24 Rue Mayet 75006.
Map 15 B1.
Tel 01 40 65 94 35.

Village Voice
6 Rue Princesse 75006.
Map 12 E4.
Tel 01 46 33 36 47.
www.villagevoicebookshop.
com

W H Smith
248 Rue de Rivoli 75001.
Map 11 C1.
Tel 01 44 77 88 99.

FLOWERS

**Art Nature
Harmonie**
1 Rue Abbé de l'Epée
75005.
Map 16 F1.
Tel 01 44 07 15 00.

Christian Tortu
6 Carrefour de l'Odéon
75006. **Map** 12 F4.
Tel 01 43 26 02 56.
www.christian-tortu.com

Hervé Gambs
9 bis Rue des Blancs
Manteaux 75004.
Map 13 C3.

Tel 01 44 59 88 88.

Monceau Fleurs
84 Blvd de Raspail 75006.
Map 12 D4.
Tel 01 45 48 70 10.
www.monceaufleurs.com
One of several branches.

SPECIALIST SHOPS

A La Civette
157 Rue St-Honoré 75001.
Map 12 F2.
Tel 01 42 96 04 99.

A L'Olivier
23 Rue de Rivoli 75004.
Map 13 C3. **Tel** 01 48 04
86 59. **www**.alolivier.com

Au Nain Bleu
5 Blvd Malesherbes 75008.
Map 5 B3. **Tel** 01 42 63
20 00. **www**.aunainbleu.
com *One of several branches.*

Calligrane
4 Rue du Pont-Louis-
Philippe 75004. **Map** 13
B4. **Tel** 01 48 04 31 89.

Cassegrain
422 Rue St-Honoré 75008.
Map 5 C5. **Tel** 01 42 60
20 08. **www**.cassegrain.fr

Deyrolle
46 Rue du Bac 75007.
Map 12 D3.
Tel 01 42 22 30 07.

Jeux Descartes
52 Rue des Écoles 75005.
Map 13 A5.
Tel 01 43 26 79 83.
One of three branches.

La Maison du Miel
24 Rue Vignon 75009.
Map 6 D5.
Tel 01 47 42 26 70.
www.maisondumiel.com

Mariage Frères
30 Rue du Bourg-Tibourg
75004. **Map** 13 C3.
Tel 01 42 72 28 11.
www.mariagefreres.com
One of several branches.
(See p286).

Pep's
Passage de l'Ancre (30 Rue
Turbigo) 75003. **Map** 13
B1. **Tel** 01 42 78 11 67.
www.peps-paris.com.fr

Wolff et Descourtis
18 Galerie Vivienne
75002. **Map** 12 F1.

Tel 01 42 61 80 84.

Food and Drink

Paris is as famous for food as it is for fashion. Gastronomic treats include *foie gras*, cold meats from the *charcuterie*, cheese and wine. Certain streets are so overflowing with food shops that you can put together a picnic for 20 in no time: try the Rue Montorgueil *(see p339)*. The Rue Rambuteau, running on either side of the Pompidou Centre, has a marvellous row of fishmongers, cheese delicatessens and shops selling prepared foods. *(See also* What to Eat and Drink in Paris *pp296–9* and Light Meals and Snacks *pp316–19.)*

BREAD AND CAKES

There is a vast range of breads and pastries in France's capital. The *baguette* is often translated as "French bread"; a *bâtard* is similar but thicker, while a *ficelle* is thinner. A *fougasse* is a crusty, flat loaf made from *baguette* dough, often filled with onions, cheese, herbs or spices. Since most French bread contains no fat it goes stale quickly: the sooner you eat it, the better. The French would never eat day-old bread so be sure to be up in time to make it to the bakery for breakfast!

Croissants can be bought *ordinaire* or *au beurre* – the latter is flakier and more buttery. *Pain au chocolat* is a chocolate-filled pastry eaten for breakfast and *chausson aux pommes* is filled with apples. There are also pear, plum and rhubarb variations. A *pain aux raisins* is a bread-like wheel filled with custard and raisins.

Poilâne sells perhaps the only bread in Paris known by the name of its baker (the late Lionel, brother of Max) and his hearty wholewheat loaves are tremendously popular, with freshly baked loaves being jetted around the world to satisfy the cravings of certain film stars. There are always big queues at the weekend and around 4pm when a fresh batch comes out of the oven.

Many think **Ganachaud** bakes the best bread in Paris. Thirty different kinds, including ingredients such as walnuts and fruit, are made in the old-fashioned ovens.

Although **Les Panetons** is part of a larger chain, it is one of the best of its kind with a broad range of breads. Favourites here include five-grain bread, sesame rolls and *mouchoir aux pommes*, a variation on the traditional *chausson*.

It is very important to remember that every Parisian has a favourite neighbourhood bakery, so when you are buying bread locally simply plump for the shop with the longest queues.

Many of the Jewish delicatessens have the best ryes and the only pumpernickels in town. One of the best known is **Sacha Finkelsztajn**.

Le Moulin de la Vierge uses a wood fire to bake organic breads and rich pound cakes. **Boulangerie de l'Ouest** is second only to **Max Poilâne** in the Montparnasse area with *baguettes*, *fougasses*, cakes and pastries. **J L Poujauran** is known for his black-olive bread and nut-and-raisin wholegrain breads. **Pierre Hermé** is to cakes what Chanel is to fashion, while **Ladurée** macaroons are legendary.

CHOCOLATE

Like all food in France, chocolate is to be savoured. **Christian Constant**'s low-sugar creations are made with pure cocoa and are known to connoisseurs. **Dalloyau** makes all types of chocolate and is not too expensive (it's also known for its pâtisserie and cold meats). **Fauchon** is world famous for its luxury food products. Its chocolates are excellent, as is the pâtisserie. **Lenôtre** makes classic truffles

and pralines. Robert Linxe at **La Maison du Chocolat** is constantly inventing fresh, rich chocolates with mouth-watering exotic ingredients. **Richart** boasts beautifully presented and hugely-expensive chocolates, which are usually coated with dark chocolate or liqueur-filled. **Debauve & Gallais** are best known for their wonderful and delicious glacé chestnut treats *(marron glacés)*.

CHARCUTERIE AND FOIE GRAS

Charcuteries often sell cheese, snails, truffles, smoked salmon, caviar and wine as well as cold meats. **Fauchon** has a good grocery, as does the department store **Le Bon Marché**. **Hédiard** is a luxury shop similar to Fauchon, and **Maison de la Truffe** sells *foie gras* and sausages as well as truffles. For Beluga caviar, Georgian tea and Russian vodka go to **Petrossian**.

The Lyon and Auvergne regions of France are the best known for their *charcuterie*. Examples can be bought from **Chrétienne Jean-Jacques**. **Aux Vrais Produits d'Auvergne** has a number of outlets where you can stock up on dried and fresh sausages and delicious Cantal cheese (rather like Cheddar). **Pou** is a sparklingly clean and popular shop selling *pâté en croute* (pâté baked in pastry), *boudins* (black and white puddings), Lyonnais sausages, ham and *foie gras*. Just off the Champs-Elysées, **Vignon** has superb *foie gras* and Lyonnais sausages as well as popular prepared foods.

Together with truffles and caviar, *foie gras* is the ultimate in gourmet food. The quality (and price) depends upon the percentage of liver used. Though most specialist food shops sell *foie gras*, you can be sure of quality at **Comtesse du Barry**, which has six outlets in Paris. **Divay** is relatively inexpensive and will ship overseas. **Labeyrie** has a range of beautifully-packaged *foie gras* suitable for giving as presents.

CHEESE

Although Camembert is undoubtedly a favourite, there is an overwhelming range of cheeses available.

A friendly *fromager* will help you choose. **Marie-Anne Cantin** is one of the leading figures in the fight to protect traditional production methods, and her fine cheeses are available from the shop that she inherited from her father. Some say that **Alléosse** is the best cheese delicatessen in Paris – the façade may be in need of renovation, but all the cheeses are made according to traditional methods. **Fromagerie Quatrehomme** sells farm-made cheeses, many of which are in danger of becoming extinct; these include a rare and delicious truffle Brie (when in season). **Boursault** is one of the best shops in Paris for all types of cheese – the *chèvre* (goat's cheese) is particularly good, and outside on the pavement the daily specials are offered at remarkably reasonable prices. **Barthelemy** in the Rue de Grenelle has a truly exceptional Roquefort. **Androuet** is a Parisian institution with several branches across the city. Try a pungent Munster or a really ripe Brie. A charming cheese shop on the bustling Rue Montorgeuil market street, **La Fermette**, offers a dazzling array of dairy products, which the helpful and friendly staff will happily encase in plastic for the journey home. This is imperative when bringing cheese through customs, so don't forget to ask your *fromager* to wrap it for you. Well-heeled locals queue in the street to buy oozing *livarot* and sharp *chèvre* from **La Fromagerie d'Auteuil**.

WINE

The chain store which has practically cornered the every-day tippling market is **Nicolas** – there's a branch in every neighbourhood with a range of wines to suit all pockets. As a rule, the sales-people are knowledgeable and helpful. Try the charming **Legrand Filles et Fils** *(see p319)* for a carefully chosen selection. **Caves Taillevent** on the Rue du Faubourg-St-Honoré is worth a sightseeing tour. It is an enormous, overwhelming cellar with some of the most expensive wine. **Cave Péret** on the Rue Daguerre has a vast selection of wines and can offer personal advice to help you with your purchase. The beautiful **Ryst-Dupeyron**, in the St-Germain quarter, displays whiskies, wines, ports, and Monsieur Ryst's own Armagnac. He will even personalize a bottle for that special occasion.

Other great wine stores include **Lavinia** *(see p319)*, which is the largest in Europe, and **Renaud Michel** at Nation, whose small boutique is well stocked and well connected. The staff in **Les Caves Augé** are also very knowledgeable and friendly.

CHAMPAGNE

Fabulous fizz can be found at most wine stores, but some know their bubbles better than others. The **Nicolas** chain, mentioned above, frequently has great offers on well-known brands so this is a good place to come and stock up on your favourite famous tipple. **La Cave des Martyrs** on the Rue des Martyrs is a friendly and well-stocked wine shop with charming staff to help you with your selection. The **Repaire du Bacchus** on the Rue d'Auteuil is a good place to go for hard-to-find vintages. The *sommelier* here is very knowledgeable and able to provide excellent alternative advice if your preferred brand is out of stock. **Legrand Filles et Fils**, on the Rue de la Banque, is one of the few shops in Paris to stock Salon, a rare high-end champagne. They also sell champagne by Jacques Selosse which is little-known but well-loved by champagne connoisseurs. **Les Caves du Panthéon** on the Rue Saint Jacques, is a small, but, lovely wine shop which has a particularly interesting selection of champagnes. Close by is **Ex Cellar France**, a corner wine-shop which is distinguished both by its charming and helpful staff and also by its frequent deals on champagne. The climate-controlled section of **Hédiard** at Place de la Madelaine is a good place to find rare, fine sparkling wines. **Caprices de l'Instant** is a fashionable wine store which stocks good quality champagne including bottles by some lesser-known producers. A stroll along the Boulevard St-Germain can be enhanced with a visit to **La Maison du Millésimes**, a wonderful store carrying excellent vintages of household-name champagnes.

OYSTERS

The ultimate aphrodisac for some, a slippery sea creature for others, there is no doubt that the once humble oyster can cause heated debate. In Paris, the argument tends to be over the best place to purchase these creatures, with every seafood fan worth his platter claiming a favourite spot and it is, of course, important to get it right. A deciding factor for some is the grace with which your fishmonger will agree to open them for you. In general, a polite request will be hon-oured, although sometimes you may have to wait a while before being presented with a platter perfect for a picnic. The fishmonger on the Rue Cler market street, **La Sablaise Poissonnerie**, has an excellent reputation as does the **Poissonnerie du Dôme** in the city's 14th arrondissement. Over in the traditionally rough-and-ready area around the Rue Oberkampf, you can find excellent oysters at the **Poissonnerie Lacroix**. If you prefer to eat your oysters on the spot then head to an *huitrerie* (oyster shop) such as the **Huîtrerie Garnier** on the Avenue Mozart in the chic 16th arrondissement, where you can tuck into your shellfish straight away at the few tables tucked into the corner of the store.

DIRECTORY

BREAD AND CAKES

**Boulangerie
de l'Ouest**
4 Pl Constantin Brancusi
75014. **Map** 15 C3.
Tel 01 43 21 76 18.

Ganachaud
226 Rue des Pyrénées
75020.
Tel 01 43 58 42 62.

J L Poujauran
20 Rue Jean-Nicot 75007.
Map 10 F2.
Tel 01 43 17 35 20.

Max Poilâne
29 Rue de l'Ouest 75014.
Map 15 B3.
Tel 01 43 27 24 91.

**Le Moulin de
la Vierge**
105 Rue Vercingétorix
75014. **Map** 15 A4.
Tel 01 45 43 09 84.
One of several branches.

Les Panetons
113 Rue Mouffetard
75005. **Map** 17 B2.
Tel 01 47 07 12 08.

Pierre Hermé
72 Rue Bonaparte 75006.
Map 12 E4.
Tel 01 43 54 47 77.

Poilâne
8 Rue du Cherche-Midi
75006. **Map** 12 D4.
Tel 01 45 48 42 59.

Sacha Finkelsztajn
27 Rue des Rosiers 75004.
Map 13 C3.
Tel 01 42 72 78 91.
www.laboutiquejaune.fr

CHOCOLATE

Christian Constant
37 Rue d'Assas 75006.
Map 16 E1.
Tel 01 53 63 15 15.

Dalloyau
101 Rue du Faubourg-
St-Honoré 75008. **Map** 5
B5.
Tel 01 42 99 90 00.

Debauve & Gallais
30 Rue des Saints-Pères
75007. **Map** 12 D4.
Tel 01 45 48 54 67.
One of two branches.

Fauchon
26 Pl de la Madeleine
75008. **Map** 5 C5.
Tel 01 70 39 38 00.
www.fauchon.com

Lenôtre
36 Ave de la Motte Picquet
75007. **Map** 10 F4. *Tel 01
45 55 71 25.*

**La Maison du
Chocolat**
225 Rue du Faubourg-St-
Honoré 75008. **Map** 4 E3.
Tel 01 42 27 39 44. www.
maisonduchocolat.com

Richart
258 Blvd St-Germain
75007. **Map** 11 C2.
Tel 01 45 55 66 00.

CHARCUTERIE
AND FOIE GRAS

**Chrétienne
Jean-Jacques**
58 Rue des Martyrs 75009.
Map 6 F2.
Tel 01 48 78 96 45.

Comtesse du Barry
1 Rue de Sèvres 75006.
Map 12 D4. *Tel 01 45 48
32 04.* www.
comtessedubarry.com
One of several branches.

Divay
4 Rue Bayen 75017. **Map**
4 D2. *Tel 01 43 80 16 97.*

Fauchon
26 Pl de la Madeleine
75008. **Map** 5 C5.
Tel 01 70 39 38 00.

Hédiard
21 Pl de la Madeleine
75008. **Map** 5 C5.
Tel 01 43 12 88 88.

Labeyrie
11 Rue d'Auteuil 75016.
Tel 01 42 24 17 62.

Maison de la Truffe
19 Pl de la Madeleine
75008. **Map** 5 C5.
Tel 01 42 66 10 01.

Petrossian
18 Blvd Latour-Maubourg
75007. **Map** 11 A2.
Tel 01 44 11 32 22.

Pou
16 Ave des Ternes 75017.
Map 4 D3. *Tel 01 43 80
19 24.*

Vignon
14 Rue Marbeuf 75008.
Map 4 F5.
Tel 01 47 20 24 26.

CHEESE

Alléosse
13 Rue Poncelet 75017.
Map 4 E3.
Tel 01 46 22 50 45.

Androuët
134 Rue Mouffetard
75005. **Map** 17 B1.
Tel 01 45 87 85 05.
www.androuet.com

Barthelemy
51 Rue de Grenelle 75007.
Map 12 D4.
Tel 01 45 48 56 75.

Boursault
71 Ave du Général-Leclerc
75014. **Map** 16 D5.
Tel 01 43 27 93 30.

La Fermette
86 Rue Montorgueil
75002. **Map** 13 A1.
Tel 01 42 36 70 96.

**La Fromagerie
d'Auteuil**
58 Rue d'Auteuil 75016.
Tel 01 45 25 07 10.

**Fromagerie
Quatrehomme**
62 Rue de Sèvres 75007.
Map 11 C5.
Tel 01 47 34 33 45.

Marie-Anne Cantin
12 Rue du Champ-de-
Mars 75007. **Map** 10 F3.
Tel 01 45 50 43 94.

WINE

Les Caves Augé
116 Blvd Haussman
75008. **Map** 5 C4.
Tel 01 45 22 16 97.

Cave Péret
6 Rue Daguerre 75014.
Map 16 D4.
Tel 01 43 22 08 64.

Caves Taillevent
199 Rue du Faubourg-
St-Honoré 75008. **Map** 4
F3. *Tel 01 45 61 14 09.*

Nicolas
35 Blvd Malesherbes
75008. **Map** 5 C5.
Tel 01 42 65 00 85.
www.nicolas.com

Renaud Michel
12 Pl de la Nation 75012.
Map 9 A3.
Tel 01 43 07 98 93.

Ryst-Dupeyron
79 Rue du Bac 75007. **Map**
12 D3. *Tel 01 45 48 80 93.*

CHAMPAGNE

Caprices de l'Instant
12 Rue Jacques Coeur
75004. **Map** 14 E4.
Tel 01 40 27 89 00.

La Cave des Martyrs
39 Rue des Martyrs
75009. **Map** 6 F3.
Tel 01 40 16 80 27.

**Les Caves du
Panthéon**
174 Rue St Jacques
75005. **Map** 13 A5.
Tel 01 46 33 90 35.

Ex Cellar France
25 Rue des Ecoles 75005.
Map 13 A5.
Tel 01 43 26 99 43.

Hédiard
21 Place de la Madeleine
75008. **Map** 5 C5.
Tel 01 43 12 88 88.

**La Maison de
Millésimes**
137 Boulevard St-Germain
75006. **Map** 12 F4.
Tel 01 40 46 80 01.

Repaire du Bacchus
1 Rue de Maistre 75018.
Tel 01 46 06 80 84.

OYSTERS

Huîtrerie Garnier
114 Avenue Mozart
75016. **Map** 9 A3.
Tel 01 40 50 17 27.

**Poissonnerie du
Dôme**
4 Rue Delambre 75014.
Map 16 D2.
Tel 01 43 35 23 95.

Poissonnerie Lacroix
44 Rue Oberkampf 75011.
Map 14 E1.
Tel 01 47 00 93 13.

La Sablaise
28 Rue Cler 75007.
Map 10 F3.
Tel 01 45 51 61 78.

Art and Antiques

In Paris you can either buy art and antiques from shops and galleries with established reputations, or from flea markets and avant-garde galleries. Many of the prestigious antiques shops and galleries are located around the Rue du Faubourg-St-Honoré and are worth a visit even if you can't afford to buy. On the Left Bank is Le Carré Rive Gauche, an organization of 30 antiques dealers. *Objets d'art* over 50 years old, worth more than a given amount (values vary for all categories of art object), will require a *Certificat pour un bien culturel* to be exported anywhere in the world (provided by the vendor), plus a *licence d'exportation* for non-EU countries. Seek professional advice from the large antique shops.

EXPORTING

The Ministry of Culture designates *objets d'art*. Export licences are available from the **Centre Français du Commerce Extérieur**. The **Centre des Renseignements des Douanes** has a booklet, *Bulletin Officiel des Douanes*, with all the details.

MODERN CRAFTS AND FURNITURE

One of the best places for furniture and *objets d'art* by up-and-coming designers is **Sentou**, where you can find objects and textiles, as well as furniture by contemporary designers. Another essential venue is the showroom of the Italian designer, **Giulio Cappellini**. **Le Viaduc des Arts** (*see pp270–71*) is a railway viaduct, each arch of which has been transformed into a shop front and workshop space. A great place for contemporary metal-work, tapestry, sculpture, ceramics and much more.

ANTIQUES AND OBJETS D'ART

If you wish to buy antiques, you might like to stroll around the areas that boast many galleries – in Le Carré Rive Gauche around Quai Malaquais, try **L'Arc en Seine** and **Anne-Sophie Duval** for Art Nouveau and Art Deco. Rue Jacob is still one of the best places to seek beautiful objects, antique or modern.
Close to the Louvre, the **Louvre des Antiquaires** (*see p120*) sells expensive, quality furniture. On the Rue du Faubourg-St-Honoré you will find **Didier Aaron**, expert on furniture from the 17th and 18th centuries. **Village St-Paul** between the Quai des Célestins, the Rue Saint Paul and the Rue Charlemagne, is the most charming group of antiques shops and is also open on Sundays.
La Calinière has a superb range of *objets d'art* and old lighting fixtures. Glassware from the 19th century to the 1960s is sold at **Verreglass**. **Le Village Suisse** in the south of the city also groups many art and antiques dealers.

REPRODUCTIONS, POSTERS AND PRINTS

A beautiful, contemporary art gallery called **Artcurial** on the Place des Champs-Elysées has one of the best selections of international art periodicals, books and prints. On the Boulevard Saint Germain, **La Hune** is a popular bookshop, particularly for art publications. The museum bookshops, especially those in the Musée d'Art Moderne (*see p203*), Louvre (*see p123*), Musée d'Orsay (*see p145*) and Pompidou Centre (*see p111*) are good for recent art books and posters.
Galerie Documents on the Rue de Seine sells original antique posters. Or leaf through the second-hand book stalls along the banks of the Seine.

ART GALLERIES

Established art galleries are located on or around the Avenue Montaigne. The **Louise Leiris** gallery was founded by D H Kahnweiler, the dealer who "discovered" both Georges Braque and Pablo Picasso. The gallery still shows Cubist masterpieces.
Artcurial holds many exhibitions and has an impressive permanent collection of 20th-century art, including works by Joan Miró, Picasso, Alberto Giacometti and Max Ernst. **Galerie Lelong** is devoted to contemporary artists.
On the Left Bank **Adrian Maeght** has a tremendous stock of paintings at prices to suit most budgets; he also publishes fine art books. **Galerie 1900–2000** specializes in works by Surrealist and Dada artists, and **Galerie Jeanne Bucher** represents post-war Abstraction with artists like Nicolas de Staël and Vieira da Silva. **Dina Vierny** is a bastion of Modernism, founded by sculptor Aristide Maillol's famous model of the same name.
Rue Louise-Weiss has become an area for cutting-edge creativity and innovation known as "Scène Est". The **Air de Paris** gallery is also popular. In the Marais try **Yvon Lambert, Galerie Templon** – specializing in American art, **Galerie Emmanuel Perrotin** and **Galerie du Jour Agnès B**, and in the Bastille, **Levignes-Bastille** and **L et M Durand-Dessert**, also a fashionable place to buy catalogues on new artists, if not their actual works.

AUCTIONS AND AUCTION HOUSES

The great Paris auction centre, in operation since 1858, is **Drouot-Richelieu** (*see p218*). Bidding can be intimidating since most of it is done by dealers. Beware of the auctioneer's high-speed patter. *La Gazette de L'Hôtel Drouot* tells you what auctions are coming up when. Drouot-Richelieu has its own auction catalogue as well. The house only accepts cash and French cheques, but there is an exchange desk in house. A 10–15 per cent commission to the house is charged, so add it on to any price you hear. You may view from 11am to 6pm on the day before the sale, and from 11am to noon on the morning of the sale. Items considered not good enough for the main house are sold at **Drouot-Nord**. Here auctions take place from 9am to noon and viewing is just 5 minutes before the sales begin. The most prestigious auctions are held at **Drouot-Montaigne**.

The **Crédit Municipal** holds around 12 auctions a month, and almost all the items on sale are small objects and furs off-loaded by rich Parisians. The rules follow those at Drouot. Information can also be found in *La Gazette de L'Hôtel Drouot*.

Service des Domaines sells all sorts of odds and ends, and here you can still find bargains. Many of the wares come from bailiffs and from Customs and Excise *(see p374)* confiscations. Viewing is from 10am to 11.30am on the day of the sale.

DIRECTORY

EXPORTING

Centre Français du Commerce Extérieur
22 Ave Franklin Roosevelt 75008.
Map 5 A4.
Tel 01 53 83 92 92.
www.cfce.fr

Centre des Renseignements des Douanes
84 Rue d'Hauteville 75010.
Tel 08 25 30 82 63.
www.douane.gouv.fr

MODERN CRAFTS AND FURNITURE

Cappellini
4 Rue des Rosiers 75004.
Map 13 C3.
Tel 01 42 78 39 39.
www.cappellini.it

Sentou
24 Rue du Pont-Louis-Philippe 75004. **Map** 13 C3. *Tel 01 42 71 00 01.*

Le Viaduc des Arts
Ave Daumesnil 750012.
Map 14 F5.
Tel 01 43 40 75 75.
This comprises a series of shops on the Avenue.

ANTIQUES AND OBJETS D'ART

Anne-Sophie Duval
5 Quai Malaquais 75006.
Map 12 E3. *Tel 01 43 54 51 16.* www.
annesophieduval.com

L'Arc en Seine
31 Rue de Seine 75006.
Map 12 E3.
Tel 01 43 29 11 02.

La Calinière
68 Rue Vieille-du-Temple 75003. **Map** 13 C3.
Tel 01 42 77 40 46.

Didier Aaron
118 Rue du Faubourg-St-Honoré 75008. **Map** 5 C5.
Tel 01 47 42 47 34.
www.didieraaron-cie.com

Louvre des Antiquaires
2 Pl du Palais Royal 75001.
Map 12 E2.
Tel 01 42 97 27 27.

Verreglass
32 Rue de Charonne 75011. **Map** 14 F4
Tel 01 48 05 78 43.

Village St-Paul
Between the Quai des Célestins, the Rue St-Paul and the Rue Charlemagne 75004. **Map** 13 C4.

Le Village Suisse
78 Ave de Suffren 75015.
Map 10 E4.
www.levillagesuisseparis.com

REPRODUCTIONS, POSTERS, PRINTS

Artcurial
7 Pl des Champs-Elysées 75008.
Map 5 A5.
Tel 01 42 99 16 16.

Galerie Documents
53 Rue de Seine 75006.
Map 12 E4.
Tel 01 43 54 50 68.

La Hune
170 Blvd St-Germain 75006.
Map 12 D4.
Tel 01 45 48 35 85.

ART GALLERIES

Adrian Maeght
42 Rue du Bac 75007.
Map 12 D3.
Tel 01 45 48 45 15.

Air de Paris
32 Rue Louise-Weiss 75013. **Map** 18 E4.
Tel 01 44 23 02 77.

Dina Vierny
36 Rue Jacob 75006.
Map 12 E3.
Tel 01 42 60 23 18.
www.galeriedinavierny.com

Galerie 1900–2000
8 Rue Bonaparte 75006.
Map 12 E3.
Tel 01 43 25 84 20.

Galerie Emmanuel Perrotin
76 Rue de Turenne 75003.
Map 14 D2.
Tel 01 42 16 79 79.

Galerie Jeanne Bucher
53 Rue de Seine 75006.
Map 12 E4.
Tel 01 44 41 69 55.

Galerie du Jour Agnès B
44 Rue Quincampoix 75004.
Map 13 B2.
Tel 01 44 54 55 90.

Galerie Lelong
13 Rue de Téhéran 75008. **Map** 5 A3.
Tel 01 45 63 13 19.

Galerie Templon
30 Rue Beaubourg 75003.
Map 13 B1.
Tel 01 42 72 14 10.
Open by appt only.

L et M Durand-Dessert

28 Rue de Lappe 75011.
Map 14 F4.
Tel 01 48 06 92 23.

Levignes-Bastille
27 Rue de Charonne 75011. **Map** 14 F4.
Tel 01 47 00 88 18.

Louise Leiris
47 Rue de Monceau 75008.
Map 5 A3.
Tel 01 45 63 28 85.

Rue Louise Weiss
75013.

Yvon Lambert
108 Rue Vieille-du-Temple 75003. **Map** 14 D2.
Tel 01 42 71 09 33.

AUCTION HOUSES

Crédit Municipal
55 Rue des Francs-Bourgeois 75004.
Map 13 C3.
Tel 01 44 61 64 00.
www.creditmunicipal.fr

Drouot-Montaigne
15 Ave Montaigne 75008.
Map 10 F1.
Tel 01 48 00 20 80.
www.drouot.fr

Drouot-Nord
64 Rue Doudeauville 75018.
Tel 01 48 00 20 20.

Drouot-Richelieu
9 Rue Drouot 75009.
Map 6 F4.
Tel 01 48 00 20 20.

Service des Domaines
Tel 01 44 64 50 00.

Markets

For eye-catching displays of wonderful food and a lively shopping atmosphere, there is no better place than a Paris market. There are large covered food markets; markets where stalls change regularly; and permanent street markets with a mixture of shops and stalls which are open on a daily basis. Each has its own personality reflecting the area in which it is located. A list of some of the more famous markets, with approximate opening times, follows. For a complete list of markets contact the Paris Office du Tourisme (*see p280*). And while you're enjoying browsing round the stalls remember to keep an eye on your money – and be prepared to bargain.

FRUIT AND VEGETABLE MARKETS

The French treat food with the kind of reverence usually reserved for religion. Most still shop on a daily basis to be sure of buying the freshest produce possible, so food markets tend to be busy. The majority of fruit and vegetable markets are open from around 8am to 1pm and from 4pm to 7pm Tuesday to Saturday, and from 9am to 1pm Sunday.

Watch what you buy in the food markets or you may find you have purchased a kilo of fruit or vegetables from a marvellous display only to discover later that all the produce hidden underneath is rotten. To avoid this, try to buy produce loose rather than in boxes. Most outdoor stalls prefer to serve you rather than allow you to help yourself, but you can point to the individual fruit and vegetables of your choice. A little language is useful for specifying *pas trop mûr* (not too ripe), or *pour manger ce soir* (to be eaten tonight). If you go to the same market every day you'll become familiar to the stall holders and are far less likely to be cheated. You will also get to know the stalls worth buying from and the produce worth buying. Seasonal fruit and vegetables are, of course, usually a good buy, tending to be fresher and cheaper than at other times of the year. Finally, go early in the day when the food is freshest and the queues are shortest.

FLEA MARKETS

It's often said that you can no longer find bargains at the Paris flea markets. Though this may be true, it's still worth going to one for the sheer fun of browsing. And bear in mind that the price quoted is not the one that you are expected to pay – it's generally assumed that you will bargain. Most flea markets are located on the city's boundaries. Whether you pick up any real bargains has as much to do with luck as with judgement. Often the sellers themselves have little or no idea of the true value of their goods – which can work either for or against you. The biggest and most famous market, incorporating several smaller ones, is the Marché aux Puces de St-Ouen. Keep your eye on your wallet, as pickpockets frequent these markets.

SPECIALIST MARKETS

Try the Marché aux Fleurs Madeleine, the Marché aux Fleurs on the Ile de la Cité (*see p81*) or the Marché aux Fleurs Ternes in the Champs-Elysées district for fresh flowers. On the Ile de la Cité on Sundays the Marché aux Oiseaux bird market replaces the flower market. Stamp collectors will enjoy the permanent Marché aux Timbres where you can also buy old postcards. In Montmartre the Marché St-Pierre, famous for cheap fabrics, is patronized by professional designers.

Marché d'Aligre

(See p235.)

Reminiscent of a Moroccan bazaar, this must be the cheapest and liveliest market in the city. Here traders hawk ingredients such as North African olives, groundnuts and hot peppers and there are even a few halal butchers. The noise reaches a crescendo at weekends when the cries of the market boys mingle with those of militants of all political persuasions as the latter petition and protest in the Place d'Aligre. The stalls on the square sell mostly second-hand clothes and bric-à-brac. This is a less affluent area of town with few tourists and many Parisians.

Rue Cler

(See p190.)

This high-class, pedestrianized food market is patronized mainly by the politicians and captains of industry who live and work in the vicinity, so it's good for people-spotting! The produce is excellent – there's a Breton delicatessen and some good *fromageries*.

Marché Enfant Rouges

39 Rue de Bretagne 75003. **Map** 14 D2. **M** Temple, Filles-du-Calvaire. 🕐 8.30am–1pm, 4–7.30pm Tue–Sat (to 8pm Fri, Sat); 8.30am–2pm Sun.

This long-established, charming fruit and vegetable market on the Rue de Bretagne is part covered, part outdoors and dates from 1620. The items on sale are famous for their freshness, and on Sunday mornings street singers, performers and accordionists sometimes enliven the proceedings.

Marché aux Fleurs Madeleine

Pl de la Madeleine 75008. **Map** 5 C5. **M** Madeleine. 🕐 8am–7.30pm Mon–Sat.

Marché aux Fleurs Ternes

Pl des Ternes 75017. **Map** 4 E3. **M** Ternes. 🕐 8am–7.30pm Tue–Sun.

Marché St-Pierre

Pl St-Pierre 75018. **Map** 6 F1. **M** Anvers. 🕐 2–7pm Mon, 9am–7pm Tue–Sat.

Marché aux Timbres

Cour Marigny 75008. **Map** 5 B5. **M** Champs-Elysées. 🕐 8am–7pm Thu, Sat, Sun & public hols.

Marché St-Germain

4–6 Rue Lobineau 75006. **Map 12 E4.** M Mabillon. ◯ 8.30am–1pm, 4–8pm Tue–Fri; 8am–1.30pm, 3.30–8pm Sat; 8am–1.30pm Sun.

St-Germain is one of the few covered markets left in Paris and has been enhanced by renovation. Here you can buy Italian, Mexican, Greek, Asian and organic produce and other goods.

Rue Lepic

75018. **Map 6 F1.** M Blanche, Lamarck-Caulaincourt. ◯ 8am–2pm Tue–Sun.

The Rue Lepic fruit and vegetable market is situated conveniently close to the sights of Montmartre in this refreshingly unspoilt winding road. The market is at its liveliest at the weekend.

Rue de Lévis

Blvd des Batignolles 75017. **Map 5 B2.** M Villiers. ◯ 8am–1pm, 4pm–7pm Tue–Sat; 9am–2pm Sun.

Rue de Lévis is a bustling, popular food market near the Parc Monceau with a number of good pâtisseries, an excellent cheese delicatessen and a charcuterie which is known for its savoury pies. The part of the street that leads to the Rue Legendre sells haberdashery and fabrics.

Rue Montorgueil

75001 & 75002. **Map 13 A1.** M Les Halles. ◯ usually 9am–7pm Tue–Sun.

The Rue Montorgueil is what remains of the old Les Halles market. The street has now been repaved and restored to its former glory. Here you can buy exotic fruit and vegetables like green bananas and yams from the market gardeners' stalls, or sample offerings from the delicatessens or from the Stohrer pastry shop. Alternatively pick up some of the pretty Moroccan pottery for sale.

Rue Mouffetard

(See p166.)

Rue Mouffetard is one of the oldest market streets in Paris. Although it has become touristy and somewhat overpriced, it's still a charming winding street full of quality food products. It's worth queuing for the freshly-made bread at Les Panetons bakery at No. 113 (see pp333–5.) There is also a lively African market down the nearby side street of Rue Daubenton.

Rue Poncelet

75017. **Map 4 E3.** M Ternes. ◯ 8am–noon, 4pm–7.30pm Tue–Sat; 8am–12.30pm Sun.

The Rue Poncelet food market is situated away from the main tourist areas of Paris but is worth visiting for its authentic French atmosphere. Choose from the many bakeries, pâtisseries and charcuteries or enjoy authentic Auvergne specialities from Aux Fermes d'Auvergnes.

Marché de la Porte de Vanves

Ave Georges-Lafenestre & Ave Marc-Sangnier 75014. M Porte-de-Vanves. ◯ 7am–7.30pm Sat & Sun.

Porte de Vanves is a small market selling good-quality bric-à-brac and junk as well as some second-hand furniture. It's best to get to the market early on Saturday morning for the best choice of wares. Artists exhibit nearby in the Place des Artistes.

Marché Président-Wilson

Situated in Ave du Président-Wilson, between Pl d'Iéna & Rue Debrousse 75016. **Map 10 D1.** M Alma-Marceau. ◯ 7am–2.30pm Wed, 7am–3pm Sat.

This very chic food market on Avenue Président-Wilson is close to the Musée d'Art Moderne and the Palais Galliera fashion museum. It has become important because there are no other food shops nearby. It is best for meat.

Marché aux Puces de Montreuil

Porte de Montreuil, 93 Montreuil 75020. M Porte-de-Montreuil. ◯ 7am–7.30pm Mon, Sat & Sun.

Go early to the Porte de Montreuil flea market, where you'll have a better chance of picking up a bargain. The substantial second-hand clothes section attracts many young people. There's also a wide variety of items including used bicycles, bric-à-brac and an exotic spices stand.

Marché aux Puces de St-Ouen

(See p233.)

This is the most well known, the most crowded and the most expensive of all the flea markets, situated on the northern outskirts of the city. Here you'll find a range of markets, locals dealing from their car boots and a number of extremely large buildings packed with stalls. Some of them are very

upmarket, others sell junk. The flea market is a 10–15 minute walk from Clignancourt metro – don't be put off by the somewhat sleazy Marché Malik which you have to pass through on your way from the metro. A Guide des Puces (guide to the flea markets) can be obtained from the information kiosk in the Marché Biron on the Rue des Rosiers. The more exclusive markets will take credit cards and arrange for goods to be shipped home. New stock arrives on Friday, the day when professionals come from all over the world to sweep up the best buys.

Among the markets here the Marché Jules Vallès is good for turn-of-the-19th century objets d'art. Marché Paul-Bert is more expensive, but charming. Items on sale include furniture, books and prints. Both markets deal in second-hand goods rather than antiques.

In a different league, Marché Biron sells elegant, expensive antique furniture of very high quality. Marché Vernaison is the oldest and biggest market, good for collectables such as jewellery as well as lamps and clothes. No information about the Marché aux Puces is complete without mentioning Chez Louisette in the Vernaison market. This café is always full of locals enjoying the home cooking and the well-intentioned renditions of Edith Piaf songs. Marché Cambo is a fairly small market with beautifully-displayed antique furniture. Marché Serpette is popular with the dealers: everything sold here is in mint condition.

Marché Raspail

Situated on Blvd Raspail between Rue du Cherche-Midi & Rue de Rennes 75006. **Map 12 D5.** M Rennes. ◯ 7am–2.30pm Tue, Fri; 9am–3pm Sun.

The Raspail market sells typical French groceries as well as Portuguese produce on Tuesdays and Fridays. But Sunday is the day for which it's famous, when health-conscious Parisians turn up in droves for the organically-grown produce. Marché Raspail is not a cheap market, but it is very good.

Rue de Seine and Rue de Buci

75006. **Map 12 E4.** M Odéon. ◯ 8am–1pm, 4–7pm Tue–Sat; 9am–1pm Sun.

The stalls here are expensive and crowded but sell quality fruit and vegetables. There is also a large florist's and two excellent pâtisseries.

ENTERTAINMENT IN PARIS

Whether you prefer classical drama or cabaret, leggy showgirls or ballet, opera or jazz, cinema or dancing the night away, Paris has it all. Free entertainment is aplenty as well, from the street performers outside the Pompidou Centre to musicians busking in the metro. Parisians themselves enjoy strolling along the boulevards or sitting at a pavement café, and nursing a drink. Of course, for the ultimate "oh-la-la!" experience, showgirls await you at celebrated cabarets while supermodels pose in nightclubs. For fans of spectator sports there is tennis, the Tour de France, horse racing, football or rugby. Recreation centres and gyms cater to the more active, while the municipal swimming pools delight waterbabies. And for those disposed either way, there's always the popular type of bowls played in Paris, *pétanque*.

PRACTICAL INFORMATION

For the visitor in Paris there is no shortage of information about what's on offer.

The **Office du Tourisme** near the Tuileries and Opera is the city's main tourism distribution point for leaflets and schedules of events. It has a recorded information telephone service giving details of free concerts and exhibitions along with information on transport to the venues. Its website is also extremely useful. Your hotel reception desk or concierge should also be able to help you with any such information. They usually keep a wide range of brochures and leaflets for guests, and will generally be more than happy to make reservations for you.

BOOKING TICKETS

Depending on the event, tickets can be bought at the door, but for blockbuster concerts it is necessary to book well in advance. For most major events, including some classical music concerts and museum shows, tickets can be purchased at the **FNAC** chain or **Virgin Megastore**. For popular events be sure to book well in advance, Parisians can be very quick off the mark for hot tickets. However, for theatre, opera and dance performances, you can often buy inexpensive tickets at the last minute. If the tickets are marked *sans visibilité* you will be able to see the stage only partially, or perhaps not at all. Often, obliging ushers

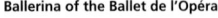
Ballerina of the Ballet de l'Opéra

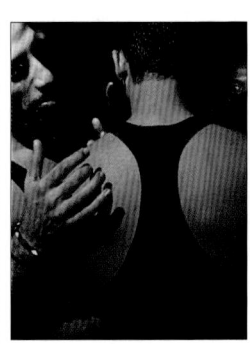
Nightclubbing in Paris

will put you in a better seat, depending on availability, but don't forget to tip.

Theatre box offices are open daily from approximately 11am–7pm. Most box offices accept credit card bookings made by phone or in person, but you may have to arrive early to pick up your tickets if you booked by telephone, as they may be sold to someone else at the last minute. If you

LISTINGS MAGAZINES

Paris has several good listings magazines. Among them are *Pariscope* and *L'Officiel des Spectacles*. They are published every Wednesday. *Le Figaro* has a good listings section on Wednesdays. The English publication, *Paris Voice* is available at newsstands or **WH Smith** *(see p332)* and free papers such as *A Nous Paris*, distributed in the metro, also give the lowdown.

Concert at Opéra National de Paris Garnier *(see p348)*

Buying tickets at the box office of a comedy club

are really keen and can't get hold of tickets, you can always turn up at the box office just before the performance in case there are unclaimed or returned tickets.

TICKET TOUTS

If you must have a ticket to a sold-out performance, do as the French do: stand at the entrance with a sign that says *cherche une place (or deux,* etc). Many people have an extra ticket to sell. Often the people selling the extra tickets are simply doing so because a person in their party cannot come and they will simply sell the ticket on at face value. It is fine to buy these tickets, but do watch out for touts and be sure you don't buy a counterfeit or overpriced ticket.

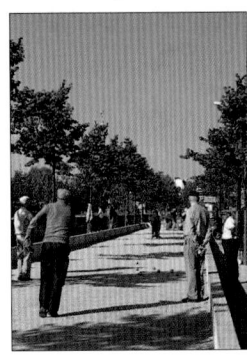

Pétanque players

CUT-PRICE TICKETS

Half-price tickets to current plays are sold on the day of performance at **Kiosque Théâtre**. Credit cards are not accepted and a small commission is charged per ticket. There is a booth on the Place de la Madeleine *(see p216)*, open 12.30–8pm, Tuesday–Saturday, 12.30–4pm Sunday, and in the Parvis de la Gare Montparnasse 12.30–6pm Tuesday–Saturday. This is a great way to buy tickets without booking weeks or even months in advance and, of course, has the added benefit of costing less. The *kiosque* is a Parisian institution and often has passes for the season's top shows.

DISABLED VISITORS' FACILITIES

Where facilities do exist, they are either very good or dreadful. Many venues have wheelchair space, but always phone in advance to make sure it's properly equipped. As far as public transport is concerned, the metro, with its long stairways, is completely inaccessible to wheelchairs. Some bus lines are equipped with ramps to make them accessible to wheelchairs; check with the city's transport authority, the RATP, to find out which lines have facilities.

USEFUL ADDRESSES

FNAC
Forum des Halles, 1 Rue Pierre-Lescot 75001. **Map** 13 A2. **Tel** *0825 020 020.*

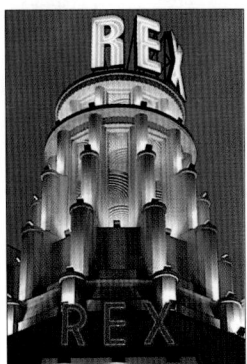

The Grand Rex cinema *(see p354)*

FNAC
26 Ave des Ternes 75017.
Map 4 D3. **Tel** *0825 020 020.*

G7 Taxis
Tel *01 47 39 47 39.*

Office du Tourisme
25 Rue des Pyramides 75001.
Map 12 E1. **Tel** *08 92 68 30 00.*
www.parisinfo.com

Taxis Bleus
Tel *01 49 36 10 10.*

Virgin Megastore
52–60 Ave des Champs-Elysées 75008. **Map** 4 F5.
Tel *01 49 53 50 00.*

Theatre

From the grandeur of the Comédie Française to slapstick farce and avant-garde drama, theatre is flourishing in Paris and the suburbs – the training ground for the best young actors and directors. The city also has a long tradition of playing host to visiting companies, and it attracts many foreign productions, often in the original languages.

There are theatres scattered throughout the city and the theatre season runs from September to July; national theatres close during August but many commercial ones stay open. For complete listings of what's on read *Pariscope* or *L'Officiel des Spectacles (see p340).*

NATIONAL THEATRES

Founded in 1680 by royal decree, the **Comédie Française** *(see p120),* with its strict conventions regarding the style of acting and interpretation, is the bastion of French theatre. Its aim is to keep classical drama in the public eye and also to perform works by the best modern playwrights.

The Comédie Française (inextricably linked in the national consciousness to Molière) is the oldest national theatre in the world and one of the few institutions of *ancien-régime* France to have survived the Revolution. It settled into its present home after players occupied the Palais-Royal during the Revolution. The traditionally-styled red velvet auditorium has a vast stage equipped with the latest technology.

The majority of the repertoire is classical, dominated by Corneille, Racine and Molière, followed by second strings Marivaux, Alfred de Musset and Victor Hugo. The company also performs modern plays by French and foreign playwrights.

The **Odéon Théâtre de l'Europe**, also known as the Théâtre National de l'Odéon *(see p140),* was at one time the second theatre of the Comédie Française. It now has two sites and specializes in performing plays from other countries in their original languages.

Next door the **Petit Odéon** features new plays and those in foreign languages.

The **Théâtre National de Chaillot** is a huge underground auditorium in the Art Deco Palais de Chaillot *(see p200).* It stages lively productions of mainstream European classics and, occasionally, musical revues. The theatre also contains a studio, the **Salle Gémier,** for more experimental work.

The **Théâtre National de la Colline** has two performance spaces and specializes in contemporary dramas.

FURTHER AFIELD

A thriving multi-theatre complex in the Bois de Vincennes, the **Cartoucherie** houses five separate avant-garde theatres, including the internationally famous **Théâtre du Soleil.**

INDEPENDENT THEATRES

Among the most important of the serious independents are the **Comédie des Champs-Elysées,** the **Hébertot** and the **Atelier,** which aims to be experimental. Other notable venues include the **Théâtre Marigny,** for excellent modern French drama, the **Montparnasse** and the **Théâtre Antoine** which pioneered the use of realism on stage. The **Madeleine** maintains consistently high standards and the **Huchette** specializes in Ionesco plays. The avant-garde producer/director Peter Brook has a loyal following at the **Bouffes-du-Nord.**

For over a hundred years the **Palais Royal** has been the temple of risqué farce. With fewer French Feydeau-style farce writers these days, translations of English and American sex comedies are

filling the gap. Other notable venues include the **Bouffes-Parisiens**, **La Bruyère,** the **Michel** and the **St-Georges.** The **Théâtre Marie Bell** presents popular one-man comedy shows.

CAFE-THEATRES AND CHANSONNIERS

There is a long tradition of entertainment in cafés, but the café-theatres of today have nothing in common with the "café-concerts" of the late 19th century. These modern entertainments have originated because young actors and new playwrights could not find work, while drama students were unable to pay to hire out established theatres. Don't be surprised if there is an element of audience participation, or alternatively, in small venues, if the actors can sometimes seem a little too close for comfort. This form of theatre is now so popular in Paris that one can often see posters advertising classes for café-theatre or notices inviting people to join small troupes. Café-theatres rose to prominence during the 1960s and 70s, when unknowns such as Coluche, Gérard Depardieu and Miou-Miou made their debut at the **Café de la Gare** before going on to success on the screen, so who knows who you might see at your local café.

Good venues for seeing new talent include the **Théâtre d'Edgar** and **Au Bec Fin,** while **Chez Michou** is an old-fashioned spot which is very popular and tends to specialize in broad caricature. Traditional *chansonniers* – cabarets where ballads, folk songs and humour abound – include **Au Lapin Agile** *(see p225),* in the heart of Montmartre. Political satire is on offer at the **Caveau de la République** and the **Deux Anes,** also in Montmartre. Another form of café entertainment that often veers towards the theatrical is café-philosophique. These are philosophical discussions or debates, held on topics such as justice, war or love, in which skilled orators take to the floor to declaim their positions. Audience participation is encouraged. Such evenings are held in many locations, but the best known are held at **Le 7 Lézards**. Although debates take place in French, English language events also exist: the monthly play-reading at the **Café de Flore** is a fine example of the genre.

CHILDREN'S THEATRE

Some Paris theatres, such as the **Gymnase-Marie Bell**, the **Porte St-Martin** and the **Café d'Edgar**, have children's matinees on Wednesdays and weekends. In the city parks there are several tiny puppet theatres (marionnettes), which are sure to delight children and adults alike. *(See Independent Theatres p344.)* The **Lido** also has a new show for children.

OPEN-AIR THEATRE

During the summer, weather permitting, open-air performances of Shakespeare in French and classic French plays are held in the Shakespeare Garden in the Bois de Boulogne. There are also occasional performances in the Tuileries and in Montmartre as part of Paris's summer festival; check listings magazines for these events.

ENGLISH-LANGUAGE THEATRE IN PARIS

The On Stage Theatre Company and The Dear Conjunction Theatre are both Paris-based companies who perform in English (details in listings magazines). There are also several English-language poetry societies which host poetry and play readings, the best is the Live Poets Society. **Kilometre Zero** is an interesting English-language arts collective that performs plays, publishes a magazine and hosts open-mike recital evenings. **La Java** puts on excellent stand-up comedy acts in English each month, courtesy of Anything Matters.

An historic venue, it is much-loved by expatriates and plays host to some of the finest comic talent on the circuit at the moment.

STREET THEATRE

Street theatre thrives during the summer. Jugglers, mime artists, fire-eaters and musicians can be seen in tourist areas such as the Pompidou Centre *(see pp110–11)*, St-Germain-des-Prés and Les Halles.

CABARET

The music hall revue is the entertainment form most associated with late 19th-century Paris. It evokes images of bohemian artists and champagne-induced debauchery. Today, most of the girls are likely to be non-French and the audience is made up mainly of foreign businessmen and tour groups.

When it comes to picking a cabaret the rule of thumb is simple: the better-known places are the best. Lesser-known shows resemble nothing so much as Grade-B strip shows. All the cabarets listed here *(see p344)* guarantee topless women sporting outrageous feather- and sequin-encrusted headpieces, an assortment of vaudeville acts and, depending on your point of view, spectacularly entertaining evening or an exercise in high kitsch.

The **Lido** is the most Las Vegas-like of the cabarets and stars the legendary Bluebell Girls. The **Folies-Bergères** is renowned for lively entertainment. It is the oldest music hall in Paris and probably the most famous in the world.

The **Crazy Horse** features some of the more risqué costumes and performances, and dancers with names such as Betty Buttocks, Fila Volcana and Nouka Bazooka. It has been transformed from its Wild West bar-room into a jewel-box theatre with a champagne bucket fastened to each seat. Here, the lowly striptease of burlesque shows has been refined into a vehicle for comedy sketches and international beauties.

Paradis Latin is the most "French" of all the city's cabaret shows. It has variety acts with remarkable special effects and scenery in a beautiful, old Left Bank theatre, partially designed by Gustave Eiffel.

The **Don Camillo Rive Gauche** has more elegant, less touristy shows, with excellent *chanson* singers, comedians and all sorts of other variety acts. The **Moulin Rouge** *(see p228)*, once the haunt of Toulouse-Lautrec, is the birthplace of the cancan. Today, the Moulin Rouge is less extravagant than the screen version portrayed in the famous film, but cabaret fans can still be certain of an evening of glamour, glitz and good times. Outrageously camp, transvestite parodies of these showgirl reviews can be seen at **Chez Madame Arthur**.

BOOKING TICKETS

Tickets can be bought at the box office, by telephone or through theatre agencies. Box offices are open daily from about 11am–7pm; some accept credit card bookings by telephone or in person.

TICKET PRICES

Ticket prices generally range from 7€–30€ for the national theatres and 8€–38€ for the independent. Reduced-price tickets and student stand-bys are available in some theatres 15 minutes before curtain-up. For cabaret, expect to pay from 23€–60€; 68€–105€ with dinner.

The **Kiosque Théâtre** offers half-price tickets on the day-of-performance: credit cards are not accepted and a small commission is charged for each ticket sold. There is a ticket booth in the Place de la Madeleine and one in front of Gare Montparnasse.

DRESS

These days, evening clothes are only worn to gala events at the Opéra National de Paris Garnier, the Comédie Française or the premiere of an up-market play.

DIRECTORY

NATIONAL THEATRES

Comédie Française
Salle Richelieu, 1 Pl Colette 75001. Map 12 E1.
Tel 08 25 10 16 80.
www.comedie-francaise.fr

Odéon Théâtre de l'Europe
Ateliers Berthier, 8 Blvd Berthier 75017. Map 12 F5. Tel 01 44 85 40 40.
Théâtre de l'Odéon, Pl de l'Odéon 75006.
Map 12 F4.
www.theatre-odeon.fr

Théâtre National de Chaillot
Pl du Trocadéro 75016.
Map 9 C2.
Tel 01 53 65 31 00.

Théâtre National de la Colline
15 Rue Malte-Brun 75020.
Tel 01 44 62 52 52.
www.colline.fr

FURTHER AFIELD

Cartoucherie
Route du Champ-de-Manoeuvre 75012.
Tel 01 43 74 24 08.

Théâtre de l'Aquarium
Tel 01 43 74 72 74.

Théâtre de l'Epée de Bois
Bois de Vincennes
Tel 01 48 08 39 74.

Théâtre de la Tempête
Tel 01 43 28 36 36.

Théâtre du Chaudron
Tel 01 43 28 97 04.

Théâtre du Soleil
Tel 01 43 74 24 08.

INDEPENDENT THEATRES

Bouffes-du-Nord
37 bis Blvd de la Chapelle 75010.
Map 7 C1.
Tel 01 46 07 34 50.
www.bouffesdunord.com

Bouffes-Parisiens
4 Rue Monsigny 75002.
Map 6 E5. Tel 01 42 96 92 42. www.
bouffesparisiens.com

La Bruyère
5 Rue La Bruyère 75009.
Map 6 E3.
Tel 01 48 74 76 99.

Comédie des Champs-Elysées
15 Ave Montaigne 75008. Map 10 F1.
Tel 01 53 23 99 10.

Gaiété Montparnasse
26 Rue de la Gaiété 75014. Map 15 C2.
Tel 01 43 20 60 56.

Hébertot
78 bis Blvd des Batignolles 75017.
Map 5 B2.
Tel 01 43 87 23 23.

Madeleine
19 Rue de Surène 75008.
Map 5 C5.
Tel 01 42 65 07 09.

Marigny
7 Ave de Marigny 75008.
Map 5 A5.
Tel 0892 222 333.

Michel
38 Rue des Mathurins 75008.
Map 5 C4.
Tel 01 42 65 35 02.

Montparnasse
31 Rue de la Gaîté 75014. Map 15 C2.
Tel 01 43 22 77 30.

Palais Royal
38 Rue Montpensier 75001. Map 12 E1.
Tel 01 42 97 40 00.

Porte St-Martin
16 Blvd St-Martin 75010.
Map 7 C5.
Tel 01 42 08 00 32.

St-Georges
51 Rue St-Georges 75009. Map 6 E3.
Tel 01 48 78 63 47.

Théâtre Antoine
14 Blvd de Strasbourg 75010. Map 7 B5.
Tel 01 42 08 77 71 & 01 42 08 76 58.

Théâtre de l'Atelier
Pl Charles Dullin 75018.
Map 6 F2.
Tel 01 46 06 49 24.
www.theatre-atelier.com

Théâtre de la Huchette
23 Rue de la Huchette 75005.
Map 13 A4.
Tel 01 43 26 38 99.

Théâtre Marie Bell
38 Blvd Bonne-Nouvelle 75010.
Map 7 A5.
Tel 01 42 46 94 82.

Théâtre Sudden
14 bis Rue Sainte-Isaure 75018.
Map 2 F4.
Tel 01 42 62 35 00.

CAFE-THEATRES AND CHANSONNIERS

Au Bec Fin
6 bis Rue Thérèse 75001.
Map 12 E1.
Tel 01 42 96 29 35.

Au Lapin Agile
22 Rue des Saules 75018.
Map 2 F5.
Tel 01 46 06 85 87.

Café de Flore
See p139.

Café de la Gare
41 Rue du Temple 75004.
Map 13 B2.
Tel 01 42 78 52 51.

Caveau de la République
23 Place République 75003.
Map 8 D5.
Tel 01 42 78 44 45.

Chez Michou
80 Rue des Martyrs 75018.
Map 6 F3.
Tel 01 46 06 16 04.

Deux Anes
100 Blvd de Clichy 75018. Map 6 D1.
Tel 01 46 06 10 26.

La Java
105 Rue du Faubourg du Temple 75010. Map 8 E5.
Tel 01 53 19 98 88. www.
anythingmatters.com

Le Point Virgule
7 Rue St-Croix-de-la-Bretonnerie 75004.
Map 13 C3.
Tel 01 42 78 67 03.

Le 7 Lézards
10 Rue des Rosiers 75004.
Map 13 C3.
Tel 01 48 87 08 97.

Théâtre d'Edgar
58 Blvd Edgar-Quinet 75014. Map 16 D2.
Tel 01 42 79 97 97.

CABARET

Chez Madame Arthur
75 bis Rue des Martyrs 75018. Map 6 F2.
Tel 01 42 54 15 92.
www.madamearthur.com

Crazy Horse
12 Ave George V 75008.
Map 10 E1. Tel 01 47 23 15 92. www.
lecrazyhorseparis.com

Don Camillo Rive Gauche
10 Rue des Sts-Pères 75007. Map 12 E3.
Tel 01 42 60 82 84.

Folies-Bergères
32 Rue Richer 75009.
Map 7 A4.
Tel 0892 681 650.
www.foliesbergere.com

Lido
116 bis Ave des Champs-Elysées 75008.
Map 4 E4.
Tel 01 40 76 56 10.
www.lido.fr

Moulin Rouge
82 Blvd de Clichy 75018.
Map 6 E1.
Tel 01 53 09 82 82.
www.moulinrouge.fr

Paradis Latin
28 Rue du Cardinal Lemoine 75005.
Map 13 B5. Tel 01 43 25 28 28

Classical Music

The music scene in Paris has never been so busy and exciting. Government spending has ensured that there are many first-class venues with an excellent range of opera, and classical and contemporary music productions. There are also numerous concerts in churches and many music festivals.

Information about what's on is listed in *Pariscope* and *L'Officiel des Spectacles*. A free monthly listing of musical events is given out at most concert halls. Also, try the Office du Tourisme in the Rue des Pyramides (*see pp340–41*) for details of many free and open-air classical music performances.

OPERA

Opera lovers will find themselves well catered for, with many productions mounted at the Bastille and the beautifully renovated **Opéra National de Paris Garnier**. Opera is also an important part of the programming at the Théâtre du Châtelet, as well as being produced intermittently by a variety of small organizations, and there are occasional large-scale lavish productions at the **Palais Omnisports de Bercy** or POB (*see p359*).

The Opéra de Paris's ultramodern home is the **Opéra National de Paris Bastille** (*see p98*), where performances have finally begun to make full use of the house's mindboggling array of high-tech stage mechanisms. There are 2,700 seats, all with a good view of the stage, and the accoustics are excellent.

Productions feature classic and modern operas, and its interpretations are often avant-garde: Philippe Mamoury's *K..*; Bob Wilson's production of *The Magic Flute*, done in the style of Japanese Noh, with some of the cast delivering their lines while balancing on one leg; Messiaen's *St Francis of Assisi*, with video screens and neon added to bring the story up to date. At Thursday lunchtimes they also offer free concerts, lectures and films as part of a programme known as *Casse-Croûte à l'Opéra*.

There are also occasional dance performances, when the Bastille plays host to the ballet company from the Opéra National de Paris Garnier (*see p217*). The house includes two smaller spaces, the **Auditorium** (500 seats) and the **Studio** (200 seats) for smaller-scale events connected to the current productions on the main stages here and at the Opera Garnier.

The **Opéra Comique** (also known as the Salle Favart), now run by Jérôme Savary, no longer has opera, but stages a wide range of eccentric, lightweight productions, including some popular music-hall-style work and operetta. Savary is also behind several large-scale musicals at the Palais des Congrès exhibition space and some municipal events (such as a public ball held to celebrate the 50th anniversary of the liberation of Paris.)

CONCERTS

Paris is the home of three major symphony orchestras, and a good half-dozen other orchestras; it is also a major venue for touring European and American orchestras. Chamber music is also flourishing, either as part of the programming of the major venues, or in smaller halls and churches.

The **Salle Pleyel** is Paris's principal concert hall. After extensive renovation, it has become part of the Cité de la Musique and now houses the Orchestre de Paris, directed by Christoph Eschenbach, as well as Radio France's Philharmonic Orchestra, led by Myung-Whun Chung. Guest orchestras and jazz and world-music ensembles complete the concert season, which tends to run from September to July. Over the next few years, the Salle's owner will invest a further 23 million euros in the refurbishment of the hall (in lieu of tax payments); then, in 2056, this legendary concert hall will become property of the French state.

The **Théâtre du Châtelet** has become one of the city's principal venues for all kinds of concerts, opera and dance. The high-quality programme includes opera classics from Mozart's *Così fan tutte* to Verdi's *La Traviata*, and more modern works, such as Boessman's *Contes d'Hiver*, and occasional concerts by international opera stars. Great attention is also devoted to 20th-century music here, and throughout the season there are lunchtime concerts and recitals in the foyer.

The beautiful Art Deco **Théâtre des Champs-Elysées** is a celebrated classical music venue which also produces some opera and dance. Radio-France is part-owner of the theatre, and its Orchestre National de France gives concerts here, as do many touring orchestras and soloists. The Orchestre des Champs-Elysées, directed by Philippe Herreweghe, is in residence here, and gives period-instrument performances.

Radio-France is the biggest single concert organizer in Paris, with a musical force that includes two major symphony orchestras: the Orchestre National de France and the Orchestre Philharmonique. Many of its concerts are given in Paris's other concert halls, but the **Maison de Radio-France** has a large hall and several smaller studios that are used for concerts and broadcasts open to the public (*see p202, Musée de Radio France*).

The **Cité de la Musique** is a massive cultural centre devoted entirely to music – of all genres and from all eras. Classical music features heavily on its programme, with lots of chamber music and recitals, as well as more ambitious orchestral concerts.

The **Auditorium du Louvre** was built as part of the ongoing expansion of the Louvre (see pp122–9) and it is used mostly for chamber music recitals. The Musée d'Orsay's (see pp144–7) **Auditorium du Musée d'Orsay** is a medium-sized auditorium, with an active concert programme. Concerts are usually held once or twice a week, and prices vary.

Other museums often hold concerts as part of an exhibition theme – such as troubadours at the Musée National du Moyen Age (see p154–7) – so do check the listings magazines.

The Musique à la Sorbonne holds a concert series in the **Grand Amphithéâtre de la Sorbonne** and the **Amphithéâtre Richelieu de la Sorbonne**. Productions have included the Slavonic Music festival, featuring the works of East European composers.

Occasionally concerts are given in the **Conservatoire d'Art Dramatique**, where Beethoven was introduced to Paris audiences in 1828 and where Hector Berlioz's major work, *La Symphonie Fantastique*, was first performed. Otherwise, it's not usually open to public.

CONTEMPORARY MUSIC

Contemporary music in Paris has a high profile and is definitely alive and kicking. Although no longer at the head of any orchestra, Pierre Boulez is still a major figure in the capital's contemporary music scene. Jonathan Nott now directs the experimental Ensemble InterContemporain, which is lavishly supported by the French state in its home at the Cité de la Musique (see pp234–5). **IRCAM**, the vast laboratory of "digital signal processing" underneath the Pompidou Centre, is still the envy of the world, architecturally at least. Musically, it is beginning to live up to its promise.

Other bright stars among the many talented composers include Pascal Dusapin, Philippe Fénelon, George Benjamin and Philippe

Manoury, as well as Georges Aperghis, who specializes in musical theatre.

The fabulously designed **Cité de la Musique** complex at Parc de la Villette includes both a spectacularly domed *salle de concerts* surrounded by a glass-roofed arcade, and the **Conservatoire National de Musique** with its opera theatre and two small concert halls. The Chamber Orchestra of Europe is in residence here. Both venues are used for regular performances, including jazz, ethnic and contemporary music, as well as *chansons* and early music.

For details either phone the venue concerned or consult the listings magazines. For those interested in contemporary music, the quarterly magazine *Résonance* is published by IRCAM at the Pompidou Centre.

FESTIVALS

Some of the most important music festivals are the result of the work of the **Festival d'Automne à Paris**, which acts as a behind-the-scenes stimulator, commissioning new works, subsidizing others and in general enlivening the Parisian musical, dance and theatrical scene from September to December.

The **Festival St-Denis** running throughout June and July holds concerts, with an emphasis on choral works. Most performances are given in the Basilique St-Denis.

The **Musique Baroque au Château de Versailles**, from around the middle of September to the middle of October, is an offshoot of the Baroque Music Centre, founded in Versailles in 1988. Operas, concerts, recitals, chamber music, dance and theatre are on offer in the fabulous surroundings of Versailles (see pp248–53).

Other interesting festivals include the Chopin festival, held in the Orangerie in the Bois de Boulogne from mid-June to mid-July, and the Quartier d'Eté festival, which host a series of outdoor classical music concerts. For tickets, it is

usually necessary to go to the theatre box office or venue concerned, though some festivals may run an advance postal booking service.

CHURCHES

Music is everywhere in Paris's churches, in the form of classical concerts, organ recitals or religious services. The most outstanding churches which hold regular concerts include **La Madeleine** (see p216), **St-Germain-des-Prés** (see p138), **St-Julien-le-Pauvre** (see p152) and **St-Roch** (see p121). Music is also performed in the **Eglise des Billettes**, **St-Sulpice** (see p172), **St-Gervais–St-Protais** (see p99), **Notre-Dame** (see pp82–5), **St-Louis-en-l'Ile** (see p87) and **Sainte-Chapelle** (see pp88–9).

A great proportion, but not all, of these concerts are free. If you have any difficulty contacting the church in question, try the Office du Tourisme for information (see pp340–41).

EARLY MUSIC

A number of early-music ensembles have taken up residence in Paris. The Chapelle Royale gives a concert series at the **Théâtre des Champs-Elysées** with programmes ranging from Renaissance vocal music to Mozart. Their enchanting sacred music concerts (look out for Bach cantatas) take place at **Notre-Dame-des-Blancs-Manteaux** (see p102).

Baroque opera is more the domain of Les Arts Florissants, founded and directed by American-born William Christie, who perform French and Italian operas from Rossi to Rameau, and Les Musiciens du Louvre, directed by Marc Minkowski. Both companies perform regularly at the Théâtre du Châtelet and the Opera National Garnier. The **Théâtre de la Ville** is also an excellent venue in which to hear Baroque chamber music, as is the pretty **Eglise Saint-Germain l'Auxerrois**.

BOOKING TICKETS

For tickets, it's always best to deal directly with the relevant box office. Booking tickets at the main venues is possible by post up to two months before the performance and by telephone two weeks to a month in advance. If you want a good seat, it's best to book in advance as tickets tend to sell quickly. Last-minute tickets may also be available at the box office, and certain venues, such as the Opéra National de Paris Bastille, keep some tickets for the cheaper seats aside for the purpose. Ticket agents, notably in the **FNAC** stores *(see p341)*, and a good hotel concierge can also help. These agencies accept credit card bookings – a useful service as not all venues are guaranteed to accept them.

Half-price tickets on the day of performance can be bought at the **Kiosque Théâtre** *(see p341)* which is found in the Place de la Madeleine and also at the RER station at Parvis de la Gare Montparnasse. However, these agencies usually only deal for performances taking place at private theatres.

Note, however, that many theatres and concert halls may be closed during the holiday season in August, so inquire first to avoid disappointment.

TICKET PRICES

Ticket prices can range from 8€–85€ for the Opéra de Paris Bastille and the principal classical music venues, and from 5€–25€ for the smaller halls and concerts in churches around the city, such as Sainte-Chapelle.

DIRECTORY

CLASSICAL MUSIC VENUES

Amphithéâtre Richelieu de la Sorbonne
17 Rue de la Sorbonne 75005.
Map 12 F5.
Tel 01 42 62 71 71.

Auditorium
See Opéra National de Paris Bastille.

Auditorium du Louvre
Musée du Louvre, Rue de Rivoli 75001.
Map 12 E2.
Tel 01 40 20 84 00.

Auditorium du Musée d'Orsay
102 Rue de Lille 75007.
Map 12 D2.
Tel 01 40 49 49 66.

Centre de Musique Baroque de Versailles
22 Ave de Paris, Versailles.
Tel 01 39 20 78 10.

Cité de la Musique
Parc de La Villette, 221 Ave Jean-Jaurès 75019.
Tel 01 44 84 44 84.
www.cite-musique.fr

Conservatoire d'Art Dramatique
2 bis Rue du Conservatoire 75009. **Map** 7 A4.
Tel 01 42 46 12 91.

Eglise des Billettes
24 Rue des Archives 75004. **Map** 13 C2.
Tel 01 42 72 37 08.

Eglise St-Germain l'Auxerrois
2 Place du Louvre 75001.
Map 12 F2
Tel 01 42 60 13 96.

Festival d'Automne
156 Rue de Rivoli 75001.
Map 12 F2 5
Tel 01 53 45 17 00.

Festival Chopin
Orangerie de Bagatelle Bois de Boulogne 75016.
Map 3 A4.
Tel 01 45 00 22 19.

Grand Amphi-théâtre de la Sorbonne
45 Rue des Ecoles 75005.
Map 13 A5.
Tel 01 42 62 71 71.

IRCAM
1 Pl Igor Stravinsky 75004.
Map 13 B2.
Tel 01 44 78 48 43.

La Madeleine
Pl de la Madeleine 75008.
Map 5 C5.
Tel 01 42 50 96 18.

Maison de Radio-France
116 Ave du Président-Kennedy 75016.
Map 9 B4.
Tel 01 42 20 42 20.

Notre-Dame
Pl du Parvis-Notre-Dame 75004.
Map 13 A4.
Tel 01 42 34 56 10.

Notre-Dame-des-Blancs-Manteaux
12 Rue des Blancs-Manteaux 75004.
Map 13 C3.
Tel 01 42 72 09 37.

Opéra Comique
(Salle Favart) 5 Rue Favart 75002.
Map 6 F5.
Tel 08 25 00 00 58.

Opéra National de Paris Bastille
120 Rue de Lyon 75012.
Map 14 E4.
Tel 08 92 89 90 90.
www.operadeparis.fr

Opéra National de Paris Garnier
Place de l'Opéra 75009.
Map 6 E4.
Tel 08 92 89 90 90.

Pompidou Centre
19 Rue Beaubourg 75004.
Map 13 B2.
Tel 01 44 78 12 33.

Quartier d'Eté Festival
Various venues.
Tel 01 44 94 98 00.

Sainte-Chapelle
4 Blvd du Palais.
Map 13 A3.
Tel 01 53 73 78 50.

St-Germain-des-Prés
Pl St-Germain-des-Prés 75006.
Map 12 E4.
Tel 01 55 42 81 33.

St-Gervais– St-Protais
Pl St-Gervais 75004.
Map 13 B3.
Tel 01 48 87 32 02.

St-Julien-le-Pauvre
1 Rue St-Julien-le-Pauvre 75005. **Map** 13 A4.
Tel 01 42 26 00 00.

St-Louis-en-l'Ile
19 bis Rue St-Louis-en-l'Ile 75004. **Map** 13 C5.
Tel 01 46 34 11 60.

St-Roch
296 Rue St-Honoré 75001.
Map 12 D1.
Tel 01 42 44 13 20.

St-Sulpice
Pl St-Sulpice 75006.
Map 12 E4.
Tel 01 46 33 21 78.

Salle Pleyel
252 Rue du Faubourg St-Honoré 75008. **Map** 4 E3.
Tel 01 42 56 13 13.
www.sallepleyel.fr

Studio
See Opéra National de Paris Bastille.

Théâtre de la Ville
2 Pl du Châtelet 75004.
Map 13 A3.
Tel 01 42 74 22 77.

Théâtre des Champs-Élysées
15 Ave Montaigne 75008.
Map 10 F1.
Tel 01 49 52 50 50.

Théâtre du Châtelet
1 Pl du Châtelet 75001.
Map 13 A3. *Tel 01 40 28 28 40.*

Dance

When it comes to dance, Paris is more a cultural crossroads than a cultural centre. Due to a deliberate government policy of decentralization, many of the top French dance companies are based in the provinces, although they frequently visit the capital. In addition, the greatest dance companies from all over the world perform here. Paris has a well-deserved reputation as a centre of excellence for modern and experimental dance, and has numerous workshops and places in which to learn its many forms.

CLASSICAL BALLET

The opulent **Opéra National de Paris Garnier** (see p217) is the home of the Ballet de l'Opéra de Paris, which is earning a reputation as one of the world's best classical dance companies.

Since the Opéra National de Paris Bastille opened in 1989, the Opéra National de Paris Garnier has been used almost exclusively for dance. It is one of the largest theatres in Europe, with performance space for 450 artists and a seating capacity of 2,200.

Modern dance companies such as the Martha Graham Company, Paul Taylor, Merce Cunningham, Alvin Ailey, Jerome Robbins and Roland Petit's Ballet de Marseille also regularly perform here.

The Opéra National de Paris Garnier, extensively restored both inside and out, now shares operatic productions with the **Opéra National de Paris Bastille**.

MODERN DANCE

Government support has helped the **Théâtre de la Ville** (once run by Sarah Bernhardt) to become Paris's most important venue for modern dance, with subsidies keeping ticket costs relatively low. Through performances at the Théâtre de la Ville, modern choreographers such as Jean-Claude Gallotta, Regine Chopinot, Maguy Marin and Anne Teresa de Keersmaeker have gained international recognition. Here you may also see troupes such as Pina Bausch's Wuppertal Dance Theatre, whose tormented, existential choreography may not be to everyone's taste, but is always popular with Parisian audiences.

Music performances also run throughout the season and include chamber music, recitals, world music and jazz.

The **Maison des Arts de Créteil** presents some of the most interesting dance works in Paris. It is located in the Paris suburb of Créteil, where the local council gives strong support to dance. Créteil's company choreographer, Maguy Marin, has won consistent praise for her darkly expressive work.

The Maison des Arts also brings in such innovative companies as the Sydney Ballet, and the Kirov from St Petersburg, which is more inclined towards the classical.

Set amid the opulent *couture* shops and embassies, the elegant Art Deco **Théâtre des Champs-Élysées** has 1,900 seats. It is frequented by an upmarket audience who watch major international companies perform here. It was here that Nijinsky first danced Stravinsky's iconoclastic *The Rite of Spring*, which led to rioting among the audience.

The theatre is more famous as a classical music venue, but recent visitors have included the Harlem Dance Company and London's Royal Ballet, and it is here that Mikhail Baryshnikov and American choreographer Mark Morris perform when they are in Paris. It also sponsors the popular *Géants de la Danse* series, an evening-length sampling of international ballet. The lovely old **Théâtre du**

Châtelet is a renowned opera and classical music venue, but it is also host to international contemporary dance companies such as the Tokyo Ballet and the Birmingham Royal Ballet.

Experimental dance companies perform in the **Théâtre de la Bastille**, where innovative theatre is also staged. Many directors and companies start here, then go on to international fame.

New companies to look out for include La P'tit Cie and L'Esquisse, but they have no fixed venue.

EVENTS LISTINGS

To find out what's on, read the inexpensive weekly entertainment guides *Pariscope* and *L'Officiel des Spectacles*. Posters advertising dance performances are widely displayed in the metro and on the streets, especially on the green advertisement columns, the *colonnes Morris*.

TICKET PRICES

Expect to pay 10€–100€ for tickets to the Opéra de Paris Garnier (5€–60€ for a ballet), 6€–75€ for the Théâtre des Champs-Élysées, and anything from 9€–30€ for other venues.

DANCE VENUES

Maison des Arts et de la Culture de Créteil
Pl Salvador Allende 94000 Créteil.
Tel 01 45 13 19 19.

Opéra National de Paris Garnier
See pp216–7.

Opéra National de Paris Bastille See p98.

Théâtre de la Bastille
76 Rue de la Roquette 75011.
Map 14 F3.
Tel 01 43 57 42 14.

Théâtre de la Ville
See p334.

Théâtre des Champs-Elysées
See p334.

Théâtre du Châtelet
See p334.

Rock, Jazz and World Music

Music lovers will find every imaginable form of music in Paris and its environs, from international pop stars in major venues to buskers of varying degrees of talent in the metro. There's a huge variety of styles on offer, with reggae, hip-hop, world music, blues, folk, rock and jazz – Paris is said to be second only to New York in the number of jazz clubs and jazz recordings and there is always an excellent selection of bands and solo performers.

On the summer solstice (21 June) each year, the Fête de la Musique takes place, when anyone can play any form of music, anywhere, without a licence, and when the whole city parties all night. Ears may be assailed by a heavy metal rock band or lulled by an accordionist playing traditional French songs.

For complete listings of what's happening, buy *Pariscope* (published every Wednesday) at any kiosk. For jazz fans there's the monthly *Jazz* magazine for schedules and in-depth reviews.

MAJOR VENUES

The top international acts are often at the enormous arenas: **Palais Omnisports** at Bercy, **Stade de France** at St-Denis or the **Zénith**. Other venues such as the legendary *chanson* centre of the universe, the **Olympia**, or the **Grand Rex** (also a cinema), have assigned seating and a more intimate atmosphere. They host everyone from bewigged and cosmetically enhanced iconic first ladies of country to acid jazz stars. (*See* Directories *p350 & p359*).

ROCK AND POP

Until recently, Paris's indigenous rock groups (Les Négresses Vertes are probably the best-known, and are still going strong) drew foreign attention precisely because they were French. For too long, Paris pop meant Johnny Hallyday and insipid covers of US and UK hits, or Serge Gainsbourg and his brand of faintly naughty decadence. Paris rock traditionally (and deservedly) attracted either patronizing praise or outright mockery.

That is no longer the case. The international success of the groups Daft Punk and Air and the contribution to the music scene of producer, songwriter and musician Bertrand Burgalat have led to a growth in confidence in the local music scene. The phrase French Touch often describes hip producers, writers or singers, now in demand all over the world. Banlieue- (suburb-) based rap, raï and reggae no longer sound like French versions of imported forms, instead they now have their own identity.

There is no shortage of gigs. The latest bands usually play at **La Cigale** and its downstairs den of din, **La Boule Noire**, the **Divan du Monde** and the **Elysée-Montmartre**, while the **Bataclan** and the **Rex** club are the best places for R&B. The **Olympia** is the city's most famous rock venue, attracting top acts. Many nightclubs also double up as live music venues (*see pp351–3*).

JAZZ

Paris is still jazz-crazy. Many American musicians have made the French capital their home because of its receptive atmosphere. All styles, from free-form to Dixieland and swing, and even hip-hop-jazz crossover, are on offer. Clubs range from quasi-concert halls to piano bars and pub-like venues. One of the most popular places, though not the most comfortable, is the **New Morning**. It's hot and smoky, and the table service can be a little erratic, but all the great jazz musicians continue to perform here, as they have in the past. Arrive early to ensure a good seat. **Le Duc des Lombards** is a lively jazz club in Les Halles, which also features salsa.

Many jazz clubs are also cafés, bars or restaurants. The latter includes the intimate **Bilboquet**, with its Belle Epoque interior. This stylish place is favoured by film stars. Dining might not be a requirement, but it's always wise to check first.

Other hotspots are **Le Petit Journal Montparnasse** for modern jazz, **Le Petit Journal St-Michel** for Dixieland and the **Sunset**. A trendy crowd is drawn to the **7 Lézards**, in the Marais. **Caveau de la Huchette** looks like the archetypal jazz joint, but today it favours swing and big-band music, and is popular with students. The **Caveau des Oubliettes** has a growing reputation for cutting-edge jazz.

For a change, try the local talent at small, friendly bars such as the less expensive **Bistrot d'Eustache**, or the trendy **China Club**, with its 1940s *film noir* decor. The **Jazz-Club Lionel Hampton** in the Méridien hotel is a well-respected venue which features Sunday jazz brunch. On the other side of town, the renovated **Trabendo** has an intriguing mix of up-and-comers and down-and-outers.

Paris does not neglect blues fans either. The **Quai du Blues** is the best-known haunt, hosting concerts by established performers.

Paris has two international jazz festivals in summer: the Paris Jazz Festival (*see p63*) which is the mainstay of the summer calendar, and the JVC Halle That Jazz at the **Grande Halle de la Villette** in July, with films on jazz, debates and discussions and *boeufs* (jam sessions).

WORLD MUSIC

With its large populations from West Africa and the countries of the Maghreb, the Antilles and Latin America, Paris is a natural centre for world music. The **Chapelle des Lombards** has played host to top acts; it also has jazz, salsa and Brazilian music. **Aux Trois Maillets** is a medieval cellar with everything from blues to tango and rock and roll covers, while **Kibélé** is a great place for North African sounds. Many jazz clubs intersperse their programmes with ethnic music. These include **New Morning**, which also has shows with South American artists, and **Baiser Salé**, for popular acts including Makossa, Kassav, Malavoi and Manu Dibango.

World music in a stunning setting can be found at the Institut du Monde Arabe, a wonderful architectural feat (see p164) which draws stars from the Arab music world to its concert hall.

TICKET PRICES

Prices at jazz clubs can be steep, and there may be a cover charge of over 15€ at the door, which usually includes the first drink. If there is no cover charge, the drinks will be expensive and at least one must be bought.

Tickets can be bought from FNAC outlets and Virgin Megastore (see p341), or directly from venue box offices and at the door of the clubs themselves.

DIRECTORY

MAJOR VENUES

Grand Rex
1 Blvd Poissonnière 75002.
Map 7 A5.
Tel 01 42 36 56 91.

Olympia
28 Blvd des
Capucines 75009.
Map 6 D5.
Tel 08 92 68 33 68.
www.olympiahall.com

**Palais Omnisports
de Paris-Bercy**
8 Blvd de Bercy 75012.
Map 18 F2.
Tel 08 92 39 04 90.
www.bercy.fr

Zénith
211 Ave de Jean-Jaurès
75019. **Tel** 08 90 71 02
07. **www**.le-zenith.com/
paris

ROCK AND POP

Bataclan
50 Blvd Voltaire
75011.
Map 14 E1.
Tel 01 43 14 00 30.

**La Cigale/
La Boule Noire**
120 Blvd Rochechouart
75018.
Map 6 F2.
Tel 01 49 25 81 75.

Divan du Monde
75 Rue des Martyrs 75018.
Map 6 F2.
Tel 01 42 52 02 46.

Elysée-Montmartre
72 Blvd Rochechouart
75018. **Map** 6 F2.
Tel 01 44 92 45 36.

Rex Club
5 Blvd Poissonnière 75002.
Map 7 A5.
Tel 01 42 36 83 93.

JAZZ

Baiser Salé
58 Rue des Lombards
75001.
Map 13 A2.
Tel 01 42 33 37 71.

Bilboquet
13 Rue St-Benoît 75006.
Map 12 E3.
Tel 01 45 48 81 84.

Bistrot d'Eustache
37 Rue Berger, Carré des
Halles 75001.
Map 13 A2.
Tel 01 40 26 23 20.

**Caveau de la
Huchette**
5 Rue de la Huchette
75005.
Map 13 A4.
Tel 01 43 26 65 05.

**Caveau des
Oubliettes**
52 Rue Galande 75005.
Map 13 A4.
Tel 01 46 34 23 09.

China Club
50 Rue de Charenton
75012. **Map** 14 F5.
Tel 01 43 43 82 02.

**Le Duc des
Lombards**
42 Rue des Lombards
75001.
Map 13 A2.
Tel 01 42 33 22 88.

**La Grande Halle
de la Villette**
211 Ave Jean-Jaurès
75019.
Map 8 F1
Tel 01 40 03 75 75.

**Jazz-Club Lionel
Hampton**
Hôtel Méridien,
81 Blvd Gouvion-St-Cyr
75017.
Map 3 C3.
Tel 01 40 68 34 34.
www.jazzclub-paris.com

New Morning
7–9 Rue des
Petites-Écuries
75010.
Map 7 B4.
Tel 01 45 23 51 41.

Paris Jazz Festival
Parc Floral Bois de
Vincennes 75012.
www.
parisjazzfestival2008.com

**Le Petit Journal
Montparnasse**
13 Rue du Commandant-
Mouchotte
75014.
Map 15 C2.
Tel 01 43 21 56 70.

**Le Petit Journal
St-Michel**
71 Blvd St-Michel
75005.
Map 16 F1.
Tel 01 43 26 28 59.

7 Lézards
10 Rue des Rosiers
75004.
Map 13 C3.
Tel 01 48 87 08 97.

Sunset
60 Rue des Lombards
75001.
Map 13 A2.
Tel 01 40 26 46 60.

Trabendo
211 Ave Jean-Jaurès
75019.
Map 8 F1.
Tel 01 42 01 12 12.

WORLD MUSIC

Aux Trois Maillets
56 Rue Galande
75005.
Map 13 A4.
Tel 01 43 54 42 94.

Baiser Salé
See Jazz.

**Chapelle des
Lombards**
19 Rue de Lappe
75011. **Map** 14 F4.
Tel 01 43 57 24 26.

**Institut du
Monde Arabe**
See p164.

Kibélé
12 Rue de l'Echiquier
75010. **Map** 7 B5.
Tel 01 48 24 57 74.

New Morning
7 Rue des Petites-Ecuries
75010.
Map 7 B4
Tel 01 45 23 51 41

Quai du Blues
17 Blvd Vital-Bouhot
92200.
Neuilly sur Seine.
Tel 01 46 24 22 00.
www.quaidublues.com

Nightclubs

The club scene in Paris is now somewhat under siege as government legislation on noise levels slightly hampers establishments' *modus operandi*. The city council is waging war on noise pollution and whilst this suits those with neighbours who possess large stereos, it's bad news for people who like to dance till dawn. They carry on regardless, albeit with fewer decibels, and you will still find every type of sound (and a great deal of creativity) on the club scene. There are clubs to suit every taste and it's worth noting that bouncers often treat foreign would-be entrants preferentially, so be sure to stand proud, ditch the attempts at French and speak English when you get near the door. The English website www.gogoparis. com reviews some of the capital's trendiest establishments. Alternatively, read the posters at the Bastille metro station or listen to Radio NOVA 101.5 FM, which gives details of the night's best raves. Flyers advertising what's on at which clubs can be found on café, bar and shop counters. Popular nighttime options for the more mature set include ballroom dancing and visits to suave piano bars. If you're wondering about what to wear, the smart side of the smart-casual approach is usually the safest bet. Attire for nightclubs varies; for upscale venues be sure to put your designer-labelled best foot forward, whilst more relaxed ones will accept an urban look, but generally, tracksuits, jeans and trainers are definite no-nos.

MAINSTREAM

A vast yet convivial venue, **Le Bataclan** is a showcase for current bands. After the show on Saturday nights, it becomes one of the best nightclubs in Paris, legendary for its mouth-watering choice of funk, soul and new jack swing.

Les Etoiles gives salsa lessons, while the inexpensive **La Scala** attracts a large, young crowd, and has recently played host to ultra-fashionable party producers la Johnson. Linked to the **Alcazar**, which is a fashionable Terence Conran bar and restaurant very popular with a pre-club crowd, **WAGG** just next door is a wonderful spot for some uninhibited dancing. WAGG is unpretentious although the door staff are discriminating, and the disco and soul played in the stone cellars make for a great night out.

Les Bains-Douches, a former Turkish bath, may have lost some of its glitterati appeal but it is still a place to go to be seen. Its upstairs restaurant, now serving Thai food, is a popular place for private dinner parties. This is the place to be, so book a table for dinner if you're concerned about gaining entry and getting a much-coveted seat. The dance floor is tiny and music is mainly house, with 1970s and 80s disco on Mondays, and R&B on Wednesdays. Gay night is *Café con Leche* on Sundays. Legendary promoters and Parisian nightowls David and Cathy Guetta left Les Bains a while ago and took some of their regulars with them, but the club is still a flash place to be and there is always the possibility of spotting a film star. A mix of ages and trends frequent the **Rex Club**. Despite the essentially conservative nature of the clientele, the music on different nights ranges from glam rock and house to "exotique" – funk, reggae and world music. Sounds are mainly rock and roll at the smart and non-ageist **Zed Club**. The vast **La Loco** caters to mainstream tastes most nights, with rock, house, groove and dance music each occupying a different floor.

Utterly unpretentious, **Club Med World** is the place to go for 1980s classics and unselfconscious dancing.

EXCLUSIVE

Being rich, beautiful and famous may not be enough to get you into **Castel's**, but it could help. It is a strictly private club and the happy few who make it, dine in one of two very good restaurants before heading down to the dance floor.

Regine's is mostly full of besuited executives and wealthy foreigners who dine and dance to the easy-listening music. However, it is now enjoying something of a renaissance, especially on ladies nights, when a trained physiognomist picks out only the best looking women to come in for a girls-own session for a few hours, complete with male strip show. Predictably, when the doors open to men later in the evening, it becomes one of Paris's top nightspots for seeing and being seen.

The wood-panelled, cosy **Ritz Club** in the legendary Ritz hotel is open only to members and hotel guests, though the chic and elegant are welcome. The ambience is upmarket and the music makes for easy listening. A younger, glamorous set have recently begun to make the Ritz Club their home, attracted, no doubt, by its old-fashioned star quality.

La Suite is currently one of the hardest places to get into in Paris. Run by the Guettas formerly of Les Bains, the smooth decor sets off the expensive tans sported by the jetsetters, supermodels and film stars who come here. Booking a table at the expensive, but decent, restaurant is a good way to ensure access. Equally, posh, **Le VIP** is populated by wannabes attracted by the name. Private parties are often held here, so it's a good idea to call ahead.

Showcase is the latest event on Paris's night-scene with over 3,000 square metres of space below the Pont Alexandre III. It triples as a bar, nightclub and concert hall. Another extremely upscale spot is **L'Etoile** situated near the Arc de Triomphe. Be prepared to make the effort to look your best (and most-solvent) to get in here.

The most popular of the posh clubs and the most laid-back and friendly once you're inside, is **Le Cab** (formerly known as Cabaret). The interior has recently been redesigned by Ora Ito, and today, anybody who's any-body comes here to dance like crazy or lay back and take it all in on one of the sumptuous mattresses in the chillout area.

TRENDY

Once a working-class music hall frequented by famous Parisians Edith Piaf and Jean Gabin, **Balajo** has now gone upmarket although it still emits a friendly vibe and remains one of the best clubs in Paris for dancing; they even hold ballroom dancing nights. It's also one of the few clubs open on Mondays.

An ultra-hip young crowd (and a few drag queens) flock to the small and cosy **Folie's Clubbing**, one-time strip joint and present-day venue for live music. Its original theme nights make for some of the best fun clubbing around. For a top dancing night out, try the fortnightly "Bal" with live big band at the **Elysée Montmartre**. Here too, look out for "Return to the Source", Goa-trance nights that come all the way from London's Fridge.

Paris's trendy clubs seem to have a longer shelf-life than those in some other cities and another hip venue that's still going strong is **Le**

Gibus which offers different dance styles throughout the week. Check the flyers to pick your own style of party.

The **Batofar**, the scarlet lighthouse ship moored on the Seine in the 13th arrondissement, is now a mainstay of the Paris club scene. The music here varies from underground techno to reggae depending on the night of the week, but the crowd are always friendly and relaxed. In the summer, try not to miss their wonderfully chilled-out afternoon sessions on the quayside.

The **Nouveau Casino** behind the ever trendy Café Charbon (see p319) in Oberkampf pulls in an eclectic crowd for events varying from dub to air-guitar competitions. Newcomer **Le Triptyque** has made an impressive mark on the Paris club scene with its mixed programming and excellent live music agenda.

Old-timer **La Flèche d'Or** also offers an eclectic array of concerts, DJ nights and concept evenings. Whilst if it's just a large dance floor that's needed, then **Mix Club** should suffice.

WORLD MUSIC

A stylish and expensive African-Antillean club, **Keur Samba** is popular with the jetset. Things get going after 2am and last long into the night. **Le Casbah** is exclusive, jazzy and one of the best established venues on the Paris club scene. Its African-Middle Eastern decor has always been a magnet for models and trendies who, in between dances, do a little nocturnal shopping in the club's downstairs boutique. Le Casbah is currently enjoying something of a renaissance of its 'chicest of the chic' reputation.

If your nervous system responds favourably to the heaving rhythms and throbbing beat of authentic Latin music, you should head for **La Java**, which combines glorious sounds with the

quaint appeal of a Belleville dance hall. **Les Etoiles** definitely is the place to go for salsa with soul. **Mood** on the other hand, is a more upmarket venue with a distinctive Japanese theme. Other lively world music nights are held at **Trottoirs de Buenos-Aires**, **Chapelle des Lombards** and the cellar bar at **Aux Trois Maillets** (see Rock, Jazz and World Music pp349–50).

GAY AND LESBIAN

The gay scene in Paris is thriving. **Le Queen** boasts a great line-up of DJs. Monday is disco night, Friday and Saturday are garage and soul and the rest of the week is drum and bass and house. Some of the raunchier events are men-only. Girls should go with pretty boys. Some nights at **La Locomotive** draw in a gay crowd. **Le Champmeslé**, one of the most venerable fixtures of Paris's ever more upfront and confi-dent lesbian scene, continues to evolve and attract a new clientele. **Pulp** is the city's biggest and best lesbian club. Men are admitted in the week, but the weekend is strictly for ladies. For a pre-club venue, lesbian bar **Le Troisième Lieu** is the hippest and busiest. **Le Day Off** is a favourite haunt for afterwork drinks. Scream is the gay night at the **Elysée Montmartre**. **Le Depôt** is rumoured to be one of the most fun gay clubs in Paris, with a much-talked about backroom. Their Gay Tea Dance, held every Sunday, is legendary.

ADMISSION CHARGES

Some clubs are strictly private, others have a more generous admission policy. Prices can range from 12€ to 15€ or 30€, or more, and may be higher after midnight and on week-ends. But quite often there are concessions for women.

In general, one drink (une consommation) is included in the entry price; thereafter it can become an extremely expensive evening.

DIRECTORY

DISCO AND CLUB VENUES

Alcazar
62 Rue Mazarine 75006.
Map 12 F4.
Tel 01 53 10 19 99.

Les Bains-Douches
7 Rue du Bourg-
L'Abbé 75003.
Map 13 B1.
Tel 01 48 87 01 80.

Balajo
9 Rue de Lappe 75011.
Map 14 E4.
Tel 01 47 00 07 87.

Le Bataclan
50 blvd Voltaire 75011.
Map 13 E1.
Tel 01 43 14 35 35.

Batofar
Moored opposite 11
Quai Francois Mauriac
75013.
Tel 01 56 29 10 00.

Le Cab
2 Pl de Palais Royal
75001.
Map 12 E1.
Tel 01 58 62 56 25.

Le Cabaret Milliardaire
68 rue Pierre Charon
75008.
Map 4 F5.
Tel 01 42 89 44 14.

Castel's
15 Rue Princesse 75006.
Map 12 E4.
Tel 01 40 51 52 80.

Club Med World
39 Cour St-Emilion
75012.
Tel 08 10 81 04 10.

Dancing de la Coupole
102 Boulevard
Montparnasse 75014.
Map 15 C1
Tel 01 43 27 56 00.

Le Duplex
2 Bis Avenue Foch 75116.
Map 4 D4.
Tel 01 45 00 45 00.
www.leduplex.fr

Elysée Montmartre
72 Blvd Rochechouart
75018.
Map 6 F2.
Tel 01 44 92 45 36.

L'Etoile
12 Rue de Presbourg
75016.
Map 4 D4.
Tel 01 45 00 78 70.

Les Etoiles
61 Rue du Château d'Eau
75010.
Map 7 C5.
Tel 01 47 70 60 56.
www.etoiles-salsa.com

La Flèche d'Or
102 bis Rue de Bagnolet
75002.
Tel 01 44 64 01 02.
www.flechedor.fr

Folie's Clubbing
11 Pl Pigalle 75009.
Map 6 E2.
Tel 01 48 78 63 56.

Le Gibus
18 Rue du Faubourg-du-
Temple 75011.
Map 8 E15.
Tel 01 47 00 78 88.

Hammam Club
94 Rue d'Amsterdam
75009.
Map 6 D2.
Tel 01 55 07 80 00.

La Locomotive
90 Blvd de Clichy 75018.
Map 4 E4.
Tel 01 53 41 88 88.

Mix Club
24 Rue de l'Arrivée 75015.
Map 15 C1.
Tel 01 56 80 37 37.

Nouveau Casino
109 Rue Oberkampf
75011. **Map** 14 E1.
Tel 01 43 57 57 40.

Les Planches
40 Rue Colisée 75008.
Map 5 A4.
Tel 01 42 25 11 68.

Pulp
25 Blvd Poissonière
75002.
Map 7 A5.
Tel 01 40 26 01 93.

Regine's
49–51 Rue Ponthieu
75008.
Map 5 A5.
Tel 01 43 59 21 13.

Rex Club
5 Blvd Poissonnière
75002.
Map 7 A5.
Tel 01 42 36 10 96.

Ritz Club
Hôtel Ritz, 15 Pl
Vendôme 75001.
Map 6 D5.
Tel 01 43 16 30 30.
www.ritzparis.com

La Scala
188 bis Rue de Rivoli
75001.
Map 12 E2.
Tel 01 42 61 64 00.

Showcase
Port des Champs-Elysées
75008.
Map 11 A1. *Tel 06 28 28
82 88.*

La Suite
40 Ave George V 75008.
Map 4 E5.
Tel 01 53 5 49 49.

Triptyque
142 rue Montmartre
75002.
Map 13 A1.
Tel 01 40 28 05 55.

VIP
76 Ave des Champs-
Elysées 75008.
Map 4 E4.
Tel 01 56 69 16 66.

WAGG
62 Rue Mazarine 75006.
Map 12 F4.
Tel 01 55 42 22 00.

Zed Club
2 Rue des Anglais 75005.
Map 13 A5.
Tel 01 43 54 93 78.

WORLD MUSIC

Le Casbah
18-20 Rue de la Forge-
Royale 75011.
Tel 01 43 71 04 39.

Les Etoiles
61 Rue Château d'Eau
75010.
Map 7 C5.
Tel 01 47 70 60 56.

La Java
105 Rue du Faubourg-du-
Temple 75010.
Map 8 E5.
Tel 01 42 02 20 52.

Latina Café
114 Ave des Champs-
Elysées 75008.
Map 4 E4.
Tel 01 42 89 98 89.

Keur Samba
79 Rue de la Boétie
75008.
Map 5 A4.
Tel 01 43 59 03 10.

GAY AND LESBIAN VENUES

La Champmeslé
4 Rue Chabanais 75001.
Map 12 E1.
Tel 01 42 96 85 20.

Le Day Off
10 Rue de l'Islay 75008.
Map 5 C4.
Tel 01 45 22 87 90.

Le Depôt
10 Rue aux Ours 75003.
Map 13 B2.
Tel 01 44 54 96 96.

Le Queen
102 Ave des Champs-
Elysées 75008.
Map 4 E4.
Tel 0892 707 330.

Le Troisième Lieu
62 Rue Quincampoix
75004.
Map 13 B2.
Tel 01 48 04 85 64.

Cinema

Paris can justifiably claim to be the world's capital of film appreciation. With more than 370 screens within the city limits, distributed among over 100 cinemas and multiplexes, a fabulous cornucopia of films are screened, both brand-new and classic. Although American movies dominate the market more than ever, virtually every filmmaking industry in the world has found a niche in the city's art houses. Cinemas change their programmes on Wednesdays. The cheapest practical guides to what's on are *Pariscope* and *L'Officiel des Spectacles (see p340)* with complete cinema listings and timetables for some 300 films. Films shown in subtitled original language versions are coded "VO" *(version originale)*; dubbed films are coded"VF" *(version française)*. The Fête du Cinéma is held for three days in June. The system is that you pay full price for one film and then every film seen subsequently in any cinema on that day costs around two euros. Film buffs think nothing of taking in six or seven screenings on the day.

MOVEMENTS IN CINEMA

Paris was the cradle of the cinematograph over 100 years ago, when Auguste and Louis Lumière invented the early film projector. Their screening of *L'Arrivée d'un Train en Gare de la Ciotat* (Arrival of a Train at la Ciotat Station) in Paris in 1895 is considered by many to mark the birth of the medium. The French reverence for film as a true art form is based on a theory of one of the world's first film critics, Ricciotto Canudo, an Italian intellectual living in France, who dubbed cinematography "the Seventh Art" in 1922. The title holds true even today. The city was of course also the incubator of that very Parisian vanguard movement, the New Wave, when film directors such as Claude Chabrol, François Truffaut, Jean-Luc Godard and Eric Rohmer in the late 1950s and early 60s revolutionized the way films were made and perceived. The exploration of existential themes, the use of long tracking shots and the rejection of studios for outside locations are some of the characteristics of New Wave film. In 2001, the success of *Amélie Poulain* revitalized the Parisian filmmaking scene; many of its locations are easy to spot

as you walk around town. The same is true of *The Da Vinci Code*, also featuring *Amelie* star Audrey Tautou.

CINEMA ZONES

Most Paris cinemas are concentrated in several cinema belts, which enjoy the added appeal of nearby restaurants and shops.

The Champs-Elysées remains the densest cinema strip in town, where you can see the latest Hollywood smash hit or French *auteur* triumph, as well as some classic reissues, in subtitled original language versions. Cinemas in the Grands Boulevards, in the vicinity of the Opéra de Paris Garnier, show films in both subtitled and dubbed versions. The Place de Clichy is the last Parisian stronghold of Pathé, which operates no less than 13 screens there, all showing dubbed versions. A major hub of Right Bank cinema activity is in the Forum des Halles shopping mall.

The Left Bank, historically associated with the city's intellectual life, remains the centre of the art and repertory cinemas. Yet, it has equally as many of the latest blockbusters. Since the 1980s, many cinemas in the Latin Quarter have closed down and the main area for Left Bank theatres is now the Odéon-

St-Germain-des-Prés area. The Rue Champollion is an exception. It has enjoyed a revival as a mini-district for art and repertory films.

Further to the south, Montparnasse remains a lively district of new films in both dubbed and subtitled prints.

BIG SCREENS AND PICTURE PALACES

Among surviving landmark cinemas are two Grands Boulevards venues, the 2,800-seat **Le Grand Rex** with its Baroque decor, and the **Max Linder Panorama**, which was refurbished by a group of independent film buffs in the 1980s for both popular and art film programming.

The massive new 14-screen **MK2 Bibliothèque** cinema (plus bar, shops and exhibition space), recently opened up in the revitalised 13th arrondissement and just across the river, the **Bercy** cinema complex is well worth a visit too.

In the Cité des Sciences et de l'Industrie at La Villette, scientific films are shown at **La Géode** *(see p237)*. This has a hemispheric screen (once the world's largest) and an "omnimax" projector which uses 70-mm film shot horizontally to project an image which is nine times larger than the standard 35-mm print. Along the Canal St-Martin, **MK2**'s twin cinema complexes – **Quai de la Loire** and **Quai de la Seine** – are linked by a canal boat.

REVIVAL AND REPERTORY HOUSES

Each week, more than 150 titles representing the best of world cinema can be seen. For old Hollywood films, the independent **Grand Action** mini-chain can't be beaten. Other active and thoughtful repertory and reissue venues include the excellent **Reflets Médicis** screens in the Rue Champollion and the **Pagode**. The latter is particularly striking; the Oriental pagoda was constructed in 1895 and has been recently renovated.

Studio 28 in Montmartre is a lovely old movie house with lights in the theatre designed by Jean Cocteau and a charming garden bar full of fairy lights and kitsch cut-outs of old film stars. Opened in the 1920s, Studio 28 claims to be the first ever avant-garde cinema and once played host to film greats such as Luis Buñuel and Abel Gance. They screen everything from the latest releases through to Fellini festivals and documentary shows. There are at least ten films screened here each week, including art-house classics and pre-releases. The cinema also holds regular debates with well-known directors and actors. Another Parisian institution, **Studio Galande** has shown the *Rocky Horror Picture Show* to costumed movie-goers every Friday night for over 20 years.

CINÉMATHÈQUE FRANÇAISE

The private "school" of the New Wave generation, this famous film archive and repertory cinema was created by Henri Langlois in 1936 (*see p200*). It has lost its monopoly on classic film screenings, but it is still a must for cinephiles in search of that rare film no longer in theatrical circulation or, perhaps, recently restored or rescued. The association is now housed at 51 Rue de Bercy in a wonderfully futuristic-looking building designed by Frank Gehry. The sail-like façade has given the building its nickname: "dancer revealing her tutu". The film library has more than 18,000 digitalized movies, and there are enough exhibitions, projections, lectures and workshops to satisfy the appetite of any film enthusiast.

NON-THEATRICAL VENUES

In addition to the Cinémathèque Française, film programmes and festivals are integral parts of two highly popular Paris cultural institutions, the Musée d'Orsay (*see pp144–5*) and the Pompidou Centre (*see pp110–11*) with its two screening rooms. The Musée d'Orsay regularly schedules film programmes to complement current art exhibitions and is usually restricted to silent films. The Pompidou Centre organizes vast month-long retrospectives, devoted to national film industries and on occasion to some of the major companies.

Finally, the **Forum des Images** (*see p109*) in the heart of Les Halles is a hi-tech film and video library with a vast selection of films and documentaries featuring the city of Paris from the late 19th century to the present day. The archives here are amazing and include news-reels and advertisements featuring Paris alongside the feature films and documentaries. The Forum has three cinemas, all of which run daily screenings of feature films, beginning at 2.30pm. One ticket allows the visitor access to both the video library and to the cinema screenings. In the video library it is possible to search the database of over 6,000 films and then watch your choice on your own personal screen. The cinema screenings are frequently grouped according to theme or director, making it possible to spend several hours enjoying a mini-retrospective.

TICKET PRICES

Expect to pay around 9€ at first-run venues or even more for films of unusual length or special media attention. However, exhibitors practise a wide array of collective discount incentives, including cut-rate admissions for students, the unemployed, the elderly, old soldiers and large families. Wednesday is discount day for everybody at some cinemas – prices are slashed to as low as 4€.

France's three exhibition giants, Gaumont, UGC and MK2, also sell special discount cards and accept credit card reservations for their flagship houses, while repertory houses issue "fidelity" cards.

FILMS WITH STRONG IMAGES OF PARIS

Historical Paris (studio-made)

An Italian Straw Hat
(*René Clair, 1927*)

Sous les toits de Paris
(*René Clair, 1930*)

Les Misérables
(*Raymond Bernard, 1934*)

Hôtel du Nord
(*Marcel Carné, 1937*)

Les Enfants du Paradis
(*Marcel Carné, 1945*)

Casque d'Or
(*Jacques Becker, 1952*)

La Traversée de Paris
(*Claude Autant-Lara, 1956*)

Playtime
(*Jacques Tati, 1967*)

New Wave Paris (location-made)

Breathless
(*Jean-Luc Godard, 1959*)

Les 400 coups
(*François Truffaut, 1959*)

Documentary Paris

Paris 1900
(*Nicole Vedrès, 1948*)

La Seine a rencontré Paris
(*Joris Ivans, 1957*)

Paris as seen by Hollywood

Seventh Heaven
(*Frank Borzage, 1927*)

Camille
(*George Cukor, 1936*)

An American in Paris
(*Vincente Minnelli, 1951*)

Gigi
(*Vincente Minnelli, 1958*)

Irma La Douce
(*Billy Wilder, 1963*)

Paris when it Sizzles
(*Richard Quine, 1964*)

Frantic
(*Roman Polanski, 1988*)

French Kiss
(*Lawrence Kasdan, 1995*)

The Ninth Gate
(*Roman Polanski, 1999*)

Moulin Rouge
(*Baz Luhrmann, 2001*)

The Bourne Identity
(*Doug Liman, 2002*)

Le Divorce
(*James Ivory, 2003*)

Before Sunset
(*Richard Linklater, 2004*)

Cinema Festivals

Film festivals are a way of life for Parisian movie buffs. There are several major events each year and lots of small themed festivals happening at any given time around the city. The annual Paris Film Festival, held at the end of March, may be dwarfed by its glitzier sister in Cannes, but the capital's version is a far friendlier event for the public to attend – and there are still more than enough opportunities to spot celebrities.

OPEN AIR FESTIVALS

There are several outdoor cinema festivals throughout the summer, including the Festival Silhouette which shows short films in the lovely Buttes Chaumont (see p234), the Cinéma au Clair du Lune festival which has projections of films at Parisian sites which are relevant to the movie and Le Cinéma en Plein Air which draws crowds to a lawn in La Villette (see pp236-7), where a giant inflatable screen shows old and contemporary classics. This is one of the summer's most popular events so be sure to get there early and don't forget to take a hamper full of goodies to nibble on throughout the movie.

INDOOR FESTIVALS

During the annual Paris Film Festival, over 100 films are shown at the Gaumont Marignon on the Champs-Elysées. The city's gay and lesbian film festival at the Forum des Images usually takes place in November. Paris Tout Court is an impressive short film festival held at the Arlequin in St-Germain which also stages lectures and meetings with renowned directors and artists. Other film festivals include the Les Etranges festival which shows weird and wonderful offbeat films from around the world to enthusiastic audiences.

DIRECTORY

CINEMAS

Action Christine Odeon
4 Rue Christine 75006.
Map 12 F4.
Tel 0892 680 598.

Action Ecoles
23 Rue des Ecoles 75005.
Map 13 A5.
Tel 0892 680 591.

Arlequin
76 Rue de Rennes 75006.
Map 12 E4.
Tel 01 45 44 28 80.

Le Balzac
1 Rue Balzac 75008.
Map 4 E4.
Tel 08 92 68 31 23.

Centre Georges Pompidou
19 Rue Beaubourg 75004.
Map 13 B2.

Le Champo
51 Rue des Ecoles 75005.
Map 13 A5.
Tel 01 43 29 79 89.

Cinémathèque Française
51 Rue de Bercy 75013.
Tel 01 71 19 33 33.
www.cinemateque.fr

Cinema Studio Galande
42 Rue Galande 75005.
Map 13 A4.
Tel 08 92 68 06 24.

Cine Sorbonne
9 Rue Champollion 75005.
Map 13 A5.
Tel 01 43 26 84 65.

Forum des Images
Porte St-Eustache,
Forum des Halles 75001.
Map 13 A2.
Tel 01 44 76 62 00.

Gaumont Marignan
27 Ave Champs-Elysées 75008.
Map 5 A5.
Tel 01 42 89 12 74.

La Géode
26 Ave Corentin-Cariou 75019.
Tel 08 92 68 45 40.
www.lageode.fr

Grand Action
Action Rive Gauche,
5 Rue des Ecoles 75005.
Map 13 B5.
Tel 01 43 54 47 62.

Le Grand Rex
1 Blvd Poissonnière 75002.
Map 7 A5.
Tel 01 42 36 83 93.

Images d'Ailleurs
21 Rue de la Clef 75005.
Map 13 B2.
Tel 01 45 87 18 09.

Latina
20 Rue du Temple 75004.
Map 7 C2.
Tel 01 42 78 47 86.

Lucenaire
53 Rue Notre-Dame-des-Champs 75006.
Map 16 E2.
Tel 01 45 44 57 34.

Max Linder Panorama
24 Blvd Poissonnière 75009. Map 7 A5.
Tel 08 92 68 00 31.

Majestic Bastille
4 Blvd Richard Lenoir 75011.
Map 14 E4.
Tel 01 47 00 02 48.

MK2 Beaubourg
50 Rue Rambuteau 75003.
Map 7 B2.
Tel 08 92 69 84 84.

MK2 Bibliothèque
128-162 Ave de France 75013. Map 18 F4.
Tel 08 92 69 84 84.

MK2 Quai de la Seine/Quai de la Loire
75019. Map 8 F1.
Tel 08 92 69 84 84.

Pagode
57 bis Rue de Babylone 75007. Map 11 C4.
Tel 01 45 55 48 48.

Racine Odeon
6 Rue de l'Ecole de Médecine 75006.
Map 12 F4.

Reflets Médicis
3-7 Rue Champollion 75005.
Map 12 F5.
Tel 01 46 33 25 97.

St-Andre des Arts
30 Rue St Andre des Arts 75006.
Map 12 F4.
Tel 01 43 26 48 18.

Studio 28
10 Rue Tholozé 75018.
Map 6 E1.
Tel 01 46 06 36 07.

UGC Ciné Cité Bercy
2 Cour St-Emilion 75012.
Tel 0892 700 000.

UGC Cine-Cite les Halles
7 Place de la Rotonde 75001.
Map 7 A2.
Tel 08 92 70 00 00.

Sport and Fitness

There is no end of sporting activities in Paris. Certain events such as the Roland Garros tennis tournament and the Tour de France bicycle race are national institutions. The only drawback is that many of the facilities are on the outskirts of the city.

For details regarding all sporting events in and around Paris contact **Paris Infos Mairie** – a free information service run by the Town Hall. The weekly entertainment guides *L'Officiel des Spectacles*, *Pariscope* and the Wednesday edition of *Le Figaro* also have good listings of the week's sporting events *(see p340)*. For in-depth sports coverage there is the daily paper *L'Equipe*. See also *Children's Paris* on page 362.

OUTDOOR SPORTS

The annual Tour de France bicycle race finishes in July in Paris to city-wide frenzy, when the French president awards the coveted *maillot jaune* (yellow jersey) to the winner. For over twenty years now the final stage of the tour has taken place on the Champs-Elysées with the riders racing up the famous avenue. Traffic across the city grinds to a halt and sports fans and couch potatoes alike flock to cheer on the cyclists. Finding a spot to watch can be extremely tough, it's best to hunt down your speck several hours before the riders are expected.

For those brave enough to tackle cycling through the city traffic, bikes may be hired throughout Paris, including at **Paris Vélo** in the Rue du Fer-à-Moulin and **Maison Roue Libre** in Passage Mondétour, headquarters of the RATP's bicycle rental service, Roue Libre *(see p359)*. In summer (weekends and bank holidays only), old RATP buses hire out bicycles from five locations (Place de la Concorde, Stalingrad, Place du Châtelet, Porte d'Auteuil and Parc Floral de Vincennes). The **Fédération Française de Cyclotourisme** in the Rue Louis Bertrand will give you information on over 300 cycling clubs around Paris. Things are gradually improving for those who favour pedal power; all year round, the city council shuts down some of the quaysides on Sundays and national holidays to allow cyclists freewheeling next to the Seine. The city has also undertaken a programme of expansion for its cycle lanes. Be aware though that Paris traffic is heavy and Parisian drivers not especially two-wheel friendly. Those who can't wait for the quais along the Seine to be closed on Sundays should head over to the Bois de Vincennes or the Bois de Boulogne for a leisurely bike ride through the woods. The more ambitious can pick up a copy of the free Paris à Vélo map from a tourist office to find details of all the city's cycle lanes. If you'd prefer to take an organized cycle tour through the city, there are several organizations who run fun trips. **Fat Tire Bike Tours** in the Rue Edgar Faure are expensive but have daily trips in spring and summer in which knowledgeable guides shepherd cyclists around the streets whilst imparting interesting information on the city's landmarks. **Paris à Vélo c'est Sympa** runs multi-lingual tours to offbeat parts of the city.

Roller bladers can enjoy parades through the city on Friday nights. The police close off boulevards around the city allowing thousands of skate fans to join the trip every week. The parade usually starts at Place de la Bastille at 10pm, but you can join the route at any point if the whole circuit seems a little much. Contact www.pari-roller.com for details of the route. Beginners can enjoy free tuition prior to the departure of the parade if they arrive at the start point at 8pm. There are many good outlets in the city for roller-blade rental. The parade's website provides useful links to recommended outlets. As a safety precaution the trip is cancelled if the weather is inclement and the roads wet.

Parisians enjoy Sunday afternoon boating in the Bois de Vincennes *(see p235)*, the Bois de Boulogne *(see p254)* and the Parc des Buttes-Chaumont *(see p234)*. Just queue up to hire a boat.

All the golf courses are outside Paris. Many are private clubs, but some will admit non-members – for further information contact the **Fédération Française du Golf** in the Rue Anatole-France. Otherwise try the **Golf de Chevry, Golf de Villeray, Golf de St-Quentin en Yvelines** or the **Golf de Villennes**. Expect to pay at least 25€ each time you want to play.

You can go horse-riding in both the Bois de Boulogne and the Bois de Vincennes. For details, contact the **Comité Departemental d'Equitation de Paris** in the Rue Laugier.

Tennis can be played at municipal courts such as the **Tennis Luxembourg** in the Jardin du Luxembourg. Courts are available every day on a first-come first-served basis. **Tennis de la Faluère** in the Bois de Vincennes has some of the better courts, but these must be booked at least 24 hours in advance.

INDOOR SPORTS

There are plenty of gyms in Paris which you can use with a day pass. Expect to pay 20€ or more, depending on the facilities.

Club Med Gym is a well-equipped, popular chain of gyms with more than twenty sites in Paris and the suburbs. Good choices include the branches in Rue de Berri and Rue de Rennes. **Club Jean de Beauvais** in the Rue Jean de Beauvais, is a state-of-the-art gym with personalized fitness programmes. The **Ken Club** on Avenue President Kennedy is an upmarket gym complete with pool and sauna in the chic 16th arronssissement. Its proximity next to a major radio studio means French media personalities are often to be found there working out on their lunch break. In theory the **Ritz Gym**, which has the finest indoor swimming pool in Paris, is for guests or members only, but if the hotel is not too full you can buy a day pass.

Skating is a cheap pastime and can be enjoyed year-round at the **Patinoire d'Asnières-sur-Seine** located on Boulevard Pierre de Coubertin.

Squash can be played at **Squash Club Quartier Latin** in the Rue de Pontoise, where options also include billiards, gym and a sauna. Other good clubs include the **Squash Montmartre** and the **Squash Front de Seine**.

SPECTATOR SPORTS

A day out at the races is a chance to see the rich in all their finery. The world-famous Prix de l'Arc de Triomphe is held at the **Hippodrome de Longchamp** in the Bois de Boulogne on the first Sunday in October. More flat racing takes place at the **Hippodrome de St-Cloud** and **Maisons Lafitte**, which are a short drive west of Paris. For steeple-chasing go to the **Hippodrome d'Auteuil** in the Bois de Boulogne. The **Hippodrome de Vincennes** on Route de la Ferne hosts the trotting races. For detailed information on all of these, consult **France Galop** by phone or check their website.

The 24-hour car race at Le Mans, 185 km (115 miles) southwest of Paris, is one of the best-known road races in the world. It takes place every year in mid-June. Contact the **Automobile Club de l'Ouest** for details. The **Palais Omnisports de Paris-Bercy** sports stadium in Boulevard Bercy is the venue for a vast range of events, including the

Paris tennis open, the six-day cycling race, showjumping, world-class martial arts demonstrations, tournaments in everything from figure skating to handball and major rock concerts.

Parc des Princes can hold 50,000 people. It is home to the main Paris football team, Paris St-Germain, and hosts the rugby internationals.

Despite its glorious baptism in 1998 with France's World Cup victory, the **Stade de France** has failed to win a home team; meanwhile, it makes do with the Six Nations Trophy, Tina Turner and Johnnie Halliday.

The **Stade Roland Garros** in Avenue Gordon-Bennett is famous for its international tennis tournament. From late May to mid-June everyone lives and breathes tennis. Business meetings are transferred from the conference room to the stadium. Apply for tickets several months ahead. Don't miss a trip to the stadium's excellent museum of tennis featuring everything from prototype rackets to a Bjorn Bjorg headband. Also, be sure to book a table at one of the swanky restaurants here, which are transformed into a place to see and be seen during the tournament. Tennis fans should also be sure to catch the mens' masters series at the Palais Omnisports de Paris Bercy in November and the womens' tournament 'open Gaz de France', which takes place at the **Stade Pierre de Coubertin** on Avenue Georges Lafont, in March.

SWIMMING

There is a massive aquatic fun park, known as **Aquaboulevard**, in south Paris (see p362). Besides an exotic artificial beach, swimming pools, water toboggans and rapids, there are tennis and squash courts, golf, bowling, table tennis, billiards, a gym, bars and shops.

Of the many municipal swimming pools, one of the best is the **Piscine des Halles** in Place de la Rotonde, with an Olympic-sized swimming pool in the

underground shopping complex. For a lovely 1930s mosaic décor with two levels of private changing cabins, a whirlpool, sauna and water jets, go to the **Piscine Pontoise-Quartier Latin**. This complex also has a small gym overlooking the pool, where fitness fans can pump a little iron before taking a dip. The **Piscine Henry de Montherlant** is part of a municipal sports complex that includes tennis courts and a gym. The beautiful Art Nouveau pool in the Butte aux Cailles (see pp272-3) is a treat for serious swimmers and sunbathers. A decent-sized indoor pool is perfect for laps whilst the two outdoor swimming areas are great for lounging. The villagey atmosphere of the surrounding area only serves to reinforce the feeling of relaxing on holiday miles away from the city. A fantastic view of the Eiffel Tower can be spied mid-crawl at the **Piscine Emile-Anthoine**. Some of the smarter hotels and gyms also have their own pools. It is possible to buy a day pass to the chic **Sofitel Paris Club Med Gym** in the Rue Louis Armand and have access to their 15-metre pool. Similarly at the **Novotel Tour Eiffel**, non-guests are welcomed to their health club and pool which has a retractable roof for swimming under the sun in spring and summer. It is important to note that all municipal pools and some private ones insist that bathers wear swimming caps and that male swimmers wear swimming trunks rather than baggy shorts.

MISCELLANEOUS

Baseball, fencing, jogging in the parks, volleyball, windsurfing at La Villette (see pp236–9) and bowling are just some of the other sporting activities that can be enjoyed during your stay.

Fishing on the Seine is fast becoming a popular pastime with Parisiens. Due to a clean-up operation the Seine is now home to a variety of freshwater fish.

DIRECTORY

OUTDOOR SPORTS

Comité Départemental d'Equitation de Paris
69 Rue Laugier 75017.
Tel 01 42 12 03 43.

Fat Tire Bike Tours
24 Rue Edgar Faure 75015.
Map 10 D4. *Tel 01 56 58 10 54.* **www.**
fattirebiketoursparis.com

Fédération Française de Cyclotourisme
12 Rue Louis Bertrand 94200, Ivry-sur-Seine.
Tel 01 56 20 88 88.

Fédération Française du Golf
68 Rue Anatole France, 92300 Levallois Perret.
Tel 01 41 49 77 00.

France Galop
Tel 01 49 10 20 30.
www.france-galop.com

Golf de Chevry
91190 Gif-sur-Yvette.
Tel 01 60 12 40 33.

Golf de St-Quentin en Yvelines
78190 Trappes.
Tel 01 30 50 86 40.

Golf de Villennes
Route d'Orgeval, 78670 Villennes-sur-Seine.
Tel 01 39 08 18 18.

Golf de Villeray
91380 St-Pierre du Perray.
Tel 01 60 75 17 47.
www.bluegreen.com

Maison Roue Libre
1 Passage Mondétour 75001. **Map** 13 B2.
Tel 08 10 44 15 34.
www.rouelibre.fr

Paris à Vélo c'est Sympa
37 Blvd Bourdon 75004.
Map 14 E4.
Tel 01 48 87 60 01.

Paris Infos Mairie
(Mon–Fri: 8am–7pm; Sat: 8:30am–1pm).
Tel 08 20 00 75 75.

Paris Vélo
2 Rue du Fer-à-Moulin 75005. **Map** 17 C2.
Tel 01 47 07 67 45.

Tennis de la Faluère Route de la Pyramide
Bois de Vincennes 75012.
Tel 01 43 74 40 93.

Tennis Luxembourg Jardins du Luxembourg
Blvd St-Michel 75006.
Map 12 E5.
Tel 01 43 25 79 18.

INDOOR SPORTS

Club Jean de Beauvais
5 Rue Jean de Beauvais 75005. **Map** 13 A5.
Tel 01 46 33 16 80.

Club Med Gym
26 Rue de Berri 75008.
Map 4 F4.
Tel 01 43 59 04 58.
149 Rue de Rennes 75006. **Map** 15 C1.
Tel 01 45 44 24 35.
www.clubmedgym.com

Ken Club
100 Ave President Kennedy 75016.
Tel 01 46 47 41 41.

Patinoire d'Asnières-sur-Seine
Blvd Pierre de Coubertin, 92600 Asnières.
Tel 01 47 99 96 06.

Ritz Gym
Ritz Hotel, Pl Vendôme 75001. **Map** 6 D5.
Tel 01 43 16 30 30.

Squash Club Quartier Latin
19 Rue de Pontoise 75005.
Map 13 B5.
Tel 01 55 42 77 88.

Squash Front de Seine
21 Rue Gaston-de-Caillavet 75015.
Map 9 B5.
Tel 01 45 75 35 37.

Squash Montmartre
14 Rue Achille-Martinet 75018.
Map 2 E4.
Tel 01 42 55 38 30.

SPECTATOR SPORTS

Automobile Club de l'Ouest
Tel 02 43 40 24 24.

Hippodrome d'Auteuil
Bois de Boulogne 75016.
Tel 01 42 88 85 30.

Hippodrome de Longchamp
Bois de Boulogne 75016.
Tel 01 44 30 75 00.

Hippodrome Maisons Lafitte
1 Ave de la Pelouze, 78600 Maisons Lafitte.
Tel 01 39 62 06 77.

Hippodrome de St-Cloud
1 Rue de Camp Canadien, 92210 St-Cloud.
Tel 01 47 71 69 26.

Hippodrome de Vincennes
2 Route de la Ferme, 75012 Vincennes.
Tel 01 49 77 17 17.

Palais Omnisports de Paris-Bercy
8 Blvd Bercy 75012.
Map 18 F2.
Tel 0892 390 490.

Parc des Princes
24 Rue du Commandant-Guilbaud 75016.
Tel 08 25 07 50 77.

Stade de France
93210 La Plaine St-Denis.
Tel 01 55 93 00 00.

Stade Pierre de Coubertin
82 Ave Georges Lafont 75016.
Tel 01 45 27 79 12.

Stade Roland Garros
2 Ave Gordon-Bennett 75016.
Tel 01 47 43 48 00.
www.fft.fr

SWIMMING

Aquaboulevard
4 Rue Louis-Armand 75015.
Tel 01 40 60 10 00.

Piscine Butte-aux-Cailles
5 Pl Paul-Verlaine 75013.
Map 17 A5.
Tel 01 45 89 60 05.

Piscine des Amiraux
6 Rue Hermann-Lachapelle 75018.
Tel 01 46 06 46 47.

Piscine des Halles
10 Pl de la Rotonde, Niveau 3, Entrance Porte St Eustache, Les Halles 75001. **Map** 13 A2.
Tel 01 42 36 98 44.

Piscine Emile-Anthoine
9 Rue Jean Rey 75015.
Map 10 D3.
Tel 01 53 69 61 59.

Piscine Henry de Montherlant
32 Blvd de Lannes 75016.
Tel 01 40 72 28 30.

Piscine Pontoise-Quartier Latin
19 Rue de Pontoise 75005.
Map 13 B5.
Tel 01 55 42 77 88.

Piscine St Germain
12 Rue Lobineau 75006.
Map 12 E4.
Tel 01 56 81 25 40.

Piscine Saint-Merri
16 Rue de Renard 75004.
Map 13 B3.
Tel 01 42 72 29 45.

Sofitel Paris Club Med Gym
8 Rue Louis Armand 75015.
Tel 01 45 54 79 00.

Novotel Tour Eiffel
61 Quai de Grenelle 75015. **Map** 9 B5.
Tel 01 40 58 20 00.

CHILDREN'S PARIS

It's never too early to instil a lifelong taste for this magical city in your children. A trip to Disneyland Resort Paris *(see pp242–5)* or down the Seine *(see pp72–3)*, the dizzy heights of the Eiffel Tower *(see pp194–5)* or a visit to Notre-Dame *(see pp82–5)* are fun at any age, and with children in tow you will see old haunts through new eyes. The historic parks are probably best appreciated by older children and adults, but everyone will love the technological wizardry of the Disneyland Paris theme park. During the summer, funfairs, circuses and all sorts of impromptu events are staged in gardens and parks, notably in the Bois de Boulogne *(see pp254–5)*. Or, take children to an entertainment centre, museum or adventure playground, or to a show at one of the café theatres.

La Cité des Enfants at La Villette

PRACTICAL ADVICE

Paris welcomes young families in hotels *(see p278)* and most restaurants *(see p295)*. Many sights and attractions offer child reductions, while infants under three or four enter free. The upper age limit for reductions is usually about 12 but can vary considerably. Many museums are free on Sundays; others allow children under 18 in free at any time. Ask at the Office du Tourisme *(see p280)* for full details of child reductions, or check in the weekly entertainment guides such as *Pariscope, L'Officiel des Spectacles* and *Paris Mômes.*

A lot of the children's activities are geared to end-of-school times, including Wednesday afternoons when French children have time off. For information on museum workshops, contact the **Ministère de la Culture** or visit **www.paris-frimousse.com**, which has information on events for 2–12-year olds.

Babychou and **Au Paradis des Petits** are specialist babysitting organizations, as well as offering a wide range of other services.

MUSEUMS

Top of the museum list for children is undoubtedly the Cité des Sciences et de l'Industrie *(see pp236–9)* at Parc de la Villette. Hands-on activities and changing exhibitions illuminate many aspects of science and modern tech-nology in this immense complex. There are sections for children called La Cité des Enfants and Techno Cité. In central Paris, the Palais de la Découverte, within the Grand Palais *(see p208)*, is an old-fashioned but lively science museum where staff adopt the role of mad inventors.

The Louvre *(see pp122–9)* organizes special sessions designed to introduce children to various aspects of art, while the Galerie des Enfants at the Pompidou Centre *(see pp110–13)* does the same with modern art.

Other enjoyable museums for children include the Musée de la Marine *(see p201)* and the Musée de la Poupée *(see p114)*. The former covers the history of the French maritime tradition and includes scale models. The latter displays hand-made dolls dating from the mid-19th century, and also offers doll-making classes for both adults and children.

USEFUL CONTACTS

Au Paradis des Petits

Tel 01 43 65 58 58.

www.auparadisdespetits.com

Babychou Services

Tel 01 43 13 33 23.

www.babychou.com

Ministère de la Culture

www.culture.gouv.fr

The Café d'Edgar theatre

The Guignol marionnettes

PARKS, ZOOS AND ADVENTURE PLAYGROUNDS

The best children's park within Paris is the Jardin d'Acclimatation in the Bois de Boulogne *(see pp254–5)*, with a children's theatre and circus, a pony club, a mini railway and boats. The Musée en Herbe *(see p254)* is a museum created especially for children offering entertaining educational activities.

France Miniature recreates France on a small scale, complete with all its monuments.

The Bois de Vincennes *(see p235)* has simple amusements for children in the

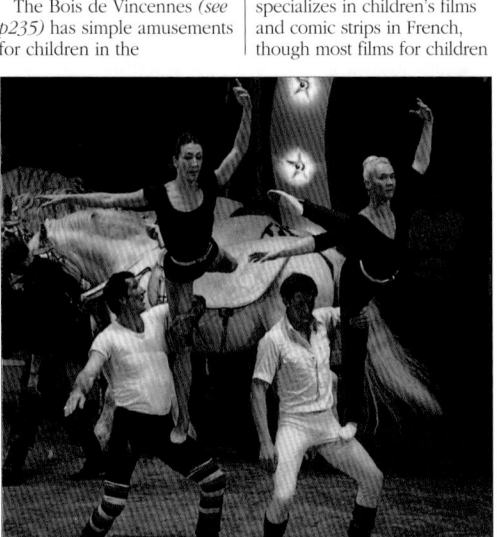

Pony rides, Jardin d'Acclimatation

inexpensive Parc Floral. It also has the largest funfair in France, open from Palm Sunday through to the end of May. Perhaps the most appealing zoo is the small Ménagerie in the Jardin des Plantes *(see p164)*.

ENTERTAINMENT CENTRES

There are many supervised children's activity centres in Paris. The Atelier des Enfants in the Pompidou Centre *(see pp110–11)* has a workshop on Wednesday and Saturday afternoons from 2.30 to 4pm. The medium of instruction is French but the circuses, mime-shows, marionnettes and craft or museum workshops focus on actions rather than words.

Several café-theatres, including Café d'Edgar *(see p343)* and Au Bec Fin *(see p342)*, offer children's shows where mime, dance or music form part of the content. The most spectacular cinematic experience is in La Géode at the Cité des Sciences et de l'Industrie (see p237). The cinema **Le Saint Lambert** specializes in children's films and comic strips in French, though most films for children

Lion in the Bois de Vincennes zoo

will not have English subtitles. Cinema tickets are cheaper on Wednesdays, with no child reductions at weekends.

Une Journée au Cirque offers children a day's entertainment when they can meet the animals, put on clown make-up or practise tightrope walking. Shows are in the afternoon, after lunch with the *artistes*.

The Guignol marionnette puppet shows are a summer tradition in Paris. The themes are similar to the traditional English Punch and Judy shows. Most of the main parks hold Guignol shows in summer on Wednesday afternoons and at weekends. Consult the entertainment guides such as *Pariscope*, *L'Officiel des Spectacles* and *Paris Mômes*.

ADDRESSES

Une Journée au Cirque
115 Blvd Charles de Gaulle, 92390 Ville-neuve-la-Garenne. **Tel** *01 47 99 40 40*.
www.journeeocirque.com

France Miniature
25 Route du Mesnil, 78990 Elancourt.
Tel *08 26 30 20 40*.
www.franceminiature.com

Le Saint Lambert
6 Rue Peclet 75015. **Tel** *08 92 68 96 99*.

Circus acrobats training at Une Journée au Cirque

Fireworks over Sleeping Beauty Castle, Disneyland Resort Paris

THEME PARKS

The two parks of Disneyland Resort Paris (see pp242–5) are the biggest and most spectacular of the Paris theme parks. Seven hotels, each with a different, imaginative theme, and a campsite provide on-site accommodation. The complex also includes a golf course, shops and restaurants.

Parc Asterix is a French theme park centring around the legendary world of Asterix the Gaul. Here six themed "worlds" feature gladiators, slave auctions and rides among the many attractions. The park is situated 38 km (24 miles) northeast of Paris. Take the RER line B to Charles de Gaulle Airport then the shuttle bus to Parc Asterix.

Donald Duck

SPORTS AND RECREATION

The giant waterpark **Aquaboulevard** is one of the best places to take energetic youngsters. Also good is the indoor pool at **Forum des Halles**. The weekly entertainment guide *Pariscope* lists the swimming pools in and around Paris. Remember that it is compulsory to wear a swimming cap. Accomplished roller-skaters and skateboarders practise outside the Palais de Chaillot (see p200). On Sundays, in summer, the roads along the Seine (between Chatelêt and Bercy) are closed to traffic. Bikers and rollerbladers descend en masse. Disneyland Resort Paris (see pp242–5) has ice-skating rinks and a range of other sports facilities.

Old-fashioned fairground carousels are situated near Sacré-Coeur (see pp226–7) and Forum des Halles (see p109). A great way of inspiring interest in the city's history, and great fun too, is a boat trip. Several companies compete (see pp72–3) from different departure points, and pass a host of waterfront sites including Notre-Dame, the Louvre and the Musée d'Orsay. Boats departing from La Villette travel along the Paris canal system. Radio-controlled model boats are popular on the ponds of the Jardin du Luxembourg (see p172). Or, take the family boating on the lakes of the Bois de Boulogne (see pp254–5) or the Bois de Vincennes (see p235). Riding is also popular in these parks (see p357 Directory).

ADDRESSES

Aquaboulevard
4 Rue Louis Armand 75015.
Tel *01 40 60 10 00.* ⬜ *9am–11pm Mon–Thu, 9am–midnight Fri, 8am–midnight Sat, 8am–11pm Sun.*

La Piscine des Halles
Forum des Halles, 10 Pl de la Rotonde, Les Halles 75001. **Map** 12 F2. ***Tel*** *01 42 36 98 44.* ⬜ *11.30am–10pm Mon–Fri, 9am–7pm Sat–Sun.*

Parc Asterix
BP8 Plailly 60128. 🚻 *08 26 30 10 40, 08 26 68 30 10.* ⬜ *Apr–mid-Oct: 10am–6pm Mon–Fri, 9.30am–7pm w/e & hols.* **www**.parcasterix.fr

Apache
56 Rue du Commerce 75015.
Map 10 E5. ***Tel*** *01 40 43 10 04. One of several branches.*

CHILDREN'S SHOPS

There is no shortage of chic children's fashion in Paris. A good place to start is the Rue du Jour in Beaubourg and Les Halles which has a number of children's boutiques. The city has many appealing toy shops such as Au Nain Bleu (see p331) or the branches of Apache (see Addresses), but, like the clothes shops, they can be prohibitively expensive. (See also p326.)

Characters from the book *Tintin*, in Au Nain Bleu toy shop

Roller-skaters near the Eiffel Tower

Carousel near Sacré-Coeur

STREET LIFE AND MARKETS

Outside the Pompidou Centre (see pp110–11) street entertainers draw the crowds on sunny afternoons. Musicians, conjurors, fire-eaters and artists of all kinds perform here. In Montmartre there is a tradition of street-painting, predominantly in the Place du Tertre (see p224) where

Model boats for hire in the Jardin du Luxembourg

someone will always be willing to draw your child's portrait. It's also fun to take the funicular up the hill to Sacré-Coeur (see pp226–7), then walk down through the pretty streets.

Parisian markets are colourful and animated. Try taking children to the Marché aux Fleurs on the Ile de la Cité (see p81) or to the food markets on the Rue Mouffetard, in the Jardin des Plantes Quarter (see p166 and p339), or the Rue de Buci in St-Germain-des-Prés. The biggest flea market, Marché aux Puces de St-Ouen, is at weekends (see p233 and p339).

Alternatively take children to the quiet Ile de la Cité or Ile St-Louis on the Seine.

VIEWPOINTS AND SIGHTSEEING

Top of the sightseeing list for children is a trip up the Eiffel Tower (see pp194–5). On a clear day spectacular views over Paris will enable you to point out a number of sights, and at night the city is magically lit up. Lifts run until 11pm and queues are much shorter in the evenings. If you are pushing a baby buggy, bear in mind that the ascent is in three stages, using two separate lifts.

Other interesting sights for children include Sacré-Coeur (see pp226–7) with its ovoid dome – the second highest point in Paris after the Eiffel Tower – and Notre-Dame cathedral (see pp82–3) on the Ile de la Cité. Children will enjoy feeding the pigeons in the cathedral square, counting the 28 kings of Judah on the West Front and listening to you recount the story of the hunchback of Notre-Dame. There are incomparable views from the towers. Children and adults alike will appreciate the enchanting Sainte-Chapelle (see pp88–9), also on the Ile de la Cité. There are reductions for children under the age of 18.

Contrast ancient and modern Paris with a visit to the Pompidou Centre (see pp110–13) and enjoy a ride on the caterpillar-like escalators outside, or go to the café on the roof terrace for the views. There is also the 56-storey Montparnasse Tower (see p178) with some spectacular telescopic views from the top terrace; and there is the huge arch at La Défense (see p255) which has lifts to exhibition platforms where visitors can overlook the whole complex.

OTHER INTERESTS

Children are quick to see the funny side of unusual spectacles. Les Egouts, Paris's sewers, now welcome apprehensive visitors for a

Escalators at the Pompidou Centre

short tour of the city's sewerage system (see p190). Display boards in several languages explain the processes.

The Catacombes (see p179) are a long series of quarry tunnels built in Roman times, now lined with ancient skulls.

On the Ile de la Cité is the Conciergerie (see p81), a turreted prison where many hapless aristocrats spent their final days. The Grévin waxworks are in Boulevard Montmartre (see p218). The museum's Revolution rooms will especially appeal to older children, with gruesome scenes and grisly sound effects, demonstrating the reality of social upheaval.

EMERGENCIES

Enfance et Partage is a free 24-hour child helpline (also for adults). One of Paris's largest children's hospitals is **Hôpital Necker**.

Enfance et Partage Tel 08 00 05 12 34. **www**.enfance-et-partage.org

Hôpital Necker 149 Rue de Sèvres 75015. **Map** 15 B1. **Tel** 01 44 49 40 00. **www**.aphp.fr

A young visitor to Paris

SURVIVAL GUIDE

PRACTICAL INFORMATION 366–375

GETTING TO PARIS 376–381

GETTING AROUND PARIS 382–389

PRACTICAL INFORMATION

As in most large cities, it's easy to waste your limited sightseeing time in Paris on transport and in queues. A little forward planning can minimize this. Ring in advance to confirm the sight is open, and isn't closed for refurbishment or holidays – a phonecard, or *télécarte,* is a wise investment *(see p372).* Purchase a *carnet* or travel pass to economize and simplify transport on the buses and metro *(see pp384– 7).* Buying a *Paris Museum Pass* will give unlimited access to museums and monuments, and cuts down on queues. Beware the Paris lunch break (around 1–3pm), since many essential services shut down, as well as some museums. Guided tours are often the best way to see the essential sights before you get your bearings. If you're on a tight budget, admission prices are sometimes lower at certain times of day, or on Sundays; card-carrying students can obtain discounts on some tickets and admissions *(see p374).*

MUSEUMS AND MONUMENTS

There are more than 170 museums and monuments open to the public in Paris. Most are open Monday (or Tuesday) to Sunday, and from 10am to 6pm. Most ticket counters close 30–45 minutes before the official closing time. To avoid queues and packed museums take advantage of the *nocturnes* (late-night opening) that many of the major museums offer or visit on weekday mornings. The national museums are closed on Tuesdays, except Versailles and the Musée d'Orsay, which are closed on Mondays. The municipal museums, such as those run by the city of Paris (Ville de Paris) are usually closed on Mondays.

An admission fee is usually charged, or a donation is expected. The entrance fee to some national museums is waived on the first Sunday of each month. Those under 18 are usually admitted free, and those 18–25 and over 60 sometimes pay a reduced rate, although not automatically. The municipal museums, and some other museums, do not charge a fee to see their permanent collections on Sundays. To obtain the discounts you will have to provide absolute proof of who you are and how old you are.

The *Paris Museum Pass* gives the bearer unlimited access to more than 60 museums and monuments for 2, 4 or 6 days, without having to queue – a significant advantage. It does not allow entry to temporary exhibitions and is only a cheap deal if you are planning to visit many listed attractions on consecutive days. The pass can be purchased at any of the city's museums as well as main metro stations, Batobus stops, FNAC ticket counters and at the headquarters of the **Office du Tourisme** or **Paris Convention and Visitors' Bureau**.

OPENING HOURS

Most Paris shops and businesses are open from 9am to 7pm. While many stay open all day, others close for an hour or two from noon or 12.30. Some smaller food shops open earlier, around 7am, and take a longer midday break. Most businesses are closed on Sunday, and many shops are also closed on Monday. Some restaurants close at least one day a week. It is not unusual for many shops to close for a month or more during summer. Banks are open from around 9am to 4.30– 5.15pm Mon–Fri, 9am–noon Sat. Some banks are closed noon–2pm while on the day before a public holiday some close at noon.

Train station sign for information services

TOURIST INFORMATION

The main tourist office in Paris, the **Office du Tourisme et des Congrès de Paris**, is near the Tuileries garden. It provides the latest maps, information and brochures, and gives a comprehensive picture of events in the city. There are also tourist offices near the Champs-Elysées (corner of ave Marigny), the Carrousel du Louvre, at Place du Tertre in Montmartre, at the Gare du Nord and Gare de Lyon, in front of Anvers metro station and at the Paris Expo exhibition centre (Porte de Versailles). A 24-hour English-speaking tourist information line can be reached on 118 247.

PARIS Convention and Visitors Bureau

Tourist Office logo

ENTERTAINMENT

The main listings magazines in Paris, available at all newsagents, are *Pariscope* and *L'Officiel des Spectacles (see p340).* Each Wednesday they present full information on the week's current theatre,

◁ River view of Pont Neuf and the Ile de la Cité

Paris sightseeing tour bus

cinema and exhibits, as well as on cabarets, dinner clubs and some restaurants. FNAC ticket agencies book all the entertainment venues, including temporary museum shows. There are FNAC branches throughout Paris. For more information call one of their branches *(see p341)*.

For booking the theatre only, the Kiosque Théâtre sells same-day tickets at 50% discount. The two locations are Place de la Madeleine and the Parvis de la Gare Montparnasse *(see p341)*.

Smoking is prohibited in theatres and cinemas.

Kiosque Théâtre booking kiosk

GUIDED TOURS

Double-decker bus tours with commentaries in English, Italian, Japanese and German

are organized by **France Tourisme**, **Cityrama** and **Paris Vision**. The tours begin from the city centre and take about two hours. They pass the main sights but do not stop at all of them. Departure times vary. **Les Cars Rouges** runs British double-decker bus tours, stopping at many of the sights in Paris, which allow you to leave the bus at any of the stops and to continue later (ticket valid for 2 days). **Paris Balades** (**www**.paris balades.com) offers guided walking tours.

DISABLED ACCESS

Services for disabled people in Paris are still comparatively limited. Although most pavements are contoured to allow wheelchairs an easier

passage, many restaurants, hotels, and even museums are poorly equipped (they may claim otherwise). However, better facilities are being incorporated into all renovated and new buildings. For up-to-date information on public facilities for the disabled, contact the **Groupement pour l'Insertion des Personnes Handicapées Physiques (GIHP)**.

DISABILITY INFORMATION

Les Compagnons du Voyage

163 bis Ave de Clichy 75017.
Tel 01 53 11 11 12.
🕒 7am–8pm Mon–Fri; 9.30am–5.30pm Sat; 1–9pm Sun (9.30am–5.30pm Jul & Aug). 7-day escort services on all transport. Costs vary.
www.compagnons.com

Association des Paralysés de France

9 Blvd Auguste Blanqui 75013.
Map 17 B5. *Tel 01 53 62 84 00.*
Fax 01 45 89 08 54.
13 Place Rungis 75013. *Tel 01 53 80 92 97.* **www**.apf.asso.fr

GIHP

10 Rue Georges de Porto-Riche 75014. *Tel 01 43 95 66 36.*
Fax 01 45 40 40 26.
www.gihpnational.org

DIRECTORY

CITY CENTRE TOURIST OFFICES	**Clémenceau**	**FOREIGN FRENCH TOURIST OFFICES**	**BUS TOUR OPERATORS**

CITY CENTRE TOURIST OFFICES

Office du Tourisme et des Congrès de Paris

25 Rue des Pyramides 75001. **Map** 12 E1.
Tel 08 92 68 30 00.
🕒 10am–7pm daily (from 11am Sun).
www.parisinfo.com

Anvers

72 Blvd Rochechouart 75018. **Map** 7 A2.
🕒 10am–6pm daily.

Carrousel du Louvre

99 Rue de Rivoli 75001.
Map 13 A2.
🕒 10am–6pm daily.

Clémenceau
cnr of Ave des Champs-Elysées & Ave Marigny 75008. **Map** 5 B5.
🕒 3 Apr–15 Sep: 9am–7pm daily.

Gare de Lyon

20 Blvd Diderot 75012.
Map 18 F1. 🕒 8am–6pm Mon–Sat.

Gare du Nord

18 Rue de Dunkerque 75010. **Map** 7 B2.
🕒 8am–6pm daily.

Montmartre

21 Place du Tertre 75018.
Map 6 F1.
🕒 10am–7pm daily.

Paris Expo

1 Place Porte de Versailles 75015. 🕒 11am–7pm during trade fairs.

FOREIGN FRENCH TOURIST OFFICES

Australia

Level 13, 25 Bligh St, Sydney NSW 2000.
Tel (2) 92 31 52 44.

Canada

1800 Ave McGill College, Suite 490, Montréal QUE H3A 3J9. *Tel 514 288 2026.* @ canada@franceguide.com

United Kingdom

178 Piccadilly, London W1J 9AL. *Tel (0906) 8244 123 (within UK).* @ info.uk@franceguide.com

United States

444 Madison Ave, New York, NY 10022.
Tel (212) 838 7800.

BUS TOUR OPERATORS

Cityrama

2 Rue des Pyramides 5001. **Map** 12 E1.
Tel 01 44 55 61 00.
www.pariscityrama.com

France Tourisme

33 Quai des Grands Augustins 75006. **Map** 12 F4. *Tel 01 45 02 88 50.*
www.francetourisme.fr

Les Cars Rouges

17 Quai de Grenelle 75015.
Map 9 C4. *Tel 01 53 95 39 53.* **www**.carsrouges.com

Paris Vision

214 Rue de Rivoli 75001.
Map 12 D1.
Tel 01 42 60 30 01.
www.parisvision.com

Personal Security and Health

Paris is as safe or as dangerous as you make it – common sense is usually sufficient to stay out of trouble. If, on the other hand, you fall sick during your visit, pharmacists are an excellent source of advice. In France pharmacists can diagnose many health problems and suggest appropriate treatment. For more serious medical help, someone at the emergency numbers below will be able to deal with most enquiries. There are many specialist services available, including a general advice line for English-speakers in crisis, an English-speaking Alcoholics Anonymous group, and a phoneline for psychiatric help.

French pharmacy sign

Emergency button at metro stations

EMERGENCY NUMBERS

SAMU (ambulance)
Tel 15 (freecall).

Police
Tel 17 (freecall).

**Pompiers
(fire department)**
Tel 18 (freecall).

European Emergency Call
Tel 112 (freecall).

**SOS Medecin
(doctor, house calls)**
Tel 01 47 07 77 77/0820 33 24 24.

SOS Dentaire (dentist)
Tel 01 43 37 51 00.

Burn Specialists
Hôpital Cochin 75014.
Tel 01 58 41 41 41.

**SOS Help (English
language crisis line)**
Tel 01 46 21 46 46.

**SOS Dépression
(for psychiatric help)**
Tel 01 40 47 95 95.

Sexual Disease Centre
Tel 01 40 78 26 00.

Family Planning Centre
Tel 01 48 88 07 28/0800 803 803.

Anti Poison Centre
Tel 01 40 05 48 48.

PERSONAL SECURITY

For a city of over 2 million people, Paris is surprisingly safe. The centre of the city in particular has little violent crime. Muggings and brawls do occur, but they are rare compared to many other world capitals. However, do try to avoid poorly lit or isolated places. Beware of pickpockets, especially on the metro during the rush hour. Keep all valuables securely concealed and if you carry a handbag or case, never let it out of your sight.

When travelling late at night, avoid long transfers in metro stations, such as Montparnasse and Châtelet-Les Halles. Generally, areas around RER train stations tend to attract groups of youths from outlying areas who come to Paris for entertainment, and may become unruly. The last runs each night of RER trains to and from outlying areas should also be avoided. In an emergency in the metro, call the station agent by using the yellow telephone marked *Chef de Station* on all metro and RER platforms, or go to the ticket booth at the entrance. Most metro stations also have emergency buttons. Carriages also have alarm pulls. If there is a problem outside stations, or at bus stops, telephone the police by dialling 17.

PERSONAL PROPERTY

Take great care with your personal property at all times. Make sure you insure your possessions before arrival. On sightseeing or entertainment trips do not carry valuables with you. Also, only take as much cash as you think you will need. Most places accept credit cards. Travellers' cheques are the safest method

Paris fireman

Policewoman

Policeman

Typical Paris police car

Paris fire engine

Paris ambulance

of carrying large sums of money. You should never leave your luggage unattended in metro or train stations – it may be stolen or cause a bomb scare. For missing persons, or in the case of robbery or assault, call the police or go to the nearest police station (*Commissariat de Police*). For lost or stolen passports call your consulate (*see p375*).

MEDICAL TREATMENT

All European Union nationals are entitled to French Social Security coverage. However, treatment must be paid for, and hospital rates vary widely. Reimbursements may be obtained if you have a European Health Insurance Card, EHIC (available free to EU citizens), but the process is lengthy. All travellers should consider purchasing travel insurance, and obtain an EHIC in case of

emergencies. Non-EU nationals must carry their own medical insurance.

In the case of a medical emergency, call **SAMU** (*see box on facing page*) or the **Pompiers** (fire department). Fire department ambulances are often the quickest to arrive at an emergency. First-aid and emergency treatment is provided at all fire stations.

Hospitals with casualty departments are shown on the Street Finder (*see p390*). For English-language visitors, there are two hospitals with English-speaking staff and doctors: the **American Hospital** and the **British Hospital**.

There are many pharmacies throughout the city, and a short list is provided here. Pharmacies are recognized by the green crosses on the shop front. At night and on Sundays, pharmacies show in their doorway the address of the nearest one open.

DIRECTORY

LOST PROPERTY BUREAU

Service des Objets Trouvés, 36 Rue des Morillons 75015.
◐ 8.30am–5pm Mon–Thu, 8.30am–4.30pm Fri.
Tel 08 21 00 25 25.

MEDICAL CENTRES

American Hospital
63 Blvd Victor-Hugo, 92200 Neuilly sur Seine.
Tel 01 46 41 25 25.
Private hospital. Enquire about insurance and costs.

British Hospital
3 Rue Barbès 92300 Levallois-Perret.
Tel 01 46 39 22 22.
A private hospital.

Centre Médical Europe
44 Rue d'Amsterdam 75009.
Map 6 D3. *Tel* 01 42 81 93 33.
For dentists *Tel* 01 42 81 80 00.
◐ 8am–8pm Mon–Sat.
An inexpensive private clinic. Appointments, or walk-in.

PHARMACIES

British and American Pharmacy
1 Rue Auber 75009.
Map 6 D4. *Tel* 01 42 65 88 29.
◐ 8.30am–8.30pm Mon–Fri, 10am–8pm Sat.

Pharmacie Bader
12 Blvd St-Michel 75006.
Map 12 F5.
Tel 01 43 26 92 66.
◐ 9am–9pm Mon–Sat, 11am–9pm Sun.

Pharmacie Anglo-Americaine
37 Ave Marceau 75116.
Map 10 E1.
Tel 01 47 20 57 37.
◐ 8.30am–7.30pm Mon–Fri, 9am–5pm Sat.

Pharmacie des Halles
10 Blvd Sebastopol 75004.
Map 13 A3.
Tel 01 42 72 03 23.
◐ 9am– midnight Mon–Sat, 9am–10pm Sun.

Pharmacie Les Champs
84 Ave des Champs-Elysées 75008. **Map** 4 F5.
Tel 01 45 62 02 41.
◐ 24 hours daily.

Banking and Local Currency

Visitors to Paris will find that the banks usually offer them the best rates of exchange. Privately owned bureaux de change, on the other hand, have variable rates, and care should be taken to check small print details relating to commission and minimum charges before any transaction is completed.

USING BANKS

There is no restriction on the amount of money or currency you may bring into France. It is wise to carry large sums in the form of travellers' cheques. To exchange travellers' cheques or cash, bureaux de change are located at airports, large railway stations, and in some hotels and shops.

Many bank branches in central Paris have their own bureaux de change. They generally offer the best exchange rates but also charge a commission for doing the exchange. Most banks also have ATMs (outside or in an indoor area) which accept credit cards in the Carte Bleue/Visa or Mastercard groups and debit cards (Switch, Maestro, Cirrus). This is the quickest and easiest way of obtaining money in local currency, although a small charge will be deducted from your account for this service.

Many independent, non-bank exchange offices do not charge commission, but they offer poorer rates of exchange. Central Paris non-bank exchanges are usually open 9am–6pm Mon–Sat, and are found along the

CHANGE
CAMBIO-WECHSEL

Sign at bureau de change

Champs-Elysées, around the Opéra and Madeleine, and near some tourist attractions and monuments. They can also be found at all main railway stations, open 8am–9pm daily. Note that the bureaux located at Gare St-Lazare and Gare d'Austerlitz

are closed on Sunday. Airport offices tend to open 7am–11pm daily.

CARDS AND CHEQUES

Travellers' cheques can be obtained from **American Express, Travelex** or from your bank. If you know that you will spend most of them, have them issued in Euros. American Express cheques are widely accepted and, if the cheques are exchanged at an

Credit card cash dispenser

Amex office, no commission will be charged. In the case of theft, your cheques will be replaced at once.

Because of the high commissions charged, many French businesses do not accept the American Express credit card. The most commonly used credit card is Carte Bleue/Visa. Eurocard/Mastercard is also widely accepted.

Most credit cards are now "smart cards", with a *puce* (a microchip capable of storing data) as well as a magnetic strip on the back. Many retailers have machines designed to read both smart cards and magnetic strips. Conventional non-French cards cannot be read in the smart card slot. Ask the cashier to swipe the card through the magnetic reader (*bande magnétique*). You may also be asked to tap in your PIN code (*code confidentiel*) and press the green key (*validez*) on a small keypad by the cash desk.

DIRECTORY

AFTER-HOURS BUREAUX DE CHANGE

Le Comptoir des Tuileries
27 Rue de l'Arbre Sec 75001.
Map 12 F2.
Tel 01 42 60 17 16.
◻ *10am–7pm Mon–Fri, 1–7pm Sat.*

Global Change
134 Blvd St-Germain 75006.
Map 12 F4.
Tel 01 40 46 87 75.
◻ *9am–10.30pm daily.*

HSBC
123 Ave des Champs-Elysées 75008. **Map** 4 E4.
Tel 01 40 70 19 54.
◻ *9am–7.15pm Mon–Fri, 9.45am–6.15pm Sat.*

Travelex
Gare du Nord
(opposite Eurostar arrivals).
Map 7 B2.
Tel 01 42 80 11 50.
◻ *6.30am–11.30pm Mon–Thu, Sun (to 11.45pm Fri, 11.15pm Sat).*

FOREIGN BANKS

American Express
11 Rue Scribe 75009.
Map 6 D5.
Tel 01 47 77 70 00.

Barclays
24 bis Ave de l'Opéra 75001.
Map 6 E5.
Tel 01 44 86 00 20.
One of several branches.

HSBC
22 Pl de la Madeleine 75008.
Map 5 C5.
Tel 01 44 71 10 00.

Travelex
8 Place de l'Opéra 75009.
Tel 01 47 42 46 52.

LOST CARDS AND TRAVELLERS' CHEQUES

American Express
Tel 01 47 77 70 00 **Cards**.
Tel 08 00 90 86 00 **Cheques**.

Mastercard
Tel 01 45 67 53 53 **Cards**.

Visa/Carte Bleue
Tel 08 92 70 57 05 **Cards**.

THE EURO

The euro (€), the single European currency, is now operational in 13 of the member states of the EU. Austria, Belgium, Finland, France, Germany, Greece, Ireland, Italy, Luxembourg, Netherlands, Portugal, Slovenia and Spain all chose to join the new currency; Denmark, the UK and Sweden chose to stay out, with an option to review their decision. France's Overseas Departments (Réunion etc) also all now use the euro.

Euro notes are identical throughout all 13 countries, bearing architectural drawings of fictitious monuments. The coins, however, have one side identical (the value side), and one side unique to each country. Both notes and coins are valid and interchangeable within each of the 13 countries.

Bank Notes

Euro bank notes have seven denominations. The 5€ note (grey in colour) is the smallest, followed by the 10€ note (pink), 20€ note (blue), 50€ note (orange), 100€ note (green), 200€ note (yellow) and 500€ note (purple). All notes show the stars of the European Union.

5 euros

10 euros

20 euros

50 euros

100 euros

200 euros

500 euros

2 euros

1 euro

50 cents

20 cents

10 cents

Coins

The euro has eight coin denominations: 1€ and 2€; 50 cents, 20 cents, 10 cents, 5 cents, 2 cents and 1 cent. The 1€ and 2€ coins are both silver and gold in colour. The 50-, 20- and 10-cent coins are gold. The 5-, 2- and 1-cent coins are bronze.

5 cents

2 cents

1 cent

Telephone and Postal Service

The French telecommunications agency is called France Télécom, the postal service is La Poste. Both work efficiently, though the customer services of the post offices may not. So, be prepared to wait in queues. There are many *bureaux de poste* scattered throughout the city. These are identified by the blue-on-yellow La Poste sign *(see p373)*. Public telephones are located in most public places, including on the streets and in railway and metro stations. If you are dialling abroad from Paris, the best way is to purchase a telephone card *(télécarte)*, then find a quiet location to call from.

Telephone Boxes
Coin-operated telephone boxes are now rare. Card-operated telephones are cheap and easy to use, but you must buy a télécarte *first.*

Modern, card-operated phonebox

Older-style phonebox

USING A PHONECARD (TELECARTE) TELEPHONE

1 Lift the receiver and wait for a dialling tone.

2 Holding the *télécarte* with the arrow side up, insert it into the slot in the direction that the arrow is pointing.

3 Wait for the display screen to indicate how many units are stored on the card. The screen will then tell you to dial.

4 Dial the number and wait to be connected.

5 If you want to make another call do not replace the receiver, simply press the green follow-on call button.

6 When you have finished the call, replace the receiver. The card will emerge from the slot. Remove it.

FRANCE TELECOM
600 AGENCES
PARTOUT
EN FRANCE
TELECARTE 50

FRANCE TELECOM

Télécarte phonecard

USING THE TELEPHONE

To use a Paris payphone, you generally need a phone card *(télécarte)*, though some accept credit cards. Sold in *tabacs*, post offices and some newsagents, *télécartes* are available in 50 or 120 telephone units. Remember to buy a new card before the old one runs out! Coin telephones have virtually disappeared from the streets of Paris. Reverse charge calls are known as *PCV* in France. Most telephone boxes can be called from anywhere. The telephone box number is displayed above the telephone unit.

French telephone numbers have ten digits. The first two digits indicate the region: 01 for Paris and the Ile de France; 02, the northwest; 03, the northeast; 04, the southeast; and 05, the southwest. Do not dial the initial zero when phoning from abroad.

Most new mobile phones brought from another European or Mediterranean country can be used in France. Alert your network in good time that you plan to use the phone abroad so that they can enable it. However, US-based mobiles need to be "triple band" to be used in France. Remember that the making and receiving of international mobile calls can be very expensive.

INTERNET ACCESS

Internet access is widely available in Paris, including WiFi access in many hotels, bars and cafés. Note that the French modem socket is incompatible with US and UK plugs, although adaptors are available.

REACHING THE RIGHT NUMBER

- **In the case of emergencies,** dial 17.
- **Directory enquiries** dial 118 712.
- **International directory enquiries**, for all countries, dial 32 12.
- **International telegrams** dial 0800 33 44 11; for telegrams in France, dial 36 55.
- **Home Direct** (reverse charge), dial 0800 99, then the country code (preceded by 00).
- To make direct international calls, dial 00, wait for the tone, then dial the country code, area code (omit the intital 0) and the number.

- The country codes for the following are: **Australia**: 61; **Canada and USA**: 1; **Eire**: 353; **New Zealand**: 64; **UK**: 44.
- **Low-rate period** (for most places): 7pm–8am Mon–Fri, all day Sun and public holidays.
- The middle pages of the telephone directory give the cost of calls per minute for each country and list their country codes, Home Direct codes, etc.
- To telephone **France** from your home country, dial: from the UK 00 33; from the US 011 33; from Australia: 00 11 33. Omit the first 0 of the French area code.

Mail and Postal Services – Using La Poste

Post office sign

In addition to all normal services – telegrams, postage stamps, registered letters, special delivery, delivery of packages and books – the post office also sells collectors' stamps, and will cash or send international money orders. Fax and telex services, as well as public telephones and Minitel, are available in all main offices.

SENDING A LETTER

Common postage stamps *(timbres)* are sold singly or in *carnets* of ten. These are valid for letters and postcards up to 20 g (approximately an ounce) to most EU countries. Stamps can often be bought in *tabacs*. Paris post office hours are 8am–7pm (or 8pm) Mon–Fri, 8am–noon Sat. At post offices you can consult the phone book *(annuaire)*, buy phonecards *(télécartes)*, send or receive money orders *(mandats)* and call anywhere in the world.

Letters are dropped into yellow mail boxes.

For poste restante (mail holding), the sender should write the recipient's name in block letters, then "Poste Restante", then the address of the Paris-Louvre post office.

When sending a letter *poste restante*, it is wise to underline the surname, as French officials otherwise may assume the first name is the family name.

MAIN POST OFFICES

Paris-Louvre
52 Rue de Louvre 75001.
Map 12 F1. **Tel** 01 40 28 76 00.
◷ 24 hrs daily.

Paris-Forum des Halles
Forum des Halles 75001. **Map** 13 A2. **Tel** 01 44 76 84 60. ◷ 8am–6pm Mon–Fri, 8am–noon Sat.

Paris-Champs Elysées
71 Ave des Champs Elysées 75008.
Map 4 F5.
Tel 01 53 89 05 80.
Fax 01 42 56 13 71.
◷ 9am–7.30pm Mon–Fri, 10am–7pm Sat.

Destinations

Paris letter box

Paris Arrondissements
The districts or arrondissements of Paris are numbered from 1 to 20 (see p390). The first three numbers of the postcode – 750 (sometimes 751) – indicate Paris; the last two give the arrondissement number. The first arrondissement's postcode is 75001.

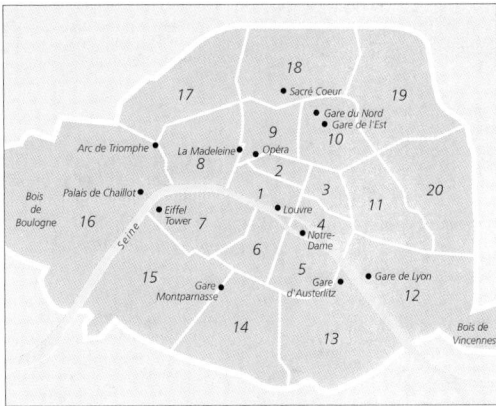

CUSTOMS AND IMMIGRATION

For travellers coming from within the EU's "Schengen" zone (ie. those that agreed to the Schengen Treaty), in theory no documentation at all is needed to enter France. However, in these days of greater security it is wise to carry a passport at all times. For "non-Schengen" nationals, including the UK, a passport (or similar) is required. Visitors from the US, Canada, Australia and New Zealand do not need a visa if staying under 3 months. However, for a trip over 3 months, a visa must be applied for from the French consulate in the visitor's own country before leaving.

TAX-FREE GOODS

The purchase of goods "Duty Free" for export to another EU country is no longer possible. Visitors resident outside the European Union can reclaim the sales tax (TVA, or VAT; *see p320*) they pay on French goods if they spend more than 175€ in the same shop in one day and take the goods out of France.

Détaxe receipts can be issued on purchase to reclaim the tax paid, and reimbursements are collected when exiting the EU, which must be within 3 months of purchase. There are some goods you cannot claim a rebate on, namely food and drink, medicines, tobacco, cars and motorbikes.

DUTY-PAID AND DUTY-FREE GOODS

There are no longer any restrictions on the quantities of duty-paid and VAT-paid goods you can take from one EU country to another, as long as they are for your own use and not for resale. You may be asked to prove the goods are for your own use if they exceed the EU suggested quantities. If you cannot do so, the entire amount of the goods (not just the deemed excess) may be confiscated. The suggested limits are: 10 litres of spirits (i.e. drinks over 22° proof), 90 litres of wine (of which a maximum of 60 litres can be sparkling), 110 litres of beer and five multipacks of cigarettes. Some dangerous goods are illegal. Visitors under the age of 17 are not allowed to import duty-paid tobacco or alcohol.

Bottle of scent

IMPORTING OTHER GOODS

In general, all personal goods (eg. car or bicycle) may be imported to France if they are obviously for personal use and not for sale. The brochure *Voyagez en toute liberté* clarifies this. It is available from the **Centre** below, which also gives advice on import regulations (usually in French).

CUSTOMS INFORMATION

Centre des Renseignements des Douanes
84 Rue d'Hauteville 75010. **Tel** 08 20 02 44 44. ◷ 8.30am–6pm Mon–Fri.
www.douane.gouv.fr

ELECTRICAL ADAPTORS

The voltage in France is 220 volts. Plugs have two small round pins; heavier-duty installations have two large round pins. Better hotels offer built-in adaptors for shavers only or will lend you an adaptor. Adaptors can be bought at department stores, such as BHV *(see p321)*.

French two-pin electrical plug

STUDENT INFORMATION

Students with valid ID cards benefit from discounts of 25–50% at theatres, museums, cinemas and many public monuments. An ISIC card (the International Student ID card) may be purchased from main travel agencies, Office de Tourisme de l'Université offices (**OTU**) and the Centre d'Information et de Documentation Jeunesse (**CIDJ**). CIDJ provides information on student life in Paris and can furnish a list of inexpensive accommodation, including the Bureau Voyage Jeunesse (**BVJ**), which has 2 hostels in central Paris with double rooms and dormitory accommodation at reasonable prices *(see pp279-80 and 375)*.

PUBLIC TOILETS IN PARIS

Most old-fashioned urinals and toilets have been replaced by modern pay toilets. They are found on pavements all over the city. In some units, classical music is played. It is crucial that children under 10 are not allowed into these toilets on their own. They have an automatic cleaning function which can be a danger to small children.

1 Put the amount indicated in the slot.

2 Press button to open sliding door.

3 The light indicates vacant or engaged.

INTERNATIONAL BOOKSHOPS

Brentano's
37 Ave de l'Opéra 75002.
Map 6 E5. **Tel** 01 42 61 52 50.
◐ 10am–7.30pm Mon–Sat.

Gibert Jeune
5 Place St-Michel 75005.
Map 13 A4. **Tel** 01 56 81 22 22.
◐ 9.30am–7.30pm Mon–Sat.

WH Smith
248 Rue de Rivoli 75001. **Map** 11
C1. **Tel** 01 44 77 88 99. ◐ 9am–
7.30pm Mon–Sat, 1–7.30pm Sun.

TV, RADIO, PRESS

British and other European papers can be bought on the day of publication at *maisons*

Foreign newspapers from kiosks

de la presse (newsagents) or *kiosques* (news-stands) throughout the city. Some are European or international editions, such as *The Sun, Financial Times Europe* and the *Guardian International, The Weekly Telegraph, USA Today, The Economist,* and *The International Herald Tribune.*

The main French national dailies are – from right to left on the political spectrum – *Le Figaro, France Soir, Le Monde, Libération* and *L'Humanité.* The weeklies include satirical *Le Canard Enchaîné,* news magazines *Marianne, Le Nouvel Observateur* and *L'Express,* and numerous titles devoted to fashion, gossip and gastronomy.

The French TV channels are *TF1* and *France 2,* both with a lightweight mix, *France 3,* with documentaries, debate and classic films, *5* ("La Cinquième") and the Franco-German high-culture *ARTE,* which share a channel special-ising in arts, classical music and films, and *M6* which devotes a lot of time to pop and rock. Cable and satellite channels include CNN, Sky, a variety of BBC channels and the English- and French-language news channel France 24.

BBC Radio 4 can be picked up during the day, while at night, *BBC World Service* uses the same channel (648AM or 198 Long Wave). *Radio France International* (738AM) gives excellent daily news in English on their web site www.rfi.fr.

PARIS TIME

Paris is one hour ahead of Greenwich Mean Time (GMT) all year round. The French use the 24-hour clock, therefore, 9am is 09.00, 9pm is 21.00. New York is 6 hours behind Paris, Los Angeles 9 hours behind and Auckland 11 hours ahead.

CONVERSION CHART

Imperial to metric
1 inch = 2.54 centimetres
1 foot = 30 centimetres
1 mile = 1.6 kilometres
1 ounce = 28 grams
1 pound = 454 grams
1 pint = 0.6 litre
1 gallon = 4.6 litres

Metric to imperial
1 millimetre = 0.04 inch
1 centimetre = 0.4 inch
1 metre = 3 feet 3 inches
1 kilometre = 0.6 mile
1 gram = 0.04 ounce
1 kilogram = 2.2 pounds
1 litre = 1.8 pints

DIRECTORY

STUDENT INFO

OTU Voyages
119 Rue St-Martin 75004.
Map 13 B2.
Tel 01 40 29 12 22.

1 Pl du Mchl. de Lattre de
Tassigny 75016.
Map 3 A4.
Tel 01 47 55 03 07.

CIDJ
101 Quai Branly 75015.
Map 10 E2.
Tel 01 44 49 12 00.
◐ 9.30am–6pm Mon–Fri
(7pm Tue & Thu), 9.30am–
1pm Sat. www.cidj.com

BVJ
20 Rue Jean-Jacques
Rousseau 75001. **Map** 12
F2. **Tel** 01 53 00 90 90.

44 Rue des Bernardins
75005. **Map** 13 B5.
Tel 01 43 29 34 80.

EMBASSIES

Australia
4 Rue Jean Rey 75015.
Map 10 D3.
Tel 01 40 59 33 00.

Canada
35 Ave Montaigne 75008.
Map 10 F1.
Tel 01 44 43 29 00.

Great Britain
35 Rue du Faubourg
St-Honoré 75008.
Map 5 C5.
Consulate (visas) 18bis
Rue d'Anjou 75008.
Tel 01 44 51 31 01.

Ireland (Eire)
12 Ave Foch 75016. **Map**
3 B4. **Tel** 01 44 17 67 00.

New Zealand
7 ter Rue Léonard de Vinci
75116. **Map** 3 C5.
Tel 01 45 01 43 43.

USA
2 Ave Gabriel 75008.
Map 5 B5.
Tel 01 43 12 22 22. *Visa
services* 0810 26 46 26.

RELIGIOUS SERVICES

PROTESTANT

American Church
65 Quai d'Orsay 75007.
Map 10 F2.
Tel 01 40 62 05 00.

Church of Scotland
17 Rue Bayard 75008.
Map 10 F1.
Tel/Fax 01 40 70 09 59.

St George's Anglican Church
7 Rue Auguste Vacquerie
75116. **Map** 4 E5.
Tel 01 47 20 22 51.

CATHOLIC

Basilique du Sacré-Coeur
35 Rue du Chevalier de la
Barre 75018.
Map 6 F1.
Tel 01 53 41 89 00.

Cathédrale de Notre-Dame
Pl du Parvis Notre-Dame
75004. **Map** 13 A4.
Tel 01 42 34 56 10.

JEWISH

Synagogue Nazareth
15 Rue Notre Dame de
Nazareth 75003. **Map**
7 C5. **Tel** 01 42 78 00 30.

MUSLIM

Grande Mosquée de Paris
Place du Puits de l'Ermite
75005. **Map** 17 B2.
Tel 01 45 35 97 33.

GETTING TO PARIS

Paris is a major hub of European air, road and rail travel. Direct flights from around the world serve the French capital's two main international airports. Paris is also at the centre of Europe's growing high-speed rail network, with arrivals throughout the day of Eurostar from London, Thalys from Brussels, Amsterdam and Cologne, and TGVs from Marseille and Geneva. Approaching by road, *auto-routes* (motorways) converge on Paris from all directions, including – via Eurotunnel's Channel rail shuttle – the UK.

Boeing 737 passenger jet

ARRIVING BY AIR

The main British airlines with regular flights to Paris are **British Airways** and **British Midland**. The main French airline is **Air France**. From the United States there are regular flights direct to Paris mainly on **American**, **United**, **Northwest**, **Continental** and **Delta**. From Canada, **Air France** and **Air Canada** fly direct to Paris. **Qantas** is one of the few providing connecting flights from Australia and New Zealand.

Easyjet (from Liverpool, Luton, Newcastle, Bristol and Belfast), **BmiBaby** (Durham, East Midlands, Leeds and London) and **Jet2** (Leeds-Bradford and Manchester) offer an inexpensive CDG service. **Ryanair** flies from Dublin, Shannon and Glasgow (Prestwick) to Beauvais, an hour's bus journey north of Paris. For airline offices in Paris, see page 379.

The peak summer season in Paris is from July to September. Airline fares are at their highest during this time. Different airlines, however, may have slightly different high summer season periods, so check with the airlines or an agent as to which months are covered by these fares.

Generally speaking, airlines offer their lowest fares to passengers booking on the internet via their websites. It often pays to book far in advance. However, last minute deals are sometimes available.

Addresses of reputable discount agencies in Paris are listed on page 379. You will find that these agencies offer charters and regular scheduled flights at extremely competitive prices. Many of them also have representatives in other countries.

Flight Times
Listed here are some examples of flight times to Paris from various cities in different parts of the world:
London 1 hour;
Dublin 90 minutes;
Montreal 7.5 hours;
New York 8 hours;
Los Angeles 12 hours;
Sydney 23 hours.

CHARLES DE GAULLE AIRPORT

T3
CDG1
CDG2
The airport complex

The terminals CDG1, CDG2 and T3 are linked by shuttle buses. The main transport services to Paris are shown below. Check door numbers as they are subject to change.

CDG1 is used for international flights, except those of Air France (see CDG2).

Taxis (Door 20)
Car-hire agencies (Doors 10, 18 & 20)
Roissybus & Disneyland Paris bus (Door 30)
Air France buses (Door 34)
Shuttle buses (Shopping Level)

CDG2 is used for all Air France flights and for short-hop international flights by other carriers.

Air France & shuttle buses (Doors 2 & 6)
CDG2B
Disneyland Paris bus (Door 11)
Air France bus to Etoile & shuttle buses (Doors 5 & 8)
CDG2A
Taxis (Door 6)
Roissybus (Door 9)
Air France buses to Montparnasse & Orly; & shuttle buses (Doors 2, 5 & 8)
CDG2C
Roissybus (Door 11)
Taxis (Door 7)
CDG2D
TGV and RER stations
Air France bus to Etoile & shuttle buses (Door 6)
CDG2F
CDG2E

ORLY AIRPORT

The two terminals Orly Sud and Orly Ouest are linked by shuttle bus, but they are within walking distance of one another.

Orly Ouest

Orly Sud

The airport complex

Orlyval (Departure Level, Hall 2 Door W)

Air France buses (Arrival Level, Door D)

Orlyrail (Arrival Level, Door G)

Taxis (Arrival Level, Doors H & D)

Air France buses (Door K, platform 6)

Orlybus (Door H, platform 4) Jetbus (Door H, platform 2)

Jetbus (Arrival Level, Door C)

Taxis (Doors L & M)

Orlybus (Arrival Level, Door J)

Orly Ouest is largely used for domestic flights.

Orlyval (Door K)

Orly Sud is used for a wider range of services, handling international, regular and charter flights.

Orlyrail (Door G, platform 1)

CHARLES DE GAULLE (CDG) AIRPORT

Paris's main airport lies 30 km (19 miles) north of the city. It has two main terminals, CDG1 and CDG2, and a charter flight terminal, T3. CDG2 straddles the TGV-RER station and comprises six linked halls: CDG2A, CDG2B, CDG2C, CDG2D, CDG2E and CDG2F.

Getting into Town

Buses, trains and taxis all run to central Paris. Air France operates two services from CDG1 and CDG2: one goes to Porte Maillot and Charles de Gaulle-Etoile (about every 12mins; journey time about 40mins); the other to the Gare de Lyon and Montparnasse TGV train station (every 30mins; journey time about 50mins). From T3 it is a short walk to the RER station, where you can catch a train to central Paris. The RATP Roissybus, serving all three terminals, takes travellers to Opéra (every 20mins 6am–11pm; journey time about 50mins).

Disneyland Paris runs the VEA bus service (8.30am–7.45pm daily, to 10pm Fri, to 9.30pm Sun) every 30–45 minutes from CDG1 and CDG2.

The TGV station is in CDG2, and there are RER

train stations (Line B) at CDG1 (linked via a shuttle bus) and CDG2. Trains leave every 5–15 minutes and take about 35 minutes to reach the city centre, at the Gare du Nord, Châtelet, St-Michel, Luxembourg and Port Royal.

Airport Shuttle (Tel: 0825 09 20 92) provides door-to-door service in a small minibus for both airports and Beauvais, for 27€ for one person, or 17€–20€ each for two or more (book at least 48 hours ahead, then call them after landing to confirm your journey). Normal taxis to the centre run between 36€ (daytime) and 45€, often with long queues.

ORLY AIRPORT (ORY)

This is Paris's second airport, which is located 15 km (9 miles) south of the capital. It has two terminals, Orly Sud and Orly Ouest.

Getting into Town

Transport services go to the southern part of the city, and a special bus (VEA shuttle) links the airport with Disneyland Resort Paris (every 45mins 8.30am–7.30pm).

Travellers arriving at Orly can take a taxi, bus or train to central Paris. The buses are run by Air France and RATP (Orlybus). Air France buses

take about 30 minutes to reach the city centre, stopping at Les Invalides and Gare de Montparnasse. The Orlybus (every 12–20mins) takes about 25 minutes to reach the city centre at Denfert-Rochereau. The Jet Bus service takes travellers from the airport to Villejuif-Louis Aragon metro station every 15–20 minutes.

A bus called Orlyrail links the airport with RER Line C at Pont de Rungis. Trains leave from here every 15 minutes (30 mins after 9pm), taking 25 minutes to reach the Gare d'Austerlitz. An automatic train, Orlyval, links the airport with RER Line B at Antony station, from where trains leave every 4–8 minutes for Châtelet (35-minute total journey).

Taxis to the city centre take 25–45 minutes, depending on the traffic, and cost 25€–30€.

Orlyval train leaving Orly Airport

CROSSING THE CHANNEL

A long-haul coach

Travellers coming to Paris from Britain by road will need to cross the English Channel. The simplest and most popular way is on the vehicle-carrying train shuttles through the Channel Tunnel. Operated by **Eurotunnel**, these run between the terminals at Folkestone and Calais. You are directed onto the trains and remain with your vehicle, though you may get out of your car and walk about inside the train.

The journey through the Tunnel takes about 30 minutes, is unaffected by sea conditions or weather, and trains depart every 15–30 minutes, depending on demand. On both the English and the French side, the Tunnel terminal has direct motorway access.

There are also several ship or catamaran car ferries across the Channel. On the short Dover–Calais route alone, there are up to 100 crossings per day, operated by several operators running frequent, fast services. **SeaFrance** takes 90 minutes to cross, for example. **Transmanche Ferries**, part of Corsica Ferries, runs the route between Newhaven and Dieppe, which takes nearly 4 hours. **Norfolkline** has a 2-hour Dover to Dunkerque crossing.

Two companies ply the longer western routes across the Channel. **Brittany Ferries** crossings from Plymouth to Roscoff take up to 8 hours, and from Poole to Cherbourg they take 4¼ hours on conventional ferry, or 3 hours on the Condor Vitesse (fast ferry). From Portsmouth, Brittany take 6 hours to Caen, and 11 hours overnight to St-Malo. **P&O** has reduced its ferry routes to just Dover–Calais. **LD Lines** now runs from Portsmouth to Le Havre in 5½ hours. Driving to Paris from Cherbourg takes 4–5 hours; from Dieppe or Le Havre, about 2½–3 hours; from Calais, 2 hours.

ARRIVING BY COACH

The main coach operator to Paris is **Eurolines**, based at the Gare Routière Internationale in eastern Paris. Its coaches travel to Belgium, Holland, Ireland, Germany, Scandinavia, United Kingdom, Italy and Portugal.

Their terminus in London is Victoria Coach Station, from where there are between three and five daily departures for Paris, depending on the season. The journey from London to Paris takes between 8 and 9 hours.

USEFUL CONTACTS

Eurostar
Tel 08705 186 186 *(UK)*.
www.eurostar.com

Eurotunnel
Tel 08705 35 35 35 *(UK)*.
www.eurotunnel.com

Brittany Ferries
Tel 0870 90 76 103 *(UK)*.
www.brittany-ferries.co.uk

LD Lines
www.ldlines.com

Norfolkline
Tel 08708 701 020 *(UK)*.

P&O
Tel 08 92 89 90 91.

SeaFrance
Tel 08705 711 711 *(UK)*.

Transmanche Ferries
Tel 08009 171 201 *(UK)*.

Eurolines
Ave de Général de Gaulle, Bagnolet.
Tel 08 92 89 90 91.
Victoria Coach Station, London SW1.
Tel 08705 808 080.
www.eurolines.com

ARRIVING BY RAIL

Eurostar trains travel directly from central London (St Pancras) and Ashford (Kent) to central Paris (Gare du Nord) in 2hrs and 35mins. There are up to 24 departures daily. Other high-speed services into Paris

The high-speed TGV train

THE TGV

Trains à Grande Vitesse, or TGV high-speed trains, travel at speeds up to 300 km/h (186mph). TGVs for northern France leave from the Gare du Nord, for the Atlantic Coast and Brittany from Gare Montparnasse, and for Provence and the southeast from Gare de Lyon. The network serves a large number of stations on routes to these destinations, and the number of stations served is growing all the time, making this an ever-more convenient form of transport (see pp380–81).

include **Thalys**, from Brussels, Amsterdam and Cologne, and **TGVs** from throughout France. These services must be pre-booked, though reservations can be made up to the last moment. Prices are much cheaper booked ahead.

As the railway hub of France and the Continent, Paris has five major international railway stations operated by the French state railways, known as SNCF *(see p388)*. The Gare de Lyon in eastern Paris is the city's main station, serving the south of France, the Alps, Italy and Switzerland. The Gare de l'Est serves eastern France, Austria, Switzerland and Germany.

Arriving at the Gare du Nord are trains from Britain, Holland, Belgium and Scandinavia. Trains from some Channel ports arrive at the Gare St-Lazare. The termini for trains from Spain, as well as from the Brittany ports, are the Gare Montparnasse and Gare d'Austerlitz. The other main stations are: Gare de Bercy; Massy-Palaiseau (SW of city); Marne-la-Vallée for Disneyland Resort Paris (E); Aeroport Charles-de-Gaulle (NE).

There is a tourist office at the Gare de Lyon where you can book accommodation *(see p367)*. All the railway stations are served by city buses, the metro and RER trains. Directional signs show where to make connections to the city transport system.

ARRIVING BY CAR

Paris is an oval-shaped city. It is surrounded by an outer ring road called the Boulevard Périphérique. All motorways leading to the capital link in to the Périphérique, which separates the city from the suburbs. Each former city gate, called a *porte*, now corresponds to an exit from (or entrance to) the Périphérique. Arriving motorists should check their destination address and consult a map of central Paris to find the closest corresponding *porte*. For example, a motorist who wants to get to the Arc de Triomphe should exit at Porte Maillot.

DIRECTORY

MAIN AIRLINES SERVING PARIS

Aer Lingus
Tel 0870 876 5000 (UK).
www.aerlingus.com

Air Canada
Tel 0825 880 881.
www.aircanada.ca

Air France
49 Ave de l'Opéra 75002.
Map 6 E5.
Tel 0820 820 820.
www.airfrance.fr

American Airlines
Charles de Gaulle airport.
Tel 0810 872 872.
www.aa.com

bmibaby
Tel 0870 607 0555 (UK).
www.bmibaby.com

British Airways
Tel 0825 825 400.
www.ba.com

British Midland
Tel 01 41 91 87 04.
www.flybmi.com

Delta Airlines
Tel 0811 640 005.
www.delta.com

Easyjet
Tel 08 99 70 00 41.
www.easyjet.com

Jet2
Tel 0871 226 17 37 (UK).
Tel 0818 200 017
(Ireland).
Tel +44 207 17 00 737
(overseas).
www.jet2.com

Qantas Airways
Tel 08 11 98 00 02.
www.qantas.com

Ryanair
Tel 08 18 30 30 30 (UK).
www.ryanair.com

DISCOUNT TRAVEL AGENCIES

Directours
90 Ave des Champs-Elysées 75008. **Map** 4 E4.
Tel 01 45 62 62 62.
www.directours.com

Forum Voyages
1 Rue Cassette 75006.
Map 12 D5.
Tel 01 45 44 38 61.
www.forumvoyages.com

Jet Tours
29 Ave de la Motte Picquet 75007. **Map** 10 F4.
Tel 01 47 05 01 95.
www.jettours.com

Nouvelles Frontières
12 Rue Auber 75009.
Map 6 D4. *Tel* 08 25 00 08 25. **www**.nouvelles-frontieres.fr

USIT Voyages
Tel 08 25 08 25 25.
www.usitconnections.fr

AIRPORT INFORMATION

www.adp.fr

Information/paging
Tel 01 48 62 22 80 (CDG).
Tel 01 49 75 15 15 (Orly).
Tel 0892 681 515 (CDG & Orly: same day flight info).

Disabled Assistance
To order free guide *Guide Passager à mobilité réduite* and further information:
Tel 01 48 62 22 80 (CDG).
Tel 01 49 75 15 15 (Orly).

Air France Buses
Tel 0892 350 820.
www.cars-airfrance.com

RATP (Roissybus/Orlybus)
Tel 08 92 68 77 14
(French); 08 92 68 41 14
(English).
www.ratp.fr

RER Trains
Tel 0892 687 714.

TGV & SNCF
Tel 36 35.
www.sncf.com

Airport Shuttle
Tel 01 53 39 18 18.
www.parishuttle.fr

CDG Airport Hotels

Ibis
Tel 01 49 19 19 19.
www.ibishotel.com

Holiday Inn
Tel 01 34 29 30 00.
www.holidayinn.co.uk

Novotel
Tel 01 49 19 27 27.
www.accorhotels.com

Sofitel
Tel 01 49 19 29 29.
www.sofitel.com

ORLY SUD AIRPORT HOTELS

Ibis
Tel 01 56 70 50 50.
@ H1413@accor.com

Hilton Hotel
Tel 01 45 12 45 12.
@ oryhitwRM@hilton.com. **www**.hilton-paris.com

Mercure
Tel 01 49 75 15 50.
@ H1246@accor.com
www.accorhotels.com

Arriving in Paris

This map depicts the bus and rail services between the two main airports and the city. It shows the ferry-rail links from the UK, the main railway links from other parts of France and Europe, and the long-haul coach services from other European countries. It also shows the main city railway and coach termini, the airport shuttle connections and the airport bus and rail stops. The frequency of services and journey times from the airport are provided, as are the approximate times of rail journeys from other cities. Metro and RER line connections to other parts of Paris are indicated at the termini and route stops.

🚢 CALAIS
Ferry and Eurotunnel links with Dover and Folkestone. Eurostar train from London to Paris Gare du Nord (3 hrs) passes through here on the way to St Pancras and Ashford from Paris. SNCF train to Gare du Nord (2 hrs–2 hrs 45 mins).

Porte Maillot M (1) RER (A)(C)

Charles de Gaulle-Etoile M (1)(2)(6) RER (A)

Champs-Elysées

Chaillot Quarter

Gare St-Lazare M (3)(1)

Invalides M (8)(13) RER (C)

Invalides and Eiffel Tower Quarter

🚢 LE HAVRE
Ferry links with Portsmouth. SNCF train to Gare St-Lazare (2 hrs).
🚢 DIEPPE
Ferry links with Newhaven (summer). SNCF train to Gare St-Lazare (2 hrs 20 mins).
🚢 CAEN
Ferry links with Portsmouth. SNCF train to Gare St-Lazare (1 hr 50 mins).
🚢 CHERBOURG
Ferry links with Portsmouth and Poole. SNCF train to Gare St-Lazare (3 hrs).

GARE ST-LAZARE
Rouen (1 hr 30 mins).

GARE MONTPARNASSE
Bordeaux (3 hrs 30 mins)
Brest (4 hrs 30 mins)
Lisbon (21 hrs)
Madrid (16 hrs)
Nantes (2 hrs 15 mins)
Rennes (2 hrs 20 mins)

Montparnasse

Gare Montparnasse M (4)(6)(12)(13)(14)

Porte de Orléans M (4)

KEY
— SNCF see pp378–9
— Coaches see p378
— Roissybus see p377
— Air France bus see p377
— RER B see p377
— Orlyrail see p377
— Orlyval see p377
— Orlybus see p377
— Jet Bus see p377
M Metro station
RER RER station

0 kilometres 1
0 miles 0.5

GARE TGV DE MASSY-PALAISEAU
Bordeaux (3 hrs 30 mins)
Lille (1 hr 40 mins)
London (3 hrs 40 mins)
Lyon (2 hrs)
Nantes (2 hrs 30 mins)
Rennes (2 hrs 10 mins)

Antony RER (B)

GARE DU NORD
Amsterdam (4 hrs 30 mins)
Bonn (4 hrs 30 mins–5 hrs)
Brussels (Thalys) (1 hr 25 mins)
Cologne (3 hrs 50 mins)
Lille (1 hr)
London (Eurostar) (2hrs 35 mins)

CHARLES DE GAULLE
Bus and train services to the city every 15 mins.
Air France to
Porte Maillot/Etoile (40 mins);
Gare de Lyon/
Montparnasse (50 mins);
Orly
(50 mins–1 hr 15 mins).
Roissybus to *Opéra*
(50 mins).
RER *Line B* to *Gare du*
Nord (35 mins).

GARE TGV AEROPORT
CHARLES-DE-GAULLE
Bordeaux (4 hrs 30 mins)
Brussels (1 hr 15 mins–2 hrs)
Disneyland Paris (10–15 mins)
Lille (50 mins)
London (3 hrs 30 mins)
Lyon (2 hrs)
Marseille (3 hrs 30 mins–4 hrs 30 mins)
Nantes (3 hrs 15 mins)
Rennes (3 hrs 30 mins)

GARE DE L'EST
Basel (6 hrs–6 hrs 30 mins)
Frankfurt (6 hrs 30 mins)
Luxembourg (3 hrs 30 mins)
Nancy (2 hrs 40 mins)
Strasbourg (5 hrs)
Vienna (14 hrs)
Zurich (6 hrs 40 mins)

Galliéni M ③

GARE INTERNATIONALE
DE PARIS-GALLIENI
All international bus services arrive
and depart from this station.

GARE DE LYON
Geneva (3 hrs 30 mins)
Lausanne (3 hrs 40 mins–
4 hrs 50 mins)
Lyon (2 hrs)
Marseille (3 hrs)
Milan (6 hrs 40 mins–8 hrs)
Rome (12 hrs 30 mins–14 hrs)
Zurich (6 hrs)

ORLY
There are direct bus and train services
to the city every 12–15 minutes.
Air France to *Les Invalides* (30 mins); *Montparnasse* (30 mins);
Charles de Gaulle (50mins–1hr15 mins).
Orlybus to *Denfert-Rochereau*
(25 mins).
RER *Orlyrail* to *Pont de Rungis & RER*
Line C to *Gare d'Austerlitz* (35 mins).
RER *Orlyval* to *Antony & RER Line B*
to *Châtelet* (35 mins).
Jet Bus to *Villejuif* (15 mins).

GARE D'AUSTERLITZ
Barcelona (12 hrs)
Limoges (3 hrs)
Madrid (13 hrs 30 mins–16 hrs)
Toulouse (6 hrs 30 mins)

GARE TGV DE MARNE-
LA-VALLEE
For Disneyland Paris
Bordeaux (4 hrs)
Brussels (1 hr 30 mins)
Lille (1 hr)
London (3 hrs 30 mins)
Lyon (1 hr 50 mins)
Marseille (3 hrs 50 mins)
Nantes (3 hrs)
Rennes (2 hrs 50 mins)

GETTING AROUND PARIS

Central Paris is compact. The best way to get around is to walk. Cycling and roller-blading are increasingly popular with Parisians and tourists alike but they are not without risk. Visitors unfamiliar with the motoring code and undisciplined French driving need to take care.

Driving a car in the city centre is not fun. Traffic is often heavy, there are many one-way streets, and parking is notoriously difficult and expensive. The bus, metro and RER train system operated by the RATP makes getting around cheap and easy. The city is divided into five travel zones: zones 1 and 2 corresponding to the centre and zones 3, 4 and 5 to the suburbs and the airport. The city is also divided into 20 arrondissements, which will help visitors in their search for addresses (see p373).

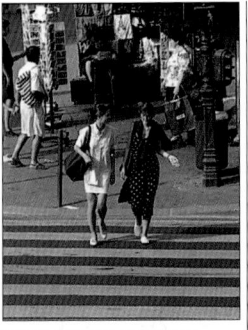

Parisian drivers do not always respect pedestrian crossings.

Stop sign

Walk sign

WALKING IN PARIS

Australian, British, Irish and New Zealand visitors need to remember that cars drive on the right-hand side of the road. There are many two-stage road crossings where pedestrians wait on an island in the centre of the road before proceeding. These are marked *piétons traversez en deux temps*.

Walking tours are cited in the weekly listings magazines (see p340).

CYCLING IN PARIS

Paris is an excellent city for cyclists. It's reasonably flat, manageably small, has many backstreets where car traffic is restricted, and about 150 km (103 miles) of cycle lanes (*pistes cyclables*). Parisian motorists are increasingly respectful of cyclists as more

and more of their fellow citizens turn to two wheels.

The RATP's own cycling centre, the **Maison Roue Libre**, in the heart of Paris, is most helpful for rental and organized tours, as well as for repairs and storage. The free map *Paris à Vélo* (Paris by Bike), available here and in most RATP metro, RER and bus stations, is a useful starting point. Bicycles may be taken on SNCF trains, and

A Parisian cyclist

TICKETS AND TRAVEL PASSES

The tickets and passes on offer in Paris will suit most tourists. Tickets can be purchased at all main metro and RER stations, at the airports and several tourist offices. Individual tickets are relatively cheap and you can buy a block of ten (*carnet*) at a discount. The *Paris Visite* pass for one, two, three or five days includes discounted entry to some sights but is comparatively expensive unless you intend to travel fairly extensively. To get a *Carte Orange*, you will need ID and a passport photo. Write your French address on the back of the main card and then the number of the card on the ticket. Visitors can also buy a one-day *Mobilis* card or a Monday–Sunday weekly (*hebdomadaire*) or monthly *Carte Orange* for selected zones.

Paris Visite pass and one-day ticket

Tickets for use on metro, RER or bus

Mobilis card

Carte Orange

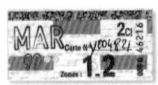

Carte Orange one-month travel ticket for zones 1 and 2

some suburban train stations rent bicycles.

There are now bicycle shops throughout Paris, most of them renting bikes from about 14€ a day, and many also organize guided tours. **Fat Tire Bike Tours** offers tours in English, departing from near the Eiffel Tower, as do **Paris Vélo** and others (*see Directory*).

No entry sign

INTERDIT
SUR TOUTE LA LONGUEUR DE LA VOIE

Parking Interdit (no parking)

DRIVING IN PARIS

Though driving and parking can be difficult in central Paris, a hire car can be useful for visiting outlying areas. To hire a car, a valid driving licence and passport are required (most firms also require one major credit card). For payment by cheque or cash, additional ID may be required (including air tickets and credit cards). International driving licences are not needed for drivers from the EU, North America, Australia and New Zealand.

Cars drive on the right-hand side of the road and must yield to traffic merging from the right, even on thoroughfares, unless marked by a *priorité* sign, which indicates right of way. Cars on a roundabout usually have right of way, though one exception is the Arc de Triomphe where cars yield to traffic from the right – one of Paris's most hair-raising experiences!

ARRÊT GÊNANT
ARTICLE A 37.1 DU CODE DE LA ROUTE

Tow-away zone

30

Speed limit sign in km/h

PARKING

Parking in Paris is difficult and expensive. Never park where there are *Parking (Stationnement) Interdit* signs. Park only in areas with a large "P" or a *Parking Payant* sign on the pavement or road, and pay at the *horodateur* machine. For towed or clamped cars, phone or go to the nearest police station (*Commissariat de Police*). For towing away there is a fine, plus a fee for each day the car is held. There are 7 car pounds (*perfourrières*) in Paris, where cars are kept for 48 hours, then sent to outlying long-term garages (*fourrières*).

USING AN HORODATEUR MACHINE

Horodateurs (parking meters) operate from 9am–7pm Mon–Fri. Unless otherwise indicated, parking is free Sat–Sun, public holidays and in August.

Card-only machine

PARIS CARTE

1 If using coins, insert according to the tariff shown. If using a card, see step 2.

MAIRIE DE PARIS **1**
PARIS CARTE

Parking card

2 If using a card, insert and press blue button for each 15 minutes required.

3 Press green button for ticket.

4 Remove ticket and place inside car windscreen.

BICYCLE HIRE/REPAIR & TOURS

Fat Tire Bike Tours
24 Rue Edgar Faure 75015.
Map 10 D3.
Tel 01 56 58 10 54.
www.fattirebiketoursparis.com
English-language bicycle tours.

Maison Roue Libre
1 Passage Mondétour 75001.
Map 13 B2.
Tel 0810 44 15 34.
www.rouelibre.fr
Bicycle rental, storage, repair.

Paris à vélo c'est sympa!
22 Rue Alphonse Baudin 75011.
Tel 01 48 87 60 01.
www.parisvelosympa.com
Bicycle rental and tours.

Paris Vélo
2 Rue du Fer-à-Moulin 75005.
Map 17 C2. **Tel** 01 43 37 59 22.
www.paris-velo-rent-a-bike.fr
Bicycle rental, tours.

RATP Information
Tel 08 92 68 77 14.
www.ratp.fr

SNCF Information
Tel 36 35.
www.sncf.fr

CAR HIRE AGENCIES

Car hire agencies abound in Paris. Here is a list of major firms with agencies at Charles de Gaulle and Orly airports, main railway stations and city-centre locations. Telephone for reservations and pick-up and drop-off information.

ADA
Tel 08 92 68 40 02.

Avis
Tel 0820 05 05 05.

Budget
Tel 0825 003 564.

Europcar
Tel 0825 358 358.

Hertz
Tel 0825 861 861.

National Citer
Tel 0825 161 212.

Sixt-Eurorent
Tel 0820 007 498.

Travelling by Metro

The RATP (Paris transport company) operates 14 metro lines, referred to by their number and terminus names, criss-crossing Paris and its suburbs. This is often the fastest and cheapest way to get across the capital, as there are dozens of stations scattered around the city. Metro stations are easily identified by their logo, a large circled "M", and sometimes their Art Nouveau entrances.

RATP logo

Neighbourhood maps are found in all stations. The metro and RER (Paris rail network) systems operate in much the same way. The first trains leave their termini at 5.30am and the last return between 00.40am and 1.15am (1 hour later on Saturday and the night before bank holidays).

Art Nouveau metro sign

Modern metro sign

Reading the Metro Map

Metro and RER lines are shown in various colours on the metro map. Metro lines are identified by a number, which is located on the map at either end of a line. Some metro stations serve only one line, others serve more than one. There are stations sharing both metro and RER lines and some are linked to one another by interconnecting passages.

Metro and RER stations with inter-connecting passage

RER and metro station serving the same lines

Metro line

Metro station serving two lines

Metro station serving one line

RER line

Metro line identification number

USING THE RER

The RER is a system of commuter trains, travelling underground in central Paris and above ground in outlying areas. Both metro tickets and passes are valid on it. There are five lines, known by their letters: A, B, C, D and E. Each line forks. For example, Line C has six forks, labelled C1, C2 etc. All RER trains bear names (for example, ALEX or VERA) to make it easier to read RER timetables in the station halls and on platforms. Digital panels on all RER platforms indicate train name, direction of travel (terminus) and upcoming stations.

RER stations are identified by a large circled logo. The main city stations are: Charles de Gaulle-Etoile, Châtelet-Les-Halles, Gare de Lyon, Nation, St-Michel-Notre-Dame, Auber-Haussmann St-Lazare and the Gare du Nord-Magenta.

The RER and metro systems overlap in central Paris. It is often quicker to take an RER train to a station served by both, as in the case of La Défense and Nation. However, getting into the RER stations, which are often linked to the metro by a maze of corridors, can be very time-consuming.

The RER is particularly useful for getting to Paris airports and to many of the outlying towns and tourist attractions. Line B serves Charles de Gaulle airport and Orly airport; Line A goes to Disneyland Resort Paris; and Line C runs to Versailles and Orly airport.

RER logo

BUYING A TICKET

Ordinary metro and RER tickets can be bought either singly or as a *carnet* of 10, from ticket booths or ticket machines in the booking halls (carry some 1 and 2 Euro coins). The useful **Paris Visite** bus, metro and RER pass *(see p382)* is widely available, and you can also buy it in advance at certain travel agencies and rail ticket agents abroad (eg. Rail Europe in London). One metro ticket "section urbaine" entitles you to travel anywhere on the metro, and on RER trains in central Paris. RER trips outside the centre (such as to airports) require special tickets. Fares to suburbs and nearby towns vary. Consult the fare charts posted in all RER stations. Passengers on all city transport must retain their tickets during the trip, as regular inspections are made and fines can be imposed for not having a ticket.

MAKING A JOURNEY BY METRO

1 To determine which metro line to take, travellers should first find their destination on a metro map. (Maps can be found inside stations and also on the inside back cover of this book.) Trace the metro line by following the colour coding and the number of the line. At the end of the line you will see the number of the terminus – remember this, as it will help you to find the correct train.

Insert the train ticket in the first barrier.

Remove the ticket from the second barrier.

2 Metro tickets are sold at all stations. Some stations are equipped with coin-operated automatic machines. All metro tickets are second class. One ticket allows the bearer travel for one journey and any transfers on the metro system.

3 To enter the platform area, insert the metro ticket, with the magnetic strip facing down, into the first barrier slot. Remove the ticket from the second slot, then push through the turnstyle, or step through the barrier if automatic.

← DIRECTION
Ⓜ① CHÂTEAU DE VINCENNES

GARE DE LYON
REUILLY-DIDEROT
NATION
PORTE DE VINCENNES
SAINT-MANDÉ-TOURELLE
BÉRAULT
CHÂTEAU DE VINCENNES

4 At the entrance to each station platform, or in the station corridors, there is a list of upcoming stations corresponding to a given terminus. Terminus names are also indicated on the platform and should be checked before boarding the train.

DIRECTION
Ⓜ①
CHÂTEAU DE VINCENNES

5 To change lines, get off at the appropriate transfer station and follow the *correspondance* (connections) signs on the platform indicating the appropriate direction.

6 On older trains there are door handles which have to be lifted to open the door. On more modern trains there is a release button which you press to open the door. Before the doors open and close, a single tone will sound.

7 Inside the trains are charts of the line being served by the train. The station stops are plotted on the chart, so travellers can track their journeys.

← SORTIE

8 The "Sortie" sign indicates the way out. At all metro exits there are neighbourhood maps.

Travelling by Bus

The bus is an excellent way to see the great sights of Paris. The bus system is run by the RATP, as is the metro, so you can use the same tickets for both. There are over 200 bus lines in greater Paris and over 3,500 buses in daily circulation at rush hour. This is often the fastest way to travel short distances. However, buses can get caught up in heavy traffic and are often crowded during peak hours. Visitors should check the times for the first and last buses as they vary widely, depending on the line. Most buses run from Monday to Saturday, from early morning to mid-evening (6am–8.30pm).

Ticket-cancelling machine

Bus terminus sign

Night bus sign

Bus stop

Bus Stop Signs
Signs at bus stops display route numbers. A white background indicates a service every day all year; a black one means no service on Sundays or public holidays.

TICKETS AND PASSES

A single bus ticket entitles the bearer to a single journey on a single line. If you want to make a change, you'll need another ticket. (Exceptions to this rule are the buses Balabus, Noctambus, Orlybus and Roissybus, and lines 221, 297, 299, 350 and 351.) Children under four travel for free, and those aged between four and ten may travel at half price.

You can purchase a *carnet* of 10 tickets, each of them valid for a single bus or metro journey (or RER too). However, a *carnet* can only be obtained at the metro stations, not on the buses. Metro tickets may be used for bus travel. Bus-only tickets are purchased from the bus driver and must be cancelled to be valid. To do this, insert the ticket into the cancelling machine inside the bus. Hold on to your ticket until the end of the journey. Inspectors do

Red exit button

Cancelling a Bus Ticket
Insert the ticket into the machine in the direction of the arrow, then withdraw it.

make random checks and are empowered to levy on-the-spot fines if you cannot produce a valid cancelled ticket for your journey.

Travel passes are a good idea if you are planning a number of journeys during your stay. For a set fee, you can enjoy unlimited travel on Paris buses (*see p382*). Never cancel these as it will render them invalid. They should be shown to the bus driver whenever you board a bus, and to a ticket inspector on request. If you have a *Carte Orange*, attach a passport photograph and write the card number on the ticket.

Paris's Buses
Passengers can identify the route and destination of a bus from the information on the panels at the front. Some buses have open rear platforms, although these are becoming more rare.

Bus route number

Bus destination

Passengers enter the bus at the front door

Bus front displaying information

Bus route number on rear of bus

Open rear platform

Bus map showing the route of an individual line, with bus stops, metro stations and other major features also marked | Bus stop | Metro Station

USING THE BUSES

Bus stops and shelters are identified by the number shields of the buses that stop at them, and by the distinctive RATP logo. Route maps at bus stops indicate transfers and nearby metro and RER stops. Bus stops also display timetables, and show first and last buses. Neighbourhood maps are also displayed at most bus shelters.

Most buses must be flagged down. Some models have multiple doors which must be opened by pressing a red button inside the bus to exit, or outside the bus to enter. All buses have buttons and bells to signal for a stop. Some buses do not go all the way to their terminus; in that case, there will be a slash through the name of the destination on the front panel.

Buses are gradually being equipped with access for wheelchairs, and all buses already have some seats reserved for disabled and elderly persons. These seats are identified by a sign and must be given up on request.

NIGHT AND SUMMER BUSES

There are 35 night bus lines, called Noctilien, for Paris and its suburbs (running 1–5.30am daily). The terminus for most lines is Châtelet, at Avenue Victoria or Rue St-Martin. Noctilien stops are identified by a letter "N" set in a white circle on a blue background. Noctilien buses must be flagged down. Travel passes are valid, as are normal metro tickets, which must be cancelled on board. Fares vary according to destination. Travellers may buy tickets on board the bus.

The RATP also operates buses in the Bois de Vincennes and Bois de Boulogne during the summer. The **RATP Information** is extremely helpful on these services and on the best and cheapest ways to get around the city.

RATP Information
54 Quai de la Rapée 75012.
Tel 08 92 68 77 14
www.ratp.fr
www.noctilien.fr

USEFUL BUS ROUTES

Here is a selection of the best sightseeing bus routes around the centre of Paris, taking in some of the great sights of the city. The routes show the major bus stops, the nearest metro stations and locations of some of the notable sights.

Gare St-Lazare Ⓜ
Opéra National de Paris Garnier
Opéra Ⓜ
Bourse Ⓜ
Eiffel Tower
Dôme Church
Invalides Ⓜ
Musée du Louvre
Rambuteau Ⓜ
Champs de Mars Ⓜ
Pont du Carrousel
Pompidou Centre
Turenne
Francs-Bourgeois

KEY
— Route 29
— Route 69
— Route 96
Ⓜ Metro station

Hôtel de Ville Ⓜ
Ⓜ St-Germain-des-Prés
St-Paul Ⓜ
Bastille Ⓜ
Tour Montparnasse
Cluny Ⓜ
Musée de Cluny
Gare Montparnasse Ⓜ
Opéra National de Paris Bastille

Using the SNCF Trains

The French state railway, Société Nationale des Chemins de Fer (**SNCF**), has two kinds of service in Paris: the Banlieue suburban service and the Grandes Lignes, or long-distance service. The suburban services all operate within the five-zone network (*see p382*). The long-distance services operate throughout France. These services allow visitors to visit parts of France close to Paris in a day round trip. The TGV high-speed service is particularly useful for such journeys, as it is capable of travelling about twice as fast as the normal trains (*see pp378–9*).

Gare de l'Est railway station in 1920

RAILWAY STATIONS

As the railway hub of France, Paris boasts six major inter-national railway stations operated by the SNCF: the Gare du Nord, Gare de l'Est, Gare de Lyon, Gare d'Austerlitz, Gare St-Lazare and Gare Montparnasse.

All the main train stations have long-distance and suburban destinations. Some of the main suburban locations, such as Versailles and Chantilly, are served by both long-distance and suburban services.

Rail traveller with luggage trolley

The stations have departures and arrivals boards showing the train number, departure and arrival time, delay, platform number, provenance, and main stops en route. For those with heavy luggage, there are trolleys, requiring a 1€ coin (refunded when the trolley is returned).

TICKETS

Tickets to suburban destinations can often be purchased at coin-operated automatic machines located inside station halls, so it is useful to carry coins (the machines give change; most also take credit cards). Otherwise you can buy tickets at the ticket counters.

Before boarding a train, travellers must time-punch (*composter*) their tickets and reservations in a *composteur* machine. Inspectors do check travellers' tickets and anyone who fails to time-punch their ticket can be fined.

Ticket booths are marked with panels indicating the kind of tickets (*billets*) sold: *Banlieue* for suburban tickets, *Grandes Lignes* for mainline tickets, and *Internationale* for international tickets.

Substantial fare discounts of 25-50% are offered to the over-60s (*Découverte Senior*), those under 26s (*Découverte 12-25*), up to four adults

Composteur Machine
The composteur *machines are located in station halls and at the head of each platform. Tickets and reservations must be inserted face up.*

A time-punched ticket

travelling with a child under the age of 12 (*Découverte Enfant Plus*), or anyone booking more than 30 days in advance.

Advance Internet bookings also offer a limited number of cheaper tickets called *prems*. Payment for these tickets (which you print from your computer) must be made online. Be aware that these tickets are not covered by an exchange or reimbursement policy.

Some last-minute offers are also available online. Visit **www.voyages-sncf.com** for more information.

SUBURBAN TRAINS

Suburban lines are found at all main Paris train stations and are clearly marked Banlieue. Tickets for city

A double-decker Banlieue train

transport cannot be used on Banlieue trains, with the exception of some RER tickets to stations with both SNCF and RER lines. Several tourist destinations are served by Banlieue trains, including Chantilly, Chartres, Fontaine-bleau, Giverny and Versailles (*see pp248–53*). Telephone the SNCF for details on 36 35 or try their website: **www.sncf.fr**

Travelling by Taxi

Taxis are more expensive than trains or buses, but they are an advantage after 1am, when the metro has stopped running. There are taxi ranks (*station de taxis*) throughout the city; a short list is provided below.

A Paris taxi rank sign

CATCHING A TAXI

There are over 10,000 taxis operating in central Paris. Yet there never seem to be enough of them to meet demand, particularly during rush hours and on Friday and Saturday nights.

Taxis can be hailed in the street, but not within 50 m (165 ft) of a taxi rank. Since ranks always take priority over street stops, the easiest way to get a cab is to find a rank and join the queue. Ranks are found at many busy cross-roads, at main metro and RER stations, and at all hospitals, train stations and airports. An illuminated white light on the roof shows that the taxi is available. A small light lit below means that the taxi is occupied. If the white light is covered the taxi is off duty. Taxis on their last run can refuse to take passengers.

The meter should have a specified initial amount showing at the taxi rank, or when it is hailed. Initial charges on radio taxis vary widely, depending on the distance the taxi covers to arrive at the pick-up point. Payment by cheque is not accepted but some cars take credit cards.

Rates vary with the part of the city and the time of day. Rate A, in the city centre, is charged per kilometre. The higher rate B applies in the city centre on Sundays, holidays and at night (7pm–7am), or daytime in the suburbs or airports. Even higher rate C applies to the suburbs and airports at night. Taxis charge for each piece of luggage. There's no need to give a tip.

Fare — **Tariff rate**

The taxi fare is recorded on the meter in the cab

Taxi roof sign — **A** **B**

The light indicates tariff rate and that the taxi is occupied

A typical Paris taxi

DIRECTORY

TAXI RANKS

Charles de Gaulle-Etoile
1 Ave Wagram 75017.
Map 4 D4.
Tel 01 43 80 01 99.

Eiffel Tower
Quai Branly 75007.
Map 10 D3.
Tel 01 45 55 85 41.

Metro Concorde
252 Rue de Rivoli 75001.
Map 11 C1.
Tel 01 42 61 67 60.

Place de Clichy
Pl de Clichy 75009.
Map 6 D1.
Tel 01 42 85 00 00.

Place Denfert-Rochereau
297 Blvd Raspail 75014.
Map 16 E3.
Tel 01 43 35 00 00.

Place de la Madeleine
8 Blvd Malesherbes 75008.
Map 5 C5.
Tel 01 42 65 00 00.

Place de la République
1 Ave de la République 75011.
Map 14 D1.
Tel 01 43 55 92 64.

Place St-Michel
29 Quai St-Michel 75005.
Map 13 A4.
Tel 01 43 29 63 66.

Place du Trocadéro
1 Ave D'Eylau 75016.
Map 9 C1.
Tel 01 47 27 00 00.

Rond Point des Champs-Elysées
7 Ave Matignon 75008.
Map 5 A5.
Tel 01 42 56 29 00.

St-Paul
10 Rue de Rivoli 75004.
M St-Paul. **Map** 13 C3.
Tel 01 48 87 49 39.

TAXIS BOOKED BY TELEPHONE

Alpha
Tel 01 45 85 85 85.

Artaxi
Tel 01 42 06 67 10.

G7
Tel 01 47 39 47 39, 01 47 39 00 91 (special needs).

Les Taxis Bleus
Tel 08 91 70 10 10.

SNCF INFORMATION

General Information and Ticket Reservations
Tel 36 35.
www.sncf.fr

Autotrain (Car trains)
Tel 36 35 (within France) or +33 892 35 35 33 (from abroad).

STREET FINDER

The map references given with all sights, hotels, restaurants, shops and entertainment venues described in this book refer to the maps in this section (*see* How the Map References Work *opposite*). A complete index of street names and all the places of interest marked on the maps can be found on the following pages. The key map shows the area of Paris covered by the *Street Finder*, with the arrondissement numbers for each district. The maps include not only the sightseeing areas (which are colour-coded), but the whole of central Paris with all the districts important for hotels, restaurants, shopping and entertainment venues. The symbols used to represent sights and features on the *Street Finder* maps are listed opposite.

Paris is divided into 20 arrondissements, outlined in orange and numbered on this map.

0 kilometres 1
0 miles 0.5

KEY

--- Arrondissement boundary

HOW THE MAP REFERENCES WORK

The first figure tells you which *Street Finder* map to turn to.

Hôtel de Ville ⓳

4 Pl de l'Hôtel-de-Ville 75004.
Map 13 B3. *Tel* 01 42 76 50 49.
M Hotel de Ville. ⬤ groups: by
arrangement. ⬤ public hols, official
functions ⬤ ⬤

The letter and number give the grid reference. Letters go across the map's top and bottom; figures on its sides.

The map continues on page 17 of the *Street Finder.*

KEY TO STREET FINDER

▨	Major sight
▨	Other sight
▨	Other building
M	Metro station
RER	RER station
🚍	Main bus stop
⛴	Boat service boarding point
P	Main car parks
🛈	Tourist information office
✚	Hospital with casualty unit
🚓	Police station
✝	Church
✡	Synagogue
⊠	Post office
═	Railway line
▓	Autoroute
⋯	Pedestrian street
◄130	House number (main street)

SCALE OF MAP PAGES

0 metres	200
▬▬▬▬▬	1:11,000
0 yards	200

Street Finder Index

A

Abbaye, Rue de l' (6)   12 E4
Abbé Carton, Rue
de l' (14)   15 B5
Abbé de l'Epée, Rue
de l' (5)   16 F1
Abbé Gillet, Rue de l' (16)   9 B3
Abbé Grégoire, Rue
de l' (6)   11 C5
Abbé J Lebeuf, Pl
de l' (15)   15 B3
Abbé Migne, Sq de l' (4)   16 E4
Abbé Patureau, Rue
de l' (18)   2 F5
Abbé Roger Derry,
Rue de l' (15)   10 E5
Abbesses, Pl des (18)   6 F1
Abbesses, Rue des (18)   6 E1
Abbeville, Rue d' (9, 10)   7 B3
Abel, Rue (12)   14 F5
   continues   18 F1
Abel Hovelacque,
Rue (13)   17 B4
Abel Rabaud, Rue (11)   8 E5
Abel Truchet, Rue (17)   5 C2
Abel Varet, Passage (17)   1 B3
Aboukir, Rue d' (2)   7 B5
   continues   12 F1
Abreuvoir, Rue de l' (18)   2 F5
Abulet, Villa (17)   4 D2
Acacias, Passage des (17)   4 D3
Acacias, Rue des (17)   4 D3
Académie Nationale de
Médecine (6)   12 E3
Achille Martinet, Rue (18)   2 E4
Adanson, Sq (5)   17 B2
Adolphe Adam, Rue (4)   13 A3
Adrienne, Villa (14)   16 D4
Adrienne Lecouvreur,
Allée (7)   10 E3
Affre, Rue (18)   7 C1
Agar, Rue (16)   9 A4
Agent Bailly, Rue de l' (9)   6 F3
Agrippa d'Aubigné,
Rue (4)   14 D5
Aguesseau, Rue d' (8)   5 B5
Aide Sociale,
de l' (14)   15 C4
Aimé Maillart, Pl (17)   4 E2
Aix, Rue d' (10)   8 E5
Ajaccio, Sq d' (7)   11 A3
Alain, Rue (14)   15 B3
Alasseur, Rue (15)   10 E4
Alban Satragne, Sq (10)   7 B4
Albert, Rue (13)   18 E5
Albert Bayet, Rue (13)   17 C4
Albert Besnard, Sq (17)   4 E1
Albert Camus, Rue (10)   8 E3
Albert de Mun, Ave (16)   10 D2
Albert Premier, Cours (8)   10 F1
   continues   11 A1
Albert Premier de
Monaco, Ave (16)   9 C2
Albert Samain, Rue (17)   4 D1
Albert Schweitzer, Sq (4)   13 C4
Albert Thomas, Rue (10)   7 A4
   continues   8 D5
Alboni, Rue de l' (16)   9 C3
Alboni, Sq de l' (16)   9 C3
Alembert, Rue d' (14)   16 E5
Alençon, Rue d' (15)   15 C1
Alésia, Rue d' (14)   16 E5
   continues   15 B4
Alésia, Villa d' (14)   15 C5
Alésia Ridder, Sq (14)   15 A5
Alexandre Cabanel,
Rue (15)   10 F5

Alexandre Charpentier,
Rue (17)   3 C1
Alexandre Dumas,
Rue (11, 20)   2 D1
Alexandre Parodi,
Rue (10)   8 D2
Alexandre III, Pont (8, 7)   11 A1
Alexandrie, Rue d' (2)   7 B5
Alexis Carrel, Rue (15)   10 E4
Alfred Bruneau, Rue (16)   9 A3
Alfred de Vigny, Rue (8)   4 F3
Alfred Roll, Rue (17)   4 E1
Alfred Stevens, Rue (9)   6 F2
Alger, Rue d' (1)   12 D1
Alibert, Rue (10)   8 E4
Aligre, Pl d' (12)   14 F5
Aligre, Rue d' (12)   14 F5
Allées L Gambetta   1 A2
Allent, Rue (7)   12 D3
Alleray, Rue d' (15)   15 A3
Alliance Française (6)   16 D1
Alma, Cité de l' (7)   10 E2
Alma, Pl de l' (8, 16)   10 E1
Alma, Pont
de l' (7, 8, 16)   10 E2
Alombert, Passage (3)   13 C1
Alphand, Ave (16)   3 C4
Alphand, Rue (13)   17 A5
Alphonse Baudin,
Rue (11)   14 E2
Alphonse Bertillon,
Rue (15)   15 A3
Alphonse de Neuville,
Rue (17)   4 F1
Alphonse Laveran,
Pl (5)   16 F2
Alphonse XII, Ave (16)   9 B3
Alsace, Rue d' (10)   7 C3
   continues   8 D3
Amboise, Rue d' (2)   6 F5
Ambroise Paré, Rue (10)   7 B2
Amélie, Rue (7)   10 F3
Amelot, Rue (11)   14 D1
American Cathedral
in Paris (8)   4 E5
Amiral Bruix, Blvd
de l' (16)   3 B3
Amiral Bruix, Sq
de l' (16)   3 B3
Amiral Courbet, Rue
de l' (16)   3 B5
Amiral de Coligny,
Rue de l' (1)   12 F2
Amiral d'Estaing, Rue
de l' (16)   10 D1
Amiral de Grasse, Pl (16)   4 D5
Ampère, Rue (17)   4 E1
Amsterdam, Rue d' (8, 9)   6 D2
   continues   6 D3
Amyot, Rue (5)   17 A1
Anatole de la Forge,
Rue (17)   4 D3
Anatole France, Ave (7)   10 E3
Anatole France, Quai (7)   11 C2
   continues   12 D2
Ancienne Comédie,
Rue de l' (6)   12 F4
Ancre, Passage de l' (3)   13 B1
André Antoine, Rue (18)   6 F2
André Barsacq, Rue (18)   6 F1
André Bréchet, Rue (17)   2 D3
André Citroën, Quai (15)   9 B5
André del Sarte, Rue (18)   7 A1
André Dubois, Rue (6)   12 F4
André Gide, Rue (15)   15 A3
André Honnorat, Pl (6)   16 E1
André Lichtenberger,
Sq (14)   15 A5
André Malraux, Pl (1)   12 E1

André Maurois, Blvd (16)   3 A3
André Messager, Rue (18)   2 F4
André Tardieu, Pl (7)   11 B4
Andrienne Simon,
Villa (14)   16 D3
Andrieux, Rue (8)   5 B2
Androuet, Rue (18)   6 F1
Angélique Compoint,
Rue (18)   2 E3
Angoulême, Cour d' (11)   14 F1
Anjou, Quai d' (4)   13 C4
Anjou, Rue d' (8)   5 C4
Ankara, Rue d' (16)   9 B4
Annibal, Cité (14)   16 E5
Annonciation, Rue
de l' (16)   9 B3
Anselme Payen,
Rue (16)   15 A3
Antin, Chaussée d' (9)   6 E4
Antin, Cité d' (9)   6 E4
Antin, Impasse d' (8)   11 A1
Antin, Rue d' (2)   6 E5
Antin, Rue de la
Chaussée d' (9)   6 E4
Antoine Bourdelle,
Rue (15)   15 B1
Antoine Chantin,
Rue (14)   15 C5
Antoine Vollon,
Rue (12)   14 F5
Anvers, Pl d' (9)   7 A2
Anvers, Sq d' (9)   7 A2
Apennins, Rue des (17)   1 C5
Appert, Rue (11)   14 E3
Aqueduc, Rue de l' (10)   8 D2
Arago, Blvd (13)   17 A3
Arago, Blvd (14)   16 F3
Arago, Rue (13, 14)   1 C2
Arbalète, Rue de (5)   17 A2
Arbre Sec, Rue d' (1)   12 F2
Arbustes, Rue des (14)   15 A5
Arc de Triomphe (17)   4 D4
Arc de Triomphe, Rue
de l' (17)   4 D3
Arc de Triomphe du Carrousel
(1)   12 E2
Arcade, Rue de l' (8)   5 C4
Archevêché, Pont
de l' (4, 5)   13 B4
Archevêché, Quai
de l' (4)   13 B4
Archives, Rue des (3, 4)   13 C2
Archives, Rue des (4)   13 B3
Arcole, Pont d' (4)   13 B3
Arcole, Rue d' (4)   13 B4
Arènes, Rue des (5)   17 B1
Arènes de Lutèce (5)   17 B1
Arènes de Lutèce,
Sq des (5)   17 B1
Argenson, Rue d' (8)   5 B4
Argenteuil, Rue d' (1)   12 E1
Aristide Briand, Rue (7)   11 B2
Aristide Bruant, Rue (18)   6 E1
Armaillé, Rue d' (17)   4 D3
Armand Carrel, Rue (19)   8 F2
Armand Gauthier,
Rue (18)   2 E5
Armand Moisant,
Rue (15)   15 B2
Armée d'Orient, Rue
de l' (18)   6 E1
Armenonville, Rue
d' (17)   3 B2
Armorique, Rue de
l' (15)   15 B2
Arnault-Tzanck,
Place (17)   1 C3
Arquebusiers, Rue
des (3)   14 D2

Arras, Rue d' (5)   13 B5
Arrivée, Rue de l' (15)   15 C1
Arsenal, Rue de l' (4)   14 D4
Arsène Houssaye, Rue (8)   4 E4
Arsonval, Rue d' (15)   15 B2
Arthur Brière, Rue (17)   2 D4
Arthur Groussier,
Rue (10)   8 E4
Arthur Ranc, Rue (18)   2 E3
Artois, Rue d' (8)   4 F4
   continues   5 A4
Arts, Passage des (14)   15 C3
Arts, Passerelle des (6)   12 E3
Asile Popincourt, Rue
de l' (11)   14 F2
Aspirant Dunand, Sq
de l' (14)   16 D4
Assas, Rue d' (6)   12 D5
   continues   16 E1
Asseline, Rue (14)   15 C3
Assemblée
Nationale (7)   11 B2
Assomption, Rue
de l' (16)   9 A4
Astorg, Rue d' (8)   5 B4
Astrolabe, Impasse
de l'   15 B1
Athènes, Rue d' (9)   6 D3
Atlas, Rue de l' (19)   8 F4
Au Lapin Agile (18)   2 F5
Auber, Rue (9)   6 D4
Aubervilliers, Rue
d' 18 (19)   8 D1
Aublet, Villa (17)   4 D2
Aubriot, Rue (4)   13 C3
Aubry le Boucher,
Rue (4)   13 B2
Aude, Rue d' (14)   16 E5
Audran, Rue (18)   6 E1
Augereau, Rue (7)   10 F3
Auguste Barbier,
Rue (11)   8 E5
Auguste Bartholdi,
Rue (15)   10 D5
Auguste Blanqui,
Blvd (13)   17 A4
Auguste Comte, Rue (6)   16 E1
Auguste Mie, Rue (14)   15 C3
Auguste Vacquerie,
Rue (16)   4 D5
Aumale, Rue d' (9)   6 E3
Aumont Thiéville,
Rue (17)   3 C2
Aurelle de Paladines,
Blvd d' (17)   3 B2
Austerlitz, Pont
d' (5, 12, 13)   18 D1
Austerlitz, Port d' (13)   18 E2
Austerlitz, Quai d' (13)   18 E2
Auteuil, Port d' (16)   9 A5
Autonome de Paris,
Port (15)   9 C4
Ave Maria, Rue de l' (4)   13 C4
Ave Maria, Sq de l' (4)   13 C4
Avre, Rue de l' (15)   10 E5
Azais, Rue (18)   6 F1

B

Babylone, Rue de (7)   11 C4
Bac, Rue du (7)   11 C4
   continues   12 D3
Bachaumont, Rue (2)   13 A1
Baillet, Rue (1)   12 F2
Bailleul, Rue (1)   12 F2
Bailly, Rue (3)   13 C1
Ballu, Rue (9)   6 D2
Balny d'Avricourt,
Rue (17)   4 E2

Balzac, Maison (16) **9 B3**
Balzac, Rue (8) **4 F4**
Banque, Rue de la (2) **12 F1**
 continues **6 F5**
Banque de France (1) **12 F1**
Banquier, Rue du (13) **17 C5**
Baptiste Renard,
 Rue (13) **18 D5**
Barbes, Blvd (18) **7 A1**
Barbet de Jouy, Rue (7) **11 4**
Barbette, Rue (3) **13 C3**
Barbey d'Aurevilly,
 Ave (7) **10 E3**
Bardinet, Rue (14) **15 B4**
Bargue, Rue (15) **15 A3**
Baron, Rue (17) **1 C1**
Barrault, Passage (13) **17 A5**
Barrault, Rue (13) **17 A5**
Barrelet de Ricou,
 Rue (19) **8 F3**
Barres, Rue des (4) **13 B3**
Barrier, Impasse (12) **14 F5**
Barrois, Passage (3) **13 C1**
Barthélémy, Passage (10) **8 1**
Barthélémy, Rue (15) **15 A1**
Barye, Rue (17) **4 F2**
Barye, Sq (4) **13 C5**
Basfour, Passage (2) **13 B1**
Basfroi, Passage (11) **14 F3**
Basfroi, Rue (11) **14 F3**
Bassano, Rue de (8, 16) **4 E5**
Bassompierre, Rue (4) **14 D4**
Baste, Rue (19) **8 F2**
Bastille, Blvd de la (12) **14 E5**
Bastille, Pl de la (12) **14 E4**
Bastille, Rue de la (4) **14 E4**
Bataillon Français de
 L'O.N.U. en Corée,
 Place du (4) **13 C4**
Bateau Lavoir (18) **6 F1**
Bateaux Pompes (6) **12 F3**
Batignolles, Blvd
 des (8, 17) **5 C2**
Batignolles, Rue des (17) **5 C1**
Batignolles, Sq des (17) **5 C1**
Bauches, Rue des (16) **9 A3**
Baudoin, Rue (13) **18 E4**
Baudoyer, Pl (4) **13 B3**
Baudricourt, Rue (13) **18 D5**
Bauer, Cité (14) **15 B4**
Baume, Rue de la (8) **5 A4**
Bayard, Rue (8) **10 F1**
Bayen, Rue (17) **4 D2**
 continues **4 D3**
Bazeilles, Rue de (5) **17 B2**
Béarn, Rue de (3) **14 D3**
Béatrix Dussane,
 Rue (15) **10 D5**
Beaubourg, Impasse (3) **13 B2**
Beaubourg, Rue (3, 4) **13 B2**
Beauce, Rue du (3) **13 C2**
Beaucour, Ave (8) **4 F3**
Beaugrenelle, Rue (15) **9 C5**
Beaujolais, Rue de (1) **12 F1**
Beaujon, Rue (8) **4 E4**
Beaujon, Sq (8) **5 A3**
Beaumarchais,
 Blvd (3, 4, 11) **14 E3**
Beaune, Rue de (7) **12 D3**
Beauregard, Rue (2) **7 B5**
Beaurepaire, Rue (10) **8 D5**
Beautreillis, Rue (4) **14 D4**
Beaux Arts, Rue
 des (6) **12 E3**
Beccaria, Rue (12) **14 F5**
Becquerel, Rue (18) **2 F5**
Beethoven, Rue (16) **9 C3**
Béla Bartók, Sq (15) **9 C4**
Belfort, Rue de (11) **1 B2**
Belhomme, Rue (18) **7 A1**
Belidor, Rue (17) **3 C2**
Bellanger, Rue **3 A2**

Bellechasse, Rue de (7) **11 C3**
Bellefond, Rue (9) **7 A3**
Belles Feuilles, Rue
 des (16) **3 B5**
 continues **9 B1**
Belleville, Blvd
 de (11, 20) **8 F5**
Belleville, Rue
 de (19, 20) **8 F4**
Belliard, Rue (18) **2 E3**
Belliard, Villa (18) **2 D4**
Bellièvre, Rue de (13) **18 E3**
Bellini, Rue (16) **9 B2**
Bellot, Rue (19) **8 E1**
Belloy, Rue de (16) **4 D5**
Belzunce, Rue de (10) **7 B3**
Ben Aïad, Passage (2) **13 A1**
Bénard, Rue (14) **15 C4**
Benjamin Franklin,
 Rue (16) **9 C2**
Benouville, Rue (16) **3 A5**
Béranger, Rue (3) **14 D1**
Bérard, Cour (4) **14 D4**
Berbier du Mets,
 Rue (13) **17 B3**
 continues **17 B4**
Bercy, Allée de (12) **18 F1**
Bercy, Blvd de (12) **18 F2**
Bercy, Pont de (12, 13) **18 F3**
Bercy, Port de (12, 13) **18 3**
Bercy, Quai de (12) **18 F3**
Bercy, Rue de (12) **14 E5**
 continues **18 E1**
Berger, Rue (1) **12 F2**
 continues **13 A2**
Bergerat, Villa (16) **3 A2**
Bergère, Cité (9) **7 A4**
Bergère, Rue (9) **7 A4**
Berie Albrecht, Ave (8) **4 E3**
Bérite, Rue de (6) **11 C5**
Berlioz, Rue (16) **3 B4**
Berlioz, Sq (9) **6 D2**
Bernard de Clairvaux,
 Rue (3) **13 B2**
Bernard de Ventadour,
 Rue (14) **15 B3**
Bernard Palissy, Rue (6) **12 E4**
Bernardins, Rue des (5) **13 B5**
Berne, Rue de (8) **5 C2**
Bernouilli, Rue (8) **5 C2**
Berri, Rue de (8) **4 F4**
Berryer, Rue (8) **4 F4**
Berteaux Dumas, Rue **3 A2**
Berthe, Rue (18) **6 F1**
Berthier, Blvd (17) **1 A4**
 continues **4 E1**
Berthollet, Rue (5) **17 A2**
Bertie Albrecht (8) **4 E4**
Bertin Poirée, Rue (1) **13 A3**
Berton, Rue (16) **9 B3**
Bervic, Rue (18) **7 A1**
Berzélius, Rue (17) **1 B4**
Beslay, Passage (11) **14 F1**
Bessières, Blvd (17) **1 C3**
Bessières, Rue (17) **1 B4**
Béthune, Quai de (4) **13 C5**
Beudant, Rue (17) **5 B2**
Bezout, Rue (14) **16 D5**
Bibliothèque
 Nationale (1, 2) **12 E1**
Bibliothèque
 Nationale (2) **6 F5**
Bichat, Rue (10) **8 D4**
Bienfaisance, Rue de
 la (8) **5 B3**
Bienvenue, Pl (15) **15 C2**
Bièvre, Rue de (5) **13 B5**
Bigorre, Rue de (14) **16 D5**
Bineau, Blvd **3 B1**
Biot, Rue (17) **6 D1**
Bir Hakeim, Pont
 de (15, 16) **9 C3**

Birague, Rue de (4) **14 D4**
Biron, Rue **2 F2**
Biron, Villa **2 F2**
Biscornet, Rue (12) **14 E5**
Bixio, Rue (7) **11 A4**
Bizerte, Rue de (17) **5 C1**
Blainville, Rue, (5) **17 A1**
Blaise Cendrars,
 Allée (1) **12 F2**
Blaise Desgoffe,
 Rue (6) **15 C1**
Blanche, Pl (9, 18) **6 E1**
Blanche, Rue (9) **6 D2**
Blanche, Villa **3 A2**
Blancs Manteaux, Rue
 des (4) **13 C3**
Blanqui, Rue **2 F1**
Bleue, Rue (9) **7 A3**
Blomet, Rue (15) **15 A1**
Blondel, Rue (2) **7 B5**
Bobillot, Rue (13) **17 B5**
Boccador, Rue du (8) **10 F1**
Bochart de Saron,
 Rue (9) **6 F2**
Boétie, Rue la (8) **4 F5**
Boieldieu, Place (2) **6 F6**
Bois de Boulogne **3 A4**
Bois de Boulogne, Rue
 du (16) **3 C4**
Bois le Prêtre, Blvd
 du (1) **1 C3**
Bois le Vent, Rue (16) **9 A3**
Boissière, Rue (16) **10 D1**
 continues **3 C5**
Boisseau, Rue (18) **7 A1**
Boissonade, Rue (14) **16 E2**
Boissy d'Anglas, Rue (8) **5 C5**
Boiton, Passage (13) **17 B5**
Bologne, Rue (16) **9 B3**
Bonaparte, Rue (6) **12 E3**
 continues **12 E4**
Bonne Graine, Passage
 de la (11) **14 F4**
Bonne Nouvelle, Blvd
 de (10) **7 B5**
Bonne Nouvelle, Impasse
 de (10) **7 B5**
Bonnet, Rue (18) **2 E3**
Bonnet, Rue **1 A3**
Bons Enfants, Rue
 des (1) **12 F2**
Bord de l'Eau, Terrasse
 du (1) **12 D2**
Borda, Rue (3) **13 C1**
Bosquet, Ave (7) **10 F2**
 continues **10 F3**
Bosquet, Rue **10 F3**
Bosquet, Villa (7) **10 F2**
Bossuet, Rue (10) **7 B3**
Bouchardon, Rue (10) **7 C5**
Bouchut, Rue (15) **15 A1**
Boucicaut, Sq (7) **12 D4**
Boudreau, Rue (9) **6 D4**
Boulainvilliers, Hameau
 de (16) **9 A4**
Boulainvilliers, Rue
 de (16) **9 A4**
Boulangers, Rue des (5) **17 B1**
Boulard, Rue (14) **16 D4**
Boulay, Passage (17) **1 B4**
Boulay, Rue (17) **1 B4**
Boule Blanche, Passage
 de la (12) **14 E4**
Boule Rouge, Rue
 de la (9) **7 A4**
Boulitte, Rue (14) **15 B5**
Boulle, Rue (11) **14 E3**
Bouloi, Rue du (1) **12 F1**
Bouquet de Longchamp, Rue
 du (16) **10 D1**
Bourbon, Quai de (4) **13 B4**
Bourdaloue, Rue (9) **6 F3**

Bourdon, Blvd (4) **14 D5**
Bourdonnais, Ave
 de la (7) **10 E3**
Bourdonnais, Port
 de la (7) **10 D2**
Bourdonnais, Rue
 des (1) **13 A2**
Bouret, Rue (19) **8 F2**
Bourg l'Abbé, Passage
 du (2) **13 B1**
Bourg l'Abbé, Rue
 du (3) **13 B1**
Bourg Tibourg, Rue
 du (4) **13 C3**
Bourgogne,
 Rue de (7) **11 B3**
Boursault, Rue (17) **5 B1**
Bourse, Pl de la (2) **6 F5**
Bourse, Rue de la (2) **6 F6**
Bourse de
 Commerce (1) **12 F2**
Bourse des Valeurs (2) **6 F5**
Boutarel, Rue (4) **13 B4**
Boutebrie, Rue (5) **13 A4**
Boutin, Rue (13) **16 F5**
Boutron, Impasse (10) **8 D3**
Bouvard, Ave (7) **10 E3**
Boyer Barret, Rue (14) **15 B4**
Brady, Passage (10) **7 B4**
Branly, Quai (7) **10 E2**
Brantôme, Passage (3) **13 B2**
Braque, Rue de (3) **13 C2**
Brazzaville, Place de (15) **9 C5**
Bréa, Rue (6) **16 D1**
Bréguet, Rue (11) **14 F3**
Bréguet Sabin,
 Sq (11) **14 E3**
Brémontier, Rue (17) **4 F1**
Brésil, Pl du (17) **4 F1**
Bretagne, Rue de (3) **14 D2**
Breteuil, Ave de (7) **11 A5**
Breteuil, Ave de (15) **15 A1**
Breteuil, Pl de (7, 15) **11 A5**
Brey, Rue (17) **4 D3**
Brézin, Rue (14) **16 D4**
Bridaine, Rue (17) **5 B1**
Brie, Passage de la (19) **8 E2**
Brignole, Rue (16) **10 D1**
Brignole Galliera,
 Sq (16) **10 E1**
Briquet, Rue (18) **7 A2**
Briqueterie, Impasse de
 la (14) **1 B3**
Brisemiche, Rue (4) **13 B2**
Broca, Rue 5 (13) **17 A3**
Brochant, Rue (17) **1 B5**
Brosse, Rue de (4) **13 B3**
Broussais, Rue (14) **16 E5**
Brown Séquard,
 Rue (15) **15 B2**
Bruant, Rue (13) **18 D3**
Brun, Rue le (13) **17 B3**
Brune, Blvd (14) **15 A5**
Brunel, Rue (17) **3 C3**
Brunoy, Passage (12) **18 F1**
Bruxelles, Rue de (9) **6 D2**
Bruyère, Rue la (9) **6 E3**
Bruyère, Sq la (9) **6 E3**
Bucherie, Rue de la (5) **13 A4**
Buci, Rue de (6) **12 E4**
Budapest, Pl de (8, 9) **6 D3**
Budapest, Rue de (9) **6 D3**
Budé, Rue (4) **13 C4**
Buffault, Rue (9) **6 F3**
Buffon, Rue (5) **18 D1**
Bugeaud, Ave (16) **3 B5**
Buisson St-Louis, Passage
 du (10) **8 E4**
Buisson St-Louis, Rue
 du (10) **8 F4**
Bullourde, Passage (11) **14 F4**
Buot, Rue (13) **17 B5**

Each place name is followed by its arrondissement number, and then by its Street Finder reference.

Burnouf, Rue (19) 8 F3
Burq, Rue (18) 6 E1
Butte aux Cailles, Rue
de la (13) 17 B5

C

C Dain, Rue 2 E1
Cabanis, Rue (14) 16 F5
Cadet, Rue (9) 6 F4
  continues 7 A3
Caffarelli, Rue (3) 14 D1
Cail, Rue (10) 7 C2
Caillié, Rue (18) 8 D1
Caire, Passage du (2) 7 B5
Caire, Rue du (2) 7 B5
Calais, Rue de (9) 6 D2
Calmels, Impasse (18) 2 F4
Calmels, Rue (18) 2 F4
Calmels Prolongée,
Rue (18) 2 F4
Calvaire, Pl du (18) 6 F1
Cambacérès, Rue (8) 5 B4
Cambon, Rue (1) 6 D5
Cambronne, Pl (15) 10 F5
Cambronne, Sq (15) 10 F5
Camille Blaisot, Rue (17) 2 D3
Camille Flammarion,
Rue (18) 2 F3
Camille Jullian, Pl (6) 16 E2
Campagne Première,
Rue (14) 16 E2
Campo Formio, Rue
de (13) 17 C3
Canada, Pl du (8) 11 A1
Canettes, Rue des (6) 12 E4
Cange, Rue du (14) 15 B4
Cantagrel, Rue (13) 18 F5
Cantal, Cour du (11) 14 E4
Capitaine Glarner,
Ave du 2 D1
Capitaine Scott, Rue
du (15) 10 D4
Capitan, Sq (5) 17 B1
Caplat, Rue (18) 7 B1
Capron, Rue (18) 6 D1
Capucines, Blvd
des (2, 9) 6 D5
Capucines, Rue des (1, 2) 6 D5
Cardan, Rue (17) 1 B4
Cardinal Amette, Pl
du (15) 10 E5
Cardinal Guibert, Rue
du (18) 6 F1
Cardinal Lemoine, Cité
du (5) 13 B5
Cardinal Lemoine, Rue
du (5) 17 B1
Cardinal Mercier, Rue (9) 6 D2
Cardinet, Passage (17) 5 A1
Cardinet, Rue (17) 1 B5
  continues 4 F2
  continues 5 A1
Carmes, Rue des (5) 13 A5
Carnot, Ave (17) 4 D3
Carnot, Rue (17) 2 D2
Caroline, Rue (17) 5 C2
Caron, Rue (4) 14 D4
Carpeaux, Rue (18) 2 D5
Carpeaux, Rue du Sq (18) 2 E4
Carpeaux, Sq (18) 2 E4
Carreau du Temple (3) 14 D1
Carrée, Cour (1) 12 F2
Carrousel, Pl du (1) 12 E2
Carrousel, Pont
du (1, 6, 7) 12 E2
Casimir Delavigne,
Rue (6) 12 F5
Casimir Périer, Rue (7) 11 B3
Cassette, Rue (6) 12 D5
Cassini, Rue (14) 16 E3

Castagnary, Rue (15) 15 A3
Castellane, Rue de (8) 5 C4
Castex, Rue (4) 14 D4
Castiglione, Rue de (1) 12 D1
Catacombs (14) 16 E3
Catalogne, Pl de (15) 15 B3
Catulle Mendès, Rue (17) 4 D1
Cauallotti, Rue (18) 6 D1
Cauchois, Rue (18) 6 E1
Caulaincourt, Rue (18) 2 E5
  continues 6 D1
Caumartin, Rue de (9) 6 D4
Cavalerie, Rue de
la (15) 10 E5
Cavalière Fortunée,
Allée (16) 3 A4
Cavalière St Denis,
Allée (16) 3 A4
Cavallotti, Rue (18) 6 D1
Cave, Rue (18) 7 B1
Cazotte, Rue (18) 7 A1
Cel Scott, Rue du (15) 10 D4
Célestins, Port des (4) 13 C4
Célestins, Quai des (4) 13 C4
Cels, Rue (14) 15 C3
Censier, Rue (5) 17 B2
Centre de Conférences
Internationales (16) 4 D5
Cerisaie, Rue de la (4) 14 D4
Cerisoles, Rue de (8) 4 F5
Cernuschi, Rue (17) 4 F1
César Caire, Ave (8) 5 B3
Chabanais, Rue (1) 12 E1
Chabrol, Cité de (10) 7 B3
Chabrol, Rue de (10) 7 B3
Chaillot, Rue de (16) 4 E5
  continues 10 E1
Chaise, Rue de la (7) 12 D4
Chaise Récamier, Sq (7) 12 D4
Chalet, Rue du (10) 8 F4
Chalgrin, Rue (16) 3 C4
Chalon, Cour de (12) 18 F1
Chalon, Rue de (12) 18 F1
Chambiges, Rue (8) 10 F1
Chambre de Commerce et
d'Industrie de Paris (8) 4 F4
Champ de l'Alouette,
Rue du (13) 17 A4
Champ de Mars, Rue
du (7) 10 F3
Champ Marie, Passage du 2 F3
Champagny, Rue de (7) 11 B3
Champaubert, Ave
de (15) 10 E4
Champerret, Allée de
la Porte de (17) 3 C1
Champerret, Porte de (17) 3 C1
Champfleury, Rue (7) 10 E4
Championnet, Rue (18) 2 E4
Champollion, Rue (5) 12 F5
Champs, Galerie de (8) 4 F4
Champs-Elysées, Ave
des (8) 11 B1
  continues 4 E4
  continues 5 A5
Champs-Elysées,
Carré (8) 11 B1
Champs-Elysées, Port
des (8) 11 A1
Champs-Elysées, Rond
Point des (8) 5 A5
Chanaleilles, Rue de (7) 11 B4
Chancelier Adenauer,
Pl du (16) 3 B5
Change, Pont au (1) 13 A3
Chanoine Viollet, Sq
du (14) 15 C4
Chanoinesse, Rue (4) 13 B4
Chantier, Passage du (12) 14 F4
Chantiers, Rue des (5) 13 B5
Chantilly, Rue de (9) 7 A3

Chapelle, Ave
de la (17) 3 C2
Chapelle, Blvd de
la (10, 18) 7 C1
Chapelle, Cité
de la (18) 7 C1
Chapelle, Pl de la (18) 7 C1
Chapelle de la
Sorbonne (5) 13 A5
Chapon, Rue (3) 13 C1
Chappe, Rue (18) 6 F1
Chaptal, Cité (9) 6 E2
Chaptal, Rue (9) 6 E2
Charbonnière, Rue de
la (18) 7 B1
Charbonniers, Passage
des (15) 15 A1
Charcot, Rue (13) 18 E4
Chardin, Rue (16) 9 C3
Charenton, Rue de (12) 14 F5
Charlemagne, Rue (4) 13 C4
Charles Albert,
Passage (17) 2 D3
Charles Baudelaire,
Rue (12) 14 F5
Charles Bernard,
Place (18) 2 F4
Charles Dallery,
Passage (11) 14 F3
Charles de Gaulle, Ave 3 A2
Charles de Gaulle, Pl (16) 4 D4
Charles de Gaulle,
Pont (12, 13) 18 E2
Charles Dickens, Rue (16) 9 C3
Charles Dickens, Sq (16) 9 C3
Charles Divry, Rue (14) 16 4
Charles Dullin, Pl (18) 6 F1
Charles V, Rue (4) 14 D4
Charles Fillion, Pl (17) 1 B5
Charles Floquet, Ave (7) 10 E4
Charles Garmer, Rue 2 F1
Charles Girault, Ave (8) 11 B1
Charles Godon, Cité (9) 6 F3
Charles Laffitte, Rue 3 A3
Charles Lamoureux,
Rue (16) 3 B5
Charles Luizet, Rue (11) 14 E2
Charles Moureu,
Rue (13) 18 D5
Charles Nodier, Rue (18) 7 A1
Charles Risler, Ave (7) 10 E4
Charles Schmidt, Rue 2 E1
Charles Weiss, Rue (15) 15 A4
Charlet, Rue (15) 15 B2
Charlot, Rue (3) 14 D1
Charonne, Rue de (11) 14 F4
Charras, Rue (9) 6 D4
Chartière, Impasse (5) 13 A5
Chartres, Rue de (18) 7 B1
Chartres, Rue de 3 B2
Chartreux, Rue des (6) 16 E2
Chassaigne-Goyon,
Pl (8) 5 A4
Chasseurs, Ave
des (17) 4 F1
Château, Rue du (14) 15 C4
Château d'Eau, Rue
du (10) 7 C5
Château des Rentiers,
Rue du (13) 18 D5
Château Landon, Rue
du (10) 8 D2
Château Rouge,
Pl du (18) 7 B1
Châteaubriand, Rue
de (8) 4 E4
Châteaudun, Rue de (9) 6 E3
Châtelet, Pl du (1, 4) 13 A3
Châtillon, Rue de (14) 15 C5
Chauchat, Rue (9) 6 F4
Chaudron, Rue (10) 8 D2

Chaufourniers, Rue
des (19) 8 E3
Chaumont, Rue de (19) 8 E2
Chauveau Lagarde,
Rue (8) 5 C5
Chazelles, Rue de (17) 4 F2
Chemin Vert, Passage
du (11) 14 F2
Chemin Vert,
Rue du (11) 14 F3
Chénier, Rue (2) 7 B5
Cherche Midi, Rue
du (6) 11 C5
  continues 12 D5
Cherche Midi, Rue
du (15, 6) 15 B1
Chernoviz, Rue (16) 9 B3
Chéroy, Rue de (17) 5 B2
Chérubini, Rue (2) 6 E5
Cheval Blanc, Passage
du (11) 14 E4
Chevaleret, Rue du (13) 18 F5
Chevert, Rue (7) 11 A3
Cheverus, Rue de (9) 6 D3
Chevet, Rue du (11) 8 E5
Chevreuse, Rue de (6) 16 E2
Choiseul, Passage (2) 6 E5
Choiseul, Rue de (2) 6 E5
Choisy, Ave de (13) 17 C5
Chomel, Rue (7) 12 D4
Chopin, Pl (16) 9 A3
Choron, Rue (9) 6 F3
Christiani, Rue (18) 7 A1
Christine, Rue (6) 12 F4
Christophe Colomb,
Rue (16) 4 E5
Cicé, Rue de (6) 16 D1
Cimarosa, Rue (16) 3 C5
Cimetière de
Montmartre (18) 2 D5
  continues 2 D5
Cimetière de Passy (16) 9 C2
Cimetière des
Batignolles, Ave de 1 A3
Cimetière du
Montparnasse (14) 16 D3
Cimetière Parisien des
Batignolles (17) 1 B3
Cimetière St Benoît,
Rue du (5) 13 A5
Cimetière St Vincent (18) 2 F5
Cino del Duca, Rue (17) 3 B1
Cinq Diamants, Rue
des (13) 17 B5
Cinq Martyrs du Lycée Buffon,
Pont
des (14, 15) 15 B3
Cirque, Rue du (8) 5 B5
Ciseaux, Rue des (6) 12 E4
Cité, Rue de la (4) 13 A4
Civiale, Rue (10) 8 F4
Clairaut, Rue (17) 1 C5
Clapeyron, Rue (8) 5 C2
Claridge, Galerie du (8) 4 F5
Claude Bernard, Rue (5) 17 A2
Claude Debussy, Rue (17) 3 C1
Claude Debussy, Sq (17) 5 A1
Claude Pouillet, Rue (17) 5 B1
Claude Vellefaux, Ave (10) 8 E4
Claude-Nicolas Ledoux,
Sq (14) 16 E4
Clauzel, Rue (9) 6 F3
Clef, Rue de la (5) 17 B2
Clément, Rue (6) 12 E4
Clément Marot, Rue (8) 4 F5
Cler, Rue (7) 10 F3
Cléry, Rue de (2) 7 A5
Clichy, Ave de (17, 18) 6 D1
Clichy, Ave de (17) 1 B4
Clichy, Ave de la Porte
de (17) 1 A4

Clichy, Blvd de (9, 18)   6 E2
Clichy, Passage de (18)   6 1
Clichy, Place de (18)   6 D1
Clichy, Porte de   1 A3
Clichy, Porte de (17)   1 A4
Clichy, Rue de   1 C1
Clichy, Rue de (9)   6 D2
Clignancourt, Rue de (18)   7 A1
Clisson, Rue (13)   18 E4
Cloche Perce, Rue (4)   13 C3
Clodion, Rue (15)   10 D4
Cloître Notre-Dame,
   Rue du (4)   13 B4
Cloître St Mérri,
   Rue du (4)   13 B2
Clotaire, Rue (5)   17 A1
Clotilde, Rue (5)   17 A1
Clovis, Rue (5)   17 B1
Clovis Hugues, Rue (19)   8 F2
Cloys, Passage des (18)   2 E4
Cloys, Rue des (18)   2 F4
Cluny, Rue de (5)   13 A5
Cochin, Rue (5)   13 B5
Coëtlogon, Rue (6)   12 D5
Cognacq Jay, Rue (7)   10 F2
Colbert, Rue (2)   6 F5
Colette, Pl (1)   12 E1
Colisée, Rue du (8)   5 A4
Collégiale, Rue de la (5)   17 B3
Collet, Villa (15)   15 B5
Collette, Rue (17)   2 D4
Colombe, Rue de la (4)   13 B4
Colonel Bonnet, Ave
   du (16)   9 A3
Colonel Combes, Rue
   du (7)   10 F2
Colonel Debussy,
   Rue (17)   3 C1
Colonel Driant, Rue
   du (1)   12 F1
Colonel Fabien, Pl
   du (10, 19)   8 E3
Colonel Manhès, Rue
   de (17)   1 C4
Colonel Marot, Rue (8)   10 F1
Colonels Renard, Rue
   des (17)   4 D3
Colonne de
   Juillet (4, 12)   14 E4
Comédie Française (1)   12 E1
Comète, Rue de la (7)   11 A3
Commaille, Rue de (7)   11 C4
Commandant Charles
   Martel, Passage du (17)   5 B1
Commandant Lamy,
   Rue du (11)   14 F3
Commandant Marchand, Rue
   du (16)   3 B3
Commandant Pilot,
   Rue du   3 A2
Commandant Puegeot,
   Rue du (17)   3 C1
Commandant Rivière,
   Rue du (8)   5 A4
Commandant Schloesing, Rue
   du (16)   9 C2
Commandeur,
   Rue du (14)   16 D5
Commendant René
   Mouchotte,
   Rue du (14, 15)   15 C2
Commerce, Rue du (15)   10 E5
Commerce St Martin, Passage
   du (3)   13 B2
Commines, Rue (3)   14 D2
Commun, Passage (8)   10 F1
Commun, Passage (8)   5 A3
Commun, Passage (8)   5 A4
Commun, Passage (8)   6 D3
Commun, Passage (12)   14 F5
Commun, Passage (17)   2 D3

Compiègne, Rue de (10)   7 B2
Comtesse, Allée (8)   5 A3
Conciergerie (1)   13 A3
Concorde, Pl de la (8)   11 C1
Concorde, Pont de
   la (7, 8)   11 B1
Condé, Rue de (6)   12 F5
Condorcet, Cité (9)   7 A3
Condorcet, Rue (9)   6 F2
   continues   7 A2
Conférence, Port de
   la (8)   10 F1
Conseiller Collignon,
   Rue du (16)   9 A2
Conservatoire, Rue
   du (9)   7 A4
Conservatoire des Arts
   et Métiers (3)   13 B1
Conservatoire National
   Supérieur d'Art Dramatique
   (9)   7 A4
Constance, Rue (18)   6 E1
Constant Coquelin,
   Ave (7)   11 B5
Constantin Brancusi,
   Pl (14)   15 C3
Constantine, Rue de (7)   11 B2
Constantinople, Rue
   de (8)   5 B2
Conté, Rue (3)   13 C1
Conti, Quai de (6)   12 F3
Contrescarpe, Pl de
   la (5)   17 A1
Copenhague, Rue de (8)   5 C2
Copernic, Rue (16)   3 C5
Coq Héron, Rue (1)   12 F1
Coquillère, Rue (1)   12 F1
Corbusier, Pl le (6)   12 D4
Cordelières, Rue
   des (13)   17 A3
Corderie, Rue de la (3)   14 D1
Corneille, Rue (6)   12 F5
Corse, Quai de la (4)   13 A3
Cortambert, Rue (16)   9 B2
Corvetto, Rue (8)   5 B3
Corvisart, Rue (13)   17 A4
Cossonnerie, Rue de
   la (1)   13 A2
Costa Rica, Pl de (16)   9 C3
Cotentin, Rue du (15)   15 A3
Cothenet, Rue (16)   3 A5
Cottages, Rue des (18)   2 F5
Cotte, Rue de (12)   14 F5
Couche, Rue (14)   16 D5
Couédic, Rue du (14)   16 D5
Couperin, Sq (4)   13 B3
Cour de Commerce
   St-André (7)   12 F4
Cour des Fermes (1)   12 F1
Courcelles, Blvd
   de (8, 17)   4 F3
   continues   5 A2
Courcelles, Porte de (17)   4 D1
Courcelles, Rue de (8)   5 A4
Courcelles, Rue de (17)   4 E2
Courty, Rue de (7)   11 C2
Coustou, Rue (18)   6 E1
Coutellerie, Rue de
   la (4)   13 B3
Coutures St Gervais,
   Rue des (3)   14 D2
Coypel, Rue (13)   17 C4
Coysevox, Rue (18)   2 D5
Crébillon, Rue (6)   12 F5
Crémieux, Rue (12)   18 E1
Cretet, Rue (9)   6 F2
Crevaux, Rue (16)   3 B5
Crillon, Rue (4)   14 D5
Croce Spinelli, Rue (15)   15 B3
Croissant, Rue du (2)   7 A5

Croix des Petits Champs, Rue
   (1)   12 F1
Croix Rouge, Carrefour
   de la (6)   12 D4
Croulebarbe, Rue
   de (13)   17 B4
Crozatier, Impasse (12)   14 F5
Crozatier, Rue (12)   14 F5
Crussol, Rue de (11)   14 E1
Crypte
   Archéologique (4)   13 A4
Cujas, Rue (5)   13 A5
   continues   12 F5
Cunin Gridaine, Rue (3)   13 B1
Curton, Rue   1 A3
Cuvier, Rue (5)   17 C1
Cygne, Rue du (1)   13 B2
Cygnes, Allée
   des (15, 16)   9 B4
Cyrano de Bergerac,
   Rue (18)   2 F5

D

D Templier, Parvis (14)   15 C3
Daguerre, Rue (14)   15 C3
continues   16 D3
Dalayrac, Rue (2)   6 E5
Dalou, Rue (15)   15 B2
Dames, Rue des (17)   5 C1
Dames Augustines,
   Rue des   3 B1
Damiette, Rue de (2)   7 A5
Damoye, Cour (11)   14 E4
Damrémont, Rue (18)   2 E4
Damrémont, Villa (18)   2 F4
Dancourt, Rue (18)   6 F2
Daniel Leseuer, Ave (7)   11 B5
Daniel Stern, Rue (15)   10 D4
Danielle Casanova,
   Rue (1, 2)   6 E5
Dante, Rue (5)   13 A4
Dantec, Rue le (13)   17 A5
Danton, Rue (6)   12 F4
Danton, Rue   3 C1
Danville, Rue (14)   16 D4
Darboy, Rue (11)   8 E5
Darcet, Rue (17)   5 C1
Dardanelles, Rue
   des (17)   3 C2
Dareau, Passage (14)   16 E4
Dareau, Rue (14)   16 F4
Daru, Rue (8)   4 F3
Darwin, Rue (18)   2 F5
Daubenton, Rue (5)   17 B2
Daubigny, Rue (17)   5 A1
Daumesnil, Ave (12)   14 F5
   continues   18 F1
Daunay, Passage (18)   2 D4
Daunou, Rue (2)   6 D5
Dauphine, Pl (1)   12 F3
Dauphine, Rue (6)   12 F4
Dautancourt, Rue (17)   1 C5
Daval, Rue (11)   14 E4
Daviel, Rue (13)   17 A5
Davy, Rue (17)   1 C5
De Grenelle, Blvd (15)   10 E5
Débarcadère, Rue
   du (17)   3 C3
Debelleyme, Rue (3)   14 D2
Debilly,
   Passerelle (7, 16)   10 E2
Debilly, Port (16)   10 E1
Debrousse, Rue (16)   10 E1
Decamps, Rue (16)   9 B1
Déchargeurs, Rue
   des (1)   13 A2
Decrès, Rue (15)   15 B4
Degas, Rue (16)   9 A5
Deguerry, Rue (11)   8 E5
Dejean, Rue (18)   7 B1

Delacroix, Rue (16)   9 A2
Delambre, Rue (14)   16 D2
Delambre, Sq (14)   16 D2
Delanos, Passage (10)   7 C3
Delbet, Rue (14)   15 C5
Delcassé, Ave (8)   5 B4
Delessert, Blvd (16)   9 C3
Delessert, Passage (10)   8 D3
Delta, Rue du (9)   7 A2
Demarquay, Rue (10)   7 C2
Denain, Blvd de (10)   7 B3
Denfert Rochereau,
   Ave (14)   16 E3
Denfert Rochereau,
   Pl (14)   16 E3
Denis Poisson, Rue (17)   3 C3
Denis Poulot, Sq (11)   14 F3
Dénoyez, Rue (20)   8 F4
Denys Bülher, Sq (7)   11 A3
Déodat de Séverac,
   Rue (17)   5 A1
Deparcieux, Rue (14)   16 D3
Départ, Rue du (14, 15)   15 C2
Département, Rue
   du (18)   8 D1
Desaix, Rue (15)   10 D4
Desaix, Sq (15)   10 D4
Desargues, Rue (11)   8 F5
Desbordes Valmore,
   Rue (16)   9 A2
Descartes, Rue (5)   17 A1
Descombes, Rue (17)   4 D1
Desgenettes, Rue (7)   11 A2
Deshayes, Villa (15)   15 B5
Désir, Passage du (10)   7 C4
Désiré Ruggieri, Rue (18)   2 E4
Desprez, Rue (15)   15 B3
Dessous des Berges,
   Rue du (13)   18 F5
Detaille, Rue (17)   4 F2
Deux Anges, Impasse
   des (6)   12 E4
Deux Avenues, Rue
   des (13)   17 C5
Deux Gares, Rue
   des (10)   7 C3
Deux Nèthes, Impasse
   des (18)   6 D1
Deux Ponts, Rue
   des (4)   13 C4
Deux Sœurs, Passage
   des (9)   6 F4
Diaghilev, Pl (9)   6 D4
Diard, Rue (18)   2 F5
Diderot, Blvd (12)   18 F1
Diderot, Cour (12)   18 F1
Didot, Rue (15)   15 B5
Dieu, Rue (10)   8 D5
Direction Générale
   SNCF (9)   6 D3
Direction RATP (6)   12 F3
Dixmude, Blvd de (17)   3 C2
Dobropol, Rue du (17)   3 C2
Docteur Alfred Fournier,
   Pl du (10)   8 D4
Docteur Babinski,
   Rue du (18)   2 E2
Docteur Bauer,
   Rue du   2 F1
Docteur Brouardel,
   Ave du (7)   10 D3
Docteur Calmette,
   Rue du   1 A3
Docteur Charles Richet,
   Rue du (13)   18 D4
Docteur Finlay, Rue
   du (15)   10 D4
   continues   9 C4
Docteur Germain Sée,
   Rue de (16)   9 B4

Each place name is followed by its arrondissement number, and then by its Street Finder reference.

Docteur Hayem, Pl du (16) **9 A4**
Docteur Heulin, Rue du (17) **1 C5**
Docteur Lancereaux, Rue du (8) **5 A3**
Docteur Magnan, Rue du (13) **18 D5**
Docteur Navarre, Pl du (13) **18 D5**
Docteur Paul Brousse, Rue du (17) **1 B4**
Docteur Roux, Rue du (15) **15 A2**
Docteur Roux, Rue du (17) **1 A3**
Docteur Victor Hutinel, Rue du (13) **18 D4**
Dolomieu, Rue (5) **17 B2**
Domat, Rue (5) **13 A5**
Dome, Rue du (16) **4 D5**
Dôme des Invalides (7) **11 A4**
Domrémy, Rue de (13) **18 E5**
Dosne, Rue (16) **3 B5**
Douai, Rue de (9) **6 E2**
Douaumont, Blvd de (17) **1 A3**
Double, Pont au (4, 5) **13 A4**
Dragon, Rue du (6) **12 D4**
Drevet, Rue (18) **6 F1**
Drouot, Rue (9) **6 F4**
Dubail, Passage (10) **7 C4**
Duban, Rue (16) **9 A3**
Dublin, Pl de (8) **5 C2**
Dubois, Rue (6) **12 F4**
Duc, Rue (18) **2 F4**
Duchefdelaville, Rue (13) **18 E4**
Dufrénoy, Rue (16) **9 A1**
Duguay Trouin, Rue (6) **16 D1**
Duhesme, Rue (18) **2 F4**
Dulac, Rue (15) **15 B1**
Dulong, Rue (17) **5 B1**
Duméril, Rue (13) **17 C3**
Dumont d'Urville, Rue (16) **4 D5**
Dunkerque, Rue de (9, 10) **7 B2**
Dunois, Rue (13) **18 E4**
Duperré, Rue (9) **6 E2**
Dupetit Thouars, Cité (3) **14 D1**
Dupetit Thouars, Rue (3) **14 D1**
Duphot, Rue (1) **5 C5**
Dupin, Rue (6) **11 C5**
Duplan, Cité (16) **3 C3**
Dupleix, Pl (15) **10 E4**
Dupleix, Rue (15) **10 E4**
Dupont, Villa (16) **3 B4**
Dupont des Loges, Rue (7) **10 F3**
Dupuis, Rue (3) **14 D1**
Duquesne, Ave (7) **10 F4**
continues **11 A4**
Durantin, Rue (18) **6 E1**
Duras, Rue de (8) **5 B5**
Durel, Cité (18) **2 E3**
Duret, Rue (16) **3 C4**
Duroc, Rue (7) **11 B5**
Durouchoux, Rue (14) **16 D4**
Dussoubs, Rue (2) **13 A1**
Dutot, Rue (15) **15 A2**
Duvivier, Rue (7) **10 F3**

E

Eaux, Rue des (16) **9 C3**
Eaux-Vives, Passage des (11) **14 E2**

Eblé, Rue (7) **11 B5**
Echaude, Rue de l' (6) **12 E4**
Echelle, Rue de l' (1) **12 E1**
Echiquier, Rue de l' (10) **7 B5**
Ecluses St-Martin, Rue des (10) **8 D3**
Ecole, Pl de l' (1) **12 F3**
Ecole de Mars, Rue de l' **3 A2**
Ecole de Médicine, Rue de l' (6) **12 F4**
Ecole Nationale d'Administration (7) **12 D3**
Ecole Nationale Supérieure des Beaux Arts (6) **12 E3**
Ecole Normale Supérieure (5) **17 A2**
Ecole Polytechnique, Rue de l' (5) **13 A5**
Ecole Supérieure des Mines (6) **16 F1**
Ecole Militaire (7) **10 F4**
Ecole Militaire, Pl de l' (7) **10 F4**
Ecoles, Rue des (5) **13 B5**
Ecouffes, Rue des (4) **13 C3**
Edgar Poe, Rue (19) **8 F3**
Edgar Quinet, Blvd (14) **16 D2**
Edgar Quinet, Rue **2 E1**
Edimbourg, Rue d' (8) **5 C2**
Edison, Ave (13) **18 D5**
Edmond About, Rue (16) **9 A2**
Edmond Flamand, Rue (13) **18 E3**
Edmond Gondinet, Rue (13) **17 A4**
Edmond Guillout, Rue (15) **15 B2**
Edmond Michelet, Pl (4) **13 B2**
Edmond Rostand, Place (6) **12 F5**
Edmond Valentin, Rue (7) **10 F2**
Edouard Colonne, Rue (1) **13 A3**
Edouard Denis, Place (6) **16 E2**
Edouard Detaille, Rue (17) **4 F2**
Edouard Jacques, Rue (14) **15 C3**
Edouard Lockroy, Rue (11) **14 F1**
Edouard Manet, Rue (13) **17 C4**
Edouard Pailleron, Rue (19) **8 F2**
Edouard Quenu, Rue (5) **17 B2**
Edouard Vaillant, Rue **2 E2**
Edward Tuck, Ave (8) **11 B1**
Eglise de la Sorbonne (5) **13 A5**
El Salvador, Pl (7) **11 A5**
Elisabeth, Passage **1 C2**
Elisée Reclus, Ave (7) **10 F3**
Elysée, Rue de l' (8) **5 B5**
Elzévir, Rue (3) **14 D3**
Emeriau, Rue (15) **9 C5**
Emile Acollas, Ave (7) **10 E4**
Emile Allez, Rue (17) **3 C2**
Emile Blémont, Rue (18) **2 F4**
Emile Chautemps, Sq (3) **13 B1**
Emile Deschanel, Ave (7) **10 E3**
Emile Deslandres, Rue (13) **17 B3**
Emile Dubois, Rue (14) **16 E4**
Emile Duclaux, Rue (15) **15 A2**
Emile Gilbert, Rue (12) **18 F1**
Emile Level, Rue (17) **1 B4**

Emile Ménier, Rue (16) **3 B5**
Emile Pouvillon, Ave (7) **10 E3**
Emile Zola, Rue **2 D2**
Emile Augier, Blvd (16) **9 A2**
Emile Richard, Rue (14) **16 D3**
Emilio Castelar, Rue (12) **14 F5**
Emmanuel Chabrier, Sq (17) **5 A1**
Enfer, Passage d' (14) **16 E2**
Enghien, Rue d' (10) **7 B4**
Epée de Bois, Rue de l' (5) **17 B2**
Eperon, Rue de l' (6) **12 F4**
Epinettes, Impasse des (17) **1 C3**
Epinettes, Rue des (17) **1 C4**
Erables, Route des (16) **3 A3**
Erasme Brossolette, Rue (5) **17 A2**
Erckmann Chatrian, Rue (18) **7 B1**
Ernest Cresson, Rue (14) **16 D4**
Ernest Gouin, Rue (17) **1 B4**
Ernest Renan, Rue (15) **15 A1**
Ernest Roche, Rue (17) **1 C4**
Esclangon, Rue (18) **2 F3**
Espace Pierre Cardin (8) **11 B1**
continues **5 B5**
Esquirol, Rue (13) **17 C3**
Essai, Rue de l' (5) **17 C2**
Estienne d'Orves, Pl d' (9) **6 D3**
Estrapade, Pl de l' (5) **17 A1**
Estrées, Rue d' (7) **11 A4**
Etats Unis, Pl des (16) **4 D5**
Etex, Rue (18) **2 D5**
Etienne Marcel, Rue (1, 2) **12 F1**
continues **13 A1**
Etoile, Route de l' (16) **3 A4**
Etoile, Rue de l' (17) **4 D3**
Eugène Fournière, Rue (18) **2 F3**
Eugène Carrière, Rue (18) **2 E5**
Eugène Flachat, Rue (17) **4 E1**
Eugène Manuel, Rue (16) **9 B2**
Eugène Varlin, Rue (10) **8 D3**
Eugène Varlin, Sq (10) **8 D3**
Euler, Rue (8) **4 E5**
Eure, Rue de l' (14) **15 C4**
Europe, Pl de l' (8) **5 C3**
Euryale Dehaynin, Rue (19) **8 F1**
Exposition, Rue de l' (7) **10 F3**
Eylau, Ave d' (16) **9 C1**

F

Fabert, Rue (7) **11 A2**
Fabriques, Cour des (11) **14 F1**
Fagon, Rue (13) **17 C4**
Faisanderie, Rue de la (16) **3 A5**
continues **9 A1**
Falaise, Cité (18) **2 E3**
Falconet, Rue (18) **7 A1**
Falguière, Cité (15) **15 A2**
Falguière, Pl (15) **15 A3**
Falguière, Rue (15) **15 A2**
Fallempin, Rue (15) **10 D5**
Fanny, Rue **1 B3**
Faraday, Rue (17) **4 D2**
Farcot, Rue **2 D1**
Faubourg du Temple, Rue du (10, 11) **8 E5**
Faubourg Montmartre, Rue du (9) **6 F4**

Faubourg Poissonnière, Rue du (9, 10) **7 A3**
Faubourg St-Antoine, Rue du (11, 12) **14 F4**
Faubourg St-Denis, Rue du (10) **7 C2**
Faubourg-St-Honoré, Rue du (8) **4 E3**
continues **5 A4**
Faubourg St-Jacques, Rue du (14) **16 F3**
Faubourg St-Martin, Rue du (10) **7 C4**
continues **8 D2**
Fauconnier, Rue du (4) **13 C4**
Faustin Hélie, Rue (16) **9 A2**
Fauvet, Rue (18) **2 D5**
Favart, Rue (2) **6 F5**
Fédération, Rue de la (15) **10 D4**
Félibien, Rue (6) **12 E4**
Félicien David, Rue (16) **9 A5**
Félicité, Rue de la (17) **5 A1**
Félix Desruelles, Sq (6) **12 E4**
Félix Pécaut, Rue (18) **2 D4**
Félix Ziem, Rue (18) **2 E5**
Fénelon, Rue (10) **7 B3**
Fer à Moulin, Rue du (5) **17 B2**
Ferdinand Brunot, Pl et Sq (14) **16 D4**
Ferdinand Duval, Rue (4) **13 C3**
Ferdousi, Ave (8) **5 A3**
Férembach, Cité (17) **3 C3**
Ferme St Lazare, Cour de la (10) **7 B3**
Fermiers, Rue des (17) **5 A1**
Fernand de la Tombelle, Sq (17) **5 A1**
Fernand Forest, Pl (15) **9 B5**
Fernand Labori, Rue (18) **2 F3**
Fernand Pelloutier, Rue (17) **1 C3**
Férou, Rue (6) **12 E5**
Ferronnerie, Rue de la (1) **13 A2**
Ferrus, Rue (14) **16 F4**
Feuillantines, Rue des (5) **16 F2**
Feuillants, Terrasse des (1) **12 D1**
Feutrier, Rue (18) **7 A1**
Feydeau, Galerie (2) **6 F5**
Feydeau, Rue (2) **6 F5**
Fidélité, Rue de la (10) **7 C4**
Figuier, Rue du (4) **13 C4**
Filles du Calvaire, Blvd des (3, 11) **14 D2**
Filles du Calvaire, Rue des (3) **14 D2**
Filles St Thomas, Rue des (2) **6 F5**
Finlande, Pl de (7) **11 A2**
Firmin Gémier, Rue (18) **2 D4**
Flandre, Passage de (19) **8 F1**
Flandre, Rue de (19) **8 E1**
Flandrin, Blvd (16) **3 A5**
continues **9 A1**
Flatters, Rue (5) **17 A3**
Fléchier, Rue (9) **6 F3**
Fleurs, Cité des (17) **1 C4**
Fleurs, Quai aux (4) **13 B4**
Fleurus, Rue de (6) **12 D5**
Fleury, Rue (18) **7 B1**
Floréal, Rue **1 C2**
Florence Blumenthal, Rue (16) **9 A5**

Florence Blumenthal, Sq (13)	**18 E5**	
Florimont, Impasse (15)	**15 B4**	
Flourens, Passage (17)	**2 D3**	
Foch, Ave (16)	**3 B4**	
Foch, Sq de l'Ave (16)	**3 B4**	
Foin, Rue du (3)	**14 D3**	
Folie Méricourt, Rue de la (11)	**14 E1**	
continues	**8 E5**	
Folies Bergères (9)	**7 A4**	
Fondary, Rue (15)	**10 D5**	
Fonderie, Passage de la (11)	**14 F1**	
Fontaine, Rue (9)	**6 E2**	
Fontaine au Roi, Rue de la (11)	**8 F5**	
Fontaine de l'Observatoire (6)	**16 E2**	
Fontaine de Médicis (6)	**12 F5**	
Fontaine des Innocents (1)	**13 A2**	
Fontaine du But, Rue de la (18)	**2 F5**	
Fontaines du Temple, Rue des (3)	**13 C1**	
Fontenoy, Pl de (7)	**10 F5**	
Forest, Rue (18)	**6 D1**	
Forez, Rue du (3)	**14 D1**	
Fortuny, Rue (17)	**4 F2**	
Forum des Halles (1)	**13 A2**	
Fossés St-Bernard, Rue des (5)	**13 B5**	
Fossés-St Marcel, Rue des (5)	**17 C2**	
Foucault, Rue (16)	**10 D1**	
Foucault, Rue (17)	**1 A2**	
Fouquet, Rue (17)	**1 A3**	
Four, Rue du (6)	**12 E4**	
Fourcroy, Rue (17)	**4 E2**	
Fourcy, Rue de (4)	**13 C4**	
Foyatier, Rue (18)	**6 F1**	
Fragonard, Rue (17)	**1 B4**	
Française, Rue (1, 2)	**13 A1**	
France, Ave de (13)	**18 F4**	
Francis de Pressensé, Rue (15)	**15 B4**	
Francis Garnier, Rue (18)	**2 D3**	
Francis Jammes, Rue (10)	**8 E3**	
Francis Poulenc, Sq (6)	**12 E5**	
Francisque Sarcey, Rue (16)	**9 B2**	
Franco Russe, Ave (7)	**10 E2**	
Francoeur, Rue (18)	**2 F5**	
François Millet, Rue (16)	**9 A5**	
François Miron, Rue (4)	**13 C3**	
François Ponsard, Rue (16)	**9 A3**	
François Premier, Place (8)	**10 F1**	
François Premier, Rue (8)	**10 F1**	
continues	**11 A1**	
continues	**4 F5**	
François-Aug Mariette, Sq (5)	**13 A5**	
Francs Bourgeois, Rue des (3, 4)	**13 C3**	
continues	**14 D3**	
Franklin D Roosevelt, Ave (8)	**11 A1**	
continues	**5 A5**	
Franz Liszt, Pl (10)	**7 B3**	
Frédéric Bastiat, Rue (8)	**4 F4**	
Frédéric Brunet, Rue (17)	**1 C3**	
Frédéric Le Play, Ave (7)	**10 F4**	
Frédéric Lemaître, Sq (10)	**8 D5**	

Frédéric Sauton, Rue (5)	**13 A5**	
Frédéric Schneider, Rue (18)	**2 F3**	
Fremicourt, Rue (15)	**10 E5**	
Frémiet, Ave (16)	**9 C3**	
Frères Périer, Rue des (16)	**10 E1**	
Fresnel, Rue (16)	**10 D1**	
Freycinet, Rue (16)	**10 E1**	
Friedland, Ave 8	**4 E4**	
Frochot, Ave (9)	**6 F2**	
Frochot, Rue (9)	**6 E2**	
Froidevaux, Rue (14)	**15 C3**	
continues	**16 D3**	
Froissart, Rue (3)	**14 D2**	
Froment, Rue (11)	**14 E3**	
Fromentin, Rue (9)	**6 E2**	
Fructidor, Rue (17)	**1 C2**	
Fulton, Rue (13)	**18 E3**	
Fürstenberg, Rue de (6)	**12 E4**	
Fustel de Coulanges, Rue (5)	**16 F2**	

G

Gabriel, Ave (8)	**5 B5**	
Gabriel, Villa (15)	**15 B1**	
Gabriel Fauré, Sq (17)	**5 A1**	
Gabriel Laumain, Rue du (9)	**7 A4**	
Gabriel Péri, Ave (18)	**2 D2**	
Gabriel Péri, Pl (8)	**5 C4**	
Gabriel Pierné, Sq (6)	**12 E3**	
Gabrielle, Rue (18)	**6 F1**	
Gaby Sylvia, Rue (11)	**14 E3**	
Gaillon, Pl (2)	**6 E5**	
Gaillon, Rue (2)	**6 E5**	
Gaîté, Rue de la (18)	**2 E2**	
Gaîté, Rue de la (14)	**15 C2**	
Gal Aube, Rue du (16)	**9 A3**	
Gal Camou, Rue du (7)	**10 E3**	
Gal de Castelnau, Rue du (15)	**10 E5**	
Gal Detrie, Ave de (7)	**10 E4**	
Gal Lambert, Rue du (7)	**9 D3**	
Galande, Rue (5)	**13 A4**	
Galerie National du Jeu de Paume (1)	**11 C1**	
Galilée, Rue (8, 16)	**4 E5**	
Galliera, Rue de (16)	**10 E1**	
Galvani, Rue (17)	**4 D1**	
Gambetta, Rue	**2 E1**	
Gambey, Rue (11)	**14 E1**	
Ganneron, Rue (18)	**2 D5**	
continues	**6 D1**	
Garabaldi, Rue	**2 D1**	
Garancière, Rue (6)	**12 E5**	
Gardes, Rue des (18)	**7 B1**	
Gare, Port de la (13)	**18 F3**	
Garibaldi, Blvd (15)	**10 F5**	
Garnier, Villa (15)	**15 B1**	
Garreau, Rue (18)	**6 E1**	
Gassendi, Rue (14)	**16 D3**	
Gastion de St-Paul, Rue (16)	**10 E1**	
Gaston Baty, Sq (14)	**15 C2**	
Gaston Couté, Rue (18)	**2 F5**	
Gaston de Caillavet, Rue (15)	**9 B5**	
Gaston Paymal, Rue	**1 A2**	
Gauthey, Rue (17)	**1 C4**	
Gavarni, Rue (16)	**9 B3**	
Gay Lussac, Rue (5)	**16 F1**	
Geffroy Didelot, Passage (17)	**5 B2**	
Général Anselin, Rue du (16)	**3 A3**	
Général Appert, Rue (16)	**3 A5**	

Général Aubé, Rue du (16)	**9 A3**	
Général Bertrand, Rue du (7)	**11 A5**	
continues	**15 B1**	
Général Brucard, Pl (8)	**4 F3**	
Général Camou, Rue du (7)	**10 E3**	
Général Catroux, Pl du (17)	**5 A2**	
Général Clergerie, Rue du (16)	**3 B5**	
Général Cordonnier, Rue du	**3 A2**	
Général de Castelnau, Rue du (15)	**10 E5**	
Général de Larminat, Rue du (15)	**10 E5**	
Général Détrie, Ave de (7)	**10 E4**	
Général Foy, Rue du (8)	**5 B3**	
Général Gouraud, Pl du (7)	**10 E3**	
Général Henrys, Rue du (17)	**2 D3**	
Général Ingold, Pl (10, 19)	**8 F4**	
Général Koenig, Pl du (17)	**3 C2**	
Général Lambert, Rue du (7)	**10 D3**	
Général Langlois, Rue du (16)	**9 B2**	
Général Lanrezac, Rue du (17)	**4 D3**	
Général Leclerc, Ave du (14)	**16 D4**	
Général Leclerc, Blvd du	**1 B2**	
Général Lemonnier, Ave du (1)	**12 D2**	
Général Mangin, Ave du (16)	**9 B4**	
Général Monclar, Pl du (15)	**15 A4**	
Général Morin, Sq du (3)	**13 B1**	
Général Roguet, Rue du	**1 A1**	
Geoffroy l'Angevin, Rue (4)	**13 B2**	
Geoffroy l'Asnier, Rue (4)	**13 C4**	
Geoffroy Marie, Rue (9)	**7 A4**	
Geoffroy-St-Hilaire, Rue (5)	**17 C2**	
George Bernanos, Ave (5)	**16 F2**	
George Eastman, Rue (13)	**17 C5**	
George F Haendel, Rue (10)	**8 D3**	
George V, Ave (8)	**4 E5**	
continues	**10 E1**	
Georges Berger, Rue (17)	**5 A2**	
Georges Bizet, Rue (16)	**10 E1**	
continues	**4 E5**	
Georges Boisseau, Rue	**1 B1**	
Georges Caïn, Sq (3)	**14 D3**	
Georges Desplas, Rue (5)	**17 B2**	
Georges Guillaumin, Pl (8)	**4 E4**	
Georges Lamarque, Sq (14)	**16 D3**	
Georges Lardennois, Rue (19)	**8 F3**	
Georges Mandel, Ave (16)	**9 B1**	
Georges Pitard, Rue (15)	**15 A3**	
Georges Pompidou, Pl (4)	**13 B2**	

Georges Pompidou, Voie (1, 4)	**13 A3**	
Georges Pompidou, Voie (16)	**9 B4**	
Georges Saché, Rue (14)	**15 C4**	
Georges Ville, Rue (16)	**3 C5**	
Georgette Agutte, Rue (18)	**2 E4**	
Gérando, Rue (9)	**7 A2**	
Gérard, Rue (13)	**17 B5**	
Gérard de Nerval, Rue (18)	**2 E3**	
Gergovie, Passage de (14)	**15 A4**	
Gergovie, Rue de (15)	**15 B4**	
Germain Pilon, Cité (18)	**6 E1**	
Germain Pilon, Rue (18)	**6 E1**	
Gesvres, Quai de (4)	**13 A3**	
Giffard, Rue (13)	**18 E3**	
Gilbert Perroy, Pl (14)	**15 C4**	
Ginoux, Rue (15)	**9 C5**	
Giordano Bruno, Rue (15)	**15 B5**	
Girardon, Rue (18)	**2 F5**	
Gît le Cœur, Rue (6)	**12 F4**	
Glacière, Rue de la (13)	**16 F5**	
continues	**17 A3**	
Gluck, Rue (9)	**6 E4**	
Gobelins, Ave des (5, 13)	**17 B3**	
Gobelins, Rue des (13)	**17 B3**	
Godefroy, Rue (13)	**17 C4**	
Godot de Mauroy, Rue (9)	**6 D4**	
Goethe, Rue (16)	**10 E1**	
Goff, Rue le (5)	**16 F1**	
Goncourt, Rue des (11)	**8 E5**	
Goüin, Rue (17)	**1 B4**	
Gounod, Rue (17)	**4 E2**	
Gourgaud, Ave (17)	**4 E1**	
Goutte d'Or, Rue de la (18)	**7 B1**	
Gouvion-St-Cyr, Blvd (17)	**3 C2**	
Gouvion-St-Cyr, Sq (17)	**3 C2**	
Gracieuse, Rue (5)	**17 B2**	
Graisivaudan, Sq du (17)	**3 C1**	
Gramont, Rue de (2)	**6 E5**	
Grancey, Rue de (14)	**16 D4**	
Grand Cerf, Passage du (2)	**13 A1**	
Grand Palais (8)	**11 A1**	
Grand Prieuré, Rue du (11)	**14 E1**	
Grand Veneur, Rue du (4)	**14 D3**	
Grande Armée, Ave de (17, 16)	**3 C3**	
continues	**4 D4**	
Grande Chaumière, Rue de la (6)	**16 D2**	
Grande Truanderie, Rue de la (1)	**13 A2**	
Grands Augustins, Quai des (6)	**12 F3**	
Grands Augustins, Rue des (6)	**12 F4**	
Grands Degrés, Rue des (4)	**13 B4**	
Grange aux Belles, Rue de la (10)	**8 D4**	
Grange Batelière, Rue de la (9)	**6 F4**	
Gravilliers, Passage des (3)	**13 C1**	
Gravilliers, Rue des (3)	**13 C1**	
Greffulhe, Rue (8)	**5 C4**	

Gregoire de Tours,
Rue (6) **12 F4**
Grenelle, Blvd
de (15) **10 D4**
Grenelle, Pont
de (15, 16) **9 B5**
continues **9 C4**
Grenelle, Port de (15) **9 C4**
Grenelle, Quai de (15) **9 C4**
Grenelle, Rue de (7) **10 F3**
continues **11 A3**
Grenelle, Villa
de (15) **10 D5**
Greneta, Rue (2) **13 A1**
Grenier St-Lazare,
Rue du (3) **13 B2**
Grenier sur l'Eau,
Rue (4) **13 B3**
Grétry, Rue (2) **6 E5**
Greuze, Rue (16) **9 B1**
Gril, Rue du (5) **17 B2**
Grisel, Impasse (15) **10 F5**
Gros Caillou, Port
du (7) **10 F2**
Gros Caillou, Rue
du (7) **10 F3**
Gros, Rue (16) **9 A4**
Grosse Bouteille,
Impasse de la (18) **2 F4**
Guatemala, Pl du (8) **5 B3**
Guelma, Villa de (18) **6 E2**
Guéménée,
Impasse (4) **14 D4**
Guénégaud, Rue (6) **12 F3**
Guerry, Rue de (11) **8 F5**
Guersant, Rue (17) **3 C2**
continues **4 D2**
Guesclin, Passage
du (15) **10 E4**
Guibert, Villa (16) **9 A2**
Guichard, Rue (16) **9 A3**
Guillaume Apollinaire,
Rue (6) **12 E4**
Guillaume Tell,
Rue (17) **4 D1**
Guillaumont, Rue (12) **18 F1**
Guilleminot, Rue (15) **15 B3**
Guillemites, Rue
des (4) **13 C3**
Guisarde, Rue (6) **12 E4**
Guizot, Villa (17) **4 D3**
Gustane Nadaud,
Rue (16) **9 A2**
Gustave Charpentier,
Rue (17) **3 B2**
Gustave Courbet,
Rue (16) **9 B1**
Gustave Doré, Rue (17) **4 F1**
Gustave Eiffel,
Ave (7) **10 D3**
Gustave V de Suède,
Ave (16) **10 D2**
Gustave Flaubert,
Rue (17) **4 E2**
Gustave Geffroy,
Rue (13) **17 B3**
Gustave Mesureur,
Sq (13) **18 D4**
Gustave Rouanet,
Rue (18) **2 F3**
Gustave Zédé,
Rue (16) **9 A3**
Guttin, Rue (17) **1 B4**
Guy de la Brosse,
Rue (5) **17 C1**
Guy de Maupassant,
Rue (16) **9 A2**
Guy Môquet, Rue (17) **1 C4**
Guy Patin, Rue (10) **7 B2**
Guynemer, Rue (6) **12 E5**
continues **16 E1**

H

Halévy, Rue (9) **6 E4**
Hallé, Rue (14) **16 E4**
Halles, Rue des (1) **13 A2**
Hamelin, Rue (16) **10 D1**
continues **4 D5**
Hanovre, Rue de (2) **6 E5**
Harlay, Rue de (1) **12 F3**
Harpe, Rue de la (5) **13 A4**
Haudriettes, Rue
des (4) **13 C2**
Haussmann, Blvd (8, 9) **6 D4**
Haussmann, Blvd (8) **5 A4**
Hautefeuille, Rue (6) **12 F4**
Hautes Formes,
Rue (13) **18 D5**
Hauteville, Cité d' (10) **7 B3**
Hauteville, Rue d' (10) **7 B3**
Havre, Cour du (8) **6 D3**
Havre, Pl du (8, 9) **6 D4**
Havre, Rue du (8, 9) **6 D4**
Hector Malot, Rue (12) **14 F5**
continues **18 F1**
Hégésippe Moreau,
Rue (18) **6 D1**
Helder, Rue du (9) **6 E4**
Hélène, Rue (17) **5 C1**
Héliopolis, Rue d' (17) **4 D1**
Héloïse et Abélard,
Sq (13) **18 E4**
Henri Barbusse, Rue **1 A2**
Henri Barbusse, Rue (5) **16 F2**
Henri Brisson, Rue (18) **2 E3**
Henri Christiné,
Sq (3, 10) **8 D5**
Henri Delormel,
Sq (14) **16 D4**
Henri Duparc,
Sq (17) **5 A1**
Henri Feulard, Rue (10) **8 E4**
Henri IV, Blvd (4) **14 D4**
Henri IV, Port (4) **14 D5**
Henri IV, Quai (4) **14 D5**
Henri Galli, Sq (4) **14 D4**
Henri Huchard, Rue (18) **2 E3**
Henri Huchard, Square **2 D3**
Henri Martin, Ave (16) **9 A1**
Henri Moissan, Rue (7) **10 F2**
Henri Monnier, Rue (9) **6 E2**
Henri Murger, Rue (19) **8 F3**
Henri Poincaré, Rue **1 B2**
Henri Queuille, Pl (15) **15 A1**
Henri Robert, Rue (1) **12 F3**
Henri Rochefort, Rue (17) **4 F2**
Henri Turot, Rue (19) **F3**
Henry de Jouvenel,
Rue (6) **12 E5**
Henry de Montherlant,
Pl (7) **11 C2**
Hérault de Séchelles,
Rue (17) **1 C2**
Héricart, Rue (15) **9 C5**
Héricart, Sq (15) **9 C5**
Hérold, Rue (1) **12 F1**
Herran, Rue (16) **9 B1**
Herran, Villa (16) **9 A1**
Herschel, Rue (6) **16 F1**
Hesre, Rue de (3) **14 D2**
Hippolyte Lebas, Rue (9) **6 F3**
Hippolyte Maindron,
Rue (14) **15 C4**
Hittorff, Rue (10) **7 C4**
Hoche, Ave (8) **4 F3**
Honoré Champion,
Sq (6) **12 E3**
Honoré Chevalier,
Rue (6) **12 E5**
Hôpital, Blvd
de l' (5, 13) **17 C3**
continues **18 D2**
Hôpital Broca (13) **17 A3**

Hôpital Broussais la
Charité (14) **15 A5**
Hôpital Cochin (14) **16 F3**
Hôpital de Paris (4) **13 B3**
Hôpital Fernand
Widal (10) **7 C2**
Hôpital Laennec (6) **11 C5**
Hôpital Necker Enfants
Malades (15) **15 B1**
Hôpital St-Louis, Rue
de l' (10) **8 D4**
Hôpitalier Pitié
Salpêtrière (13) **18 D3**
Horloge, Quai de l' (1) **12 F3**
continues **13 A3**
Hôtel Colbert, Rue
de l' **13 A4**
Hôtel de Lamoignan (4) **14 D3**
Hôtel de Lauzun (4) **13 C4**
Hôtel de Matignon (7) **11 C4**
Hôtel de Rohan (3) **13 C2**
Hôtel de Sully (4) **14 D4**
Hôtel de Ville (4) **13 B3**
Hôtel de Ville, Bazar
de l' (4) **13 B3**
Hôtel de Ville, Pl
de l' (4) **13 B3**
Hôtel de Ville, Port
de l' (4) **13 B4**
Hôtel de Ville, Quai
de l' (4) **13 B4**
Hôtel de Ville, Rue
de l' (4) **13 C4**
Hôtel des Invalides (7) **11 A3**
Hôtel des Monnaies (6) **12 F3**
Hôtel des Sens (4) **13 C4**
Hôtel Dieu (4) **13 A4**
Hôtel Guénégaud (3) **13 C2**
Hôtel Libéral Bruand (3) **14 D3**
Hôtel Soubise (3) **13 C2**
Houdon, Rue (18) **6 F2**
Huchette, Rue de la (5) **13 A4**
Humblot, Rue (15) **10 D5**
Huyghens, Rue (14) **16 D2**
Huysmans, Rue (6) **16 D1**

I

Iéna, Ave d' (16) **4 D5**
continues **10 D1**
Iéna, Pl d' (16) **10 D1**
Iéna, Pont d' (7) **10 D2**
Ile de France, Sq
de l' (4) **13 B4**
Ile de la Cité (4) **13 A4**
Ile de Seine, Pl de l' (14) **16 E4**
Ile St-Louis (4) **13 C4**
Impasse de l'enfant
Jesus (15) **15 B1**
Industrie, Passage
de l' (10) **7 B5**
Ingénieur, Rue de l' (15) **9 B5**
Inkermann, Blvd d' **3 A1**
Innocents, Rue des (1) **13 A2**
Innocents, Square
des (1) **13 A2**
Institut, Pl de l' (6) **12 E3**
Institut de France (6) **12 E3**
Institut du Monde
Arabe (5) **13 C5**
Institut Géographique National
(7) **11 B3**
Institut Pasteur (15) **15 A2**
Invalides, Blvd des (7) **11 B5**
Invalides, Esplanade
des (7) **11 A2**
Invalides, Pl des (7) **11 A3**
Invalides, Pont
des (7, 8) **11 A1**
Irlandais, Rue des (5) **17 A1**
Islettes, Rue des (18) **7 B1**

Israel, Place d' (17) **4 F1**
Italie, Ave d' (13) **17 C5**
Italie, Pl d' (13) **17 C5**
Italiens, Blvd des (2, 9) **6 F4**
Italiens, Rue des (9) **6 E4**

J

Jacob, Rue (6) **12 E3**
Jacquard, Rue (11) **14 E1**
Jacquemont, Rue (17) **1 C5**
Jacques Antoine, Sq (14) **16 E3**
Jacques Bainville, Pl (7) **11 C3**
Jacques Bingen, Rue (17) **5 A2**
Jacques Cartier, Rue (17) **2 D4**
Jacques Coeur, Rue (4) **14 D4**
Jacques Coeur, Rue (4) **14 E4**
Jacques Callot, Rue (6) **12 E3**
Jacques Dulud, Rue **3 A2**
Jacques Froment,
Place (18) **2 E5**
Jacques Ibert, Rue (17, 18) **3 C1**
Jacques Kablé, Rue (18) **8 D1**
Jacques Louvel Tessier,
Rue (10) **8 E5**
Jacques Rouché, Pl (9) **6 E4**
Jacques Rueff, Pl (7) **10 E3**
Jacques Vigués,
Cour (11) **14 F4**
Jacquier, Rue (15) **15 B5**
Jadin, Rue (17) **4 F2**
Jamot, Villa (15) **15 B5**
Jardin Alleray
Labrouste (15) **15 A3**
Jardin de Babylone (7) **11 C4**
Jardin de l'Amérique
Latine (17) **3 C1**
Jardin de l'Infante (1) **12 E2**
Jardin de l'Intendant (7) **11 A4**
Jardin de Navarre (7) **13 B5**
continues **17 B1**
Jardin des Plantes (5) **17 C1**
Jardin des Tuileries (1) **12 D1**
Jardin du Carrousel (1) **12 E2**
Jardin du
Luxembourg (6) **12 E5**
continues **16 E1**
Jardin du Moulin de
la Vierge (15) **15 B4**
Jardin du Palais
Royal (1) **12 E1**
Jardin Marco Polo (6) **16 E2**
Jardin R Cavelier-de-
la-Salle (6) **16 E1**
Jardin St-Aignan (3) **13 B2**
Jardin Villemin (10) **8 D4**
Jardinet, Rue du (6) **12 F4**
Jardins du
Trocadéro (16) **10 D2**
Jardins, Rue des (4) **13 C4**
Jarente, Rue de (4) **14 D3**
Jarry, Rue (10) **7 C4**
Javel, Port de (15) **9 B5**
Jean Baptiste Dumas,
Rue (17) **4 D2**
Jean Bart, Rue (6) **12 D5**
Jean Beausire,
Impasse (4) **14 E3**
Jean Beausire, Rue (4) **14 E4**
Jean Bologne, Rue (16) **9 B3**
Jean Bouton, Rue (12) **18 F1**
Jean Calvin, Rue (5) **17 A2**
Jean Carriès, Rue (7) **10 E4**
Jean Colly, Rue (13) **18 E5**
Jean de Beauvais,
Rue (5) **13 A5**
Jean Dolent, Rue (14) **16 F4**
Jean Dollfus, Rue (18) **2 E3**
Jean du Bellay, Pl (1) **13 A2**
Jean du Bellay, Rue (4) **13 B4**
Jean Ferrandi, Rue (6) **15 C1**

Jean François Gerbillon, Rue (6) **11 C5**
Jean François Lépine, Rue (18) **7 C1**
Jean Giraudoux, Rue (16) **4 E5**
Jean Goujon, Rue (8) **10 F1**
continues **11 A1**
Jean Henri Fabre, Rue (18) **2 F2**
Jean Hugues, Rue (16) **3 A5**
Jean Jacques Rousseau, Rue (1) **12 F2**
continues **13 A1**
Jean Jaurès, Ave (19) **8 F1**
Jean Lantier, Rue (1) **13 A3**
Jean Leclaire, Rue (17) **2 D3**
Jean Mermoz, Rue (8) **5 A5**
Jean Moinon, Rue (10) **8 E4**
Jean Monnet, Pl (16) **3 B5**
Jean Moréas, Rue (17) **4 D1**
Jean Moulin, Rue (14) **16 D5**
Jean Nicot, Rue (7) **10 F2**
Jean Poulmarch, Rue (10) **8 D4**
Jean Rey, Rue (15) **10 D3**
Jean Richepin, Rue (16) **9 A2**
Jean Rostand, Pl (10, 19) **8 F4**
Jean Sébastien Bach, Rue (13) **18 D4**
Jean Varenne, Rue (18) **2 E3**
Jean XXIII, Sq (4) **13 B4**
Jean Zay, Rue (14) **15 C3**
Jean-Pierre Timbaud, Rue (11) **14 F1**
Jeanne d'Arc, Pl (13) **18 E5**
Jeanne d'Arc, Rue (13) **17 C3**
continues **18 D4**
Jehan Rictus, Sq (18) **6 F1**
Jemmapes, Quai de (10) **8 D3**
continues **8 E2**
Jenner, Rue (13) **18 D3**
Jérome Bellat, Sq (17) **4 D1**
Jessaint, Rue de (18) **7 C1**
Jessaint, Sq de (18) **7 C1**
Jeûneurs, Rue des (2) **7 A5**
Jocelyn, Villa (16) **9 A1**
Joffre, Place (7) **10 F4**
Johann Strauss, Pl (10) **7 C5**
Jolivet, Rue (14) **15 C2**
Jonquière, Rue de la (17) **1 C4**
Jonquilles, Rue des (14) **15 A4**
Jonquoy, Rue (15) **15 B5**
José Marti, Place (16) **C2**
Joseph Bara, Rue (6) **16 E2**
Joseph Bouvard, Ave (7) **10 E3**
Joseph de Maistre, Rue (18) **6 E1**
Joseph de Maistre, Rue **2 D5**
Joseph et Marie Hackin, Rue (16) **3 B3**
Joseph Granier, Rue (7) **11 A4**
Joseph Sansboeuf, Rue (8) **5 C4**
Josset, Passage (11) **14 F4**
Joubert, Rue (9) **6 D4**
Jouffroy, Passage (9) **6 F4**
Jouffroy, Rue (17) **4 F2**
continues **5 A1**
Jour, Rue du (1) **13 A1**
Jouy, Rue de (4) **13 C4**
Juge, Rue (15) **10 D5**
Juges Consuls, Rue des (4) **13 B3**
Juin 18 1940, Pl du (16) **15C1**
Juillet 29, Rue du (1) **12 D1**
Jules Breton, Rue (13) **17 C3**
Jules César, Rue (12) **14 E5**

Jules Chaplain, Rue (6) **16 D1**
Jules Claretie, Rue (16) **9 A2**
Jules Cloquet, Rue (18) **2 E3**
Jules Ferry, Sq (11) **8 E5**
Jules Guesde, Rue (14) **15 C3**
Jules Janin, Ave (16) **9 A2**
Jules Lefebvre, Rue (9) **6 D2**
Jules Renard, Pl (17) **3 C1**
Jules Romains, Rue (19) **8 F4**
Jules Sandeau, Blvd (16) **9 A2**
Jules Vallès, Rue **2 F2**
Jules Verne, Rue (11) **8 E5**
Jules Verne, Rue (7) **2 D1**
Juliette Dodu, Rue (10) **8 E4**
Junot, Ave (18) **2 E5**
Jura, Rue du (13) **17 C3**
Jussienne, Rue de la (2) **13 A1**
Jussieu, Pl (5) **17 B1**
Jussieu, Rue (5) **17 C1**

K

Keller, Rue (11) **14 F4**
Keller, Rue (15) **9 B5**
Keppler, Rue (16) **4 E5**
Kléber, Ave (16) **4 D5**
continues **9 C1**
Kléber, Rue **2 E1**
Klock, Rue **1 A**

L

L Gambetta, Allées **1 A2**
L Vaudoyer, Rue (7) **11 A5**
La Boétie, Rue (8) **4 F5**
continues **5 A4**
La Condamine, Rue (17) **5 C1**
La Fayette, Rue (9, 10) **7 A3**
La Fayette, Rue (9) **6 E4**
La Fayette, Rue (10) **8 D2**
La Fontaine, Rue (16) **9 A4**
La Fontaine, Rue **2 D2**
La Madeleine (8) **5 C5**
La Pérouse, Rue (16) **4 D5**
La Sorbonne (5) **12 F5**
continues **13 A5**
La Vrillière, Rue (1) **12 F1**
Labie, Rue (17) **3 C3**
Laborde, Rue de (8) **5 C3**
Labrouste, Rue (15) **15 A3**
Lacaille, Rue **1 C4**
Lacépède, Rue (5) **17 B1**
Lacharrière, Rue (11) **14 F2**
Lacombe, Passage **1 B3**
Lacour, Passage **1 C2**
Lacroix, Rue (17) **1 C5**
Lacuée, Rue (12) **14 E5**
Laferrière, Rue (9) **6 F3**
Laffitte, Rue (9) **6 F4**
Lagarde, Rue (5) **17 A2**
Lagille, Rue (17) **2 D4**
Lagrange, Rue (5) **13 A4**
continues **13 A5**
Lahire, Rue (13) **18 D5**
Lalande, Rue (14) **16 D3**
Lallier, Rue (9) **6 F2**
Lally Tollendal, Rue (19) **8 F2**
Lalo, Rue (16) **3 B4**
Lamandé, Rue (17) **5 B1**
Lamarck, Rue (18) **2 E5**
continues **7 A1**
Lamartine, Rue (9) **6 F3**
Lamartine, Sq (16) **9 A1**
Lamballe, Ave de (16) **9 B4**
Lamennais, Rue (8) **4 F4**
Lancry, Rue de (10) **8 D4**
Landrieu, Passage (7) **10 F2**
Landy, Rue du **1 A1**
Lanneau, Rue de (5) **13 A5**
Lannes, Blvd (16) **3 A5**
Lantiez, Rue (17) **1 C4**

Laos, Rue du (15) **10 E5**
Lapeyrère, Rue (18) **2 F5**
Lappe, Rue de (11) **14 E4**
Largillière, Rue (16) **9 A3**
Larochelle, Rue (14) **15 C2**
Laromiguière, Rue (5) **17 A1**
Larrey, Rue (5) **17 B2**
Larribe, Rue (8) **5 B2**
Las Cases, Rue (7) **11 C3**
Lasteyrie, Rue de (16) **3 C5**
Laterale, Rue **1 C2**
Lathuille, Passage (18) **6 D1**
Latran, Rue de (5) **13 A5**
Laugier, Rue (17) **4 D2**
Laugier, Villa (17) **4 D2**
Laurent Pichat, Rue (16) **3 B4**
Lauriston, Rue (16) **3 C5**
continues **4 D5**
continues **9 C1**
Lauzin, Rue (19) **8 F3**
Lavoir, Passage du (18) **2 D5**
Lavoisier, Rue (8) **5 C4**
Le Châtelier, Rue (17) **4 D1**
Le Sueur, Rue (16) **3 C4**
Lebon, Rue (17) **4 D2**
Lebouis, Rue (14) **15 C3**
Lebouteux, Rue (17) **5 B2**
Léchevin, Rue (11) **14 F1**
Leclerc, Rue (14) **16 E4**
Lécluse, Rue (17) **5 C1**
Lecomte, Rue (17) **1 C5**
Lecourbe, Rue (15) **15 A1**
Lécuyer, Rue **2 E2**
Ledion, Rue (15) **15 B5**
Ledru Rollin, Ave (12) **14 F5**
continues **18 E1**
Legendre, Rue (17) **1 C5**
continues **5 B1**
Léger, Impasse (17) **5 A1**
Legouvé, Rue (10) **8 D4**
Legraverend, Rue (12) **18 F1**
Leibnitz, Rue (18) **2 E3**
Leibnitz, Sq (18) **2 E3**
Lekain, Rue (16) **9 B3**
Lemercier, Cité (17) **5 C1**
Lemercier, Rue (17) **1 B5**
continues **5 C1**
Lemoine, Passage (2) **7 B5**
Lemon, Rue (20) **8 F4**
Leneveux, Rue (14) **16 D5**
Léningrad, Rue de (8) **5 C2**
continues **6 D2**
Lentonnet, Rue (9) **7 A2**
Léo Delibes, Rue (16) **9 C1**
Léon, Passage (18) **7 B1**
Léon, Rue (18) **7 B1**
Léon, Sq du Passage (18) **7 B1**
Léon Cogniet, Rue (17) **4 F2**
Léon Bonnet, Rue (11) **8 F5**
Léon Cladel, Rue (2) **6 F5**
Léon Cosnard, Rue (17) **5 A1**
Léon Droux, Rue (17) **5 B2**
Léon Jost, Rue (17) **4 F2**
Léon Jouhaux, Rue (10) **8 D5**
Léon Maurice Nordmann, Rue (13) **17 A4**
Léon Paul Fargue, Pl (7, 6, 15) **15 B1**
Léon Serpollet, Sq (18) **2 F4**
continues **2 F5**
Léonard de Vinci, Rue (16) **3 C5**
Léonce Reynaud, Rue (16) **10 E1**
Léonidas, Rue (14) **15 C4**
Léopold Achille, Sq (3) **14 D3**
Léopold Bellan, Rue (2) **13 A1**
Lepage, Cité (19) **8 E2**
Lepic, Rue (18) **6 E1**
Leredde, Rue (13) **18 F5**
Leroux, Rue (16) **3 C5**

Les Colonnes (15) **15 B3**
Lesdiguières, Rue de (4) **14 D4**
Letellier, Rue (15) **10 D5**
Letort, Rue (18) **2 F4**
Lévis, Rue de (17) **5 A1**
Lhomond, Rue (5) **17 A1**
Liancourt, Rue (14) **16 D4**
Lido, Arcades du (8) **4 F4**
Liège, Rue de (8, 9) **6 D3**
Liège, Rue de (8) **5 C3**
Lille, Rue de (7) **11 B2**
continues **12 D3**
Lincoln, Rue (8) **4 F5**
Linné, Rue (5) **17 B1**
Linois, Rue (15) **9 B5**
Lions St-Paul, Rue des (4) **14 D4**
Lisbonne, Rue de (8) **5 A3**
Littré, Rue (6) **15 C1**
Livingstone, Rue (18) **7 A1**
Lobau, Rue de (4) **13 B3**
Lobineau, Rue (6) **12 E4**
Logelbach, Rue de (17) **4 F2**
continues **5 A2**
Loing, Rue du (14) **16 D5**
Loire, Quai de la (19) **8 F1**
Lombards, Rue des (4) **13 A2**
Londres, Cité de (9) **6 D3**
Londres, Rue de (8, 9) **6 D3**
Londres, Rue de (8) **5 C3**
Longchamp, Allée de (16) **3 A3**
Longchamp, Rue de (16) **3 A5**
continues **9 B1**
continues **10 D1**
Lord Byron, Rue (8) **4 E4**
Losserand Suisses, Sq (14) **15 A4**
Lota, Rue de (16) **9 A1**
Louis Armand, Cour (12) **18 E1**
Louis Blanc, Rue (10) **8 D2**
Louis Blériot, Quai (16) **9 A5**
Louis Codet, Rue (7) **11 A4**
Louis David, Rue (16) **9 B2**
Louis le Grand, Rue (2) **6 E5**
Louis Lépine, Pl (4) **13 A3**
Louis Morard, Rue (14) **15 C5**
Louis Murat, Rue (8) **5 A3**
Louis Pasteur-Vallery-Radot, Rue (18) **2 E2**
Louis Philippe, Passage (11) **14 F4**
Louis Philippe, Pont (4) **13 B4**
Louis Robert, Rue (14) **16 D2**
Louis Thuillier, Rue (5) **17 A2**
Louis XIII, Sq (4) **14 D3**
Louis XVI, Sq (8) **5 C4**
Louise Labé, Allée (19) **8 F4**
Louise Michel, Rue **3 C1**
Louise Weiss, Rue (13) **18 E4**
Lourmel, Rue de (15) **10 D5**
Louvois, Rue de (2) **6 E5**
Louvre, Pl du (1) **12 F2**
Louvre, Port du (1) **12 E2**
Louvre, Quai du (1) **12 E2**
Louvre, Rue du (1) **12 F2**
Lowendal, Ave de (7) **10 F5**
continues **11 A4**
Lowendal, Sq (15) **10 F5**
Lt-Col Dax, Rue du (18) **2 F2**
Lübeck, Rue de (16) **10 D1**
Lucien Gaulard, Rue (18) **2 F5**
Lucien Herr, Pl (5) **17 A2**
Lucien Sampaix, Rue (10) **8 D4**
Lunain, Rue du (14) **16 D5**
Lune, Rue de la (2) **7 B5**
Lutèce, Rue de (5) **13 A4**
Luynes, Rue de (7) **12 D4**

Each place name is followed by its arrondissement number, and then by its Street Finder reference.

Lyautey, Rue (16) **9 B3**
Lycée Henry IV (5) **17 A1**
Lycée Louis le Grand (5) **13 A5**
Lycée Technique Roger
 Verlomme (15) **10 D5**
Lyon, Rue de (12) **14 E5**
 continues **18 E1**
Lyonnais, Rue des (5) **17 A3**

M

Mabillon, Rue (6) **12 E4**
Mac Mahon, Ave (17) **4 D3**
Madame de Sanzillon,
 Rue **1 B2**
Madame, Rue (6) **12 E5**
 continues **16 E1**
Madeleine, Blvd de
 la (1, 9) **6 D5**
Madeleine, Galerie de
 la (8) **5 C5**
Madeleine Michelis, Rue **3 B1**
Madrid, Rue de (8) **5 B3**
Magdebourg, Rue de (16) **9 C1**
Magellan, Rue (8) **4 E5**
Magenta,
 Blvd de (10) **7 B3**
 continues **8 D5**
Mai 8 1945, Rue
 du (10) **7 C3**
Mai 8 1945, Rue
 du **1 A3**
Mail, Rue du (2) **12 F1**
Maillot, Blvd (16) **3 A3**
Maillot, Pl de la
 Porte (16) **3 B3**
Maillot, Porte (16) **3 B3**
Main d'Or, Passage de
 la (11) **14 F4**
Maine, Ave du (14) **15 C3**
Maine, Rue du (14) **15 C2**
Maire, Rue au (3) **13 C1**
Mairie de Paris (4) **13 B3**
Maison de Radio-
 France (16) **9 B4**
Maison Dieu, Rue (14) **15 C3**
Maison Victor Hugo (4) **14 D4**
Maître Albert, Rue (5) **13 B5**
Mal du Harispe,
 Rue (7) **10 E3**
Malakoff, Ave de (16) **3 C4**
Malakoff, Impasse
 de (16) **3 B3**
Malaquais, Quai (6) **12 E3**
Malar, Rue (7) **10 F2**
Malebranche, Rue (5) **16 F1**
Malesherbes, Blvd (8) **5 B3**
Malesherbes,
 Blvd (17) **4 F1**
Malesherbes, Cité (9) **6 F2**
Maleville, Rue (8) **5 A3**
Malte, Rue de (11) **14 E1**
 continues **8 D5**
Malus, Rue (5) **17 B1**
Mandar, Rue (2) **13 A1**
Manin, Rue (19) **8 F3**
Mansart, Rue (9) **6 E2**
Manuel, Rue (9) **6 F3**
Manufacture des
 Gobelins (13) **17 B3**
Manutention, Rue de
 la (16) **10 D1**
Marbeau, Blvd (16) **3 B4**
Marbeau, Rue (16) **3 B4**
Marbeuf, Rue (8) **4 F5**
Marcadet, Rue (18) **2 D4**
Marceau, Ave (8, 16) **10 E1**
 continues **4 E5**
Marceau, Rue **2 F2**
Marcel Pagnol, Sq (8) **5 C3**
Marcel Proust, Ave (16) **9 B3**

Marcel Renault, Rue (17) **4 D2**
Marcel Sembat, Rue (18) **2 F3**
Marcel Sembat, Sq (18) **2 F3**
Marcès, Villa (11) **14 F3**
Marché, Pl du **3 A2**
Marché aux Puces de
 St-Ouen **2 F2**
Marché d'Aligre (12) **14 F5**
Marché Neuf, Quai
 du (4) **13 A4**
Marché Popincourt,
 Rue du (11) **14 F1**
Marché St-Honoré, Rue
 du (1) **12 D1**
 continues **12 E1**
Marché Ste-Catherine,
 Place du (4) **14 D3**
Maréchal de Lattre de Tassigny,
 Pl du (16) **3 A4**
Maréchal Fayolle,
 Ave du (16) **3 A5**
Maréchal Gallieni, Ave
 du (7) **11 A2**
Maréchal Juin, Pl du (17) **4 E1**
Marguerin, Rue (14) **16 D5**
Margueritte, Rue (17) **4 E2**
Margueritte de Navarre,
 Pl (1) **13 A2**
Maria Deraismes,
 Rue (17) **2 D4**
Marie, Pont (4) **13 C4**
Marie Curie, Rue **2 F2**
Marie Curie, Sq (13) **18 D2**
Marie du 6e Arr (6) **12 E5**
Marie et Louise,
 Rue (10) **8 D4**
Marietta Martin,
 Rue (16) **9 A3**
Marignan, Passage (8) **4 F5**
Marigny, Ave de (8) **5 B5**
Mariniers, Rue des (14) **15 A5**
Marinoni, Rue (7) **10 E3**
Mario Nikis, Rue (15) **10 F5**
Mariotte, Rue (17) **5 C1**
Maria Stuart, Rue (2) **13 A1**
Mariton, Rue **2 F1**
Marivaux, Rue de (2) **6 E5**
Maroc, Pl du (19) **8 E1**
Maroc, Rue du (19) **8 E1**
Marronniers, Rue
 des (16) **9 A4**
Marseille, Rue de (10) **8 D4**
Marsollier, Rue (2) **6 E5**
Martel, Rue (10) **7 B4**
Martignac, Cité (7) **11 B3**
Martignac, Rue de (7) **11 B3**
Martissot, Rue **1 B2**
Martre, Rue **1 A3**
Martyrs, Rue des (9) **6 F3**
Marx Dormoy,
 Rue (18) **7 C1**
Maspéro, Rue (16) **9 A2**
Massenet, Rue (16) **9 B3**
Massenet, Rue **1 C2**
Masseran, Rue (7) **11 B5**
Mathurin Moreau,
 Ave (19) **8 F3**
Mathurins, Rue des (8, 9) **6 D4**
Mathurins, Rue des (8) **5 C4**
Matignon, Ave (8) **5 A5**
Matthieu, Rue (18) **2 F1**
Maubert, Pl (5) **13 A5**
Maubeuge, Rue de (9) **6 F3**
Maubeuge, Rue de (10) **7 B2**
Mauconseil, Rue (1) **13 A1**
Maure, Passage du (3) **13 B2**
Maurice Bourdet,
 Rue (16) **9 B4**
Maurice Quentin, Pl (1) **13 A2**
Maurice Ripoche,
 Rue (14) **15 C4**

Maurice Rouvier,
 Rue (14) **15 A4**
Maurice de la Sizeranne,
 Rue (7) **11 B5**
Mauvais Garçons, Rue
 des (4) **13 B3**
Max Hymans, Sq (15) **15 B2**
Mayet, Rue (6) **15 B1**
Mayran, Rue (9) **7 A3**
Mazagran, Rue de (10) **7 B5**
Mazarine, Rue (6) **12 F4**
Mazas, Pl (12) **18 E1**
Mazas, Voie (12) **18 D1**
Meaux, Rue de (19) **8 F2**
Méchain, Rue (14) **16 F3**
Médéric, Rue (17) **4 F2**
Médicis, Rue de (6) **12 F5**
Mégisserie, Quai de
 la (1) **13 A3**
Meissonier, Rue (17) **4 F2**
Melun, Passage de (19) **8 F1**
Mémorial de la Shoah (4) **13 C4**
Ménageries (5) **17 C1**
Ménars, Rue (2) **6 F5**
Mérimée, Rue (16) **3 B5**
Meslay, Passage (3) **7 C5**
Meslay, Rue (3) **7 C5**
Mesnil, Rue (16) **3 C5**
Messageries, Rue
 des (10) **7 B3**
Messine, Ave de (8) **5 A3**
Messine, Rue de (8) **5 A3**
Metz, Rue de (10) **7 B5**
Mexico, Pl de (16) **9 B1**
Meyerbeer, Rue (9) **6 E4**
Mézières, Rue de (6) **12 E5**
Michal, Rue (13) **17 A5**
Michel Chasles,
 Rue (12) **18 F1**
Michel le Comte,
 Rue (3) **13 C2**
Michel Peter, Rue (13) **17 B3**
Michelet, Rue (6) **16 E2**
Michodière, Rue de la (2) **6 E5**
Midi, Rue du (18) **6 E2**
Midi, Rue du **3 B2**
Mignard, Rue (16) **9 A1**
Mignon, Rue (6) **12 F4**
Mignot, Sq (16) **9 B2**
Milan, Rue de (9) **6 D3**
Milton, Rue (9) **6 F3**
Minimes, Rue des (3) **14 D3**
Ministère de
 l'Intérieur (8) **5 B4**
Ministère de la
 Justice (1) **9 D5**
Ministère de l'Economie
 des Finances (12) **18 F2**
Mirbel, Rue de (5) **17 B2**
Mire, Rue de la (18) **6 F1**
Miromesnil, Rue de (8) **5 B3**
Missions Etrangères,
 Sq des (7) **11 C4**
Mizon, Rue (15) **15 B2**
Mogador, Rue de (9) **6 D4**
Moines, Rue des (17) **1 C5**
Molière, Passage (3) **13 B2**
Molière, Rue (1) **12 E1**
Mollien, Rue (8) **5 A3**
Monceau, Rue de (8) **4 F3**
 continues **5 A3**
Monceau, Villa (17) **4 E2**
Moncey, Rue (9) **6 D2**
Moncey, Sq (9) **6 D2**
Mondétour, Rue (1) **13 A2**
Mondovi, Rue de (1) **11 C1**
Monge, Pl (5) **17 B2**
Monge, Rue (5) **13 B5**
 continues **17 B1**
Mongolfier, Rue (3) **13 C1**

Monnaie, Rue de la (1) **2 F2**
Monseigneur Rodhain,
 Rue (10) **8 D3**
Monsieur le Prince,
 Rue (6) **12 F5**
Monsieur, Rue (7) **11 B5**
Monsigny, Rue (2) **6 E5**
Mont Cenis, Rue du (18) **2 F5**
Mont Dore, Rue du (17) **5 C2**
Mont Thabor, Rue
 du (1) **12 D1**
Mont Tonnerre, Impasse
 du (15) **15 B1**
Montagne Ste-
 Geneviève, Rue de
 la (5) **13 A5**
Montaigne, Ave (8) **10 F1**
 continues **5 A5**
Montalembert, Rue (7) **12 D3**
Montalivet, Rue (8) **5 B5**
Montbrun, Passage (14) **16 D5**
Montbrun, Rue (14) **16 D5**
Montcalm, Rue (18) **2 E4**
Montebello, Port de (5) **13 B4**
Montebello, Quai
 de (5) **13 A4**
Montenotte, Rue de (17) **4 D3**
Montespan, Ave de (16) **9 A1**
Montesquieu, Rue (1) **12 F2**
Montevideo, Rue de (16) **3 A5**
 continues **9 A1**
Montfaucon, Rue de (6) **12 E4**
Monthiers, Cité (9) **6 D2**
Montholon, Rue de (9) **7 A3**
Montholon, Sq de (9) **7 A3**
Montmartre, Rue de la
 Porte de (18) **2 E3**
Montmartre, Blvd (2, 9) **6 F4**
Montmartre, Galerie (2) **6 F5**
Montmartre, Rue (1, 2) **13 A1**
Montmartre, Rue (2) **6 F5**
Montmorency, Rue
 de (4) **13 C2**
Montorgueil, Rue (1, 2) **13 A1**
Montparnasse, Blvd
 du (6, 14, 15) **15 C1**
Montparnasse, Blvd
 du (6, 14) **16 E2**
Montparnasse,
 Passage (14) **15 C2**
Montparnasse, Rue
 du (6, 14) **16 D1**
Montpensier, Rue de (1) **12 E1**
Montrosier, Rue de **3 B2**
Monttessuy, Rue de (7) **10 E2**
Montyon, Rue de (9) **7 A4**
Mony, Rue (16) **9 A1**
Morand, Rue (11) **8 F5**
Moreau, Rue (12) **14 E5**
Morel, Rue **1 B2**
Morice, Rue **1 A2**
Morland, Blvd (4) **14 D5**
Morlot, Rue (9) **6 D3**
Mornay, Rue (4) **14 D5**
Moro Giafferi, Pl de (14) **15 C4**
Moscou, Rue de (8) **5 C2**
Moselle, Passage
 de la (19) **8 F1**
Moselle, Rue de la (19) **8 F1**
Moskowa, Cité de la (18) **2 E3**
Mosquée de Paris (5) **17 C2**
Motte Picquet, Ave
 de la (7) **10 F4**
 continues **11 A3**
Mouffetard, Rue (5) **17 B1**
Mouffetard Monge,
 Galerie (5) **17 B2**
Moufie, Rue (11) **14 F2**
Moulin de la
 Galette (18) **2 E5**

Moulin de la Vierge, Rue du (15) 15 B4
Moulin des Prés, Rue du (13) 17 B5
Moulin Joly, Rue du (11) 8 F5
Moulin Rouge (18) 6 E1
Moulin Vert, Rue du (14) 15 C4
Moulinet, Rue du (13) 17 C5
Moulins, Rue des (1) 12 E1
Mousseau, Impasse 2 E2
Moussy, Rue de (4) 13 C3
Mouton Duvernet, Rue (14) 16 D4
Mozart, Ave (16) 9 A3
Mulhouse, Rue de (2) 7 A5
Muller, Rue (18) 7 A1
Murillo, Rue (8) 4 F3
 continues 5 A3
Musée Adam Mickiewicz (4) 13 C4
Musée Bouilhet Christofle (8) 5 C4
Musée Bourdelle (15) 15 B1
Musée Carnavalet (3) 14 D3
Musée Cernuschi (8) 5 A3
Musée d'Arménien (16) 3 B5
Musée d'Art Moderne (16) 10 E1
Musée d'Ennery (16) 3 B5
Musée d'Orsay (7) 12 D2
Musée de Cluny (5) 12 F5
 continues 13 A5
Musée de Cristal (10) 7 B4
Musée de l'Armée (7) 11 A3
Musée d'Art et d'Histoire du Judaïsme (3) 13 B2
Musée de l'Holographie (1) 13 A2
Musée de l'Orangerie (1) 11 C1
Musée de l'Ordre de la Libération (7) 11 A4
Musée de la Contrefaçon (16) 3 B5
Musée de la Mode et du Costume Palais Galliera (16) 10 D1
Musée de la Musique Méchanique (3) 13 B2
Musée de la Poste (15) 15 B2
Musée de la Sculpture en Plein Air (5) 13 C5
Musée de Minéralogie (5) 13 B5
Musée Delacroix (6) 12 E4
Musée des Arts Décoratifs (1) 12 E2
Musée des Arts et Metiers (3) 13 B1
Musée de la Mode et des Textiles (1) 12 E2
Musée des Plan-Reliefs (7) 11 B3
Musée du Louvre (1) 12 E2
Musée du Montmartre (18) 2 F5
Musée du Vin (16) 9 C3
Musée Grévin (3) 13 A2
Musée Grévin (9) 6 F4
Musée Gustave Moreau (9) 6 E3
Musée Légion d'Honneur (7) 11 C2
Musée Maillol (7) 11 C4

Musée National des Arts Asiatiques Guimet (16) 10 D1
Musée National d'Histoire Naturelle (5) 17 C2
Musée Nissim de Camondo (8) 5 A3
Musée Picasso (3) 14 D2
Musée Radio-France (16) 9 A4
Musée Rodin (7) 11 B3
Musée Zadkine (6) 16 E1
Myrha, Rue (18) 7 A1
 continues 7 B1
Myron Timothy Herrick, Ave (8) 5 A4

N
N20 (14) 16 D5
N306 (14) 15 C5
Nadar, Sq (18) 6 F1
Nancy, Rue de (10) 7 C4
Naples, Rue de (8) 5 B3
Napoléon, Cour (1) 12 E2
Narvik, Pl de (8) 5 A3
Nationale du Jeu de Paume, Galerie (1) 11 C1
Nationale, Pl (13) 18 D5
Nationale, Rue (13) 18 D4
Nations Unies, Ave des (16) 10 D2
 continues 9 C2
Navarin, Rue de (9) 6 F2
Navarre, Rue de (5) 17 B1
Navier, Rue (18) 2 D4
Necker, Rue (4) 14 D3
Nélaton, Rue (15) 9 C4
Nemours, Rue de (11) 14 E1
Nesle, Rue de (6) 12 F3
Neuf, Pl du Pont (1) 12 F3
Neuf, Pont (1, 6) 12 F3
Neuilly, Ave de (16) 3 B3
Neuve Pierre Curie, Rue 2 E2
Neuve Popincourt, Rue (11) 14 F1
Neuve St-Pierre, Rue (4) 14 D4
Neuve Tolbiac, Rue (13) 18 F4
Néva, Rue de la (17) 4 E3
Nevers, Rue de (6) 12 F3
New York, Ave de (16) 10 D2
 continues 9 C2
Newton, Rue (16) 4 E5
Ney, Blvd (18) 2 E3
Nicolas Flamel, Rue (4) 13 A3
Nicolas Fortin, Rue (13) 17 C5
Nicolas Houël, Rue (5) 18 D2
Nicolas Roret, Rue (13) 17 B3
Nicolay, Sq (17) 5 B1
Nicolo, Rue (16) 9 A2
Niel, Ave (17) 4 E2
Niel, Villa (17) 4 E2
Niepce, Rue (15) 15 B3
Nil, Rue du (2) 7 A5
Nobel, Rue (18) 2 F5
Nocard, Rue (15) 9 C4
Noisiel, Rue de (16) 3 B5
Nollet, Rue (17) 1 B5
 continues 5 C1
Nollez, Cité (18) 2 E4
Nonnains d'Hyères, Rue des (4) 13 C4
Nordling, Rue 3 A3
Normandie, Rue de (3) 14 D1
Norvins, Rue (18) 6 F1

Nôtre, Rue le (16) 9 C2
Notre-Dame (18) 13 B4
Notre-Dame, Pl du Parvis (4) 13 A4
Notre-Dame, Pont (4) 13 A3
Notre-Dame de Bonne Nouvelle, Rue (2) 7 B5
Notre-Dame de Lorette, Rue (9) 6 E3
Notre-Dame de Nazareth, Rue (3) 13 C1
 continues 7 B5
Notre-Dame de Recouvrance, Rue (2) 7 A5
Notre-Dame des Champs, Rue (6) 16 E2
Notre-Dame des Victoires, Rue (2) 12 F1
 continues 6 F5
Nov 8 1942, Pl du (10) 7 B3
Nov 11 1918, Pl du (10) 7 C3

O
Obelisque (8) 11 C1
Oberkampf, Rue (11) 14 E1
Observatoire, Ave de l' (14) 16 E3
Observatoire de Paris, l' (14) 16 E3
Octave Gréard, Ave (7) 10 D3
Odéon, Carrefour de l' (6) 12 F4
Odéon, Pl de l' (6) 12 F5
Odéon, Rue de l' (6) 12 F5
Odessa, Rue d' (14) 15 C2
Olivet, Rue d' (7) 11 B5
Olivier Noyer, Rue (14) 15 C4
Olympia (9) 6 D5
Opéra, Ave de l' (1) 12 E1
Opéra, Ave de l' (2) 6 E5
Opéra, Pl de l' (2, 9) 6 E5
Opéra de Paris Bastille, l' (12) 14 E4
Opéra de Paris Garnier (9) 6 D4
Oratoire, Rue de l' (1) 12 F2
Orchampt Ravignan, Rue d' (18) 6 E1
Ordener, Rue (18) 2 E4
Orée du Bois, l' (16) 3 B3
Orfèvres, Quai des (1) 12 F3
Orfèvres, Rue des (1) 13 A3
Orgues, Passage des (3) 7 C5
Orillon, Rue de l' (11) 8 F5
Orléans, Quai d' (4) 13 B4
Orléans, Rue d' 3 A2
Orléans, Villa d' (14) 16 D5
Ormesson, Rue d' (4) 14 D3
Orsay, Quai d' (7) 10 F2
 continues 11 B2
Orsel, Rue d' (18) 6 F2
 continues 7 A1
Ortolan, Rue (5) 17 B1
Ortolan, Sq (5) 17 B1
Oslo, Rue d' (18) 2 D4
Oudinot, Rue (7) 11 B5
Oudry, Rue (13) 17 C3
Ouessant, Rue d' (15) 10 E5
Ouest, Rue de l' (15) 15 B3
Ours, Rue aux (3) 13 B2
Ozanam, Pl et Sq (6) 16 D1

P
P Langevin, Square (5) 13 B5
Pablo Picasso, Place (14) 16 D2
Paix, Rue de la (1, 2) 6 D5
Pajol, Rue (18) 7 C1

Pajou, Rue (16) 9 A3
Palais, Blvd du (1, 4) 13 A3
Palais Abbatial (6) 12 E4
Palais Bourbon (7) 11 B2
Palais Bourbon, Pl du (7) 11 B2
Palais de Chaillot (16) 9 C2
Palais de Justice (1) 13 A3
Palais de l'Elysée (8) 5 B5
Palais de la Découverte (8) 11 A1
Palais de Tokyo (16) 10 E1
Palais des Congrès (17) 3 B3
Palais du Luxembourg (6) 12 E5
Palais Omnisports de Paris Bercy (12) 18 F2
Palais Royal (1) 12 E1
Palatine, Rue (6) 12 E5
Palestro, Rue de (2) 13 B1
Palloy, Rue 1 A2
Palouzie, Rue 2 D1
Panoramas, Passage des (2) 6 F5
Panthéon (5) 17 A1
Panthéon, Pl du (5) 17 A1
Pape Carpentier, Rue (6) 12 E5
Papillon, Rue (9) 7 A3
Papin, Rue (3) 13 B1
Paradis, Cité (10) 7 B4
Paradis, Rue de (10) 7 B4
Paraguay, Pl du (16) 3 A4
Parc du Champ de Mars (7) 10 E3
Parc Monceau (8) 4 F3
 continues 5 A3
Parc Municipal (17) 1 A1
Parc Océanique Cousteau (1) 13 A2
Parc Royal, Rue du (3) 14 D3
Parchappe, Cité (11) 14 E4
Parcheminerie, Rue de la (5) 13 A4
Parme, Rue de (9) 6 D2
Parmentier, Ave (10, 11) 8 E5
Parmentier, Ave (11) 14 F1
Parmentier, Pl 3 B2
Parmentier, Rue 3 B1
Parrot, Rue (12) 14 F5
Pas de la Mule, Rue du (3, 4) 14 D3
Pascal, Rue (5, 13) 17 A3
Pasdeloup, Pl (11) 14 E1
Pasquier, Rue (8) 5 C4
Passy, Pl de (16) 9 A3
Passy, Port de (16) 10 D2
 continues 9 B4
Passy, Rue de (16) 9 B3
Pasteur, Blvd (15) 15 A1
Pasteur, Rue (11) 14 F2
Pasteur, Rue (17) 2 D2
Pasteur M Boegner, Rue du (16) 9 B2
Pastourelle, Rue (3) 13 C2
Patay, Rue de (13) 18 E5
Patriarches, Rue des (5) 17 B2
Patrice Boudart, Villa (16) 9 A4
Pâtures, Rue des (16) 9 A5
Paul Adam, Ave (17) 4 E1
Paul Albert, Rue (18) 7 A1
Paul Baudry, Rue (8) 4 F4
Paul Bert, Rue (11) 2 F2
Paul Bodin, Rue (17) 1 B4
Paul Cézanne, Rue (8) 5 A4
Paul Claudel, Pl (6) 12 F5

Each place name is followed by its arrondissement number, and then by its Street Finder reference.

Paul Delaroche, Rue (16) 9 A3
Paul Déroulède, Rue 3 A3
Paul Deschanel, Allée (7) 10 D2
Paul Doumer, Ave (16) 9 B2
Paul Dupuy, Rue (16) 9 A5
Paul Escudier, Rue (9) 6 E2
Paul Feval, Rue (18) 2 F4
Paul Gervais, Rue (13) 17 A4
Paul Léautaud, Pl (17) 4 E1
Paul Lelong, Rue (2) 6 F5
Paul Louis Courier, Rue (7) 11 C3
Raul Painlevé, Sq et Pl (5) 13 A5
Paul Saunière, Rue (16) 9 B2
Paul Séjourné, Rue (6) 16 E2
Paul Valéry, Rue (16) 3 C4
continues 4 D5
Paulin Méry, Rue (13) 17 B5
Pauline Borghese, Rue 3 A1
Pauly, Rue (14) 15 A4
Pavée, Rue (4) 14 D3
Pavillon d'Armenonville, Chemin du (16) 3 A3
Pavillon, Ave des (17) 3 C2
Pavillons, Impasse des (18) 2 E3
Payenne, Rue (3) 14 D3
Pecquay, Rue (4) 13 C2
Péguy, Rue (6) 16 D1
Pelée, Rue (11) 14 E2
Peletier, Rue le (9) 6 F4
Pélican, Rue du (1) 12 F2
Pelouze, Rue (8) 5 B2
Penel, Passage (18) 2 F3
Penthièvre, Rue de (8) 5 B4
Pépinière, Rue de la (8) 5 C4
Perche, Rue du (4) 13 C2
Percier, Ave (8) 5 B4
Perdonnet, Rue (10) 7 C2
Père Guérin, Rue (13) 17 B5
Père Teilhard de Chardin, Pl de (4) 14 D5
Pereire (Nord), Blvd (17) 3 C3
Pereire (Nord), Blvd (17) 4 D2
Pereire (Sud), Blvd (17) 3 C3
Pereire (Sud), Blvd (17) 4 D2
Pergolèse, Rue (16) 3 B4
Pérignon, Rue (7, 15) 15 A1
Perile, Rue de la (3) 14 D1
Périphérique, Blvd 1 B3
Périphérique, Blvd (16) 3 A2
Perle, Rue de la (4) 13 C2
Pernelle, Rue (4) 13 B3
Pernette du Guillet, Allée (19) 8 F4
Pernety, Rue (15) 15 B3
Perrault, Rue (1) 12 F2
Perrée, Rue (3) 14 D1
Perrichont, Ave (16) 9 A5
Perronet (7) 12 D3
Perronet, Rue 3 A1
Perronet, Sq 3 A1
Pershing, Blvd (17) 3 C2
Pestalozzi, Rue (5) 17 B2
Pétiet, Rue (18) 2 D4
Petit Cerf, Passage (17) 1 B4
Petit Luxembourg (6) 12 E5
Petit Moine, Rue du (5) 17 B3
Petit Musc, Rue du (4) 14 D4
Petit Palais (8) 11 B1
Petit Pont (4, 5) 13 A4
Petit Pont, Pl du (5) 13 A4
Petit Pont, Rue du (5) 13 A4

Petite Truanderie, Rue de la (2) 13 A1
Petites Ecuries, Cour des (10) 7 B4
Petites Ecuries, Passage des (10) 7 B4
Petites Ecuries, Rue des (10) 7 B4
Petits Champs, Rue des (1, 2) 12 E1
Petits Hôtels, Rue des (10) 7 B3
Pétrarque, Rue (16) 9 B2
Pétrarque, Sq (16) 9 B2
Petrelle, Rue (9) 7 A2
Petrelle, Sq (9) 7 A2
Phalsbourg, Rue de (17) 4 F2
continues 5 A2
Philibert Delorme, Rue (17) 4 E1
Philip Le Boucher, Ave 3 A2
Philippe de Champagne, Rue (13) 17 C4
Philippe de Girard, Rue (18) 7 C1
Philippe Hecht, Rue (19) 8 F3
Picardie, Rue de (3) 14 D1
Piccini, Rue (16) 3 C4
Picot, Rue (16) 3 B5
Pierrard, Rue 3 A1
Pierre, Passage 2 D2
Pierre Bullet, Rue (10) 7 C4
Pierre Charron, Rue (8) 4 F5
Pierre Chausson, Rue (10) 7 C5
Pierre Cherest, Rue 3 B2
Pierre Curie, Rue 1 B2
continues 2 F1
Pierre Demours, Rue (17) 4 D2
Pierre Dupont, Rue (10) 8 D3
Pierre et Marie Curie, Rue (5) 17 A1
Pierre Ginier, Rue (18) 6 D1
Pierre Gourdault, Rue (13) 18 E4
Pierre Haret, Rue (9) 6 D1
Pierre Lafue, Pl (6) 16 D1
Pierre Lampué, Pl (5) 17 A2
Pierre Larousse, Rue (15) 15 B5
Pierre Le Grand, Rue (8) 4 E3
Pierre l'Ermite, Rue (18) 7 B1
Pierre Leroux, Rue (7) 11 C4
Pierre Lescot, Rue (1) 13 A2
Pierre Levée, Rue de la (11) 14 E1
continues 8 E5
Pierre Loti, Ave (7) 10 E3
Pierre Louÿs, Rue (16) 9 A5
Pierre Nicole, Rue (5) 16 F2
Pierre Picard, Rue (18) 7 A1
Pierre Premier de Serbie, Ave (16) 10 E1
Pierre Rebière, Rue (17) 1 B3
Pierre Reverdy, Rue (19) 8 F1
Pierre Sarrazin, Rue (6) 12 F5
Pierre Semard, Rue (9) 7 A3
Pierre Villey, Rue (7) 10 F2
Pigalle, Cité (9) 6 E2
Pigalle, Pl (9, 18) 6 E2
Pigalle, Rue (9) 6 E2
Pillet Will, Rue (9) 6 E4
Pilleux, Cité (18) 2 D5
Pinel, Pl (13) 18 D4
Pinel, Rue (13) 17 C4

Pirandello, Rue (13) 17 C3
Piver, Passage (11) 8 F5
Place Clément Ader (16) 9 A4
Place de la République (3, 10, 11) 8 D5
Place du Palais Royale (1) 12 E1
Place du Pyramides (1) 12 E2
Place Vendôme (1) 12 D1
Plaisance, Rue de (15) 15 B4
Plaisance de Paris Arsenal, Rue de (12) 14 E5
Plantes, Rue des (14) 15 C5
Platon, Rue (15) 15 A3
Plâtre, Rue du (4) 13 B2
Plumet, Rue (15) 15 A2
Poinsot, Rue (14) 15 C2
Poissonnière, Blvd (2, 9) 7 A5
Poissonnière, Rue (2) 7 A5
Poissonniers, Rue des (18) 7 B1
Poissy, Rue de (5) 13 B5
Poitevins, Rue des (6) 12 F4
Poitiers, Rue de (7) 12 D3
Poitou, Rue de (3) 14 D2
Pôle Nord, Rue du (18) 2 F4
Poliveau, Rue (5) 17 C2
Pologne, Ave de (16) 3 A5
Polonceau, Rue (18) 7 B1
Pomereu, Rue de (16) 3 B5
Pompe, Rue de la (16) 3 B5
continues 9 A2
Pompidou, Centre (4) 13 B2
Poncelet, Passage (17) 4 E2
Poncelet, Rue (17) 4 E3
Pondichéry, Rue de (15) 10 E5
Pont à Mousson, Rue de (17) 1 C3
Pont aux Biches, Passage du (3) 7 C5
Pont aux Choux, Rue du (3) 14 D2
Pont de Lodi, Rue du (6) 12 F4
Pont Louis-Philippe, Rue du (4) 13 B3
Pont Neuf, Rue du (1) 13 A2
Ponthieu, Rue de (8) 4 F4
continues 5 A5
Pontoise, Rue de (5) 13 B5
Popincourt, Cour (11) 14 F2
Popincourt, Impasse (11) 14 F3
Popincourt, Rue (11) 14 F3
Port des Saints Pères (7) 12 E3
Port Mahon, Rue de (2) 6 E5
Port Royal, Blvd de (5, 13) 17 A3
Port Royal, Blvd de (5, 14) 16 F2
Port Royal, Sq de (13) 16 F3
Portalis, Rue (8) 5 B3
Portefoin, Rue (3) 13 C1
Portugais, Ave des (16) 4 D5
Possoz, Pl (16) 9 A2
Postes, Passage des (5) 17 A2
Pot de Fer, Rue du (5) 17 A2
Poteau, Passage du (18) 2 E3
Poteau, Rue du (18) 2 F4
Pouchet, Ave de la Porte (17) 1 C3
Pouchet, Passage (17) 1 C3
Pouchet, Porte (17) 1 C3
Pouchet, Rue (17) 1 C4
Poulet, Rue (18) 7 A1

Poulletier, Rue (4) 13 C4
Pouy, Rue de (13) 17 B5
Poyer, Rue 1 A2
Prague, Rue de (12) 14 F5
Pré aux Chevaux, Sq du (16) 9 A4
Pré aux Clercs, Rue du (7) 12 D3
Précheurs, Rue des (1) 13 A2
Préfecture de Paris (12) 18 E1
Presbourg, Rue de (16) 4 D4
Présentation, Rue de la (11) 8 F5
Présidence du Conseil (7) 11 C4
Président Ed Herriot, Pl du (7) 11 B2
Président-Kennedy, Ave du (16) 9 B4
Président-Mithouard, Pl du (7) 11 B5
President-Wilson, Ave du (16) 10 D1
Presles, Rue de (15) 10 E4
Prêtres, Impasse des (16) 9 B1
Prêtres St-Séverin, Rue des (5) 13 A4
Prêtres St-Germain l'Auxerrois, Rue des (1) 12 F2
Prévôt, Rue du (4) 13 C4
Primatice, Rue (13) 17 C4
Princesse, Rue (6) 12 E4
Printemps, Rue du (17) 5 A1
Procession, Rue de la (15) 15 A3
Prony, Rue de (17) 4 F2
continues 5 A2
Prosper Goubaux, Pl (8, 17) 5 B2
Provence, Rue de (8, 9) 6 D4
Puget, Rue (18) 6 E1
Puits de l'Ermite, Rue du (5) 17 B2
Pusy, Cité de (17) 5 A1
Puteaux, Rue (17) 5 C2
Puvis de Chavannes, Rue (17) 4 E1
Pyramide (1) 12 E2
Pyramides, Pl des (1) 12 E1
Pyramides, Rue des (1) 12 E1

Q

Quai de la Gare (13) 18 F3
Quai Voltaire (7) 12 D3
Quatre Frères, Place des (18) 2 E5
Quatre Septembre, Rue du (2) 6 E5
Quatre Vents, Rue des (6) 12 F4
Quatrefages, Rue de (5) 17 B1
Quatres Fils, Rue des (4) 13 C2
Quentin Bauchart, Rue (8) 4 E5
Quincampoix, Rue (3) 13 B2

R

Rabelais, Rue (8) 5 A5
Rachel, Ave (18) 6 D1
Racine, Rue (6) 12 F5
Radziwill, Rue (1) 12 F1
Raguinot, Passage (12) 18 F1

Rambuteau, Rue (3, 4)	**13 B2**	Richard Lenoir,		Roux, Impasse (17)	**4 E2**	St-Fiacre, Rue (2)	**7 A5**
Rameau, Rue (2)	**6 E5**	Blvd (11)	**14 E1**	Roy, Rue (8)	**5 B4**	St-Florentin, Rue (1, 8)	**11 C1**
Ramey, Rue (18)	**7 A1**	Richard Lenoir,		Royal, Pont (1, 7)	**12 D2**	St-Georges, Rue (9)	**6 E3**
Rampon, Rue (11)	**14 D1**	Sq (11)	**14 E2**	Royale, Rue (8)	**5 C5**	St-Germain, Blvd (7)	**11 C2**
Ranelagh, Rue du (16)	**9 A4**	Richelieu, Rue de (1)	**12 E1**	Royer Collard,		St-Germain, Blvd (5)	**13 A5**
Raoul Dautry, Pl (15)	**15 C2**	Richelieu, Rue de (2)	**6 F5**	Impasse (5)	**16 F1**	St-Germain-des-Prés (6)	**12 E4**
Raoul Follereau, Pl (10)	**8 D3**	Richemont, Rue		Royer Collard, Rue (5)	**16 F1**	St-Germain-l'Auxerrois (1)	**12 F2**
Rapée, Port de la (12)	**18 E1**	de (13)	**18 E5**	Rubens, Rue (13)	**17 C4**	St-Gervais–St-Protais (4)	**13 B3**
Rapée, Quai de la (12)	**18 E1**	Richepance,		Rude, Rue (16)	**4 D4**	St-Germain, Blvd (6, 7)	**12 D4**
Rapp, Ave (7)	**10 E2**	Rue (1, 8)	**5 C5**	Ruelle, Passage (18)	**7 C1**	St-Germain, Blvd (7)	**11 C3**
Raspail, Blvd (6, 7)	**12 D4**	Richer, Rue (9)	**7 A4**	Ruelle Sourdis (3)	**13 C2**	St-Gervais, Pl (4)	**13 B3**
Raspail, Blvd (6, 14)	**16 D2**	Richerand, Ave (10)	**8 D4**	Ruhmkorff, Rue (17)	**3 C2**	St-Gilles, Rue (3)	**14 D3**
Raspail, Rue	**2 D1**	Richomme, Rue (18)	**7 B1**	Ruisseau, Rue du (18)	**2 F4**	St-Gothard, Rue du (14)	**16 E5**
Rataud, Rue (5)	**17 A2**	Ridder, Rue de (14)	**15 A4**	Rutebeuf, Pl (12)	**18 F1**	St-Guillaume, Rue (7)	**12 D3**
Raymond Losserand, Rue (15)	**15 B4**	Rigny, Rue de (8)	**5 B4**	Ruysdaël, Ave (8)	**5 A3**	continues	**12 D4**
Raymond Poincaré, Ave (16)	**3 C5**	Rimbaut, Passage (14)	**16 D5**			St-Hippolyte, Rue (13)	**17 A3**
continues	**9 C1**	Rio de Janeiro, Pl de (8)	**5 A3**	**S**		St-Honoré, Rue (1, 8)	**5 C5**
Raynouard, Rue (16)	**9 B3**	Riverin, Cité (10)	**7 C5**	Sablière, Rue de la (14)	**15 C4**	St-Honoré, Rue (1)	**13 A2**
Réaumur, Rue (2, 3)	**13 B1**	Rivoli, Rue de (1, 4)	**13 A2**	Sablons, Rue des (16)	**9 B1**	continues	**12 D1**
Réaumur, Rue (2)	**6 F5**	Rivoli, Rue de (1)	**11 C1**	Sablons, Villa des	**3 A2**	St-Hyacinthe, Rue (1)	**12 D1**
continues	**7 A5**	Robert de Flers, Rue (15)	**9 B5**	Sablons à la Porte Maillot; Route de la Porte des (16)	**3 A3**	St-Jacques, Blvd (14)	**16 E4**
Rébeval, Rue (19)	**8 F4**	Robert Desnos, Pl (10)	**8 E3**	Sablonville, Rue de	**3 B2**	St-Jacques, Pl (14)	**16 E4**
Rébeval, Sq de (19)	**8 F4**	Robert Esnault Pelterie, Rue (7)	**11 B2**	Sabot, Rue du (6)	**12 D4**	St-Jacques, Rue (5)	**13 A5**
Récamier, Rue (7)	**12 D4**	Robert Houdin, Rue (11)	**8 F5**	continues	**12 E4**	continues	**16 F1**
Récollets, Passage des (10)	**7 C4**	Robert Le Coin, Rue (16)	**9 A3**	Sacré-Coeur (18)	**6 F1**	St-Jacques, Villa (14)	**16 E4**
Récollets, Rue des (10)	**7 C4**	Robert Montagne, Sq (5)	**17 B2**	Sacy, Ave de (7)	**10 E3**	St-Jean, Rue (17)	**1 C5**
Récollets, Sq des (10)	**8 D4**	Robert Planquette, Rue (18)	**6 E1**	Sadi Lecointe, Rue (19)	**8 F2**	St-Jérôme, Rue (18)	**7 B1**
Recteur Poincaré, Ave du (16)	**9 A4**	Roberval, Rue (17)	**1 C4**	Saïd, Villa (16)	**3 B4**	St-Joseph, Rue (2)	**7 A5**
Reculettes, Rue des (13)	**17 B4**	Robespierre, Passage	**2 D2**	Saïgon, Rue de (16)	**4 D4**	St-Joseph des Carmes (6)	**12 D5**
Regard, Rue du (6)	**12 D5**	Rochambeau, Rue (9)	**7 A3**	Saillard, Rue (14)	**16 D4**	St-Joseph, Cour (11)	**14 F4**
Régis, Rue (6)	**11 C5**	Rochechouart, Blvd de (9, 18)	**6 F2**	St-Alexander Nevsky Cathedral (8)	**4 E3**	St-Julien le Pauvre, Rue (5)	**13 A4**
Regrattier, Rue le (4)	**13 B4**	Rochechouart, Blvd de (9)	**7 A2**	St-Amand, Rue (15)	**15 A4**	St-Just, Rue	**1 A3**
Reims, Rue de (13)	**18 E5**	Rochechouart, Rue de (9)	**7 A2**	St-Ambroise, Passage (11)	**14 F2**	St-Laurent, Rue (10)	**7 C3**
Reine, Cours la (8)	**11 A1**	Rochefoucauld, Rue de la (9)	**6 E3**	St-Ambroise, Rue (11)	**14 F2**	St-Lazare, Rue (9)	**6 D3**
Reine Astrid, Pl de la (8)	**10 F1**	Rocher, Rue du (8)	**5 C3**	St-André des Arts, Pl (6)	**12 F4**	St-Louis (10)	**8 E4**
Reine Blanche, Rue (10)	**8 D3**	Rocroy, Rue de (10)	**7 B2**	St-André des Arts, Rue (6)	**12 F4**	St-Louis-des-Invalides (7)	**11 A3**
Reine Blanche, Rue de la (13)	**17 B3**	Rodier, Rue (9)	**6 F3**	St-Ange, Passage (17)	**2 D3**	St-Louis-en-l'Île (4)	**13 C4**
Reine de Hongrie, Passage de la (1)	**13 A1**	continues	**7 A2**	St-Anne Popincourt, Passage (11)	**14 E3**	St-Louis-en-l'Île, Rue (4)	**13 C4**
Rémi-Belleau, Villa (19)	**8 F1**	Rodin, Ave (16)	**9 A1**	St-Antoine, Passage (11)	**14 F4**	St-Louis, Cour (11)	**14 E4**
Rémusat, Rue de (16)	**9 A5**	Roger, Rue (14)	**16 D3**	St-Antoine, Rue de (4)	**14 D4**	St-Louis, Pont (4)	**13 B4**
Rémy de Gourmont, Rue (19)	**8 F3**	Roger Bacon, Rue (17)	**3 C2**	St-Augustin, Pl (8)	**5 B4**	St-Luc, Rue (18)	**7 B1**
Rémy Dumoncel, Rue (14)	**16 D5**	Roger Verlomme, Rue (3)	**14 D3**	St-Augustin, Rue (2)	**6 E5**	St-Marc, Rue (2)	**6 F5**
Renard, Rue du (4)	**13 B3**	Rohan, Rue de (1)	**12 E2**	St-Benoît, Rue (6)	**12 E3**	St-Marcel, Blvd (5, 13)	**17 C3**
Renaudes, Rue des (17)	**4 E2**	Roi de Sicile, Rue du (4)	**13 C3**	St-Bernard, Port (5)	**13 C5**	St-Martin, Blvd (3, 10)	**7 C5**
René Binet, Rue (18)	**2 F3**	Roi Doré, Rue du (3)	**14 D2**	continues	**18 D1**	St-Martin, Canal (10)	**8 D3**
René Boulanger, Rue (10)	**8 D5**	Rollin, Rue (5)	**17 B1**	St-Bernard, Quai (5)	**13 C5**	St-Martin, Porte	**7 C5**
René Boylesve, Ave (16)	**9 C3**	Rome, Cour de (8)	**5 C3**	continues	**18 D1**	St-Martin, Rue (3, 4)	**7 B5**
René Cassin, Pl (1)	**13 A2**	Rome, Rue de (17)	**5 B1**	St-Bernard, Sq (18)	**7 C1**	St-Martin, Rue (3)	**13 B1**
René Coty, Ave (14)	**16 E4**	Ronsard, Rue (18)	**7 A1**	St-Bon, Rue (4)	**13 B3**	St-Mathieu, Rue (18)	**7 C1**
René Panhard, Rue (13)	**17 C2**	Roquépine, Rue (8)	**5 B4**	St-Bruno, Rue (18)	**7 B1**	St-Maur, Passage (11)	**14 F1**
René Viviani, Sq (5)	**13 A4**	Roquette, Rue de la (11)	**14 F3**	continues	**7 C1**	St-Maur, Rue (10, 11)	**8 E4**
Rennequin, Rue (17)	**4 E2**	Rosa Bonheur, Rue (15)	**15 A1**	St-Charles, Place (15)	**9 C5**	St-Maur, Rue (11)	**14 F1**
Rennes, Rue de (6)	**16 D1**	Rosiers, Rue des (4)	**13 C3**	St-Charles, Rue (15)	**10 D4**	St-Médard (5)	**17 B2**
République, Ave de la (11)	**14 E1**	Rosiers, Rue des	**2 E1**	continues	**9 C5**	St-Mérri (4)	**13 B3**
République, Pl de la (3, 11)	**14 D1**	Rossini, Rue (9)	**6 F4**	St-Chaumont, Cité (19)	**8 F4**	St-Mérri, Rue (4)	**13 B3**
République, Pl de la	**1 A2**	Rotrou, Rue (6)	**12 F5**	St-Claude, Rue (3)	**14 D2**	St-Michel, Blvd (6)	**12 F5**
République Dominicaine, Pl de la (8, 17)	**5 A2**	Roubaix, Pl de (10)	**7 B2**	St-Denis, Blvd (2, 3, 10)	**7 B5**	continues	**16 F2**
Résistance, Pl de la (7)	**10 F2**	Rouelle, Rue (15)	**9 C5**	St-Denis, Impasse (2)	**13 A1**	St-Michel, Pl (5)	**13 A4**
Retiro, Cité de (8)	**5 C5**	Rouen, Rue de (19)	**8 F1**	St-Denis, Porte (2)	**7 B5**	St-Michel, Quai (5)	**13 A4**
Ribouté, Rue (9)	**7 A3**	Rougemont, Cité (9)	**7 A4**	St-Denis, Rue (1, 2)	**7 B5**	St-Michel, Pont (1, 4, 5, 6)	**13 A4**
Ricaut, Rue (13)	**18 D5**	Rougemont, Rue (9)	**7 A4**	continues	**13 B1**	St-Michel, Villa (18)	**2 D5**
Richard Baret, Pl (17)	**5 C1**	Rouget de l'Isle, Rue (1)	**12 D1**	St-Denis, Rue (4)	**13 B3**	St-Nicolas, Rue (12)	**14 F5**
		Rouget de l'Isle, Rue (1)	**1 A3**	St-Didier, Rue (16)	**9 C1**	St-Ouen, Ave de (18)	**2 D4**
		Roule, Ave du	**3 A2**	St-Dominique, Rue (7)	**10 F2**	St-Ouen, Ave de la Porte de (17, 18)	**2 D3**
		Roule, Sq du	**3 B1**	continues	**11 A2**	St-Paul, Rue (4)	**14 D4**
		Roule, Villa du	**3 A2**	continues	**11 C3**	St-Paul–St-Louis (4)	**14 D4**
		Rousselet, Rue (7)	**11 B5**	St-Etienne-du-Mont (5)	**17 A1**	St-Philippe, Rue (2)	**7 B5**
				St-Ephrem (5)	**13 A5**	St-Philippe du Roule, Rue (8)	**5 A4**
				St-Eustache (1)	**13 A1**		
				St-Ferdinand, Rue (17)	**3 C3**		
				St-Ferdinand, Pl (17)	**3 C3**		

Each place name is followed by its arrondissement number, and then by its Street Finder reference.

St-Pierre Amelot, Passage (11)	**14 E2**	Santiago du Chili, Sq (7)	**11 A3**
St-Pierre de Montmartre (18)	**6 F1**	Saône, Rue de la (14)	**16 D5**
St-Placide, Rue (6)	**11 C5**	Sarrette, Rue (14)	**16 D5**
continues	**12 D5**	Sauffroy, Rue (17)	**1 C4**
St-Quentin, Rue (10)	**7 C3**	Saules, Rue des (18)	**2 F5**
St-Roch (1)	**12 E1**	Saulnier, Rue (9)	**7 A4**
St-Roch, Passage (1)	**12 E1**	Saussaies, Pl des (8)	**5 B4**
St-Roch, Rue (1)	**12 E1**	Saussaies, Rue des (8)	**5 B5**
St-Romain, Rue (6)	**11 C5**	Saussier Leroy, Rue (17)	**4 E2**
St-Rustique (18)	**6 F1**	Saussure, Rue de (17)	**1 A5**
St-Sabin, Passage (11)	**14 E3**	*continues*	**5 B1**
St-Sabin, Rue (11)	**14 E3**	Sauval, Rue (1)	**12 F2**
St-Saëns, Rue (15)	**10 D4**	Savoie, Rue de (6)	**12 F4**
St-Sauveur, Rue (2)	**13 A1**	Savorgnan de Brazza, Rue (7)	**10 F4**
St-Sébastien, Impasse (11)	**14 E2**	Saxe, Ave de (7)	**10 F5**
St-Sébastien, Passage (11)	**14 E2**	*continues*	**11 A5**
St-Sébastien, Rue (11)	**14 E2**	Saxe, Ave du 15 (7)	**15 A1**
St-Senoch, Rue de (17)	**4 D2**	Saxe, Villa de (7)	**11 A5**
St-Séverin (5)	**13 A4**	Say, Rue (9)	**6 F2**
St-Séverin, Rue (5)	**13 A4**	Scheffer, Rue (16)	**9 B2**
St-Simon, Rue de (7)	**11 C3**	Schoelcher, Rue (14)	**16 D3**
St-Spire, Rue (2)	**7 B5**	Schomberg, Rue de (4)	**14 D5**
St-Sulpice (6)	**12 E5**	Schutzenberger, Rue (15)	**9 C5**
St-Sulpice, Pl (6)	**12 E4**	Scipion, Rue (5)	**17 B3**
St-Sulpice, Rue (6)	**12 E4**	Scipion, Sq (5)	**17 B3**
St-Thomas d'Aquin, Pl (7)	**12 D3**	Scribe, Rue (9)	**6 D4**
St-Victor, Rue (5)	**13 B5**	Sébastien Bottin, Rue (7)	**12 D3**
St-Vincent, Rue (18)	**2 F5**	Sébastopol, Blvd de (1, 2, 3. 4)	**7 B5**
St-Vincent de Paul (14)	**16 E3**	Sébastopol, Blvd de (2, 3)	**13 B1**
St-Vincent de Paul, Rue (10)	**7 B2**	Secrétan, Ave (19)	**8 E2**
St-Vincent de Paul, Sq (10)	**7 B3**	Sedaine, Rue (11)	**14 F3**
Ste-Anastase, Rue (3)	**14 D2**	Sedillot, Rue (7)	**10 E3**
Ste-Anne, Rue (1)	**12 E1**	Séguier, Rue (6)	**12 F4**
Ste-Anne, Rue (2)	**6 E5**	Ségur, Ave de (7, 15)	**11 A4**
Ste-Apolline, Rue (2)	**7 B5**	*continues*	**10 F5**
Ste-Beuve, Rue (6)	**16 D1**	Ségur, Villa de (7)	**11 A5**
Ste-Cécile, Rue (9)	**7 A4**	Seine, Quai de la (19)	**8 F1**
Ste-Chapelle (1)	**13 A3**	Seine, Rue de (6)	**12 E4**
Ste-Clotilde (7)	**11 B3**	Séminaire, Allée du (6)	**12 E5**
Ste-Croix de la Bretonnerie, Rue (4)	**13 B3**	Sentier, Rue du (2)	**7 A5**
continues	**13 C3**	Senus, Rue de (17)	**4 E1**
Ste-Croix de la Bretonnerie, Sq (4)	**13 B3**	Sergent Hoff, Rue du (17)	**4 D2**
Ste-Elisabeth, Passage (3)	**13 C1**	Serpente, Rue (6)	**12 F4**
Ste-Elisabeth, Rue (3)	**13 C1**	Servandoni, Rue (6)	**12 E5**
Ste-Foy, Rue (2)	**7 B5**	Severo, Rue (14)	**15 C4**
Ste-Geneviève, Pl (5)	**17 A1**	Sèvres, Rue des (6)	**11 C5**
Ste-Hélène, Sq (18)	**2 F3**	Seveste, Rue (18)	**7 A2**
Ste-Leonie, Sq (14)	**15 C4**	Sévigné, Rue de (3, 4)	**14 D3**
Ste-Marthe, Impasse (10)	**8 E4**	Sèvres, Rue de (6, 7, 15)	**11 C5**
Ste-Marthe, Rue (10)	**8 E4**	*continues*	**11 D4**
Ste-Odile, Sq (17)	**4 D1**	Sèvres, Rue de (1, 7)	**15 B1**
Ste-Opportune, Pl (1)	**13 A2**	Sextius Michel, Rue (15)	**9 C4**
Sts-Pères, Port des (6, 7)	**12 E3**	Sèze, Rue de (9)	**6 D5**
Sts-Pères, Rue des (6, 7)	**12 D4**	Sfax, Rue de (16)	**3 C5**
Saintonge, Rue de (3)	**14 D1**	Siam, Rue de (16)	**9 A2**
continues	**14 D2**	Sibour, Rue (10)	**7 C4**
Salardier, Passage (11)	**14 F3**	Silvestre de Sacy, Ave (7)	**10 E3**
Salneuve, Rue (17)	**5 B1**	Simón Bolívar, Ave (19)	**8 F3**
Salonipue, Ave de (17)	**3 B2**	Simon Dereure, Rue (18)	**2 E5**
Sambre et Meuse, Rue de (10)	**8 E4**	Simon le Franc, Rue (4)	**13 B2**
Samson, Rue (13)	**17 B5**	Simonet, Rue (13)	**17 B5**
Samuel Rousseau, Sq (7)	**11 B3**	Simonneau, Rue (1)	**1 B3**
Santé, Rue de la (13, 14)	**16 F3**	Singer, Passage (16)	**9 A3**
Santeuil, Rue (5)	**17 B2**	Singer, Rue (16)	**9 A3**
		Sivel, Rue (14)	**16 D4**

Soeur Rosalie, Ave de la (13)	**17 B4**	Tarbé, Rue (17)	**5 A1**
Sofia, Rue de (18)	**7 A1**	Tardieu, Rue (18)	**6 F1**
Soissons, Rue de (19)	**8 E1**	Tasse, Rue le (16)	**9 C2**
Solférino, Passerelle (1, 7)	**11 C2**	Taylor, Rue (10)	**7 C5**
Solférino, Port de (7)	**11 C2**	Téhéran, Rue de (8)	**5 A3**
Solférino, Rue de (7)	**11 C2**	Temple, Blvd du (3, 11)	**14 D1**
Somme, Blvd de la (17)	**4 D1**	Temple, Rue du (3, 4)	**13 C2**
Sommerard, Rue du (5)	**13 A5**	Temple, Sq du (3)	**13 C1**
Sontay, Rue de (16)	**3 C5**	Tennis, Rue des (18)	**2 D4**
Sophie Germain, Rue (14)	**16 D4**	Ternaux, Rue (11)	**14 E1**
Sorbonne, Pl de la (5)	**12 F5**	Ternes, Ave de la Porte des (17)	**B2**
Sorbonne, Rue de la (5)	**12 F5**	Ternes, Ave des (17)	**3 C2**
Soudan, Rue du (15)	**10 E5**	*continues*	**4 D3**
Soufflot, Rue (5)	**17 A1**	Ternes, Pl des (17)	**4 E3**
Souham, Pl (13)	**18 E5**	Ternes, Porte des (17)	**3 B2**
Sourdière, Rue de la (1)	**12 E1**	Ternes, Rue des (17)	**3 C2**
Souvenir Français, Esplanade du (7)	**11 A4**	Ternes, Villa des (17)	**3 C2**
Spontini, Rue de (16)	**3 B5**	Terrage, Rue du (10)	**8 D3**
Spontini, Villa (16)	**3 A5**	Terrasse, Rue de la (17)	**5 A2**
Spuller, Rue (3)	**14 D1**	Terrasse Modigliani (14)	**15 C2**
Sq Village Suisse (15)	**10 E4**	Tertre, Pl du (18)	**6 F1**
Square du Vert-Galant (1)	**12 F3**	Tesson, Rue (10)	**8 E5**
Stade Bertrand Dauvin (18)	**2 F2**	Texel, Rue du (14)	**15 C3**
Stade Emile Anthoine (15)	**10 D3**	Thann, Rue de (17)	**5 A2**
Stade Max Rousie (18)	**2 D3**	Théâtre, Rue du (15)	**10 D5**
Stade Paul Faber (17)	**3 C1**	*continues*	**9 C5**
Staël, Rue de (15)	**15 A1**	Théâtre de Banville, Rue (17)	**4 E2**
Stalingrad, Pl de (10, 19)	**8 E2**	Théâtre des Champs-Elysées (8)	**10 F1**
Stanislas, Rue (6)	**16 D1**	Théâtre National de l'Odéon (6)	**12 F5**
Statue de la Liberté (15, 16)	**9 B5**	Thénard, Rue (5)	**13 A5**
Steinlen, Rue (18)	**2 E5**	Théodule Ribot, Rue (17)	**4 E2**
Stéphane Mallarmé, Ave (17)	**4 D1**	*continues*	**4 E3**
Stéphen Pichon, Ave (13)	**17 C4**	Théophile Gautier, Ave (16)	**9 A5**
Stephenson, Rue (18)	**7 C1**	Théophile Roussel, Rue (12)	**14 F5**
Stockholm, Rue de (8)	**5 C3**	Thérèse, Rue (1)	**12 E1**
Strasbourg, Blvd de (10)	**7 C4**	Thermopyles, Rue des (14)	**15 B4**
Stuart Merrill, Pl (17)	**4 D1**	Thibaud, Rue (14)	**16 D5**
Suez, Rue de (18)	**7 B1**	Thiéré, Passage (11)	**14 F4**
Suffren, Ave de (7, 15)	**10 E4**	Thierry de Martel, Blvd (16)	**3 B3**
Suffren, Port de (15)	**9 C3**	Thiers, Rue (16)	**9 A1**
Suger, Rue (6)	**12 F4**	Thiers, Sq (16)	**9 B1**
Suisses, Rue des (15)	**15 B4**	Thimonnier, Rue (9)	**7 A2**
Sully, Pont de (4)	**13 C5**	Thoirigny, Pl de (3)	**14 D3**
Sully, Rue de (4)	**14 D5**	Tholozé, Rue (18)	**6 E1**
Sully Prudhomme, Ave (7)	**11 A2**	Thomy Thierry, Allée (7)	**10 E3**
Surcouf, Rue (7)	**11 A2**	Thorel, Rue (2)	**7 A5**
Surène, Rue de (8)	**5 C5**	Thorigny, Rue de (3)	**14 D2**
Suzanne Buisson, Sq (18)	**2 E5**	Thouin, Rue (5)	**17 A1**
		Tilsitt, Rue de (8)	**4 E4**
T		Tilsitt, Rue de (16)	**4 D4**
Tacherie, Rue de la (4)	**13 B3**	Tino Rossi, Sq (5)	**18 D1**
Taillandiers, Passage des (11)	**14 F4**	Tiphaine, Rue (15)	**10 D5**
Taitbout, Rue (9)	**6 E3**	Tiquetonne, Rue (2)	**13 A1**
Talma, Rue (16)	**9 A3**	Tiron, Rue (4)	**13 C3**
Tandou, Rue (19)	**8 F1**	Titien, Rue (13)	**17 C3**
Tanger, Rue de (19)	**8 E1**	Tocqueville, Rue de (17)	**5 A1**
Tanneries, Rue des (13)	**17 A4**	Tolbiac, Rue de (13)	**18 E5**
		continues	**18 F5**
		Tombe Issoire, Rue de la (14)	**16 E4**
		Tombouctou, Rue de (18)	**7 C1**
		Torricelli, Rue (17)	**4 D2**
		Toulouse-Lautrec, Rue (17)	**2 D2**
		Tour d'Auvergne, Rue de la (9)	**6 F2**
		continues	**7 A3**

Tour d'Auvergne, Rue de la (9)	**6 F2**	Tuileries, Quai des (1)	**12 D2**	Verdeau, Passage (9)	**6 F4**	Villersexel, Rue de (7)	**11 C3**
continues	**7 A3**	Tulipes, Villa des (18)	**2 F3**	Verdun, Ave de (10)	**8 D3**	Villette, Bassin de la (19)	**8 E1**
Tour de Jean Sans Peur (2)	**13 A1**	Turbigo, Rue de (1, 2)	**13 A1**	Verdun, Pl de	**3 B3**	*continues*	**8 F1**
Tour de Vanves, Passage de la (14)	**15 C3**	*continues*	**13 B1**	Vergniaud, Rue (13)	**17 A5**	Villette, Blvd de la (10, 19)	**8 E2**
Tour des Dames, Rue de la (9)	**6 E3**	Turbigo, Rue de (3)	**13 C1**	Vergniaud, Rue	**3 B1**	Villiers, Ave de (17)	**4 F2**
Tour Eiffel (7)	**10 D3**	Turenne, Rue de (3)	**14 D2**	Vermenouze, Sq (5)	**17 A2**	*continues*	**5 A2**
Tour Maubourg, Blvd de la (7)	**11 A2**	Turgot, Rue (9)	**7 A2**	Vernet, Rue (8)	**4 E4**	Villiers, Ave de la Porte de (17)	**3 C1**
Tour Maubourg, Sq de la (7)	**11 A3**	Turin, Rue de (8)	**5 C2**	Verneuil, Rue de (7)	**12 D3**	Villiers, Porte de (17)	**3 C2**
Tour Montparnasse (15)	**15 C2**	**U**		Vernier, Rue (17)	**4 D1**	Villiot, Rue (12)	**18 F2**
Tour, Rue de la (16)	**9 B2**	Ulm, Rue d' (5)	**17 A1**	Verniquet, Rue (17)	**4 E1**	Vinaigriers, Rue des (10)	**8 D4**
Tour St-Jacques (1, 4)	**13 A3**	UNESCO (5)	**10 F5**	Véron, Cité (18)	**6 E1**	Vincent Auriol, Blvd (13)	**18 D4**
Tour St-Jacques, Sq de la (4)	**13 A3**	Union, Passage de l' (7)	**10 F3**	Véron, Rue (18)	**6 E1**	Vincent Compoint, Rue (18)	**2 F4**
Tourlaque, Rue (18)	**2 E5**	Université Paris IV (8)	**11 A1**	Véronèse, Rue de (13)	**17 B4**	Vincent Scotto, Rue (19)	**8 F1**
Tournefort, Rue (5)	**17 A1**	Université Paris VI et VII (5)	**13 C5**	Verrerie, Rue de la (4)	**13 B3**	Vineuse, Rue (16)	**9 C2**
Tournelle, Pont de la (4, 5)	**13 C5**	*continues*	**17 C1**	Verrier, Rue le (6)	**16 E2**	Vintimille, Rue de (9)	**6 D2**
continues	**13 B5**	Université, Rue de l' (7)	**10 E2**	Versailles, Ave de (16)	**9 A5**	Violet, Rue (15)	**10 D5**
Tournelle, Quai de la (4, 5)	**13 B5**	Ursins, Rue des (4)	**13 B4**	Vertbois, Rue du (3)	**13 C1**	Viollet le Duc, Rue (9)	**6 F2**
Tournelles, Rue des (3, 4)	**14 D3**	Ursulines, Rue des (5)	**16 F2**	Verte, Allée (11)	**14 E2**	Visconti, Rue (6)	**12 E3**
Tournon, Rue de (6)	**12 E5**	Uzès, Rue d' (2)	**7 A5**	Verzy, Ave de (17)	**3 C2**	Visitation, Passage de la (7)	**11 C3**
Tourville, Ave de (7)	**11 A4**	**V**		Vésale, Rue (5)	**17 B3**	Vital, Rue (16)	**9 B2**
Toussaint Féron, Rue (13)	**17 C5**	Val de Grâce (5)	**16 F2**	Vézelay, Rue de (8)	**5 B3**	Vivarais, Sq du (17)	**3 C1**
Toustain, Rue (6)	**12 E4**	*continues*	**17 A2**	Viaduc des Arts (12)	**14 F5**	Vivienne, Rue (2)	**12 F1**
Touzet-Gaillard, Rue (17)	**1 C2**	Val de Grâce, Rue du (5)	**16 F2**	Viala, Rue (15)	**10 D5**	*continues*	**6 F5**
Tracy, Rue de (2)	**7 B5**	Valadon, Rue (7)	**10 F3**	Viarmes, Rue de (1)	**12 F2**	Volney, Rue (2)	**6 D5**
Traktir, Rue de (16)	**4 D4**	Valence, Rue de (5)	**17 B3**	Vicq d'Azir, Rue (10)	**8 E3**	Volontaires, Rue des (15)	**15 A2**
Traversière, Rue (12)	**14 F5**	Valenciennes, Pl de (10)	**7 B3**	Victoire, Rue de la (9)	**6 E4**	Volta, Rue (3)	**13 C1**
continues	**18 E1**	Valenciennes, Rue de (10)	**7 B3**	Victoires, Pl des (1, 2)	**12 F1**	Voltaire, Blvd (11)	**14 E1**
Treilhard, Rue (8)	**5 A3**	Valette, Rue (5)	**13 A5**	Victor Basch, Pl (14)	**16 D5**	Voltaire, Rue (18)	**2 F2**
Trémoille, Rue de la (8)	**10 F1**	Valeurs, Bourse des (2)	**6 F5**	Victor Considérant, Rue (14)	**16 D3**	Vosges, Pl des (4)	**14 D3**
Trésor, Rue du (4)	**13 C3**	Valhubert, Pl 5 (13)	**18 D1**	Victor Cousin, Rue (5)	**12 F5**	Vouillé, Rue de (15)	**15 A4**
Trétaigne, Rue de (18)	**2 F5**	Valmy, Quai de (10)	**8 D3**	Victor Hugo, Ave (16)	**3 B5**	Vrillière, Rue de la (1)	**12 F1**
Trévise, Cité de (9)	**7 A4**	*continues*	**8 E2**	*continues*	**3 C5**	Vulpian, Rue (13)	**17 A4**
Trévise, Rue de (9)	**7 A4**	Valois, Rue de (1)	**12 F1**	*continues*	**9 A1**	**W**	
Trinité (4)	**13 B2**	Van Dyck, Ave (8)	**4 F3**	Victor Hugo, Blvd	**1 B2**	Wagram, Ave de (8, 17)	**4 F3**
Trinité, Rue de la (9)	**6 D3**	Van Gogh, Rue (13)	**18 E1**	Victor Hugo, Blvd	**2 D1**	Wagram, Pl de (17)	**4 F1**
Trinité, Sq de la (9)	**6 D3**	Vandamme, Rue (14)	**15 C2**	Victor Hugo, Blvd	**3 B1**	Waldeck Rousseau, Rue (17)	**3 C2**
Tristan Bernard, Pl (17)	**4 D3**	Vandrezanne, Rue (13)	**17 B5**	Victor Hugo, Pl (16)	**3 C5**	Wallons, Rue des (13)	**17 C3**
Trocadéro, Sq du (16)	**9 B2**	Vaneau, Cité (7)	**11 B4**	Victor Hugo, Villa (16)	**3 B5**	Washington, Rue (8)	**4 F4**
Trocadéro et du Novembre, Pl du (16)	**9 C2**	Vaneau, Rue (7)	**11 B4**	Victor Marchand, Passage (13)	**16 F5**	Weber, Rue (16)	**3 B4**
Trois Bornes, Rue des (11)	**14 E1**	*continues*	**11 C5**	Victor Massé, Rue (9)	**6 E2**	Winston Churchill, Ave (8)	**11 A1**
Trois Couronnes, Rue des (11)	**8 F5**	Varenne, Rue de (7)	**11 C3**	Victoria, Ave (4)	**13 A3**	Winston Churchill, Pl	**3 A2**
Trois Frères, Cour des (11)	**14 F4**	Varsovie, Pl de (7, 16)	**10 D2**	*continues*	**13 B3**	Wurtz, Rue (13)	**17 A5**
Trois Frères, Rue des (18)	**6 F1**	Vauban, Pl (7)	**11 A4**	Vieille du Temple, Rue (3, 4)	**13 C3**	**X**	
Trois Portes, Rue des (5)	**13 A4**	Vaucanson, Rue (3)	**13 C1**	Vieille du Temple, Rue (3)	**14 D2**	Xaintrailles, Rue (13)	**18 E5**
Tronchet, Rue (8)	**5 C5**	Vaucouleurs, Rue de (11)	**8 F5**	Vienne, Rue de (8)	**5 C3**	Xavier Privas, Rue (5)	**13 A4**
Tronchet, Rue (8)	**6 D4**	Vaugirard, Blvd de (15)	**15 B2**	Viète, Rue (17)	**4 F1**	**Y**	
Tronson du Coudray, Rue (8)	**5 C4**	Vaugirard, Galerie (15)	**15 B2**	Vieuville, Rue de la (18)	**6 F1**	Yéo Thomas, Rue (13)	**18 D4**
Trouillet, Rue	**1 A2**	Vaugirard, Rue de (6)	**12 E5**	Vieux Colombier, Rue du (6)	**12 D4**	Yorktown, Sq (16)	**9 C2**
Trousseau, Sq (12)	**14 F5**	Vaugirard, Rue de (15, 6)	**15 B1**	Vigée Lebrun, Rue (15)	**15 A2**	Yser, Blvd de l' (17)	**3 C1**
Troyon, Rue (17)	**4 D3**	Vauquelin, Rue (5)	**17 A2**	Vignes, Rue des (16)	**9 A3**	Yves du Manoir, Ave (17)	**3 C2**
Trudaine, Ave (9)	**6 F2**	Vauvenargues, Rue (18)	**2 E4**	Vignon, Rue (8, 9)	**6 D4**	Yves Toudic, Rue (10)	**8 D5**
continues	**7 A2**	Vavin, Ave (6)	**16 E1**	Villars, Ave de (7)	**11 A4**	Yvon et Claire Morandat, Place (17)	**3 C3**
Truffaut, Rue (17)	**1 B5**	Vavin, Rue (6)	**16 D1**	Ville, Pl de (6)	**12 D5**	Yvon Morandat, Pl (17)	**3 C3**
continues	**5 C1**	Velasquez, Ave (8)	**5 A2**	Ville l'Evêque, Rue de la (8)	**5 B4**	Yvon Villarceau, Rue (16)	**3 C5**
Truillot, Impasse (11)	**14 F2**	Velpeau, Rue (7)	**11 C4**	Ville Neuve, Rue de la (2)	**7 A5**	Yvonne Le Tac, Rue (18)	**6 F1**
Tuileries, Quai des (1, 8)	**11 C1**	Vendôme, Passage (3)	**14 D1**	Villebois Mareuil, Rue (17)	**4 D3**		
		Vendôme, Pl (1)	**6 D5**	Villedo, Rue (1)	**12 E1**		
		Venezuela, Pl du (16)	**3 C4**	Villehardouin, Rue (3)	**14 D3**		
		Venise, Rue de (4)	**13 B2**	Villemain, Ave (15)	**15 B4**		
		Vercingétorix, Rue (14)	**15 A4**	Villeneuve, Rue	**1 A1**		
				Villeneuve, Rue	**1 B1**		

Each place name is followed by its arrondissement number, and then by its Street Finder reference.

General Index

A

A la Civette 331, 332
A l'Olivier 331, 332
Aaron, Didier 336, 337
Les Abbesses 228
Abbesses, Place des
    see Place des Abbesses
Abbey Bookshop 331, 332
Abou d'Abi Bazar 324, 325
Abstract expressionism 113
Académie Française 44, **141**, 166
Académie Royale de Peinture et
    de Sculpture 35, 60
Action Ecoles cinema 356
Action Christine Odeon cinema
    356
ADA 383
Adelaide of Savoy 224
Admission charges
    museums 366
    nightclubs 352
Aer Lingus 379
African art 58
Agatha 328, 329
The Age of Bronze (Rodin)
    265
Agnès B 11, 324, 325, 327
Agrippa 129
Air Canada 376, 379
Air France 376, 377, 379
Air de Paris 10, 336, 337
Air travel 376–7, 379
Airport Shuttle 377, 379
Airports
    Charles de Gaulle 376–7, 379,
        380 –81
    Orly 377, 379, 381
    transport to city 380–81
Alberola, Jean-Michel 113
Alcohol, customs and excise 374
Alechinsky, Pierre 113
Alexander II, Tsar 232
Alexander III, Pope 82, 83
Alexander III, Tsar 208
Aligre, Marché d' see Marché
    d'Aligre
Allegory of the Republic (Papety)
    17
Alléosse 334, 335
Allo Logement Temporaire
    280, 282
Alpha taxis 389
Alphand, Adolphe
    Bois de Boulogne 53
    Bois de Vincennes 53, 246
    Parc des Buttes-Chaumont 234,
        268
    Parc Monceau 232
    Parc Montsouris 246
Alsace wines 301
Alternatives (store) 326, 327
Amboise, Jacques d', Abbot of
    Cluny 154, 155
Ambulances 368, 369
American Airlines 376, 379
American Church 375
American Express 370
American Hospital 369
Les Amis des Livres 140
Amphithéâtre Richelieu de la
    Sorbonne 346, 347
Andouillettes à la Lyonnaise 297
André Citroën, Parc 247
Androuët 334, 335
Angel Traveller (Moreau) 231

Angelico, Fra 126
Angélina 11, 130, 293, 294
Angers, David d' 158
Anti-Poison Centre 368
Antiques 336–7
Apache 362
Apartments, self-catering 278, 279
Apéritifs 299
A-Poc 324, 325
Apollinaire, Guillaume 137, 223
Apple tarts 297
Aquaboulevard 358, 359, 362
Aquarium du Trocadero **200**
Arc de Triomphe
    43, 205, **210–11**
    architectural features 210–11
    history 34–5
    Napoleon's nuptial parade 211
    reliefs 146
    timeline 210
    Tomb of the Unknown Soldier
        38, 210
Arc de Triomphe du Carrousel
    33, 122, 130
L'Arc en Seine 336
Arcades see Les Galeries
The Archer (Bourdelle) 178
Architecture, museums 58–9
Arènes de Lutèce 21, 163, **165**
L'Argonaute 237
Arlequin cinema 356
Armani, Giorgio 326, 327
Armée, Musée de l'
    see Musée de l'Armée
Armenian Museum
    see Musée Arménien
Art Deco 38
    antique shops 336
    Café de Flore 136, 139
    glass 330
    Musée des Arts Décoratifs 130
    Musée Bouilhet-Christofle 132
    Quai de Jemmapes 261
    Rue Campagne-Première 178
    Rue de La Fontaine 264
    La Samaritaine 115
Art galleries 336, 337
    see also individual galleries
    and museums
Art Moderne, Musée National d'
    see Musée National d'Art
    Moderne
Art Moderne de la Ville de Paris,
    Musée d' see Musée d'Art
    Moderne de la Ville de Paris
Art Nature Harmonie 331, 332
Art Nouveau 36, 37
    antique shops 336
    Auteuil 264, 265
    Avenue Rapp, No. 29 193
    Fouquet Jewellery Boutique 97
    Galerie Royale 132
    glass 330
    Grand Palais 208
    metro stations 228, 266, 384
    Musée des Arts Décoratifs
        118, 130
    Musée d'Orsay 146
    Notre-Dame du Travail 247
    Pont Alexandre III 208
    Rue Cler 190
    Rue de la Fontaine 254
    St-Jean l'Evangéliste 49, 226,
        266–7
    La Samaritaine 115

Artaxi 389
Artcurial 336, 337
L'Artisan Parfumeur 330, 332
Artois, Comte d' 255
Arts Décoratifs, Musée des see
    Musée des Arts Décoratifs
Arts de la Mode, Musée des
    see Musée des Arts de la Mode
Asian art 58
ASLOM 278, 280
Assemblée Nationale Palais-
    Bourbon 69, **192**
Association des Paralysés de
    France 367
Asterix the Gaul 362
Atelier des Enfants 361
At Home in Paris 278, 280
Au Bec Fin 342, 344, 361
Au Bon Marché 333, 335
Au Lapin Agile 222, **225**,
    267, 342, 344
Au Nain Bleu 331, 332, 362
Au Paradis des Petits 360
Au Petit Marguery 11
Au Printemps 10, 321
Auberge de la Bonne Franquette
    267
Auberge de la Reine Blanche 263
Auctions and auction houses
    336–7
Auditorium du Louvre 346, 347
Auditorium du Musée
    d'Orsay 346, 347
Austerlitz, Battle of (1805) 33,
    208, 209
Australian tourist office 367
Auteuil 34, 39
    racecourse 358, 359
    walks 257, 264–5
Automatic tellers, banks 370
Automobile Club de l'Ouest 358
Aux Trois Mailletz 350
Aux Vrai Produits
    d'Auvergne 333, 335
Avenue de l'Opéra 219
Avenue des Champs-Elysées
    see Champs-Elysées
Avenue du Président Wilson 197
Avenue Junot 229
Avenue Montaigne 206, **209**
Avenue Rapp 191
Averbode altarpiece 156
Avis 383
Avril, Jane 228
Axel, Michel 326, 327
Azéma 200

B

Babychou Services 360
Baby Dior 326, 327
Baccarat crystal 203, 323, 330, 332
Bagatelle gardens, Bois de
    Boulogne 50, 53, 133, **255**
Bags, shops 328, 329
Baguettes (bread) 296, 333
Les Bains-Douches 351, 353
Baiser Salé 350
Baker, Josephine 38, 112, 178
Balajo 352, 353
Baldaccini, César 164
Balenciaga 203
Ballet 345, 348
Baltard, Victor-Louis 49, 106, 144, 259
Balthus 61
Ban, Shigeru 113

Le Balzac cinema 356
Balzac, Honoré de 146
  Maison de Balzac 201
  statue 177
  tomb 240
Bank notes 371
Banking 370
Banlieue (suburban trains) 388
Banque de France 34, 132–3
Barbizon School 208
Barillet-Deschamps 232
Baroque art 60
Baroque churches 48–9
La Barque (Monet) 254
Barrière de la Villette 260
Barry, Comtesse du 333, 335
Bars 292, 316–17, 318–19
Barthélemy 334, 335
Bartholdi, Frédéric-Auguste,
  tomb 180
Bartholomé, Paul Albert 240
Bas et Haut 328, 329
Baseball 358
Basilique St-Denis 156, 233
Basquiat, Jean-Michel 113
Bassin de l'Arsenal 53
Bassin de la Villette 72, 73, 234,
  260
Bastien-Lepage, Jules 147
Bastille 23
  fall of 30–31, 41
Bastille, Opéra de see Opéra de
  Paris Bastille
Bastille, Place de la see Place
  de la Bastille
Bastille area
  art galleries 336
  cafés 292
Bastille Day 63, 131
Bataclan 349, 350, 351, 353
Bateau-Lavoir 44, 223, 228, 267
Bateaux Mouches 72, 73, 362
Bateaux Parisiens 72
Bateaux Vedettes 73
The Bathers (Picasso) 101
Baths
  Gallo-Roman 154
  Turkish 167
Batifol 264
Batobus 72, 73
The Battle of Austerlitz
  (Gechter) 211
Batofar 353
Baudelaire, Charles 34, 87,
  142, 145, 180, 181
  Cenotaph 180
  tomb 181
Baudot, Anatole de 49, 228
Bazille, Frédéric 146
BBC World Service 375
Beach, Sylvia 45, 140
Beads, Gallo-Roman 20
Beaubourg and Les Halles
  104–15
  area map 105
  Street-by-Street map 106–7
  Street Finder map 13
  see also Pompidou Centre
Beaujolais Nouveau 64
Beaujolais wine 298
Beaumarchais 140
Beauvais tapestries 232
Beauveau St-Antoine 235
Beauvilliers 293
Beauvoir, Simone de 40, 136,
  139, 143
  tomb 181

Beckett, Samuel, tomb 180
Beer 299, 316–17
Beethoven, Ludwig van 346
Belgrand 34
Belle Epoque 36–7, 108, 240,
  258, 293
Belleville 293
Belmondo, Jean-Paul 44
Belts, shops 328, 329
Belzunce 142
Benedictine Order 138, 224
Benet, Eugène, Christ 223
Bercy 246
Berlioz, Hector 44, 186, 227,
  346
Berluti 328, 329
Bernard, Émile 147
Bernhardt, Sarah 348
  tomb 240
Bernini, Giovanni Lorenzo
  173
Berthillon 262, 263
  Homogenous Infiltration 113
Beuys, Joseph 113
BHV (Le Bazaar de
  l'Hôtel de Ville) 331, 332
Bibliothèque Nationale 217
Bibliothèque Nationale de France
  40, 246
Bicloune 383
Bicy-Club 383
Bicycles 382
  hiring 357, 383
  repairs 383
  Tour de France 357
Bilboquet 349, 350
Billettes, Cloîtres des
  see Cloître des Billettes
Bird market
  see Marché aux Oiseaux
Bismarck, Otto von 226
Bistros 292, 293
Bistrot d'Eustache 109
Bizet, Georges 44–5
Blanche, J E, Proust 45
Blue Water Lilies (Monet) 147
Blute-fin see Moulin de la Galette
BNP Parisbas Masters Tennis
  64
Boats
  boat trips 67–73, 357, 362
  cross-Channel ferries 378
  model 169, 362, 363
Boileau, Louis-Auguste 200
Boileau, Nicolas, tomb 138
Bois de Boulogne 35, 43, 231,
  254–5
  Bagatelle gardens 50, 53, 133,
  255
  buses 387
  Jardin d'Acclimatation 361
  lakes 362
  open-air theatre 343
  Paris's Best 50–53
  sports 357
Bois de Vincennes 64, 235, 271
  buses 387
  Cartoucherie 342, 344
  lakes 362
  Parc Floral 361
  Paris's Best 50–53
  sports 357
  zoo 233, 361
La Boîte à Bas 328, 329
Bon Marché 10, 321, 335
Bonaparte, Joseph, tomb 188,
  189

Bonaparte, Napoleon
  see Napoleon Bonaparte,
  Emperor
Bonaparte, Pierre 241
Bonbec Tower, Conciergerie 81
Bonnard, Pierre 56, 57, 61, 113,
  147
Bonpoint 326, 327
Bonton 326, 327
Books
  Les Bouquinistes 67
  international bookshops 375
  Shakespeare & Co. 140, 151,
  331, 332
  shops 331, 332, 336
Books of Hours 23, 155
Bordeaux wines 298, 299
Bosch, Hieronymus 126
Botanski, Christian 113
Bouchardon, Edme, Fontaine des
  Quatre Saisons 187
Boucher, François 60, 103, 207
Boucheron 117, 328, 329
Bouffes-du-Nord theatre 344
Bouffes-Parisiens 342, 344
Boufflers, Comtesse de 264
Bouilhet-Christofle, Charles 57
Boulangerie de l'Ouest 333, 335
Boules (game) 169
Boulevard des Capucines 214, 215
Boulevard des Italiens 217
Boulevard des Italiens
  (Grandjean) 34
Boulevard Haussmann 217
Boulevard St-Germain 136, 139
Boulevard St-Michel (Boul'Mich)
  149, 150, 152, 169
Boulez, Pierre 45, 346
Boulle, André-Charles 26, 129
Boulogne, Bois de
  see Bois de Boulogne
Les Bouquinistes 67
Bourbon, Duchesse de 190
Bourbon dynasty 19, 99, 130,
  188
Bourdelle, Antoine 68, 146
  The Archer 178
  bust of Gustave Eiffel 195
  Musée Antoine Bourdelle
  57, 178
  Penelope 57
Bourgeois, Louise 113
Bourgogne, Duc de 114
Boursault 334, 335
Bourse du Commerce 115, 293
Bouvier collection 97
Bowling 358
Box offices 340–41
Brancusi, Constantin 44, 61, 112,
  164, 178, 247
  The Kiss 180
  Miss Pogany 112
Brandy 299
Braque, Georges 36, 38, 44, 57,
  61, 112, 113, 201, 228, 336
  Le Duo 111
Brasserie Lipp 136, 139
Brasseries 292, 293
  menus 294
Bread 321
  baguettes 296, 333
  shops 333, 335
Breakfast
  cafés 316
  in hotels 277, 278
Brentano 331, 332, 375
Breton, André 38, 112

Breton Peasant Women
  (Gauguin) 147
Bricard, Musée
  see Musée Bricard
Briçonnet 142
Bridges
  Passerelle des Arts 70, 77
  Passerelle Solférino 70
  Pont Alexandre III 67, 69, 206,
    207, 208
  Pont de l'Alma 362
  Pont Bir-Hakeim 68
  Pont de la Concorde 62, 70,
    139
  Pont de Grenelle 62
  Pont d'Iéna 199, 201
  Pont Louis-Philippe 262
  Pont Marie 263
  Pont Neuf 18, 24, 25, 40, 41,
    77, 86
  Pont Notre-Dame 24
  Pont Royal 27
  Pont St-Michel 149
  Pont Sully 70
  Pont de la Tournelle 262
Brie de Meaux cheese 297
Brioches 296
Bristol hotel 276
British Airways 376, 379
British and American Pharmacy
  369
British Hospital 369
British Midland 376, 379
British tourist office 367
Brittany Ferries 378
Broodthaers, Marcel 113
Brosse, Salomon de
  48, 171, 172
Bruand, Aristide 225
Bruand, Libéral
  Hôtel des Invalides 187
  Hôtel Libéral Bruand 93, 98
  St-Louis-des-Invalides 49, 186
  Pitié-Salpêtrière Hospital 49,
    167
Brueghel, Peter 57
Brunet, P, *Virgin Mary and
  Child* 226
Bruno, Vanessa 11, 324, 327,
  328, 329
La Bruyère theatre 342, 344
Budé, Guillaume 153
Budget car hire 383
Buffet, Bernard 61
Buffon, Comte de **166**, 167
Bureaux de change 370
Bureaux de postes 372
Bureau Voyage Jeunesse (BVJ)
  279, 280
Buren, Daniel 120
Burgundy wines 298, 299
The Burial at Ornans 61
Burne-Jones, Edward 147
Buses
  airport 377
  bus stops 386, 387
  coaches 378, 380–81
  from airport to city 380–81
  night buses 341, 387
  route maps 387
  sightseeing routes 387
  sightseeing tours 367
  summer season 387
  tickets 386
  travelling on 386–7
La Butte Bergèyre 268
La Butte-aux-Cailles 272–3

Buttes-Chaumont, Parc des
  see Parks and Gardens
By Terry 330, 332

C

Le Cab 352, 353
Cabaret 343
Cabaret des Assassins 225
Le Cabaret Milliardaire 353
Cabinet des Médailles et des
  Antiques **219**
Cacharel 133
Cadente, Stella 326, 327
Cadolle 328, 329
Caen 380
Caesar, Julius 77
Café de l'Abreuvoir 224
Café Cluny 152
Café Cyrano 44
Café Drouant 217
Café d'Edgar 342, 344, 350, 361
Café de Flore 136, 137, **139**,
  143, 293, 343, 344
Café de la Gare 342, 344
Café de la Mairie 172
Café Marly 10
Café d'Orsay 142
Café de la Paix 142, 212, 213
Café de Paris 142
Café-theatres 342, 344
Café Tortini 142
Cafés 142–3, 316
  Bastille area 292
  history 29
  Left Bank, 142, 143
  Luxembourg Quarter 292
  Marais 292
  Montmartre 36
  Montparnasse 143, 175, 292–3
  St-Germain-des-Prés 135, 136
  smoking in 295
  types 293
  where to find 292–3
  wine 298
Cake shops 333, 335
Calais 380
Calder, Alexander 112
  Mobile on Two Planes 113
Calendar, Republican 30
Calendar of events 62–5
La Calinière 336, 337
Camembert cheese 297, 334
Camondo, Isaac de 129
Camondo, Comte Moise de 232
Camping du Bois de Boulogne/
  Ile de France 279, 280
Camus, Albert 143
Canal de l'Ourcq 73
Canal St-Martin 44, **234**
  boat trips 73
  walks 257, 260–61
Canaletto 56
Canals
  boat trips 73, 362
  shuttle services 72
Canauxrama 73
Cantin, Marie-Anne 334, 335
Capet, Hugh 18, 44
Capetian dynasty 18, 78
Cappellini 336, 337
Caprice de l'Instant 334, 335
Caravaggio, *The Fortune
  Teller* 126
Caravanning 279, 280
Cardenas, *Large Window* 164
Cardin, Pierre 324, 325,
  326, 327

Carel 328, 329
Carmontelle, Louis 232
Carnavalet, Hôtel *see* Hôtel
  Carnavalet
Carnavalet, Musée *see* Musée
  Carnavalet
Carné, Marcel 44
Carnet (bus ticket) 386
Carolingian dynasty 18
Carpeaux, Jean-Baptiste 53, 61,
  146
  The Dance 144
  Fontaine de l'Observatoire 173
  Four Quarters of the World 54
  Le Pêcheur à la coquille 54
Le Carré des Feuillants 294
Carré Rive Gauche 62, 336
Carrousel, Jardin du
  see Jardin du Carrousel
Carrousel du Louvre 122
Cars
  Centre International
    d'Automobile 234
  driving in Paris 382, 383
  driving to Paris 378, 379
  hiring 383
  parking 383
Cars Rouges 367
Carte Orange 382
Carte Paris Visite 382
Cartier 117, 200, 323, 328,
  329
Cartoucherie 342, 344
Le Casbah 352, 353
Cassatt, Mary 147
Castel Béranger **254**, 264, 265
Castel's 351, 353
Castro, Jean-Pierre de 336, 337
Catacombes 29, **179**, 363
Cathedrals
  Notre-Dame 11, 43, 47, 48, 78,
    79, 80, 82–5, 198, 346, 347,
    363, 375
  St-Alexandre-Nevsky 232
  St-Denis 157, 200
  see also Churches
Catherine de Médicis 52, 231
Catholic Church 46, 223, 375
Catholic League 99
Caveau des Echansons 201
Caveau de la Huchette 349, 350
Caveau des Oubliettes 349
Caveau de la République
  342, 344
La Cave des Martyrs 334, 335
Les Caves Augé 334, 335
Les Caves du Panthéon 334, 335
Caves Taillevent 334, 335
Cellini, Benvenuto 127
Celts 20, 78, 81
Cemeteries
  Catacombes 179
  Cimetière de Montmartre 229
  Cimetière du Montparnasse
    175, 176, 180–81
  Cimetière du Père Lachaise
    233, 240–41
Centre de Création Industrielle
  58, 110
Centre des Reseignements
  Douanes 336, 337
Centre Français du Commerce
  Extérieur 336, 337
Centre d'Information et de
  Documentation Jeunesse
  374, 375
Centre Médical Europe 369

Centre des Monuments
Nationaux (MONUM) 95, 367
Centre des Renseignements des
Douanes 374
Ceramics, Gallo-Roman 20
Cézanne, Paul 38, 56, 59,
61, 131, 147
Chablis wine 298
Chabrol, Claude 354
Chagall, Marc 44, 61, 112, 178,
215, 227, 247
*To Russia, the Asses and the
Others* 111
Chaillot, Palais de *see* Palais de
Chaillot
Chaillot Quarter 196–203
area map 197
Street-by-Street map 198–9
Street Finder maps 3, 9–10
Chain hotels 279, 280
La Chaise Longue 330, 332
Chalgrin, Jean-François 140, 171
Arc de Triomphe 209, 210
Chalus, Pierre de, Abbot of
Cluny 154
Chamberlain, John 113
Chambre des Députés 69
Champ-de-Mars 11, 52, **191**
Champ-de-Mars massacre (1791)
30
Champagne 299, 334, 335
Champaigne, Philippe de
Last Supper 60
Portrait of Cardinal Richelieu
44
Le Champo cinema 356
Champs-Elysées
area map 205
Avenue des 35, 131, 205,
207, 209
cinemas 354
Street-by-Street map 206–7
Street Finder maps 3–4, 5, 11
Chanel 41, 322, 324, 317, 328
Channel ferries 378
Chansonniers 342, 344
Chantilly, rail services 388
Chapelier, Hervé 328, 329
Chapelle des Lombards 350
Chapelle du Martyre 225
Chaput 328, 329
Charcuterie 333, 335
Chardin, Jean-Baptiste-Siméon
56, 60
Charlemagne, Emperor 18, 22
statue of 78
Charles I, King of England 126
Charles I the Bald, King 18
Charles II, King of England
142
Charles II the Fat, King 18
Charles III the Simple,
King 18
Charles IV the Fair, King 19
Charles V, Emperor 129
Charles V the Wise, King 19, 23,
86, 92, 123, 129
Charles VI the Fool, King 19
Charles VII the Victorious, King
19
Charles VIII, King 19, 88
Charles IX, King 19
Charles X, King 19, 179
Musée de la Marine 201
Charles de Bourbon 138
Charles de Gaulle airport 376–7,
379, 380–81

Chartres, rail services 388
Chartres Cathedral 193, 200
Charvet 326, 327
Chasse et de la Nature,
Musée de
see Musée de la Chasse et de la
Nature
Chat Noir 266
Château de Bois-Préau 255
Château des Brouillards 229
Château de Malmaison 32, 33, **255**
Château de Vincennes 235
Châteauneuf-du-Pape
wine 298
Cheese 296, 297
shops 334
Chelles, Jean de 48
Cherbourg 380
Le Cheval Majeur
(Duchamp-Villon) 110
Chez Madame Arthur
343, 344
Chez Michou 344
Childebert I, King 18, 138
Childebert II, King 18
Childéric I, King 18
Childéric II, King 18
Childéric III, King 18
Chilpéric I, King 18
Chilpéric II, King 18
China Club 350
Chinese restaurants 292, 293
Chirac, Jacques 40
Chirico, Giorgio de 112
Chocolate pots 29
Chocolate shops 333, 335
Chopin, Frédéric 87, 132
monument 258
tomb 240
Chou En-Lai 45
Christ (Benet) 223
Christ in the Garden of Olives
(Delacroix) 99
Christmas illuminations 65
Christo 40, 41
Christofle 330, 332
Churches
Basilica de St-Denis 48
Chapelle du Martyre 225
Dôme 14, 27, 43, 46, 48–9,
159, 184, 185, 187, 188–9
Eglise de la Sorbonne 48, 153
Eglise des Billettes 346, 347
La Madeleine 33, 46, 49, 214,
216, 346, 347
music 346, 347
Notre-Dame de l'Assomption
265
Notre-Dame d'Auteuil 264
Notre-Dame des Blancs
Manteaux 102
Notre-Dame du Travail 247
Panthéon 29, 46, 49, 158–9, 262
Paris's Best 46–9
Sacré-Coeur 15, 44, 47, 49,
221, 223, 226–7, 363, 375
St-Augustin 49, 259
St-Etienne-du-Mont 25, 48, 153
St-Eustache 25, 44, 47, 48,
105, 114

Churches (cont)
St-Germain-des-Prés 48, 135,
136, 138, 139, 152, 157,
346, 347
St-Germaine l'Auxerrois 48,
115
St-Gervais–St-Protais 38, 44,
46, 48, 71, 99, 346, 347
St-Jean l'Evangéliste 49,
226, 266–7
St-Joseph-des-Carmes 49, 173
St-Julien-le-Pauvre 48, 151,
152, 346, 347
St-Louis-des-Invalides 49,
185, 186, 187
St-Louis-en-l'Ile 87, 263, 346,
347
St-Médard 162, 166
St-Merry 48, 107, 108
St-Paul–St-Louis 47, 49, 99
St-Pierre de Montmartre 223,
224
St-Roch 49, 118, 121, 346,
347
St-Séverin 47, 48, 150, 151,
152
St-Sulpice 29, 48, 49, 138,
142, 152, 170, 172, 346, 347
Sainte-Chapelle 17, 41, 46,
48, 88–9, 219, 346, 347, 363
Sainte-Clothilde 48, 49, 187
Salpêtrière 49
Tour St-Jacques 25, 48
tourist information 375
Val-de-Grâce 48, 49, 173
Churchill, Winston 186, 283
La Cigale 349, 350
Cigarettes, customs and excise
374
Cigars 331
Cimabue 126
Cimetière de Montmartre 229
Cimetière de Montparnasse 175,
176, **180–81**
Cimetière de Passy **202**
Cimetière du Père Lachaise 233,
240–41
Cine Sorbonne 356
Cineiffel 194
Cinema 354–6
festivals 356
for children 361
history 37, 44
Musée du Cinéma Henri
Langlois 201
Cinema Studio Galande 356
Cinémathèque Française
355
Circus 361
Les Citadines 280
Cité de l'Architecture et du
Patrimoine 58, 199, **200**
Cité de la Musique 236, 237, 346,
347
La Cité des Enfants 360
Cité des Sciences et de
l'Industrie 11, 40, 59, 237,
238–9, 360, 361
Explora 238, 238–9
La Géode 239, 354
Cité Universitaire 247
Cithéa 350
Citroën, André, tomb 180
Citroën cars 37, 39
Citron pressé 299
Cityrama 367
Classical churches 48–9

Claude Alain café 143
Claudel, Camille 146
Clergerie, Robert 328, 329
Clock Quarter
  see Quartier de l'Horloge
Clocks 32
  Le Défenseur du Temps 107
  109
  Eglise de la Sorbonne 153
  Tour de l'Horloge 71
  Versailles 251
Cloîtres des Billettes 102
La Closerie des Lilas 143, **179**
Clotaire I, King 18
Clotaire II, King 18
Clotaire III, King 18
Clothes
  children's 326, 327, 362
  fashion shows 65
  hat shops 328, 329
  haute couture 322, 324
  lingerie shops 328, 329
  men's 326, 327
  museums 57
  in restaurants 294
  shoe shops 328, 329
  shops 324–29
  size chart 328
Cloud, St 152
Clovis I, King 18, 21, 22
Clovis II, King 18
Clovis III, King 18
Club des Haschischines 87
Club Med World 351, 353
Cluny, Musée de see Musée de
  Cluny
Coach travel 378, 380–81
Cocteau, Jean 121, 143, 176
  Space Conquest 239
Cognacq, Ernest 94, 115
Cognacq-Jay, Musée see Musée
  Cognacq-Jay
Coins 371
  Musée de la Monnaie 141
Colbert, Jean-Baptiste 26
Colette (novelist) 39
Colette (store) 326
Collection des Minéraux de
  l'Université 165
Collège de France 25, **153**
Colonial Exhibition (1931) 39,
  235
Colonne de Juillet 98
Coltelli, Procopio dei 140
Comédie des Champs-Elysées
  342, 344
Comédie Française 28–9, 45,
  119, **120**, 140, 342, 344
Comité Départemental
  d'Equitation de Paris 357, 359
Comme des Garçons 324, 325
Committee of Public Safety 31
Commune 122, 150, 241, 272
Les Compagnons du Voyage
  367
Composteur machines 388
Comptoir des Cotonniers 324, 325
Le Comptoir des Tuileries 370
Conceptual art 113
Concerts 345–6, 349
Conciergerie 71, 76, 78, 81, 363
Concorde, Place de la see Place
  de la Concorde
Conservatoire d'Art Dramatique
  346, 347
Constable, John 59
Constitutional Council 120

Contrefaçon, Musée de la see
  Musée de la Contrefaçon
Contrescarpe, Place de la see
  Place de la Contrescarpe
Conversion chart 375
Coquilles Saint-Jacques 296
Le Corbusier
  Cité Universitaire 247
  Fondation Le Corbusier 59,
  254, 265
  Villa La Roche 58–9, 59, 254, 265
Corday, Charlotte 81
Corn Exchange
  see Bourse du Commerce
Corneille, Pierre 120, 121
Corot, Camille 222
Cortot, J P,
  Triumph of Napoleon 210
Cosmetics 330
Cosmo Paris 328, 329
Costes, Jean-Louis 108
Côte de Beaune wine 298
Côte de Nuits wine 298
Côte-Rôtie wine 298
Council of State 120
Couperin, François 99
Couperin family 44
La Coupole 143, 176, **178**, 292
Cour d'Honneur, Hôtel des
  Invalides 185
Cour Carrée du Louvre 316
Cour du Commerce St-André 141
Cour du Mai, Palais de Justice 78
Cour de Rohan 140
Courbet, Gustave 56, 58, 208
  The Burial at Ornans 61
Courtonne, Jean 187
Couscous restaurants 292
Coustou, Guillaume, *Marly
  Horses* 123, 125, 127
Coustou, Nicolas, *Pietà* 84, 85
Couture 324
  area map 322
  see also Fashion
Couture, Thomas 146
Coysevox, Antoine 60, 84, 127,
  253
  statue of Louis XIV 93
Cranach, Lucas 126
Crazy Horse 343, 344
Crèche 65
Credit cards 370
Crêpes 317
Crêpes Suzettes 297
Créteil 348
Crime 368
Croissants 296, 333
Crottin de Chavignol cheese 297
Crown jewels 129
Crypte Archéologique 21, 56,
  79, **81**
Cubism 38, 57, 100, 110, 111,
  112, 226, 336
Curie, Marie 37, 45, 159, 263
Curie, Pierre 37, 45, 159
Currency 371
Customs and immigration 374
Cuvier, Georges 163
Cuvier Fountain 163
Cycling see Bicycles

D

Dada 112, 181
Dagobert I, King 18
Dagobert III, King 18
Daillion, H,
  Génie du Sommeil Eternel 181

Dalí, Salvador 44, 112, 143
  Espace Dalí Montmartre
  222, 224
Dalloyau 333, 335
Dalou, Jules 170
Dance 348
The Dance (Carpeaux) 144
Dancing de la Coupole 353
*Dancing at the Moulin
  de la Galette* (Renoir) 145, 147
*Dante and Virgil in the
  Underworld* (Delacroix) 56
Danton, Georges 31, 81, 97, 131,
  152
  statue 137
Darius, King of Persia 128
Daughters of Charity convent
  263
Daumesnil, Lac 246
Daumier, Honoré 61, 146
Dauphine, Place
  see Place Dauphine
David, Jacques-Louis 29, 33, 171,
  252
  The Oath of the Horatii 60
Davioud 150, 269
Le Day Off 352, 353
Debauve & Gallais 333, 335
De Gaulle, Charles 91
  history 40, 41, 83
  Liberation of Paris 210
  Musée de l'Ordre de la
  Libération 210
  Palais de l'Elysée 209
  Place Charles de Gaulle 209
  Place du 18 Juin 1940 178
De Max, *The Separation of a
  Couple* 176
Dead Poet (Moreau) 56
Debussy, Claude 45
Declaration of the Rights of Man
  and the Citizen 30
Découverte, Palais de la
  see Palais de la Découverte
La Défense 40–41, 43, 110, 211,
  255, 363
Le Défenseur du Temps 107, **109**
Degas, Edgar 56, 59, 61, 147
  Young Dancer of Fourteen 146
Dehillerin, E. 331, 332
Le Déjeuner sur l'Herbe (Manet)
  61, 144, 146
Delacroix, Eugène 61, 146, 208
  Christ in the Garden of Olives
  99
  *Dante and Virgil in the
  Underworld* 56
  Jacob Wrestling with the Angel
  137, 172
  Liberty Leading the People 61
  monument 170
  Musée Eugène Delacroix 56,
  137, 138
  The Tiger Hunt 145
Delanoë, Bertrand 102
Delaunay, Robert 57, 61
Delors, Jacques 133
Delta Air Lines 376, 379
Delville, Jean 147
Demidoff, Elizabeth, tomb 241
Deneuve, Catherine 44
Denis, Maurice 146
Denis, St 21, 225
Dentists, emergencies 368
Department stores 321
*Departure of the Volunteers in
  1792* (Rude) 61

Le Depôt 353
Depôt-Vente de Buci-Bourbon 326, 327
Derain, André 57, 61
  The Two Barges 112
Descartes, René 136
  tomb 138
Desportes, Alexandre-François 57
Détaxe 374
Deux Anes 342, 344
Les Deux Magots 135, 136, 138, 143, 293
Deyrolle 331, 332
Diaghilev, Serge 37, 101
Dialling codes 372, 373
Diane de France 94
Diane de Poitiers 127, 140
Diderot, Denis 28, 45, 121, 127
  monument 159
Diehl 190
Dieppe 380
Digestifs 299
Dinh Van 328, 329
Diptyque 331, 332
Dior, Christian 206, 324, 325
Directory 30, 31
Directours 379
Disabled travellers 367
  airport information 379
  on buses 387
  entertainments 341
  hotels 278
  information 367
  restaurants 295
Discotheques 351
Discount travel agencies 379
Disney, Walt 243, 245
Disneyland Resort Paris 242–5, 360, 362
  Adventureland 244–5
  bus services 377
  Discoveryland 245
  Fantasyland 245
  Frontierland 244
  Main Street, USA 244
  map 242–3
Le Divan 331, 332
Divan du Monde 349, 350
Divay 333, 335
Dix, Otto, *Portrait of the Journalist Sylvia von Harden* 110
Doctor Paul Gachet (Van Gogh) 145
Doctors, emergencies 368
Dolet, Etienne 152
DOM 330, 332
Dôme Church 14, 27, 43, 159, 187
  architectural features 188–9
  floorplan 188–9
  Napoleon's tomb 184, 189
  Paris's Best 46, 48–9
  Street-by-Street map 185
Dormitory accommodation 279, 280
Dragon Fountain 248
Les Drapeaux de France 330, 332
Dreyfus, Alfred 37
  tomb 180
Drinks, what to drink in Paris 298–9
  see also Wine
Drouot, Comte de 216

Drouot (Hôtel des Ventes) **216**, 336–7
Drouot-Montaigne 337
Drouot-Nord 337
Du Pareil au Même 326, 327
Dubois, François, *The St Bartholomew's Day Massacre* 115
Dubreuil, Toussaint, *Hyante and Climente* 25
Dubuffet, Jean 57, 61
Le Duc des Lombards 349, 350
Duchamp, Marcel 38, 61, 112
Duchamp-Villon, Raymond, *Le Cheval Majeur* 110
Dufy, Raoul 127
Dumas, Alexandre 120
Duncan, Isadora, tomb 240
Le Duplex 353
Dupont, Karine 328, 329
Dupuis, Nicolas 96
Durand-Dessert, L et M 336, 337
La Durée 333, 335
Dürer, Albrecht 126
Duty-free/duty paid limits 374
The Dying Slave (Michelangelo) 125

E

The Eagle of Suger 129
Easyjet 379
Eaux-de-vie 299
L'Eclaireur 324, 325
Ecole de Médecine 139
Ecole de Paris 131, 227
Ecole Militaire 29, 52, 183, **193**
Ecole Nationale d'Administration 142
Ecole Nationale Supérieure des Beaux-Arts 141
Ecole Nationale Supérieure des Mines 152, 173
L'Ecoute (Miller) 105
Eglise de la Sorbonne 48, **153**
Eglise des Billettes, concerts 346, 347
Les Egouts **192**, 363
Egyptian art 128
Eiffel, Gustave 343
  Le Bon Marché 321
  Eiffel Tower 45, 108, 194–5
Eiffel Shopping 330, 332
Eiffel Tower 11, 14, 43, 52, 53, 110, 183, 362, 363
  architectural features **194–5**
  history 36, 36, 193
  river view 68, 72
  statistics 195
  Street-by-Street map 198
  tourist office 366, 367
Eisenhower, General Dwight 186
Electrical adaptors 374
Ely 12 12/ 280, 281
Elysée-Montmartre 266, 352, 353
Elysée Palace
  see Palais de l'Elysée
Embassies 375
Emergencies
  children 363
  telephone numbers 368, 383
English-language theatre 343
Enlightenment 27, 30, 48
Ennery, Adolphe d', Musée National d'Ennery 202
Entertainment 340–59
Epstein, Jacob 61, 241
Eres 326 327

Ernst, Max 61, 112, 336
Escargots à la Bourguignonne 297
Espace Dalí Montmartre 222, **224**
Espace Pierre Cardin 52
Espace Vit'halles 358, 359
Esplanade des Invalides 50
Estates Council 26, 30
Etex, Antoine 188
L'Etoile 352, 353
Les Etoiles 351, 353
Etruscan art 128–9
Eugénie, Empress 35
Euro 370–71
Euro Disney *see* Disneyland Resort Paris
Eurolines 378
Europcar 383
Ex Cellar France 334, 335
Exchange rates in hotels 277
Existentialism 45, 136, 139, 143
Exports, *objets d'art* 336, 337
Exposition des Arts Décoratifs (1925) 38

F

Fabrics 330, 338
Fainsilber, Adrien 236
Fairgrounds 362
Falconet, Etienne-Maurice 60
Falguière, Alexandre 146
Family Planning Centre 368
Fashion
  20th century 39, 41
  area map 322
  fashion shows 65
  Musée Galliera 39, 57, 203
  Musée de la Mode et du Textile 118, 121
  see also Clothes
Fast food 374
Fat Tire Bike Tours 359, 383
Faubourg St-Antoine 270–71
Fauchon 10, 213, 214, 216, 333, 335
Fautrier, Jean 113
Fauves 57, 61, 110, 112, 127
Fédération Française de Camping-Caravanning 279, 280
Fédération Française du Cyclotourisme 358, 359
Fédération Française du Golf 358, 359
Fédération Unie des Auberges de Jeunesse (FUAJ) 279, 280
Fenestrier 328, 329
Féraud, Louis 324, 325
La Fermette 334, 335
Fernand, Armand Pierre *Home Sweet Home II* 113
Ferries, Channel 378
Festival d'Art Sacré 64
Festival d'Automne à Paris 64, 346, 347
Festival Chopin 346, 347
Festival du Cinema en Plein Air 63
Festival St-Denis 63, 346
Festival Quartier d'Eté 346, 347
Festivals, music 346
Fête du Cinéma 63, 356
Fêtes de Nuit 63
Feydeau de Brou, Denis 142
Feydeau de Brou, Paul-Espirit 142
Fifi Chachnil 328, 329

Filliou, Robert 113
Films *see* Cinema
Finkelsztajn, Sacha 333, 335
Fire services 368, 369
Fitzgerald, Scott 45, 140, 143, 179, 215
Flamboyant Gothic style, St-Séverin 152
Flamel, Nicolas 114
Flea markets 233, 338, 339, 363
La Flèche d'Or 352, 353
Fleury, Rohault de 226
Le Flore en l'Ile 262
Flower market
  see Marché aux Fleurs
Flower shops 331, 332
Flower shows 62, 63
FNAC 321, 340, 341, 366, 367
FNAC Micro-informatique 321
Foch, Marshal Ferdinand 188, 211
  statue 198
  tomb 189
Foie gras 296, 333, 335
Foire Internationale d'Art Contemporain 64
Folies Bergères 343, 344
Folies Clubbing 352, 353
The Follies, Parc de la Villette 236
Fondation Cartier 179
Fondation Le Corbusier 39, 58, **254**, 265
Fontaine Igor Stravinsky (Tinguely and Saint-Phalle) 61, 105, 107
Fontaine des Innocents 106, **108**
Fontaine de Médicis 171, **172**
Fontaine Molière 119, **121**
Fontaine de l'Observatoire 173
Fontaine des Quatre Points Cardinaux 170
Fontaine des Quatre Saisons 28, 187
Food and drink
  the flavours of Paris 296–97
  light meals and snacks 316–19
  markets 338–9
  shops 333–5
  see also Restaurants; Wine
Football 62, 358
Forestier, Gabriel 127
Forney fine arts library 99
The Fortune Teller (Caravaggio) 126
Forum des Halles 104–15, 144, 179
  area map 105
  cinemas 354, 355
  gardens 53
  history 23, 34, 40
  Musée Grevin 216
  Street-by-Street map 106–7
  Street Finder map 13
Forum des Images 106, **109**, 355
Forum Voyages 379
Fountains 35
  Cuvier Fountain 163
  Dragon Fountain 248
  Fontaine des Innocents 106, 108
  Fontaine de Médicis 171, 172
  Fontaine Molière 119, 121
  Fontaine de l'Observatoire 173
  Fontaine des Quatre Points Cardinaux 170

Fountains (cont)
  Fontaine des Quatre Saisons 28, 187
  Fountain of Latona 248
  Fountain of Neptune 249
  Fountain of the Four Bishops 172
  Place Igor Stravinsky 61, 105, 107
  Place St-Michel 150
  Pot de Fer 162
  Trocadéro fountains 199, 200
Fouquet Jewellery Boutique 97
Four Quarters of the World (Carpeaux) 54
Four Seasons George V hotel 276
Fragonard, Jean-Honoré 44, 56, 60, 127, 209
France Appartements 280
France Galop 358, 359
France-Lodge 278, 279, 280
France Miniature 361
France Télécom 372
France Tourisme 367
Francesca, Piero della 126
Franchini, Gianfranco 110
Franco-Prussian War 35, 36, 226
François I, King 172
  Collège de France 153
  history 19, 24, 25
  and Leonardo da Vinci 127
  Musée du Louvre 122, 124
François II, King 19
Francs 371
Franks 17, 78
Frédéric Malle 330, 332
Frémiet, Emmanuelle 118, 121
French Revolution *see* Revolution
French Tennis Open 62, 63
Frey, Pierre 330, 332
Frigidarium, Gallo-Roman 154, 157
Frisoni, Bruno 328, 329
La Fromagerie d'Auteuil 334, 335
Froment-Leroyer 326, 327
Fruit markets 338–9
Funiculaire, Montmartre 223, 363
Furla 328, 329
Furniture
  antiques 336–7
  medieval 22
  modern 336, 337
  Musée du Louvre 129
  museums 57
  Renaissance 25
  Revolutionary 31
  17th century 26
Futurism 112

G

Gabin, Jean 260
Gabriel, Jacques-Ange 45, 131, 193
Gabrielle (Renoir) 59
Gachet, Dr Paul 145, 147
Gaëlle Barré 326, 327
Gaiéte Montparnasse 344
Gainsborough, Thomas 126
  tomb 181
Galerie 1900–2000 336, 337
Galerie des Bijoux 130
Galerie Documents 336
Galerie Emmanuel Perrotin 336, 337

Galerie Jeanne Bucher 336, 337
Galerie du Jour Agnès B 336, 337
Galerie Lelong 336, 337
Galerie Marian Goodman **109**
Galerie Nationale du Jeu de Paume 95, **131**, 146
Galerie Noemi 330, 332
Galerie Sentou 336, 337
Galerie Templon 337
Galerie Vivienne 216
Galeries Lafayette 37, 321
Galeries Nationales du Grand Palais 208
Galignani 331, 332
Gallé, Emile 130
Galleries
  see Art galleries; Museums
Galliera, Duchesse Maria de Ferrari 203
Galliera, Palais
  see Musée Galliera
Gallo-Roman remains 20–22
  Arènes de Lutèce 165
  Crypte Archéologique 81
  Musée de Cluny 154, 157
  Musée de Notre-Dame de Paris 80
Ganachaud 333, 335
Gance, Abel 38
Gardens
  see Parks and Gardens; Squares
Gare d'Austerlitz 379, 381, 388
Gare de l'Est 379, 381, 388
Gare de Lyon 276, 378–9, 381, 388
  tourist office 367
  Le Train Bleu 295
Gare Montparnasse 380, 388
Gare du Nord 276, 379, 381, 388
Gare Routière 381
Gare St-Lazare 379, 388
Garnier, Charles
  Café de la Paix 215
  Opéra de Paris Garnier 35, 98, 217
The Gates of Hell (Rodin) 54, 144
Gau, Franz Christian 49, 187
Gauguin, Paul 56, 61, 147
  Breton Peasant Women 147
Gaultier, Jean-Paul 213, 325, 326
Gaumont Marignan 356
Gautier, Théophile 87
Gay and lesbian clubs 352
Gay Pride 63
La Gazette 26
Gechter, *The Battle of Austerlitz* 211
Gehry, Frank 198, 246
Geneviève, Sainte 21, 22, 153, 158
  statue 171
Génie du Sommeil Eternel (Daillion) 181
La Géode **237**, 354
George VI, King of England 186
Géricault, Théodore 61, 222
  The Raft of the Medusa 124, 240
  tomb 240
Gervase, St 99
Giacometti, Alberto 112, 113, 176, 336
  Standing Woman II 61
Gibert Joseph 331, 332

Le Gibus 353
Gide, André 140, 169
Gift shops 330–31, 332
Gill, André 225
Gilles (Watteau) 126
La Gioconda see Mona Lisa
Giotto 126
Girardon, François 60, 85, 153, 234
Girault, Charles 206
Givenchy 57, 324, 325
Giverny, rail services 388
Glasgow School 146
Glassware 330
    Musée du Cristal de Baccarat 203
Global Change 370
Gloriette de Buffon, Jardin des Plantes 52, 53
Glory of Paradise (La Fosse) 189
Goat's cheese 296, 297
Gobelins tapestries
    see La Manufacture des Gobelins
Godard, Jean-Luc 44, 200, 354
Golden Rose of Basel 154, 157
Goldenberg, Jo 95
Golf 357
Golf de Chevry 358, 359
Golf de St-Quentin en Yvelines 358, 359
Golf de Villennes 358, 359
Golf de Villeray 358, 359
Goncourt Prize 219
González, Julio 112
Good Morning Paris 279, 280
Gothic Revival 49
Goujon, Jean 106, 123
Gounod, Charles, monument 258
Goutal, Annick 330, 332
Goya y Lucientes, Francisco José de 126
Goyard 328, 329
Grace, Princess of Monaco 203
Grand Amphithéâtre de la Sorbonne 346, 347
Grand Café 215
Grand Camée 219
Le Grand Hôtel Intercontinental 283
Grand Hôtel d'Entragues 171
Grand Louvre *see* Musée du Louvre
Grand Palais **208–9**
    history 36, 37
    river view 68, 69
    Street-by-Street map 206
Grand Rex 349, 350, 354
Le Grand Siècle 26
Grand, Toni 113
Grand Trianon, Versailles 26, 45, **249**
Grand Trianon (cinema) 266
Le Grand Véfour 119, 293
La Grande Arche 40, 133, **255**
Grande Armée 130
La Grande Epicerie 10
Grande Halle de la Villette 236, 350
Grande Mademoiselle 152

Grandjean, Edmond Georges, *Boulevard des Italiens* 34
Grands Boulevards 142, 213, 216, **217**, 355

Grands Eaux Musicales 62, 249
Grands Magasins du Louvre 120
Grands Travaux 40, 255
Grape Harvest (tapestry) 156
Graves wine 298
Great Mosaic of Christ (Merson) 226
Greco, Juliette 136, 143
Greek art 56, 128
Greek Orthodox Church 152
Greenhouses, Cité des Sciences 239
Greuze, Jean-Baptiste 60
Grevi 328, 329
Grévin 11, 58, 218, 363
Gris, Juan 61, 228
Gros, Antoine Jean 60
Grosse, Katharina 113
Groupe Hospitalier Pitié-Salpêtrière 49, 161, **167**
Groupement pour l'Insertion des Personnes Handicapées Physiques (GIHP) 278, 367
Gruyn des Bordes, Charles 87
G7 taxis 341
Gucci 328, 329
Gudea, Prince of Lagash 128
Guénégaud, Hôtel
    see Hôtel Guénégaud
Guénégaud des Brosses, Henri de 103
Guerlain 330, 332
Guided tours 367
Guignol marionette shows 361
Guilbert, Yvette 228
Guillaume, Eugène 146
Guillaume, Paul 57, 131
Guillaumin, Armand 229
Guillotin, Dr 141
Guillotine 31, 131, 141
Guimard, Hector
    Auteuil houses 264, 265
    Castel Béranger 254, 264
    metro stations 37, 146, 228, 266
Guimet, Emile, Musée National des Arts Asiatiques Guimet 203
Guise family 99
Guitry, Sacha 183
Guston, Philip 113
Guyot, G 201
Gymnase-Marie Bell 342, 344
Gyms 358–9

H

Hadrian, Emperor 129
Halle St-Pierre **225**
Les Halles *see* Beaubourg and Les Halles
Hals, Frans 126
Hammam Club 353
Hammurabi, Code of 55, 128
Hanska, Madame 202
Harden, Sylvia von 110
Hardouin-Mansart, Jules 45
    Dôme Church 48–9, 187, 188
    Place Vendôme 132
    Place des Victoires 133
    St-Louis-des-Invalides 186
    St-Roch 121
    Versailles 248–51
Hari, Mata 283
Harry's Bar 215
Harvesting (Pissarro) 58
Hat shops 328, 329

Haussmann, Baron 17, 49, 246
    Bois de Boulogne 255
    Boulevard St-Germain 139
    Les Egouts 190
    Grands Boulevards 34–5, 45, 71, 81, 142, 219, 259
Haussmann, Baron (cont)
    Opéra Quarter 213, 215
    Parc des Buttes-Chaumont 234
    Place Charles de Gaulle 209
Haussmann, Raoul 112
Haute couture 118, 324
Health services 369
Hébertot theatre 342, 344
Hédiard 10, 213, 334, 335
Heine, Heinrich, tomb 227
Héloïse 23
Helplines, children 363
Hemingway, Ernest 38, 45, 136, 138, 140, 143, 176, 179, 215
Hennes 325, 326
Henri I, King 18
Henri II, King 19, 25, 94, 127, 140
Henri III, King 19, 25, 86
Henri IV, King 19, 83, 127
    assassination 25, 81, 99, 102, 106
    Hôpital St-Louis 261
    Place Dauphine 86
    Place Royale 24
    Place des Vosges 25
    Pont Neuf 18, 86
    Square du Vert-Galant 87
    statue 87
    wedding 115
Henri of Navarre *see* Henri IV
Henry V, King of England 246
Henry VI, King of England 23
Herbe, Musée en
    see Musée en Herbe
Hermès 324, 325, 328
Hérouard, Jean 162, 167
Hertz 383
Hervé Gambs 331, 332
Hilton 379
Hippodrome d'Auteuil 358, 359
Hippodrome de Longchamp 358, 359
Hippodrome Maisons Lafitte 358, 359
Hippodrome de St-Cloud 358, 359
Hippodrome de Vincennes 358, 359
Hiring
    bicycles 357, 383
    cars 383
Histoire Naturelle, Muséum National d' *see* Muséum National d'Histoire Naturelle
History of Paris 17–39
Hitler, Adolf 194
Hittorff, Jacques 206
Hoffmann, Josef 146
Holbein, Hans, *Portrait of Erasmus* 126
Holiday Inn 379
Holiday on Ice 62
Holidays, public 65
Homage to Apollinaire (Picasso) 137
Home Sweet Home II (Fernand) 113
Homogenous Infiltration (Beuys) 113

Hôpital Necker 363
Hôpital St-Louis 261
Horodateurs (parking meters) 383
Horse and Pony Show 65
Horse racing 358
Horses of Apollo (Le Lorrain) 102
Horses of St Mark's 130
Hospitals 369
  children's 363
Hostels 279, 280
L'Hôtel 276, 283
Hôtel de l'Abbaye 283
Hôtel Biron 27, 263
Hôtel de Bourgogne 114
Hôtel de Broglie 97
Hôtel Carnavalet 27, 29, 92, **96**
Hôtel Chernizot 263
Hôtel de Cluny 25, 156
Hôtel de Condé 140
Hôtel de Coulanges 95
Hôtel de Crillon 276, 282
Hôtel Dieu 79, **81**
Hôtel Donon 94
Hôtel Four Seasons George V 276, 277
Hôtel des Grands Hommes 278
Hôtel Guénégaud 57, **103**
Hôtel des Invalides 27, 98, 99, 184–5, **187**
  see also Jardin des Invalides
Hôtel Jassaud 263
Hôtel du Jeu de Paume 283
Hôtel Lambert 27, 263
Hôtel de Lamoignon 92, **94**
Hôtel de Lauzun **87**, 263
Hôtel Libéral Bruand 93, **98**
Hôtel Matignon 187
Hôtel Meurice 277
Hôtel Mezzara 254
Hôtel des Monnaies 70, **141**
Hôtel du Nord 261
Hôtel le Peletier de St-Fargeau 93, **96**, 97
Hôtel Prince de Galles Sheraton 279
Hôtel Relais Christine 277
Hôtel Richelieu 263
Hôtel de la Rivière 96
Hôtel de Rohan **102**, 103
Hôtel Rohan-Guéménée 95
Hôtel Rolland 262, 263
Hôtel Salé 100
Hôtel de Salm 143
Hôtel de Sens 99
Hôtel de Soubise 40, 58, 94, 102, **103**
Hôtel de Sully 93, **95**
Hôtel d'Uzès 96
Hôtel des Ventes 216
Hôtel de Ville 25, **102**, 258
Hôtel de la Villette 142
Hôtel de Wendel 97
Hotels 276–91
  airport 379
  chain hotels 279, 280
  children in 278, 360
  deposits 281
  directory 280
  disabled travellers 278, 367
  facilities 277
  grading 277
  hidden extras 277
  how to book 281
  Paris's Best 282–3

Hotels (cont)
  prices 276–7
  restaurants 277
  special breaks 278
  what to expect 278
  where to look 276
Hôtels (mansions) 27, 92
Hôtels de charme 276, 282
Houdon, Jean-Antoine 60, 127, 159
Household goods shops 330–31, 332
HSBC bank 370
Hugo, Victor 33, 35, 47, 115, 119, 165, 187, 217, 262, 342
  house in Rue du Dragon 139
  Maison de Victor Hugo 93, 95
  marble bust of 95
  Place des Vosges 94
  tomb 159
  waxworks 108
Huguenots 115
Huîtrerie Garnier 334, 335
Hulten, Pontus 113
Hundred Years' War 24
La Hune 331, 332
Hunting Museum *see* Musée de la Chasse et de la Nature
Hyante and Climente (Toussaint Dubreuil) 25

I

Ice cream 317
Ile de la Cité 77–89
  area map 77
  Gallo-Roman remains 20, 21
  history 17, 18
  medieval remains 22, 165
  river view 70, 71
  Street-by-Street map 78–9
  Street Finder maps 12, 13
Ile de France 40, 72
Ile St-Louis 77–9, 139
  river view 71
  walks 257, 262–3
Images d'Ailleurs 356
Impression: Sunrise (Monet) 58, 61
Impressionists 36, 44, 56, 58–9, 60, 61, 208
  Galerie National du Jeu de Paume 131
  Musée d'Orsay 146, 147
Information offices 340, 366, 367
Ingres, Jean-Auguste-Dominique 60, 127, 146, 208
Institut Catholique de Paris 173
Institut de France 141, 254
Institut du Monde Arabe 164–5
Institut Pasteur 45, **247**
Insurance 369
International Herald Tribune 331
International Style 265
Invalides, Hôtel des
  see Hôtel des Invalides
Invalides gardens
  see Jardins des Invalides
Invalides and Eiffel Tower Quarter 182–195
  area map 183
  history 33
  river trip 69
  Street-by-Street map 184–5
  Street Finder maps 9–10, 11
IRCAM 45, 106
  concerts 346, 347

Isabelle Marant 325, 326
ISIC card 374
Islam 164–5, 166–7, 375

J

Jacadi 326, 327
Jacob, Nina 324, 325
Jacob Wrestling with the Angel (Delacroix) 137, 172
Jacobin Club 31
Jacquemart-André, Musée
  see Musée Jacquemart-André
Janniot, A 235
Japanese restaurants 293
Jardin d'Acclimatation 361
Jardin des Halles 361
Jardin des Plantes Quarter 11, 160–67
  area map 161
  botanical gardens 167
  markets 363
  Paris's Best 51, 52, 53
  Street-by-Street map 162–3
  Street Finder map 17–18
Jardin des Tuileries 11, 65, 117, **130**, 132–3
  Paris's Best Gardens, Parks and Squares 50
  river view 70
  Street-by-Street map 118
Jardin du Carrousel 122
Jardin du Luxembourg 11, 43, 63, 132, 149, **172**
  Fontaine de l'Observatoire 173
  model boats 169, 362, 363
  Paris's Best 50–3
  Pot de Fer fountain 162
  Street-by-Street map 170
Jardin du Palais Royal 52, 119, **121**, 132
Jardins des Champs-Elysées 52, **207**
Jardins des Invalides 52, **185**
Jardins du Trocadéro 53, 198, 199, **201**
La Java 343, 344, 353
Jay Ahr 325, 326
Jazz 349–50
Jazz-Club Lionel Hampton 350
Jean II the Good, King 19
Jean XXIII, Square du
  see Square du Jean XXIII
Jean de Beauvais 358, 359
Jean Sans Peur, Tour de
  see Tour de Jean Sans Peur
Jena, Battle of (1806) 216
Jérôme, King of Westphalia, tomb 189
Jesuits (Society of Jesus) 25, 99, 225
Jet-Set 328, 329
Jeu de Paume *see* Galerie National du Jeu de Paume
Jeux Descartes 331, 332
Jewellery 24
  Musée de Cluny 157
  shops 328, 329
Jews 91
  delicatessens 333
  history 23
  Mémorial de la Shoah 99
  Musée d'Art et de l'Histoire du Judaïsme 103
  Rue des Rosiers 95
  synagogues 375
Joan of Arc 23
  statues 118, 121, 225, 259

John, St 156
John XXII, Pope 154
John XXIII, Pope 80
John Casimir, King of Poland, tomb 136, 138
John-Paul II, Pope 41
Jonak 328, 329
Jordaens, Jacob 126
Josephine, Empress 32, 33, 211
Château de Malmaison 255
Jourdan, Charles 328, 329
Journée du Patrimoine 64
Jouve, P. 201
Joyce, James 45, 140
Judah, Kings of 155
Le Jules Verne 195
Julian the Hospitaller, St 152
Julien, Emperor 21
Julius II, Pope 125
Jumping International de Paris 62
Junot, Avenue see Avenue Junot

K

Kahnweiler, D H 336
Kandinsky, Vassily
With the Black Arc 112
Kardec, Allan, tomb 240
Kenzo 133, 322, 324, 325, 326, 327
Kéroualle, Louise de 142
Keur Samba 352, 353
Kibélé 350
Kid Services 360
Kiffer, Charles 233
Kings 18–19
Kiosque de l'Empereur 255
Kiosque Théâtre 347, 367
Kir 299
The Kiss (Brancusi) 180
The Kiss (Picasso) 100
The Kiss (Rodin) 187
Knights Hospitallers of St John 103
Knights Templar 103
Kong 11
Kookai 325, 326
Kusama, Yayoï 113

L

La Brosse, Guy de 162, 167
LA City 325, 326
La Fosse, Charles de, Glory of Paradise 189
La Roche, Raoul 59, 254
La Tour, Georges de 127
La Vrillière, Louis de 132–3
Labienus 20
The Lacemaker (Vermeer) 124
Lacroix, Christian 324, 325, 328
Lady with the Unicorn (tapestries) 154, 156, 157
Lafayette, Marquis de 30
Lagerfeld, Karl 324, 325, 326
Laitié 208
Lalique, René 146, 330, 332
Laloux, Victor 144
Lamb 297
Lambert, Yvon 336, 337
Lamoignon, Hôtel de
see Hôtel de Lamoignon
Lamorisse, Albert 199
Landowski, Paul 189
Langlois, Henri 354
Lanvin, Jeanne 54, 130, 326, 327
Laprade, Albert 235
Lardat, R 199
Large Window (Cardenas) 164
Larizzi, Sidonie 328, 329

Lasserre 206
Last Supper (Champaigne) 60
Late-night transport 341
Latin Quarter 148–59
area map 149
cinemas 354
Street-by-Street map 150–51
Street Finder maps 12, 13, 17
student riots 40, 41
Latina cinema 356
Laurens, Henri, tomb 181
Lauzun, Duc de 87
Lavier, Bertrand 113
Lavinia 334, 335
LD Lines 378
Le Bon Marché 328, 329
Le Brun, Charles 60
Hôtel Carnavalet ceilings 27, 96
Hôtel de Lauzun ceilings 87
"May" Paintings 84
tapestries 167
Versailles 248, 251–3
Le Fin Gourmet 263
Le Havre 380
Le Lorrain, Robert, Horses of Apollo 102
Le Mans car race 358
Le Moiturier, Antoine 127
Le Nôtre, André
Avenue des Champs-Elysées 207
Jardin des Tuileries 52, 118, 130
Jardins des Champs-Elysées 52
tomb 121
Versailles 26, 132, 248, 249
Le Rhinocéros (Veilhan) 113
Le Saint Jean 266
Le Sueur, Eustache 60
Le Vau, Louis 45
Château de Vincennes 246
Hôtel de Lauzun 87
Institut de France 141
Musée du Louvre 123
Versailles 248, 250, 251
Leather shops 328, 329
Leclerc, General 178
Ledoux, Claude Nicolas 96, 258, 260
Lefèbvre, H 225
Left Bank 67, 68
antique dealers 336
cafés 142, 143
cinemas 354
hotels 276
restaurants 292
see also St-Germain-des-Prés
Legentil, Alexandre 224
Léger, Fernand 57, 61, 112, 247
Légion d'Honneur, Musée
Nationale de la see Musée
Nationale de la Légion
d'Honneur
Legion of Honour 32
Legrand 10, 334, 335
Leiris, Louise 336, 337
Lemercier, Jacques 48, 121, 153
Lemot 130
Lempicka, Lolita 324, 325
Lenin, Vladimir Ilyich 45, 143, 179
Lenôtre 333, 335
Leonardo da Vinci 56, 126, 127, 243
Mona Lisa 24, 124, 125, 127
Self-portrait 127
Leroux, Paul 215
Lesbian clubs 352
Lescot building 106
Lesseps, Ferdinand de 36

Levignes-Bastille 336, 337
Libéral Bruand, Hôtel
see Hôtel Libéral Bruand
Liberty Flame 69
Liberty Leading the People
(Delacroix) 61
Libraries
Bibliothèque Nationale 219
Bibliothèque Nationale de France (Tolbiac) 246
Forney fine arts library 99
Hôtel de Lamoignon 94
Hôtel de Sens 99
Institut Pasteur 247
Lido 343, 344
Lifestyle stores 326, 327
Limoges enamels 157
Limonaire brothers 114
Lingerie shops 328
Listings magazines 340, 366–7
Liszt, Franz 44
Little Athens 150
"Little Russia" 230
Loft Design By (store) 326, 327
Le Loir dans la Théière 293
Loire wines 298, 299
Lollipops 328, 329
Lombard moneylenders 108
Longchamp 328, 329
Longchamp, Hippodrome de 358, 359
Loos, Adolf 227
Lost property 369
Lothaire, King 18
Louis I the Debonair, King 18
Louis II the Stammerer, King 18
Louis III, King 18
Louis IV the Foreigner, King 18
Louis V, King 18
Louis VI the Fat, King 18, 224
Louis VII, King 18
Louis VIII, King 19
Louis IX, King (St Louis) 19, 23, 153
Sainte-Chapelle 48, 88
relics 89
statues 87, 225
Louis X, King 19
Louis XI the Spider, King 19, 24, 152
Louis XII, King 19
Louis XIII, King 19, 26, 44, 48, 162
marriage 26
Place Dauphine 86
St-Paul–St-Louis 99
statue 85
Louis XIV, King 17, 19, 26–7, 58, 87, 240
Dôme Church 185, 188
Ecole Nationale Supérieure des Mines 173
Gobelins 167
Hôtel des Invalides 184, 187
Notre-Dame 83
Observatoire de Paris 179
Palais Royal 120
Place des Victoires 117, 133
St-Roch 121
Salpêtrière hospital 167
statues 27, 84, 93, 117, 133, 250
Val-de-Grâce 48, 173
Versailles 44, 248–53
Louis XV, King 19, 27
Bois de Vincennes 246
crown jewels 129

Louis XV, King (cont)
  Ecole Militaire 191
  Hôtel de Crillon 282
  Mint 141
  Panthéon 158
  statues 131
  Versailles 28, 44, 250, 251
Louis XVI, King 19
  commemorative mass for 65
  execution 131, 251
  Revolution 30, 31, 103, 191
  Versailles 44, 251, 252
Louis XVIII, King 19, 155
  Jardin du Luxembourg 170
  Versailles 249
Louis-Philippe, King 18, 19, 132,
    170
  Arc de Triomphe 210
  Napoleon's tomb 188, 189
  Palais Royal 120
  Versailles 250, 251
Louboutin, Christian 328, 329
Louvre, Musée du
  see Musée du Louvre
Louvre des Antiquaires 119, **120**,
    336, 337
Louvre Palace 18, 23, 24, 25, 27,
    33, 92, 141, 245
Louvre-Rivoli area, restaurants
    293
Loyola, Ignatius de 25, 223
Lucenaire 356
Ludot, Didier 326, 327
Lumicristal 323, 330, 332
Lumière brothers 37, 213, 215
Lutetia (Lutèce) 20, 21, 165, 81,
    166
Lutétia hotel 283
Luxembourg Gardens
  see Jardin du Luxembourg
Luxembourg Palace
  see Palais du Luxembourg
Luxembourg Quarter 168–73
  area map 169
  Street-by-Street map 170–71
  Street Finder maps 12, 16
Lycée Henri IV 149
Lycée Louis le Grand 149

M

Mac Douglas 325, 326
Mackintosh, Charles Rennie 144,
    146
La Madeleine 33, 46, 49, 214, 216
  concerts 346, 347
La Madeleine, Place de
  see Place de la Madeleine
Madeleine theatre 342, 344
Magazines
  listings 340, 366–7
  shops 331, 332
Maillol, Aristide 50, 52, 187,
    336
Maintenon, Madame de 27, 249
Maison des Arts de Créteil 348
Maison de Balzac 201
La Maison du Cantal 387
La Maison du Chocolat 333, 335
La Maison du Miel 331, 332
Maison Internationale de la
  Jeunesse et des Etudiants 279,
    280
La Maison de Millésimes 334, 335
Maison de la Poésie 109
Maison Quatrehomme 334, 335
Maison de Radio-France 68, 200,
    265, 345, 347

Maison Rouc Libre 357, 382, 383
Maison de la Truffe 333, 335
La Maison de l'UCRIF 280
Maison de Victor Hugo 93, **95**
Maison de la Villette 237
Maje 324, 325
Majestic Bastille cinema 356
Malatesta, Sigismondo 126
Mallet-Stevens, Robert 265
Malmaison, Château de
  see Château de Malmaison
Malraux, André 40, 103, 120, 159
Mamynoo 360
Man with a Guitar (Braque) 111
Manet, Edouard 35, 56, 58,
    146, 147
  Le Déjeuner sur l'Herbe 61,
    144, 146
  Olympia 147
Mansard roofs 26
Mansart, François
  Banque de France 132
  Hôtel Guénégaud 103
  Val-de-Grâce 48, 173
Mansart, Jules Hardouin
  see Hardouin-Mansart, Jules
Mantegna, Andrea 56, 209
La Manufacture des Gobelins 24,
    167
Maps
  bus routes 387
  metro 384, see back endpaper
  Street finder 390–423
The Marais 40, 86, 90–103, 183
  area map 91
  art galleries 336
  Street-by-Street map 92–3
  Street Finder map 13-14
Marais, Jean 121
Marant, Isabelle 11
Marat, Jean-Paul 31, 81
Marceau, General 211
Marché d'Aligre 235, 338
Marché Enfant Rouges 338
Marché aux Fleurs 79, **81**,
    338, 363
Marché aux Fleurs Madeleine 338
Marché aux Fleurs Ternes 338
Marché aux Oiseaux 79, 81
Marché de la Porte de Vanves
    322, 339
Marché Président-Wilson 339
Marché aux Puces de Montreuil
    339
Marché aux Puces de St-Ouen,
    233, 339, 363
Marché Raspail 339
Marché Rue Cler 338
Marché Rue Lepic 339
Marché Rue de Levis 339
Marché Rue Montorgueil 339
Marché Rue Mouffetard 339
Marché Rue Poncelet 339
Marché Rue de Seine et Rue de
    Buci 339
Marché St-Germain 137, 339
Marché St-Pierre 338
Marché aux Timbres 338
Marden, Brice 113
Margaux wine 298
Margiela, Martin 324, 325
Mariage Frères 292, 293, 331
Marie-Antoinette, Queen 129
  Bagatelle 255
  execution 31, 131, 251
  In Mourning (Kucharski) 96

Marie-Antoinette, Queen (cont)
  in the Revolution 81, 103, 253
  Versailles 249, 251
Marie-Louise, Empress 32, 209
Marie de Médicis 26, 52, 162, 172
Marie-Thérèse, Queen 251
Marine, Musée de la
  see Musée de la Marine
Marionnette shows 343, 361
Markets 338–9
  Beauveau St-Antoine 233
  for children 363
  Paris's Best 322–3
  Rue Cler 190, 338
  Rue Lepic 229, 339
  Rue Mouffetard 161, 162, 166,
    339
  see also Marché
Marly Horses (Coustou) 123, 125,
    127
Marmottan, Paul,
  Musée Marmottan 254
Marne, Battle of the 38
Marne-la-Vallée 41, **242**
Marochetti, Charles, *Mary
  Magdalene Ascending to
  Heaven* 216
La Marseillaise
  (Arc de Triomphe reliefs)
    146
La Marseillaise
  (national anthem) 30, 31
Marsy, Balthazar, Fountain of
  Latona 248
Martin, Etienne 164
Martin, Raymond 198
Martyr Juif Inconnu, Mémorial
  du see Mémorial du Martyr
  Juif Inconnu
*Mary Magdalene Ascending to
  Heaven* (Marochetti) 216
Mastercard 370
Matif (futures market) 219
Matignon, Hôtel
  see Hôtel Matignon
Matisse, Henri 36, 57, 61, 110,
    112, 113, 127, 131, 167, 176
  Sorrow of the King 111
Maubert-Mutualité market square
    139
Mauboussin 328, 329
Maupassant, Guy de
  monument 258
  tomb 180
Max Linder Panorama 354
MaxMara 324, 325
"May" Paintings (Le Brun) 84
Mazarin, Cardinal 26, 219
Médard, St 166
Médéric, St 108
Medical treatment 369
Medieval Paris 22–23, 48, 56
Méliès, Georges 200
Mémorial de la Shoah
    99
Ménagerie **164**, 361
Men's clothes 326
Mercié, Marie 328, 329
La Mère Catherine 222, 224
Merovingian dynasty 18
Merson, Luc-Olivier 47
  Great Mosaic of Christ 226
Mesopotamian art 128
Metal Pointu's 328, 329
Metro 36
  Art Nouveau stations 37, 146,
    228, 266, 384

Metro (cont)
  late-night travel 341
  making a journey on 385
  maps 384, back endpaper
  safety 368
  tickets 382, 384, 385
Meurice hotel 276
Michel theatre 342, 344
Michelangelo 127
  The Dying Slave 125
Mickey Mouse 233, 243
Mickiewicz, Adam, Musée **87**,
  262
Mickiewicz, Ladislas 87
Mignard, Pierre 173
Mikimoto 328, 329
Milinkov, L, *L'Opéra de Paris*
  223
Military Academy
  see Ecole Militaire
Military Hospital *see* Musée du
  Service de Santé des Armées
  173
Miller, Henri de, *L'Ecoute* 105
Millet, Jean-François 56
Mineral water 299
Minéralogie, Musée de
  see Musée de Minéralogie
Minéraux de l'Université,
  Collection des *see* Collection
  des Minéraux de l'Université
Mines, School of *see* Ecole
  Nationale Supérieure des Mines
Minimalist painting 113
Ministry of Culture 118, 120,
  360
Ministry of Defence 139
Mint *see* Hôtel des Monnaies
Minucchio da Siena 154
Mirabeau, Honoré 159
Miró, Joan 61, 110, 112, 178, 193,
  255, 336
  postage stamps 179
Miss Pogany (Brancusi) 112
Mistinguett 67
Mitterrand, François 40, 133, 139,
  255
Mix Club 352, 353
MK2 Beaubourg cinema 356
MK2 Quai de Seine/Quai de la
  Loire cinemas 354, 356
Mobile on Two Planes (Calder)
  113
Mobilis card 382
Model boats 169, 362, 363
Modernism 265, 336
Modigliani, Amedeo 44, 57, 61,
  131, 176, 178, 181, 228, 247
  Portrait of a Woman 223
Molière, Jean-Baptiste 45, 81,
  114, 120, 142, 223, 264
  Fontaine Molière 119, 121
  tomb 241
Mona Lisa (Leonardo da Vinci)
  24, 124, 125, 127
Monastier, Jacques 109
Monceau Fleurs 331, 332
Le Monde 211
Monde Arabe, Institut du
  see Institut du Monde Arabe
Mondrian, Piet 61
Monep (traded options market)
  219
Monet, Claude 36, 44, 56, 58–9,
  60, 103, 146, 147
  La Barque 254
  Blue Water Lilies 147

Monet, Claude (cont)
  Impression: Sunrise 58, 61
  Musée Marmottan 254
  Water lily series 131
Money
  banking 370
  credit cards 370
Money (cont)
  currency 371
  Revolutionary 31
  safety 368–9
  travellers' cheques 370
Monnaie, Musée de la
  see Musée de la Monnaie
Monory, Jacques 238
Monroe, Marilyn 109, 201
Montagne Sainte-Geneviève 152
Montagnier, Professor Luc 45,
  247
Montaigne, Avenue 209
Montand, Yves 44
  tomb 240
Montesquieu 28
Montfaucon gallows 261
Montgolfier brothers 29
Montmartre 110, 145, 219–29
  area map 221
  cafés 36
  Street-by-Street map 222–23
  Street Finder maps 2, 6, 7
  street-painting 363
  walks 257, 266–7
Montmartre, Cimetière de
  see Cimetière de Montmartre
Montmartre, Musée de
  see Musée de Montmartre
Montparnasse 174–81
  area map 175
  cafés 143, 175, 292–3
  cinemas 354
  musée de 179
  Street-by-Street map 176–7
  Street Finder map 15–16
Montparnasse theatre 342, 344
Montparnasse Tower 41, 363
Montreuil, Pierre de 45, 48
Montrouge 179
Montsouris 179
Montsouris, Parc
  see Parc Montsouris
Monuments
  Charles Baudelaire Cenotaph
    180
  Colonne de Juillet 98
  Delacroix 170
  Mémorial de la
    Shoah 99
  Mémorial des Martyrs et de la
    Déportation 80
  Monument aux Morts 240
  Parc Monceau 258
  practical information 366
  to Oscar Wilde 241
  see also Statues
Monuments Français, Musée des
  see Musée des Monuments
    Français
Moore, Henry, *Reclining Figure*
  193
Moreau, Gustave
  Angel Traveller 233
  Musée Gustave Moreau 56,
    233
Morellet, François 113
Morgan 325, 326
Morrison, Jim, tomb 240, 241
Moser, Koloman 146

Mosquée de Paris 47, 49, **166–7**,
  375
Motels 279
Moucha, Alphonse 97
Moules marinières 296
Moulin, Hyppolyte 146
Moulin, Jean 159
Moulin de la Galette 229, 267
Moulin du Radet 229, 267
Moulin de la Vierge 333, 335
Moulin Rouge 37, **228**, 267, 343,
  344
Le Mouton à Cinq Pattes 326,
  327
Movies *see* Cinema
Mugler, Thierry 65, 133
Murat, Caroline 209
Murat, Joachim 209
Le Musée (shop) 330, 332
Musée des Années 30 255
Musée Antoine Bourdelle 57,
  178
Musée de l'Armée 58, 184, **186**
Musée Arménien 202
Musée d'Art et d'Histoire du
  Judaïsme 58, 103
Musée d'Art Moderne de la Ville
  de Paris **203**, 336
Musée des Arts Décoratifs 54, 57,
  118, 130
Musée des Arts et Metiers 103
Musée des Beaux-Arts de la Ville
  de Paris 208
Musée Carnavalet 94, 214
  Empire style 33
  Enlightenment Paris 29
  floorplan 96–7
  Paris's Best 55, 57, 58
  shop 330
  statue of Louis XIV 27
  Street-by-Street map 93
Musée Cernuschi 58, **233**
Musée de la Chasse et de la
  Nature 103
Musée Cognacq-Jay 56, 57, 92, **94**,
  115
Musée de la Contrefaçon 57, 202
Musée du Cristal de Baccarat 203
Musée Dapper 58, **202**
Musée Delacroix 56, 137, **138**
Musée Galliera 39, 57, **203**
Musée Edith Piaf 234
Musée Guimet 54
Musée Gustave Moreau 56, **233**
tMorellet, François 113
Musée en Herbe **225**, 361
Musée de l'Histoire de France
  58, **93**
Musée de l'Holographie 106,
  109
Musée de l'Homme 59, 198,
  201
Musée Jacquemart-André 56, 57,
  209
Musée du Louvre 10, 14, 60, 117,
  122–9
  architectural features 122–3
  Arts from Africa, Asia, Oceania
    and the Americas 124
  concerts 346, 347
  European paintings 126–7
  European sculpture 127
  floorplan 124–5
  Musée des Arts de la Mode
    121
  objets d'art 129
  Oriental, Egyptian, Greek,

Musée du Louvre (cont)
Etruscan and Roman
antiquities 128–9
Paris's Best 55, 56, 57
Pyramid 41, 43, 122, 123, 129
river view 70
shop 330, 336
Street-by-Street map 119
Visitors' Checklist 123
Musée Maillol 57, **187**
Musée de la Marine 59, 198, **201**, 360
Musée Marmottan-Claude Monet 56, 57, **254**
Musée de Minéralogie 173
Musée de la Mode et du Textile 10, 118, **121**
Musée de Montmartre 58, 223, **224**, 267
Musée de la Monnaie de Paris 57, **141**
Musée du Montparnasse 179
Musée National d'Art Moderne 57, 110
Musée National des Arts Asiatiques Guimet 58, **203**
Musée National d'Histoire Naturelle 59, **167**
Musée Nationale de la Légion d'Honneur 143
Musée National du Moyen Age 139, **154–7**
carvings 156
floorplan 154–5
Gallo-Roman ruins 21, 157
Lady with the Unicorn tapestries 157
metalwork 157
Paris's Best 55, 56
sculpture 157
stained glass 149, 156
Street-by-Street map 150
tapestries 154, 156, 157
Visitors' Checklist 155
Musée Nissim de Camondo 57, **232**, 259
Musée de Notre-Dame de Paris 79, **80**
Musée de l'Opéra 215, **218**
Musée de l'Orangerie 56, 57, 70, **131**
Musée de l'Ordre de la Libération 184, **186**
Musée d'Orsay 37, 40, 43, 126, 131, **144–7**, 366
Art Nouveau 146
concerts 346, 347
films 355
floorplan 144–5
Impressionism 147
Naturalism and Symbolism 147
Neo-Impressionism 147
painting before 1870 146
Paris's Best 54, 56, 57
river view 70
sculpture 146
shop 330, 336
Visitors' Checklist 145
Musée Picasso 10, 55, 57, 93, **100–101**
Musées des Plans-Reliefs 58, 184, **186**
Musée de la Poste 57, **179**
Musée de la Prefecture de Police 152
Musée de la Publicité 130

Musée du Quai Branly 58, **192–3**
Musée de Radio-France 202
Musée Rodin 10, 52, 54, 56, 184, 185, **187**
Musée de la Sculpture en Plein Air 164
Musée du Service de Santé des Armées 173
Musée du Vin 201
Musée Zadkine 57, **178**
Museums and galleries
cafés 316
children in 360
Paris's Best 54–9
practical information 366
shops 330, 332, 336
Music
churches 346, 347
concerts 345–7
contemporary 346
early music 346–7
festivals 346, 347
jazz 349–50
musicians 44–5
opera 345
rock and pop 349, 350
world music 349–350
Muslims 164–5, 166–7, 375
Musset, Alfred de 187
monument 258

N

Napoleon Bonaparte, Emperor 17, 19, 44, 83, 119
Abel Gance's film 38
Arc de Triomphe 18, 210–11
Arc de Triomphe du Carrousel 122, 130
Avenue des Champs-Elysées 209
Banque de France 132
Château de Malmaison 255
Château de Vincennes 246
Cimetière du Montparnasse 180–81
Cimetière du Père Lachaise 240
crown jewels 129
Ecole Militaire 191
Jardin des Tuileries 133
Legion of Honour 143
La Madeleine 49
Musée de l'Armée 186
Napoleonic Paris 32–33
Notre-Dame 84
Palais de la Bourse 219
Palais de Chaillot 198
Palais de Justice 86
Panthéon 158
Pont d'Iéna 199
at Le Procope 140
Rue de Rivoli 130
La Sorbonne 153
statues 132, 185
Temple of Glory 216
tomb 46, 121, 184, 185, 188
Versailles 252
Napoleon III, 19, 132, 189, 190
Bois de Boulogne 255
Bois de Vincennes 246
Drouot 218
Le Grand Hôtel 283
Jeu de Paume 131
parks and squares 52–3
Legion of Honour 143
Opéra de Paris Garnier 217
Sebastopol bell 247
transformation of Paris 34–5

National Natural History Institute
see Musée National d'Histoire Naturelle
Nazis 39, 80
Nefertiti, Queen of Egypt 128
Neo-Classicism 49, 60
Neo-Impressionism 59, 147
Nerval, Gérard de 229
Netscher, Caspar, *Madame de Maintenon* 27
New Morning 349, 350
New Realists 113
New Wave cinema 44, 200, 354
Newspapers 375
shops 331, 332
Nicholas, St 156
Nicolas (wine stores) 334, 335
Night buses 341, 387
Nightclubs 351–3
Nijinsky, Vaslav 218, 229, 348
tomb 229
Nissim de Camondo, Musée
see Musée Nissim de Camondo
Noctilien 387
Norfolkline 378
Normandy hotel 118
Normans 22
North African restaurants 292, 293, 294
Notre-Dame 23, 43, 80, **82–5**, 114, 157, 200
address 375
architectural features 82–3
for children 363
concerts 346, 347
floorplan 84–5
Paris's Best 47, 48
river view 71, 72
stained glass 84–5
Street-by-Street map 78, 79
timeline 83
Visitors' Checklist 83
walks 262
see also Musée de Notre-Dame de Paris
Notre-Dame de l'Assomption 265
Notre-Dame d'Auteuil 264
Notre-Dame des Blancs Manteaux 102
concerts 346, 347
Notre-Dame du Travail 247
Nouveau Casino 353
Nouveau Drouot 216
Nouvelles Frontières 379
Novotel 280, 379
Novotel Tour Eiffel 359
Nuit Blanche 64
Nureyev, Rudolf 45

O

The Oath of the Horatii (David) 60
Obelisks 117, 131, 264
Objets d'art 57, 336, 337
Observatoire de Paris 179
Oceanian art 58, 124, 235
Octagonal Lake, Jardin du Luxembourg 171
Odéon 135
Odéon Théâtre de l'Europe 45, **140**, 342, 344
Odo, Count of Paris 18
Offenbach, Jacques, tomb 229
The Offering of the Heart (tapestry) 156

Office du Tourisme et des
  Congrès de Paris 278, 280, 281,
  340, 341, 367
L'Officiel des Spectacles 331, 360,
  366–7
Oil lamps, Roman 21
Olympia 349, 350
Olympia (Manet) 147
Olympic Games (1924) 38
Open-air theatre 343
Opera 345
  baroque 346
  Musée de l'Opéra 215, 218
Opéra 212–19
  area map 213
  Street-by-Street map 214–15
  Street Finder map 5-6
Opéra, Avenue de l'
  see Avenue de l'Opéra
L'Opéra, Versailles 250, 251
Opéra Comique 345, 347
L'Opéra de Paris (Milinkov) 223
Opéra National de Paris Bastille
  40, 41, **98**, 217, 345, 347
Opéra National de Paris Garnier
  35, 44, 98, 213, 215, **216–17**,
  219, 345, 347
Orange pressée 278, 299
Orangerie, Musée de l' *see* Musée
  de l'Orangerie
Orb, Ron 326, 327
Ordre de la Libération, Musée de
  see Mémorial de l'Ordre de la
  Libération
Orléans, Ducs d' 114, 120, 232
Orly Airport 377, 379, 381
Orsay, Musée d' *see* Musée
  d'Orsay
OTU Voyages 374, 375
Oudry, Jean-Baptiste 57, 60, 103
Our Lady of Consolation 138
Oysters 334, 335

P

P&O 378
Pagoda, Parc Monceau 259
Pagode 354, 356
Pain au chocolat 296, 333
Painter with Palette and Easel
  (Picasso) 101
Palais Abbatial 137, **138**
Palais-Bourbon **192**, 216
Palais de la Bourse 219
Palais de Chaillot 39, 200, 362
  Jardins du Trocadéro 53
  Musée de la Marine 201
  restaurants 293
  river trip 68
  Street-by-Street map 198
Palais de la Découverte 59, 206,
  208, 360
Palais de l'Elysée 44, 108, 205, **209**
Palais des Etudes 161
Palais Galliera *see* Musée Galliera
Palais de l'Industrie 204
Palais de Justice 78, 81, **86**
Palais du Luxembourg 27, 171,
  172
Palais d'Omnisports de Paris-
  Bercy 349, 350, 358, 359
Palais de la Porte Dorée 235
Palais Royal 44, 118, 119, **120**
  Jardin du 52, 119, 121, 132
Palais Royal theatre 342, 344
Palais de Tokyo
  Musée d'Art Moderne de la
  Ville de Paris 10, 203

Palais des Tuileries
  see Tuileries Palace
Palladio, Andrea 49
Les Panetons 333, 335
Panthéon 29, 46, 49, **158–9**, 262
Papety, Dominique Louis,
  Allegory of the Republic 17
Paradis Latin 343, 344
Parc André Citroën 11, 247
Parc Asterix 362
Parc de la Villette 11, **236–9**
  boat trips 362
  Cité de la Musique 236, 237,
    346, 347
  Cité des Sciences 238–9
  gardens 53
  La Géode 239
Parfums Caron 330, 332
Paris à Velo c'est Sympa! 359, 383
Paris Air and Space Technology
  Show 65
Paris Appartements Services 278,
  280
Paris Canal Company 73
Paris Convention and Visitors'
  Bureau 366, 367
Paris Exhibition (1937) 200
Paris Industrial Tribunal 261
Paris International Boat Show 65
Paris Infos Mairie 357, 359
Paris International Marathon 62
Paris Jazz Festival 64
Paris Mémorial de la Déportation 80
Paris Mômes 360
Paris Museum Pass 366
Paris-Plage 63
Paris Quartier d'Eté 63
Paris School 44
Paris-Séjour-Réservation 278, 280,
  281
Paris Vélo 357, 359, 383
Paris Vision 367
Paris Voice 340
Pariscope 331, 357, 361, 366
Parisii tribe 17, 20, 78, 81
Parks and gardens 132–3
  Bagatelle gardens, Bois de
    Boulogne 50, 53, 255
  Bois de Boulogne 35, 50, 53,
    231, 254–5, 357, 361, 362
  Bois de Vincennes 51, 52,
    53, 64, 246, 357, 361, 362
  Boulevard Jules Ferry 261
  Champ-de-Mars 52, 193
  children in 361
  Esplanade des Invalides 50
  Forum des Halles 53
  Hôpital St-Louis 261
  Hôtel Biron 52
  Hôtel Guénégaud 103
  Jardin d'Acclimatation 361
  Jardin du Carrousel 122
  Jardin des Halles 361
  Jardin du Luxembourg 50-53,
    63, 132, 162, 169, 170, 172,
    173, 362, 363
  Jardin du Palais Royal 52, 119,
    121, 132
  Jardin des Plantes 51, 52, 53,
    166, 167
  Jardin des Tuileries 50, 52,
    65, 70, 118, 130, 132, 133
  Jardins des Champs-Elysées
    52, 207
  Jardins des Invalides 52, 185
  Jardins du Trocadéro 53, 198,
    199, 201

Parks and gardens (cont)
  Parc André Citroën 11, 247
  Parc des Buttes-Chaumont 51,
    53, 232, 268–9, 357, 362
  Parc du Champ de Mars 183
  Parc Floral, Bois de Vincennes
    361
  Parc Monceau 50, 52, 232, 257,
    258–9, 362
  Parc Montsouris 53, 246
  Parc des Princes 358, 359
  Parc de la Villette 11, 53,
    234–5
  Paris's Best 50–53
  Place Jean-Baptiste Clément
    267
  St-Médard 166
  Square Barye 263
  Versailles 26, 132, 248–9
  Villandry 132
Parliament *see* Assemblée
  Nationale
Pascal, Blaise 115, 153
Les Passages **218**, 323
Passage Galerie Vivienne 213
Passage des Panoramas 213, 218,
  323
Passage des Postes 162
Passage des Princes 213
Passage Verdeau 213
Passages (arcades) 213, 218
Passerelle des Arts 70, 77
Passerelle Solferino 70
Passports, lost 369
Pasteur, Louis 36, 45
  Institut Pasteur 247
  tomb 247
Pastis 299
Patinoire d'Asnières-sur-Seine
  358, 359
Pâtisseries 292
Pauillac wine 298
Pavarotti, Luciano 345
Le Pavillon Montsouris 294
Pavillon Richelieu 123
Le Pêcheur à la Coquille
  (Carpeaux) 54
Pedestrian crossings 382
Pei, I M 45, 123, 129
Penelope (Bourdelle) 57
Pep's 331, 332
Père Lachaise,
  Cimetière du
  see Cimetière du Père Lachaise
Père Lachaise taxi rank 389
Perfume 330, 332
Périphérique 379
Perry, Michel 328, 329
Pessac-Léognan wine 298
Pétain, Marshal, tomb 180
Pétanque (boules) 86, 341, 357
Petit Bâteau 326, 327
Le Petit Journal Montparnasse
  349, 350
Le Petit Journal St-Michel 349,
  350
Le Petit Opportun 349, 350
Petit Palais 37, **208**
  Paris's Best 54, 56
  river view 68, 69
  Street-by-Street map 206, 207
Petit Trianon, Versailles 232, **249**,
  250
Petrossian 333, 335
Peyre, Marie-Josephe 140
Pharamond 37
Pharmacie Anglo-Americaine 369

Pharmacie Bader 369
Pharmacie des Halles 369
Pharmacie Les Champs 369
Pharmacists 368–9
Philippe I, King 18
Philippe III the Bold, King 19
Philippe IV the Fair, King 19, 103
Philippe V, King 19
Philippe VI, King 19
Philippe-Auguste, King 18, 19, 83, 122, 123
Philippe de Champaigne 114
Phonecards 372
Piaf, Edith 45, 260
  Musée Edith Piaf 234
  tomb 241
Piano, Renzo 110
Piaski, O 229
Picasso, Pablo
  Au Lapin Agile 225
  Bateau-Lavoir 228, 267
  The Bathers 101
  Les Demoiselles d'Avignon 37
  Guernica 37
  Homage to Apollinaire 137
  The Kiss 100
  Musée Picasso 55, 57, 93, 100–101
  Painter with Palette and Easel 101
  Pompidou Centre 110, 112, 113
  Sculptor and Model 55
  Self-portrait 100
  The Two Brothers 100
  Two Women Running on the Beach 101
  UNESCO mural 191
  Violin and Sheet Music 100
  Woman Reading 101
  Woman with a Mantilla 100
Pickpockets 368
Pierlot, Claude 11, 324, 325
Pierot (Watteau) 126
Pierre et Vacances 280
Pierre Hermé 333, 335
Piffaretti, Bernard 113
Pigalle 276
Pigalle, Jean-Baptiste 60, 172
Pigeon, Charles, Family Tomb 180
Pisanello 126
Piscine des Amiraux 359
Piscine Deligny 67
Piscine des Halles 362
Piscine Henry de Montherlant 358, 359
Piscine Pontoise-Quartier Latin 359
Piscine St-Germain 359
Piscine St-Merri 359
Pissarro, Camille 59, 61, 147, 254
  Harvesting 58
Pitié-Salpêtrière *see* Groupe Hospitalier Pitié-Salpêtrière
Place des Abbesses **228**, 266
Place de la Bastille 32, **98**, 234
Place Charles de Gaulle (l'Etoile) 35, **209**, 211
Place de Clichy, taxi rank 389
Place de la Concorde 29, 117, **131**
Place de la Contrescarpe 162, **166**
Place Dauphine 77, **86**

Place Denfert-Rochereau, taxi rank 389
Place de l'Etoile
  see Place Charles de Gaulle
Place Igor Stravinsky 105, **107**
Place Jean-Baptiste Clément 267
Place de la Madeleine 214, **216**, 322
  taxi rank 389
Place Maubert 152
Place de l'Opéra 214, **215**
Place des Pyramides 118, **121**
Place de la République 217, 261
  taxi rank 389
Place Royale 24–5
Place St-Michel 150
  taxi rank 389
Place St-Sulpice 170, **172**
Place du Tertre 221, 222, **224**, 228
Place du Théâtre Français 29
Place du Trocadéro 197, **198**
  taxi rank 389
Place Vendôme 117, **132**
Place des Victoires 117, **133**
Place des Vosges 25, 93, **94**
Les Planches 353
Planetarium, Cité des Sciences 238, 240
Plans-Reliefs, Musée des
  see Musée des Plans-Reliefs
Plantes, Jardin des
  see Jardin des Plantes
Playgrounds, Parc de la Villette 236
Plaza Athénée hotel 276, 278, 282
Pleats Please 324, 325
La Pléiade 166
Plein Sud 324, 325
Poilâne, Max 10, 333, 335
Le Point Virgule 344
Point Zéro 79
Poiray 328, 329
Poissonnerie du Dôme 334, 335
Poissonnerie Lacroix 334, 335
Polanski, Roman 178
Police 78, 368, 369
  telephone numbers 383
Police Museum *see* Musée de la Préfecture de Police
Political leaders 44
Pollock, Jackson 110, 113
Pomerol St-Emilion wine 298
Pommier 200
Pompadour, Marquise de 29, 114
Pompidou Centre **110–13**
  architectural features 110–11
  Atelier Brancusi 112
  Atelier des Enfants 361
  cafés 316
  Centre de la Création Industrielle 58
  concerts 347
  films 355
  Four Great Days in Paris 10
  Musée de l'Art Moderne 41, 57, 110, 112–13
  Paris's Best 55, 56
  shop 336
  Street-by-Street map 106–7
  street entertainers 363
  see also Beaubourg
Pompiers 368, 369
Pont Alexandre III 67, 69, 206, 207, **208**

Pont de l'Alma 362
Pont Bir-Hakeim 68
Pont de la Concorde 62, 70, 139
Pont de Grenelle 62
Pont d'Iéna 66, **199**, 201
Pont Louis-Philippe 262
Pont Marie 263
Pont Neuf 18, 24, 25, 40, 41, 77, **86**
Pont Notre-Dame 24
Pont Royal 27
Pont St-Michel 149
Pont de Sully 70, 164
Pont de la Tournelle 262
Porcelain 330
Porcelainor 323
Port de l'Arsenal 98, 232
Port de Plaisance 270
Porte de Charenton 381
Porte de Clignancourt 233
Porte St-Denis 234
Porte St-Martin 234
Porte St-Martin theatre 344
Portes (former city gates) 379
Portrait of Cardinal Richelieu (Champaigne) 44
Portrait of Erasmus (Holbein) 126
Portrait of the Journalist Sylvia von Harden (Dix) 110
Portrait of a Woman (Modigliani) 223
Post-Impressionism 56, 60, 61
Post offices 373
Postage stamps 373
Postal services 372, 373
Postcodes 373
La Poste 372, 373
Poste, Musée de la
  see Musée de la Poste
Poste restante 373
Posters 36
  shops 336, 337
Pot, Philippe, tomb 127
Pot de Fer fountain 162
Pou 333, 335
Poujauran, J.L. 333, 335
Poulbot, Francisque 222, 229
Pound, Ezra 140
Poussin, Nicolas 60, 127
Prada 324, 325
Pradier, James 138, 187
Pradier, Jean-Jacques 142
Pré Catelan 255
Préfecture de Police 78
The Presentation in the Temple (Vouet) 60
Prévost, Abbé 150
Princess Tam Tam 328, 329
Le Printemps des Rues 62
Printing presses 24
Print shops 336, 337
Private homes, staying in 279, 280
Prix d'Amérique 65
Prix de Diane Hermés 63
Prix de l'Arc de Triomphe 64
Le Procope 25, 27, **140**, 142
Profile of a Model (Seurat) 59
Promod 325, 326
Property, safety 368–9
Protase, St 99
Protestants 152
Proust, Marcel 37, 45, 52, 58, 205, 216, 219
  tomb 240
Proust (Blanche) 45
Public holidays 65

Pubs 317
Puech, Jamin 328, 329
Puget, Pierre 127
Pulp 353
Puppet shows 343, 361
Puvis de Chavannes, Pierre 158
Pygmalion (Silva) 109
Pyramid *see* Musée du Louvre
Pyramides, Place des
　see Place des Pyramides

Q

Qantas 376, 379
Quai de Jemmapes 260–61
Quai des Orfèvres 78
Quai St-Bernard 164
Quai de Valmy 261
Quai Voltaire 142
Quartier d'Eté Festival 346, 347
Quartier de l'Horloge 109
Quarton, Enguerrand 127
Le Queen 353

R

Rabanne, Paco 324, 325
Rabelais, François 166
Racecourses 358
Racine, Jean 45, 79, 81, 120, 153,
　240, 342
Racine Odeon cinema 356
Radio 375
Radio-France 40, 345, 347
　see also Musée de Radio-France
The Raft of the Medusa (Géricault)
　124, 240
Rag Time 325, 326
Rail services 33, 378–9
　from airport to city 377, 380–81
　RER 368, 377, 382, 384
　SNCF 378, 382, 383, 388, 389
　stations 388
　suburban 388
　TGV high-speed trains 179,
　　378, 379, 388
　tickets 384, 388
　tourist offices 366, 367
Rainfall 65
Rambuteau 80
Rameau, Jean-Philippe 44
Rapp, Avenue 193
Raphael 56
Raspail, François, tomb 241
RATP 377, 382, 383, 384, 386–7
RATP Voyages Accompagnés 367
Ravaillac, François 25, 81, 102,
　106
Ravy, Jean 83, 84
Ray, Man 38
　tomb 181
Raynaud, Jean-Pierre 113
Raysse, Martial 113
Realism 56, 61, 147
Rech, Georges 324, 325
Récipon, *Quadriga* 209
Réciproque 324, 325, 326
Reclining Figure (Moore) 193
The Red Wheelbarrow Bookstore
　331, 332
Redon, Odilon 147
Reflets Médicis 354, 356
Regent diamond 129
Regine's 351, 353
Reichelt (birdman) 194
Relais Christine 279, 283
Rembrandt 56, 103, 126
Renaissance 17, 24–5, 48
Renaud-Barrault Company 206

Renaud Michel 334, 335
Renée, Jean-Marie 45
Renoir, Pierre-Auguste 36, 44, 56,
　59, 61, 131, 146, 147, 229,
　254, 266, 267
　*Dancing at the Moulin de la
　Galette* 145, 147
　Gabrielle 59
Repaire du Bacchus 334, 335
Reproductions 336, 337
RER 368, 377, 382, 384
Résidence Internationale de Paris
　280
Résidence du Roy 280
Resistance movement 69, 152, 179
Resnais, Alain 200
Résonances 330, 332
Restaurants 292–319
　children in 295, 360
　dress code 294
　Eiffel Tower Quarter 293
　ethnic food 292
　the flavours of Paris 296-97
　Les Halles 293
　in hotels 277
　Les Invalides 293
　Left Bank 293
　Louvre-Rivoli area 293
　Madeleine area 292
　Montmartre 293
　Opéra Quarter 293
　Palais de Chaillot 293
　prices 294
　reading the menu and ordering
　　294–5
　reservations 294
　service 295
　smoking in 295
　St-Germain-des-Prés 292
　types 293
　vegetarian food 294
　what to eat 292
　wheelchair access 295
　where to find 292–3
　wine 298–9
Restout, Jean 103
Revolution (1789) 15, 30–31, 32,
　48
　Bicentenary celebrations 41, 131
　Conciergerie 78, 81
　guillotine 31, 131, 141
　Hôtel de Lamoignon 94
　The Marais 91
　Marie-Antoinette 31, 81, 103,
　　131, 251, 253
　Musée Carnavalet 97
　Place de la Bastille 98
　St-Germain-des-Prés 138
　September Massacres 30, 173
　La Sorbonne 153
　Square du Temple 103
Revolution (1830) 33, 98
Revolution (1848) 17, 34, 98
Revolutionary Tribunal 86
Rex Club 349, 350, 351, 353
Reynolds, Sir Joshua 126
Rhône wines 298
Ribera, José de 126
Ricci, Nina 324, 325
Richart 10, 333, 335
Richelieu, Cardinal 44, 94
　Eglise de la Sorbonne 48, 153
　Institut de France 141
　Palais Royal 26, 52, 118, 120,
　　121
　St-Eustache 114
　St-Paul–St-Louis 47

Richter, Gerhard 113
Riemenschneider, Tilman 127
Rigaud, Hyacinthe 60
　Louis XIV 253
Right Bank 67
Rilke, Rainer Maria 87
Ritz 117, 132, 276
Ritz, César 132
Ritz Club 351–2, 353
Ritz Gym 358, 359
River trips 67–71, 362
Rivoli, Battle of (1797) 32
Robert II the Pious, King 18
Robespierre, Maximilien 30, 31,
　81, 131, 159
Rock music 349, 350
Rockefeller, John D 247
Rococo artists 60
Rodenbach, George, tomb 241
Rodin, Pierre Auguste 44, 57,
　61, 146
　The Age of Bronze 265
　Balzac 177
　bust of Victor Hugo 95
　The Gates of Hell 54, 144
　The Kiss 187
　Musée Rodin 54, 56, 184, 185,
　　187
Rogers, Richard 110
Rohan, Hôtel de *see* Hôtel de
　Rohan
Rohan, Princesse de 103
Rohan-Soubise, Armand de 102
Rohmer, Eric 354
Roland Garros tennis tournament
　358
Roller skating 362
Romanesque sculpture 157
Romans 17, 20–21, 56, 78, 129
　see also Gallo-Roman remains
Romantic artists 61
Rond Point des Champs-Elysées
　205
　taxi rank 389
Rondelet, Guillaume 49, 158
Roofs, mansard 26
Roque, Jacqueline 100
Rosa, Sabbia 328, 329
Rosimond, Roze de 224
Rothschild, Baronne Hélène de
　203
La Rotonde 143, 292
Rotonde de la Villette 234
Rotundas 52–3
Rouault, Georges 57, 61, 113,
　127
Rouen, archbishops of 140
Rousseau, Henri (Le Douanier)
　61, 131, 147
Rousseau, Jean-Jacques 28, 29, 96
　tomb 159
Roux, Dr Emile, tomb 247
Royal Garden St-Honoré 280
Royal Monceau 276
Rubens, Peter Paul 57, 103
Rude, François 146, 210,
　211, 216
　*Departure of the Volunteers
　in 1792* 61
Rue des Arènes, No. 5 163
Rue Bréa 177
Rue de Buci 137, 339, 363
Rue Campagne-Première
　177, 178
Rue Chanoinesse 79
Rue du Chat qui Pêche 151
Rue Cler **192**, 338

Rue du Dragon 139
Rue de Fouarre 151
Rue des Francs-Bourgeois **94**, 323
Rue de Fürstenberg 137
Rue de la Ferronnerie 106
Rue la Fontaine 254
Rue Galande 151
Rue de Montmorency, No. 51 114
Rue Mouffetard 162, **166**, 323, 339, 363
Rue de l'Odéon 140
Rue de Paradis 323
Rue Quincampoix 107
Rue de Rivoli **130**, 322
Rue des Rosiers 92, **95**
Rue St-Séverin, No.12 150
Rue de Tournon 171
Rugby 358
Russian Orthodox Church 232
Ryanair 376, 379
Rykiel, Sonia 283, 324, 326, 327
Ryst-Dupeyron 334, 335

S

La Sablaise Poissonnerie 334, 335
Sacré-Coeur 15, **226–7**
  for children 363
  floorplan 226–7
  gardens 266
  Paris's Best 47, 49
  Street-by-Street map 223
Sacré-Coeur (Utrillo) 44
Safety 368–9
St-Alexandre-Nevsky Cathédral 232
St-André des Arts cinema 356
St-Augustin 49, 259
St Bartholomew's Day Massacre (1572) 25, 115
The St Bartholomew's Day Massacre (Dubois) 115
Sainte-Beuve, Charles Augustin 175
  tomb 180
Sainte-Chapelle 23, 43, **88–9**
  architectural features 88–9
  Cameo 219
  for children 363
  concerts 346, 347
  history 17, 22
  Paris's Best 46, 48
  river view 71
  St Louis's relics 89
  stained glass 88, 89, 156
  statues 157
  Street-by-Street map 78
Sainte-Clothilde 48, 49, **187**
St-Cloud 25
St-Denis 157, 200
St Denis Preaching to the Gauls (Vien) 121
St-Emilion wine 298
St-Estèphe wine 298
St-Etienne-du-Mont 25, 48, **153**
St-Eustache 25, 44, 47, 48, 105, **114**
St George's Anglican Church 375
St-George's theatre 342, 344
St-Germain, Boulevard
  see Boulevard St-Germain
St-Germain l'Auxerrois 48, **115**, 346, 347
St-Germain-en-Laye 33
St-Germain-des-Prés 134–47, 138, 152, 157
  area map 135

St-Germain-des-Prés (cont)
  cafés 143
  church 48
  cinemas 354
  concerts 346, 347
  history 22
  Street-by-Street map 136–7
  Street Finder map 11–12
St-Gervais–St-Protais 99
  concerts 346, 347
  history 38, 44
  Paris's Best 46, 48
  river view 71
St-Jean l'Evangéliste 49, **228**, 266–7
St-Joseph-des-Carmes 49, **173**
St-Julien-le-Pauvre 48, 151, **152**
  concerts 346, 347
St-Julien wine 298
Le Saint Lambert 361
Saint Laurent, Yves 57, 135, 324, 326, 327
St-Louis-en-l'Ile **87**, 263
  concerts 346, 347
St-Louis-des-Invalides 49, 185, **186**, 187
St-Martin area, walks 257
St-Médard 162, **166**
St-Merry 48, 107, **108**
St-Paul, taxi rank 389
St-Paul–St-Louis 47, 49, **99**
Saint-Phalle, Niki de 61, 107
  Fontaine Igor Stravinsky 61
St-Pierre fabrics market 225
St-Pierre de Montmartre 223, **224**
St-Roch 49, 118, **121**
  concerts 346, 347
Saint-Saëns, Camille 140
  tomb 180
St-Séverin 47, 48, 150, 151, **152**
St-Sulpice
  Chapel of the Holy Angels 138
  concerts 346, 347
  history 29
  Paris's Best 48, 49
  Street-by-Street map 170
St-Victor suburb 162
St-Vincent cemetery 229
Sales 320
Sales tax (TVA) 320, 374
Salle Garance 355
Salle Pleyel 345, 347
Salm-Kyrbourg, Prince de 143
Salon 59, 60
Salon de l'Automobile 64
Salon des Indépendents 225
Salon International d'Agriculture 62
Salon des Refusés 58, 61
Salons du Palais Royal 330, 331
Salpêtrière 49, 161, **167**
La Samaritaine 10, 94, **115**
SAMU 369
Sancerre wine 298
Sand, George 138, 262
Sargon II, King of Assyria 128
Sarkis 113
Sartre, Jean-Paul 40, 136, 139, 143, 178
  tomb 181
Sarut, Corinne 324, 325
Satie, Erik 267
Sausages 297
Savonnerie carpets 232
Sax, Adolphe 209
La Scala 351, 353

Scallops 296
Scène Est 10
Schiaparelli, Elsa 121
The School (woodcarving) 156
Science City *see* Cité des Sciences
Science museums 59
Scientists 45
Scooter 328, 329
Sculptor and Model (Picasso) 55
Sculpture en Plein Air *see* Musée de la Sculpture en Plein Air
Seacat 378
Seafrance 378
Sebastopol bell 247
Seberg, Jean 44
  tomb 181
Second Empire 34–5, 197
Second-hand clothes shops 326, 327
Seine, River 20
  boat trips 67–73, 362
  Ile de la Cité 77, 78
  quays 53, 257
  see also Bridges
Le Sélect 143, 292
Self-catering 278, 279, 280
Senate 172
Sens, Hôtel de *see* Hôtel de Sens
Sentou Gallery 331, 332
The Separation of a Couple (de Max) 176
Sephora 330, 332
September Massacres (1792) 30, 173
Sert y Badia, José Maria 97
Servandoni, Giovanni Niccolo 49, 170
Service des Domaines 337
Seurat, Georges 56, 59, 61, 147, 267
  Profile of a Model 59
Seurre the Elder 185, 210
Sévigné, Madame de 94, 96
Sèvres porcelain 232
Sewers 34, 190, 363
Sexual Disease Centre 368
Shakespeare, William 120, 342
Shakespeare Garden Festival 62
Shimada, Junko 324, 325
Shoe shops 328, 329
Shops 320–39
  art galleries 336, 337
  auction houses 336–7
  books, magazines and newspapers 331
  bread and cakes 333, 335
  charcuterie and *foie gras* 333, 335
  cheese 334, 335
  for children 328, 329, 362
  chocolate 333, 335
  clothes and accessories 324–9
  department stores 321
  flowers 331, 332
  food and drink 333–5
  gifts and souvenirs 330–32
  hats 328, 329
  household goods 330–31, 332
  how to pay 320
  international bookshops 375
  jewellery 328, 329
  lifestyle stores 326, 327
  lingerie 328, 329

Shops (cont)
markets 338–9
men's clothes 326, 327
modern furniture 336, 337
objets d'art 336, 337
opening hours 320
Paris's Best 322–3
perfume 330, 332
reproductions, posters and prints 336, 337
sales 320
second-hand clothes 326, 327
shoes, bags and belts 328, 329
specialist 331
VAT exemption 320
wine 334, 335
Showcase 352, 353
Sibelius, Jean 142
Sickert, Walter 87
Siege of Paris (1870–71) 36, 164, 226, 229
Sightseeing tours 367
Signac, Paul 147
Signoret, Simone 44
tomb 240
Silva, Julio, *Pygmalion* 109
Sinéquanone 326, 327
Sirops à l'eau 299
Sisley, Alfred 44, 59, 61, 146, 147, 254
Six Nations Trophy 65
Six Pieds Trois Pouces 326, 327
Sixt-Eurorent (car hire) 383
Skate-boarding 362
Skating 362
Smalto, Francesco 326, 327
Smith, W H 341, 375
Smoking regulations 295, 367
Snails 297, 321
SNCF 378, 382, 383, 388, 389
Société Historique et Littéraire Polonaise **77, 87**
Sofitel 379
Sofitel Paris Club Med Gym 359
Sommerard, Alexandre du 155, 156
Son et Lumière 62
Sorbon, Robert de 153
Sorbonne 153
concerts 346, 347
Street-by-Street map 150
Sorrow of the King (Matisse) 111
SOS Dentaire 368
SOS Dépression 368
SOS Help 368
SOS Médecin 368
Soubise, Hôtel de
see Hôtel de Soubise
Soufflot, Jacques-Germain 49, 158
Soulages, Pierre 113
Soulange-Boudin, Father 247
Soutine, Chaim 61, 112, 131
tomb 181
Souvenir shops 330–31, 332
Sparkling wines 299
Specialist museums 57
Specialist shops 330–31
Spectator sports 358
Sports 357–9, 362
Spreckelsen, Otto von 255
Spree 326, 327
Spring, calendar of events 62
Squares 52–3
Paris's Best 50–53
Place des Abbesses 228, 266
Place de la Bastille 32, 98
Place Charles de Gaulle (l'Etoile) 35, 209, 211

Squares (cont)
Place Charles Dullin 266
Place de la Concorde 29, 131
Place de la Contrescarpe 166
Place Dauphine 77, 86
Place Jean-Baptiste Clément 267
Place de la Madeleine 214, 216, 322
Place Maubert 152
Place de l'Opéra 215
Place des Pyramides 118, 121
Place de la République 261
Place Royale 24–5
Place St-Michel 150
Place St-Sulpice 170, 172
Place du Tertre 221, 222, 224, 228
Place Vendôme 132
Place des Victoires 133
Place des Vosges 51, 93, 94
Square Barye 263
Square Frédéric Lemaître 261
Square Georges Caïn 91
Square Jean XXIII 79, 80
Square du Temple 103
Square du Vert-Galant 51, 53, 77, 87
Square Willette 223
Squash 358
Squash Club Quartier Latin 358, 359
Squash Front de Seine 358, 359
Squash Montmartre 358, 359
Squatting Scribe (Egyptian) 129
Stade de France 358, 359
Stade Pierre de Coubertin 359
Stade Roland Garros 358, 359
Stael, Nicolas de 61
Stained glass 22
Musée de Cluny 156
Notre-Dame 82–5
Sainte-Chapelle 88, 89
Stamps
markets 338
postage 373
Standing Woman II (Giacometti) 61
Starck, Philippe 108, 113
Stationery shops 331, 332
Stations *see* Metro; Rail services; and individual stations
Statues
Ambroise Thomas 258
Charlemagne 78
Danton 137
Diderot 159
Henri IV, 87
Homage to Apollinaire (Picasso) 137
Joan of Arc 118, 121, 227, 259
Louis XIII 85
Louis XIV 27, 84, 85, 93, 133, 250
Marly Horses 123, 125
Marshal Foch 198
Napoleon 132
Pygmalion (Silva) 109
Sainte-Geneviève 171
St Louis 227
Statue of Liberty 68
Victor Noir 241
Voltaire 159
The Zouave 69
see also Fountains; Monuments

Stein, Gertrude 38
Stella Cadente 326, 327
Stern, H. 328, 329
Stevenson, Robert Louis 245
Stock Exchange 219
Stodtz brothers 107
Stravinsky, Igor 346
Street entertainers 363
Strelli, Olivier 326, 327
Students
information 374
riots (1968) 40, 41
travel tickets 388
Studio 28/ 356
Suburban trains 388
Suger, Abbot of St-Denis 129
La Suite 352, 353
Sully, Bishop Maurice de 48
Sully, Duc de 95
Sully, Hôtel de *see* Hôtel de Sully
Summer, calendar of events 63
Sun King *see* Louis XIV
Sunset (jazz club) 349, 350
Sunshine hours 63
Surface to Air 326, 327
Surrealists 38, 44, 53, 61, 101, 110, 112, 138, 143, 224
Swarovski, Daniel 328, 329
Swimming 67, 358, 362
Symbolists 147, 233
Synagogue Nazareth 375

T
La Table d'Anvers 293
Take-away food 316
Talleyrand, Charles Maurice de 187
Tanaka, Atsuko 113
Tapestries
Gobelins 26, 167
Musée de Cluny 154, 156, 157
Tarte Alsacienne 297
Tarte Tatin 297
Tartine et Chocolat 326, 327
Tax, sales (TVA) 320, 374
Taxis 341, 377, 389
Les Taxis Bleus 341, 389
Tea and Tattered Pages 331, 332
Tea salons 316
Teddy's 326, 327
Tehen 324, 327
Télécartes 372
Telephone services 372–3
emergency 368, 383
Television 361, 375
Temperature, weather 64
Templon, Galerie 336, 337
Tennis 357
Tennis de la Faluère 357, 359
Tennis Luxembourg 357, 359
Terrier 333, 335
Terroir, Alphonse 159
Tessin, Count 142
TGV (*Trains à Grande Vitesse*) 179, 378, 379, 388
The City 340
Theatre 342–4
Theatre Antoine 342, 344
Théâtre de l'Aquarium 344
Théâtre de l'Atelier 266, 342, 344
Théâtre de la Bastille 348
Théâtre des Champs-Elysées 178, 345, 346, 347, 348
Théâtre du Châtelet 345, 347, 348
Théâtre du Chaudron 344
Théâtre de l'Epée de Bois 344
Théâtre Française 28

Théâtre de La Huchette 342, 344
Théâtre Montparnasse 176
Théâtre du Grévin 347
Théâtre National de Chaillot 199, **200**, 342, 344
Théâtre National de la Colline 342, 344
Théâtre du Rond Point 206
Théâtre du Soleil 342, 344
Théâtre Sudden 344
Théâtre de la Tempête 344
Théâtre de la Ville 347
Theme parks 362
Thierri III, King 18
Thierri IV, King 18
Thierry, Alexandre 186
Third Republic 36, 147
Thomas, Ambroise, statue 258
Thomas, Petit 95
Tickets
   buses 386
   cinemas 355
   cut-price 341
   dance 348
   entertainments 340–41, 367
   jazz clubs 349–50
   metro 384, 385
   opera and concerts 347
   public transport 382
   RER trains 384
   SNCF trains 388
   theatre 343
   touts 341
Tiepolo, Giovanni Battista 209
The Tiger Hunt (Delacroix) 145
Time 375
Tinguely, Jean 61, 107
   Fontaine Igor Stravinsky 61
Tipping
   in hotels 277
   in restaurants 294
Titian 56
To Russia, the Asses and the Others (Chagall) 111
Tobacco, customs and excise 374
Toilets, public 374
Tomb of the Unknown Soldier 38, 210
Toni Pato 328, 329
Tortu, Christian 331, 332
Toulouse, Comte de 133
Toulouse-Lautrec, Henri de 36, 44, 61, 147, 225
   Moulin Rouge 228
   waxworks 108
La Tour d'Argent 293
Tour Eiffel *see* Eiffel Tower
Tour de France 63, 357
Tour de l'Horloge 71
Tour de Jean Sans Peur 114
Tour Montparnasse 175, 176, **178**, 181
Tour St-Jacques 25, 48, **115**
Tourist information desks 281
Tourist offices 340, 366, 367
Town Hall
   see Hôtel de Ville
Toyshops 331, 332
Trabendo 349, 350
Traffic wardens 383
Train Bleu restaurant 295
Trains *see* Rail services
Transmanche Ferries 378
Transports Urbains, Musée des
   see Musée des Transports Urbains

Travel 382–73
   air 376–7, 379
   from airport to city 380–81
   buses 386–7
   cars 382, 383
   coaches 378, 380–81
   cross-Channel ferries 378
   cycling 382, 383
   driving to Paris 379
   late-night 329
   metro 384–5
   railways 378–3
   RER trains 384
   safety 368
   SNCF trains 388, 389
   taxis 341, 377, 389
   tickets and travel passes 382, 386
   walking 382
Travelex 370
Travellers' cheques 320, 368–9, 370
Traverse, P 201
Tremblot, F, *The Wall* 225
Très Riches Heures du Duc de Berri 23
Tresca 28
Triptique 353
Triquet, Henri 114
Triqueti, Henri de 216
Triumph of Napoleon (Cortot) 210
Trocadéro 39
   see also Palais de Chaillot
Trocadéro fountains 199, 200
Trocadéro gardens
   see Jardins du Trocadéro
Les Trois Belles (Zadkine) 178
Le Troisième Lieu 352, 353
Trotsky, Leon 143, 179
Truffaut, François 180, 200, 354
   tomb 229
Tuileries gardens
   see Jardin des Tuileries
Tuileries 116–33
   area map 117
   Street-by-Street map 118–19
   Street Finder maps 6, 11–12
Tuileries Palace 26, 30, 31, 32, 122, 130, 209
Turkish baths 167
Turner, J M W 59, 126
TVA (sales tax) 320, 374
The Two Barges (Derain) 112
The Two Brothers (Picasso) 100
Two Women Running on the Beach (Picasso) 101
Tzara, Tristan 229, 267
   tomb 181

U

Uccello, Paolo 56, 126, 209
UCRIF 279
UGC Ciné-Cité Bercy cinema 356
UGC Ciné-City les Halles cinema 356
UK tourist office 367
Une Journée au Cirque 361
UNESCO 40, 191
Universal Exhibition (1889) 52, 192
Universal Exhibition (1900) 144, 191, 206, 208, 247
Universal Exhibition (1937) 53
University of Paris 23, 152, **153**
   Cité Universitaire 247
   Collection des Minéraux de l'Université 165
   see also Sorbonne
Unknown Soldier, tomb of 38, 210

USIT Voyages 379
Utrillo, Maurice 57, 61, 222, 224, 229
   Sacré-Coeur 44

V

Val-de-Grâce 48, 49, **173**
Valéry, Paul 140, 200
Valmy, Battle of (1793) 31
Valois dynasty 19
Valois, Marguerite de 83, 99, 115
Van Dyck, Anthony 126
Van Eyck, Jan 126
Van Gogh, Theo 266
Van Gogh, Vincent 56, 61, 147, 178, 227, 266, 267
   Doctor Paul Gachet 145
VAT 320, 374
Vauban, Sébastien le Prestre de 46, 186, 188
Vedettes pleasure boats 72–3, 87
Vedettes du Pont Neuf 73, 87
Vegetable markets 338–9
Vegetarian food 294
Veilhan, Xavier 113
Vendôme, Place *see* Place Vendôme
Ventes, Hôtel des *see* Drouot
Ventilo 324, 327
Venus de Milo 124, 128
Verlaine, Paul 169, 194
Verlor 328, 329
Vermeer, Jan, *The Lacemaker* 124
Vermouth 299
Verne, Jules 108
Verreglas 336, 337
Versace, Gianni 324, 325, 326, 327
Versailles **248–53**, 366
   Château 26, 27, 43, 57, 167, 250–53
   floorplan 252–3
   gardens 26, 52, 132
   Grand Trianon 26, 45, 249
   map 248–9
   Petit Trianon 232, 249, 250
   Royal menagerie 164
   trains 388
Versailles, Musique Baroque au Château de 64, 346, 347
Versailles Treaty (1919) 38, 251, 253
Vert-Galant, Square du *see* Square du Vert-Galant
Le Viaduc des Arts 53, 270–71, 336, 337
Vian, Boris 143
Victoire 324, 327
Victoires, Place des *see* Place des Victoires
Victor, Michel-Louis 171
Victoria, Queen of England 115
Vien, Joseph-Marie,
   St Denis Preaching to the Gauls 121
Vierny, Dina 187, 336, 337
Vietnamese restaurants 292, 293
Viewpoints 363
Vignon, Pierre 216
Vignon, Claude 60
Vignon 333, 335
Vigouroux, P. 163
Vikings 122
Villa du Docteur Blanche 265
Villa Jeanneret 254, 265
Villa Montmorency 264
Villa La Roche 38–9, 59, 254, 265

Village Royal 132
Village St-Paul 336, 337
Village Suisse 191, 336, 337
Village Voice 331, 332
Villandry 132
Ville, Hôtel de *see* Hôtel de Ville
La Villette *see* Parc de la Villette
La Villette Jazz Festival 64
Vin, Musée du *see* Musée du Vin
Vincennes, Bois de
  see Bois de Vincennes
Vincennes, Château de
  see Château de Vincennes
Vineyard, Montmartre 221, **222**
Vintage chart, wine 298
Vintage clothes shops 326, 327
Violin and Sheet Music
  (Picasso) 100
Viollet-le-Duc, Eugène 83, 84,
  200
Le VIP 352, 353
Virgin Mary and Child
  (Brunet) 226
Virgin Megastore 321, 340, 341
Visa credit cards 370
Visas 374
Visconti, Joachim 172, 184
Visconti, Louis 119, 121
Vlaminck, Maurice de 112
Volleyball 358
Voltaire 28, 29, 96, 127, 140, 142
  tomb 159
Vosges, Place des
  see Place des Vosges
Vouet, Simon, *The Presentation
  in the Temple* 60
Vuillard, Edouard 56, 61
Vuitton, Louis 202

W

WAGG 351, 353
Wagner, Otto 146
Wagner, Richard 44, 87, 142
Walks 257–73, 382
  Auteuil 264–5
  Butte-aux-Cailles 272–3
  Canal St-Martin 260–61
  Faubourg St-Antoine 270–71

Walks (cont)
  Ile St-Louis 262–3
  Montmartre 266–7
  Parc des Buttes-Chaumont
  268–9
  Parc Monceau 258–9
Wallace, Richard 35, 264
Walter-Guillaume collection
  131
Warhol, Andy 113
Water, drinking 299
Water lily series (Monet) 131
Waterloo, Battle of (1815) 32, 130
Waterparks 362
Watteau, Jean-Antoine 44, 56, 60,
  127
  Gilles 126
Waxworks, Musée Grévin 58,
  108, 218, 363
Weather
  rainfall 65
  sunshine hours 63
  temperature 64
Wederkinch 68
Weill (art dealer) 145
Wheelchair access
  see Disabled travellers
Whistler, James Abbott McNeill 61
Why (accessories) 330, 332
Wilde, Oscar 45, 142, 276
  tomb 241
Wilmotte, Jean-Michel 191
Windmills, Montmartre 229, 267
Windsor, Duchess of 45
Windsor, Duke of 45
Windsurfing 358
Wine
  customs and excise 374
  Musée du Vin–Caveau des
  Echansons 201
  in restaurants 293, 295
  shops 334, 335
  vintage chart 298
  what to drink in Paris 298–9
  wine bars 298, 316–17
Winged Bull with Human Head
  (Assyrian) 128
Winged Victory of Samothrace 128

Winston, Harry 328, 329
Winter, calendar of events 65
With the Black Arc (Kandinsky)
  112
Wolff et Descourts 331, 332
Woman Reading (Picasso) 101
Woman with a Mantilla (Picasso) 100
Women
  clothes 324–7
  safety 368
World Bar 10–11
World Fair (1855) 34, 206
World Fair (1867) 35, 246
World Fair (1889) 36, 193
World Fair (1900) 196, 208
World Fair (1937) 196, 208
World fairs 244
World music 350
World War I 38, 112, 207
World War II 38, 39, 69, 80, 113,
  179, 207
Wren, Christopher 49
Wright, Frank Lloyd 146
Writers 45

Y

Yamamoto, Yohji 326, 327
Yoba 328, 329
Young Dancer of Fourteen
  (Degas) 146
Youth discount tickets 388
Youth hostels 279, 374
Yves Delorme 330, 332

Z

Zadig et Voltaire 324, 327
Zadkine, Ossip 44, 61
  Musée Zadkine 57, 178
  Les Trois Belles 178
Zara 326, 327
Zed Club 351, 353
Zénith 235, 349, 350
Zola, Emile 106, 142
  tomb 159
Zoos
  Bois de Vincennes 246, 361
  Ménagerie 164, 361
Zouave (statue) 69
Zurbarán, Francisco de 126, 166

Acknowledgments

Dorling Kindersley would like to thank the many people whose help and assistance contributed to the preparation of this book.

Main Contributor

Alan Tillier has lived in all the main areas of Paris for 25 years, during which time he has been Paris correspondent for several journals including Newsweek, The Times and the International Herald Tribune. He is the author of several Herald Tribune guides for business travellers to Europe.

Contributors

Lenny Borger, Karen Burshtein, Thomas Quinn Curtiss, David Downie, Fiona Dunlop, Heidi Ellison, Alexandre Lazareff, Robert Noah, Andrew Sanger, Martha Rose Shulman, David Stevens, Ian Williams, Jude Welton.

Dorling Kindersley wishes to thank the following editors and researchers at Websters International Publishers: Sandy Carr, Siobhan Bremner, Valeria Fabbri, Gemma Hancock, Sara Harper, Annie Hubert, Celia Woolfrey.

Additional Photography

Andy Crawford, Michael Crockett, Lucy Davies, Mike Dunning, Philip Gatward, Steve Gorton, Alison Harris, Andrew Holligan, Chas Howson, Britta Jaschinski, Dave King, Ranald MacKechnie, Oliver Knight, Eric Meacher, Neil Mersh, Ian O'Leary, Stephen Oliver, Poppy, Susannah Price, Tim Ridley, Philippe Sebert, Steve Shott, Peter Wilson, Steven Wooster.

Additional Illustrations

John Fox, Nick Gibbard, David Harris, Kevin Jones Associates, John Woodcock.

Cartography

Andrew Heritage, James Mills-Hicks, Suresh Kumar, Alok Pathak, John Plumer, Chez Picthall (DK Cartography). Advanced Illustration (Cheshire), Contour Publishing (Derby), Euromap Limited (Berkshire). Street Finder maps: ERA-Maptec Ltd (Dublin) adapted with permission from original survey and mapping by Shobunsha (Japan).

Cartographic Research

Roger Bullen, Tony Chambers, Paul Dempsey, Ruth Duxbury, Ailsa Heritage, Margeret Hynes, Jayne Parsons, Donna Rispoli, Andrew Thompson.

Design and Editorial

Managing Editor Douglas Amrine
Managing Art Editor Geoff Manders
Senior Editor Georgina Matthews
Series Design Consultant Peter Luff
Editorial Director David Lamb
Art Director Anne-Marie Bulat
Production Controller Hilary Stephens

Picture Research Naomi Peck
Production Controller Hilary Stephens
Proofreader Stewart Wild
DTP Designer Andy Wilkinson
Janet Abbott, Emma Ainsworth, Vandana Bhagra, Hilary Bird, Anna Brooke, Vanessa Courtier, Maggie Crowley, Lisa Davidson, Guy Dimond, Nicola Erdpresser, Elizabeth Eyre, Simon Farbrother, Fay Franklin, Eric Gibory, Paul Hines, Fiona Holman, Gail Jones, Nancy Jones, Stephen Knowlden, Chris Lascelles, Delphine Lawrance, Sam Merrell, Rebecca Milner, Fiona Morgan, Lyn Parry, Shirin Patel, Pamposh Raina, Philippa Richmond, Philippe Rouin, Sands Publishing Solutions, Andrew Szudek, Alka Thakur, Dora Whitaker.

Special Assistance

Miranda Dewer at Bridgeman Art Library, Editions Gallimard, Lindsay Hunt, Emma Hutton at Cooling Brown, Janet Todd at DACS.

Photographic Reference

Musée Carnavalet, Thomas d'Hoste.

Photography Permissions

Dorling Kindersley would like to thank the following for their kind permission to photograph at their establishments: Aéroports de Paris, Basilique du Sacré-Coeur de Montmartre, Beauvilliers, Benoit, Bibliothèque Historique de la Ville de Paris, Bibliothèque Polonaise, Bofinger, Brasserie Lipp, Café de Flore, Caisse Nationale des Monuments Historiques et des Sites, Les Catacombes, Centre National d'Art et de Culture Georges Pompidou, Chartier, Chiberta, La Cité des Sciences et de l'Industrie and L'EPPV, La Coupole, Les Deux Magots, Fondation Cousteau, Le Grand Colbert, Hôtel Atala, Hôtel Liberal Bruand, Hôtel Meurice, Hôtel Relais Christine, Kenzo, Lucas-Carton, La Madeleine, Mariage Frères, Memorial de la Shoah, Thierry Mugler, Musée Armenien de France, Musée de l'Art Juif, Musée Bourdelle, Musée du Cabinet des Medailles, Musée Carnavalet, Musée Cernuschi: Ville de Paris, Musée du Cinema Henri Langlois, Musée Cognacq-Jay, Musée de Cristal de Baccarat, Musée d'Ennery, Musée Grévin, Musée Jacquemart-André, Musée de la Musique Méchanique, Musée National des Châteaux de Malmaison et Bois-Préau, Collections du Musée National de la Légion d'Honneur, Musée National du Moyen Age-Thermes de Cluny, Musée de Notre-Dame de Paris, Musée de l'Opéra, Musée de l'Ordre de la Libération, Musée d'Orsay, Musée de la Préfecture de la Police, Musée de Radio France, Musée Rodin, Musée des Transports Urbains, Musée du Vin, Musée Zadkine, Notre-Dame du Travail, A l'Olivier, Palais de la Découverte, Palais de Luxembourg, Pharamond, Pied de Cochon, Lionel Poilaêne, St Germain-des-Prés, St Louis en l'Ile, St Médard, St Merry, St Paul–St-Louis, St-Roch, St-Sulpice, La

Société Nouvelle d'Exploitation de La Tour Eiffel, La Tour Montparnasse, Unesco, and all the other museums, churches, hotels, restaurants, shops, galleries and sights too numerous to thank individually.

Picture Credits

t=top; tc=top centre; tr=top right; cla=centre left above; ca=centre above; cra=centre right above; cl=centre left; c=centre; cr=centre right; clb=centre left below; cb=centre below; crb=centre right below; bl=bottom left; bc=bottom centre; br=bottom right.

Works of art have been reproduced with the permission of the following copyright holders: © Succession H Matisse/DACS 2006: 111ca; © ADAGP/SPADEM, Paris and DACS, London 2006: 44cl; © ADAGP, Paris and DACS, London 2006: 61br, 61tr, 105tc, 107cb, 109b, 111tc, 111cb, 112bl, 112t, 112br, 113bl, 113br, 119c, 120b, 179tl, 180bc, 181cr, 211tc; © DACS 2006: 38tl, 45cr, 50br, 55cr, 57tl, 100t, 100br, 100clb, 100cl, 100ca, 101t, 101ca, 101cr, 101bl, 104, 107cra, 113c, 137tl, 178cl, 178ca, 208br.

Christo–The Pont Neuf wrapped, Paris, 1975-85: 40cla; © Christo 1985, by kind permission of the artist. Photos achieved with the assistance of the EPPV and the CSI pp 234-9; Courtesy of Erben Otto Dix: 110bl; Photos of Disneyland ® Paris: 242tr, 243bl, 243cr. The characters, architectural works and trademarks are the property of The Walt Disney Company. All rights reserved; Fondation Le Corbusier: 59t, 254b; Courtesy of The Estate of Joan Mitchell: 113t; © Henry Moore Foundation 1993: 191b. Reproduced by kind permission of the Henry Moore Foundation; Beth Lipkin: 241t; Courtesy of the Maison Victor Hugo, Ville de Paris: 95cl; Courtesy of the Musée d'Art Naïf Max Fourny Paris: 223b, 225b; Musée Carnavalet: 214b; Musée de L'Histoire Contemporaine (BDIC), Paris: 210br; Musée de L'Orangerie: 130tr; Musée du Louvre: 125br, 128c; Musée National des Châteaux de Malmaison et Bois-Préau: 255cr; Musée Marmottan: 58c, 58cb, 59c, 60tl, 131tr; Musée de la Mode et du Costume Palais Galliera: 57br; Musée de Montmartre, Paris: 223t; Musée des Monuments Français: 199tc, 200cr; Musée National de la Légion d'Honneur: 32bc, 143bl; Musée de la Ville de Paris: Musée du Petit Palais: 54cl, 207cb; © Sundancer: 362bl.

The Publishers are grateful to the following individuals, companies and picture libraries for permission to reproduce their photographs:

ADP, 377b; Alamy: Bertrand Collet 269cl; Glenn Harper 212tl; Image State 270br; Allsport UK: Sean Botterill 41br; Allvey & Towers: 378bl; The Ancient Art and Architecture Collection: 22clb; James Austin: 88t.

Banque de France: 133t; Nelly Bariand: 165c; Gérard Boullay: 84tl, 84tr, 84bl, 84br, 85t, 85cra, 85crb, 85br, 85bl; Bridgeman Art Library, London: (detail) 21br, 22cr, 23cl, 30cr–31cl, (detail) 35br; British Library, London (detail) 18br, (detail) 23bl, (detail) 24tl, (detail) 31tl; B N, Paris 19bl, (detail) 23tc, (detail) 23cr; Château de Versailles, France 19tr, 19bc, (detail) 19br, (detail) 30br, (detail) 155b; Christie's, London 8–9, (detail) 24cb, 34cla, 36tl, 44c; Delomosne, London 32clb; Giraudon 16, (detail) 26bl, (detail) 26clb, (detail) 27br, (detail) 30bl, (detail) 30cla, (detail) 31bl, 33cb, 58br, (detail) 60bl, 60ca, 60c; Lauros– Giraudon 23tr; Louvre, Paris 56t, 60br, 61bl, 61tl; Roy Miles Gallery 27tr; Musée de L'Armée, Paris (detail) 83br; Musée Condé, Chantilly (detail) 4tr, 18bl, 19tcl, (detail) 19tcr, (detail) 19c, (detail) 22tl, (detail) 26bc; Musée Crozatier, Le Puy en Velay, France (detail) 25bl; Musée Gustave Moreau, Paris 56b, 233tr; National Gallery (detail) 29tl, (detail) 44b; Musée de la Ville de Paris, Musée Carnavalet (detail) 30bc, (detail) 31tr, 31crb, 97t. CineAqua: 200bl. Collection Painton Cowen 40cla; Palais du Tokyo, Paris 59b; Temples Newsham House, Leeds 25cr; Uffizi Gallery, Florence (detail) 24br; © British Museum: 31tc.

Cité de la Musique: Eric Mahondieu 237br; Cité des Sciences et de l'Industrie: Michel Lamoureux 238cb, 238b, 239tl, 239tr, 238c, 239br; Pascal Prieur 238tr; Natacha Soury 238tl; Michel Viard 238clb, 239tl; Corbis: Burnstein Collection 229b; Ray Juno 10cl; Richard List 11cl; Sylvain Saustier 268b; Tom Craig: 273t, 273br.

R Doisneau: Rapho 143t

Espace Montmartre: 222bl; European Commission 371; Mary Evans Picture Library: 38bl, 81br, 89tl, 94b, 130b, 141cl, 191c, 194cr, 195crb, 211b, 226bl, 247br, 251t, 253b, 388t.

Getty Images: Fred Dufour 192clb; Giraudon (detail) 22bl, (detail) 23crb; Lauros–Giraudon (detail) 33bl; Musée de la Ville de Paris: Musée Carnavalet (detail) 213t; Le Grand Véfour 293t; Philippe Guignard: 193br.

Roland Halbe: 192tr; La Halle Saint Pierre 225bc; Robert Harding Picture Library: 22br, 26tl, 29ca, 29br, 36cla, 38tl, 41tl, 45cr, 65br, 240cb, 381cr; B M 27ca; B N 191tr, 210bc; Biblioteca Reale, Turin 127t; Bulloz 210cb; P Craven 380b; R Francis 82clb; I Griffiths 376t; H Josse 210br; Musée National des Châteaux de Malmaison et Bois-Préau 33tc; Musée de Versailles 26cl; R Poinot 361b; P Tetrel 251crb; Explorer 12bl; F. Chazot 341b; Girard 65c; P Gleizes 62bl; F Jalain 378b; J Moatti 340bl, 340cl; Walter Rawlings 43bc; A Wolf 123br, 123tl; Alison Harris: Musée de Montparnasse 179cl; Pavillon des Arts 108br; Le Village Royale 132tl; John Heseltine Photography:

174; Hulton Getty: 45cl, 101br, 181tc, 233bl, 234c; Charles Hewitt 40clb; Lancaster 181tc.

© IGN Paris 1990 Authorisation N° 90–2067: 13b; Institut du Monde Arabe: Georges Fessey 165tr; InterContinental Hotels Group: 215crb.

The Kobal Collection: 44t, 140b; Columbia Pictures 181br; Société Générale de Films 38tc; Les Films du Carrosse 109t; Kong: Patricia Bailer 10b.

The Lebrecht Collection: 229br; François Lequeux 194cl.

Magnum: Bruno Barbey 64b; Philippe Halsmann 45b; Ministère de L'Economie et des Finances: 371c; Ministère de L'Intérieur SGAP de Paris: 368bc, 368br, 369t; Collections du Mobilier National-Cliché du Mobilier National: 167cr; © photo Musée de L'Armée, Paris: 189cr; Musée des Arts Décoratifs, Paris: L Sully Jaulmes 54t, *Cabinet* (1922-1923) Jacques-Emile Ruhlmann 57tr; Musée des Arts de la Mode-Collection UCAD–UFAC: 121b; Musée Bouilhet-Christofle: 132t; Musée Cantonal des Beaux-Arts, Lausanne: 115b; Musée Carnavalet: Dac Karin Maucotel 97b; Musée d'Art et d'Histoire du Judaïsme/Christophe Fouin 103br; Musée National de L'Histoire Naturelle: D Serrette 167cl; © Musée de L'Homme, Paris: D Ponsard 198cb, 201c; © Photo Musée de la Marine, Paris: 32bl, 196cl; Musée National d'Art Moderne – Centre Georges Pompidou, Paris: 61tr, 110br, 110bl, 111t, 111ca, 111cb, 112t, 112bl, 112br, 113t, 113c, 113bl, 113br; Musée des Plans-Reliefs, Paris: 186crb; Musée de la Poste, Paris: 179tl; Musée du Quai Branly: Patrick Gries/Bruno Descoings 54cb, 192br.

© Paris Tourist Office: Catherine Balet 270cl; David Lefranc 268c, 269t, 269br, 270tr, 271t, 271br, 272cl, 272bl, 272br; Philippe Perdereau: 132b, 133b; Cliché Photothèque des Musées de la Ville de Paris –© DACS 1993: 21ca, 21crb, 28cr–29cl, 96tr; courtesy of Poilâne: 321bl; Popperfoto: 229t.

Paul Raferty 246b; RATP.SG/G.I.E. Totheme 54; 386; Redferns: W Gottlieb 38clb; © Photo Réunion des Musées Nationaux: Grand Trianon 26crb; Musée Guimet 202tr; Musée du Louvre: 27cb, (detail) 32cr–33cl, 55tl, 123bl, 124t, 124c, 124b, 125t, 125c, 126c, 126bl, 126br, 127b, 128t,

128b, 129t, 129c; Musée Nationaux d'Art Moderne 111crb; Musée Picasso 55cr, 100t, 100c, 100cl, 100clb, 100br, 101bl, 101cr, 101ca, 101t; Roger-Viollet: (detail) 24clb, (detail) 39bl, (detail) 194bc, (detail) 211t; Ann Ronan Picture Library: 173cr; Philippe Ruault: Fondation Cartier 179bl.

La Samaritaine, Paris: 115c; Photo Scala, Florence: Musée du Quai Branly/Patrick Gries/Valérie Torre 193cr,/Patrick Gries/Bruno Descoings 193c; Sealink Plc: 378cl; Sipapress: 224c; SNCF – Service Presse Voyages France Europe: 388bl; Frank Spooner Pictures: F Reglain 64ca; P Renault 64c; Sygma: 35crb, 240cl; F Poincet 40tl; Keystone 40bc, 241cra; J Langevin 41br; Keler 41crb; J Van Hasselt 41tr; P. Habans 62c; A Gyori 63cr; P Vauthey 65bl; Y Forestier 188t; Sunset Blvd 241br; Water Carone 340t.

Tallandier: 25cb, 25tl, 28cl, 28clb, 28bl, 29bl, 30tl, 31cr, 31ca, 32tl, 32cb, 32br, 38cla, 39ca, 39br, 40cb, 52cla; B N 28br, 32crb, 38bc; Brigaud 39crb; Brimeur 34bl; Charmet 36cb; Dubout 17b, 20br, 24ca, 25br, 26br, 30c, 33cr, 33tr, 34br, 35bl, 36clb, 36bl, 36br, 37bl, 37br, 37clb, 37tl, 38crb; Josse 20cla, 20tc, 20c, 20clb, 21tl, 36bc; Josse-B N 20bl; Joubert 38c; Tildier 37ca; Vigne 34clb; Le Train Bleu: 295t.

Vidéothèque de Paris: Hoi Pham Dinh 106lb Agence Vu: Didier Lefèvre 340cr.

Front Endpaper: John Heseltine Photography br. © DACS 1993: cra. Back endpaper: RATP CML Agence Cartographique.

Jacket:
Front - DK Images: Eric Meacher bl;
Tips Images: Chad Ehlers main image.
Back - DK Images: Max Alexander tl, clb, bl;
Le Grand Vefour: cla.
Spine - DK Images: b; Tips Images: Chad Ehlers t.

Phrase Book

In Emergency

Help!	**Au secours!**	*oh sekoor*
Stop!	**Arrêtez!**	*aret-ay*
Call a doctor!	**Appelez un médecin!**	*apuh-lay uñ medsañ*
Call an ambulance!	**Appelez une ambulance!**	*apuh-lay oon oñboo-loñs*
Call the police!	**Appelez la police!**	*apuh-lay lah pob-lees*
Call the fire brigade!	**Appelez les pompiers!**	*apuh-lay leh poñ-peeyay*
Where is the nearest telephone?	**Où est le téléphone le plus proche?**	*oo ay luh teblehfon luh ploo prosh*
Where is the nearest hospital?	**Où est l'hôpital le plus proche?**	*oo ay l'opeetal luh ploo prosh*

Communication Essentials

Yes	**Oui**	*wee*
No	**Non**	*noñ*
Please	**S'il vous plaît**	*seel voo play*
Thank you	**Merci**	*mer-see*
Excuse me	**Excusez-moi**	*exkoo-zay mwah*
Hello	**Bonjour**	*boñzhoor*
Goodbye	**Au revoir**	*oh rub-vwar*
Good night	**Bonsoir**	*boñ-swar*
Morning	**Le matin**	*matañ*
Afternoon	**L'après-midi**	*l'apreb-meedee*
Evening	**Le soir**	*swar*
Yesterday	**Hier**	*eeyehr*
Today	**Aujourd'hui**	*oh-zboor-dwee*
Tomorrow	**Demain**	*dubmañ*
Here	**Ici**	*ee-see*
There	**Là**	*lah*
What?	**Quoi, quel, quelle?**	*kwab, kel, kel*
When?	**Quand?**	*koñ*
Why?	**Pourquoi?**	*poor-kwab*
Where?	**Où?**	*oo*

Useful Phrases

How are you?	**Comment allez-vous?**	*kom-moñ talay voo*
Very well, thank you.	**Très bien, merci.**	*treb byañ, mer-see*
Pleased to meet you.	**Enchanté de faire votre connaissance.**	*oñsboñ-tay dub febr votr kon-ay-sans*
See you soon.	**A bientôt.**	*byañ-toh*
That's fine	**C'est bon**	*say bon*
Where is/are...?	**Où est/sont...?**	*ooay/soñ*
How far is it to...?	**Combien de kilometres d'ici à...?**	*kom-byañ dub keelo-metr d'ee-see ab*
Which way to...?	**Quelle est la direction pour...?**	*kel ay lah deer-ek-syoñ poor*
Do you speak English?	**Parlez-vous anglais?**	*par-lay voo oñg-lay*
I don't understand.	**Je ne comprends pas.**	*zhub nuh kom-proñ pab*
Could you speak slowly please?	**Pouvez-vous parler moins vite s'il vous plaît?**	*poo-vay voo par-lay mwañ veet seel voo play*
I'm sorry.	**Excusez-moi.**	*exkoo-zay mwah*

Useful Words

big	**grand**	*groñ*
small	**petit**	*pub-tee*
hot	**chaud**	*show*
cold	**froid**	*frwah*
good	**bon/bien**	*boñ/byañ*
bad	**mauvais**	*mob-veb*
enough	**assez**	*assay*
well	**bien**	*byañ*
open	**ouvert**	*oo-ver*
closed	**fermé**	*fer-meb*
left	**gauche**	*gobsh*
right	**droit**	*drwah*
straight on	**tout droit**	*too drwah*
near	**près**	*preb*
far	**loin**	*lwañ*
up	**en haut**	*oñ ob*
down	**en bas**	*oñ bab*
early	**de bonne heure**	*dub bon urr*
late	**en retard**	*oñ rub-tar*
entrance	**l'entrée**	*l'on-tray*
exit	**la sortie**	*sor-tee*
toilet	**les toilettes, le WC**	*twab-let, vay-see*
free, unoccupied	**libre**	*leebr*
free, no charge	**gratuit**	*grab-twee*

Making a Telephone Call

I'd like to place a long-distance call.	**Je voudrais faire un appel à l'étranger.**	*zhub voo-dreb febr uñ apel a laytroñ-zhay*
I'd like to make a reverse charge call.	**Je voudrais faire une communication en PCV.**	*zhub voo-dreb febr oon komoonikab-syoñ oñ peb-seb-veb*
I'll try again later.	**Je rappelerai plus tard.**	*zhub rapel-eray ploo tar*
Can I leave a message?	**Est-ce que je peux laisser un message?**	*es-keb zhub pub leh-say uñ mehsazh*
Hold on.	**Ne quittez pas, s'il vous plaît.**	*nuh kee-tay pab seel voo play*
Could you speak up a little please?	**Pouvez-vous parler un peu plus fort?**	*poo-vay voo par-lay uñ pub ploo for*
local call	**la communication locale**	*komoonikab-syoñ low-kal*

Shopping

How much does this cost?	**C'est combien s'il vous plaît.**	*say kom-byañ seel voo play*
I would like ...	**je voudrais...**	*zhub voo-dray*
Do you have?	**Est-ce que vous avez?**	*es-kub voo zavay*
I'm just looking.	**Je regarde seulement.**	*zhub rubgar sublmoñ*
Do you take credit cards?	**Est-ce que vous acceptez les cartes de crédit?**	*es-kub voo zaksept-ay leb kart dub kreb-dee*
Do you take travellers' cheques?	**Est-ce que vous acceptez les cheques de voyages?**	*es-kub voo zaksept-ay leb shek dub vuayazb*
What time do you open?	**A quelle heure vous êtes ouvert?**	*ah kel urr voo zet oo-ver*
What time do you close?	**A quelle heure vous êtes fermé?**	*ah kel urr voo zet fer-may*
This one.	**Celui-ci.**	*suhl-wee-see*
That one.	**Celui-là.**	*suhl-wee-lah*
expensive	**cher**	*shebr*
cheap	**pas cher, bon marché**	*pab shebr, boñ mar-sbay*
size, clothes	**la taille**	*tye*
size, shoes	**la pointure**	*pwañ-tur*
white	**blanc**	*bloñ*
black	**noir**	*nwabr*
red	**rouge**	*roozb*
yellow	**jaune**	*zbobwn*
green	**vert**	*vebr*
blue	**bleu**	*blub*

Types of Shop

antique shop	**le magasin d'antiquités**	*maga-zañ d'oñteekee-tay*
bakery	**la boulangerie**	*booloñ-zhuree*
bank	**la banque**	*boñk*
book shop	**la librairie**	*lee-brebree*
butcher	**la boucherie**	*boo-sbebree*
cake shop	**la pâtisserie**	*patee-sree*
cheese shop	**la fromagerie**	*fromazb-ree*
chemist	**la pharmacie**	*farmab-see*
dairy	**la crémerie**	*krem-ree*
department store	**le grand magasin**	*groñ maga-zañ*
delicatessen	**la charcuterie**	*sbarkoot-ree*
fishmonger	**la poissonnerie**	*pwasson-ree*
gift shop	**le magasin de cadeaux**	*maga-zañ dub kadob*
greengrocer	**le marchand de légumes**	*mar-sboñ dub lay-goom*
grocery	**l'alimentation**	*alee-moñta-syoñ*
hairdresser	**le coiffeur**	*kwafubr*
market	**le marché**	*marsb-ay*
newsagent	**le magasin de journaux**	*maga-zañ dub zboor-no*
post office	**la poste, le bureau de poste, le PTT**	*pobst, boorob dub pobst, peb-teb-teb*
shoe shop	**le magasin de chaussures**	*maga-zañ dub show-soor*
supermarket	**le supermarché**	*soo pebr-marsbay*
tobacconist	**le tabac**	*tabab*
travel agent	**l'agence de voyages**	*l'azhoñs dub vwayazb*

Sightseeing

abbey	**l'abbaye**	*l'abay-ee*
art gallery	**la galerie d'art**	*galer-ree dart*
bus station	**la gare routière**	*gabr roo-tee-yehr*

English	French	Pronunciation
cathedral	la cathédrale	katay-dral
church	l'église	l'aygleez
garden	le jardin	zhar-dañ
library	la bibliothèque	beebleeo-tek
museum	le musée	moo-zay
railway station	la gare (SNCF)	gahr (es-en-say-ef)
tourist information office	les renseignements touristiques, le syndicat d'initiative	roñsayn-moñ toorees-teek, sandee-ka d'eenee-syateev
town hall	l'hôtel de ville	l'otel duh veel
closed for public holiday	fermeture jour férié	fehrmeh-tur zhoor febree-ay

Staying in a Hotel

Do you have a vacant room?	Est-ce que vous avez une chambre?	es-kuh voo-zavay oon shambr
double room, with double bed	la chambre à deux personnes, avec un grand lit	shambr ah duh pehr-son avek un gronñ lee
twin room	la chambre à deux lits	shambr ah duh lee
single room	la chambre à une personne	shambr ah oon pehr-son
room with a bath, shower	la chambre avec salle de bains, une douche	shambr avek sal duh bañ, oon doosh
porter	le garçon	gar-soñ
key	la clef	klay
I have a reservation.	J'ai fait une réservation.	zbay fay oon rayzehrva-syoñ

Eating Out

English	French	Pronunciation
Have you got a table?	Avez-vous une table de libre?	avay-voo oon tahbl duh leebr
I want to reserve a table.	Je voudrais réserver une table.	zhub voo-dray rayzehr-vay oon tahbl
The bill please.	L'addition s'il vous plaît.	l'adee-syoñ seel voo play
I am a vegetarian.	Je suis végétarien.	zhub swee vezhay-tehryañ
Waitress/ waiter	Madame, Mademoiselle/ Monsieur	mah-dam, mah-demwahzel/ mub-syuh
menu	le menu, la carte	men-oo, kart
fixed-price menu	le menu à prix fixe	men-oo ah pree feeks
cover charge	le couvert	koo-vehr
wine list	la carte des vins	kart-deh vañ
glass	le verre	vehr
bottle	la bouteille	boo-tay
knife	le couteau	koo-toh
fork	la fourchette	for-shet
spoon	la cuillère	kwee-yehr
breakfast	le petit déjeuner	pub-tee deb-zhub-nay
lunch	le déjeuner	deb-zhub-nay
dinner	le dîner	dee-nay
main course	le plat principal	plab prañsee-pal
starter, first course	l'entrée, le hors d'oeuvre	l'oñ-tray, or-dubvr
dish of the day	le plat du jour	plab doo zhoor
wine bar	le bar à vin	bar ab vañ
café	le café	ka-fay
rare	saignant	say-noñ
medium	à point	ab pwañ
well done	bien cuit	byañ kwee

Menu Decoder

English	French	Pronunciation
apple	la pomme	pom
baked	cuit au four	kweet oh foor
banana	la banane	banan
beef	le boeuf	bubf
beer, draught	la bière, bière	bee-yehr, bee-yehr
beer	à la pression	ab lab pres-syoñ
boiled	bouilli	boo-yee
bread	le pain	pan
butter	le beurre	burr
cake	le gâteau	gab-toh
cheese	le fromage	from-azh
chicken	le poulet	poo-lay
chips	les frites	freet
chocolate	le chocolat	shoko-lab
cocktail	le cocktail	cocktail
coffee	le café	kah-fay
dessert	le dessert	deb-ser
dry	sec	sek
duck	le canard	kanar
egg	l'oeuf	l'uf
fish	le poisson	pwah-ssoñ
fresh fruit	le fruit frais	frwee freb
garlic	l'ail	l'eye
grilled	grillé	gree-yay
ham	le jambon	zhoñ-boñ
ice, ice cream	la glace	glas
lamb	l'agneau	l'anyoh
lemon	le citron	see-troñ
lobster	le homard	omahr
meat	la viande	vee-yand
milk	le lait	leb
mineral water	l'eau minérale	l'ob meeney-ral
mustard	la moutarde	moo-tard
oil	l'huile	l'weel
olives	les olives	leb zoleev
onions	les oignons	leb zonyoñ
orange	l'orange	l'oroñzh
fresh orange juice	l'orange pressée	l'oroñzh press-eb
fresh lemon juice	le citron pressé	see-troñ press-eb
pepper	le poivre	pwavr
poached	poché	posh-ay
pork	le porc	por
potatoes	les pommes de terre	pom-dub tehr
prawns	les crevettes	krub-vet
rice	le riz	ree
roast	rôti	row-tee
roll	le petit pain	pub-tee pañ
salt	le sel	sel
sauce	la sauce	sobs
sausage, fresh	la saucisse	sohsees
seafood	les fruits de mer	frwee dub mer
shellfish	les crustaces	kroos-tas
snails	les escargots	leb zes-kar-goh
soup	la soupe, le potage	soop, pob-tazh
steak	le bifteck, le steack	beef-tek, stek
sugar	le sucre	sookr
tea	le thé	tay
toast	pain grillé	pan greeyay
vegetables	les légumes	lay-goom
vinegar	le vinaigre	veenaygr
water	l'eau	l'ob
red wine	le vin rouge	vañ roozh
white wine	le vin blanc	vañ bloñ

Numbers

Number	French	Pronunciation
0	zéro	zeb-rob
1	un, une	uñ, oon
2	deux	dub
3	trois	trwab
4	quatre	katr
5	cinq	sañk
6	six	sees
7	sept	set
8	huit	weet
9	neuf	nerf
10	dix	dees
11	onze	oñz
12	douze	dooz
13	treize	trebz
14	quatorze	katorz
15	quinze	kañz
16	seize	sebz
17	dix-sept	dees-set
18	dix-huit	dees-weet
19	dix-neuf	dees-nerf
20	vingt	vañ
30	trente	tront
40	quarante	karoñt
50	cinquante	sañkoñt
60	soixante	swasoñt
70	soixante-dix	swasoñt-dees
80	quatre-vingts	katr-vañ
90	quatre-vingt-dix	katr-vañ-dees
100	cent	soñ
1,000	mille	meel

Time

English	French	Pronunciation
one minute	une minute	oon mee-noot
one hour	une heure	oon urr
half an hour	une demi-heure	oon dub-mee urr
Monday	lundi	luñ-dee
Tuesday	mardi	mar-dee
Wednesday	mercredi	mehrkrub-dee
Thursday	jeudi	zhub-dee
Friday	vendredi	voñdrub-dee
Saturday	samedi	sam-dee
Sunday	dimanche	dee-moñsh

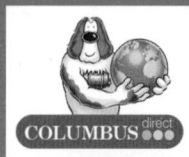

Paris Metro and Regional Express Railway (RER)